THE BIRTH
OF THE
CHRISTIAN
RELIGION

AND

THE ORIGINS
OF THE NEW
TESTAMENT

by Alfred Loisy

Les Mystères païens et le Mystère chrétien,
deuxième édition, 1930, 1 vol. gr. in-8, 352 pages.
Essai historique sur le sacrifice.
1920, 1 vol. gr. in-8, 552 pages.
Les Livres du Nouveau Testament,
traduit du grec en français avec introduction générale et notices, 1922,
1 vol. gr. in-8, 711 pages.
L'Evangile selon Marc
1912, 1 vol. in-12, 500 pages.
L'Evangile selon Luc
1924, 1 vol. gr. in-8, 600 pages.
Le quatrième Evangile,
deuxième édition, 1921, 1 vol. gr. in-8, 602 pages.
Les Actes des Apôtres
1920, 1 vol. gr. in-8, 963 pages.
L'Epitre aux Galatés
1916, 1 vol. in-12, 204 pages.
L'Apocalypse de Jean
1923, 1 vol. gr. in-8, 406 pages.
Le Mandéisme et les Origines chrétiennes
1934, 180 pages.
Remarques sur la littérature épistolaire du Nouveau Testament
1935, 202 pages.
Les Origines du Nouveau Testament
1936, 393 pages.
Histoire et Mythe à propos de Jésus-Christ
1938, 260 pages.
Un Mythe apologétique
1939, 192 pages.
La Religion,
deuxième édition, 1924, 1 vol. in-12, 406 pages.
La Morale humaine,
deuxième édition, 1928, 1 vol. in-12, 306 pages.
L'Eglise et la France
1925, 1 vol. in-12, 237 pages.
Religion et Humanité
1926, 1 vol. in-12, 266 pages.
Mémoires pour servir à l'Histoire religieuse de notre Temps,
1931, trois vol. gr. in-8, 589, 664 et 607 pages.
Y a-t-il deux sources de la religion et de la morale?
1933, 1 vol. in-12, 204 pages.
La Religion d'Israël,
troisième édition, 1933, in-8, 328 pages.
Etudes bibliques,
troisième édition, 1903, 1 vol. in-8, 336 pages.
L'Evangile et l'Eglise,
cinquième édition, 1930, 1 vol. in-12, XLIV, 277 pages.

THE BIRTH OF THE CHRISTIAN RELIGION

(La Naissance du Christianisme)

AND

THE ORIGINS OF THE NEW TESTAMENT

(Les Origines du Nouveau Testament)

by

ALFRED FIRMIN LOISY

Authorized translation from the French by L. P. Jacks

UNIVERSITY BOOKS   *New Hyde Park, New York*

Manufactured in the United States of America

INTRODUCTION

by

W. NORMAN PITTENGER, S.T.D.

The two books here made available for the first time to American readers were Loisy's last notable contributions to the history of early Christian thought.

Alfred Loisy was born in 1857 and died in 1940. From his appointment in 1889 to the professorship of Sacred Scripture at the *Institut Catholique* in Paris until his excommunication from the Roman Catholic Church in 1908, he was one of the acknowledged leaders—perhaps one might say was *the* leader—of that movement in the Roman Church which is known as "Catholic Modernism," although he must share this title with George Tyrrell in England and with Ernesto Buonaiuti in Italy. Noted Old and New Testament scholar, brilliant master of the French language, he died at the very time when the German Army under Hitler was overrunning his beloved France.

In order to understand Loisy, it is necessary to see the situation in France which provided a background for much of his thinking. At the time when he was establishing his reputation as a distinguished biblical scholar and a member of the faculty of the celebrated *Institut Catholique*, the French republic was largely in the hands of a series of clerically minded royalist leaders, and the Roman Catholic Church exercised a very considerable control over many aspects of the life of the nation, not least in the educational field. Church and state were no longer separated and genuine freedom of thought was hardly possible under governments which combined an excessive loyalty to the dictates of the Roman Church with a reactionary political and social programme. It is obvious that a scholar of Loisy's calibre, who believed that no study could be conducted objectively if the conclu-

v

sions were dictated either by ecclesiastical pressure or by secular authority, would find himself unhappy in such a situation. During the eighties and nineties of the century, Loisy—with many other scholars in all fields—became convinced that only free institutions of learning could possibly perform the necessary task of research and enquiry which sound scholarship demands and the cause of truth expects.

One of the important factors in the Modernist Movement, to which we shall turn shortly, was its concern with such matters as these. While the note of "social reform," with all that accompanies it, was heard more loudly from Italian Modernists such as Murri, Minnocchi, and Buonaiuti, it was by no means without voice in France; Loisy's *Memoirs* are full of references to his concern for the educational issue, the necessity for a state free from ecclesiastical control, and the ancient French cry of "freedom" from interference from outside the nation.

The discontent in France reached its climax in what has become known as the Dreyfus Affair. Alfred Dreyfus was an officer in the French Army who was connected with the General Staff; he was also a Jew. In 1894, the very year after Loisy was obliged to leave the faculty of the *Institut Catholique* because of his critical studies of the Old Testament, Dreyfus was court-martialled on a charge of high treason. It was alleged that he had sold military secrets to a great foreign power. After a secret trial he was sentenced to military degradation and to solitary confinement on the infamous *Ile du Diable*, off French Guiana. In a ceremony in the *Ecole Militaire* in Paris, he was stripped of his military insignia and his sword broken, and he was then transported to his place of imprisonment.

Dreyfus had denied his guilt and this denial was supported by most of the distinguished literary leaders of the republic. Men like Zola and the statesmen Clemenceau and Jaurès were among his defenders. The French nation was in an uproar. Not only was there the matter of the probable injustice of the condemnation of the man himself; there was also the fact that because he was a Jew his arrest and trial had led to an outbreak of anti-Semitic feeling in France and pogroms in Algeria—and there was considerable suspicion that the combination of royalist and ecclesiastical power was not free from condoning this outbreak. Eventually, a Colonel Henry, a functionary of the General Staff, confessed to having forged the documents against Dreyfus; and after much further legal action, and new elections favorable to the Dreyfusards, the prisoner was pardoned in 1899 by the President of the republic. After still another trial—in which the unrepentant military caste condemned Dreyfus again!—the Court of Cassation annulled the sentence altogether and restored Dreyfus to his place in the Army. The Chamber of Deputies raised him to the rank of major. Later, Dreyfus served with distinction in the French Army during the First World War, receiving the decoration of the Cross of the Legion of Honor.

What has all this to do with Loisy, the priest and teacher? The answer is simply that it was the incident which taught him, and many other scholars in France, that a reactionary government, in close assocation with ecclesiastical interests, is fatal to the life of freedom in every area, not least in the religious and educational realms. Loisy became a dedicated advocate of the separation of Church and State and did all in his power, often through influential friends, to bring about separation and the freedom of education in France. When separation was accomplished in 1905, control of the University of Paris, the Sorbonne, was no longer in the hands of reaction. It was this change which made it possible for Loisy to teach, from 1909 until his retirement in 1930, at the *College de France*. Otherwise he would have been deprived of all possibility of exercising his profession as an expert in the field of history of religions.

What concerned Loisy and other educators, including many in the Church itself, was the need for the establishment of a reasonable and open approach to questions of historical origins and every other aspect of scholarly study. Without understanding the background which has just been sketched altogether too briefly, it is impossible for the contemporary reader of men like Loisy to see that, however objectionable some of their views may have been to Church leaders, their battle was essentially a battle for freedom of thought. To the end of his days, Loisy was pursued by ecclesiastical hatred, even though some of his friends, like Monsignor Mignot, were loyal to him so far as they could be so while remaining highly placed in the hierarchy. The writer of this Introduction has been told by a friend of Loisy that the old man was not able to have his beard trimmed by the barber in the small village where he lived in retirement. Loisy was *vitandus,* a heretic to be "avoided," and the barber did not dare serve his neighbor in this small way. Loisy was obliged to make the trip to Paris for a haircut.

Nor is it fanciful to say that the forces which were at work in the kind of treatment accorded Loisy were precisely the forces which helped to bring about the collapse of European civilization at the time of the First World War and hence to provide the backdrop against which the Second World War and its aftermath must be seen. Whenever the cause of freedom is lost sight of, and whenever reactionary powers, whether civil or churchly, gain control, demons are unloosed on the world, and the results are always disastrous.

Americans will not easily have a grasp of the Modernist Movement with which Loisy was associated. In the United States, the word "Modernism" has been used with a considerable variety of meanings, some of which are precisely the opposite of that position to which Loisy and his associates gave their best years in the Roman Catholic Church.

Perhaps the best way to begin is to point out that the type of Christian thought which in this country is described as "Modernism" is in truth the view which as a matter of historical fact is associated with the liberal Protestant thinking of continental scholars like the great Adolf von Harnack of

Berlin, whose point of view Loisy attacked and demolished in his first widely read book, *L'Evangile et l'Eglise (The Gospel and the Church)*, published in 1902 as a reply to Harnack's work *Das Wesen des Christentums (The Meaning of Christianity)*, which appeared in German in 1900 and was translated into English in 1903 with the title *What is Christianity?*

Harnack sought to show that Christianity, properly understood, is the religion which Jesus taught and practiced. It can be summed up as including the fatherhood of God, the brotherhood of man, the leadership of Jesus, and the possibility of living "the eternal life in the midst of time." The theological interpretation of Jesus as in some profound sense truly divine as well as human, the existence of the Church as an institution, and the sacramental rites of the Christian community, are to be interpreted (Harnack asserted) as examples of the "acute Hellenization" of the simple gospel which Jesus taught. What we should do, if we wish to be authentic Christians, is return to the simplicities of Jesus' teaching, for *this* is essential Christianity. All the rest is addition to, or unnecessary complication of, the essential thing.

Anyone who is familiar with the history of religious thought in the United States will at once recognize that Harnack here states what was common teaching in many American Protestant churches during the period from 1900 to 1930. But it was precisely this interpretation of the meaning of Christianity which Loisy—and with him, the rest of the Catholic Modernists—regarded as entirely mistaken. They insisted that a sound historical analysis of the New Testament as a whole, including the gospels and the epistles, will show that Christianity was *never* such a simple following of the teaching of the Prophet of Nazareth. From the earliest period of which we have any knowledge, Christianity has been a religion which has seen the presence of God in Jesus; it has been a religion which has been embodied in, and conveyed by, a community of believers or a Church; it has celebrated sacramental rites and has regarded these as integral to the Christian profession. Loisy's *The Gospel and the Church* is a sustained demonstration, on strictly historical grounds, of the truth of this statement. And there are very few scholars today who would disagree with Loisy, however they may feel about the truth or falsehood of Christianity as a religious possibility for modern man.

What the Modernists maintained was that there was *that* in Jesus which inevitably led to the development of belief about him; and that the development of Church, sacraments, and other institutional agencies was the inevitable consequence of taking seriously the *that* which was present in this historical Man of Nazareth. The notion of *development*, therefore, was at the heart of the whole Modernist picture. This notion, which Loisy says that he had come to see from historical study, was confirmed for him by his reading of Cardinal Newman's work on *The Development of Doctrine*, the essay which brought Newman from the Church of England to the Roman Catholic Church. "In another world it may be otherwise," Newman had said, "but in this world to live is to change . . ." And this conception of change or development was central to the interpretation of Christianity which Loisy and his associates accepted.

Furthermore, Loisy insisted that the way in which Jesus interpreted his own mission, teaching the imminent advent of the Kingdom of God, was entirely in line with this view. Jesus' own outlook was necessarily conditioned by the patterns of thought of his own time; hence he believed that God's Kingdom was to come to men and he also believed that he was both the proclaimer of that Kingdom and in some way closely related to its coming. What came, in fact, was the Church. The death of Jesus, the conviction of his disciples that although dead he was yet alive with them in his "risen life," and the empowering which the primitive Christians felt through what they called "the Holy Spirit"—all these were the historical factors which brought about the appearance of the Church and its rites; and all these were the developmental source of that new community which is the Catholic Church and which has continued to the present day.

It was this interpretation of the origins of Christianity which Modernism believed to be required by a study of history; it was this interpretation which, in their judgment, could guarantee the importance and value of the Catholic way of worship and of life. Harnack's portrayal was not only unhistorical, it was also destructive of the integrity of Catholic Christianity. So it was that Loisy believed that his work was very far from being destructive. In his view, he had established the only ground upon which a sound, true, and defensible presentation of Christianity could be maintained in the modern age.

At first there was some acceptance of Loisy's criticism of Harnack and defense of Catholic Christianity. But very soon the Roman Catholic Church, through its hierarchy, came to the conclusion that Loisy's position was utterly unacceptable to it. The story of his "duel" with the Vatican, which begins at this point, continued for a decade. As the attacks on him continued, as he was more and more harassed by authority, as he found that the project so dear to his heart—the defense of Catholic Christianity by scholarly methods of historical enquiry—failed to commend itself to his superiors, he came to feel that he had no place in the Church which he loved and wished to serve. A certain bitterness crept into his attitude and long before most of his associates recognized that Rome had no place for them, Loisy saw that he himself could not continue the struggle. This is the tragedy of his life, as his friend Maude Petre has shown in her beautifully perceptive book *Alfred Loisy, His Religious Significance* (1944). His heart was broken, as he himself wrote after one of his encounters with Vatican intransigeance, and it was with a certain relief that he found himself, in 1908, excommunicated from the Church—he had already ceased, for two years, to exercise his priestly functions.

After this, he continued his study and his teaching. From 1909 to 1930, when he retired, he served as a professor at the *College de France*. During this period, he continued writing on New Testament origins, his last important works on this subject appearing in 1933 under the title *La Naissance du Christianisme* (The Birth of The Christian Religion) and in 1936 *Les Origines du Nouveau Testament*. The two have been translated by L. P. Jacks, the English scholar, commissioned by the Hibbert Trust. These are the books which are reprinted in the present volume. Loisy also published his several-volumed *Memoirs*, in which he gives what might be described as a "blow-by-blow" account of his struggle with ecclesiastical authority, but in which he also writes beautifully and pathetically of his childhood and early days as a seminarist and as a priest and student. He also published a series of works in which he sought to work his way through to a new understanding of the meaning and place of religion in the life of men—and the astounding thing, as Miss Petre has remarked in her study, is that as he grew older he came more and more to react from his earlier bitterness and to feel that in Christianity, in its essential meaning, there is much that will provide precisely that religious orientation which man requires if he is to live as truly human and not as a sophisticated animal.

Loisy was a complex personality. He was a great scholar. Like many Frenchmen he had a grain of skepticism in his make-up, and it is this which may explain his sometimes over-doubtful attitude to some of the elements in the New Testament which most New Testament scholars would regard as having a very high degree of probability. He was inclined, in his critical work, to take the more extreme view on any issue. And yet he was far from being an extreme skeptic. Despite the regularly made statement that he separated completely the "Jesus of history" from the "Christ of faith," for example, he was himself entirely clear that there was a continuity between them; and the picture of his work which the late Dean Inge of St. Paul's Cathedral in London popularized—that Loisy simply reduced Jesus to an insignificant and unimportant figure in the development of Christianity—is utterly mistaken, as a reading of Loisy's own books will plainly show.

The two volumes which are here published in one volume represent the last important writing of Loisy in his own special field. The position which the author takes would not commend itself to all experts in early Christian history, but the scholarly acumen, careful examination of evidence, and willingness to adopt positions which are often revolutionary in their import, would be recognized by all. The first volume, on "the birth of the Christian religion," is an attempt to sketch the earliest history of the Christian Church from New Testament evidence and from other literature of the period; the second, on "the origins of the New Testament," is an examination of the second half of the Christian Bible from the perspective of an historian of religion and with the use of all the tools which are available to him—such as comparative study of religions and their literatures, the discipline which has now become known as "form-criticism" (here Loisy anticipated much which has later been written by scholars such as Rudolf Bultmann and others), and the usual textual and literary criticisms accepted by most scholars.

Loisy's conclusions are often radical, in the sense that they are developed with the utmost thoroughness from the scientific apparatus employed in the study of non-religious history, with no regard for the theological or devotional results which may follow. But the fact that the procedure is radical and that the conclusions are often radical, too, does not mean that the intention of the writer of the volumes was to "destroy faith." He had long since given up his allegiance to the Roman Catholic Church, of course, and he believed that the Christian faith as he had once accepted and believed it was no longer a live possibility for thinking men; but Loisy remained always a religious man and he had no use for the kind of skepticism which would say that religion is always and necessarily a fraud and a lie. Indeed the last words of the second volume, on "origins," says as much: "What matters is the fire they (Jesus, Peter, Paul, John) kindled, and it is a fire that will never die till mankind is no more. Men pass away, but humanity remains; religions die, but religion shines for ever. Man would have perished long ago, victim of his own folly, had not the religious ideal of humanity rescued him from the edge of the abyss. May he mend his ways and himself establish this law of his progress on an ever firmer foundation."

That the work of men like Loisy, and his colleague Charles Guignebert, need not totally demolish Christianity is shown by one interesting fact. In the decade after the Second World War, the then Anglican bishop of Birmingham, Ernest William Barnes, published a large volume in which he surveyed early Christian history; it was published under the title *The Rise of Christianity* (London, Longmans, 1947). In this book Bishop Barnes was able to accept and use much of the scholarly work of both Loisy and Guignebert, and to remain not only a bishop of the Church of England but a convinced and devout Christian. He was violently attacked by conservatives within his own communion and elsewhere; his book may not be representative of much that is being written today in the field, but of the good faith and integrity of the author there can be no doubt. Many of us have thought that the attacks upon him were unjust and inaccurate; yet the fact remains that Barnes was, and remained, a Christian to the day of his death. In other words, he illustrated that an honest approach to the material in question, however radical and disturbing it may be, need not lead men from a responsible Christian faith; in fact, it may lead them to a deeper and truer faith—and this, one would think, is part of what Loisy was saying in the passage quoted above.

However this may be, the fact remains that Loisy was an entirely honest and devoted student of the Bible; and that his intention, at least in the days before the Roman Church thrust him out of its priesthood and fellowship, was to find a way in which historical Christianity, in its rich devotional and sacramental life, could be maintained and defended in the modern world. In this he was at one with his associates in the Modernist Movement; and to this Movement, in its wider aspects, we must now turn in an effort to set this book in the proper context.

Modernism, in the sense in which Loisy represented it, is not confined to the Roman Catholic Church. It had, and has, its counterparts in the Anglican Communion, in many Protestant bodies, and even to some extent in the Eastern Orthodox Church. Essentially, it is the attempt to reconcile the central affirmations of Christian faith with the inescapable facts of modern research. It seeks so to understand and state this faith that a modern man can accept it, without abdicating his reason or his common sense. Unless this can be done, there is no possibility for the continuance of Christianity in our time.

There are many, of course, who would say that Christianity is over and done with. They would give it up, once and for all, as belonging to the dead past; and if they wish to find any religious faith, they will feel impelled to look elsewhere. On the other hand, there are those who feel that all this is a tempest in a teapot. For them, Christianity is entirely true and sound, precisely as they have received it; they see no problems whatever in its relationship to such modern knowledge as they are inclined to accept. But there is still a third group—and the writer of this Introduction would put himself among them—who believe that Christianity is indeed an insight into ultimate reality, without which we are without access to the deepest truth about our world and ourselves and about the Divine Reality on whom both depend, but who also are convinced that an accurate understanding of Christianity's historical origins and a serious attempt to relate it to the best currents of thought in our own time are necessary if that insight and truth are to be seen in their splendid integrity.

Roman Catholic Modernism took precisely this stand. It sought to use the best knowledge of its time in the interpretation of the history of Christianity; it sought also to use that same knowledge in the presentation of the faith to contemporary men and women. It was willing to employ the philosophical insights of a Bergson, for example, as well as the sociological understanding of, say, a Durkheim. It believed that the problem of God was, in a profound sense, the problem of man's own spiritual existence. It shirked no problems and sought no easy solutions. That its point of view was often limited by the then available knowledge was inevitable; men cannot jump out of their time and place in history and deal with eternal and unconditioned truth. But its stance was surely the only possible one for those who are serious both in their acceptance of the historical faith and in their citizenship in the world of their own period.

In recent years, we have witnessed a great reaction in the direction of theological conservatism, just as we have seen the same reaction in political, economic, and social questions. Yet there are signs that this reaction has by now spent itself, at least so far as the religious life of men are concerned. It may be—some of us are convinced that it is—the fact that when we are ready once again to concern ourselves with the relation of faith to the whole world of our experience, the labors of the Modernists, and not least those of Alfred Loisy, will have their invaluable contribution to make to our renewed wrestling with the problems that all men face as they seek to make sense of their lives and find meaning in the universe where those lives are lived.

PUBLISHER'S NOTE

Only three of the many books written by Loisy have ever been translated into English. *The Gospel and the Church* was translated and published in 1904, from the text of the third edition of *L'Evangile et l'Eglise*. It appears never to have been reprinted since. We plan to publish it in one volume with new translations of other material belonging to that period of the height of the Catholic Modernist struggle. The other two books translated are published here for the first time in the United States.

Grateful acknowledgement is made for the use of the translations here published. The rights of translation of *La Naissance du Christianisme* and *Les Origines du Nouveau Testament* into English were acquired by the Hibbert Trust under whose commission this translation was made and published in England. Thanks are also due the following libraries which provided material for reproduction purposes: Andover-Harvard Theological Library, Union Theological Seminary Library, General Theological Seminary Library. As the publishers of three books by Charles Guignebert, it is natural enough that we now publish Loisy. But we do so at the present time thanks primarily to Professor Benjamin Nelson who urged the immediate need to publish Loisy and who unerringly indicated Dr. W. Norman Pittenger as the ideal theologian to introduce Loisy today to a new audience.

CONTENTS

(*Note:* Pagination of *The Birth of the Christian Religion* ends on page 414; pagination of *The Origins of the New Testament* follows, but begins anew with page 1.)

PREFACE

by

GILBERT MURRAY

DR. JACKS has rendered a great service to religious thought by his translation of this very remarkable book, which sums up the main conclusions of M. Loisy's elaborate studies of early Christian literature. It represents the latest, and, in my judgment, the most masterly of all the attempts to understand and describe according to the normal canons of human history, without prejudice and without miracle, a movement which has shaped the whole subsequent religion of the Western World. Previous historians of Christianity have generally been theologians, convinced of the miraculous nature of their subject and consequently, however learned, compelled to be uncritical. Only a few have deliberately rejected the miraculous, and many of them, in their anxiety to be freed from a false mythology, have been betrayed into a polemical attitude and failed to appreciate the grandeur of their theme. But, apart from these considerations, the subject itself is curiously difficult and obscure. The actual Christian literature proves on examination to be so different from what it seems. The Gospels, which look at first sight like simple lives of Jesus, prove on analysis to have had quite a different purpose and also to have been exposed to varied and incalculable influences in the interests of different doctrines and communities. It is only of recent years that scholars have begun to understand how different from a modern book, printed off in a thousand or so uniform copies, was the nature of an ancient book written out copy by copy; how different again the book which, although written, is still in the main merely an instrument for oral recitation, liable to be improved or altered according to circumstances or the taste of the reciter; different again the book of devotion or edification meant to enforce or correct the rites and beliefs of a community. M. Loisy's analysis of the books of the New Testament and other early Christian literature surpasses, in my opinion, any previous analysis known to me. He writes with an intimate understanding of the problems before him which seems to me to shed a new, and I would almost

5

add a convincing, light on one of the most important movements in human history. I only hesitate to use the word "convincing" because, as he himself emphatically warns us, the evidence itself often leads only to a doubt or at most to a strong probability.

There is another advance of knowledge in recent years which explains much in the rise of Christianity and its acceptance by the Greco-Roman world which must have seemed inexplicable a generation ago. To one who, like myself, approaches the problem from the Greek side it is very significant that the language of the New Testament is Greek. The crude contrast between "Christian" and "Pagan" is really a false one. The idea of a son of God born to save the world is essentially a Greek idea. All the Greek-speaking populations of the Levant were permeated by the old agricultural worship of the Renewal of Life in the New Year after the dead winter. The Renewal was of course conceived as a person. He was the fruit of the marriage of earth with Heaven through the spring Sun and Rain; a son of God and an earthly *Kore* or maiden; a babe who will become King and make all things new, shaking off the dead impurities of the past. This theme is the subject of countless myths and rituals and forms a specially large element in the Drama and the ritual of Dionysus. From early times onward, and increasingly in the Hellenistic Age, these myths and rites were allegorized. The Τρίτος Σώτηρ, the "Saviour" who comes "Third," after the death of the Vegetation-King and of that king's slayer, became something much more than the saviour of the seed sown and the life of the ploughed field; he was to save the life of the world, and above all to save man's soul. All the philosophy of the Hellenistic age is tinged with a mysticism which comes chiefly from a sublimation of this agricultural New Life, combined with the desire for *Gnôsis*, Knowledge of God or union with God, of which there were germs in Plato and intense developments in the Egyptian and Oriental mystery-cults. There was also a wide-spread groping towards monotheism, attained not by denying any of the gods—that would have seemed impious —but by explaining them as emanations, or interpreters, or merely other names, of the One; and lastly in almost all the religious or philosophical movements one finds a tendency towards asceticism or at least a strong protest against the lusts of the flesh.

On Greek minds affected by these ideas contact with the Jews

6

seems to have had almost the effect of a revelation. The very qualities which made that strange race so unpopular, their intolerance, their denial of the gods, their contemptuous hatred of idolatry and blood-sacrifice, had for thoughtful minds an extraordinary power of attraction. Here at last, in the phrase of one Greek writer, was a φιλόσοφον ἔθνος, "a philosopher nation," in which the whole people had risen above the turmoil of vulgar superstitions and incessant religious observances which beset the Pagan world, and moreover had a clear moral standard in sexual matters. The Jews stood altogether for a cleaner and less frightened world. Besides, in place of the confused mythical legends of the Greeks, this nation had an ancient and sacred Book, of uncontested authority, containing laws and prophecies which had stood the test of time. And they were all expecting a Messiah, a Saviour.

By the time of St. Paul these influences must have become more intense, more disturbing. A new sect of Jews was saying that the Messiah had actually come and that his kingdom was about to be proclaimed; only it seemed that he had failed. He was dead, condemned by law and crucified. As M. Loisy points out, that disaster would by no means be fatal to the survival of an ordinary sect, like that of the followers of John the Baptist, disciples of a human prophet. It was a much severer blow to worshippers of a Messiah announcing the arrival of a heavenly kingdom. One who failed, it seemed obvious, could not be the Messiah. But was this objection really valid? The common people of the Hellenistic world knew that the Saviour must die; to die and be re-born was the course of his normal history. And as for the condemnation and crucifixion, the more educated men were familiar with Plato's famous description of the righteous man in an unrighteous world, who must expect "to be thrown into prison, scourged and racked, and after every kind of torment . . . be impaled or crucified." It is not difficult to imagine speculations of this sort bearing fruit in the mind of Paul during his period of conversion.

Thus Hebrew ideas influenced the Greek mind, and in return ideas that were traditional among the populations of the great cities and country villages of Greek Asia not only gave a new inspiration to the Jewish followers of Jesus but inevitably invaded and shook the narrow Jewish orthodoxy. It was not a mere

7

Jewish Messiah that the world hungered for; it was a Saviour of mankind. And such a Saviour must, according to all Greek precedent, be the son of a God by a daughter of Earth, and she, on the analogy of many myths, a Virgin of royal birth, made fruitful by the divine Touch or Breath or Spirit. The Jews might indignantly protest. Greek philosophers might cry halt. But these ideas were too wide-spread and deep-rooted to be suppressed, and soon began to lead away from strict monotheism to something more emotional and more familiar; to the immemorial worship of the Mother Goddess, to the old Trinity of Father, Mother and Child in different forms, and to various rites for entering into communion with God by the mediation of minor deities or by the mystical partaking of the divine blood. No wonder there was bitter opposition between Christian and Jew. The Jews could not but feel that these Hellenizers were trying to drag them into a swamp of mere paganism.

It was a long time before these various streams of religious emotion could be shaped into one coherent Christian creed. At first, apparently, it was enough to have received the Good News that the Saviour had come and suffered and re-risen, and now the Kingdom of God was at hand. Even when that Good News proved to be not true in its literal sense, the intense longing which inspired that unhappy generation was too strong to let it die. It was preserved as at least an allegorical truth. In the early days it seems clear that there was no exact orthodoxy. Different teachers and different parts of the Hellenistic world followed their divergent ways of thought. I suspect, however, that one binding force among Christians was the conscious misery of the subject populations of the Roman Empire after the awful series of civil wars and proletarian rebellions whose effects still persisted even after the establishment of the Augustan Peace. The early Christian literature which accepts as obvious the wickedness of *publicani* and upper-class Pharisees and the extreme improbability of any rich man entering the Kingdom of Heaven, which cries that the foxes have holes and the birds of the air have nests but the son of man has not where to lay his head, was, as Arnold Toynbee has pointed out,* repeating an old "flying word" which had been familiar to unhappy populations from the time of Tiberius

* *Study of History*, vi, p. 414.

Gracchus onward. Such a movement brought union among the oppressed and at the same time roused terror in society generally. Again and again the writers of the New Testament repeat the command "Slaves, obey your masters,"* and explain that they use no violence and seek no earthly kingdom. Those who remembered with horror the risings of Mithridates, of the Heliopolites in Asia, Spartacus in Italy, the slave-king "Antiochus" in Sicily, were mistrustful of this mysterious current of emotion among the proletariates of the eastern cities, and its occasional outbursts of unconcealed fury against the Harlot seated upon Seven Hills and drunken with the blood of saints. When one reads of the horror inspired by the name of Christian and the monstrous persecutions to which Christians were exposed in a world which did not persecute other religions, I suspect that the explanation lies chiefly in two of the new religion's noblest qualities. It represented the cry of the poor in a suffering and harshly administered world, and it proclaimed a great, if temporary, liberation of the human mind by its wholesale denial of false gods and idolatrous pietisms.

* Eph. vi, 5; Col. iii, 22; Tit. ii, 9; 1 Pet. ii, 18.

AUTHOR'S INTRODUCTION

THE present study of the origin of the Christian religion comes
in sequence to that which the author has recently published on the
religion of Israel, the mention of which suffices to render another
introduction unnecessary. A complete translation of the New
Testament has also been edited[1] which, to some extent, supplies
the documentation and critical discussion behind the present
synthesis, while the synthesis completes that volume by placing
the New Testament writings, and the other sources of primitive
Christian history, in their original setting.

Needless to say, a synthesis of this kind can be no more than an
essay, related as closely as possible to the present state of knowledge, but making no pretence to offer a definite solution of all
the problems raised by the birth of the Christian religion;
problems concerning the character of the evangelical writings and
the Epistles attributed to the apostle Paul; problems concerning
the evolution of the religion from its point of departure in Judaism
until the time when the Church, in the last quarter of the second
century, is seen building itself up, in opposition to a flood of
gnostic systems, on the base of a tradition alleged to be apostolic,
of which the New Testament is held to be the witness, and the
episcopate called catholic claims to be the authorized interpreter
or guardian.

The author of this book makes humble avowal of not having
yet discovered that Jesus never existed. The conjectures by which
some among us, in these latter days, would explain the Christian
religion without him whom that religion regards as its founder
have always seemed to him as fragile as they are vociferous. These
conjectures come, for the most part, from persons who have
arrived somewhat late at the problem of Jesus, and not all of
whom have prepared for that problem by deep study of the
history of Israel's religion or of the Christian. For them the non-
existence of Jesus forms part of a philosophical system, except
where it proceeds from polemical interests avowed or discreetly
veiled. Long ago the Christ was discovered by Dupuis to be a
solar myth; Bruno Bauer and the Dutch school (Van Manen
excepted) make him out a pure creation of Alexandrian allego-

rists, in which they are followed by W. B. Smith, Drews and Robertson. In France P. L–Couchoud (*Le mystère de Jésus*) and E. Dujardin (*Le Dieu Jésus*) have each struck out on a line of his own; Couchoud postulating a pre-Christian myth of a suffering Jahveh (!) which a vision of Simon Peter suddenly transformed into a living religion; Dujardin, a pre-Christian worship of Jesus with the fictitious crucifixion of an individual playing the part of a god, the Christian religion having its origin in the last exhibition of this pageant, which also gives the date of its birth.

These hypotheses all share in a common defect: they are air-drawn fabrics and they do not explain the birth of the Christian religion. For the part played by myth in the Christian tradition concerning Jesus is as undeniable as it was inevitable in the origins of the Christian movement; but the witness to the Christian fact does not entirely dissolve into a myth, and the fact itself is not a myth. The messianic myth supports Jesus, but Jesus together with the myth support the Christian religion; the distinctively Christian myth of Jesus–God did not exist before Christianity, but was formed inside that religion, and formed stage by stage, to the glory of Jesus. The Christian myth of salvation was, in a manner, called into being and set on foot by Jesus himself, to be afterwards elaborated in the first age of the Christian religion. The testimony and the facts being what they are, the mythical theory unduly simplifies the problem of Christian origins, which it does more to obscure than to illuminate. In the *Revue Critique*, 1925 (pp. 343–347) the present author wrote as follows: "the part played by myth in the birth of Christianity is more easily determined by the historian than is the part played by Jesus himself. While the Christian religion was not created by myth alone, so, certainly, it was not created by Jesus alone; its creator was neither Jesus without the myth, nor the myth without Jesus. Jesus the Nazorean is at once an historical person and a mythical being who, supporting the myth and supported by it, was finally made by it into the Christ, Lord and God, for the faith which so acknowledged him. To say this is not to reduce the part of Jesus to an occasional cause. On the other hand, to present, as the sole and total cause of Christianity, one human being who, considered as divine, was also the very object worshipped by that religion would only be to create another myth.'»

It is however true that the ancient testimonies do not permit us to reconstitute the human figure of Jesus, his personal doings, the meaning of his career and its chief circumstances, with full and unfaltering certitude.

That Jesus was one among a number of agitators and enthusiasts who appeared in Judea between the years 6 and 70 of our era; that his appearance is to be placed towards the middle of this period or the beginning of its third; that it had, in one form or another, a messianic character; that Jesus was crucified as a pretended Messiah by sentence of Pontius Pilate—all this has the highest degree of probability; to be more exact, the whole Christian movement becomes unintelligible if these beginnings are suppressed. No consistent argument authorizes their elimination and there is nothing to replace them. But what idea had Jesus of his mission, if even he had any precise idea? What did he hope for and aim at? What was his message and on what special charge was he condemmed to death? How were his followers grouped round him and on what grounds did they become convinced after his death that he was still alive, immortal, powerful and glorified at the right hand of God? How was Christ Jesus presently sublimated into Jesus the God-saviour? These are questions which the evidence does not permit us to answer with complete certitude and in detail. And the most brilliant hypotheses brought forward to answer them are not necessarily the best founded.

The Tradition which has preserved for us the memory of Jesus was at its origin entirely different from historical tradition. From the very beginning it was a tradition of *faith*, and almost immediately afterwards the tradition of a *cult* which grew continually more impassioned and developed until it attained complete deification of its object. Memory, in a word, was transfigured into faith and adoration. In all strictness the Gospels are not historical documents. They are catechisms for use in common worship, containing the cult-legend of the Lord Jesus Christ; that, and no other, is the content they announce; that, and no other, is the quality they claim. Even Luke, which assumes a high degree of editorial exactitude, set out to be, before all else, "sound instruction in the Word"—as we should say, "a good manual of Christian initiation" (i, 1–4). Even the teaching attributed to

Jesus is constructed, for the most part, to meet the needs of Christian propaganda, for the edification of the earliest communities, or, yet again, especially in the fourth Gospel, to elaborate a mystical theory of salvation by Jesus Christ. We cannot complacently assume that we are able clearly to recognize, behind all these elaborations of faith, the real features of Jesus, his personal activities and the precise circumstances of his ministry and death. What the historian sees directly before him in all this is the faith of the first Christian generations and the intensity of their devotion to Jesus, the Saviour.

There is nothing to make good this insufficiency of the Gospel evidence. The Acts of the Apostles, supposed to narrate the history of the first Christian age, contain the legend and, in some respects, the myth rather than the history of it, insomuch that the general perspective of the book is, in its own way, as artificial as that of the Gospels, if not more so. The Epistles known as apostolic have been edited in the same spirit as the Gospels and with likelihood hardly greater of being the work of the authors to whom they are attributed. Little by little it has perforce been admitted that the Gospels are not the personal works of individual writers, and that the traditional attribution of these books to apostles or to apostolic men is contestable in every instance. It has also at length been recognized that a false authorship has been attributed to several Epistles and that their date is uncertain: cases in point are Hebrews, Ephesians, second Thessalonians and the Epistles known as catholic. Furthermore it has become impossible not to recognize traces of compilation in the two Epistles to the Corinthians, and the conclusion has followed that they were composed by amalgamating matter drawn from a much larger number of authentic letters. Even bolder conjectures, not only for the two Epistles in question, but for Romans, first Thessalonians and perhaps others, might be reasonably defended. The obvious doctrinal incoherence between the Epistles, and often in the same Epistle, would thus find a better explanation than that afforded by the restlessness of mind with a superabundant endowment of which the Apostle is usually credited. Thus the question arises of whether the theories of redemption brought forward in the Epistles called Pauline are really those of the Apostle. Or do they represent flights of gnostic speculation later than Paul but earlier than the chief systems of heretical gnosticism?

In the next chapter we shall see how limited are the resources which other Christian documents anterior to the year 180 offer to the critical historian. We feel therefore entitled to remark, in terminating this preamble, that while every history of Christian origins rests, admittedly or not, on more or less shaky foundations, the fault is not necessarily attributable to the historian who tries to write that history, but to the condition of the evidence on which he has to base it. For that reason we here make no pretence to give a finished and balanced picture of the birth of the Christian religion. Our aim will be to show forth with simplicity what seem the most probable conclusions in this delicate matter, as they offer and prove themselves to our own mind.

CONTENTS

Chapter I

THE SOURCES

ALL indications point to the conclusion that the Christian religion, though an offspring of Judaism, did not issue from any of the great currents then dominant in Jewish thought and known under the name of Pharisee, Sadducee and Essene. It sprang from small eccentric circles and stood out so little in the history of Palestinian Judaism before the year 70 that Josephus thought himself dispensed from mentioning it in his writings.[1] Christianity was not a contagious movement of organized asceticism, still less a form of legalist pietism and least of all a school of traditional conservatism. It was distinctly a Messianist movement, carried on in conditions peculiar to itself and without the sanguinary fanaticism of the Zealots. It invoked as its head a Christ who, after dying on earth, was living at the right hand of God; his return would proceed from the higher world, that is, from his own being and nature, and in this sense it soon became a salvation-mystery of which the Christ was life and soul, the coming of this Christ progressively shifting its position to a new point and becoming realized, so to speak, in the faith of his Church. A mystery of this nature could not fail to get defined in a theology. In the beginning, however, Christianity was a religion of humble folk. Men of learning, dogmatizing theologians, contemplative dreamers were not its originators.

The Christian religion was not founded on doctrine formulated in a book. It formed its own doctrine as it grew, and the books distinctively its own, known among us as the literature of primitive Christianity, are the products and the historic witnesses of its doctrinal elaboration as this was achieved during the first hundred or hundred and fifty years in the life of the new religion. It may be said with confidence that Christianity, at its point of departure, had no other literature than that of the Judaism from which it sprang. This literature it began to interpret in a manner all its own, with reference to its Christ and in the interests of Christian propaganda, while reserving till later the creation of its own literature in answer to the needs which arose in the course of

17

its experience. This specifically Christian literature is the principal and almost the only source at our disposal for understanding Christianity in the first age of its evolution. The direct evidence of Jewish writers is relatively late, scanty, of mediocre scope and value, while that of pagan writers concerns only the outside of Christian propaganda and informs us chiefly of the impression it made on the "enlightened" opinion of that age.

In a sense very true, the history of primitive Christianity is a kind of pre-history which has to be reconstructed—one might almost say to be guessed—from documents which reflect it but were not originally conceived, nor later edited, for the purpose of putting it on record. The labours of criticism are therefore indispensable, and so much the more in need of cautious handling as the scientific examination of these documents is far from having spoken its last word.

From about the year 180 onwards the history of the Christian religion is no longer beset by great obscurity. With the writings before us of Irenaeus, Tertullian, Clement of Alexandria and Hippolytus we have enough daylight to make visible the interior organization, the exterior relations and the characteristic doctrines of the new religion. As for the earlier period, we are bound to admit that information is far from complete, indeed almost fragmentary, and too often untrustworthy and difficult to interpret. The present chapter will offer a kind of inventory of the documents in question. The chapters to follow will unfold the meaning we find in them for reconstructing the history of the Christian religion in the earliest period of its life.

1. The New Testament

To the books comprised in what is known as the New Testament, which forms a pendant to the collection of the Old, inherited from the Synagogue and from hellenizing Judaism, tradition assigns a place of their own as books divinely authorized and the work of apostles. In reality the apostolic elements in these books are not very numerous. They were canonized by and for their employment in the Christian communities for public reading in preference to others of similar character which the Church thought well, as occasion called for it, to set aside or to condemn. We may recall that the collection of the Old Testament was also fixed in Jewish tradition, derived from synagogal usage, to the depreciation of a literature, apocalyptic or otherwise, and partly more recent, of which the disqualification was judged desirable. In both cases, Old and New, the authenticity of the canonized writings, relative to those excluded from the canon, is artificial and based on theological convention; in both cases the authorship of books is falsely assigned, or partly falsified, for the purpose of guaranteeing the exceptional credit claimed for all parts alike of a collection of books thenceforth to be regarded as sacred.

Although the writings comprised in the New Testament constitute our chief source for the history of primitive Christianity, they carry no privilege in the eyes of the scientific historian, save what may be derived from their relative value as evidence, when compared with non-canonical writings. All the documents of ancient Christianity, canonical and non-canonical, will be classed in this chapter according to their kind, though not according to their literary kind precisely, since the greater number do not fall into any of the accepted classes of literature. We shall deal first with those documents which affect, more or less distinctly, the form of epistles; second, with those in the form of apocalypse; third, with those, known as Gospels, which present the sacred legend of Jesus and the apostles; fourth and last, with the sharply defined group of second century apologists. Had the writings of the second century gnostics come down to us, them also we should have to consider; but little more is known of them than what can be gathered from ecclesiastical authors who placed these writings on their list of heresies or laboured to refute them.

Pauline Epistles

Fourteen Epistles appear in the New Testament under the name of Paul. Few critics have had the hardihood to class them all as literary forgeries, and those who have done so, Bruno Bauer and the Dutch school of Van Manen, seem to have taken insufficient account of the great variety of elements which have found their way into the two Epistles to the Corinthians and the Epistle to the Romans.

To begin with, the Epistle to the Hebrews stands apart as one whose origin was matter of debate in the ancient Church. The Roman Church, while not ignoring it, long refused to recognize it as Paul's and attributed to him thirteen Epistles only. The heretic Marcion (140–150) knew, or recognized, only ten, not knowing, or rejecting, the two Epistles to Timothy and the Epistle to Titus; he accepted the so-called Epistle to the Ephesians under the name of the Epistle to the Laodiceans, a name he can have had no reason to invent. This, however, does not prove the complete authenticity of the ten. That Marcion put much of his own into them is neither proved nor even probable; he did not force his system into them any more than he put it into his Gospel; contenting himself with cutting down or retouching in the Gospel of Luke whatever was in conflict with his system, he would do the same in the Epistles with passages that displeased him. The fact remains that the ten, the thirteen, or the fourteen, whatever their connexion with Paul, were not preserved for themselves as epistles, but as providing catechetical matter and passages to be read in public for the instruction and edifying of congregations. If some of them are fictitious, as seems certain, it cannot be *a priori* improbable that compilations like the Epistles to the Romans and the Corinthians contain considerable additions to their authentic elements.

Thessalonians

The First to the Thessalonians, if authentic, as it seems to be, would date from the year 51, the oldest document of Christian literature to which an approximate date can be assigned. It is not free from editorial surcharges[2] and the long passage on the ressurrection (iv, 13–v, 11) must be a late insertion.[3]

Imitated from the First Epistle and specially co-ordinated with the insertion on the resurrection of the dead, the Second to Thessalonians is, for the most part, a theological dissertation on the conditions of the Second Advent. It is not written for the instruction of a particular community but aims rather to dissipate the general uneasiness of Christian thought in regard to the Parousia, impatiently expected and continually postponed. The author enlarges on the apocalyptic theme of the Antichrist,

perhaps identified with Nero risen from the dead, whose manifestation was to cause the ruin of the Roman Empire. The
document is conceived in the spirit of the synoptic Gospels and
is probably not earlier than the first quarter of the second century.
Since Marcion accepted it as authentic, we can hardly place it
as late as 130–135. The pains taken by the author at the end
(iii, 17) to declare his signature genuine render it the more
suspect.

Corinthians

The two Epistles contain elements bearing on the relations
of Paul with the community of Corinth, during the years 50–56
approximately, which cannot be explained on any other hypothesis than that of their authenticity. But the two Epistles in
their traditional form are not pieces of written correspondence.
They are two discourses made up of letters and instructions of
various kinds at a date considerably later than the years in which
epistolary relations existed between Paul and his Corinthian
converts.

We gather from the first Epistle that Paul, while at Ephesus
in 54 or 55, wrote to these converts with the aim of healing
divisions of whose existence in the community he had been
informed (i, 1–16);4 the final recommendations (xvi) are co-
ordinated with this opening and the interval between them
filled with ill-assorted matter of various kinds. We begin with
an eloquent outburst on the mystery of the Cross, hidden from
the heavenly powers appointed to govern the world, who
crucified the Lord in their ignorance (i, 17–ii, 8);5 of this mystery,
Paul, taught by the Spirit, is the herald (ii, 10–16); if he has not
spoken to the Corinthians as spiritual, that is because they are
carnal, as they are proved to be by their quarrels (iii, 1–4);
following this, a sublime conception of the apostolate and the
consideration of Paul's unique relation to the Corinthians. All
of which is pitched on so high a level that we cannot but ask
whether the point of view may not be that of polemical theory
rather than that of the modest reality. To the latter belongs
what we go on to read about Timothy's preliminary errand, of
Paul's impending visit to Corinth and the incestuous man whose
excommunication he decrees. Moral lessons come next, grouped

by a certain analogy of subject, but without real cohesion. Then follow a mystic couplet about the old leaven, the Christian azyme and Christ the pascal victim of the faithful (v, 6–8); a remark on keeping bad company awkwardly adjusted to what has been said about the incestuous man, which again is disastrously cut up and surcharged in a passage against lawsuits between believers; and then a moral lesson against impurity (vi, 12–20). From this point the document before us ceases to be a letter and becomes an assemblage of miscellaneous instructions: further rules of discipline later in origin than the beginning of apostolic preaching; rules on marriage and virginity (vii);[6] on the eating of meat that comes from pagan sacrifices, the passage cut in two by an editor (viii; x, 23–xi, i)[7] and doubled by mystic instruction on the same subject (x, 1–22) which contradicts the disciplinary rule first given; in the space between, an apology, mainly retrospective, for the action Paul has taken to avoid being a charge to his converts, especially to the Corinthians (ix);[8] further on (xi, 3–16) two rulings on the holding of assemblies; the first, enjoining the women to keep veiled when they prophesy in course of the meeting, inserted into the framework of the second which has to do with the good order and especially the high signification of the Eucharist (xi, 2, 17–34);[9] another instruction on spiritual gifts divided into two parts, the theory of the *charismata*, their rôle in the life of the community, and rules for speaking with tongues and prophesying in the assembly of the faithful (xii, xiv),[10] with the Song of Love (xiii, 1–12) intercalated between the two parts and coming in as a corrective to the foregoing decree;[11] followed up by a dissertation on the bodily resurrection of the Christ, type of a general resurrection of the dead and especially of believers (xv), in which there is revealed a certain development of the evangelical tradition and of the Christian gnosis. The conclusion of the original letter (xvi) then follows without further preparation.

The Second to the Corinthians was written from Macedonia in the autumn of the year 55; but this Epistle, though less complicated than the first by editorial treatment, also contains elements of various date and origin. The opening (i–ii, 13) appears to belong to a letter of reconciliation or of consolation written by Paul after experiencing a great affliction while in Asia, from which he had been delivered by the good news that Titus had brought him of better conditions in Corinth. The affliction in question was less probably persecution undergone at Ephesus than the anguish of mind into which Paul had fallen after making a visit to Corinth, which had rather aggravated the difficulties between him and the community, difficulties which the intervention of Titus had subsequently smoothed over. But even in this part of the letter certain additions tinged with mystical gnosis may have been made (i, 3–7; 12–14, 21, 22). Suddenly the flow of the original is arrested to make room for a long dithyramb in praise of the true apostleship which belongs solely to Paul, herald of the new convenant in the spirit, triumphant in weakness and suffering while waiting for eternal glory, knowing no man after the flesh, not even Christ, and announcing with unwearied zeal the message of the reconciliation of the world to God by faith in Christ risen from the dead; at this point he beseeches the Corinthians to be faithful to the grace of God and to enlarge their heart towards him, now straitened on his account (ii, 14–vi, 13). Then comes a new insertion into the flow of this fine utterance, which resumes its course a little later on (vii, 2–3) but only to lose itself immediately in a forced transition to the letter of reconciliation (vii, 4). The inserted passage is an instruction about keeping company with pagans (vi, 14–vii, 1) which connects with nothing in the Second to the Corinthians and must be a quotation from elsewhere. What follows (vii, 5–16) concerns the happy issue of the mission to the Corinthians undertaken by Titus: it forms the original conclusion of the letter. The two pieces about the collection for the saints in Jerusalem (viii, ix) hang loose from the context and cannot have been written at the same time; the older of the two (ix) has been placed second by the compiler.[12] The greater part of the last chapter is conceived in the same spirit and tone as the earlier eulogium of Paul's apostleship, except for several passages of a distinctly personal character which seem to come from the severe letter, written after Paul's second stay in Corinth, to which the letter of reconciliation makes allusion (vii, 8). The most important of these personal passages is a fighting apology against "the very chiefest of the apostles" (xi, 5)[13]—who are the elder apostles of Jerusalem and not any kind of missionaries—

to whom Paul boasts of being inferior in nothing. Here is another insertion about the disinterested conditions of Paul's Corinthian mission (xi, 6b–12a).[14] Whereupon the denunciation of the super-apostles is resumed with increased vigour, Paul sounding his own praises in abundance by recalling his labours and tribulations, nay even his visions, especially the most important which carried him up to the third heaven;[15] "a thorn in the flesh" warns him not to be overproud; but for all that he will yield in nothing to the highest of them; and his apostleship has been made plain by many a prodigy. Then, suddenly, the tone changes and the question turns to the disinterestedness Paul has shown among the Corinthians; he will not change that attitude; if he now seems to be defending himself that is because he is on the point of coming to Corinth for the third time and is unwilling to find himself in the midst of their quarrels and disorders; let them mend their ways that he may not have to employ severity. But the grandiloquent apology preceding, which shows a very precise knowledge of Paul's career, would perhaps be better understood as coming from a distance in time and from the pen of an empassioned disciple. It flows in the same current of thought and style as the praise of the apostolate in the first part of the Epistle.

Galatians

There is a question whether this Epistle, written towards the end of the year 55, before the Second to the Corinthians and the Epistle to the Romans, was addressed to the communities of Pisidia and Lycaonia[16] or rather to those of Galatia proper. Perhaps it concerned all of them. But the capital question is that of its authenticity. Paul would seem to have written to justify his apostleship against Judaizing propaganda which was meeting with success in the communities. Fundamentally, the issue concerned a matter quite other than the uselessness of the Jewish observances. Paul presents himself as an apostle sent direct from God and from Christ the redeemer (i, 1–7) and anathematizes those who would turn the Galatians from the true Gospel (i, 5–9); describes the conditions in which the revelation of this Gospel was directly imparted to him (i, 10–12); how he fulfilled his vocation of apostle to the Gentiles up to the moment when he got his doctrine and practice recognized by the Jerusalem apostles and the admission made that he was to preach to the Gentiles while the other apostles occupied themselves with the Jews; which form of the compact Peter is said to have broken at Antioch (i, 13–ii, 14).[17] But the rebuke which Paul boasts of having administered to Peter face to face is lost sight of in a formal announcement of the thesis of salvation by faith in the Christ without the works of the law (ii, 15–20). To the demonstration of this thesis by diverse arguments, all inspired by the mystic gnosis already met in certain parts of Corinthians and methodically developed in Romans, the rest of the Epistle is thenceforward devoted. Entangled with these arguments are speculations about the faith of Abraham, type of the justified man, who received the saving benediction due to faith on behalf of all believers, Jews and Gentiles (iv, 21–31). Throughout all this there is only one small fragment that bears a genuinely personal accent (iv, 11–20), where Paul describes his present anxiety and the special circumstances in which he had preached the Gospel to the Galatians. The moral counsels of the last two chapters are, for the most part, in the customary vein of mystical gnosis.[18] It is in conformity with this gnosis that the origin of Paul's career is here interpreted, a mode of interpretation under which his conversion and apostolic activity become almost unintelligible to the historian, and the authenticity of the Epistle, taken as a whole, is gravely compromised. There cannot be a doubt that Paul, in becoming converted, adhered to a gospel preached before he took it up. As a matter of fact the conversion of Paul was not the absolute beginning of hellenic Christianity, and the division of the world to be converted, Jews to Peter and Gentiles to Paul, was not realized. Whence we may infer that the division was never agreed on.

Romans

The document called the Epistle to the Romans, so far as it comes from Paul's hand, probably dates from the year 56, having been written at Corinth a little before Paul left that city to carry to Jerusalem the collection made in the communities. Whatever value we may assign to it, the Epistle, like the two to the Corinthians, is a compilation. In the preamble (i, 1–17) Paul announces an explanatory apology for his ministry to pagans. Connected with this explanation is the discussion of Abraham's righteousness realized in his faith (iii, 28-iv), a line of thought already encountered in Galatians, and here completed by the discussion of prophetical texts which the author interprets as foretelling the conversion of the Gentiles and the reprobation, at least temporary, of the Jews. The passages at the end of the Gospel, describing the projects of Paul (xv, 8–38), are equally authentic.[19] But the theory of sin and grace, of salvation by the death of Christ, which is expounded at great length (v–viii) is clearly detached from these passages, has a style peculiar to itself and makes no attempt to support the argument in detail by scriptural texts.[20] On the other hand, certain developments[21] seem to have been inserted to soften the rigour of this theory (i, 18–iii, 20) and to prevent its abuse in practice by conclusions that might be drawn from it. The moral part of the Epistle must in like manner be secondary, since it was not for Paul to offer such lessons to a community of which he had no personal knowledge; these lessons moreover were not all inserted at the same time (xii–xv, 7).[22] The formulas of conclusion, which multiply towards the end (xv, 13, 33; xvi, 16, 25), bear witness to surcharges and retouchings.

Colossians, Ephesians and Philippians

The Epistles to the Colossians and Philippians, which some critics would attach to a hypothetical captivity at Ephesus, seem rather to have been written while Paul was a prisoner in Rome between 59 and 61. But the authenticity of Colossians is contestable. In it there is developed a mystical gnosis in affinity with that in Romans, though sensibly different in its formulas,[23] and akin to the Epistle to the Hebrews (cf. Hebrews i, 1–4). This gnosis has the appearance of being affirmed in opposition to another of Judaizing tendency which may possibly be the cult of Zeus Sabazios (ii, 16–23). Certain incoherences in the editing of the Epistle lead us to think that a document of Christian gnosis was attributed to Paul, as an afterthought, by means of the additions concerning his captivity, an authentic letter being utilized at the end for establishing a close relation between the Epistle to the Colossians and that to Philemon, as we now have them (iv, 7–11, 14). The authenticity of the latter, as a whole, presents no great difficulty. But the Epistle to the Colossians should rather be referred to the beginning of the second century.

The Epistle to the Ephesians figures in Marcion's collection as the Epistle to the Laodiceans. Imitated, though in a manner more servile, from the Epistle to the Colossians, as the Second to Thessalonians was imitated from the First, it was probably presented originally as the letter to the Laodiceans mentioned in Colossians (iv, 16).[24] The style of this spurious Epistle is turbid and obscure. As to the foundation of it, the author replaces the cosmological and soteriological gnosis of Colossians by a gnosis which might be called mainly ecclesiological, integrating the myth of salvation by the Christ into his own myth of the Church. Since it was known to Marcion the composition goes back to the first third of the second century.[25]

Though of mediocre compass, the Epistle to the Philippians has the appearance of being a compilation of two letters. Towards the middle we find a clean cut, following on a vehement outburst against Judaism which recalls the fiery apology of Paul in Second Corinthians (iii, 1–iv, 1, 8–9). Moreover in the first part of the Epistle (ii, 25–30) we read that Epaphroditus, Paul's messenger to the Philippians, has just left the Apostle after being long at his side, while in the second part (iv, 18) we are told that this same Epaphroditus is just come to him, bringing the help for which Paul thanks the Philippians. Plain proof that the Epistle is a compilation made up of two short letters placed in inverted order, the first belonging approximately to 59, the second to 60. To the two letters thus brought together were added, about the beginning of the second century, certain elements of Christian gnosis and anti-Jewish polemic.[26]

Pastoral Epistles

The term "pastoral" is commonly applied to the two Epistles to Timothy and the Epistle to Titus on the ground that they are chiefly concerned with the institution of pastors and with church discipline. Conceived with the purpose of checking the growth of gnosticism, they are much later than the apostolic age. It may well be that these apocryphal compositions were not divulged in the communities till after the explosion of Marcion's heresy: Timothy vi, 20 seems aimed directly at his *Antitheses*. As to their place of origin, the Roman souvenirs apparently contained in the Second to Timothy are not decisive for preferring Rome to the East. The hypothesis of short authentic letters embedded in a later commentary applies only to the Second (iv, 10–20) and is not exempt from question. Moreover the First does not seem to have been written continuously.[27] It is possible that a body of rules claiming to be apostolic has been drawn upon by the editor of our two Epistles, which probably have a common origin.

Hebrews

The Epistle "to the Hebrews" known in Rome at an early date, is earlier than the Epistle of Clement to the Corinthians which stands to it in a relation of dependence.[28] The attribution of the authorship to Paul, long unknown at Rome, seems to have been first made in Alexandria. Keeping the date commonly assigned to the letter of Clement (about 95) the Epistle to the Hebrews could not be later than 80. If the dates be postponed to the second century it would have to be admitted that the last two verses (xiii, 23–25) are a fictitious addition intended to support the attribution of the Epistle to Paul. In the same way the title "to the Hebrews" is no more than an ancient conjecture, perhaps originally connected with the said attribution. The attribution of authorship to Barnabas professed by Tertullian (*De Pudicitia*, 20), and perhaps current at Rome in his time, cannot be sustained, since the author places himself outside the apostolic age (ii, 3, 4).[29] A treatise rather than a letter, consisting of doctrinal and moral instruction, the document is addressed to a community of converted pagans nourished on the Old Testament as the only authorized scripture.[30] But the display of quotations serves only to support a Christian gnosis of salvation by the mediation of Christ, unique priest and victim, distinguished in express terms from the elementary catechesis in which the common teaching of Christianity was summed up (vi, 1–2). The conclusions which the author draws from the

Mosaic ritual are derived from texts, not from observances then flourishing, while the moral teaching is addressed to believers already tried by persecution and liable to lose their confidence in the mystery of salvation here presented as the true fulfilment of Jewish scripture. Earlier than the explosion of the gnostic crisis and the canonization of the Gospel, the Epistle is probably of Alexandrian origin.

Incidentally, this Epistle affords a striking example of the freedom with which primitive gnosis developed the conception of the Christ, and of its independence of what is commonly called the Gospel tradition. We find it especially in the parallel instituted in chapter vii between Melchisedec and Jesus, in which the Christ, without father or mother, without beginning or end of life in this world, "rose up," like a star—allusion to the star of Numbers xxiv, 17—"from Judah," whose descendant he certainly was not in the Gospel tradition.

Peter and Jude

The first of the Epistles named after Peter would be placed under the patronage of that apostle at a time when he had become recognized as the founder of the Roman community: it is a catechism or homily in which baptism is made much of, but with a theme of wider range than baptismal instruction. Rome is here spoken of under its mystic name of Babylon (v, 13) and perhaps the mention of Mark (v, 13) is intended to promote his claim to the authorship of the second Gospel. But this writing contains little sign of influence by Gospel tradition, the sole feature, on which the writer insists complacently, as though it were well known, being the descent of the Christ into hell (iii, 19–20; iv, 6), a feature hardly hinted at in the canonical Gospels. The document is almost contemporary with the Epistle to the Hebrews, but of Roman origin, at least in its canonical edition.

The second Epistle attributed to the same apostle is perceptibly of a later date. The central part of it (ii, iii) which corresponds with the Epistle of Jude, is an attack on the gnostic movement then in full life and vigour. In the preamble[31] it refers not, as commonly supposed, to the Gospel story of transfiguration, but to the Apocalypse of Peter—which we shall discuss later on. In the conclusion (iii, 15, 16) it mentions a collection of Paul's Epistles of which certain heretics are making abusive employment; this doubtless is the collection of the ten Epistles known to Marcion. The Epistle therefore must be later than the birth of Marcionism and was most probably composed in the East, about 150 at the earliest.

Apart from its superscription (1–2) and doxology (24–25), the Epistle named after Jude embodies, in a form at least relatively primitive, the anti-gnostic writing, or fragment, which is paraphrased in Second Peter. The original writing may be dated as far on as about 130, and its working up into an Epistle to 150. The relative antiquity of this composition appears in the quotations from the Apocrypha, Enoch and the Assumption of Moses (14, 15 and 9), which Second Peter has not retained.

James

The so-called Epistle of James is a piece of simple moral instruction drawing its inspiration from a catechism rather Jewish than Christian. It makes a lively attack on the idea of faith without works which suggests that its editing took place before the time when the four Gospels, and the writings attributed to Paul, were advanced to canonical authority, that is, before 150.[32] The fictitious address to the Twelve Tribes, which transforms a collection of moral maxims into an Epistle, is symbolic, like that of 1 Peter to the "dispersed" Jews of Asia Minor. A certain affinity in tone with the Pastor of Hermas suggests that its place of origin was Rome.

John

Of the three Epistles attributed to the apostle John, the first, like the Epistle to the Hebrews, does not affect the form of a letter. It consists of instruction, dogmatic and moral, perhaps originally founded on a rhythmical discourse like those found in the Fourth Gospel. The successive editions of the Epistle seem to have been co-ordinate with those of the Gospel itself; whence it would follow that the last edition, directed against gnosticism, cannot be earlier than the middle of the second century.33 This would also be the date of the two smaller Epistles, which have only the appearance of letters, the designation of the author being deliberately vague, as well as that of the recipients. The two were intended to act as convoy to the first in its final form, the second condemning the Docetic Christology, perhaps especially that of Marcion, while the third blasts those leaders of the community who oppose the Johannine writings. All three Epistles, like the fourth Gospel, were worked into their present form in Ephesian surroundings.

Barnabas

The Epistle "of Barnabas,"' also anonymous in itself, presents a certain analogy to the Epistle to the Hebrews, and must belong to nearly the same period, to a time, that is, when the Gospel legend was in process of formation.34 The Epistle of Barnabas has no dependence on any of the canonical Epistles. In the moral part it reproduces instruction about the "two ways," the way of light and the way of darkness, a kind of Jewish catechism also made use of in the *Didache*. It was probably composed, therefore, at Alexandria in the first third of the second century.

Clement

Addressed in the name of "the community of God living in Rome to the community of God living in Corinth," the Epistle attributed to Clement is a long piece of moral teaching composed on the occasion of troubles which had broken out in the Corinthian community and intended for their remedy. The document itself is one of the most authentic, but the date commonly assigned to it, about 95, seems open to question. Although it quotes the First to the Corinthians it is more indebted for its Christology to the Epistle to Hebrews than to Paul. It speaks of Peter and Paul as founders of the Roman Church, but seemingly more on the strength of the legend to that effect than of recent memories,35 and conceives the organization of the communities after the pattern common to the Pastoral Epistles. An elder of the Roman community writing in 95, only some thirty years after the persecution of Nero, could hardly have said that the disciples of Christ set out to preach everywhere immediately after the resurrection, instituting bishops and deacons and even laying down rules for their succession and life-long tenure of office. The indications rather are that the author of the letter is the Clement mentioned by Hermas and that he wrote towards 130–135.

Of different origin and less ancient date is the homily named in tradition as the second Epistle of Clement. This composition presupposes a great development of the Gospel literature; some of its quotations appear to come from the so-called Gospel of the Egyptians. In all probability the homily is of Alexandrian origin and belongs to the second half, if not to the end, of the second century.

Ignatius and Polycarp

The authenticity of the letters attributed to Ignatius of Antioch martyred under Trajan (98–117), was at one time strongly denied, then recognized, but has recently become the object of a new attack. The fact is that these letters lose their historical background if placed in the time of Trajan, since the seven in question inculcate a system of belief and discipline which correspond to the conditions of the later period when the gnostic crisis was at its height. Moreover the Epistle of Polycarp to the Philippians seems to have been interpolated into the collection of the Ignatian letters, by their author or editor, for the purpose of recommending them; this alone would seem to prove them apocryphal and later, at least in publication, than the death of Polycarp. Irenaeus quotes the Ignatian letter to the Romans, which we must suppose in existence about 170, but without naming the author whom he seems not to know as a quasi-apostolic person connected with Polycarp. Neither can Polycarp's Epistle, when freed from its artificial attachment to the Ignatian letters, be dated in the reign of Trajan; it belongs to the last years of its author's life.[36] In this way we can explain this author's apparent knowledge of the collection of the thirteen Epistles of Paul, the Acts of the Apostles, First Peter, the synoptic tradition of Jesus' discourses, the Epistles of John and his reproval, without theological reasoning, of Marcion's Docetic gnosis by utilizing 1 John iv, 2–3. The Johannine writings, whose existence we find him attesting, have but a very slight influence on his thought and style, which would be extremely surprising if the fourth Gospel were the work of an apostle or of an apostolic person of whom Polycarp himself is said to have been the disciple.

The Didache

Here it will be in place to call attention to the type of catechesis which has come down to us under the name of *Doctrine* (*Didache*) *of the Twelve Apostles*, a work of moral and disciplinary instruction highly esteemed in the first Christian age, which seems to have been composed in Syria or in Egypt at the beginning of the second century. As already pointed out, the moral part reproduces a body of Jewish teaching on "the two ways," eternal life and eternal death, intermingled with Gospel sentences corresponding to the tradition in Matthew. The second part has to do with baptism and the communion, the good order of assemblies and the choice of ministers, overseers (bishops) and deacons. The baptismal formula and the Lord's Prayer are identical with the canonical text of Matthew (vii, 1; viii, 2). In the ordering of the communion the prophets have liberty to render thanks in their own terms (10), as an exercise outside the indicated formulas. From this we are led to assign a rather early date to the rule, seeing that, in the time of Justin, the Supper has a president who alone may pronounce the eucharistic prayers. The prayers of the *Didache*, moreover, do not give the impression that the Supper, as understood by the author, is the mystic commemoration of the death of Christ indicated in First Corinthians and in the Gospels.

2. THE CHRISTIAN APOCALYPSE

The imminent return of Christ Jesus to the earth had been proclaimed for many years before the story was told, in oral preaching and in evangelical writings, of what in detail Jesus had done, taught and suffered before ascending into heaven to prepare the day of God. The Gospel was the announcement of this coming Day before it became an account of the Christ's teaching and of his saving death. For that reason the documents

33

of Christian apocalyptic will here be considered before we come to those of the literature known as "the Gospels."

Reference has already been made to the more or less considerable elements of apocalyptic to be found in the epistolary, or rather catechical, literature we have just been considering, such as chapter xv of First Corinthians, the dissertation on the resurrection of the dead included in First Thessalonians (iv, 13–v, 11), and the central passage in Second (ii, 1–12). The *Didache*, the Doctrine of the Twelve Apostles, while containing no summary of the Gospel story, terminates in a short apocalypse closely related to the discourse on the end of the world common to the three Synoptics (16). And this discourse is itself the Christian adaptation of a Jewish apocalypse contemporary with the siege of Jerusalem by Titus. All that Christian apologetic did was to co-ordinate and interpret the elements of the Jewish apocalypse in application to the second coming of Jesus, impatiently expected and always postponed, and this it did not only with the apocalypse current before the preaching of the Gospel but with that of later date, which uttered its last cries of anguish and hope amid the death throes of nationalist Judaism.[37]

Thus it was that apocalyptic found its way into the Gospel tradition, which originally had no more of it than is contained in its general idea of the speedy coming of the Reign of God. But the Great Coming seeming ever to be further off, the delay was explained as a providential ordering of events prophesied as due to happen first. Jewish eschatology and Jewish apocalyptic contained a rich mine of allusions, no better understood, and of predictions not yet fulfilled. All this was now regarded as due to happen before the Day of God and his Christ, "the sorrows" naturally preceding the "coming." The synoptic apocalypse accordingly marks out three stages, the beginning of the sorrows, the climax of the sorrows, and then the "end." They are expressly distinguished in Mark xiii, 8, 14, 24.

The Apocalypse of John has the appearance of a methodical exposition of Jewish hopes interpreted in a Christian sense, and is conceived on the model of the Jewish apocalypses then current, which in turn professed to interpret ancient prophecies. In its groundwork the Johannine Apocalypse would seem to be a compilation, but there is an almost mathematical regularity in its logical structure and literary arrangement. The traditional date of it is probably correct; it saw the light among the communities of Asia to which it was originally addressed, most likely at Ephesus towards the end of the first Christian century. The author was probably a Jewish Christian who had fled from Palestine during the Jewish war; certainly not the apostle John; nor can he have been "John the elder" known to Papias as a witness to the Gospel tradition. To that tradition the Apocalypse pays scant attention, knowing only that Christ, as the first to be raised up, is "the first-born of the dead" (i, 5, 18); incidentally it mentions that he was crucified at Jerusalem (xi, 8). Some time must have elapsed between the publication of the Apocalypse in the Asiatic communities by the act of the prophet himself and what may be called the final edition of it for general circulation throughout all the communities as an apostolic work by the same author as the fourth Gospel and the three Epistles. This identification and the constitution of the Johannine collection of books took place towards the middle of the second century.

The Apocalypse of Peter and the Pastor of Hermas are also books of Christian prophecy, which failed however to get admission into the collection of the New Testament. But mention must first be made of other writings more closely related to the Johannine Apocalypse. These are the Christian parts of the Ascension of Isaiah, the Christian oracles annexed to the Jewish Apocalypse called the Fourth Book of Esdras and the Christian elements in the Sibylline Books.

In the Ascension of Isaiah we can recognize three writings originally distinct, of which the oldest is the Jewish legend of the prophet's martyrdom under Manasseh. The other two are Christian. The longer of these is an ecstatic vision of the Ascension of Isaiah to the seventh heaven in which he sees God and the Christ, "the Lord of all Glory," and hears the Most High dictate to the Christ the programme of his earthly manifestation and of his return.[38] The third piece, inserted into the legend of martyrdom, is a vision concerning the coming of Christ and of Antichrist, in which the resurrection of Jesus is described as in the Gospel of Peter and allusion made to Peter's martyrdom in the persecution by Nero, who is Antichrist. The two Christian fragments are relatively old, probably of the second century, the part attributed by both to the earthly life of Jesus being in harmony with the development of the Gospel literature. The author of the Ascension, who knew the substance of Matthew's Gospel, may have been a Syrian and must have written between 130 and 150: the author of the other fragment is more recent and, in virtue of its almost certain dependence on the Gospel of Peter, cannot have been written before 170–175.

Almost of the same date is the fragment of apocalypse represented by the first two chapters of the Fourth Book of Esdras in editions of the Latin Bible, a self-contained prophecy originally in Greek, but, like the book of Hermas, composed in the West when Greek was still the liturgical and literary language of the Christian communities. It consists of an indictment of the Jews and a vision of the eternal Jerusalem. The prophecy contained in the last two chapters of the same Book of Esdras is more recent and may have been originally conceived as an appendix to the book to which we find it annexed. It contains an exhortation to persecuted Christians which tells us almost nothing about the evolution of apocalyptic beliefs in the early Christian age.

The third of the Sibylline Books contains a Christian interpolation set in a Jewish context. In this interpolation Beliar, or Satan-Antichrist, appears to be identified with Simon Magus. The eighth book, wholly Christian, was composed in the last years of Marcus Aurelius; like the Johannine Apocalypse, it centres round the Antichrist Nero. The Jewish Sibyl, in the fourth of the Books, written shortly after the eruption of Vesuvius in 79, exhibits Nero, "the fugitive from Rome," crossing the Euphrates with a great army and goes on to speak of him in the fifth book. But in that book Nero is introduced as still a living man and in hiding among Parthians, whereas, in the Christian apocalyptic, Nero, still supported by the Parthians, and in the character of Antichrist, appears as a ghost or as risen from the dead.

Less ancient than these, the Apocalypse of Peter is also less preoccupied with revelation about the end of the world, and seems to aim rather at instructing believers as to the respective fates that will fall after the judgment on the wicked and on the righteous. In its treatment of that topic it comes near not only to the Ascension of Isaiah and the first two chapters of Fourth Esdras but also to the Egyptian mysteries and to the Orphic tradition. It is connected with the Gospel of Peter by the place it assigns to the cross in the second coming of the Lord. (In the Gospel the cross comes forth from the tomb behind the Christ as he rises from the dead; in the Apocalypse Jesus says that the cross will go before him when he comes in his glory.) In the Second Epistle of Peter formal reference is made to the Apocalypse in the opening chapter. It is therefore earlier than 150, and perhaps was written about 135. A Greek fragment of the apocalypse, with a passage from Enoch and a part of the Gospel of Peter, was found at Akhmim in Egypt, while the whole text, perhaps a little touched up and interpolated, has been preserved in an Ethiopian version.[39]

The scene depicted in this apocalypse presents the critic of the New Testament with a problem that demands the most careful handling. Jesus, having risen from the dead, is on the Mount of Olives with his disciples who question him about his second coming and the end of the world; Jesus answers by a short discourse which corresponds to the synoptic apocalypse, especially to Luke xvii, 20–27, and to the preliminaries of the Ascension as told in Acts; the discourse finishes with an allegorical declaration connected with the fig tree; on the request of Peter, Jesus comments on what he has just said by a paraphrase, not of the comparison with a fig tree in the synoptic apocalypse (Mark xiii, 28; Luke xxi, 29–30), but of the parable of the barren fig tree in Luke xiii, 6–9; the tree which must be cut down is Judaism with a false Jewish Messiah, a persecutor of Christians—probably Barkochba— whom the two messengers of God, Enoch and Elias, will unmask; follows a description of the Second Coming and the Last Judgment; the Christ then reveals to Peter in great detail how the wicked will be punished after the judgment;[40] the elect will be witnesses of their chastisements and will be able to obtain from the Lord pardon for those among the damned whom they have known;[41] Peter is then warned of the fate that awaits him in the capital of the West; finally Jesus and his disciples repair to the holy mountain[42] where two luminous beings, Moses and Elias, make their appearance; on Peter asking where the patriarchs are, Jesus causes him to behold the dwelling place of the blessed; Peter then declares his intention to set up three tents, for Jesus,

Moses and Elias, for which the Christ rebukes him severely (in terms corresponding to Mark viii, 33); whereupon the voice of the Father is heard saying "this is my beloved son in whom I am well pleased"; a bright cloud envelopes Jesus, Moses and Elias, who are carried to heaven in the cloud; the heavens open to receive them, and then close; the disciples descend the mountain "praising God who has written the names of the righteous in the book of life in heaven."

Here then we have gathered into one picture the transfiguration of Jesus and the apocalyptic discourse reported in the first three Gospels (Mark xiii; Matthew xxiv; Luke xxi), together with the scene of the Ascension described in Acts, not to mention the prediction of Peter's martyrdom found in the Fourth Gospel. The problem to be solved by the critic is this; how was pseudo-Peter able to dispose, apparently at his own will, of elements utilized in a manner so different by the Gospel tradition and the Acts of the Apostles? Perhaps we may answer that the arrangement of elements in the Apocalypse of Peter is no more arbitrary than that to be found in the canonical writings. The apocalyptic discourse in Mark is an extract brought in from elsewhere and substituted for another conclusion to the Jerusalem ministry— the parable of the Wicked Husbandmen, originally conceived as the end of Jesus' teaching in Jerusalem. The discourse itself may very well have been drawn up at first in the form of a revelation made by the Christ after rising from the dead, a hypothesis supported by the preamble to the Ascension in Acts (i, 6–8). In the same way it has long been suspected that the transfiguration of Jesus was originally a manifestation of the risen Christ which Mark has thrown back into the Galilean ministry.[43] What may be taken as certain is that, before the canonization of the New Testament, a great liberty was used in the dealings of tradition with the manifold material at its disposal for constructing the legend of Jesus and his ministry—material messianic, eschatological, apocalyptic and theosophic. The Apocalypse of Peter belongs to this precanonical age when the literature of the Christian religion had no stereotyped form, the religion itself being still amorphous; Marcion had not yet become active and the reaction against him and against gnosticism in general had yet to come. It is moreover evident that the second Epistle of Peter, in all it says about the revelation made to Peter on the mountain about the glory of the Christ (i, 12–19), is not based on the story of the transfiguration as told in the Synoptics, nor on Acts for what it says of the Ascension, nor on the Fourth Gospel for the prediction of the apostle's death, but entirely and exclusively on our apocryphal book. This book seems to have been written at Alexandria and Clement was making great use of it in 135, citing it largely in his *Hypolyposes*. Be it noted that Alexandria, towards 135, was using its Gospel of the Egyptians. Our pseudo-Peter in writing his apocalypse would therefore be unrestrained in breaking up and arranging at his pleasure a mass of material which the canonical Gospels and Acts arranged in a different pattern. We can well understand why in the process of definitely canonizing the Gospels and Acts, there would be no long delay in excluding a document which doubled their stories and contradicted them too plainly. We may note, however, that towards the year 200 Rome still kept the Apocalypse of Peter in its collection of the Scriptures, although there were some who contested it, along with the Apocalypse of John (Canon of Muratori).

Hermas

Hermas lived at Rome during the first half and wrote in the second quarter of the second century.44 The tradition of the Roman community made him a brother of the bishop Pius; the rest of our knowledge of him is derived from what he says of himself in his book. He was not without learning, but is generally not regarded as a man of genius. Like the Apocalypse of John, but with fewer repetitions and incoherences, his book has an almost mathematical arrangement. It is divided into three: visions, to the number of four; commandments, to the number of twelve; similitudes or parables, to the number of eight—the ninth being a summary of what has been said in the visions, and the tenth serving for conclusions. The whole book has the character of a vision, both the precepts and the parables being dictated or shown to Hermas by an angel garbed as a shepherd. The significance of the book of Hermas lies chiefly in its relation to the history of Christian discipline.

To the Epistles attributed to Paul, the Epistle to the Hebrews and the first Epistle of John, the idea of the Christian as a sinner is repugnant; they regard baptism as a final regeneration by means of which the saints acquire at once the sinlessness of the redeemed. But as the parousia came not and the Church continued its life, the question of the Christian sinner began to present itself and became urgent. Hermas, inspired to declare that God will give pardon, once but no more, to the Christian who has sinned gravely after his baptism, was the first to administer a corrective to the notion that the believer became the unconditional heir of immortality on undergoing the rite of Christian initiation. What we encounter in Hermas is no longer a vision of the Eternal Jerusalem ready to come down to earth, but the church in process of organizing itself on earth. The prophet, confronted with growing abuses, here sets out to bring them remedy by giving utterance first to the angel of the Church itself, and then to the mystical Shepherd changed into an angel of penitence.45

In his knowledge of the Gospel tradition Hermas seems little better informed than the author of the Johannine Apocalypse or Clement of Rome who, as mentioned above, was probably a contemporary of Hermas and identical with the person named in his *Vision* (ii, 4). With some of the Gospel writings he was certainly acquainted; on occasion he is inspired by their sayings and he consciously imitates the parables. But it cannot be said that the Gospel legend was his favourite theme of meditation. The salvation-myth he reduces to its simplest form of expression. All the evidence points to the conclusion that the outbreak of the gnostic crisis, with its lawless flood of speculation and fiction, compelled the church to go back on its steps, to sift its archives, to catalogue and guarantee them and to define the right faith. Hermas brings us to the eve of that decision, which he did not foresee and which finally was to turn against him.

About half a century after Hermas the author of the Canon of Muratori expounded and defended the New Testament catalogue of the Roman Church. Having closed the list with the Apocalypses of John and of Peter, and before mentioning the works of the heretics reproved by the Church, he wrote as follows: "As to the Pastor, it was written recently in our time at Rome by Hermas, his brother the bishop then occupying the chair of the Roman community. Therefore we ought indeed to read it"—for private edification—"but it may not be publicly read to the people in the church"—because it would be held of no account—"nor among the prophets, of which the number is complete"—the prophets of the Old Testament of whom the full list was long since established—"nor among the apostles, to the end of the ages"— Hermas not having been an apostle nor one of their disciples as the author believed the New Testament writers to have been. We may read between the lines that the Pastor had for some time figured on the margin of the apostolic collection and that the reaction against the Montanists may have done him as much harm in Rome as did the definition of the Canon in opposition to the gnostics. In the fourth century the book was still used for public reading by congregations in the East, but only for the instruction of catechumens and without decisive authority in matters of faith.

3. GOSPELS AND ACTS

The four Gospels and the Acts of the Apostles are traditionally regarded as the most important part of the New Testament. On first inspection they would seem to contain the history of the very beginnings of the Christian religion. Nevertheless they are far from being books of history proper, far from having been originally conceived by their authors as history, or selected by the Church, from among many other writings of similar character, on account of their historical value.

A distinction has to be made between *the* Gospel and the Gospel*s*. The word "Gospel" in the New Testament is not a name given to *books* about the life and death of Jesus; it signifies "the good news," that is, the message of salvation won by the Christ. Even in our canonical Gospels the word is applied to this salvation, as made real by Jesus, and not to what seems to have been the theme of his preaching, the theme, namely, of the imminent coming of the Reign of God and the need of repentance for those who would share in its blessedness. In the end "Gospel" came to refer to the life and teachings of Jesus, but only so far as the life and the teachings were integral parts of the saving work which reached its climax, so to say, in the death and resurrection of the Christ. Moreover, when the word came to be applied to a plurality of books, the fact that only *one* Gospel was involved, or had ever existed, was indicated in the titles used to denote their authors, which titles ran, not the Gospel *of* Matthew or *of* Mark, but *according to* Matthew and *according to* Mark. This "according to" implied no doubt or attenuation of the authorship attributed to the book. As expressly stated by Irenaeus (*Heresies*, iii, 1) it was intended to emphasize the *oneness* of *the* Gospel under the four authorized forms of its text. Each of the communities began the use of books with one short book only; this, for the community using it, was "*the* Gospel." Many of the gnostic sects, Marcion's for example, did the same.

Justin is the oldest author to employ the word "Gospels" in the plural, to designate the books of the Good News;[46] their use in liturgical reading would lead to them being so named. The oldest author to affirm that there were four, and only four books so authorized, is Irenaeus.[47] The tone he assumes leaves no doubt as to the unique and exclusive authority of these writings; but the insistence displayed both by him and by the author of the Canon of Muratori in defending their authority rouses a suspicion that the fixing of the fourfold collection was not so primitive nor so natural as their tone of assurance might suggest to the incautious reader.

From our examination of the epistolary and apocalyptic literature it seems that the Gospel literature did not acquire importance till after the close of the first century. It is evident, moreover, that the legend of Jesus and the tradition of his teaching were not fixed at the outset of the Christian movement, and that for a long time the writings to which they were consigned continued to be produced without much restraint and without being authorized or commended otherwise than by their content. It is also certain that the practice began at an early date of putting forward, under the name of the Christ, teaching about the end of the world which had been borrowed from the apocalyptic tradition of Judaism; and, further, that many a lesson reflecting the needs of the infant communities or their propaganda was ascribed to him, together with revelations about his own transcendent personality and mission. By the visionary and fervid temper of the first generations acquisitions of all kinds were made easy. The imagination of the believer was constantly in search of anything which would exalt the Christ beyond comparison with

42

the pagan gods and leave no doubt as to his relations to Judaism, whose sacred books it turned into witnesses to Jesus. There is no difficulty in perceiving, in the documents of primitive Christianity, how theories of salvation, mystical interpretations of the messianic rôle attributed from the first to Jesus, though not logically deduced from the Scriptures, were artificially supported by them, and how even the legend of the Christ was similarly constructed by attaching it to messianic texts, real or supposed, in the Old Testament. We can understand how, under these conditions, Gospel writings began to multiply from an early date. They would have continued to multiply indefinitely had not the Church laid down a rule in the matter.

It is, however, important to remark that the use of these books by congregations in meetings for worship tended to fix their theme and give authority to certain writings. The Gospels when closely examined are far less the echoes of a tradition zealous to keep intact the memories of Jesus than a didactic instrument, we might even say, a catechism of the worship rendered to the Lord Christ. Those which the Church decided to retain are small books, very sober in style, not overcharged with matter but made up of selected elements, of stories brief and full of meaning, of teachings concise and sententious. Two cycles, or centres, are discernible, the cycle of the preaching in Galilee and the cycle of the passion in Jerusalem; the instruction of catechumens and the revelation of a mystery; the baptismal catechism and the eucharistic. The whole is thus brought into co-ordination with the great rites of Christian initiation and with the Christian mystery. It is no effect of chance that the Fourth Gospel, in the story of the passion as given in its source document, is found to justify the Easter observance of the "quartodeciman" congregations of Asia, while the first three conform to the common practice of Sunday observance ordained by the Roman Church. Our Gospels were originally conceived as ritual books for both observances, and were subsequently corrected at a few points to cover up the difference between them on this. Their literary form, their liturgical and oracular style, are in keeping with the purpose they are intended to serve. The question of the New Testament style is still under examination. It is certain that the discourses in the Gospels, even those in the fourth, were originally short writings composed in the rhythmic form peculiar

43

to the poetic writings of the Old Testament, Psalms, Proverbs and the discourses in Job. It is equally certain that some parts at least of the Epistles and the entire Apocalypse were put out at first in rhythmic form. The same may well be true of the Gospel stories.

Both the history and the fortunes of the Gospels are thus explained. Originally they were anonymous writings belonging to the communities which used them. The third Gospel seems an exception, offering itself to the reader as a personal work and with a dedicatory preface in the form then customary with profane writers. But this laicization of the Gospel theme hardly goes beyond the preface; moreover the editorial elaboration of Luke and Acts reduces them to the common level of biblical historiography. At the height of the gnostic crisis Marcion, opposing the common Christianity with a Gospel which, according to him, was the one Gospel and the only true, depersonalized Luke and further lightened it of everything that he found of Judaizing tendency. Then it was that the Church replied by canonizing the Gospels most in honour among the chief communities, disdaining the others and setting them aside, especially those which the gnostic themselves had fabricated or arranged. The reason why the Church did not limit its choice to one Gospel and only one, as Marcion had done, probably lay in the fact that the canon of the four Gospels resulted from a compromise between the influential communities. These came more easily to agreement in mutual recognition of the texts they were severally familiar with than they would have done in elaborating a single Gospel and securing its acceptance by them all.

As to what followed, there can be little doubt that the canonization of the four Gospels as traditional provided the occasion for some retouchings of their already edited text. It may well have had the further effect of giving consistency to the attribution of authorship, by means of which it was hoped to render indisputable a number of books which, in reality, did not come directly from any apostle, and in which the faith, aspirations and prophetic genius of the first Christian generations chiefly found utterance. The statements of John the Elder, reported by Papias of Hierapolis, in regard to Mark and Matthew, were put into words, at the very time when the canonization of the

Gospels was under consideration, with the object of guaranteeing the application of the apostolic names to writings for whose authority that form of recommendation was judged to be indispensable. The situation these statements were intended to justify was one of fact and of right; of fact, in respect of the credit already acquired by the writings in question; of right, in respect of the eminent authority that had to be given to books about whose origin little was known, or whose real origin would not have sustained their prestige at a sufficient height. The fiction of apostolic origin was a necessity for Christian apologetic when at grips with gnosticism. The fixation of the canon, to which the apostolic fiction was linked, was itself a necessity for the same reason—as the argument of the Canon of Muratori in regard to Hermas has already shown us. The fiction is without bearing on the history of the composition of the Gospels, except at the final stage of that history and in regard to the revision of their text in the process of forming them into a canonized group.

The Gospel attributed to Mark, generally regarded as the oldest of the Four,[48] is a shortened manual of Christian catechesis, not all of one piece and not exempt from retouchings. The last of these consisted in the adding of a conclusion (xvi, 9–20) perhaps as recent as the middle of the second century.[49] The basis of Mark seems to have been a document which agreed with John in the date of the passion, that is to say, in implying the coincidence of the Christian with the Jewish Passover.[50] This document has been worked over and surcharged, one part of the alterations betraying the influence of Pauline tendencies and doctrines while others[51] reveal the knowledge of didactic elements expanded in Matthew and Luke and readjustment of the passion stories to adapt them to the practice of the Sunday Easter. The date of the fundamental document may be earlier than the year 70; the subsequent editorial revision is later than the fall of Jerusalem. The final editings of Luke and of Matthew are founded on Mark as it stands, minus the deuterocanonical conclusion. After the discovery of the empty tomb, which these Gospels take from Mark, their editors artificially introduce completely divergent stories of apparitions of the risen Jesus. Both of them agree in loosening the tongues of the women whom the editor of Mark (xvi, 8) expressly makes silent, because he was aware that his story of the empty tomb had been unheard of till he told it. This compromising feature in Mark is redressed in Matthew xxviii, 8 and in Luke xxiv, 10–11; but what the two evangelists go on to relate on their own responsibility is no less freely invented and put together than the story of the empty tomb.

Mark seems to have been a Roman Gospel of ancient date.[52] Its attribution to Mark possibly coincides with the final revision of the book and the introduction of the Sunday Easter, when the Roman community ceased to celebrate the festival of salvation on the same day as the Jews. This would be some time before 150–160, when Pope Anicetus was able to cite the tradition of his predecessors in opposing Polycarp on the question of Easter Day.[53] Disparaging references to the Galilean apostles found in Mark are the following: Peter's lack of intelligence, viii, 32, 33; his ridiculous remark, ix, 5–6; ill-judged demand of the sons of Zebedee, x, 35–40; Peter's boasting and denial, xiv, 29–31, 54, 66–72; pitiful attitude of Peter, James and John at Gethsemane. On this we may remark, but only by way of a probable hypothesis, that the revision of Mark thus characterized by ill will to these apostles was the work of parties in Rome devoted to the memory of Paul, and was finally adopted, with the observance of the Sunday Easter, when the Roman community became united towards the beginning of the second century. But the dependence of the other Gospel writings, notably Matthew, revised in the East, on a document of this nature, is enough to prove the original poverty of what we are accustomed to call the Gospel tradition.

The first of our canonical Gospels seems to have circulated to begin with among the hellenic-christian congregations in Syria and Palestine. The narrative parts are mainly founded on Mark, what is added to them being secondary fiction with apologetic bearings and sometimes romantically conceived, as in the rôle attributed to Pilate's wife in the story of the passion (xxvii, 19). The birth-stories belong to the order of mythical fictions and are studiously elaborated in connexion with texts from the prophets (i, ii). The idea of conception by the Holy Spirit, notwithstanding its superficial resemblance to Isaiah vii, 14, is thoroughly pagan; if it first saw the light in Jewish-Christian circles, they must have been considerably paganized. These birth-stories, however, seem to have come into the text at the last revision of the Gospel, and in any case proclaim themselves clearly enough to be adventitious. The special interest of the Gospel, to which it owed its high credit among the early communities, lies in the place it gives to discourses attributed to Jesus, a mass of teachings not without Jewish-Christian features and bearing, in the total, the mark of their Jewish origin, but adapted under revision to the spirit of universal Christianity. As the greater part of these teachings are repeated in the third Gospel, with variations which affect only their literary form, critics generally admit the dependence of Matthew and Luke, for the discourses, on a common source, but in two different versions both derived from a Semitic original of relatively ancient date. But the evangelical matter in Matthew, so far as it consists of teachings, does not represent a single collection of memories faithfully preserved from the apostolic age, any more than its narratives represent the legend of Jesus preserved in the same way. It contains rather a series of acquisitions successively taken over under the pressure of circumstance, of the progressive needs of Christian propaganda, and as required by the organization of Christian teaching in the communities. The original document was a *Didache* (a "teaching") afterwards worked up into a Gospel of the canonical type by amalgamation with Mark. The importance attached to the person of Peter, notably in xvi, 13–20, derives from the fact that this Gospel took form in Jewish-Christian circles with a turn for universalism. The same is true of the Peter-legend developed in the first part of Acts.

In the traditional form it now has, the first Gospel cannot be much earlier than the year 125, a date somewhat movable, like all those here indicated for the Gospels, since retouches were always possible up to the final canonization of the books and of their official text. There is no doubt that it existed before Justin and was known in Asia, as Mark also was, in the time of Papias. We are much in the dark as to the reasons for its being attributed to the apostle Matthew; we may recall what has been said above of the originally anonymous character of the Gospel revisions. The substitution of the name Matthew for Levi in the story of the calling of the publican (ix, 9) must be connected with this attribution; but, if the intention is clear, the motive is not. By a forced interpretation of the evidence of Papias, often adopted since Schleiermacher, but open to question at every point, it has been supposed that the Gospel was judged to be the work of Matthew because this apostle had composed the collection of discourses which is one of its chief sources. But that collection was an impersonal work and not apostolic.[54] Some apostolic name had to be chosen to give authority to the Gospel: the reason for the choice of Matthew the publican lying perhaps in some legend about him which made him a reciter of the Gospel.

The writings of Luke present another enigma. The preface to the third Gospel and that of Acts[55] show that the two books were originally the first and second parts of one work which professed to be composed under conditions common to the issue of books in that time, with a dedication to some eminent personage. But the preface to Acts has been mutilated, the first stage in a process of alteration which seems to have been extended to the whole of the original document; the first part, or Gospel, was apparently recast and completed in a similar manner. It seems impossible to admit the view that the author of this, the original, document was the person who writes "we" in certain narratives in Acts, and who is to be identified with Luke the companion of Paul, and that this man, arriving in Rome with Paul about the year 60, wrote the story of Christian origins about the year 80. The author of the general preface (Luke i, 1–4) does not place himself among the companions and disciples of the apostles; the underlying idea of his preface is that of an apostolic tradition transmitted in good order down to the time of those, who, like himself, have undertaken to describe the institution of the Christian faith. And the writings said to be Luke's, taken in the form in which they have come down to us, cannot go back to the apostolic age, nor even to the end of the first century; they are the prelude to the age of Christian apologetic as practised by Athenagoras and Justin. This Gospel, moreover, is no longer the mixed catechesis of Mark and Matthew, nor is it the gnosis of John. But Luke and Acts are earlier than 140, since Marcion, excommunicated from the Roman church about 144, furnished his sect with our third Gospel as an authorized version, with the matter omitted that conflicted with the heresiarch's system. The contrary hypothesis, which makes Marcion's Luke the original and our canonical Gospel the derivative, is indefensible. Marcion took the Gospel used by the Roman Church and adapted it in conformity with the needs of his doctrine. In this procedure he took no greater liberty, in principle, than the editors of our Gospel texts were wont to allow themselves.

Luke is a compilation analogous to Mark and Matthew and like them intended for reading aloud in the assemblies. Here again Mark has furnished most of the stories in the body of the book; what does not come from Mark is legendary fiction or mythical construction; examples of these are the preaching of Jesus at Nazareth (iv, 16–30), the mission of the seventy-two disciples (x, 1–12),[56] the ascension of the risen Christ (xxiv, 50–53).[57] The birth-stories, though not constructed all at once, are better put together than in Matthew, but with as little basis in tradition; though not independent of ancient prophecy they are not constructed on texts for the purpose of showing their fulfilment. The idea of virgin conception (i, 34–35) is adventitious; it is only in their source that the stories are of earlier date than Matthew's. The evangelical teachings are as abundant as in Matthew but more dispersed. Certain parables, of deeply moving character—the Rich Man and Lazarus, the Prodigal Son, the Pharisee and the Publican and others—are peculiar to Luke, where they represent an original development of tradition. By an almost mechanical device of editing the greater part of the discourses attributed to Jesus are lodged between the departure of the Christ for Jerusalem and his arrival in Judea (ix, 51–xviii, 14). The explanation is that the sayings and parables having no attachment to time and place in the traditional souvenirs, the evangelists inserted them as best they could in the course of the narratives, Matthew preferring an arrangement in long discourses and Luke in distributed pieces.

The Acts of the Apostles

This book, in the form it now has, is an amalgamation of primitive data concerning the beginnings of Christian preaching and the missions of Paul with mythical and legendary fictions, and discourses artificially composed in the manner of ancient historiography. Anti-Jewish polemic, perceptible in all the Gospels, is here outstandingly tendentious, the author having set himself the task of proving that Christianity is the most authentic form of Judaism and has the right, in that capacity, to the same tolerance by Roman authority as that enjoyed by official Judaism. Peter and Paul are in the forefront of evangelical activity, and it would seem that the author has taxed his wits to furnish them with the same miracles; each brings a dead person to life, cures a paralytic and performs miscellaneous miracles, the one with his shadow, the other with aprons snatched from his body. But, in all this, Paul is given second place to the elder apostles, especially to Peter whom we find taking the lead in preaching to the Gentiles (x–xi, 18); while every trace of old disputes and rivalries between them is carefully obliterated, and the presentation of the primitive history dominated throughout by the fictitious idea of an apostolic tradition originally guarded by the Twelve.

Both the Gospels and Acts acquired their final form in the first half of the second century—a conclusion which may be taken as guaranteed by the proceedings of Marcion and by the apologist Justin's employment of the third Gospel. The first book "to Theophilus" became, in revision, a cult-book impersonalized and enriched with the latest acquisitions of the faith, while the passion and resurrection stories were retouched and augmented, not only for the demonstration of the Christian message, but to adapt the stories to the Easter usage of the Roman congregation. On the latter point the revision of the third Gospel, like that of the first, was conformed to the revision of the second and then brought to the point by stories of the resurrection which bring the Sunday Easter into plain relief.[58] While the systematic preoccupation with prophecy betrays a development of Christian belief and apologetic in presence of Judaism and in opposition to it, it is not impossible that the ardour for the Old Testament apparent in Luke and Acts attest a reaction against those gnostics who, like Marcion and Basilides before him, repudiated the Old Testament and the God of the Jews. We have still stronger grounds for supposing that the materialization of the apparitions of the risen Christ, both in the Gospel and in Acts, is aimed at destroying the influence of the Docetism which denied his material existence, but of which Marcion was not the initiator. It should not be overlooked that, alone among the New Testament writers, the editor of Luke and Acts has had the hardihood to represent the risen Christ as eating material food (Luke xxiv, 42; Acts x, 41) and as remaining among his followers for a longish period afterwards, as some of the gnostics also did. It remains to be said that the dependence of certain passages in Luke and Acts on the so-called Johannine tradition and on the fourth Gospel,59 in the revision of which the aim at Docetic gnosticism is equally apparent, invites us to place the canonical revision of our two books near the time when the group of four Gospels was canonized as a whole.

Wherever they were composed, the third Gospel and Acts reflect the development of Christian faith and institution between the years 125 and 150. The two books were prepared and revised in a great centre of Christianity which also undertook their general diffusion. The Roman Church itself had perhaps promoted their last revision for the purpose of admitting them into its collection of the Scriptures, and therefore knew what it was about in admitting them. We can easily understand how this Church found the Gospel of Mark, which it already had, inadequate for Christian instruction; and how the original work of Luke failed to make good the inadequacy. For neither Mark, nor, probably, Luke's original related the birth of the Christ; moreover, they lacked the greater part of the sayings which were circulating among the communities at the opening of the second century as discourses of Jesus.

The Fourth Gospel

In the matter forming its groundwork the Fourth Gospel is of later date than the three Synoptics and would seem to have been conceived in another setting and on a different pattern. Perhaps, however, in its original form, the frame was not very different, though the Gospel was wholly unlike the others in spirit and doctrine. Towards the end of the first century there appeared at Ephesus, perhaps from Syria, a mystical prophet, a master of Christian gnosis rather than a preacher of the Gospel, who conceived and gave form to the sublime discourses and the symbolic visions on which the Gospel was finally built up—the style of the discourses being rhythmic, like that of the sayings and sentences in the Synoptics, but the development of the thought more spacious and the themes perceptibly different.[60] But the mystic Christ of our prophet not being born of the flesh, and his gift to those who were his being simply that of immortal life, it soon became necessary to conform his figure to the Christ of the common tradition in whom the Jewish prophecies were fulfilled and who was soon to appear in his Kingdom and raise the dead from their graves. Had not the Apocalypse, conceived in that strain, just been published at this same Ephesus? Two chief stages can be distinguished in the literary formation of this Gospel: a first official edition, about 135–140, ended by the present conclusion of chapter xx, and characterized by the greater part of the borrowings from the Synoptic tradition and by passages specially conceived to effect the adjustment, probably also by the fixation of the chronological framework and distribution of the material in accordance with it;[61] then a second edition, the canonical, about 150–160, almost contemporary with the last editions of Matthew and Luke.[62] In this second edition chapter xxi is the piece most easily recognizable as a newcomer; but various retouchings and further additions may have been made in the body of the book, notably in regard to the beloved disciple, who is given a prominence of his own as author of the book at the same time as he was being proclaimed the author of the Apocalypse and an apostle of the Lord Jesus. The object aimed at in this edition seems to have been precisely that of procuring the inclusion of the book in the authorized group of Gospels by making it acceptable to the community which apparently had the leading part in fixing the New Testament Canon, to wit, the Roman. It may be said, for example, that chapter xxi was added to make good the legend of Peter as chief shepherd of Christ's sheep, by harmonizing it, as well as might be, with the fiction of the beloved disciple. But it is important to note that during the Montanist crisis towards the end of the second century, in the time of Irenaeus, the canonization of the fourth Gospel had opponents. Not only does Irenaeus mention them in *Heresies* (iii, 11, 9) but finds it necessary to condemn them at the end of his *Exposition of Apostolic Preaching*.

The fourth Gospel agrees with the Easter usage of the "Quarto-decimans" who celebrated Passover on the same day as the Jews. Their Passover was the festival of a beneficial death, the Christ being thought to have died at the hour when the lamb of the Jewish festival was sacrificed. This being certainly the primitive custom, and implied in the foundation documents of Mark and Luke, we are bound to conclude that our Gospel supplanted one of the others, Luke probably, in Ephesian usage, and in a form not yet adapted to the Sunday observance of Easter, though doubtless the adaptation had by this time already been made in Rome. When the Easter controversy broke out about the year 190 the Roman party did not perceive, or pretended not to perceive, that while the Synoptics, in their last edition, were now supporting the common Sunday observance, the fourth Gospel fully authorized the other, the Asiatic observance. In what followed the discord on this point was at last covered up under borrowings made by the editors of John from the last edition of the Synoptics, notably those taken from the narrative which fix the passion on Friday and the resurrection on the following Sunday. The discord remains none the less, and the ill-disguised contradiction would be enough to prove that the Gospels are, before all else, a catechism of Christian initiation. It shows that even in their most important part, and the part historically the best guaranteed in the essential datum, namely the crucifixion of Jesus, we have clearly the wording of a liturgical drama, rather than a record of accurate memories of the facts commemorated in the liturgy.

THE NON-CANONICAL LITERATURE

In the period when effort was being made to fix the canon of the New Testament, other Gospels and even other Acts of the Apostles, less recommended by church usage, if not positively disqualified by heretical origin or flavour, were offered for the edification of the communities. A certain number of these writings are known to us only by their titles or in fragments, catholic tradition having either neglected or suppressed them.

Some nevertheless exercised an appreciable influence on the evolution of Christianity of which they were also a product.

As the Gospel tradition was more or less Jewish-Christian at its point of departure, it is a disaster that the Jewish-Christian Gospels have not come down to us. The most important of these, if not the oldest, seems to have been the Gospel of the Nazareans (a Jewish-Christian sect), the Gospel of which Jerome says he translated the Aramean text,[63] wrongly making it the original of canonical Matthew. It is at least true that the Gospel in question was somewhat nearly related to Matthew and, as it had a history of its own, may have been earlier than Matthew at some points and dependent on it at others. It was preserved in Jewish-Christian groups which accepted the virgin conception and were still in existence at the end of the fourth century. According to Eusebius (iii, 39, 16) it contained the incident of the woman taken in adultery, a fragment belonging to the synoptic tradition which, passed by in the first three Gospels, fell in time, and as though by chance, into John. According to Jerome (*de viris*, 2) the first apparition of the risen Christ was accorded by this Gospel to James,[64] which is not surprising in a Jewish-Christian book: after the apparition, Jesus administers the holy sacrament to James who is said to have eaten nothing since the last supper; a trait conforming to the customs of fasting at the Passover, which shows that this Jewish-Christian Gospel, like the four canonicals, was intimately connected with Easter observance.[65] The question is still discussed as to whether the Gospel according to the Hebrews, which seems to have been used by Jewish Christians in Egypt at a very early date, is to be distinguished from the Gospel of the Nazareans, or is only another name for it.

The Gospel according to the Twelve, known as the Gospel of the Ebionites, belonged to Christian groups existing in Transjordania at the time of Epiphanius; the genuine fragments of it are those given by him (*Heresies*, 30). Denying the virgin birth and professing that Jesus was made Son of God by his baptism, these Jewish-Christians were regarded as heretics; but, Jewish as its colour was, their Gospel prescribed the abolition of the sacrifices, baptism taking its place. The Christ is made to say "if you cease not your sacrifices, wrath will not cease to smite you." In general pattern the Ebionite Gospel resembles Mark; as to the contents, its affinity is with Matthew, and it professed to have been revised by that apostle. It was originally written in Greek and depended on earlier Gospels, but only on those in the synoptic tradition, chiefly Matthew and Luke. That it owes nothing to John does not prove it earlier and there seems no compelling reason to place it further back than the last quarter of the second century.[66]

The Gospel according to the Egyptians, of which it is to be regretted that we possess only a few fragments,[67] must have been more ancient and more gnostic in character. The Naasseenes quoted it; but Clement of Alexandria cites it after "the four transmitted to us"; so too, and with equal respect, does the homily known as the Second Epistle of Clement. Origen pays it no other honour than to place it at the head of the non-inspired Gospels and supposes that the prologue to Luke refers to this book and to the Gospel according to the Twelve as "attempts" preceding his own. The Gospel according to the Egyptians, so named in Egypt itself, must have been the one in use among Christians of Egyptian origin, the Gospel according to the Hebrews being that of Jewish-Alexandrian converts. The two, if as old as Origen makes them, would be of great value to the historian. It remains to add that the language of the Gospel of the Egyptians had a savour of gnosticism and that it taught a sex-mystery, an *encratism*, on which fuller information were much to be desired;[68] it is said to have been Sabellian which, however, does not diminish the interest of the problem raised by its existence. It was a Gospel parallel to the Synoptics, but edited independently of them.

The Gospel of Peter, known to us in a considerable fragment dealing with the passion and resurrection of the Christ, is an hellenic-christian Gospel of gnostic tendency on much the same line as the Gospel of the Ebionites in its relation to the canonical four, except that it depends on John as well as on the Synoptics.[69] Not without reason did Serapion, Bishop of Antioch, having found it used by a Syrian community towards the end of the second century, reject it as infected with Docetism.[70] It must have been composed about the middle of that century, perhaps in Syria, and is related to the apocryphal Apocalypse of Peter already discussed.

Basilides, a gnostic teaching in Alexandria, about 140 composed a Gospel on which he wrote a commentary. The Gospel was presented as based on the authority of Glaucias, a disciple of Peter—a case analogous to that of Mark—and in it we find the parable of the Rich Man and Lazarus. There is no reason to regard this Gospel as more freely composed than the others of which we have spoken, or that of Marcion. Like the Gospels of Valentinus and of Marcion, it was written for the use of the group of believers whom the author had gathered round him. As the church hierarchy was as yet but little organized, there was nothing abnormal in the literary experiments of these doctors and, apart from their particular tendencies in doctrine, they used no greater liberty in their method of composition than did the authors of the canonical Gospels.

Of the Gospel of Truth, used by the Valentinians, we know little more than the name. Valentinus appears to have put it out as derived from a certain Theodas, a disciple of Paul.[71] Marcion's Gospel, entitled simply *Evangelion*, with no recommending name, was presented by him as the only true, he himself having amended it in conformity to what he believed was the doctrine of Paul. (To Marcion, with his *Evangelion* and *Apostolicon* we shall return later.) Other gnostic Gospels made their appearance at the same time, such as the Gospel of Matthias, of Philip, of Judas, of Eve, of Mary, etc. It is easy to understand how, confronted with this inundation of Gospel literature, the leaders in the churches, beginning with the Roman, who had already repudiated Valentinus and Marcion, made up their minds to fix once and for all what Gospels, to the exclusion of all others, were to be retained as apostolic.

Mention must here be made of Tatian's *Diatessaron* which was in essence a Gospel remodelled by the method generally adopted from the beginning in Gospel literature. The *Diatessaron* was the first Gospel of the Church of Edessa and for long remained official among the Syrian congregations; an interesting fact as showing how little regardful these congregations were, about 170, of the canon which Irenaeus had just vaunted as fixed, and how they could arrange for themselves a Gospel not in liturgical

56

use in the congregations of the Roman world. It is however certain that Tatian's work was a harmony of the four canonical Gospels with a small number of secondary features seemingly borrowed from the non-canonical. More significant are the omissions and retouches which reveal Tatian's encratism and anti-semitic bias.[72]

The work of the Christian imagination in dealing with the birth of Jesus was not limited to the stories in Matthew and Luke. Some of the gnostics took part in it, and the idea of the virgin birth, with its mixed savour of encratism and docetism, probably came from that source.[73] Among the gospels of the infancy which have most influenced catholic tradition is the Protoevangel of James, a book written to establish the virginity of Mary *ante partum*, *in partu* and *post partum*, and in which the author has amplified both Luke and Matthew.[74] Although Justin's dependence on it is not proved, the core of the book may be dated as far back as the middle of the second century. It was written outside of Palestine and by a writer ignorant of Jewish affairs.

Very different in character is the Gospel of Thomas which tells of the miracles performed by Jesus in his infancy. The catholic version which has come down to us is apparently based on a gnostic gospel in which the story of Jesus bears a strong resemblance to that of the youth of Krishna, if not really modelled on it. The catholic versions are not very old, but the gnostic Gospel at the base was known to Irenaeus and Hippolytus, and is mentioned by Eusebius. Here, too, the date may go back to the middle of the second century.

The Acts of Pilate (the Gospel of Nicodemus) are of the fourth or fifth century and have no interest for our subject. When Justin refers his readers to the acts of Pilate for information about the passion of the Christ he is not referring to a book any more than when he refers them, for information about the birth, to the registers of the census made by Quirinius. But Tertullian, in his *Apology* (21), mentions a story told by Pilate at Tiberias about the life, death and resurrection of Jesus which seems to have been preserved as an appendix to the Gospel of Nicodemus. This document, fictitious as it is, would thus be earlier than 197. It is based on canonical Matthew.

In the literary class called "Acts" or "Travels," widely known and circulated in Hellenic antiquity (πράξεις, περίοδοι) 75 canonical Christian literature has produced only the Acts of the Apostles— a book improperly named, since it comprises only the Acts of Peter, stopped short at his imprisonment by Agrippa I and his miraculous escape, and the Acts of Paul in his missions and captivity, but not continued to his martyrdom. Other Acts were written completing the canonical book in matters regarding Peter, Paul and John, or about other apostles less important in the tradition. Needless to say, the object aimed at in recounting the apostolic travels and miracles was to edify the reader in respect of the Christian propaganda and to shed lustre by one means or another on Christian teaching. But these apocryphal Acts, in contrast to the canonical book, do not rest upon a basis having the slightest claim to be historical and inform us only of the spirit and turn of mind of those who wrote them or found them to their taste.[76] They are pious romances more recent in date than the canonical Acts which they feebly imitate. Certain of their apostolic discourses are written in the style of rhythmical chanting, and occasionally we come upon veritable hymns— precious samples of the Christian manner of worship.

Among these apocrypha, the Acts of John, incompletely preserved, seem to be the oldest. They are saturated with Docetism. They contain the Ephesian legend of John fully formed and were probably composed in Asia; in their first form before the end of the second century. In no sense is the book Marcionite, but Docetic in the highest degree: the identification of Christ with God is absolute, his humanity and death mere appearance and the whole symbolic.

The Acts of Paul, known to Hippolytus and to Origen, were widely diffused in the East. Tertullian says that the author, a priest of Asia, was dismissed when his fraud was discovered (*De Baptismale*, 17). None the less the book, constructed on canonical Acts and starting with Paul's mission to Antioch of Pisidia, continued to be widely read. Only fragments of it have survived, the most considerable and the most in favour being the piece which bears the title Acts of Paul and of Thecla. The mention of it by Tertullian places the composition towards 160–180. The author appears to belong to the region chosen for the scene of his romance and may have exploited a local tradition along with Acts and the thirteen Epistles attributed to Paul.

The Acts of Peter, which it has been possible to reconstruct from the Clementine apocrypha,77 and the Catholic Acts, in which the legend of Peter's martyrdom is developed, probably go no further back than the beginning of the third century, but they reflect some traditions and doubtless incorporate older documents.

Of all these unorthodox lucubrations the strangest is the Acts of Thomas, a Syrian work apparently composed in Syriac. It is made up of marvellous stories and liturgical hymns, all strongly impregnated with gnosis and encratism. The Greek version, if it is a version, is hardly less ancient than its Syriac original of which the date may be given about 200, without excluding the possibility of an earlier date for some of its elements.

The vogue enjoyed by all these writings of suspect origin is a point worthy of attention as proof that ancient Christianity was endowed with a singular capacity to receive what was offered to it, and even at a time when it was engaged in the war with Gnosticism.

With the apocryphal Acts we pass beyond the limit of direct witness to the Christian movement before the year 180. It remains to mention those of the Christian apologies which have come down to us from the second century, chiefly the writings of Justin, his *Apologies* and *Dialogue with Trypho*. Here we have a Christian teacher not without culture but with a mediocre range of mind, a Hermas but better versed in the Scriptures and with a tinge of philosophy. He was a moral philosopher inclined to take Christianity as moral philosophy and to make it acceptable as such to pagans. His writings enable us to grasp the position of Christianity, about 150–160, surrounded by Judaism, paganism, gnostic heresy, and the first approach of that theory of the Logos which soon, at the hands of Irenaeus, Tertullian, Clement of Alexandria, Hippolytus, in preparation for Origen, was to fix the direction of the Christian gnosis. From these doctors themselves, or by inference from their writings, we cannot fail to learn how, during the middle part of the second century, there was forged the mighty power which the Church invoked at the time, and was to evoke thenceforward, against all innovators, namely the power of *tradition*, embodied in the collection or canon of scripture, in the symbols of faith (creeds), in the episcopal magistracy—the whole, scripture, symbols and magistracy being held of apostolic origin, or rather as going back, through the apostles, to Jesus himself and his Gospel.

We shall find the testimony of profane writers valuable at certain points, but they cannot make good the insufficiency and clear up the obscurities of the Christian witness to Christian history. At least they convey to us the impression made by the new religion on the men of letters, the statesmen and the philosophers of the time. Thus Celsus, though known to us solely through Origen, gives us the impression made by Christianity on enlightened people in the time of Marcus Aurelius, and shows us how the apparently irreconcilable conflict between Christianity and paganism might have ended by the incorporation of Christianity in the imperial religion, into which all religions were admitted, if hellenized Christianity had not been strong enough to compel its final acceptance as the one religion of the Empire. The genesis of the gnostic sects, of which the Great Church disencumbered itself by condemning them, is in like manner not accessible to us in the original writings of the doctors who founded them; the men and their writings we know only from those who refuted them when the sects had already lost some of their primitive force. Thus we are less well informed about dissenting Christianity than about dominant Christianity. More strictly speaking, the general history of the Christian movement, from its point of departure to the year 180, has to be deduced from documents distinctly non-historical in the proper sense of history, but intended to serve in some way the movement which produced them, and not as a faithful record for posterity of its stages and fortunes. To sum the matter up in a sentence, all the difficulties and gropings in the dark which the interpretation of these documents imposes on the impartial historian proceed from the fact that the documents he is interpreting are something other than history.

Chapter II

THE GOSPEL OF JESUS

WHEN Tacitus, in his account of the burning of Rome in the year 64, comes to the point where mention has to be made of the Christians, he writes of them as follows:—

"The founder of this sect, Christ, was condemned to death in the reign of Tiberius by the procurator Pontius Pilate, but the disastrous superstition, repressed for a time, spread not only throughout Judea, where the evil was born, but also through the City, the place of confluence from everywhere of all sorts of abominable and shameful things, and the scene where they are practised."[1]

Tacitus has no more information to give about the career of Jesus. He conceives it as an outbreak of propaganda arrested by the death of its author, but afterwards renewed and with such vigour that, passing the frontiers of Judea, it reached Rome almost immediately. In the same way Tacitus is repeating a current opinion when he writes of Judaism, *Histories*, v, 3: "Moses, quo sibi in posterum gentem formaret, novos ritus contrariosque ceteris mortalibus indidit."

At the time when Tacitus thus evaluated the Christian religion and its founder, Pliny the Younger wrote on similar lines to Trajan that the Christians "in their meetings sing praises to Christ as to a god."[2]

From these statements we may gather the official opinion of high functionaries and educated persons, at the beginning of the second century, in regard to the Christian religion. It was to the effect that this new religion, sprung from Judaism in the time of Tiberius, had been founded by an agitator to whom Pilate had put an end and whom his followers had quickly turned into an object of worship. Neither Tacitus nor Pliny had read the Gospels. Their opinion is that which was formed by the administrative personnel of the Roman Empire after the judicial interrogation of the Christians. To be more exact, since Tacitus reflects the opinion of the time of Nero, it must be conceded that this opinion was formed as much on the basis of official information received from Judea as from the statements of Christians themselves when on trial before the Roman tribunals, beginning with the trial of Paul and the martyrs of the year 64. The Christians, then, make their entry on historical ground as claiming to be under the leadership of Jesus called Christ, who had been condemned to crucifixion by Pontius Pilate, while those who were first opposed to their propaganda admitted his historical reality, just as the Christians did.

After all, then, the difficulty encountered by the historian who has no axe to grind is not that of ascertaining whether Jesus ever existed, but of discerning what his action and teaching really were, and how this action and teaching led on to the movement which began with him. Viewed in the light of the cult devoted to him, and in Christian tradition, the Christ would be incommensurable by any standard of human greatness. But, as facts of history, the appearance of Jesus as a figure on earth and the birth of the Christian religion are neither more nor less explicable than the appearance of Mahomet and the birth of Islam. Our task is to study the conditions of that appearance and of that birth, as they are furnished by the environment and by the times which produced them. In regard to Jesus the only environment with which we are concerned is that of Palestinian Judaism; and the time is the period, probably very short, within which the career of the Galilean reformer was confined.

1. JOHN THE BAPTIST

In an earlier volume (*La Religion d'Israel*, p. 308) we have shown how the Kingdom of Herod the Great was first divided between three of his sons and how a few years later the portion of Archelaus, that is to say Judea proper with Samaria, was placed directly under the government of Rome. From this point we may date the crisis which ended in the birth of the Christian religion and the destruction of Jewish nationalism. Further back in history preparation for the crisis had begun. It was during the Babylonian captivity that Jewish eschatology began to shape itself as a project of national restoration concurrent with the religious and moral regeneration of the chosen people.

Most of all, the way had been paved by the foolish policy of Antiochus Epiphanes, which had the effect of provoking a reaction of Jewish faith, in the form of a belief in the near and decisive intervention of God for the extermination of the imperial oppressor and the establishment of his own Kingdom—a fever-heat of enthusiasm rather inflamed than allayed by the temporary establishment of a national monarchy. But the reduction of Judea to the status of a Roman province caused a shock to the Jewish mind which was only appeased, and that only for a feeble minority of the Jews, by the progressive spiritualization of their hope under the influence of the Christian Gospel, and, on the other hand, for the mass of the people, by the overthrow of Jewish nationalism. It is, however, true that both the spiritualization of the Jewish hope and the overthrow of Jewish nationalism were realized only by stages. Christian hope was still violently revolutionary when the Apocalypse appeared towards the end of the first century, while Jewish nationalism, surviving the destruction of Jerusalem in the year 70, was not finally broken down until a new revolt had been suppressed in the time of Hadrian.

It is well to remember also that in this crisis Galilee was a hotbed of Jewish nationalism. Thence came that Judas whom Josephus represents as the founder of the school of uncompromising resistance which he compares to the schools of the Pharisees, the Sadducees and the Essenes. Judas the Galilean was certainly no master of religious philosophy or of ascetic living; historically little more than the leader of a band of brigands, he is yet a representative of that spirit of blind and unyielding faith which embraced the idea of the Kingdom of God in all its rigour. It was a principle of these zealots—and on this point we can trust Josephus[3]—that the Israelites, the people and children of God, had no master on earth save their Master in heaven. Hence the Roman government was a sacrilege, its exercise an impious usurpation, and there must be no paying tribute to Caesar.[4] Insurrection against the idolatrous emperor was, of all duties, the most sacred. But Roman power being what we know, this simplest of duties became the crowning folly.

We know that not all the Jews drew the same consequences from this principle, which became, in sum, the dominant motive of Jewish faith. The Sadducees tended to regard the Kingdom of God as essentially realized in observation of the Law; the Essenes believed it attained in their Mystery and, in an eternal future, by the ascension of souls to God. A considerable party of educated Pharisees, while cherishing the idea of a Kingdom of God on earth, and accepting the resurrection of the dead, denied that there was any need to lend the aid of human violence in founding an order of things which only the power of God was able to bring about. But the various forms of the national hope, of which it would be a mistake to deny the diversity, did not come into conflict on the field of practice. They subsisted in the inner life of Judaism, rather associated than antagonistic, loosely held together by common faith in the revelation which made Israel the privileged object of divine solicitude, and by the hope of a national future which their divine protector would clothe with glory. Fundamentally, foreign rule on the soil of Palestine was an offence to all these parties. When the great revolt broke out in the time of Nero, the number of sincere believers who understood the futility of that desperate attempt seems to have been small.[5]

Under the working of this faith, to which the course of events lent its aid, the popular imagination became more and more excited and the superheated atmosphere was created in which religious movements are likely to be born.[6] It was no effect of chance that the beginning of our era witnessed the appearance of a swarm of sects in Palestine and the region of the Jordan. John the Baptist, Simon the Magician and Elchasai are witnesses, each in his own way, to the religious ferment of which the Christian religion was also an issue.[7] The sects founded by them missed the great fortune in store for the Christian movement, though they are more or less related to it. But while we can clearly see their failure to win the same success, it is not so easy to explain why it so happened, the play of circumstances and the character of the men concerned being too little known to us. Of the three we have mentioned it is John the Baptist of whom exact information would be of most value to the historian, since it was to him that the Christian religion, up to a certain point, traced its origin, while Simon and Elchasai, who also depend on John,[8] stand rather in a relation of rival movements to the Christianity of the first age.

John appeared on the scene earlier than Jesus and founded a sect, slightly anterior to the Christian, which became a rival whose claims are combated in the Gospel literature.9 But what the Gospel tells us about John is a tendentious legend, while the notice bestowed upon him by Josephus,10 though commonly accepted by critics, is of doubtful authenticity, and vague enough in any event. The Gospels are more precise but not more trustworthy. Even if the stories in Luke about the birth of John have been borrowed, as Bultmann supposes, from the Johannite sect, they are none the less fictitious on that account. The testimony which John is made to render to Jesus, in giving himself out as the precursor of the Messiah, as in the synoptic tradition, or in expressly designating Jesus as the Messiah expected, as in the fourth Gospel which contradicts Matthew xi, 2, 6 and Luke vii, 18–20, is another fiction contrived by Christian apologetic for the purpose of attenuating or disguising the original dependence of the Christian sect on the Johannite. Even the account of the martyrdom of John in the first two Gospels has few marks of historicity. Herodias is a new Jezebel persecuting the new Elijah. All the legend leaves us is the fact that John was put to death by order of Antipas.

We may take it as certain that John proclaimed himself as the messenger of God, a prophet of the end of the age with a mission subordinate to that of no other prophet, and not even to that of the Messiah; a precursor of none save of God only in his coming to judge the world, unless he be subordinate to the Son of Man, the great Envoy; but it was not thus that his sectaries seem to have understood him. It was within the Baptist sect that John was first proclaimed as "a prophet and more than a prophet"; equally from within the sect came the application to John of the text from Malachi (iii, 1) "behold I send my messenger who shall prepare my way before me"; and it was within the sect that the saying was current "among them that are born of women there has not risen up a greater than John the Baptist."11 All this was marked for correction by the Gospel tradition; but there would have been no need to correct it if it had not been professed. In like manner it is incredible that John should in advance have discredited his own baptism in favour of Christian baptism by declaring that his own was a mere symbol and that the only true and efficacious baptism was that which the Christ would give in the Holy Spirit.[12] These sayings are put into the mouth of John in order to avoid the simple avowal that the baptismal rite had been borrowed by the Christian sect from the Johannite. All these petty frauds are significant, indeed more significant than would have been the simple avowal of the truth.

Mark and Matthew have a strange manner of introducing their account of the Baptist's death and burial by making Antipas declare, as an explanation of Jesus and his miracles, that "John is risen from the dead"; and it is not impossible that we have signs here of a set purpose to confuse and discredit the faith of the Baptist sect in the survival of the prophet martyr. Mark, in relating the burial of John (vi, 14, 16, 29), has an air of suggesting that it was not followed by his resurrection. In Matthew (xiv, 1–2, 12) even John's own disciples, who come to inform Jesus of their master's death, seem to imply that his ministry has come to an end. Not thus, assuredly, was his ministry understood in the Baptist sect.

John, then, was a preacher of the Kingdom of God some time in advance of Jesus. His ministry was carried on beside the Jordan in the territories of the tetrarch Antipas.[13] He was probably an ascetic after the manner of the Essenes, although, in all probability, he did not belong to their order. For John acted on his own account and founded his own sect, his activity resembling in certain respects that of the hermit Banus mentioned by Josephus. Needless to say he was not a Sadducee. Matthew, no doubt by way of conforming him to Jesus, makes him preach against the Pharisees, adding the Sadducees at a venture (iii, 7) while Luke (iii, 7) speaks only of "crowds." He proclaimed the imminence of the Great Kingdom which he expected to be brought in by God only. He was, moreover, detached from apocalyptic preoccupations, and being a stranger, like Jesus, to the science of the schools, he engaged in no speculations concerning the preliminaries of the coming End. He insisted on repentance in preparation for God's judgment of the world and, in prevision of its coming, it may be said that he instituted, if he did not adopt, a veritable sacrament of purification,[14] which became at the same time a guarantee of salvation. This was nothing more than baptism by immersion in the waters of the Jordan. In this practice he again comes near to the Essenes, with the difference that the Essenes required many ablutions and bathings. John seems to have attached essential importance to the one total immersion he imposed on his converts, regarding it as the symbol of conversion, the effectual sign of forgiveness and regeneration.

It is remarkable that neither sacrifice, nor the bare idea of sacrifice, finds any place in this scheme of salvation, and furthermore that the death of the prophet was not interpreted as providing vicarious satisfaction for the redemption of sinners. A rite of purification at once the most significant, and the simplest, commonest, and one may add the oldest and most universally practised by mankind was enough to put the man of goodwill in a condition to face the judgment of God. It may be that John, like the Essenes, passed no condemnation on the legal sacrifices, his doctrine of salvation simply leaving them on one side as having no meaning for the religious life as he conceived it. For the rest, we cannot be certain that John's baptism allowed of no repetition. But we can hardly doubt that, like Christian baptism, it operated once and for all on every individual receiving it. Had it been a repeatable ablution there would be no ground for comparing it with the Christian rite.

At first sight it would seem that there was no reason why political authority should consider John more disturbing than the Essenes. But the Essenes did not proclaim that the Judgment Day of God was at hand. The soul, according to them, when duly purified by continence, holy washings, holy feasts and prayers would be able, after death, to reascend to the heaven whence it came down, without interfering with the order established on earth. But the universal judgment which John announced as on the point of coming implied something more than the recompense due to the righteous and the punishment that would fall on the wicked: it implied an immediate and complete revolution in which the Kingdom of God would make a clean sweep of all human governments. An outlook such as this could not be regarded with an indifferent eye by the shepherds of the people, even though the eye were that of a sceptic. It was an expectation likely to agitate the public mind in a way not conducive to the tranquillity of the ruling powers. Accordingly,

Antipas made short work of the Baptist, by casting him into prison and cutting off his head. The particular circumstances of his imprisonment and death are unknown to us, but it is safe to say that the agitation provoked by John was judged by political authority to be dangerous. In point of fact it is hardly possible that it could be long restrained within purely moral limits and that the eager longing for divine judgment could have no effect in compromising obedience to established authority. It may very well be that the Tetrarch decided to take the prophet's life on finding that his imprisonment had failed to put a final stop to the agitation.

His death, however, was not enough to discourage his followers and here his case again deserves study for the analogy it affords to that of Jesus. The sect John left behind him was rendered inoffensive by the death of its founder, but none the less it continued to exist under his name. It was perpetuated especially in Transjordania, where the Essenes, the Jewish Christians and the Elchasaites also had a footing. The signs which some have thought to find of the sect's diffusion in Alexandria and Asia are more than fragile; for the author of Acts, when he speaks of Apollos and the twelve disciples of Ephesus as "knowing only the baptism of John,"[15] does not seem to have had in mind the followers of the Baptist; and the polemic of the Fourth Gospel, which aims, through John, at the whole religious economy of the Jews, does not necessarily imply that the Baptist's sect was represented at Ephesus. In like manner the place given to John by the Mandeans in their tradition does not go back to the source; it seems to have been invented in Islamic time to give importance to the Mandean sect and to ensure its conservation. But if John was not the precursor of Jesus in the sense in which Christian tradition makes him out to be, he and his sect were historically, and in a very true sense, precursors of the Christ and of the Christian religion.

2. JESUS

Though myth and legend have considerable place in evangelical tradition, our knowledge of Jesus is somewhat fuller than of John the Baptist. But all the mythical and legendary elaboration within the tradition bears testimony, in its own way, to him from whom the Christian movement had its beginning. Whatever may have been said to the contrary, there is not a single Christian document of the first age which does not imply the historicity of Jesus. The gnostic Docetists who denied the materiality of Christ's body and the physical reality of his Passion believed, with the mass of Christians, in the historicity of Jesus and of his appearance as a figure upon the earth; their Christ, immaterial but visible, was not for them an unreal phantom, a pure image of the mind, as our mythologues would sometimes make him out to have been. And pagan writers least favourable to the Christian religion, from Tacitus to Celsus and the Emperor Julian, always regarded Jesus as an historical figure, Christ being for them the name of a Galilean agitator who came to an evil end and whom his followers had absurdly made into a god. The criticism which attempts to replace this figure by a myth will find itself involved in endless subtleties and travelling on a road which leads to nowhere. None the less it is true that Jesus has lived on in myth, and been carried by myth to the highest peak of history.

Where exactly he was born is unknown to us; we know only that he came from Galilee. The oldest legend shows him at Capernaum and in the region north-west of the Lake of Tiberias; this probably is the region of his birth. The myth which assigns his birthplace to Bethlehem and makes him of the family of David is founded on an arbitrary interpretation of prophecy and contains nothing of primitive and historical tradition. The myth, moreover, is full of contradictions. In order to fix his birthplace at Bethlehem of Judea, Matthew domiciles his parents there; then, to bring him from Judea into Galilee he imagines that Joseph, after his flight into Egypt, not daring to re-install himself in his own country, established himself at Nazareth, whence Jesus came to Capernaum; all of it presented as a fulfilment of ancient prophecies on the strength of an exegesis carried to the extreme of phantasy.[16] Luke, quite differently, supposes that the parents of Jesus had their home in Nazareth and that Jesus was born at Bethlehem by accident, his parents having been brought there in consequence of the census presided over by Quirinius; though it is far from clear why Joseph, even if he was a descendant of David, should have had to report himself at a place which his ancestors had quitted a thousand years previously. This evangelist is equally unaware that he contradicts himself by dating the birth of Jesus both under the reign of Herod, who died in the year 4 before our era, and in the year of the census, which took place after the deposition of Archilaus ten years later.[17] In reality, evangelical tradition had no knowledge either of the village in Galilee or of the year in which Jesus was born. Nor was it any clearer on the point of his Davidic descent, since the two genealogies presented mutually contradict and annul each other.[18] Jesus was made a descendant of David because that was what the Messiah had to be.[19]

The assignment of Nazareth as the family home of Jesus was an attempt made by the same tradition after the event to explain the surname "Nazorean," which was originally added to the name of Jesus and remained the name for designating Christians in Rabbinic literature and in Eastern countries. This name, Nazorean, is quite clearly the name of a sect having no connexion with the town of Nazareth, unless it be that of a common etymology. Nor has it any closer connexion with the *nazirs*, "the men under vow," mentioned in the Old Testament. It may have been the name of the Baptist's sect, of which the Christian was originally an offshoot.[20] Jesus himself, before beginning an independent ministry of his own, was probably at first a member of the Johannite sect. But the story told in the Gospels about the relations of John and Jesus belongs to legend. The message sent to Jesus from prison by John is merely a frame within which considerations are introduced for exhibiting the superiority of Jesus and the Christian Gospel to John and his preaching.[21] The story of the baptism of Jesus by John is nothing else than the myth of the institution of Christian baptism.[22] It pretends to found the complete independence of the Christian scheme of salvation, in relation to other baptist sects and to Judaism, on a decree of divine providence. Implied in the story there is a consciousness of the independence of Christianity, in regard to Judaism, which cannot have been acquired before the year 70, our texts showing signs of having been incessantly retouched in the course of handing the story on.[23] The account of the temptation in the desert has the same mythical character and the documents of the New Testament bear their witness to its evolution. The reason is obvious why the Fourth Gospel omits the temptation, as it omits the cures of demoniacs and even the baptism of Jesus by John. A single trace of service rendered by angels to the Son of God is retained in John i, 51.

In the tradition common to all the Gospels, Jesus is a wandering preacher, as John the Baptist had been before him. The two preachers are not represented as teaching in the manner of contemporary rabbis, but rather as prophets, and both as prophets of a single oracle—"the Kingdom of God is at hand" (Matthew iii, 2; iv, 17). In the Synoptic tradition Jesus is also a wonder-working exorcist—nothing more natural in those times; but in the fourth Gospel, while the wonders increase in magnitude, the exorcisms disappear, as does the story of the temptation in the desert. There is, however, no reason, so far as the personal history of Jesus is concerned, to linger over a detailed discussion of the miracles attributed to him. They represent the appanage of "powers" or "virtues" with which, in the thought of the time, a ministry such as his would be endowed.[24] They are constructed in accordance with current types and are even presented as types, arranged in a series, and, at the same time, turned by all the Gospels, but especially by the fourth, into symbols of the spiritual work accomplished by the Christ. Just as the parables in the Gospels are mystical allegories, so the miracles are "signs," σημεῖα, not only marks of divine power, but symbols of salvation.[25] As spiritual symbols they foreshadow the formation of the Christian Mystery as a whole. But there is no room to doubt that the gift of healing was attributed to Jesus in his lifetime and that he himself deliberately exercised it. The first Christian missionaries were preaching exorcists, as Jesus had been before them, and in that were doing no more than following his example.[26] The Christian religion was not born in an atmosphere of transcendent mysticism and erudite theology.

It is very remarkable that tradition never represents Jesus as preaching in large towns, except when he came to Jerusalem to meet his end. We see him going from one to another of the townlets and straggling villages of Galilee and entering their small synagogues; but there is no evidence that he ever went to Tiberias, a profane town, ordinary residence of the Tetrarch, nor to any other of importance. We must conclude that towns did not provide him with an atmosphere favourable to his message. The people with whom he sought contact were fishermen round the Lake of Gennesaret, poor craftsmen and workers on the land in his neighbourhood. The geographical frame of his ministry did not enclose a large area. Nearly all the souvenirs, if souvenirs they be, are attached to Capernaum and the surrounding country.

It was, then, in a few villages, or at most in a few districts of Galilee, to the north-west of the Lake, that we must conceive him as teaching for some time and with some measure of success. A theatre so small and, moreover, so little known can hardly have been invented by tradition as the scene of a ministry to which it attached importance so great, the connexion of it with these humble localities by means of the text in Isaiah indicated by Matthew (iv, 12–16) being surely an afterthought. The journeys outside Galilee attributed to Jesus were not preaching tours. If they ever took place, it must have been towards the end of the Galilean ministry, and they would seem to have been undertaken by Jesus to escape from the pursuit of Antipas when the attention of the Tetrarch had been drawn to the movement excited by his preaching.[27] We are told, and it is probably true, that quite early in his career Jesus recruited a certain number of companions who followed him regularly from place to place— though the stories of their vocation that have come down to us are all typical and symbolic. What the Gospels have to tell us about the crowds which pressed upon the footsteps of the preacher, and the thousands who came from all Palestine and from Transjordania to hear the Sermon on the Mount, can only be regarded as the work of pious exaggeration.[28] The preaching of Jesus could not have reverberated far beyond Galilee, and the Sermon on the Mount, a collection of didactic fragments and sentences originally distinct, was never preached.

Of what the teaching of Jesus was in reality only an approximate idea can be formed from the teaching that has been attributed to him. It may be said without a trace of paradox that of the teaching he actually gave no collection was ever made. Neither the preacher nor his most faithful hearers dreamed of fixing the tenor of his preaching for the purpose of transmitting it to posterity; every purpose of that kind was thrust aside by the imminent prospect of the Kingdom of God, the near coming of which, with the Christ in glory, was continually announced by the first apostles after the death of Jesus. It was only after the lapse of a considerable time, when groups of believers had become organized in permanent confraternities, that the need for more complete instruction began to be felt, and the teaching *about* Jesus and the teaching *of* Jesus, the latter already greatly modified and augmented, were more and more fused together to form the books of liturgical catechesis for which the name "Gospel" was retained.

Our Gospels, even the Synoptics, are more truly understood as containing the elements of the primitive Christian catechism than as representing instructions really given by Jesus in Galilee and Jerusalem. Needless to say, the mystical gnosis of the fourth Gospel was wholly outside his ken. Just as a legend has been built up for him, so too there has been built up for him a body of teaching, and it has been done by borrowings from many quarters. One part of the sayings which constitute the synoptic tradition was taken from the teaching of the Rabbis, while the whole of it, even where the spirit is that of hellenic Christianity, has the tone of Jewish hellenism.[29] It is safe to say that the teaching of the first three Gospels is conceived after the manner of Jesus and directly penetrated by his spirit. But no attempt could be more futile than that which aims to-day at reconstituting the teaching of the Christ by arranging, in an order more or less logical, the discourses and sayings scattered throughout the first three Gospels. The thought of Jesus is not more directly reflected in such a synthesis than it is in the broken order of the discourses it seeks to arrange. These discourses are constructs designed for the Christian communities, with a view to their needs, their misgivings, their sufferings, their interior difficulties, their position in the pagan world and their controversies with the Jews. It may be that the general principles of this teaching were laid down by Jesus, or merely foreshadowed by him. But, in all strictness of language, the teaching of the discourses and sayings called evangelical are one thing, and the personal preaching of Jesus was another.

Some critics, notably Schmiedel[30] and Goguel more recently, have been forward in maintaining that clearly authentic sayings of Jesus are to be recognized in certain declarations which run counter, more or less, to the early Christologies and so create embarrassment for the apologists. Examples are the following: "Why callest thou me good: there is none good but God," which seems to make the Christ a man subjèct to imperfection; the despairing outcry of Jesus on the Cross, "My God, my God, why hast thou forsaken me?";[31] "some of them that stand here shall not be dead when the Son of Man comes in his Kingdom." Others again have found a unique savour of originality in sayings such as these: "The sabbath was made for man, not man for the sabbath";[32] "not that which goeth into a man defileth him, but that which cometh out," and such like invectives against the Pharisees. It is a risky kind of argument. The saying about "goodness" as an incommunicable attribute of God is a theological subtlety the credit for which may well belong, if not to an evangelist, to some pious rabbi, the taste of whose wisdom was familiar to the Marcan tradition. The dying outcry of Jesus marks the fulfilment of Psalm xxii by the Passion of the Christ. The saying about the near approach of the parousia expresses the faith of the first community of Christians, though in a form which had lost something of its original force. The sayings about the sabbath and about the cause of defilement are as much in the tone of Jewish wisdom as in that of the Gospel; they may be in harmony with the spirit of Jesus but there are no other grounds for asserting that he was the first to formulate them in his preaching and was not repeating them after others. As to the invectives against the Pharisees, they are just as likely to have come from a Christian prophet as from Jesus himself.

Let us be content with the knowledge that while Pontius Pilate was procurator of Judea, perhaps in 28 or 29 of our era, perhaps a year or two earlier, a prophet appeared in Galilee, in the region of Capernaum. He was called Jesus, a name so common among the Jews of that time that assuredly no reason can be found for conceding to the mythologues, as Guignebert does, that the name might have been given him after his death to mark the rôle of saviour early ascribed to him by his followers. This Jesus was a man of lowly origin. It is improbable that Joseph, the name of his father, and Mary, the name of his mother, were invented by the tradition. He had brothers[33] who played a part of some importance in the life of the earliest community of believers. Doubtless he was born in some townlet or village of the region where he began to teach. There are also reasons for believing, as indicated above, that he was for some time attached to John the Baptist, or affiliated to the sect called after him, before himself beginning to preach the near approach of the Kingdom.

The Gospels probably had reasons for defining his teaching and that of the Baptist by the same general formula: "Repent, for the kingdom of God is at hand."[34] This simple though widely comprehensive indication gives us our surest knowledge of his teaching. We may regard it as certain, first because it remained the fundamental element in the faith of his earliest followers who continued his work after his death in proclaiming him Christ: and second, because the earlier elaborations of the Christian tradition, always bound to this as their initial datum, consisted in retouchings or attenuations of the same idea—the coming of the Great Kingdom. We know moreover that the hopes of the Jewish people all came to a head precisely in that idea, and that Jesus was regarded as appointed to bring the realization of these hopes to his faithful followers.

There is no reason to doubt that Jesus, like John, presented the Kingdom unencumbered by the preliminaries in which apocalyptic literature was fond of indulging. The coming of the Kingdom would be immediate and sudden as was befitting, or seemed befitting, to the majesty and might of Him who was to bring it to pass, thereby replacing at a stroke all the kingdoms of flesh, which the powers of our lower world were upholding in unjust exercise of the mandate committed to them by the Master of the universe. What would be the conditions of his coming? How would his reign be carried on? There is no proof that the mind of Jesus dwelt on this subject, which he had not studied in books, as did the apocalyptic writers from Daniel onwards. But there is no sign that he or his first disciples were preoccupied by these fantastic speculations. They were men of the people and their conception of the Great Kingdom had the same simplicity as that of the Zealots, though entirely free from the violence of their fanaticism. We may conclude, then, that Jesus proclaimed, if not the end of the world—for we should have to ask whether he had

75

an idea of the "world," and if so what—at least the end of the present age, the end that is of Satan's Kingdom and of the earthly powers set up by him, the coming of God, the reign of the just, the resurrection of the dead, and the Great Assize at which the wicked everywhere would be sentenced to extermination. With the view before him of judgment about to fall, let the wicked man repent and change his life!

Did Jesus, like John, baptize those who were converted by this message? The Synoptics do not affirm that he did, and critics are generally content to say that he required only the change of heart, thus making him the teacher of a pure religion entirely free from ritual magic. But Jesus had no intention of founding a religion; the idea never entered his mind. It is probable that his baptism by John, whether historical or not, figured at the head of the evangelical catechesis, but quite impossible to say exactly when, how, or why his disciples after him adopted a rite which, on the hypothesis favoured by the critics, Jesus himself neither recommended nor practised. Is not the silence of the Synoptics on this matter a simple consequence of the fact that the story they tell of his Galilean ministry does not aim at recording the historical actions of Jesus, but at instructing the believer about to undergo an initiation, of which the outward ritual is marked with sufficient clearness by the baptism of Jesus himself at the opening of the catechism? Strange as this idea may seem to those who insist on taking the arrangement of Gospel stories as representing the perspective of factual history, it is not impossible that adhesion or, one might say, conversion to the message of the Galilean Jesus was marked by the same rite of baptism as that which marked conversion to the message of John.35 Nor is it impossible that even the meals taken in common by his regular followers were strongly coloured, as Renan supposes,36 by a mystical element as prefiguring the banquets of the elect in the Kingdom of God.37 Preconceptions are rife as to the conditions under which Jesus delivered his message, and it is a common assumption that these differed greatly from those which attended the ministry of John. But the plain truth is that we know very little about either, the Gospels giving us no information on the subject, or informing us inexactly, even in regard to Jesus. After all, a group of believers would not have been so easily formed after the death of Jesus had

he not gathered around him during his lifetime a sort of confraternity analogous to that which we know was gathered
round John and perpetuated in a sect after the Baptist's death.

Did Jesus claim for himself an eminent place in the coming
Kingdom? In recent times many have deemed it possible to answer
this question in the negative, but without suspecting that they
might be bringing Jesus too near to their own mentality or to
their own religious ideals. In their view Jesus was a mystical
philanthropist, the Kingdom of Heaven was essentially inward
and moral, the presence of God in the soul, the revelation and
intimate awareness of the divine fatherhood and goodness, of the
law of love, of the dignity of man. And this no doubt is what the
Gospel may seem to those who try to find themselves in it and
view it, from a great distance of time, sifted by the experience of
nineteen centuries. But Christianity was not born in that transcendent atmosphere and our metaphysical universals were as
remote from the mind of Jesus as were the sceptical smiles of
Ernest Renan and the humanitarianism of Henri Barbusse. The
dominating perspective of the Gospel, and the dominating
thought of Jesus, is the concrete, real and even realistic conception
of the Kingdom of God, involving the complete renovation of the
human order both inward and outward. The value of the human
soul—still less its absolute value, the autonomy of human
personality in a transcendent individualism—is not presented in
the Gospel independently of the individual's destiny in the coming
Kingdom; the law of love is not laid down independently of the
renunciations required by the coming revolution in earthly
affairs; the relief of the poor man is not prescribed independently
of his exaltation in the everlasting Kingdom. In sober truth,
neither the revelation of Divine Goodness, nor the value of the
soul, nor the law of love, nor the dignity of the poor has the
eminent place in the primitive Gospel which many in our time
would assign to it. These are the elements of the Gospel which,
more or less magnified when seen from our point of view,
happen to be for us the least worn out by time. But, for the
historian, the sum and substance of the Gospel can always be
found, and must always be found, in the eschatological idea of the
Kingdom of God, all the rest being subordinate to that.

That being so, Jesus could hardly have overlooked himself as a figure destined to play a part in the coming Advent of God. To be sure he does not seem to have given much thought to the order that would be set up by the divine polity of the future. The saying about the thrones on which his principal disciples were to sit at his side does not go back to him, but was probably conceived by the earliest community in honour of the Twelve. There is at least an equal probability that the notion of the Son of Man, which holds so large a place in the Gospel tradition, was introduced into it for the purpose of glorifying Jesus after his death and linked to that event in order to bring out its providential significance. "The Son of Man" is a mythical conception, earlier than the Gospel tradition which so largely exploits it; earlier than the apocalypses of Daniel and Enoch, where use is made of it.[38] Its origin is pagan, probably Chaldeo-Iranian.[39] In the apocalyptic tradition it became a kind of definition for an idealized Messiah. Although the history of the myth is far from being clear, it is assuredly pre-Christian and was probably without influence on the Gospel at its point of departure, that is on Jesus and his first disciples. The idea, in short, is bound up with a redemption-gnosis which the Epistles present in a developed form but whose place in the Gospel is progressive and of secondary importance only.[40] We may agree further that Jesus never described himself in set terms as the future King of the Elect, and that even the confession of Peter at Caesarea Philippi anticipates a faith which, as so defined, was that of the first group of believers and only came into being after the catastrophe of Calvary. But it remains true that, before the final drama, this faith was in a manner existent, and to some extent explicit, among the first converts to Jesus' Gospel, and in Jesus himself as naturally involved in the initiative taken by him in proclaiming the Great Event and making preparation for its advent.

It was as an Envoy of God, not as a simple prophet, nor as a sage and a moralist, that Jesus presented himself to his contemporaries. He claimed a special and unique mission in regard to the Great Event, but did not define it with precision. "The Great Envoy" would be the equivalent in our language. So far as we can judge Zoroaster and the Buddha made similar claims; so, too, did Mani and Mahomet. There could be no question of his being the Messiah there and then, since the Messiah was the

Prince of the Great Kingdom and there could be no Messiah till the Kingdom came. Elsewhere the author of this book has argued for the view that Jesus was Messiah in expectation, Messiah presumptive, and some of his critics have condemned the idea as a theological subtilty. Perhaps it is neither as subtle nor as theological as they deem it to be. But let us keep only to this; Jesus, as the Great Herald of the coming Kingdom, certainly made claim, before the end of his life, to the rôle which would involve his becoming, after his death, the Messiah who was to come with the Kingdom. Nothing else is of import if his mortal career is to suffice as an explanation of his immortal destiny. The closer definitions of that destiny would never have come into being if the faith of Jesus and his disciples had not, in one way or another, contained their beginnings and their justification. This faith it is that also explains the culminating action of Jesus at Jerusalem; this faith it was that triumphed in his death.

3. Jesus Proclaims the Kingdom in Jerusalem

Believers, even the most liberal, and they perhaps most of all, are still loath to admit that the action of Jesus in carrying his message to Jerusalem was not, humanly speaking, more reasonable than that of the others who are commonly known as "false Messiahs": for example, Theudas who, fifteen years after the death of Jesus, recruited some thousands of followers in Perea and brought them to the side of Jordan in the belief that the river would open up its waters to facilitate their triumphal march on Jerusalem; or the Egyptian, of whom Acts also speaks (xxi, 38), who led a much more formidable body of partisans as far as the Mount of Olives, convinced in their simplicity that the walls of Jerusalem would fall down at the voice of their prophet.[41] These cases however are parallel to that of Jesus and their issue, so far as the immediate result was concerned, was much the same for him as for them.[42] But our liberal believers are not content with insisting that the personality of Jesus was loftier and purer than that of these men, who were only adventurers and visionaries; they will have it also that Jesus was less under illusion than they, or even—an absurd supposition both historically and psychologically—that he was under no illusion at all about the fate in store for him at Jerusalem, which, had illusion been absent, he would have had no motive to encounter. Jesus, they would have it, came to Jerusalem at the risk of his life to accomplish a great duty. As the interpretation of an act of faith, and, we must add, of religious illuminism, all this is too modern and rationalistic.

On this occasion Jesus was not visiting Jerusalem in the character of a simple pilgrim.[43] It is possible that he had made several pilgrimages to the city before taking up the rôle of a prophet; but it is wholly improbable, not to say quite impossible, that he was there more than this once as announcer of the Kingdom of God. The synoptic tradition gives us to understand that he presented himself with this announcement on the occasion of a Passover which, in Luke's reckoning, would probably be that of the year 29. The artificial chronology and editorial arrangements of the Fourth Gospel need not be taken into account. Being what it was, the preaching of Jesus in Galilee must have been of short duration; to make it last a few months is to give it good measure. Whether the reason was that he had seen the speedy collapse of the credit accorded his message at its first announcement, or that he had reason to think that Antipas was about to put a violent stop to his preaching,[44] or simply because Jerusalem was the appointed place for the publication of his message, as well as being the place predestined for the Great Coming, Jesus resolved to proclaim the word of the Kingdom in the Holy City.

No direct testimony has come down to us to throw light on the convictions which determined his action at this conjuncture. The Gospels present him to us as fully conscious of providential designs and as going to Jerusalem that he might there procure the fulfilment of divine intentions and ancient prophecies—a systematic and apologetic conception of which next to nothing can be retained for the psychology of Jesus. It cannot be repeated too often that the Gospel stories are the scenes of a ritual drama in which the actions of the characters, especially of the chief character, are governed by the faith which the drama is designed to represent, to fortify and, one might say, to realize. Most assuredly the young Galilean continued in Jerusalem to be animated by the faith and the hope which had led him in his own country to proclaim the speedy coming of the Great Kingdom. It was that same impulse of faith and hope, raised perhaps to a higher ardour by the obstacles already encountered, encouraged also by the measure of success already won and rendered more urgent by the necessity to proclaim the divine message to the Jewish people at the centre of the national life—that same impulse it was that drew Jesus on to his fate, but without giving him clear foreknowledge of what that fate would be.[45] Doubtless his hope was too masterful to permit him to envisage, with complete lucidity and calm, the likelihood, in reality a certainty, that death was awaiting him. What he did expect, and his followers expected with him, was the manifestation of divine power, the advent of the Kingdom foretold, the dawn of the Day of God. Neither in the messianic tradition of Judaism, nor in the message of the Kingdom as he had delivered it, was there anything to make him suppose that his own death was a necessary condition of the Great Event. He came to Jerusalem fully confident in the power of God, in the validity of the ancient promise to Israel, in the urgent need of divine intervention to establish the reign of justice on the earth.

We could not be worse informed than we are about the real events immediately preceding the tragic climax of this religious adventure. The affair of the Egyptian, above referred to, is enough to show that the messianic demonstration on the Mount of Olives, as described in the synoptics, is not in itself improbable. But the story they give us is derived from Old Testament texts.[46] The same is true of the expulsion of the traders from the temple, a story much less easy to accept as recording a real event.[47] Tradition has constructed for Jesus a Jerusalem ministry analogous to the Galilean; but the long invective against the Pharisees seems no more authentic in its substance, as the real teaching of Jesus at Jerusalem, than the discourse on the end of the world.[48] It is, moreover, improbable that Jesus would have been allowed to teach publicly in the temple for many days without suffering interference. Our choice lies practically between two hypotheses: a riot created by the followers of Jesus, if we may suppose them numerous enough to make it, immediately on their arrival in Jerusalem,[49] and the prompt arrest of their leader by the Roman authority; or a popular movement excited by the preaching of

Jesus in the temple, which would very quickly have brought on the intervention of the priests, followed at once by recourse to the procurator. In either case the affair would have borne, or would seem to bear, the character of a politico-religious demonstration which the procurator would suppress severely and without a moment's delay, as happened to the movements led by Theudas and the Egyptian. But the affair of Jesus, at the time when it occurred, seemed of less importance than theirs. He did not march on Jerusalem, as they did, with thousands of followers behind him, and his presence in the city would do no more than provoke a tumult to be suppressed at once.

All the evangelists have to record of the final evening is connected with the mystical meanings attached to the Last Supper, the Christian Passover in which the death of the Christ was commemorated. The treachery of Judas is accessory and it is by no means easy to say what, in reality, can have corresponded to this incident; it may have been invented as a mythical amplification of the punishment inflicted on Jesus.[50] The previsions attributed to the Christ on the same occasion are intended to throw a stronger light on his person; they come from the realms of drama and apologetic. One may be a fiction built up on a real fact; thus, the passing consternation of the disciples at the arrest and punishment of their Master is the basis for his prediction of their flight (Mark xiv, 27).[51] Another may be a fiction co-ordinated to another fiction or to a supposed fact; thus, the announcement of the coming betrayal[52] may be co-ordinated with Peter's denial—if, as is probable, the denial is an invention of Paul's party directed against the chief of the Galilean apostles.[53] In the same manner, but more surely, the announcement of the coming resurrection, interpolated into that of the flight (Mark xiv, 28) paves the way for the fictitious story of the discovery of the empty tomb. The words of the Eucharistic institution correspond to the interpretation of the Supper given by the First Epistle to the Corinthians:[54] they signify not only the presence of the Christ among his own at the common meal, but also the mystical relation of bread and wine to the commemoration of his saving death, of which the Supper is, in a manner, the mystical reiteration. And this interpretation, which can hardly go back to the apostolic age, is superimposed upon an older one in which the Supper is understood as a symbolic foretaste of the happiness of the elect in the Kingdom of God after the Great Event.[55] But even this earlier interpretation is the work of tradition which attached it typically to the last meal taken by Jesus who may very well have himself suggested it in the course of his ministry at the daily meals with his disciples. Finally the scene at Gethsemane[56] brings together and endows with material form the speculations of primitive Christianity concerning the great ordeal undergone by the Christ. Incidentally, the editors of Mark, followed by Matthew, have given that story a turn unfavourable to the Galilean apostles.

Of the circumstances of the arrest in the Garden of Olives not one, perhaps not even those of place and time, can be retained as historical.[57] The economy of the Gospel narratives is related to the ritual commemoration of the Passion; taking them literally we run the risk of transposing into history what are really the successive incidents of a religious drama. True it is that behind this drama lie the brutal facts, the condemnation to death and the crucifixion. But the real physiognomy of the facts has been transfigured in the drama which was conceived, not for reproducing the history reflected in it, but for its own purpose, that of bringing out its mystic significance, as well as in the interests of apologetic. Strictly speaking, it is possible, though there is nothing to make it probable, that Jesus was arrested at night, outside Jerusalem, by a sudden surprise organized by the temple police or by the Roman. If we suppose that Jesus was violently seized during an affray occasioned by him, and not without resistance by his partisans, we may be sure that tradition would have been careful to preserve no record of it. For not only has it not preserved the real circumstances of his burial, which it had perhaps an interest in falsifying, but it has no clear story to tell of his trial and condemnation.

For a long time past discussion of the Trial of Jesus has proceeded on the assumption that our texts contain an authentic account of its successive stages. What they do contain, let it once more be repeated, is the liturgical dramatization of the trial together with an apologetic commentary. Mark and Matthew report two trials and two condemnations: first, the Sanhedrim tries Jesus and condemns him;[58] then the procurator Pilate takes up the affair for confirmation, examines the case, finds Jesus innocent, tries vainly to save him and, finally, disclaiming all responsibility, ratifies the sentence of death.[59] According to Luke, the Sanhedrim prepares the accusation, then submits the affair to the Jews, passes the case on to Antipas; Antipas finding no ground for condemnation, Pilate then concedes the execution of the accused to the clamour of the Jews, after another vain attempt to pardon Jesus as in Mark and Matthew. In the fourth Gospel Jesus is first examined about his teaching by the High Priest, Annas (Hanan), who was not High Priest at that time.[60] Annas then sends Jesus to Caiaphas and the Jews carry to Pilate an accusation which they are not able to formulate (John xviii, 28–32); Jesus then explains to Pilate that his Kingdom is not of this world: Pilate pronounces him innocent and has recourse to the expedient of pardon; but the Jews persist in their demand and Pilate makes another attempt to deprive them of their victim, going so far as to present Jesus in kingly state and saying he will not crucify their King; the Jews reply they have no King but Caesar, and Pilate yields them Jesus for crucifixion. Let those who can find their way through this judicial phantasmagoria.

The one stable fact is the crucifixion, a Roman punishment reserved for rebels and inflicted on Jesus on one of the days preceding the Jewish Passover. It follows that the sentence was pronounced by Roman authority after a trial in which that authority acted in its own right,[61] and not as ratifying a sentence passed by the Sanhedrim.[62] It is easy to understand how the agitation fomented by Jesus would be construed as subversive of the sovereignty of the Emperor, even though it would not be regarded as a serious menace to the security of the Empire. Pilate would pronounce the sentence of death without a moment's hesitation; nor is it easy to see, in view of the historic circumstances and the probabilities, how he could have avoided doing so. Jesus was not condemned because he had been misunderstood. He had exposed himself to suspicion by the attitude he had openly adopted and by the tenor of his message. Only by his death did he triumph over his accusers. Had Pilate, *per impossibile*, decided to keep him in prison, the Christian religion would not have owed its birth to him.

Was there an accusation by the Sanhedrim? We cannot

84

answer in the affirmative with certainty nor even with much probability. Our texts, repeatedly cut about and surcharged, are not an historic record of the death of Christ. More than that, they are not even founded on any historic record discoverable by literary analysis. It would seem indeed that the fundamental document of Mark agreed with the fundamental document of John in the date of the Passion, that is to say in fixing the death of Jesus at the day and hour when the Jews sacrificed the paschal lamb. But the date is not historical; it proclaims itself symbolic and liturgical. It reflects the primitive Easter observance of the Christian communities retained to the end of the second century by the communities of Asia from which the others had long been divided by their custom of celebrating Easter on Sunday, as the day of the resurrection.[63] The Christian religion had its birth in history, but only began to write its history with Eusebius of Caesarea, when it was too late. Let us then recognize the simple fact that the oldest tradition now perceptible about the death of Jesus, like that about his ministry, has already become a liturgical legend, the evolution of which in the gospel literature preserves throughout the same ritual character, complicated by apologetic interests.

While the chronology of the Passion was retouched in a way which distinguishes and clearly separates the Christian Passover from the Jewish, as the two were distinguished and separated in object, in like manner the story of the trial has been given a turn for the purpose of throwing back upon the Jews the initiative and the responsibility for the sentence of death. Hence the doubling of the procedure and, in the Synoptics, the improbable nocturnal sitting of the Sanhedrim during the holy night of the Passover. At this sitting Jesus is condemned for professing a Christology which was that of the second generation of Christians.[64] But the evangelists get embarrassed by the saying in which Jesus is made to avow an intention to destroy the temple. Taking the words literally, they would, if authentic, place Jesus on the same level as Theudas and the Egyptian mentioned above. The saying may, indeed, have been brought up in evidence at the trial before Pilate, to the ruin of him who had pronounced it, but has no natural context in any of the Gospel stories. The nocturnal arrest of Jesus by servants of the

High Priest is all of a piece with the trial before the Sanhedrim. But the story in the Fourth Gospel about Judas at the head of a band of soldiers and temple rabble who fall to the ground on their backs before Jesus in the garden is in no better keeping with historical tradition.

The incident of Barabbas is a fiction of which the origin is obscure, but the purpose evident.[66] The best device its authors could find for shifting responsibility for the sentence from Pilate to the Jews was to make the procurator offer pardon to Jesus and the Jews prefer its bestowal on a brigand. In like manner the intervention of Herod is to procure an unexpected witness to the innocence of Jesus in the person of the tetrarch. Originally this fiction must have been a parallel to that of Barabbas, but bolder, in that Herod was substituted for Pilate as condemning Jesus and taking the initiative in his execution, as he is said to have done in the Gospel of Peter.[67] It is obvious that the lofty declarations of Jesus before Annas and before Pilate have interest only for the history of Christology. Generally speaking it may be said that the statements and attitudes attributed to Jesus by the Gospels on this occasion are clearly devoid of meaning except in relation to Christology and to the liturgical drama of the Passion. To the historical reality of the arrest, condemnation and crucifixion they have no relation.[68]

In regard to the place of execution the traditional indication can be retained, although there is ground to suspect that tradition in placing the tomb has taken over an ancient grotto of Adonis, as it took over the cave at Bethlehem.[69] The whole setting of the scene of the crucifixion suggests dramatization, theological and ritual, even to the incident of Simon of Cyrene who saves Jesus from the humiliation of carrying the cross.[70] Other incidents[71] are introduced for the fulfilment of prophecy: the two robbers (Isaiah liii, 12);[72] the wine mixed with spices or gall (Psalm lxix, 19); the division of the garments;[73] the insults of the passers-by (Psalm xxii, 7–9); the words of Jesus on the cross (Psalm xxii, 1).[74] In other cases these incidents have symbolic value: the darkness;[75] the rending of the temple veil;[76] the earthquake; the dead rising from their graves. Symbolism is most pronounced in the fourth Gospel which, careless of probability, brings the mother of Jesus and the beloved disciple to the foot of the cross, shows Jesus issuing instructions till his last breath and discovers the mystic economy of the Christian sacraments in the effect that followed the thrust of the lance.77 The reality of it all was on a level less exalted than this drama, but more poignant and more cruel. Jesus was promptly condemned and promptly executed; he died in torment and, save for his executioners, there can hardly have been any to witness his agony.

Chapter III

BIRTH OF THE BELIEF IN JESUS AS THE CHRIST

WE have seen that the circumstances of Jesus' death are far from being defined in their details, even in those which would be of considerable importance to the historian, such as the date, now impossible to determine not only as to the day, but equally so, and primarily, as to the year. A still deeper obscurity reigns over the question now to come before us. Under what conditions did the disciples of Jesus acquire their faith in the victory over death which they quickly came to believe had been won by the Master they had lost: under what conditions did they acquire the eager desire, the strong will, the firm resolution, to spread this faith abroad as the sole means of admission to the Kingdom of God which Jesus, now glorified as the risen Christ, would soon bring down to earth?

We may assume that Jesus was crucified in one of the years between 26 and 29 and that the event occurred a little before the feast of the Passover. How then shall we explain the reaction of the disciples to a blow which might well have shattered their faith, but which actually ended by exalting it to new heights? In what conditions did they set about the propagation of the faith thus newly enhanced? How came it to pass that the propagation of it was so promptly carried beyond the borders of Palestine? These are questions which legend and myth have answered with much assurance and equal simplicity, but to which probable answers based on certain significant traces, debris of a deposit left by a true tradition and not entirely overlaid by legend and myth, are the best answers the historian is able to offer.

1. COLLAPSE AND RECOVERY OF THE DISCIPLES' FAITH

On the evening of the day when Jesus breathed his last, no man living could have foreseen the incomparable future awaiting the unfortunate prophet whose hopes of a renovated world had received from the course of events a refutation so complete and so cruel. The executioners who took down his body from the cross doubtless flung it, perhaps after giving a finishing blow to the half-dead sufferer, into some trench reserved for those deemed unworthy of honourable burial, in conformity with the Jewish law which forbad the bodies of executed criminals to be exposed after sunset. Perhaps the place of burial was "the field of blood," Aceldama,[1] to which Christian tradition has clumsily tacked on the legend of Judas, making Judas into a substitute for him who was not to be thought of as buried for ever in such a place. However that may be, the legend of the laying-out and burial of the body by Joseph of Arimathea, conceived as the fulfilment of prophecy (probably Isaiah liii, 9) and of one piece with the apologetic fiction of the empty tomb, is also a fiction.

The usual practice was to cast the body of an executed criminal into the common grave, unless the family obtained permission to bury it in their own way. At the time when the tradition was born it was known that in the case of Jesus nobody intervened. But later on, when the need was felt to give the Christ an honourable burial, which the family was thought unable to do, tradition imagined for the part a person of consideration alike for his social standing and character. But the invention of Joseph of Arimathea to play the part of intervener is a perceptible artifice, so, too, is the invention of women, in default of the disciples then in flight, as the most likely witnesses of the burial and afterwards of the resurrection. Even in the Fourth Gospel we get glimpses of an older story in the background which represented the executioners as putting the body into a grave that chanced to be at hand near the place of execution.[2] The stories in Mark about the burial and the tomb found empty are fictions which the other evangelists have elaborated so as to give them a better consistency. The object aimed at was to furnish the resurrection with a proof hitherto unthought of. The part played by women in funeral rites suggested the Galilean women, who, having ministered to Jesus in his native province, might be supposed to have followed him to Jerusalem, been present at his passion on Calvary, then at his burial and finally to have found his tomb unoccupied. Joseph of Arimathea was the male figure indispensable for decency of burial and boldly selected as a member of the Sanhedrim. Pilate, before granting the authority demanded for the removal, is informed by the centurion that Jesus is quite dead—a point intended to meet the theory, brought forward in a controversy between Jews and Christians, that the body had been carried away before death, neither party knowing more than the other how the matter had really gone.

Mark makes Joseph buy a new winding sheet: according to the other evangelists the tomb is also a new one;[3] the Synoptics describe it as hewn out of the rock—doubtless in fulfilment of prophecies such as Isaiah xxii, 16, xxxiii, 16. The great stone blocking the entrance is intended to enhance the miracle of the resurrection.[4] John adds to Joseph a second male figure in the person of Nicodemus, a figure peculiar to this evangelist; to give the burial a higher dignity and to complete the symbolism he has Jesus embalmed, contradicting the Synoptics. All this is supposed to take place on the evening of Friday so as to keep Jesus in the tomb for the whole of the Sabbath and a few hours of the following night; this has the secondary purpose of excluding the theory that the body had been carried off. With the same purpose, but more directly, Matthew has the fantastic fiction of a guard of soldiers stationed at the tomb. But the main object of the whole arrangement is to make the resurrection take place on the day of the Sun, which thus becomes the day of the Risen Lord. Apologetic and symbolism are thus equally satisfied.[5]

The discovery of the empty tomb by women is arranged in Mark with surprising artlessness. Never has fiction more childish found so many to believe it true. The concluding statement "they said nothing to any man, because they were afraid," which suppresses the testimony invented for them, by leaving it with no guarantee but the word of the evangelist, has the simple and very evident object of explaining how the discovery of the empty tomb was unknown to anybody until the moment when here recorded by him. As this plainly will not do, the other evangelists have taken pains to improve upon it, and first of all by omitting Mark's unfortunate explanation. Matthew, Luke and John[6] all release the tied tongues of the women. But in spite of all they can do to improve on Mark it is clear enough that the whole story came into the tradition long after the accounts of visions and apparitions on

91

which the earliest faith was nourished; and equally clear that the connexion is artificial throughout between the story of the empty tomb, with its secondary purpose of authorizing the Roman custom of celebrating Easter on Sunday, and the oldest recollections, whether concerned with visions of the Risen Christ or with the beginnings of Christian preaching. A like artificiality may be discerned in the way the burial by Joseph of Arimathea is bound together with the discovery of the empty tomb. But, though of earlier date than the story of the empty tomb, that of the burial by Joseph is no better founded on reality.[7]

The dead Jesus was left to his fate. But what became of the memory of him? What became of the faith he inspired in his disciples? It is certain that his arrest and execution put a stop for the time being to the proclamation of his message, and equally certain that the preaching of it by apostles did not begin in Jerusalem till some time had elapsed after the tragic end. How long the interval was cannot be exactly discerned, for the chronology in Acts is artificial and bound up with an imaginary and tendentious account of the facts. The perspective unrolled in the first two chapters of Acts, which are continuous with the end of Luke, omits entirely what may be called the interregnum of the faith or, more strictly, its period of crisis. It reveals nothing of the confusion into which the disciples were plunged by the arrest and death of Jesus, nor of their flight into Galilee nor of the real conditions under which their faith was re-established by the conviction that Jesus, risen from the dead, was about to return in glory as the Christ. Suppressing all this, Luke and Acts keep the disciples in Jerusalem, limiting the period of their anguish almost to the time while the Christ was in his tomb, and making them the recipients of a new and higher initiation, which begins on the very evening of the resurrection, is then continued for forty days by instructions from the Risen Christ in person, and consummated by the descent of the Holy Ghost and the foundation of the Catholic and Apostolic Church on the day of Pentecost. All of which is gnosis[8] and fiction, disguising a highly complex reality, the fiction serving only to baffle our conjectures as to the real course of events.

As Jesus cannot have been allowed to teach in Jerusalem for any length of time, if indeed he was able to teach there at all, it is improbable that he recruited many followers in that city. Thus the whole future of the Gospel came to depend on the believers from Galilee, the most ardent and faithful of whom, or at least those who were his regular followers, had doubtless accompanied him to Jerusalem. The third Gospel and Acts, as we have seen, keep them in Jerusalem, under the express order of Jesus, to the hour of Pentecost when their preaching is supposed to have begun. In this way the ministry of Jesus is prolonged after his death up to the time of his ascension into heaven; some days are then passed in prayer during which a twelfth apostle is chosen by lot to fill the place of Judas until finally, on the day of Pentecost, regarded as the anniversary of the promulgation of the Law, the Spirit descends from heaven upon the apostles and opens its victorious activity in the Church by the public preaching of Peter. All this is artificial and of late origin. The institution of the Twelve is not likely to have preceded the organization of the earliest community, while the idea of the Church as the Kingdom of the Spirit and a kind of substitute for the Reign of God, whose coming it still awaits, is relatively recent and certainly later than the foundation of the first groups of hellenizing Christians. We may add that the object the apostolic preaching is said to have aimed at—that of proving the Gospel by the fulfilment of prophecies (Luke xxiv, 43–47)—is not that with which it really began, but presupposes the evangelical tradition already grown to the form represented by the common source of the Synoptics.9

The sum of the matter comes then to this: the perspective of Luke and Acts, in itself symbolic throughout, is radically false from the historian's point of view. It deliberately contradicts an older and more probable tradition according to which the followers of Jesus returned at once into Galilee. It is true that this tradition, in the form in which it has come down to us, has already taken up a legendary element in the texts which inform us that Jesus, before his death, appointed a rendezvous with his disciples in Galilee, and that the order to repair to Galilee was repeated by the angel whom the women found in the empty tomb. All that is pure fiction, conceived for the purpose of disguising the collapse of the disciples, and their flight into Galilee in presence of the catastrophe which fell on their leader, and, at the same time, of buttressing the myth of the resurrection. Had the disciples really remained in Jerusalem and there found confirmation of their faith, the tradition would not have started by localizing the apparitions of the Risen Christ in Galilee. But the fiction of the rendezvous in Galilee proved somewhat embarrassing; for, if the disciples were actually in Jerusalem on the morning of the resurrection, why were they sent to distant Galilee to get the evidence of it in apparitions of the Christ risen from the dead? Luke (xxiv, 6) gets out of the difficulty by substituting for the rendezvous in Galilee the reminder of a prediction made by Jesus in Galilee to the effect that he would suffer and rise again; after which Luke localizes all the apparitions in Jerusalem. The perspective is still further distorted in the fourth Gospel,[10] where we find it completely upset by the addition of the last chapter, an overload impossible to fit in with the setting of chapter xx. All this elaborate staging, constructed for the purpose of providing an entrance into evangelical history for the resurrection-myth, and of adjusting thereto the origin of Christian preaching, comes to one result—that of obscuring, if not rendering quite undiscoverable, the real sequence of events between the execution of Jesus and the dawn of apostolic activity in Jerusalem. The scripture version of the tradition has thus created, but without perceiving it, an irreducible gap in its own evidence, thanks to which the mythologues of our time have been able to produce their theory that Jesus never existed.

We can well believe that Jerusalem was a dangerous place for the disciples after the arrest of their Master. The circumstances of the arrest seem to have been such that none of them was caught; doubtless the affair had gone too swiftly to give the authorities time to pick them out at the prophet's side. The instant his doom was pronounced they made off in all haste to their own country, overwhelmed by the blow which had struck down their leader and having no thought for the moment but that of their own safety. To call them disillusioned by the terrible outcome would not be strictly accurate; disillusion would imply a fuller participation in the tragedy than had actually been theirs, were it only to the extent of seeing with their own eyes the ignominy of their leader's execution and burial, which they did not see. But they were in utter consternation and amazement and needed a little time and freedom from danger to pull themselves together. The shock was violent; but their faith had a deep root and was bound in course of time to assert itself against the violence of the shock. And this reaction would come the more easily inasmuch as they knew only by rumour of the horror of the crucifixion and the infamy of the burial.

According to the tradition their faith was awakened, or rather created anew, by sensible apparitions of Jesus come back to life. It is easy to see that these apparitions, fitted with time and place and given material form in the traditional stories, are based upon *visions* in which faith was able to find nourishment and confirmation, and for the good reason that faith had created them. Taken as they stand, the Gospel stories do not show us the growth of the disciples' emotions into the belief that Jesus was risen from the dead. It cannot be repeated too often that the object these stories are aimed at is to transform what was essentially an inward conviction, insight or vision of faith, into external fact attested by the witness of the senses, and so make the conviction a part of factual history. To give substance to the apparitions as external facts, pains were taken to mark the day, with all the circumstances of their occurrence co-ordinated to those of the death, and with these again adapted to the day and circumstances of the burial. In this way the inward visions were objectified into outward occurrences, into material phenomena at once verifiable and verified. This done, the facts were arranged in serial order so as to form a posthumous life of Jesus. The faith was thus defended against objectors by fictions which faith produced for its own justification, but which were not the source from which it sprang. Belief in the immortality of Jesus risen from the dead existed long before anybody imagined or professed to know the day on which he rose, or that his tomb had been found empty, or that he had afterwards given the disciples their capital instructions, conversing and eating with them as he had been accustomed to do before his death. There is, however, good reason for adding that the authors of our texts are to be credited with relative sobriety in the shaping of their work. The tradition they have handed down has deliberately avoided the worst extravagances, such as those displayed by the story of the resurrection in the Gospel of Peter.

In those who first believed in Jesus the working of faith was deep and masterful. Their belief that he had risen from the dead was the fruit of that inner process. Needless to say the process was never analysed by those in whom it worked. History knows it directly only by its results. We have seen that the violent death of John the Baptist did not prevent the survival of his sect and that his followers did not believe that he had perished in the grave. But fortunes more resounding than John's were in store for Jesus. Let us not forget how, in the last days, Jesus and his company were convinced that the Great Event was *at hand* and that to-morrow might see them enter, alive and glorified, into the felicity of the Kingdom. There is little risk in assuming that in these solemn hours the disciples believed that Jesus was about to become the Messiah promised to Israel and that Jesus himself, in one way or another, accepted the idea. Nothing is impossible to the ardours of faith. On a faith which knows not how to criticize itself, and would not if it could, disillusion has no hold. Then, too, we must remember that, to minds habituated to the belief in resurrection or in immortality, death is an accident of no significance. Jesus and his followers were in that condition: they believed that the resurrection of the just in the Kingdom of God was *at hand*. One of two things, then, was inevitable, either the faith of the disciples would founder, which it neither could nor would; or it would gather up its forces for a bolder affirmation, continuing to proclaim as before, that the Kingdom was on the point of coming, but with the addition that Jesus, now raised to glory at God's right hand, would personally bring it in.

In fact there was nothing to prevent the disciples from continuing to expect what they had expected all along. He whom they mourned was not, in their eyes, a mere teacher who had converted a few simple souls. They had lost their Master, and their Master was none other than the King of Glory into whom Jesus was now transfigured and about to reveal himself to the world in the swiftly coming Kingdom of God. The Kingdom would descend from the high heavens, whence many besides themselves had begun to look for the coming of the Messiah, whence they had always thought he would come, but now expected him with confidence raised to the highest pitch of certitude. If all the righteous would be raised from the dead at the coming of the Kingdom, was it not fitting that Jesus, its prophet and founder, should be raised in advance of the resurrection of his followers, so soon to come? Since God must needs send him with the Kingdom would He not at once take him up to His right hand instead of leaving him in the abodes of the dead? Even if we suppose that Jesus himself had predicted his death in their presence, he could not have pictured his future otherwise either to himself or to them. God would not forsake him. The Kingdom was coming and Jesus, immortal and glorious, would come with the Kingdom.

What is religious faith? Essentially nothing else than the whole mind, reason, imagination and will, putting forth their combined energy in an effort to break a way through the natural framework of existence and escape from the mechanism which seems so inexorably to govern the destiny of all things. Thanks to the force of that effort, the difficulties aroused in our modern minds by the idea of resurrection, difficulties familiar also to the mind of Greece, had no existence for these Jewish believers, accustomed as they were to thinking in plain terms of survival after death, and incapable of conceiving it otherwise. Many apologists in our time have been wont to argue as though the resurrection of Jesus had to be demonstrated to the disciples by tangible and indisputable proofs such as would satisfy impartial investigators in a scientific age. In reality the first believers accepted the resurrection precisely because they were men for whom proofs of that kind had no interest. The power of their antecedent faith made it impossible for them to think of Jesus as one to whom death had put an end; they believed that he had been raised from death because otherwise they could not think of him as living. The "how" of the raising troubled them not the least: that was God's affair. It was only at a later stage, when the Gospel was being proclaimed among people of non-Jewish mentality that objections began to arise. Then it was that the effort was made to prove the resurrection by arguments convincing to critical minds: then it was that material form was given to the fugitive visions which had been nourishment enough for the earliest faith: then it was that the story of the tomb found empty was invented in order to prove that Jesus had not remained in his grave; then it was that he was represented, in apparitions clearly characterized, as conversing with his followers, eating with them and offering to Thomas the wound in his side and the holes in his nail-pierced hands. This array of proofs, so far-fetched and yet naïve, was not imagined till long after the birth of the belief that they were intended to support. The earliest faith had not sought them; one might almost say it would have found them meaningless. It never paused to speculate on the where and when of it all; cared not to know what had happened to the dead body of Jesus; raised no questions about the re-animation of the corpse and never asked how it had been done. Had the first believers been men with a turn for scientific inquiry into these matters they would have had no belief. Those who first came forward as witnesses that Jesus was risen were indeed persuaded that they had seen him alive in their visions, but they told no stories of his resurrection as a fact materially attested.

Thus did belief in the resurrection of Jesus come to its birth, and the manner of it may be called spontaneous. The faith of the disciples in his Messianic future was too strong to admit of self-contradiction, too strong to give way under the refutation thrown upon it by the ignominy of the Cross. Faith raised Jesus into the glory he expected; faith declared him living for ever because faith itself was determined never to die. Quickened by the ordeal, faith produced out of itself visions that brought balm to its anguish and strength to its affirmations. With the fragments of a shattered hope, and building on the death of Jesus, which might well have killed their faith outright, the disciples founded the religion of Jesus the Christ. Astonishment that faith can work such a miracle will be felt only by those who know not what religious faith really is and have no experience of the realities it can summon into being when once the power of it gets hold on a group of ardent souls. Unconsciously faith procures for herself all the illusions she needs for the conservation of her present possessions and for her advance to further conquests. But, humanly speaking, the work she accomplishes in availing herself of illusion is not always illusory.

Attempts at greater precision, if only by conjecture, in defining the process by which the faith of the disciples took form, are apt to end in fantasy. Renan, working on the theme of the resurrection, made out of it a little romance. J. Weiss, pressing hard on the meaning of Mark xiv, 28 ("after my rising I will go before you into Galilee"), concludes that Jesus had promised to lead his disciples after his resurrection into Galilee where the Kingdom of God would then appear. R. Schütz, improving on this idea, describes the disciples returning to Galilee with as much enthusiasm as if Jesus were really with them; Nazareth is saturated with Hellenism; Jesus himself and his Galilean disciples are full of it; the order of the day is rejection of the Law (*Los von Gesetz*); a Hellenist-Christian community is formed with which a Jewish-Christian community enters into competition. Thus everything is explained. But the whole construction rests upon air.[11]

2. THE CONTRIBUTION OF SIMON PETER

A name which we shall find in the forefront of the apostolic propaganda must here be introduced as that of the man who, in all probability, was the first to give out that Jesus was risen. Simon called Peter is, according to the tradition, one of the earliest disciples recruited by Jesus and the head of the apostolic college established by the Christ as the foundation and guide of the Church. Round him there has grown up an imposing legend to which his admirers are not the only contributors. None the less his share in the birth of the Christian movement was assuredly of the highest importance.

Legend has made great capital out of the surname Peter which Jesus himself is said to have conferred on Simon. But legend would not be legend if it developed consistently. According to Mark (i, 14–20) Jesus, at the very beginning of his ministry, peremptorily summons to his side two brothers, Simon and Andrew, as they were fishing in the sea of Galilee, near to Capernaum, and immediately afterwards, in the same sovereign manner and under the same conditions, two more brothers, James and John, the sons of Zebedee; this done, he expressly reveals his intention to make the four fishers of fish into fishers of men. To endow the event with greater significance Luke enlarges the story with that of the miraculous draught of fishes, which the appendix to John connects with an apparition of the risen

Christ. There can be no doubt that the story of the Miraculous Draught was originally comprised in the myth which related the foundation of the Christian apostolate: in the arrangement presented by John, which is probably the earlier version of the story, the apostolate is a creation of the immortal Christ. Mark as well as Luke has antedated its institution. John, in his account of the Vocation (i, 35–42), gives precedence before Peter to Andrew and to an unnamed but doubtless the "beloved" disciple; notwithstanding this, the change of name, intended to mark Peter as the foundation apostle, is made at his first encounter with Jesus—"thou art Simon son of John; thou shalt be called Cephas"—the evangelist being at pains to explain that Cephas means Peter. From all of which the historical fact to be retained is that the Simon in question was among the first adherents of Jesus, that he lived at Capernaum and was a fisherman by trade.

In reporting the choice of the Twelve, Mark (iii, 13–19) puts Peter at the head of the list and adds, as though the surname had been given on that occasion, "and he gave him the name Peter." But the importance of this mystical title is somewhat diminished by the prominence which the evangelist immediately gives to the resounding surname Boanerges conferred on the sons of Zebedee in the same circumstances. Luke (vi, 12–16) follows Mark. Matthew (x, 1–4) in reproducing the apostolic list says simply "first Simon called Peter" without intimation that the surname was bestowed at the time. He leaves us to suspect that the surname was not chosen by Jesus. And possibly not by the Christ. It may have been a mystical development of tradition, and this is the more likely inasmuch as the incident to which Mark connects it has no historical consistency.

In the incident of the Confession at Caesarea Philippi ("thou art the Christ") Mark brings Peter to the front, the idea being that Simon Peter must be the first to proclaim that Jesus is the Messiah on occasion requiring it. The original intention in recording the confession was, no doubt, to make it a merit on Peter's part. But the evangelist, as though he would destroy this favourable impression, forthwith makes Jesus address him as "Satan" for having tried to prevent the Christ from predicting his death. "Get thee behind, Satan, thou hast no feeling for the things of God." Peter does not understand the necessity and mystical power of the Passion. Needless to say that if the Messianic confession has been antedated by the evangelist, this lightning reproach is still more so. It is a product of the Pauline tradition in its hostility to the older apostles. Luke omits it—an omission that tells its own tale. Matthew has retained it, but follows up the Messianic confession by intercalating a eulogistic response of Jesus in which the confession itself is presented as a revelation of the Spirit and Simon Peter as the man who would hold the Keys of the Kingdom of Heaven, regulate the discipline of the new community (more or less identified with the Kingdom of Heaven) and would become the foundation of the Church—the only passage in the Gospels when Jesus speaks of his Church, and assuredly not the most authentic.[12]

In all probability this development of the Confession was originally Jewish-Christian and anti-Pauline, for it was not without purpose that Peter is said to have been favoured with a revelation from on high in which flesh and blood had no part. We can almost see in it a discreet response to certain ambitious claims put out by Paul in Galatians (i, 11–12, 15–16). At all events there is enough in it to neutralize what is said, a few lines lower down, about Peter's lack of feeling for things divine. We may add that the bishops of Rome, who apply the eulogy to their order, have abstained up to now from claiming the reproach. John is content to idealize the Messianic confession, turning the profession of faith into a profession of fidelity, and avoiding the need to add either approbation or corrective (vi, 68–69).

The transfiguration of Jesus (Mark ix, 2–8) seems to have been conceived originally as the story of an apparition of the Risen Christ, afterwards antedated to his earthly life and lodged immediately after the Confession, with the insertion of a blunder made by Peter, who is judged to have no understanding of the manifestation, Mark and Luke excusing him as not knowing what he said. We have already seen that the Apocalypse of Peter connects the blunder with the rebuff administered by Jesus, which Mark has placed after the Confession and the first announcement of the passion. It is the same Peter who figures at Gethsemane in an attitude little to his glory, sleeping, spite of his Master's warning, while Jesus is at prayer in the Agony. All the evangelists, moreover, describe, with a kind of complacency,

Peter's triple denial in the High Priest's house during the trial of Jesus, and all are careful to make Jesus predict the denial before the event: in this way the offence is, as it were, palliated and then corrected by the repentance of the culprit. It is to be noted that Mark (xiv, 50) begins by saying that all the disciples took to flight, after which one hardly expects to find Peter following Jesus even "afar off" (54) as the armed band led him away. The same incoherence in Matthew. Luke omits the flight but records the denial. In John xviii, 15–18, 25–27, the denial, cut in two, seems to have begun in the house of Annas and ended in the house of Caiaphas, without Peter changing his place. On this anomaly see *Le quatrième Evangile*, 458–460; 463–464.

Exegetes have made it a merit in Peter that he himself revealed his weakness, which the world would never have known if he had held his tongue. There are better grounds for believing that the incident is in line with the other fictions invented to belittle an apostle who became the grand authority of Jewish Christianity.

Amends of a kind are made to Peter in the stories of the resurrection. The angel names him to the women for a special injunction to return to Galilee, where, it would seem, the coming manifestation of the Risen Christ is to concern him more than the other disciples (Mark xvi, 7). In Matthew there is no mention of Peter.[13] Luke changes the whole character of the angel's discourse to the women, but represents Jesus as predicting to Peter, during the Last Supper, that his faith would be unshakable in the coming torment and that his part would be to strengthen the shaken faith of his brethren. This prediction seems to have been conceived at an independent source which, if not ignorant of the story of the denial, left it aside. As Luke knew of Peter's vision (xxiv, 34) but abstains from giving an account of it, he must have known also that it was this vision that enabled Peter to revive the faith of the other disciples; and of that, too, he says nothing. In the Fourth Gospel the coming martyrdom of Peter is announced twice over (xiii, 36 and xxi, 18–19) and the Risen Christ, after the apparition on the Lake, where Peter is the leading figure, solemnly confides to him the guardianship of his flock.[14] From all of which it is clear enough that the Gospel and the Acts of the Apostles have done their best to reconcile two divergent tendencies: one, Jewish-Christian, in which the rôle of Peter was magnified; the other characteristic of certain Pauline circles, in which it was belittled: the reconciliation being effected, more or less happily, by upholding Peter as the head of the apostolate not only to the Jews, to which the Epistle to the Galatians (ii, 7–9) would limit him, but also to the world at large. The editor of Acts exhibits him in this universal character even at the risk of making him profess the doctrine of salvation by faith alone before the elders of Jerusalem after the affair of Cornelius, which symbolizes the opening of salvation to the whole world, with Peter as the opener of the door. The reality of Peter's contribution was of dimensions much more modest than this, but it led to results no less important.

Putting all these indications together we may conclude that Simon Peter was a fisherman, perhaps a master-fisherman of Capernaum, that he was an early adherent of Jesus, whom he accompanied in his wanderings and then followed to Jerusalem. If Jesus in his lifetime was not hailed by him as the Christ at Caesarea Philippi, Peter certainly entered with his whole being into the Great Expectation, and came to Jerusalem to share in the coming of God and the revelation of Messiah in that city. His faith survived the catastrophe. Returning to Galilee, to the surroundings and atmosphere whence the Great Expectation had its birth, coming back also to himself, his thought leapt to the conviction that Jesus could not have perished in death and that God had taken him to Himself that He might reveal him to the world in the day of his coming, straightway believing that he could see the Master thus, immortal with God. Such is the meaning of the firm tradition that the first vision of Jesus had come, in Galilee, to Simon Peter. No account of that first vision is to be found in any of the documents. Mark gives an advance hint of it (xvi, 7; cf. I Cor. xv, 5). Luke is content to mention the bare fact (xxiv, 34). The appendix to John (xxi) attaches it to a miraculous draught of fishes, where it is difficult to recognize, except in the symbolic meaning of the prodigy. But it may be said with confidence that the primacy of Peter's vision is implied by the whole tradition relating to apparitions of the Christ.

It may well be that Peter himself never described his vision, just as Paul never described the vision which converted him, for the triple story of the vision in Acts cannot be considered as coming directly or indirectly from Paul himself. Whatever the content of the vision may have been, its occurrence was a sudden explosion produced by the intense and inward workings of faith; out of which there leaped forth the answer to the riddle of the crucifixion. The answer was this—death has not held Jesus captive: he is alive with God, on the point of returning as the Christ with the Kingdom. What Peter was able to see in his vision escapes us and would seem to us insignificant if we knew it; what matters far more are the deductions that were made from it. The idea of a blessed survival was certainly not strange to Peter. His mind kept turning it over, and turning it over with Jesus as the focus of his thought. Then came the shining day when he thought that Jesus was visibly, and perhaps audibly, before him. His faith filled the vision with all he longed to believe and gave him the assurance that what he saw was a reality. Neither historian nor psychologist need inquire further. Even if we had before us a detailed account from Peter himself of what he believed to be a vision of Jesus clothed with immortality we should hardly know more, nor better understand the certitude of his faith.

We may be equally sure that Peter's faith immediately became contagious among those about him, the former disciples of Jesus, who, like Peter, were already prepared for it, one might even say were being carried along by it. He "strengthened the brethren"; that is, he regathered the now scattered group who had staked their hope on Jesus the Nazorean, and imparted to them his own confidence. Removed to the invisible world, the object of their faith was beyond the reach of the accidents which might otherwise have shaken belief. True, the Kingdom of God was in no haste to come; true, the Messiah delayed his appearance among the clouds. But what of that? One can always wait a little longer. They waited.

What length of time was needed to bring about this rekindling of their faith? We can only conjecture. But since a faith which hesitates or remains dormant for long is unlikely ever to revive, we are entitled to think that the interval was fairly short and the tempo rapid. We may assume that Peter had his vision in the days immediately following his return to Capernaum, days filled with the thought of his lost Master. Arrived at a clear conviction, he at once imparted it to his companions, and immediately these humble folk were back on the summit of the idealism to which Jesus had led them. More than that, they were persuaded that the Master was still alive and beyond a doubt was about to "come" again, but this time with the "Kingdom" and in "the glory of the Father." Back, then, to Jerusalem, appointed scene of the Great Event, there to wait for his coming! Only a naïve and superficial psychology would interpret this bright dawning of the faith as the product of material proof, such as the empty tomb, or of a parcel of gross illusions, and spend effort in searching for these proofs while knowing them to be false when found. Not through preoccupation with such proofs were the disciples possessed with their ardent belief that Jesus was alive with the Father. They believed it ardently because they desired it ardently and felt him near to them in the ardour of their desire, while fugitive and dreamlike visions, perhaps pure dreams, sufficed for the time to nourish and confirm their faith. Then came the discovery of confirmation in the Scriptures. Only at a still later period, when discussion had arisen, did the search begin for more palpable arguments; but it was not until the second, or possibly the third, Christian generation that the need for such arguments became urgent. This was the stage at which the story of the empty tomb was invented, but too reflectively for our liking; and then it was that the fugitive visions of the Risen One, the memory of which had sustained the faith of the first age, were transformed into apparitions and presented as tangible realities.

We have endeavoured to reconstitute the faith of Peter on lines which follow as closely as possible the faith which Jesus had, the faith which had led him to Jerusalem. In this we have been on fairly safe ground. The prompt return of these first believers to the capital of Judaism and their continued residence there have to be explained, and what other explanation can be given? The members of the pious band had no intention to make Jerusalem the centre of an apostolic mission to distant lands; it may be doubted if they had any conception of apostleship in the strict sense of the term. They came back to Jerusalem to await the Christ, and remained there for that purpose as long as they could. The last believers of this type quitted the Holy City when Roman armies were about to invest it, having doubtless come to the conclusion that Jerusalem, deaf to their warning, must be destroyed and trodden down of the Gentiles before the new and eternal Jerusalem, the true City of God, could be established in its place.

It was the march of events that first brought the apostolic office into existence and then gave direction to its work. But before we reconstitute the evolution of that office, at least hypothetically, it behoves us to weigh the importance of the forward step the disciples had now taken in raising their dead master, Jesus, to the dignity of Christ alive in heaven. Without a suspicion on their part of what was involved, their belief was already an essential transformation of the Gospel announced by Jesus; but nothing could be less intended by it than to form the followers of the Christ they were proclaiming into a particular sect either at the centre or the circumference of Judaism. Right up to the moment of Golgotha inclusive, Jesus and his companions seemed in their own eyes to be standing on the ground of a hope common to all the Jews. As to the complicity of the Jewish leaders in the sentence of death pronounced by Pilate, if complicity there were, it could be passed over as a human error and an injustice to God's Ambassador. The preaching of Jesus may well have prepared the way for a split in Judaism, but had not yet created it. But the split was bound to occur if the partisans of the crucified prophet took the line of openly proclaiming that he, their Master, now raised to life at the right hand of God, was the Christ, and that his coming was at hand. Such a profession of faith could not be a matter of indifference to the religious authorities of Judaism nor to the Jewish mass which obeyed them. The vast majority of the Jews would have refused at once to recognize the Christ in the man crucified on Calvary; he would seem to them in nowise qualified for such an honour, and the hope that, after such a prelude, he would presently descend on the clouds of heaven to judge the earth, would be counted a chimerical absurdity. True, a Christ in heaven was less of a political danger than a messianic agitator on earth but, apart from that, many would regard the partisans of the Christ as merely troublesome fanatics, while the majority, from the religious leaders downwards, would proclaim them heretics, and as such drive out of the fold whoever would persevere in such a faith. Thus condemned and driven out these obstinate believers would, without any will of their own, become a sect more or less under suspicion or even shameful and despised. That point reached, the road which led from the new Gospel to a Christian religion separate from Judaism would be opened to traffic.

3. PROCEEDINGS OF THE FIRST BELIEVERS

So Peter and his companions, brimful of their hopes, went back to Jerusalem. Whether the Feast of Pentecost had anything to do with their return to the city they had recently quitted in their extremity cannot be stated with confidence. Certainly it was not only as a pilgrimage that the return journey was undertaken. They went back with the intention of remaining in the Holy City and, so to say, of making a home there. Formed plan of active propaganda they clearly had not; perhaps it was not within their means; moreover the indications are that they were somewhat cautious at the beginning in communicating their faith. We may suppose they found lodgings with friendly people, perhaps with those who had entertained them when they came up with Jesus for the Passover. Living on little, they kept up assiduous attendance in the Temple at the hours of prayer. Without any attempt at public preaching in that neighbourhood they found opportunities to impart their hope to a few of the pious Jews whom they met in the outer court. The grand scenes of preaching described in Acts (ii, iii, iv, v) have no more reality than the sittings of the Sanhedrim convened to put a stop to the apostolic propaganda (iv, v). The conviction that had kindled the ardour of John the Baptist and of Jesus in their ministries was at work to the same effect in them, and long continued to work as the driving power of the Christian apostolate. The Kingdom being at hand, nothing could be more urgent than to warn men of goodwill, wherever they could be met, to make ready for the Great Event. And, like John in his day, and Jesus in his, they met from time to time with simple souls who believed their message and joined their little company.

It is also probable that Baptism was administered to their

proselytes in association with their profession of faith in Jesus the Messiah. For the Christian religion made its entry into the world as a baptist movement, and must have so begun since Jesus himself had turned it in that direction. It would be hard to understand why Peter and his companions decided to baptize the newcomers unless the rite had seemed a matter of course as conforming to the practice of Jesus. In like manner it was customary for the new initiates to share in the simple meals of the brethren, when the bread was broken in memory of Jesus and in lively expectation of his coming.[15]

If we are to believe the book of Acts, which at this point seems to reflect an authentic tradition of the earliest community, it was a miraculous incident which first drew the attention of the temple priests to the followers of the new faith. This was the cure of a paralytic operated by Peter in the name of Jesus the Nazorean.[16] After making whatever reserves may be needed in regard to the supernatural character of this adventure, only a paltry rationalism would deny the probability that Peter made the attempt and even succeeded, or that Jesus ever risked it and with like success. We may be sure that the Christian missionaries would not hesitate to practice exorcisms for the cure of maladies by invoking the name of Jesus. Somebody must have made a beginning: it was Peter who made it on the day in question. On seeing the paralytic walk, a crowd formed, a great uproar rose round Peter and the miraculous walker; the temple police naturally came on the scene and the priests, informed of what had happened, asked Peter "by what power or in what name" he had done that. To their utter amazement they learnt that the potent name was "Jesus-Messiah the Nazorean" and that the men before them were followers of the Galilean recently crucified at the Passover. Whereupon "they strictly commanded them not to speak at all nor teach in the name of Jesus." And "when they had further threatened them, they let them go, finding nothing that they might punish them, because of the people; for all men glorified God for that which was done. For the man was over forty years old on whom this miracle was shewed" (Acts iv, 21–22).[17]

Prodigies of this kind increase the vogue of a nascent religion. One was enough to raise the credit of our pious band in the eyes of the common people. If the editor of Acts has not multiplied the number of them—as when he makes the shadow of Peter heal the sick brought in from neighbouring towns to attend his walk (v, 15–16)—we may be sure that public rumour did. As people watched the band at prayer or conversing with adherents under the Porch of Solomon, the most part would keep at a distance knowing that the priests now regarded their doings with no friendly eye. That, however, did not prevent increasing recruitment by private propaganda (v, 52). But the anger of the authorities would certainly be roused by any rash attempt at public preaching; nothing more was needed to bring down the arm of the law.

There is evidence that cohesion was rapidly acquired by this ardent group. Tradition has it that their meals were taken in common and that each contributed of his substance for the support of the fraternity. That this was the practice of these latter day saints may well be true. The Christ might come at any hour, and what else remained to do but help one another in the brief interval before his coming, the better-off ministering to the wants of the poor and bringing provisions to the common table. "There was not among them one person in want," remarks the editor of Acts, no doubt with a touch of exaggeration. It is true, nevertheless, that the Jerusalem community was always poor. But this was not, as many have thought, the result of a communistic system established at the outset; such a system certainly never existed in the rigorous form suggested by a literal reading of Acts. The poverty of the group was due to the fact that the nucleus of Galilean believers found themselves in Jerusalem almost without resources; that the new members seldom came from the richer classes of the city's population; that the generosity of the few better-off was insufficient to overcome the general indigence; that indigence was not unwelcome, since the Kingdom was for the poor; that, in their preoccupation with the coming parousia, they had little concern for the business of this world, fell into poverty and remained poor as the inevitable consequences of neglecting it. It does not follow that any of them died of hunger. The condition in which they were is supportable enough when religious faith is intense and the needs of the body restricted to the bare minimum.[18]

Precarious and rudimentary as the organization was, it was

yet organization. This society of friends had leaders, and we know who they were. They were the Twelve, whom tradition has made into apostles, and even into apostles *par excellence*, though some of them were not very active as missionaries of the new faith. Strictly speaking, the Twelve were the administrators of the first community; this is implied in Acts iv, 34 and v, 11, whatever doubts may be felt about the passage as a whole and the adventure of Ananias and Sapphira. But the Twelve certainly had no existence as a separate group prior to the formation of the community from which they were chosen. The committee of the Twelve—if that were the real number, as it probably was— was created in order to give the little society the elementary organization that would be needful in the early stages of its growth. The number of these committee-men, assuming it to have been twelve, seems to betray a symbolic intention; it corresponded to the arrangement imagined for the Kingdom of God in which the hopes of Israel were to be fulfilled. The saying about the twelve thrones, to be occupied by the twelve apostles judging the twelve tribes bears witness to the ruling idea (Matthew xix, 28). But the function there assigned to the Twelve is one of government rather than of preaching. Quite naturally our twelve overseers would be chosen from among the original disciples of Jesus in Galilee, with Peter as some sort of President. But it cannot be said that "apostle" was their title from the very first.

Certain ecclesiastical writers long since pointed out[19] that the name "apostle" belonged to the emissaries maintained after the fall of Jerusalem by the Jewish patriarchate to carry the letters of the central authority and to collect the subscriptions paid by the Jews of the Dispersion. On the strength of this it was supposed by Harnack and many others that the function must have existed before Jerusalem fell, and that the name passed to the Christian preachers who also organized collections in the communities, as appears from the testimony and example of Paul. But, if these envoys existed before the year 70, which is possible, it is difficult to understand how their name could have been applied to the messengers of the Gospel who were not sent out to visit already established communities, nor were chiefly collectors of offerings; while, as we have just seen, the Twelve, who seem to have been the first to hold the apostolic office, were not sent out anywhere and were neither professional preachers nor collectors of alms in the strict meaning of the term. Moreover the evidence of the New Testament on the matter is confused enough to make the problem difficult of solution, apart from any question that may be raised about a connexion between the Christian apostolate and the office of the Jewish collectors.

A close examination of the Book of Acts shows clearly that it knows of no apostles save the Twelve, understanding their title of apostle as meaning that they were missionaries of the Word and qualified for the work, inasmuch as they had been witnesses of the resurrection and followers of Jesus from the beginning of his ministry to the final hour of his ascent into heaven. Though the definition is systematic, and as such not without interest, we are not entitled to transport it into history. But Paul's Epistles reveal a much wider application of the term which bestowed it on Christian missionaries in general, and first of all on Paul who, while seeming to give express recognition to the apostleship of the Twelve, claimed the title for himself also, a claim which the Twelve and their party appear to have contested. The Epistles mention "the Twelve" only once (1 Cor. xv, 5). Luke affirms that Jesus himself named the disciples "apostles" (vi, 18), and throughout his Gospel, as in Acts, the Twelve and the apostles are the same persons, while Mark, who makes Jesus not only choose them but "send them out" as well, only once calls them "apostles" (vi, 30) and speaks constantly of "the Twelve." Matthew in like manner has "the twelve apostles" once only (x, 2), but often "the twelve disciples" or "the twelve." In the fourth Gospel "the twelve" are mentioned twice, but not called apostles (vi, 67, 71; xx, 24).

From all this confusion the certainty seems to emerge that the Twelve were not called apostles at the time they were formed into a group, nor did they become apostles merely by their membership. They were elected from among "the disciples," that is, the existing body of believers, not to preach, but to order the affairs of the first community, so far as this was necessary. Their importance grew as the Gospel spread. Viewing the matter from a standpoint in the present and giving full confidence to the Pauline literature, we might be tempted to conclude, as

Edouard Meyer has done, that the attribution of the title to the Twelve only was a reaction against the claim of Paul to be an independent apostle and missionary to the Gentiles, appointed thereto directly by the Lord—a reaction which went so far as to exclude Paul from any right to the title. This would explain why, in Mark, instructions intended for all the Christian missionaries are addressed to the Twelve in particular,[20] a transference the more easily made since Peter himself turned missionary after the year 44, together with his colleagues in Jerusalem and the brothers of the Lord (1 Cor. ix, 5).

It may well be that the transference of the title to the Twelve was not made quite so simply, promptly and mechanically. When indications furnished by our sources, themselves of later origin, are interpreted as reflecting the first beginnings of the Christian movement, we run the risk of immensely shortening a development which took a much longer time to mature. It is obvious that no *missionaries* (apostles) can have been appointed until *missions* had begun, and we can see both how and why the Twelve were not instituted as apostles; for not only is it true that not all of them were missionaries at any time, but those who were missionaries, that is employed in the propagation of the Gospel, were not *missioned* (if the word may be used) from any source outside or above; properly speaking, no mission had been given them as apostles in the service, to which they were devoting themselves, of propagating the Gospel. The apostolate in the sense indicated by our texts, does not begin until the business of propaganda has an organized basis, at least of a rudimentary kind; and this, it seems, did not happen until after the dispersion of the group of hellenizing believers which we are about to consider in the next chapter. When that has happened then, to judge by what we shall see taking place at Antioch, the apostles are definitely *missioned*, delegated and approved by a group which supported them. In this way, as we shall see, Paul and Barnabas were at first appointed to the propaganda in Syria and Cilicia.

At that time Paul had not put forth his claim to a unique and special mission conferred upon him by the Christ alone. In the epistles he would seem to have first made this claim when he decided to go his own way. As one no longer *missioned* by a group, he would despise henceforth the attribution of a human commission, and proclaims himself *missioned* by the Christ. Meanwhile the number of missionaries was rapidly increasing both in Palestine and beyond, but always it would seem in the same conditions under which Paul and Barnabas had been *missioned* at Antioch, Paul remaining alone in the singularity of his claim. It must be added, however, that this claim, clothed in the absolute form given it by various passages in the epistles, does not correspond with the reality of the situation and must have been conceived after the event. It belongs to the development of the literature called apostolic. The same is true of the systematic limitation of the apostolic title to the Twelve said by the evangelists to have been *missioned* by Jesus in the course of his ministry. This last point, which reveals the opposition to the Pauline tradition, was reached only when the conditions of Christian propaganda had completely changed and the primitive apostolate had become hardly more than a memory preserved in legend and surrounded by a halo. But let us now turn to the event immediately followed by the apostolic propaganda, of which it seems to have released the spring.

4. STEPHEN AND THE HELLENISTS

From a story in Acts (vi, 1–6) superficially clear, but intentionally confused, the fact emerges that the group of Jerusalem believers, whose recruits, after its first formation, had not been all of one type, was quickly divided into two parties. It soon counted among its members a certain number of hellenizing Jews, that is, Jews whose ordinary language was Greek, and whose ways of thinking, perhaps also their manner of life, were not quite the same as those of the believers speaking Aramaic and called "Hebrews," who had been gained over in the beginning by the disciples from Galilee. The hellenizing believers presently began to hold separate meetings with an organization of their own. What Acts tells us about the choice of the seven deacons is a fiction which too thinly disguises the distinct organization set up by these messianist Jews whom we must suppose to have been better acquainted with the pagan world than were the believers from Palestine. The greater part of them had probably lived more or less in Greek or in hellenized countries and had come to Jerusalem either on temporary business or with the intention of establishing a permanent abode. It must not be forgotten that the regular relations established between Jerusalem and the communities of the Jewish Dispersion, which facilitated travel from place to place, helped greatly at the outset in spreading the Christian propaganda.

Even on the strength of the fiction arranged by the editor of Acts, one is driven to suppose that the community of Jerusalem believers found itself, after no long time, composed of two elements which were not slow to separate more or less completely. In addition to that, since it was the hellenizing group only which, compromised by the action of one of its members, was driven out and dispersed, we may take it as certain that these hellenizers already constituted a distinct body having its own directors, the seven so-called deacons, and that the propagation of the Christian religion beyond Judea was begun by the scattered members of that group. The great outburst of evangelical preaching outside Palestine, to say nothing of that already inside, did not come from the Twelve and their group of Hebraizers. This fact the editor of Acts takes pains to hide, but without succeeding; and here is the point of departure to which he co-ordinates many other fictions in the course of the book. (Later on a bolder step was taken by representing the twelve apostles as having left Jerusalem after dividing between them the world to be converted.) In order to preserve the union of the Hebrew and Hellenizing groups in a single community, as his perspective required, the editor makes out that the Twelve constituted a kind of priestly body which administered the spiritual affairs of the community, and changes the seven heads of the hellenizing party to the lower status of deacons or helpers to the Twelve, appointed for the service of tables and the distribution of alms, in other words, for the administration of the temporalities—a type of organization which was in fact adopted in the Christian community, but only at a later stage.

The list of the seven deacons is neither better nor worse guaranteed than that of the twelve apostles. But the Seven were not helpers subordinate to the Twelve. They were formed as the governing body of the hellenizing group as soon as it acquired a separate existence. The existence of the group is certain. How exactly it was formed escapes us. Some difference of opinion analogous to that mentioned in Acts may have given occasion for the split; but the cause was other and profound. And we cannot invert the chronological relation of the two groups, as if faith in Jesus had begun with the hellenizing party. All the names on the list of deacons are Greek. Only one of the seven is a pagan by origin, but circumcised; he comes from Antioch; the others are Jews by birth but not "Hebrews" by language. It should be noted that the number seven, like the number twelve, has a symbolic meaning, being the cypher for the gentile or universal world, as twelve is for Israel. For that reason a strict interpretation of the names on the list would be out of place.

One individual alone stands out before us detached from the hellenistic group as having taken the initiative in the public propagation of the Gospel message in Jerusalem, and with results of considerable importance. Stephen, whom Acts describes as "full of grace and power"—animated, that is, by a zeal outstandingly effective in preaching—seems to have been the first to carry the Gospel into the arena of public discussion, not in the Temple, but in certain synagogues of the Greek-speaking Jews in Jerusalem. According to the statement in Acts, which seems to have been tampered with, "there arose certain of the synagogue which is called the synagogue of the Libertines, and Cyrenians and Alexandrians, and of them of Cilicia and Asia, who disputed with Stephen, and they were not able to resist the wisdom and the Spirit by which he spake" (vi, 9). The text insists on the opposition to Stephen's discourse, but tells us nothing of what the preacher said to provoke it. The source-document on which the editor was working no doubt indicated this in place of the miracles attributed to Stephen in v, 8. But having just placed Stephen among the *deacons*, he would naturally be unwilling to exhibit him too plainly in the preaching function of an *apostle*. The reference to synagogues is probably to several where Stephen found opportunity for delivering his message to the congregations gathered there. It is in keeping with the sense of the above passage to assume that the disputes in question were not confined to private conversations, and that Stephen took his turn to address the congregations, as any private person, even one not recognized to be a qualified preacher, could do. That his teaching raised objections should cause no surprise; and it is not impossible that the ardour of his convictions reduced his adversaries to silence. The certain fact is that instant animosity was aroused against Stephen by these actions.

Let us recall at this point how the cautious propaganda of the Galilean disciples came into being and was allowed to continue, even for several years after the affair of Stephen, without serious interference from the authorities. If Stephen's efforts to win converts were quickly followed by forcible official reaction the reason must be sought in its publicity, and, very probably, in the character of his teaching. This, at certain points, differed from the teaching of the original disciples. They announced that Jesus was risen from the dead as the Christ and about to return with the reign of God; but they did not speculate on the economy of the coming kingdom, nor on the changes it might involve in matters concerning the established cult of Judaism. Stephen, it seems, was less reserved. The witnesses who appeared against him at his trial before the Sanhedrim are reported to have said: "This man is for ever speaking against the holy place and the Law: for we have heard him say that this Jesus the Nazorean will destroy this place and change the customs which Moses delivered to us."[21] Although the deponents are described as "false witnesses" the charge is not said to have been denied, but was rather confirmed by Stephen who, in an ecstatic outburst and with transfigured countenance, answered the question of the high priest by simply exclaiming: "I see the heavens opened and the Son of Man standing at the right hand of God." Without taking these indications for an official report of a judicial inquiry, which they are not, we are entitled to infer from them that this hellenizing Jew went to the length of saying that the temple, the bloody sacrifices, the legal observances and whatever was specifically Jewish in the established cult would pass away at the coming of the Christ. Such, we are given to suppose, was Stephen's comment on the saying attributed to Jesus concerning the temple which he would destroy and rebuild.[22]

As already pointed out, closely analogous doctrines or opinions are to be met with in certain of the baptist sects and to some extent among the Essenes. Their converts from paganism were dispensed from an array of prescriptions which, said they, were due to be abrogated under the coming Reign of God and the imposition of which was found a serious obstacle to the propagation of the faith. In the sequel, the destruction of the Temple in the year 70 was soon to give these practices and doctrines a measure of justification. Was it not clear that God, by that event, had condemned the outward and material economy of the Jewish cult?

In that lies the starting point for explaining the conduct of the missionaries who went out from Antioch, the work of Paul, and even the foundation of hellenistic Christianity. The long and curious indictment of the Jews attributed to Stephen (vii, 2–33) is conceived in the same anti-Jewish spirit. It is a digression, serving the dominant purpose of the editor of Acts, which is to prove that notwithstanding the recriminations and fury of those who are Jews by race and name, it is not these always hardened and rebellious Jews but the Christians who represent the religion which claims the authority of Abraham, Moses and the prophets. The author had an ampler experience than Stephen could have had towards the year 30 of our era.

The exact date of his martyrdom, just indicated approximately, is uncertain. Unless we abandon all the indications of time in Acts and Galatians, we are led to place the martyrdom of the sons of Zebedee in the year 44; a little earlier than that, the meeting in Jerusalem at which the question of legal observances was discussed; and the conversion of Paul about the year 30. With these data as our baseline we must place the crucifixion of Jesus in 26 or 27 and the martyrdom of Stephen in 28 or 29. This leaves the sequence of events somewhat compressed, for it is obvious that the Christian propaganda had reached Damascus and made some progress there before the conversion of Paul. It is true that the faith was rapidly contagious; nevertheless a minimum of time was needed for its formation and diffusion.

Here then is Stephen, the first martyr of the Christ and in some sense his first apostle, condemned to death, apparently after regular trial in the courts for blasphemy against the Law. He died by stoning in pursuance of the sentence pronounced by a Jewish tribunal. Until quite recent years it has been taken for granted that the Sanhedrim had no power to pronounce a capital sentence and least of all to carry it into execution without ratification by the Roman procurator, and, since there is no mention of Pontius Pilate or of his successor, it is supposed that Stephen's execution was an affair of mob-law and carried out in a riot, as the conclusion of the story gives us to understand. To this it is often added that the execution probably took place in 36 during the interval between the departure of Pilate and the arrival of his successor, as if, on anything of the kind happening, there was no representative of Roman authority in the city to give ratification. It seems certain on the contrary that the Sanhedrim retained complete jurisdiction in all religious matters and that its competence was limited on the political side only. The false perspective in which the Evangelists have set the trial of Jesus has contributed more than anything else to lead criticism astray at this point. It was only after the destruction of Jerusalem that the religious authorities of Judaism were deprived of the right to pass sentence of death, by losing the National Council which possessed the right.

Repression of the new movement was not limited to the execution of Stephen. Menaced and hunted down, the whole group to which he belonged scattered and lost no time in clearing out of Jerusalem. Whatever the editor of Acts, who contradicts himself, may say, it was not the entire community, Hebrew and Greek believers alike "except the apostles" (viii, 1), that was persecuted and driven into flight. (If they were bent on exterminating the Hebrew group why did they spare its chiefs?) It was the hellenistic group only. The Hebrew group was not disturbed, no doubt because it was less disturbing.

The story in Acts of repressive proceedings against *both* groups hangs together with the equally fictitious particulars about Saul-Paul taking part in the affair. The elements of the latter fiction are adjusted to the course of the story. By way of introducing him it opens by saying that the witnesses, who had to cast the first stones, "laid down their garments at the feet of a youth named Saul" who was "consenting to the execution."[23] A few lines further on the youth finds himself promoted, somewhat rapidly in view of his age, to the office of Grand Persecutor of Christianity in Jerusalem: it would seem, moreover, that he went about it by himself, proceeding on his own authority to search all the houses of the city in his hunt for Christians, and to take men and women to prison; while next day a commission from the High Priest charges him to continue the business at Damascus; though it is not easy to see how the Gospel could have so soon found its way into that city.

Later we shall discuss the legend of Paul's conversion. The preliminaries found in the story of Stephen's martyrdom are totally unworthy of credence. The "youth," even if we suppose him to have aged ten years as he went home after the execution of Stephen, could not have organized and carried on all alone the persecution of the Christians here ascribed to him. According to Galatians (i, 22–24) the Christian communities in Judea, prior to the Jerusalem conference, knew Paul only by reputation. Paul was not in Jerusalem when Stephen was executed. As general persecutor of the nascent Christian religion he is a creation of legend. The motive of the editor of Acts in calling him "a youth" is to present him as having been brought up at Jerusalem and a pupil of the famous Gamaliel (xxii, 3; v, 34). The editor has also made Gamaliel his victim by putting a discourse in his mouth, which the good doctor never made, on the occasion of a trial of the Twelve, which never took place. What we are told of the relations of Paul with Gamaliel has every likelihood of being no less fictitious than the rest.

From the time of the persecution onwards we find the entire community of Judaizing believers established in Jerusalem, just as it was before. There Peter and his companions remained, without any one of them being molested, till towards the end of the reign of Agrippa I. But never again was a Hellenizing group, such as Stephen's had been, formed in that city. Obviously Jerusalem was unpromising ground for the open propaganda of their Messiah— Jesus, especially if it was thought to offer any kind of threat to Jewish nationalism and the superstitious regard for the Law. But those who had driven the group of Stephen into flight turned out to have assured, by that very act, the future of the Christian religion.

Chapter IV

THE BIRTH OF
APOSTOLIC PROPAGANDA

AN ardent, regulated and almost methodical propaganda was now to be launched which, in less than thirty years, would carry the Christian religion to all the countries of the Eastern Mediterranean and as far as Rome, but under conditions which only permit us to catch glimpses of the chief stages in a mighty movement and to follow a few of its protagonists. As far as we can judge, this was not achieved by the proper and direct initiative of the Aramaic-speaking group of believers gathered in Jerusalem. The propulsive force that carried the new religion into the Mediterranean world was the force of the blow that had struck Stephen. Up to that moment the effort to make converts, in the conditions we have just studied, had been confined to Jerusalem. It is not certain, as some would have it, that small groups of believers existed in Galilee at that time, to which we might attribute the spread of the Gospel to Damascus. The invective against the Galilean towns (Matthew xi, 20–24; Luke x, 12–15) and the symbolic check to the preaching of Jesus at Nazareth (Mark vi, 1–6; Matthew xiii, 53–58; Luke iv, 15–30) would rather invite the conclusion that there were no groups of believers in Galilee in apostolic times. It may well be that the Jewish-Christian propaganda was roused into activity only by the Hellenistic-Christian, and did not become effective in North Palestine, Transjordania and Syria until after the migration thitherward of the Jerusalem community at the beginning of the Jewish war.

If the Christian religion which spoke in Aramaic was not without a future, if it was even destined to exert indirectly a profound influence on Christianity as a universal religion, that religion could not exist, and had in fact no existence, so long as the pagan world was unreached by its message. And the pagan world was not even touched so long as propagandist activity was confined to Jewish circles in Jerusalem, or even in Palestine. By the action of the Sanhedrim, the most active among the new believers, the most open minded, or if it be preferred, the least imprisoned within Judaism were driven abroad into various provinces of the Roman Empire where, in a very short time, they did a work remarkable in its results and astonishing in its success.

On evidence derived from the Epistles preserved under his name, the foundation of hellenistic Christianity, that is of the Christian Church, of the historic Christian religion, is still generally attributed to Paul. But, if his rôle was of such capital importance, how comes it that ancient Christian documents, the *Didache* and the so-called Epistle of Barnabas, seem to ignore him, and that the Apocalypse of John, though more judaizing in style than in spirit, makes his school, if not his memory, the object of attack? It is the Paul of the Epistles who is aimed at in the letters to the Asiatic Churches in Revelation ii, 2, 9, 14–15, 20–24; iii, 9. Notwithstanding that he was a contributor to founding the churches of Asia, they did not claim him, in the second century, as their founder, while the silence of the apologist Justin in regard to him is outstandingly significant. In the course of the second century, circumstances furnished him with an important collection of epistles, now gathered into the New Testament, and these, together with the combinations worked up in Acts, which give a considerable place to his missions, have made it possible to construct a scheme of Christian Origins partly false and too simple in relation to the complicated reality. Paul, for us, is the best known of the first Christian missionaries to the pagan world; but he was not the one and only missionary, nor even quite the first; he was simply the most active. The influence which his epistles came, ultimately, to acquire ought not to be credited entirely to his apostolic career; for the problem which now presents itself is just that of finding out whether the elaborate gnosis developed in the Epistles really belonged to their presumed author, to Paul. Even if that problem be set aside, it seems beyond doubt that the diffusion of the Christian religion in the pagan world had begun before Paul became a partner in the work, and that, notwithstanding his large contribution, it went on its course to a great extent independently of him.[1]

In order that our departure may be taken from a point of utmost certainty, let us fix attention on the following incomplete but trustworthy account in the Book of Acts (xi, 19–21): "They that were scattered abroad by the persecution in the time of

Stephen travelled as far as Phoenicia"—that is, to the hellenized towns of the Phoenician coast, including Caesarea, which, though the residence of the procurator of Judea, was not a Jewish town— "and to Cyprus and to Antioch, speaking the word to none save only to Jews. But there were some of them, men of Cyprus and Cyrene who, when they were come to Antioch, spake to the Greeks also, preaching the Lord Jesus. And the hand of the Lord was with them and a great number"—of uncircumcised as well as Jews—"believed and turned unto the Lord. And it was at Antioch that the disciples"—the believers in Jesus—"were first called Christians." In the pagan world the name of the sect is the name here indicated by Acts, and the foundation of the first hellenist-Christian community was the occasion of its adoption. In the Jewish, aramaic-speaking world, on the other hand, the adherents of the new faith, according to the same book of Acts, were called Nazoreans, following the title given to Jesus himself. "For we have found this man (Paul) a pestilent fellow . . . and a ringleader of the sect of the Nazoreans" (xxiv, 5).[2]

The text previously cited (xi, 19–21) comes from the same source as the account of the hellenistic group at Jerusalem and of the martyrdom of Stephen, to which it forms the natural sequel, but is here converted into a brief introduction to what the author is intent on telling about the foundation of the first community to be recruited, at least in part, from among the uncircumcised pagans. Phoenicia and Cyprus are quickly passed over, but the author's meaning is, clearly, that in these two countries, as in the first place at Antioch, the word was carried to the Jews, but "to Jews only." If the source has nothing to say about the results of this preaching, it is because its author was in haste to get on to the mission at Antioch and the exploits of Paul. The editor of Acts, for his part, presupposes, in what he has to tell of Phoenicia, the existence there of groups of Christian recruits from the Jewish population, and contents himself with a few legends about the ministry of Philip, one of the Seven, in Samaria, before his settlement at Caesarea. It is probable that some of the fugitives found their way also to Alexandria, whence Apollos was later to come, but Acts knew nothing of them, or preferred to say nothing. Believers in Jesus also came early to Rome, but we are left equally in the dark as to the conditions. Let us not overlook the fact that the missionaries who "spoke to the Greeks" were strangers to the country, this one from Cyprus, the other from Cyrene. (We shall learn their names a little later.) From this it would seem that the hellenistic believers who fled from Jerusalem after the death of Stephen did not seek refuge in the countries of their birth, and were not merely bent on saving their lives, but concerned also to carry on elsewhere a propaganda to which Jerusalem gave no support. Beyond that we cannot say what considerations and what circumstances suggested to these propagandists the choice of their destination. But it seems clear that the desire to proclaim their message held priority over personal interest. Without this ardour of apostleship it is indeed impossible to explain the prompt diffusion of the sect. To make known to the Jews of the Dispersion that Jesus was about to return as the Christ was to them a mission of extreme urgency. Nevertheless, however urgent they deemed their message to be, they believed they had time to deliver it, and that belief brought some enlargement of perspective to the hope which had caused the Galilean disciples to return to Jerusalem.

What these passages tell us about the foundation of the Antioch community contradicts the traditional legend presented elsewhere in Acts, which gives Peter the initiative in the conversion of the Gentiles; and it contradicts the legend, also traditional, but scientifically exaggerated in recent times, which makes out that Paul was the first apostle, and the universal apostle, of the Gentile world and indeed the veritable founder of the hellenistic-Christian Church.

According to the first legend, Peter, during the interval between the death of Stephen and the foundation of the mixed community at Antioch, and after the propagators of the Gospel had made some converts in Samaria and the coast towns of Phoenicia, undertook a sort of pastoral visit to the new groups there recruited by evangelists who were not apostles. In Samaria, accompanied by John, who remains a dumb figure, we find him bestowing the Holy Spirit on Philip's converts, which Philip had been unable to bestow upon them, and confounding one of the converts, the famous magician, Simon, who had offered for cash down to buy the power to confer the Spirit, so that he, Simon, might bestow the gift himself.[3] After which, we are given to understand that Peter, making a similar tour of the coast towns, where he at once performed some miracles,4 travelling this time alone, was guided to carry the Gospel to the centurion, Cornelius, a man of substance friendly to the Jews—the guidance being furnished by a paraphernalia of revelations constructed on the same model as those by which the Book of Acts prepared the baptism of Saul-Paul by Ananias, and also to be met with in the mysteries of Isis.5 The interview of Peter and Cornelius, their reciprocal explanations and the subsequent discourse of Peter are somewhat lacking in interest. The object of the discourse is to exhibit Peter as the very first to proclaim before a pagan audience the principle of universal salvation by faith in the Christ, the principle which this legend of conversion is designed throughout to illustrate and figuratively to set forth.

The third act of the pious drama is the baptism of Cornelius and his household under a kind of mandate from the Holy Spirit, who descends on the catechumens before the sacrament is administered. This legend, somewhat abbreviated, is repeated in the account of his conduct which Peter is represented as rendering to the community at Jerusalem. As the conversion of Cornelius symbolizes the conversion of the Gentiles, so the misgivings of the Jerusalem community symbolize the opposition of the Judaizing party, while Peter's answer to their complaint is designed to show that the little Pentecost of Caesarea puts the pagans on the same footing as the believers of Israel baptized in the Spirit at the great Pentecost in Jerusalem. Thus the question of the salvation of the uncircumcised, by faith alone and baptism, is answered, always symbolically, before it arose in reality. But there is matter for a smile when, after hearing Peter, under reprimand for eating with Gentiles, prove so solidly that he has done well, one goes on to read in the Epistle to the Galatians (ii, 11–14) how Paul fell foul of this same Peter for refusing to sit at the same table with the uncircumcised.

Simon Peter may well have been the leading spirit in the genesis of the faith, but his rôle in reality was always little more than that of an apostle to the circumcision. No doubt it was impossible for him to be anything else, although, when the time for it came, he did not oppose the admission of pagans into the community by baptism without circumcision—so much may be retained from Galatians ii, 9, 12. There is no evidence of his going far away from Jerusalem before the year 44. Peter, James and John, the sons of Zebedee, and "James, the brother of the Lord"[6] were the chief figures of the Jewish-Christian community in Jerusalem during the first twelve or fifteen years of its existence. The legend of Cornelius is the creation of a time considerably later when an effort was made to give Peter prominence in relation to Paul, to exhibit him as representing the authentic and primitive apostolic tradition, the founder and first appointed leader of the universal church embracing both Jewish and pagan elements.[7]

The legend of Paul has undergone a parallel amplification to that of Peter, but on two different lines: first, by his own statements or by the tradition of his Epistles designed to make him the possessor of the true Gospel and of a strictly personal mission for the conversion of the Gentile world; and then by the common tradition for the purpose of subordinating his rôle and activity to the work of the Twelve, and especially of Peter regarded as the chief instrument of the apostolate instituted by Jesus.

Relying on the Epistles and disregarding their apologetic and tendentious character, even in much that concerns the person of Paul, though this perhaps is secondary, criticism is apt to conclude that Paul from his conversion onwards had full consciousness of an exceptional calling as apostle to the pagans, and that he set to work, resolutely and alone, to conquer the world, drawing in his wake the leaders of Judaic Christianity, whether willing or not. And this, indeed, is how things happened if we take the indications of the Galatian Epistle at their face value. There we encounter an apostle who holds his commission from God only, who has a gospel peculiar to himself given him by immediate revelation, and has already begun the conquest of the whole Gentile world. No small claim! (Galatians i, 11–12, 15–17, 21–24; ii, 7–8).

But things did not really happen in that way, and could not have so happened. Paul did not arrive in Syria and Antioch in order to preside at the foundation of the first community of hellenizing Christians and to place himself at the head of missionaries who had come there before him, as Galatians ii, 1–10 might very naturally lead us to infer. Not only does the quite trustworthy account in Acts xi, 20–21 make it clear that the first conversions of the non-circumcised were made by believers from Cyprus and Cyrene, while a supplement, otherwise needing caution (xi, 22–26), sends Barnabas to seek out Paul at Tarsus[8] not till after their conversion had taken place—not only this, but another notice entirely consistent (xiii, 1–3) which enumerates the prophets and teachers in Antioch at the moment when it was determined to carry the missions abroad, heads the list with the name of Barnabas.[9] Him we may identify without hesitation as the Cypriote who had a preponderant part in the evangelization of Antioch; while the fifth and last name on the list is Saul-Paul, whom nobody would suspect of choosing the last place for himself, but who filled it quite naturally after the others who belonged to the group of founders. Barnabas, moreover, takes precedence of Paul in the mission entrusted to them jointly by the community (xiii, 3).

Interpret how we may the over-statements in the Epistle to the Galatians,[10] it is certain that Saul-Paul did not make his entry on the Christian stage as the absolute innovator, the autonomous and independent missionary exhibited by this Epistle. The believers in Damascus to whom Paul joined himself were zealous propagandists imbued with the spirit of Stephen, and there is nothing whatever to suggest that he was out of his element among them. Equally, he was quite unaware at that time of possessing a peculiar Gospel or a vocation on a different level from that of all the other Christian missionaries. That idea he certainly did not bring with him to Antioch, where he found a community which others had built up and which recruited non-Jews without imposing circumcision. For long years[11] he remained there as the helper of Barnabas rather than his chief. When the Jerusalem community took offence at what was going on at Antioch, it was Barnabas and Paul, with Barnabas in front, who went to plead the cause of liberty before the elders. Paul's only initiation into the apostolate to the Gentiles was the initiation he received at Antioch by the side of Barnabas. That apostolate was established before Paul appeared on the scene and continued to be exercised by others at the same time as by him. Paul was simply one of the greatest missionaries of the earliest period. In the conventional histories of primitive

Christianity he has eclipsed the true founders of the hellenizing movement, as well as eclipsing Barnabas, who has almost been turned into a modest companion of his missionary labours, like Timothy and Titus at a later stage. But he owes this eminence far more to the exploitation of his memory by one part of the Christian tradition, and to the writings that were assigned to his name, than to any first-hand evidence of his apostolic activity and its successes.

The legend in Acts on the other hand, while magnifying him in its own way, has unduly subordinated him, along with Barnabas, to the founders of the first Christian community. Although edited Acts tell the story of his conversion in detail[12] and has it twice told by Paul himself in speeches put in his mouth, all that we can retain from this as certain is that Paul came from Tarsus in Galicia and that suddenly, in consequence of a vision, he was converted at Damascus to faith in the Christ whom he had previously opposed. Paul's native country is not mentioned in the Epistles, but Tarsus is no invention of the editor of Acts; it is even the most certain piece of information he has left us concerning the antecedents of the great apostle. We may believe in like manner that the apostle's Semitic name was Saul and that the name Paul, always used in the Epistles, is a surname; as it is probable that Paul was a Roman citizen the surname may be a *cognomen*. Nothing is known of his family. Perhaps the trade of tentmaker, which we shall find him following at Corinth in the house of Aquila, was learnt from his father. There were flourishing schools at Tarsus, but there is nothing to prove that Paul frequented them in his youth. By education he was a Pharisee, but the editor of Acts is responsible for making him a disciple of Gamaliel, which he never was; his culture was Jewish; he read the Scriptures in the Septuagint and may have known Aramaic as the traditional speech of his family as well as from his later travels. Needless to say our assessment of the influences to be recognized as having moulded his thought depends on the credit we attach to the Epistles. The gnostic ways of salvation to be met with in the great Epistles and in Colossians and Philippians—not to speak of Ephesians—suggest many and varied contacts with the mystical thought of the period. Retaining only what is most probable, it seems that Paul was of Jewish culture and a Jew of strict observance, but, with experience of life in a pagan environment, rendered capable by that experience of embracing without repugnance the programme of evangelization adopted by the missionaries of Antioch.

The Book of Acts gives us the romance, not the psychology, of his conversion. There is every reason to believe that Paul himself never examined the process that led up to it and never analysed its motives; nor has he described the vision which seems to have suddenly changed the orientation of his being.[13] The event took place at Damascus, but we have no knowledge of what brought him to that city, nor do we know whether he had previously been a zealous opponent of Christian groups elsewhere. He was never the general commissioner in charge of an official persecution. He must have been a Messianist, bewildered at first but afterwards gained over by what the followers of Jesus had to tell of their Christ. The inner process which issued in his conversion is not to be discerned either in the Epistles or in Acts. The Epistles say nothing about it, although commentators have pretended, and often still pretend, to discover it there. The editor of Acts has run the story of his conversion into the conventional mould of miracle and interpreted it according to the notion he is bent on giving of the providential mission to be assigned to Paul.[14] That he stirred up the Jews in Damascus by preaching immediately after his conversion, the Christ he had come to oppose is contradicted by Galatians (cf. Acts ix, 20–22; Galatians i, 15–17);[15] which equally contradicts the story of his setting out at once to Jerusalem to join the old disciples and of his preaching there in the synagogues only to provoke a plot from which he escapes again by flight.[16] As to the story of Barnabas, departing under orders from the apostolic community, to meet Paul at Tarsus and to bring him to Antioch, this is only another effort to exhibit Paul as an auxiliary of considerable importance recruited and patronized by the Jerusalem apostles. All these fictions must be set aside if the movement of primitive evangelization is to recover its true physiognomy.

1. First Impacts of the Gospel on the Pagan World

The author of Acts in its original form seems to have had before him fairly precise information concerning the Jerusalem community, the foundation of the Antioch community and the missions of Paul. The editor of our canonical book has not enlarged the framework of the story; he has merely modified the contents, drowning them in his legends about Peter and Paul, and arranging them to suit the needs of his apologetic or to edify the Church. But missionary activity and the expansion of the Christian religion vastly exceeded in reality the scope assigned to it in Acts. In this respect the wholly fictitious scene of Pentecost, in its catalogue of the Mediterranean peoples, may give us a truer idea of the work accomplished during the first forty years of evangelization than can be gathered from the subsequent narratives in the book.

It is true that Acts gives summary information that the Phoenician towns and Cyprus were evangelized before Antioch (xi, 19), but tells us nothing whatever of how the preaching of the Christ came to Damascus so early in the day. The most probable conjecture is that some of Stephen's companions were able to reach that city; there is, however, the possibility that, when the Hebrew group also finally embarked on propaganda outside Jerusalem, Jewish Christianity may at once have thrown out casts in Palestine and found its way into the neighbouring countries of Transjordania and Syria. Both Egypt and "the regions of Libya round about Cyrene" are mentioned in the story of Pentecost (ii, 10). Ought we not also to recall that a Cyrenian is said to have carried the cross of Jesus to Golgotha? It is at least significant that Jews of Cyrene figure at the side of Barnabas among the founders and teachers of the Antioch community—Lucius of Cyrene and probably "Simeon called the Black" (xiii, 1).

It is a reasonable conjecture that some believer in Cyrene evangelized his own country. But the probability is very high that the faith of Jesus, having once left Jerusalem and crossed the frontiers of Palestine, quickly penetrated Egypt and found its way to Alexandria. Christian propaganda does not seem to be aimed at in express terms in a letter addressed by Claudius to the Alexandrians shortly after his accession, although many have thought the letter condemns it;[17] but it is virtually impossible that Christian propaganda was not active at that time, or soon afterwards, in Alexandrian Jewry, and the more so in view of the contact of Stephen and his group with Jews of Alexandria.[18]

It is not until near the end of the second century, at the time of the pascal controversy, that the Christian community of Alexandria makes its appearance in history. But by then it had become of considerable importance and fully formed; it had a great teacher, Clement, a profound and learned mystic; it had behind it a long and, for us, extremely obscure past, of which our chief knowledge is that it supplied the Christianity of that time with many notable heretics. Although its origin must date back to the dawn of the Christian religion, we are completely ignorant of how, when or by whom the Gospel was carried into Egypt,[19] and of the conditions under which it lived and spread in that country. We have already indicated all that is known about *the Gospel of the Egyptians*. In the highly syncretist atmosphere of Alexandria Christianity seems to have taken a strong turn towards gnosticism. It is a misfortune, doubtless attributable to that atmosphere, that the writings of the Alexandrian gnostics of the second century have not come down to us, any more than *the Gospel of the Egyptians*. The consequence is that Alexandrian Christianity eludes the grasp of the historian until the time when it was caught up in the general current of the catholic movement, into which the gnostic crisis was later canalized and compressed.

Similar observations apply to the Roman community. When Paul wrote to it about the year 56 this community was not a thing of yesterday; yet a quarter of a century earlier the Gospel propaganda had hardly begun and must therefore have been carried to Rome in the earliest period of its activity. An edict of Claudius against the Jews, issued under conditions obscure to the historian, may have been occasioned by agitation provoked in Roman Jewry by the preachers of the Christ. It seems that the edict came out in the early years of his reign and was caused by the Christian propaganda; this it chiefly aimed at repressing, but without restricting the liberty of the Jewish cult.[20] Perhaps we may consider as probable the hypothesis that the Christian propaganda was not of the inoffensive political character it affects in the writings of the New Testament, and that it led to serious messianic agitation in the great Jewries, like that of Rome and especially that of Alexandria.

Who were the first and real founders of the Roman community? Certainly no important person from the first community in Jerusalem; certainly not Peter; otherwise Paul in his letter to the Romans would have had to pay regard to such notables and would not have been able to claim the field as freely open to him. They must have been Christian Jews from Palestine, hellenistic rather than Hebrew, who had not come to Rome for the sole purpose of propaganda, but had none the less exercised it there both among the Roman Jews and among the pagan frequenters of their synagogues; and with rapid success, since the community —or, more exactly, the Christian groups in Rome—had attained considerable importance, though as yet unable to claim that importance under any apostolic name.

The time is long past when critics ought to have recognized, or at least more deeply understood, that Christian propaganda was not at first, and was not to become until more than one generation had passed, a methodically conducted enterprise for the foundation of communities planned on a model predetermined by the first missionaries, or even determined after the lapse of several years. It was the kind of agitation that arises from personal communication, one might call it a contagion, and remained so from the time when Jesus began to preach till that of the Apocalypse. The promptitude with which the propaganda was begun and its almost staggering success would be inexplicable, though without being more miraculous than a world-epidemic, unless we took into consideration the free outburst of enthusiasm which started the first migration of the Gospel on its way, together with the whole assemblage of conditions under which the preaching of the Gospel was born. As the fever of extravagant hope cooled down, system and rule came in to the same measure.

Let us never forget that the message which fired this hope was at once urgent and easy to deliver; *God and His Christ were on the point of coming.* Every Jew had an interest in knowing that. Is it likely that any Jew would not be eager to hear of it? And those who carried the message, with a simple-minded conviction of its truth, never doubted for a moment that multitudes would be ready to believe them. Their faith gave them assurance of success. Moreover the utmost alacrity was imperative for the sake of every man whom the message might reach; the Great Event was bound to come suddenly and without warning: let every man then be ready. It must be admitted, however, that some groups of Hebrew believers refused to treat the message as an article for export, and represented Jesus as commanding his missionaries not to go to the Samaritans nor to the pagans, because the Son of Man would come before they had time to make the round of the cities of Israel (Matt. x, 5, 23). Superfluous orders for propaganda already on the wing and which nothing thereafter could stop!

There is, however, no need to exaggerate the meaning of the texts just quoted. They reflect the programme of the Judaizing party. They are easily explained by saying that their authors were resolved to keep their propaganda within the regions to which Jesus had confined his own activity. But, from the fact that this programme is here turned into a precept of the Christ, it does not follow that it was intended to make the example of Jesus into a binding rule for all. We must first consider how the Great Event was understood. Certain it is that the Judaizers were not bent on excluding all the Jews of the Dispersion from the coming Kingdom of God; they believed that the accession of the Dispersed to the Kingdom would be effectively brought about after, and as a consequence of, the Event, which the original believers feverishly awaited from day to day. On the other hand, the hellenistic believers, who proclaimed Jesus as "Lord" had begun to preach the *religion* of the Christ also, and not merely his imminent advent, and were early convinced that the message of this religion ought to be carried at once to the Gentiles, and to all nations, since faith in the Christ was, for all, an indispensable condition of entry into the Kingdom. "This Gospel of the Kingdom shall be preached in all the world as a witness to all nations; and then shall the end come" (Matt. xxiv, 14). As the Second Coming did not take place the delay was explained by the necessity of completing the world-wide proclamation of the Gospel. In any case, what was now more and more aimed at was the gathering, in hope of his coming, of recruits to the faith of the Christ who was acclaimed "as a god." Thus understood, the Kingdom of God was something very different from the enthronement of the Messiah-King at Jerusalem, and came more and more to be felt as already realized in the Christian community.

In this way the evangelical message was continually passed on from one locality to the next in the Jewish colonies of all countries, where it naturally gained a hearing and then came under discussion. It was not accepted by all who heard it—how could it be?—but a certain number received it as a hope imparted by contagion. To all appearance the Jewish authorities were not as prompt in discrediting the propaganda as the Christian missionaries were in spreading it. These authorities could not measure in advance the harm which the propaganda was about to inflict upon Judaism. At first they must have thought that the execution of Jesus would suffice to break down the agitation which the Galilean preacher had started. The formation of the Jewish-Christian community took them, so to speak, off their guard; they scented no great peril in that. Disquieted, later, by the formation of the hellenistic group and the preaching of Stephen, they reassured themselves by executing the new preacher and by dispersing his associates. But this dispersion of the hellenistic believers had also the effect of spreading their belief, and when information came to the authorities of the growing success which the propagation of it everywhere was achieving, they found themselves powerless to stop it. It was doubtless at their instigation that King Agrippa I resolved to strike down the leaders of the community holding on at Jerusalem. But Peter escaped. To set the law in motion against the whole group of Hebrew believers would have been too risky, while the hellenistic preaching was beyond the reach of violent repression. Before the fall of Jerusalem in the year 70 it seems improbable that the faith of Jesus was considered in any of the Jewries as altogether incompatible with the profession of Judaism.

Considered in itself the Gospel message appealed in the main to simple souls, who awaited the day of the Lord in good faith, and to the poor, who had need of its coming. Although the Christian movement was not, strictly speaking, socialism coloured by religion, it had from the very beginning and long continued to have, indeed has never altogether lost, the character of a popular association which offered a promising asylum to the disinherited classes of contemporary society, to the Jewish plebs, to the pagan plebs and to the pagan slaves. The participation of the more fortunate classes was for a long time on a small scale, but this favoured rather than hindered the organization of the new religion as a vast mutual aid society, in which the unfortunate of all classes found moral support and material help. In short, Christianity brought to its adepts something more than an unrealizable hope continually frustrated. It brought solace to great miseries, and led on to the founding of an equalitarian society less crushing for the oppressed victims of the old civilizations.

The expansion of the constituency of the new cult was effected from the side where the synagogues themselves recruited proselytes more or less complete but fairly numerous, that is, from the pagans. That Christianity was able to make such remarkable progress in so short a time is due to the fact that Judaism had previously spread itself over the entire Mediterranean world, and that the synagogues had everywhere throughout the Roman Empire, and even beyond, become centres of active propaganda. The missionaries of Jesus made all haste to carry their message to the synagogues. Gaining them, they came, almost without premeditation, into contact with the pagan proselytes, and when the missionaries, after drawing away a large part of these, were driven out of the synagogues, they addressed themselves directly to the pagans. This first happened at Antioch and it must have repeated itself everywhere.

Although Acts (xi, 19–21) give a highly summarized version of the doings at Antioch, it leaves us with the certainty that the believers in Jesus began by addressing themselves to Jews in the synagogues; that thereby they made an impression on a few pagans friendly to Judaism, and were thus led to recruit uncircumcised persons who were willing to hear their message. But, in all this, there was no question of a rupture with the synagogue, doubtless because the preachers had done nothing to provoke it, and also because the spirit of the Antioch Jewry was not bigoted. (The protest against preaching the Gospel to the Gentiles without requiring circumcision did not come from the Jews of Antioch but from Judaizing believers sent there by Jerusalem.) No official repudiation of the Christian propaganda was issued by the Jewish authorities till long after the year 44;

for we find that Paul, to all appearances, had been everywhere able to present himself in the synagogues of Asia Minor, Macedonia and Achaia without any ban being imposed from the outset on the reception of his message, which was obstructed only by local reactions. When he was taken prisoner in Jerusalem, his person was the object of attack. The Judaizing Christians of the earliest community continued to be tolerated and to frequent the temple, perhaps also the synagogues, without constituting a group separate from traditional Judaism, as the hellenistic-Christians organized by Paul in Asia Minor had by this time become.

It may therefore be taken as certain that the Gospel would have found no easy way out of Palestine if Judaism had not established colonies in almost every part of the Roman Empire, and beyond it. Christian propaganda would have taken no hold on the pagan world had not Judaism begun the conquest of it in advance and initiated the pagans, to some extent, in the hope of the Jews. But, Judaism being there, Christianity—a Jewish heresy—was enabled to make its appearance at every centre of the ancient world where Judaism was firmly rooted. In the environment where Judaism had won victories Christianity won them also, and more easily. For the Gospel seemed to bring, and did bring, the same hope, even a better hope, for it was on the way to fulfilment; at the same time it dispensed adherents from Jewish observances repugnant to the habits of the Greco-Roman world. With the way into pagan territory thus opened, Christianity found there an immense clientele of the disinherited, to whom it offered substantial help in their present misery, moral in the first instance but material also, with the expectation of felicity in the coming age.

2. THE HEADQUARTERS AT ANTIOCH

The texts before us make it possible to see how, when once the Antioch community had been constituted, the propagation of the Gospel was organized for the countries of Syria and Cilicia. Although the members, at least the Jewish-Christian part of them, still frequented the synagogue, the community had nevertheless a life of its own, but without breaking away from

Judaism. Private meetings of believing groups for instruction and for the Eucharist had, in Antioch, a greater importance than in Jerusalem, because in the former there was no temple to serve as a common meeting place for the pious Jews and followers of Jesus.

Paul, in the Epistle to the Galatians, speaks of having preached in Syria and Cilicia for at least ten years.[21] The following notice in Acts (xiii, 1–2) concerning the initiative, taken by the Antioch community for the preaching work in question, refers to the beginning of this period.

> Now there were at Antioch,
>   in the community of that place,
>   prophets and preachers:
> (Joseph called) Barnabas (of Cyprus)[22]
>   Simeon called the Black
>   and Lucius of Cyrene
> Manaen, friend of Herod the tetrarch,
>   and Saul (called Paul, of Tarsus). . . .
> And as they worshipped the Lord and fasted,
>   The Holy Spirit said:
> "Separate me Barnabas and Saul
>   to the work whereto I have called them."

In the edited or canonical book of Acts this preamble introduces a common and prolonged mission of Barnabas and Paul to Cyprus and Asia Minor (xiii, 4–xiv) which is represented as taking place before the meeting at Jerusalem which settled the question of the legal observances. But this arrangement is contradicted both by the Epistle to the Galatians (cf. Gal. i, 21–ii, 1), which puts the Jerusalem meeting immediately after the mission into Syria-Cilicia, and by Acts themselves (xv, 23) to which, in their account of the meeting, the only hellenistic-Christian communities known are those of Syria-Cilicia. Moreover, it seems impossible to place this mission, with E. Meyer (iii, 421) and others, between the Jerusalem meeting and the subsequent conflict between Peter and Paul at Antioch, after which Paul, now separated from Barnabas, followed his personal inspirations only. Far more probably the Cyprus mission was undertaken by Barnabas alone after this separation, and the mission to Lycaonia and Galatia by Paul alone on the same occasion; the editor of Acts having thought well to combine these two missions into one, and to anticipate certain events in each of the two in the common mission he proceeds to imagine.[23]

The text just cited, then, concerns a mission of which the story is not told in canonical Acts. It can only be that of which the whole credit seems to be attributed to Paul in the Epistle to the Galatians. In fact our text supposes the mission to have been carried out under conditions very different from those implied by the Epistle. Following the latter, one might think that Paul set forth entirely alone in order to carry out a programme laid down by himself at the time of his conversion. We here see that he did nothing of the kind. At a meeting of the congregation, assembled, we must suppose, in the name of the Holy Spirit, the Spirit, doubtless with one of the prophets for spokesman, commands the congregation to make provision for the support of two missionaries, whose whole time is to be devoted to making converts, both in Antioch itself and especially in the neighbour-ing regions of Syria and Cilicia. The two missionaries selected were evidently the two judged to be most gifted for this kind of service, the first being Barnabas who heads the list of prophet-teachers as chief founders of the Antioch congregation, the second being Paul, the last on the list as having been admitted to the congregation when it was already founded, but whose zeal and gifts as a maker of converts had speedily won recognition.

It is not very difficult to see how the decision to undertake the mission came about. When the community had grown, through the adhesion of new recruits, to fairly large proportions, though the apostolic office had as yet no definite form, it became obvious that the time was ripe to organize teaching, for the furtherance of propaganda, by delegating it to those best fitted for that employment. Now the Antioch congregation was well furnished in this respect, having five "prophets and teachers." To support the home propaganda, in the conditions under which this had been carried on hitherto, half of the total force would be enough, while the most active, enterprising and—may we guess?—the youngest could then be more usefully employed on outside work. For various reasons Barnabas and Paul were the likely candidates for a travelling mission. Both of them, moreover, and Paul especially, were acquainted with the region in which their zeal was to be exercised; the purpose being to radiate outwards from Antioch and as far as Cilicia—Paul's country of origin.

We can only conjecture how the Antioch community attained the degree of development at which we find it when the apostolic expedition of Barnabas and Paul was set on foot. To begin with, a few Jews would be won over by the fugitives from Jerusalem; then the Cypriots and the Cyrenians—Barnabas, Simeon the Black and Lucius—would recruit a certain number of uncircumcised proselytes to Judaism, whom they found attached to the synagogues. Since the synagogues had accepted them without demanding circumcision our new preachers would do the same, and would have little scruple in doing so if they thought, as Stephen did, that in the Reign of the Christ the non-moral observances of the Law would be swept away. So they confined themselves to baptizing their uncircumcised converts before admitting them to fellowship, just as they also baptized the circumcised Jews. For the rest, we may conjecture that at Antioch, as at Jerusalem, the new believers, while perhaps continuing to frequent the synagogues, would in addition have meetings of their own, especially in the form of meals for the solemn breaking of bread in memory of Jesus, and in celebration of his approaching advent. Assuming that complete separation from the synagogue was not soon effected—and it is probable that the bond was not broken for a considerable time—the final result is that the new community would have a life of its own and, we may add, its own meetings for worship, as we are in effect told it had.

In these meetings at Antioch strange phenomena were produced which can hardly have been forthcoming at Jerusalem in the same degree or in the same form. For the scene at Pentecost described in Acts is entirely fictitious; so too is what the same book has to tell us elsewhere about "speaking with tongues" (ii, 1–13; x, 46; xix, 6). Moreover there is no evidence of prophets or inspired teachers appearing in Jerusalem, except casually in stories of secondary origin and poor credibility (xi, 27–30).[24] At Antioch instructors in doctrine were regarded as endowed by the Spirit with the gift of Knowledge, and as able, on occasion, to deliver true oracles under the Spirit's dictation, as happened

139

in the case of the mission entrusted to Barnabas and Paul. There seems to be no ground for dividing the list of the five "prophets and teachers" into two parts, as if the first two or three had been "prophets" and the others "teachers." A prophet does not prophesy without intermission. The same individual who at exceptional times seemed to be speaking to the direct dictation of the Spirit would, in ordinary times, deliver his teaching with its help and presence, that is, under the simple inspiration of his faith, but without emotional transports. Conversely, there were few teachers at this time who had not, at certain conjunctions, their moments of trance and prophetic revelation. In the case before us the suggestion which pointed to Barnabas and Paul was obviously the outcome of circumstances, and it matters little to know by the mouth of which prophet it was uttered, though we may be sure it did not come from either of the two persons interested.

It would no doubt be somewhat risky to assume that the spiritual gifts, which play so large a part in the history of primitive Christianity, were not first manifested at Jerusalem but had their beginning at Antioch. Mystical and visionary exaltation infectiously communicated is contemporary with faith in Christ risen from the dead, and helped to fortify it, the disposition to yield to it being strengthened by anxious expectation of the parousia. But Antioch may well have marked a stage onwards in the evolution of this mysticism, the stage of prophetical teaching, which is not said to have accompanied the delirious "speaking with tongues." Incomplete as our documentary evidence may be, it is an important fact that the Antioch community was organized under the direction of teaching prophecy.

Not less important to note at this point is the way in which the apostolate was instituted under the form of a *delegation*. Barnabas and Paul are teaching prophets at Antioch whom the community, at the suggestion of the Spirit—the Christ-Spirit—delegates for a mission abroad. This delegation clearly makes them "apostles," that is to say envoys of the community which had given them the mission at the bidding of the Spirit of Christ. "The work" referred to is a real or genuine apostolic mission, its significance as such being underlined for the sole reason that it was, at least in the writer's thought, the first of its kind;

an enterprise declared to be necessary in the name of Christ at a meeting of believers, and entrusted to delegates whom the community, while accompanying them with its prayers, provides with letters of recommendation, with money, and all else needful for the journey. Otherwise such expeditions would not have been possible. The passage before us, then (xiii, 1–2), is an account of the first institution of the travelling apostolate, the narrator being fully aware of it as such, as well as of the close collaboration of Barnabas and Paul for several years, a collaboration which the Epistle to the Galatians tends to disguise. A commission from the community to which the traveller belonged, with a contribution to the expenses of his journey, leaving the rest of his entertainment to his prospective converts, was a normal feature in the constitution of the primitive apostolate.

We lack the details of the preaching tours made by Barnabas and Paul in the regions of Syria and Cilicia.[25] All we know of it are the results. Several Christian groups were formed in these countries under the same conditions as those at Antioch. They were partly recruited from the pagans, so that now there were many communities, using the name of Jesus and sharing the Jewish hope, in which adherents were to be found who had not submitted to the obligations of the Jewish cult.

One may well ask whether the Antioch missionaries had weighed the consequences of what may perhaps be called their liberalism. No doubt the two envoys conformed to the broader tendencies of Judaism as observed in the Dispersion, putting the essentials of religion in a belief in the One God and in the salvation promised by him to Israel subject to observance of the Jewish moral law. These tendencies would be in agreement with the opinion attributed to Stephen regarding the abrogation, in the final economy of the Kingdom, of the material observances required by the Mosaic ritual. We may believe further that they had some sense, perhaps confused, of the great opportunities which the abandonment of these practices could not fail to bring for their propaganda. But neither could they disguise from themselves that these easy-going ways would give rise to opposition, and they would need to have their answer ready. What they probably did not suspect nor aim to bring about was that, in reality, they were laying the foundation of a new religion and that soon, in consequence of their exertions, the faith of Christ, the religion of Jesus would be separated for ever, and immediately, from Judaism.

3. PAUL BREAKS WITH ANTIOCH

Between the new community at Antioch, with its offshoots, and the community at Jerusalem, the first and chief centre of the faith, there existed relations, just as there were relations between the Judaism of the Dispersion and the metropolis of all the Jews. It was not very long before the saints in Jerusalem began to be alarmed by the news that groups were being formed in Syria and Cilicia of persons more or less strangers to Judaism inasmuch as they were outside its ritual economy. The problem which the liberalism of the Antioch missionaries had found so easy of solution did not seem so simple to the Hebrew believers of the original community. How, they asked, could the promises be inherited by those who bore not the mark of the chosen people, by those who were not partners in the holy covenant with its ritual conditions fixed by revelation direct from God? Perhaps the chiefs of the community hesitated to pronounce judgment in the matter, the teaching of Jesus, so far as there was any to refer to, having never touched this problem, nor furnished a principle for its solution. At an early hour in the development of primitive Christianity, Jesus was represented as having predicted the accession of the Gentiles to the Kingdom, and even as having realized it symbolically by miracles performed at the request of the Canaanite woman and of the centurion at Capernaum. But he was not made to declare that circumcision and the other observances were of no value for salvation. The Judaizers made him say the flat contrary and openly declare that he had not come to abrogate the Law (Matthew v, 17–19).

There were, however, some zealous individuals, more or less imbued with the pharisaic spirit, who pronounced against the practice of the Antioch missionaries and took upon themselves the duty of travelling to that city and catechizing the proselytes, explaining to them that salvation was impossible unless the Law of Moses was observed.[26] Perhaps the Jewish believers in Antioch were easily shaken; but the hellenistic believers resisted, and their chiefs refused to yield to the injunctions of Judaizing extremists. By way of putting an end to the trouble the community resolved to send a delegation which would go into the matter with the elders in Jerusalem. Paul in the Epistle to the Galatians gives us to understand that this step was taken under orders from the Spirit (ii, 2),[27] the text describing it, however, as a private revelation in consequence of which Paul decided to betake himself to Jerusalem. But the thing happened quite differently. There was no question either of the affairs or of the doctrines peculiar to this apostle. Either Paul, after the event, immensely exaggerated his own importance in it, making the whole negotiation centre on himself, and claiming as his personal inspiration the step taken by the community, under injunction of the Spirit, in delegating, not Paul alone, but Barnabas first and Paul second—either this, or the text, written in eulogy of Paul, is apocryphal. The Epistle also mentions a certain Titus, an uncircumcised believer, as having been chosen by Paul himself as his companion. If Titus really accompanied the delegates, he too may have been appointed by the community. The journey probably took place towards the end of the year 43. Agrippa I died in the course of 44; Peter fled from Jerusalem in the spring of that year; the apostolic meeting took place some time previously.

The problem was not settled without a clash of argument. Reading the Epistle to the Galatians one might think that Paul and his doctrines were the sole matters in the debate. In fact the whole work of the Antioch missionaries, which had not been started by Paul himself, was in question. At the general meetings of the community little was spoken of beyond the results obtained by the missionaries. But Barnabas and Paul had long private audiences with the chiefs, of whom the Epistle mentions Peter, John and James—according to the context not the brother of John, but James the brother of the Lord.[28] To them the Antioch apostles gave their reasons and defended their practice. The elders of Jerusalem were at last convinced. If we could believe what the Epistle to the Galatians has to say of the matter (ii, 7–9) it would seem that the "pillars" recognized in Paul a unique and universal vocation as apostle to the Gentiles and a parallel vocation for Peter as apostle to the circumcision.

Nothing could be less probable than such a convention. The book of Acts has no suspicion of its having ever existed. Either, then, Paul immensely overstates his own importance in describing his providential mission, or the text is not authentic. The elders of Jerusalem were hardly more capable of claiming for themselves alone the evangelization of all the Jews in the world than they were of confiding to Paul alone the evangelization of all the Gentiles. Such a division would have been an outrage upon common sense. To render it more acceptable Edouard Meyer arbitrarily supposes that the Jerusalem believers, not knowing Greek, confined themselves to the evangelization of the Jews in Palestine and left all the other countries in the world to the hellenists. This in fact is what happened, but is not what the text of the Epistle means.[29] The debate was not aimed at the theoretical object of determining the vocation of the chief apostles and their respective spheres of influence, a problem both abstract and retrospective. From beginning to end the one question at issue was whether or no salvation could be assured to the uncircumcised by virtue alone of faith in God and His Christ Jesus, along with a change of heart and observance of the Jewish moral law, but without circumcision and the ritual practices obligatory for Jews by birth. This was the only question examined and it was so important in itself that to seek another theme for the debate in the personalities that were parties to it is a gratuitous expenditure of effort. On this, the only point at issue, the Jerusalem elders finally came to terms with the Antioch missionaries. This, doubtless, was done the more easily because Jewish opinion on the necessity of circumcision for the salvation of proselytes had not been at that time determined. The Galilean believers, moreover, cannot have been very deeply versed in the problems of theology. At this period they seem to have had no thought of leaving Palestine, nor even Jerusalem, and to have willingly given consent that others should carry the Gospel to the outside world, whether Jewish or Gentile, and under the conditions which the Antioch missionaries had adopted. Their sole request was the preachers to the countries of the Dispersion should not forget "the poor"—that is, the Jerusalem community, where material poverty was common enough. The help thus to be given was doubtless understood as a sign of communion, not to say as a kind of allegiance. Notwithstanding the story in Acts (xv, 13–20)[30] it may be doubted whether the arrangement carried other conditions, such as the interdiction of blood and of "things strangled." But it is morally certain that the general picture in Acts reflects the real practice, that of a compromise adopted in mixed congregations to allay the scruples of Jewish believers, and sanctioned from the outset by apostolic authority. What the chiefs had decided the Jerusalem community accepted, and letters were written disavowing the disturbers of the peace at Antioch; they were carried by two notables of Jerusalem, Judas Barsabbas and Silas who accompanied the Antioch delegation on the return journey. Thus the danger of division at the moment when the Christian religion was in process of being born was averted, and the continuation of the propaganda on pagan soil assured. But the external peace enjoyed by the Jerusalem congregation was about to pass through a time of trouble; while the agreement reached by the missionaries was soon, by the action of Paul, to be shattered also.

In the years when these things were happening the old Kingdom of Herod the Great was provisionally reconstituted for the benefit of Herod Agrippa the First, a dependant of the Emperor Claudius, and previously the friend of Caligula. This prince, after a life of many adventures and of mediocre edification, thought to win the favour of his subjects by putting on grand airs of piety.[31] Like the procurators, he resided by preference at Caesarea, but coming to Jerusalem for the Passover in the year 44 he made it his duty to persecute the heads of the Christian congregation. It is possible that the decision to do this was not entirely his own, but was made in response to solicitation from the Jewish ecclesiastical authorities. Since his reign began in 41 it may, however, be asked why had not the priests and the Sanhedrim made an earlier appeal to him? Perhaps the success of the Christian propaganda outside Palestine was beginning at last to alarm them, and it may even be that the Antioch affair, and the solution in which it resulted, had come to their knowledge and caused them particular irritation.[32] There is also the further possibility that the attitude of Agrippa may have been determined by that of Claudius towards Jewish agitation. For the rest, it is to be noted that action was not taken against the congregation as a whole, nor against James the brother of Jesus, who enjoyed a great reputation for fidelity to the Law. To begin with, the two sons of Zebedee, James and John, were arrested and put to death, probably after trial by the Sanhedrim.33

Peter was the next to be seized and, the time of the Passover having come, was thrown into prison to await his trial at the conclusion of the solemnities; but he made his escape under conditions which the book of Acts represents as wholly miraculous, and of which the least to be said is that the romancer and the dramatist have been hard at work (xii, 3–19). The alternatives seem to be that either he took to flight under the menace of arrest and that pains have been taken to cover up his inglorious retreat, or else some influential person found means to get him out of prison, and the incident became dramatized as a miracle. In either event he left Jerusalem in haste and in all probability never returned. But whither did he go? The editor of Acts is deliberately silent about the locality to which he betook himself, and for a twofold reason; first, because his purpose was to ignore the conflict between Peter and Paul; and, second, because by postponing the discussion about legal observances till after the events just related, he made it impossible to bring Peter, whom he supposes to have reached the solution of the problems at the conversion of Cornelius, on to the ground where the discussion had its birth. It may be that Peter left the city accompanied by John-Mark34 and by Silas.35 Palestine, now almost entirely under the rule of Herod Agrippa, being no safe place for him, he betook himself to Antioch.

Then arose the conflict which was to lead Paul on a road all his own and to wholly new fields for the proclamation of his Gospel. If we are to believe the Epistle to the Galatians (ii, 11–13) Peter found the Antioch community at peace under the recent decision of Jerusalem, and lived in the city for some time, participating without scruple, among the uncircumcised believers, in the meals where bread was broken in memory of the Lord Jesus. But soon there arrived certain emissaries from James who were scandalized by this promiscuous association of the circumcised and the uncircumcised. Save for indications in the Epistle to the Galatians, which are open to suspicion, there is no evidence that these emissaries attempted to cancel the Jerusalem decision and force circumcision on pagan converts. Their intention was to make it clear that the Jewish believers ought not to evade the obligations of the Jewish Law as interpreted in Pharisaic tradition. As they had on their side a little logic and a good deal of hereditary fanaticism, Peter gave way to their reproaches; so did the other circumcised believers; so, too, even Barnabas seems to have done, thinking no doubt that separation of circumcised and uncircumcised at meal times was preferable to schism between Antioch and Jerusalem on a matter of secondary importance.

Paul judged otherwise, and, if we may believe the Epistle to the Galatians,[36] lost his temper, denouncing Peter and the other Jewish believers as hypocrites, Barnabas included. He accused them roundly of being false to the Gospel, charging Peter in particular with attempting, in contravention of the Jerusalem agreement, to force circumcision on the Gentiles. The accusation, if it was ever made, seems to have had no foundation in fact. Barnabas, who had no thought of betraying the principle he had followed in evangelizing the pagans, did not change. Christian propaganda went on as before without imposition of the legal observances. It was largely owing to the absence of any such condition that it continued to succeed on the one hand and, on the other, that official Judaism was finally brought to the point of condemning it. We do not know whether Peter and Barnabas submitted indefinitely to the pressure of the Judaizers in governing their relations with the pagan converts. It is improbable. We may suppose that a compromise was soon effected—the very compromise in fact which the editor of Acts puts into the discourse of James and the apostolic decree for allaying the scruples of the Judaizers (xv, 20, 28–29).

The Epistle to the Galatians does not inform us what the sequel was to the controversy raised by Paul.[37] But it may be conjectured from the situation of which the Epistles, that to the Galatians to begin with, give us a glimpse. In that Epistle we see Paul isolated, proud of his isolation, and glorying in the consciousness of a unique vocation for which his isolation is, as it were, the natural price he has to pay. He sees himself, and describes himself, as pursued by unrelenting hostility, which he takes pains to discredit by attributing it to a difference of opinion about the essential principles of salvation and to certain unworthy intentions, but which we may suspect was mainly personal, caused by the way in which Paul had created solely for himself a schism from the other missionaries. But the question still remains for us of how far the view of the matter thus disclosed corresponds to the reality. If account be taken of the Epistle only, Paul is never again to be found in the relations of fraternal communion, existing up to the time of the Antioch quarrel, with Barnabas, with Peter or with other leading figures of the Christian propaganda, whoever they may have been. But, though Paul's independent turn of mind made him seek a field for his apostleship where he would have no competitors, there is no evidence that the communities founded by him formed a dissenting group, or even that there was a final breach between him and the authentic representatives of Judaizing Christianity. Just as he went to Jerusalem with Barnabas to obtain guarantees for the communities in Syria and Cilicia on the principle of freedom from circumcision, so later on we find him a second time in presence of the mother-community—this time with a collection taken up from his converts, as though with object of obtaining recognition from the Jerusalem leaders of the work he had accomplished all alone. But it may well be that confidence was not complete on either side, though matters were not yet at the pitch of anathema and excommunication.

Our canonical book of Acts is deliberately circumspect about the whole of this affair and firmly resolved to say nothing of the difficulties Paul had to encounter later in consequence of his separation from the other Christian missionaries. It confines itself to falsifying the true motive which prevented Barnabas and Paul, returned to Antioch after their journey to Jerusalem, from continuing to preach together as hitherto they had been doing. Barnabas is made to express a wish that Paul and he should be accompanied by John-Mark on a projected mission to the South of Asia Minor. Paul not wanting this companion, a lively contention then arises between the two which comes to such a pass that Barnabas goes off to Cyprus with John-Mark, and Paul to Asia Minor with Silas. The two departures, which we must suppose to have been almost simultaneous, belong, no doubt, to history. But the circumstances which led to them were not those indicated by the book of Acts.[38]

For different reasons the two missionaries judged it best to abandon the Antioch community which for many years had been the centre of their apostolic activity. Barnabas, certainly, might have stayed there. But perhaps, after the quarrel that had just arisen, he preferred to deliver the Gospel message in Cyprus, his native country, whither he had probably fled after the dispersion of Stephen's followers, but where he did not remain very long (xi, 19–20). If one may believe the Epistle to the Colossians, John-Mark was his nephew (Col. iv, 10); while according to Acts the house of Mary, John-Mark's mother, was a place of rendezvous for the Jerusalem believers.[39] It was to this house that Peter came, after his escape from prison, to bid them farewell on departing for Antioch. Of what Barnabas accomplished in Cyprus we know nothing, and can only presume that this true apostle, whose action was so decisive in carrying the Gospel to the pagan world, continued to labour fruitfully in the work he had been the first to set on foot. Tradition has pitched upon him as author of the Epistle to the Hebrews and of the so-called Epistle of Barnabas. But his real work was of greater value than Epistles or any treatise in theology. As to John-Mark, he was an evangelical worker of the second rank whose relations with Peter[40] made his name useful as a commendatory title for the oldest of the canonical Gospels.

Chapter V

THE APOSTLE PAUL

In Christian tradition Saul-Paul has become a massive influence embodied in a personality ever dear to Protestants as that of a father, but not easily grasped nor understood by the critical historian. The perplexity of the critic in presence of this more or less authentic patron saint of religious individualism is due to the fact that the human figure of him whom we conventionally name "the Apostle," which seems clear-cut so long as our faith is unshaken in most of the writings that bear his name, progressively loses its outlines in proportion as we become aware of the artificial elements in the documents concerning him. The present author does not claim to reconstitute his figure but only to fix its main features by means of probable hypotheses based on the glimpses we can get of his real activities.

1. From Antioch to Corinth

We have seen how, when Barnabas went off to preach the Gospel in his own country of Cyprus, probably at the end of the year 44, Paul took the road into Asia Minor accompanied by Silas. That his expedition received the unqualified blessing of the Antioch community, as the Book of Acts affirms (xv, 40), we take leave to doubt. For never again did Paul return to that neighbourhood,[1] and never did he speak of the Antioch community as his base of operations; even in the Epistle to the Galatians he recalls no memory of his ministry in the city at the side of Barnabas. The link between him and that centre of the apostolate was finally severed; for it was there that he had broken with all his brother apostles.

His little schism, however, did not deprive him of all his friends. Silas, as we have seen, had been the bearer of the letter from Jerusalem and time had been given him to become acquainted with Paul and Barnabas. Returned now to Antioch, we find Silas, if not taking the side of Paul—for his conduct proves that he was of neither party exclusively—at least associating himself with the new work Paul was about to set on foot. This work no doubt attracted Silas, Paul himself having personally gained his goodwill. Paul, though at variance with the other missionaries, did not regard himself as excommunicated, nor was he so in fact, nor did Silas think of him as being in that condition. So, without reserve, he joined himself to this pioneer of the Gospel withhis grand projects for the cause of the Christ and his capacity for giving them effect. In the sequel Silas did not remain permanently at the side of Paul and we shall have to ask why he left it, just as we have asked why he came to be there in the first instance. It is worthy of note that Silas was a Jew by origin and that Titus, a converted pagan who had followed Paul to Jerusalem did not follow him in the mission he undertook with Silas; only after some years, and then transitorily, shall we find him at Paul's side, in Corinth. Perhaps there were certain aspects or peculiarities in Paul's character which exhausted the patience of collaborators otherwise loyal and of goodwill. After all, we have no ground whatever for interpreting his rupture with Barnabas in a sense unfavourable to that apostle. It is probable that another companion, Luke (Lucas), a convert of Antioch, and pagan by origin, joined Paul and Silas in their apostolic expedition.[2]

It was quite natural, but is also highly significant, that Paul, who was a native of Tarsus, began his work as an independent apostle in regions bordering on his native country, regions which could not have been altogether unknown to him, instead of at once proceeding to some important centre of the empire, Ephesus, Corinth, Alexandria, Rome. It suggests that he had no thought, at the beginning of his ministry, of the unique and universal mission to the human race usually attributed to him; certainly he can have had in his head no map of the Mediterranean world, with the stages marked in advance, province by province and city by city, as far as Rome and thence into Spain. His first attack was on the place nearest at hand and, keeping continually on the move, he would pass from one to the next as opportunity offered and the course of events made possible. His first thought accordingly was to make for Pamphilia and Pisidia, where he knew of Jewish communities which perhaps would give the Gospel a favourable hearing.

The first halt of our wandering preachers was at Derbe where they had some success, for a Derbe man, Gaius, is found soon afterwards in the company of believers that went on with Paul (Acts xx, 4); but Acts gives no detail about the mission there.3 From Derbe Paul made for Lystra where there was further success, this being the place where he recruited Timothy, most faithful of all his disciples and the one who followed him to the end (xvi, 1–3). If Acts are to be believed, Timothy was the son of a Jewish mother and of a pagan father, and was circumcised by Paul "because of the Jews which were in those quarters." This indication, implicitly contradicted by the Epistle to the Colossians,4 is probably a tendentious counterbalance to what is said in Galatians about the uncircumcised Titus (Gal. ii, 3).

From Lystra the apostolic company passed on to Iconium where it had to make a rather long stay, Paul preaching in the synagogue and recruiting both Jews and proselytes. But the majority of the Jews proved refractory and soon became hostile, even stirring up the pagans against the new preacher, with the result that a riot broke out and Paul was stoned.5 Quitting the scene he now conveyed himself to Antioch of Pisidia where he preached under the same conditions and had a like experience. The next project of the missionaries was to evangelize the coast towns of Asia Minor, but they were "forbidden by the Holy Spirit" (xvi, 6), by which we may understand that the obstructions they had met with suggested a dream or mystic vision which turned the steps of the apostolic group towards Phrygia and Galatia proper. If the Epistle to the Galatians can be trusted Paul fell sick and remained for some time in these regions.6 But he continued to preach and not without success, founding several communities recruited mainly from among the pagans.7

"After they were come to Mysia," the Gospel heralds, who now seem to have been steering a rather haphazard course, "assayed to go into Bithynia but"—circumstances not favouring the plan—"the Spirit of Jesus suffered them not; and passing by Mysia"—without any attempt to preach there—"they came to Troas." Painful experiences, of which no detail is given, here lie concealed. We can hardly fail to see that after his rupture with Barnabas Paul had plunged into Asia Minor somewhat at a venture, without formed plan and without great resources, and that he went on his way guided by opportunities, or turned back by difficulties, to which the revelations of the Spirit adapted themselves, as best they could. He had not come to Troas to preach, for it was only at a later date that he was to find there "an open door" and was able to form a group of Christians. His object was to get clear of regions where an ugly reception awaited the good news, and so he took ship at Troas without yet knowing where he would disembark. A vision, which we may suppose to have been occasioned by some useful information picked up on board about the Jewries of Macedonia, settled the matter. "A vision appeared to Paul in the night: a man of Macedonia appeared before him who appealed to him and said 'Come to Macedonia and help us.' And when he had seen the vision we at once endeavoured to enter Macedonia, persuaded that God so called us to preach the Gospel unto them."[8]

The travellers disembarked at Neapolis (Cavalla) whence they took the road to Philippi. Knowing nobody in the town they went on the following Sabbath to the place of prayer beside a watercourse and sitting down waited for the chance of encountering some Jews. That day the only people to come were women, among them one who was well-off, a seller of purple and a native of Thyatira "whose heart the Lord opened, so that she was interested in what Paul told her" (xvi, 11–14). Soon afterwards this Lydia, now baptized, takes the missionaries into her house and so puts them into a more favourable condition for launching their propaganda in the town, with the result that Paul gets together a considerable group of converts consisting mainly if not exclusively of pagans. But the success of their propaganda got them into difficulties. There came a day when Paul and Silas were violently laid hold of by people who dragged them before the magistrates of Philippi and charged them as follows: "these men are a serious nuisance to our town: the fellows are Jews and teach customs which it is unlawful for us Romans to have anything to do with." The two missionaries are then whipped and put in prison, but soon afterwards released on the intervention of some friendly people who go bail for them, on condition, however, that they clear out of the town forthwith.[9] The statements about the beginning of the Philippi mission (xvi, 11–15) are plain and precise, probably coming from the source of Acts:

but the sequel is cut about, the editor introducing at the start of it the incident of the pythoness, which, had it occurred, would at once have compelled Paul to quit Phillipi, where he must have remained long enough to form a numerous and very faithful group of believers. The story of the pythoness exorcised by Paul, whose cure is said to have caused his arrest (xvi, 16–19) if not invented entire by the editor, can only be his romantic version of something that really happened. The only offence charged against Paul was his propaganda and the charge must have been sustained by the evidence of that alone. The editor had his reasons for trying to put readers off the scent. For the significant point here to be remarked is that a popular rising was caused by Jewish propaganda which directly and openly ran counter to the religious foundation of the Roman empire. That was the objection brought against the Christian religion up to the moment of its final victory. That the objection was brought against it at the very beginning is entirely natural.

At Thessalonica, where Paul made his next halt, "there was a synagogue of the Jews," the Jewish colony there being much more important than at Philippi. For three sabbaths in succession the apostle was able to discourse "on the Scriptures explaining and proving that the Christ must needs suffer and rise from the dead, and that Jesus is the Christ." A few Jews were convinced by these arguments and "a much greater number of Greeks and among them several persons of quality" (xvii, 1–4).[10] But the mass of the Jews showed an ugly temper and Paul was compelled to continue his teaching outside the synagogue. By this outside preaching he had time to recruit a considerable band of believers; the difficulties which followed seem to have come chiefly from the Jews. Under similar conditions he was able to found a community at Berea.[11]

Leaving Silas in the latter town he now comes with Timothy to Athens.[12] Here he spends himself to no purpose. The editor of Acts has attempted to conceal his failure by the fiction of his speech to the Areopagus (xvii, 22–31). He would here give us a specimen of the teaching which Paul, according to him, was wont to address to audiences of highly educated pagans;[13] it is a philosophical apology in the style of those published by Aristides, Athenagoras and Justin in the second century—a trait which would suffice to date the editing of Acts. A verse from the poet Aratus is somewhat playfully quoted,[14] as though by way of replacing the quotations from the prophets with which the editor adorns Paul's other discourses, all the rest of the story being contrived to furnish this fine oration with a framework and stage-setting. The failure encountered at Athens might easily have been foreseen; nowhere else could audiences have been found less ready to be impressed by an apocalyptic message.[15] Before quitting the place Paul had received news from Thessalonica which decided him to send Timothy to that city,[16] giving him a rendezvous at Corinth and charging him to bring Silas along with him (1 Thess. iii, 2, 6; Acts xviii, 5). It will be noticed that Paul's auxiliaries move from place to place as freely as he does, and that the new Christian groups keep him informed of what is going on in their midst by messengers and correspondence. Without these frequent contacts the improvised communities might easily have dissolved.

To Corinth accordingly the apostle, travelling alone, now betakes himself, probably in course of the year 50. He seems to have arrived there without resources and in low spirits after the check he had received in Athens. Meeting Aquila, a Jew of Pontus already won over to faith in the Christ, together with his wife Prisca or Priscilla, he installed himself in their house, these people being tent-makers, which was his own trade. There he remained, working for his living, until the arrival of Silas and Timothy[17] who brought him money furnished by the communities in Macedonia—in particular, doubtless, by the group at Philippi and the good Lydia (2 Cor. xi, 9).[18] Thanks to this he was now at leisure to devote himself again to his preaching and took lodgings near to the synagogue in the house of a Judaizing pagan named Titius Justus.[19] Thus for a time he was able to teach in the synagogue and to make a fair number of conversions, including Crispus the chief ruler. As in other places, the majority of the Jews were not slow to declare themselves against the Gospel, so that Paul had to continue his teaching outside the synagogue and henceforth to make his converts for the most part among the well-disposed pagans. Here his harvest was outstandingly plentiful, insomuch that the Corinth community may well have been, at least in point of numbers, the most considerable of all his personal foundations. For eighteen months[20] his Corinth mission went on (xviii, 11). The Epistles show that, by his own activity and that of his auxiliaries, Christian groups were founded at Cenchrea, the Port of Corinth, and in some of the towns of Achaia (Rom. xvi, 1; 2 Cor. i, 1).

It is hard to say what elements of authentic reminiscence are contained in the story of the Jewish riot which is said to have resulted in Paul being haled before the pro-consul Gallio. As arranged by the editor of Acts the story comes in as a surcharge and outside that of the mission at Corinth. Gallio's proconsulate there must have covered the second half of the year 51, and the first of 52.[21] This date would be priceless for fixing the Pauline chronology, and could always be used provisionally, were it not, unfortunately, that the editor of Acts may have got his information about the Corinthian magistracy of Gallio from other sources than Luke's original document, and exploited the name for his own ends, just as he exploited the name of Sergius Paulus in his story about the mission to Cyprus which in all probability Paul never made (xiii, 4–12).[22] Taking the Gallio incident as it stands, all that is clear in it is the apologetic purpose of the editor. He had risked the conversion of Sergius Paulus, but to make Gallio turn Christian was beyond his editorial courage; so he contented himself with ascribing to him the attitude which in his, the editor's, view the Roman authorities ought to take in regard to the conflict which separated Christianity from Judaism, the attitude, namely, of refusing to be mixed up in a Jewish theological quarrel, of not confirming the excommunication of the Christians by the Jews and of leaving the former to go their own way under the official protection guaranteed to the latter. A doubt is permissible as to whether Gallio understood the matter quite in that sense.

2. From Corinth to Jerusalem

His work in Corinth nearly done, Paul, in company with Aquila and Priscilla, embarked for Ephesus, probably in the fall of the year 52, but immediately left his two companions in that city, being anxious to revisit the communities he had founded in Galatia.[23] Perhaps he had been warned that a great effort was in preparation to detach them from his Gospel. While he was absent on this business there arrived at Ephesus a disciple named Apollos, native of Alexandria, a learned and eloquent man well versed in the Scriptures, who got a hearing in the synagogue.[24] The editor of Acts seems much concerned to prevent Apollos from being regarded as the original founder of Ephesian Christianity which, in point of fact, he seems to have been. For the anecdote about the twelve disciples, found by Paul at Ephesus on his return,[25] who were unacquainted with the baptism of the Spirit must refer—if it has any historical reality—to converts made by Apollos, here fictitiously presented, along with Apollos himself, as Christians insufficiently taught and in need of further instruction—Apollos by Aquila and Priscilla and the twelve disciples by Paul himself. This distinction has probably no greater weight than the similar story by the same editor about the converts made by Philip in Samaria who, though baptized, had not received the Holy Spirit, of which we are invited to think the Jerusalem apostles were the depositaries.[26] To transform Apollos and the twelve disciples into disciples of John converted at Ephesus into disciples of the Christ, as most critics and some mythologues are eager to do, is a somewhat risky procedure. The facts are simply that Apollos, having set the evangelization of Ephesus well on foot, decided to go on to Corinth, and that "the brethren," among whom doubtless were chiefly Aquila and Priscilla, furnished him with a letter of recommendation to the community (xviii, 27).[27] At Corinth his success was as brilliant as at Ephesus and his reputation soon began to outshine that of Paul.

There may be significance in the fact that Apollos, who has had such good success at Ephesus in the absence of Paul, disappears before Paul's arrival there; and the same will happen at Corinth, whence Apollos will again depart before Paul comes back. We may suspect, but without committing ourselves to risky conclusions, that the two teachers thought it wiser not to meet on the field of their missionary activity, and that their friends encouraged them, or at least encouraged Apollos, in that precaution. On returning to Ephesus as soon as Paul was ready to quit that city for Corinth, Apollos appears to have been extremely reserved (1 Cor. xvi, 12). He cannot be represented as holding entirely with the Judaizers, but neither was he exactly on the line of Paul from the hellenic-Christian point of view. We should regard him as a teacher less jealous for his own doctrines and apostolic privilege than Paul was, and ready, like Paul and the others, to go wherever he could find an open door. His position may have been similar to that of Barnabas, inclining to hellenism, but in good relations with the old believers in Palestine; in Corinth we shall find his partisans associating with Peter's on lines somewhat opposed to Paul. He was probably urged to go to Corinth by friends he had made in Ephesus, perhaps even by Aquila and Priscilla, who knew the many advantages of the Corinthian field. Moreover, notwithstanding their relations with Paul, Aquila and Priscilla were of the same way of thinking as Apollos in regard to the common Christianity.

In this connexion it should be noted that Silas (Sylvanus), who was still with Paul at Corinth, having borne him company all the way from Antioch, is now no longer at his side. As a companion of Paul he makes no further appearance and tradition puts him later at the side of Peter (1 Peter v, 12). It was at Corinth that the two apostolic labourers took their separate ways, perhaps in consequence of some personal coolness. The source of Acts can hardly have failed to leave a record of their separation, which the editor would be very careful to omit. To remain for long the companion of Paul a docile temper was necessary, like that of the good Timothy. Luke was not always at his side; however deeply he may have been attached to his person he does not seem to have been as closely associated with his ministry.

Meanwhile Paul returned to Ephesus and preached in the synagogue for three months on end. But a lively opposition declaring itself and the Jews scoffing openly at the faith he was offering them, he carried his teaching elsewhere, and continued it for two years[28] in a room he had hired from a certain Tyrranus, where he taught daily, thus exchanging, so to say, the pulpit of the preacher for the platform of the public lecturer. From all of which we may infer that a wide currency attended this teaching, to us so extraordinary in its contents and yet indisputably successful to a degree which baffles our reason. The angry opposition it awakened, of which the detailed manifestations escape us,[29] was commensurate with the success. But, as happened in the case of Corinth, the Ephesus mission was fraught with consequence not only for the development of the Ephesian community, which owed its beginnings to Apollos, but for the evangelization of other towns in that region.

Having taught at Ephesus for two years under these conditions, Paul formed a project which, with his past achievements in view, should not strike us as too ambitious, that of carrying the Gospel to Rome, but not until he had gone to Jerusalem with the collection he would first take up from the groups of believers in Macedonia and Achaia, as well as from those he was now forming in Asia.[30] These collections were to some extent imitated from those regularly made among the Jews for the support of the temple worship; and that no doubt is the reason why the editor of Acts is perseveringly silent on the subject.[31]

The true motive which led Paul to go to Jerusalem before making for Rome is not clearly indicated in the Epistles and we can only guess what it was. During his stay at Ephesus Paul had received the news that divisions, not entirely due to the activities of Apollos, were growing apace at Corinth. It seems that believers, or wandering preachers coming from Palestine or Syria to Corinth, as also to Galatia, had given it out to the communities founded by Paul that their apostle was not a genuine apostle and was not recognized as such by the authorized custodians of the Gospel. It is impossible to say what authority these people had to denounce him in this manner, but at least there can be no doubt that they expressed the general uneasiness of the earliest formed communities as to the doings of an apostle whose independence was too pronounced for their liking.[32] It must have been for the purpose of allaying their alarm that Paul found it opportune to fulfil the promise he had made twelve years previously to the elders of Jerusalem (Gal. ii, 10).[33] But it seems likely that the state of affairs at Corinth determined him to keep this promise with the least possible delay and in a manner most likely to defeat the manœuvres of the enemy.

Reading the Epistle to the Galatians one might think that the extreme Judaizers were trying to compel the uncircumcised believers in Galatia to submit to the Jewish observances. But this conclusion falls to the ground on closer scrutiny of the facts. For the credit of Paul was being undermined in the same way at Corinth as in Galatia without the apostle saying a word to the Corinthians about the legal observances. The Epistle to the Galatians falsely accuses Peter and Barnabas of trying to impose Judaism on the uncircumcised converts at Antioch, and consequently exaggerates the danger of Judaization by which the Galatians were threatened, but about which Paul says nothing to frighten the Corinthians; moreover, while explaining to the Romans the economy of salvation by the sole means of faith in the Christ, his arguments are not in the form of a defence against high authorities who would deny the principle of that faith, but against those who have accused him of failing in respect for the Law of Moses and for the people of the Promise. (Cf. Romans ix–xi.)

His experience at Corinth could not fail to induce in him some degree of moderation. Before quitting Ephesus he had sent out two of his auxiliaries, Timothy and Erastus, to hasten the collections in Macedonia and Achaia.[34] But Timothy had promptly returned to Asia with bad news: the conflict in Corinth between Paul's party and his enemies was going from bad to worse. As he had written to the Corinthians, before sending them Timothy, and had told them that he would come to Corinth himself after visiting Macedonia, he now judged it expedient to go there immediately. He did so, and came off badly.[35] His presence in Corinth, far from causing appeasement, gave rise to a grievous dispute in which he seems to have been humiliated before an unscrupulous opponent (2 Cor. ii, 5–11).[36] Returned to Asia he wrote, in a kind of despair,[37] a severe letter which he described later on as having afflicted the Corinthians for the health of their souls.[38] What proved more useful than the letter was the mediation of Titus who happened to be at Corinth at the very moment when his help was most needed to pacify the Corinthians.[39] There are grounds for thinking that this man, a member of the Antioch community who had formerly taken part in the Jerusalem meeting (Gal. ii, 1), had come to Corinth with the original intention of pacifying Paul himself, and that, fortified by his first success, he then consented to intervene in making peace between the Corinthians and Paul who was now disposed to be more agreeable to the old missionaries and to the Jerusalem community.

Paul meanwhile was at Troas where he founded a new Christian group while he waited for Titus who was returning by way of Macedonia. Becoming impatient he went back to Macedonia himself and met Titus who had made peace with the Corinthians. The immediate result was a new letter, full of joy and consolation, and incompletely reproduced in 2 Cor. i–ii, 13; vii, 6–16. Paul pardons the wrong done him (2 Cor. ii, 5–11). Titus wishes to go a second time to Corinth to complete the collection (2 Cor. viii). The good Titus then disappears from Paul's company, having no doubt more important business on hand elsewhere. We should think of him as an effective and conscientious worker for the peace of Christianity in the time of its birth when it was threatened with schism by the doings of Paul and by his pretensions. Let us remember that Titus did not follow Paul when he went his own way after the conflict at Antioch; we must suppose him to have been on good terms with Peter, Barnabas and the Antioch headquarters.

Returning to Corinth for the last time[40] at the end of the year 55 or 56,[41] Paul spent three months in the city. Then it was that he wrote the Epistle to the Romans,[42] that is to say the authentic parts of it, the document on which the canonical Epistle is based. The letter was addressed to a community mainly recruited from uncircumcised pagans with no inclination to Judaism, not at least to the point of themselves accepting circumcision and the Jewish observances. Thus we read (i, 13–15): "I would not have you ignorant, brethren, that often I purposed to come unto you —and hitherto I have been prevented—that I might have some fruit among you, as among the other Gentiles. I owe a duty to Greeks and to barbarians, to the wise and to the ignorant. So, to the utmost of my power, I am ready to preach the Gospel to you also." On looking closely into the matter we perceive that Paul, in developing his idea that the Gentiles must share the faith of Abraham in order to share the promise made to that patriarch, was less concerned in confuting the advocates of circumcision than in establishing the authority of his own mission. And he explains why the business of the collection obliges him to go to Jerusalem before coming to Rome: "But now I go to Jerusalem to do a service to the saints. For it has pleased them of Macedonia and Achaia to make a charitable offering to the poor among the saints at Jerusalem" (xv, 25–26).

From this we gather that Paul regarded his friendly action towards the mother-community in Jerusalem as likely to raise his credit when he arrived in Rome and to ensure the support of the Roman believers for his intended mission to Spain. For to Spain he certainly meant to go. But why to Spain? Because, in his view of the world, Spain represented its uttermost limit, and that the Gospel would have been preached everywhere when he had completed the "circle" of the Mediterranean (xv, 19, 22–23)—a somewhat imaginary framework for his ever overflowing activity. Strange as these particulars are to our minds, account of them must be taken by those who would understand the man and his work.

The projects of Paul were not realized according to plan. In the spring of the year 56 (or 57) he embarked at Cenchrea with Macedonia as his first destination. The Jewish plot mentioned in Acts (xx, 3) must be an arbitrary explanation of this detour, the true reason being that the bearers of the collection from the Macedonian communities had not arrived in Corinth, as soon as Paul desired, to set out with him on his pilgrimage to Jerusalem; he would go himself, then, and gather them together. We have already seen how the editor of Acts is deliberately silent about this collection as likely to upset his apologetic aim by showing, as it would, that from the very first Christianity tended to organize itself outside Judaism. It was not Paul's intention to be himself alone the bearer of the money collected among his Gentile converts for the saints at Jerusalem, partly because he would not have it suspected that he was actuated only by his personal interest, but also because he was eager to bring the representatives of the communities he had founded in person before the elders at Jerusalem. The list of Paul's travelling companions (xx, 4) is made up, for the most part, of the gift-bearers: Sopater of Berea, Aristarchus and Secundus of Thessalonica certainly carried the subscriptions raised in their respective communities. It is surprising that no mention is made of a representative from Philippi; but it may well be that the list is not complete. The two Asiatics, Tychicus and Trophimus, would take the collection from Ephesus; they were not due to come to Corinth and Paul would pick them up at Miletus. Timothy and perhaps Gaius[43] figure as Paul's assistant missionaries, not as representatives of the Galatian communities whose collections were not to be passed through Corinth, but sent directly to Jerusalem—as mentioned incidentally in 1 Cor. xvi, 1. None the less the apostle and his associates constituted a small embassy to Jerusalem from the converted Gentile world.

As a pilgrim under a vow, to be accomplished in Jerusalem at the feast of Pentecost,[44] Paul, on departing, shaved his head. This vow has perplexed certain critics who regard Paul as no more capable of such a thing than a good Protestant would be of taking a vow to Our Lady. And it is true enough that to find the author of the Law-sin-death theory acting like a fervent *naẓir* is not what we expect. But Paul did not necessarily conform to all the theories his writings impute to him. It is certain that the information comes from the source of Acts, for the editor, either not understanding it, or thinking he might cut it into two, has made it unintelligible. While the real Paul did not impose the Law on his Gentile converts he seems himself to have meticulously observed it, at least in regard to cult practice.

The delegates from Corinth went with him, bearing the contribution from Achaia. But Paul lingered by himself among the groups in Macedonia, gathering the delegates from those regions, and, having stayed at Philippi for the week of Unleavened Bread, only after reaching Troas rejoined a part of the company which had embarked with him at Corinth;[45] there was now a Christian group at Troas to receive the travellers.[46] Thence he went on to Assos by land, his companions going by sea; after which they all kept to the sea route, sailing by short stages along the coast. "Paul," we read, "had decided to pass Ephesus by, so as to avoid losing time in Asia; for he hasted in the hope of reaching Jerusalem in time for the Day of Pentecost" (Acts xx, 16). This motive does not, by itself, explain why Ephesus was avoided, seeing that the company was making a stop at Miletus. The community at Ephesus might have put pressure on Paul to remain among them at a time when a stay there had become dangerous for him. The rendezvous for the delegates from Asia was therefore fixed at Miletus.[47] At

Patara a ship was found on the point of sailing for Phoenicia; this carried them to Tyre,[48] thence to Ptolemais, whence Paul proceeded on foot to Caesarea.

Here the whole apostolic company was entertained by Philip. This former companion of Stephen and one of the Seven had established himself at Caesarea immediately after the dispersion of Stephen's group and had gathered round him a small band of believers. A special point is made of informing us that he had four virgin daughters endowed with the gift of prophecy (xxi, 19). The purpose of the original author of Acts in mentioning them was certainly to make them utter a prophecy analogous to that which the later editor thought would be more decently placed in the mouth of a male prophet. All that concerns Agabus is fiction of the editor who has already made use of the same person for another fiction (xi, 27–28). The prophecy was that Paul would fall into enemy hands at Jerusalem.[49] Everybody, his companions no less than the local believers, now implored him to go no further. But Paul replied that he would not renounce his project, even though it meant that he would perish in the Holy City: whereupon they all abandoned themselves to the will of God. Perhaps the scene has been to some extent arranged by the original author, Luke. But the attitude ascribed to Paul is intelligible. At all costs the task to which he had committed himself in preparing his journey to Jerusalem must be carried out to the end. A few of the Caesarea believers added themselves to Paul's company and went on with him to Jerusalem where they had procured the hospitality of Mnason, an "old disciple." Evidently this Mnason, who came from Cyprus, was, like Philip, a "hellenist" and well disposed to Paul.[50] It remained to make contact with the Hebrew believers, on whose account the expedition has been undertaken.

3. From Jerusalem to Rome

Next day Paul and his retinue were received by James and the collection from the communities was presented to the Jerusalem elders.—Omitting all mention of the collection, which was the principal object of the expedition, the editor of Acts confines himself to saying that Paul, after saluting the company, proceeded at once "to set forth in detail all that God had done among the Gentiles by his ministry" (xxi, 15–16).—The offering was accepted; Paul's account of his mission was then heard and due satisfaction expressed. But the elders did not disguise from Paul the danger he was running from the Jews who regarded him as no better than the preacher of an apostasy. They then proceeded to advise him, by way of making himself less conspicuous, to join up with four *nazirs* of their community, who were on the look out for some charitable person to pay their expenses,[51] and to fulfil his vow as one of their company. Such at least seems to be the meaning of the elders' discourse as it was given by Luke in the original document. But the editor of canonical Acts would have it understood[52] that the "believing" Jews who were seeking Paul were Jewish-Christian believers, and that it was to them, Jewish Christians, that Paul must prove, by becoming a *nazir*, that he was not an apostate to the Law, as he was accused of being. All this, in the given circumstances, is wholly unintelligible and irrelevant. These Jewish Christians were not to be counted by "thousands," as the edited text declares, but were chiefly to be found in the very audience to which Paul had just recounted his triumphs. The members of that audience knew perfectly well why Paul was accused of being an apostate to the Law, but they also knew that in strictness the charge was unfounded, since Paul dispensed with the Law only in the case of Gentile converts. Apart from that, the advice to take on the character of a *nazir*, as the elders are made by the editor to recommend, would, if adopted, prove nothing by itself; in point of fact Paul's adoption of it was not proclaimed, and his recognition came about by chance. Now, since the normal observance of the vow was for thirty days,[53] the nature of the case makes it morally certain, and our texts confirm the certitude, that Paul took his vow as a *nazir* on leaving Corinth and timed it to be completed in Jerusalem; he was still under the vow on his arrival and could not do otherwise than join up with persons in the same condition,[54] not for the purpose of showing himself more openly but for the opposite purpose of being less conspicuous, as appears plainly in the course of the narrative. Perhaps the editor was unwilling to represent Paul as one who would hide himself; but his chief concern was to maintain his thesis—that Paul and the Christians were the best Jews in the

world, Christianity when rightly understood being the true
Judaism.[55]

Paul accepts the elders' advice, repairs to the temple with the
four *nazirs* of the Jerusalem community and the day is fixed for
the discharge of the vow (xxi, 26). But on that day, the seventh or
eighth after Paul's arrival, some Jews from Asia, who have met
him on the street with Trophimus of Ephesus, catching sight of
him in the holy place, cry out on the profanation, believing or
pretending that he has introduced an uncircumcised person into
the sacred precincts. The crowd rushes in; Paul is dragged out of
the temple and the priests close the gates. Paul would have been
killed had not the tribune of the cohort in barracks at the Tower
of Antonia received timely notice that a mob was gathering and
violence afoot; he hurries to the spot with his soldiers, gets
possession of Paul, puts him in chains and asks the cause of the
trouble. Getting no clear answer in the tumult he carries Paul off
to the fortress and orders him to be put to the question. Whereupon Paul declares himself a Roman citizen and his chains are at
once taken off. Meanwhile the Jewish authorities, informed of
what has happened, at once put in a claim to the prisoner demanding that, as guilty of an offence against religion, he must be
given up to them.[56] Fortified by a vision,[57] and perceiving that
his sole chance of safety lies in his status as a Roman citizen,
Paul insists on his right to be judged by Roman Law. Without further delay the tribune then despatches him to Caesarea
and tells his accusers to state their case before the procurator
Felix.[58]

This simple and well co-ordinated story has been dismembered
by the editorial fictions of canonical Acts. In the story of Paul's
arrest by the Roman soldiery, and before they carry him to the
Tower of Antonia, a gross interpolation, easily recognizable as
such,[59] has been introduced. It represents him, when half beaten to
death by the blows he had received, as capable of delivering on the
spot a long speech for the benefit of the tribune and the mob, in
which he expounds his merits as a faithful Jew and tells the whole
story of his conversion and calling to the Gentiles (xxi, 37–xxii, 22)
—a fine opportunity to represent the Jews, on hearing the latter
proposition, as lifting up their voices in protest against the
conversion of the pagans (xxii, 22)! From what follows our

interpolator would lead us to infer that Paul disclosed his status as a Roman citizen[60] only in order to escape the torture; in fact the legal conditions of the affair are thrown into confusion by any device that occurs to him, and always for the purpose of closing our eyes to the fact that Paul's manœuvres were consciously aimed from the first at escaping from the jurisdiction of the Sanhedrim, which was bringing the charge against him. He forgets to say that the Sanhedrim claimed to judge Paul, and that Paul rejected its right to judge him, not for having profaned the Temple, but as a cause of trouble in the synagogues outside Palestine. In contrast to this the editor has imagined a sitting of the Sanhedrim convoked by the tribune to get information about Paul, which ends in nothing because the Pharisees and Sadducees fall to quarrelling about the resurrection;[61] in all of which he is aiming to show that orthodox Judaism and Christianity agree in principle about the survival of the dead. But that was not the question at issue. Finally we are given to understand that Paul was transferred to Caesarea merely to put him out of range of Jewish plots on his life. At this point the editor gives the rein to his imagination and creates for Paul an unexpected nephew whose revelations induce the Tribune to despatch Paul to Caesarea.[62] The editor even goes the length of inventing an official report from the tribune Lysias to the procurator Felix containing cautious testimony to Paul's innocence.[63] To avow the simple reality of the facts would not have served the editorial purpose. He would say nothing about the Sanhedrim claiming the right to judge Paul, because, by doing so, he would have been led to admitting that Paul had denied the right of a Jewish tribunal to judge him, and that this was the reason why the tribune had referred the case to the procurator and sent Paul to Caesarea, admissions he was not willing to make. The plain fact is that Paul escaped from the clutches of the Jewish authorities only by establishing his Roman citizenship; but, for all that, he was not yet saved.

Arrived before the procurator Felix, Paul undergoes a simple interrogation as to his identity and is then remanded under guard to Herod's pretorium pending the presentation of the Sanhedrim's petition.[64] When this has been done, Felix, who was well informed about the Christian sect, adjourns the final solution of the affair and keeps Paul in custody, leaving him free to see his friends and receive their ministrations.[65]

As a political measure the adjournment had the double advantage of keeping the accused agitator quiet for the time being and of not handing over to the Sanhedrim a Roman citizen whom the procurator had no right to abandon to its jurisdiction. It is conceivable, moreover, that the question of the legitimacy of the Christian propaganda from the Jewish point of view was not clear to the first Roman magistrate called to adjudicate in the matter, even though he understood his duty no more rigorously than Felix is said to have understood his. And there was yet another question of equal if not greater import, of which Paul himself does not seem to have thought, but demanding urgent consideration. Was not this propaganda, which the Jews declared to be an infraction of the traditional law of their religion, equally condemned by the laws and fundamental principles of the Roman Empire?

It is a common practice with the editor of Acts to amplify his story by repeating an incident twice over. When, therefore, we find the judicial action taken by the Sanhedrim before Felix repeated before Festus who succeeded him as procurator, we might suspect, in view of the editor's habits that we have here another instance of his duplications. But, in the present case, the duplication seems to be only partial, the change of procurator[66] coming from the source document and the editor merely antedating to the time of Felix the fuller debate under Festus. The question at issue, which Felix had decided to adjourn, was a question of jurisdiction; this, when referred to him, Festus considered his duty required him to decide in favour of the Sanhedrim. Paul's appeal to the tribunal of the Emperor was determined by that decision, with the result that the root question, that of Paul's culpability, though touched upon during the debate on competence, was not directly examined and adjudicated till the accused arrived in Rome. Thus we may conclude that the adjournment by Felix, the change of procurator at the end of two years and the measures taken for the cusody of the prisoner in the interval come from the source. But the *mise-en-scène* of the judicial enquiry before Felix, the discourse of the accuser's advocate and Paul's defence are all in the editor's manner, though a few of the details he may very well have picked out from the source document.

Felix became procurator of Judea in the year 52. The exact date of his recall in uncertain, but not earlier than 55 and, probably, not later than 58. Festus remained procurator till his death in 61. It is not surprising that Felix, who had been some years in office, was tolerably well informed about the Christian movement, at least as the Jews understood it,[67] in contrast to Festus who found the case of Paul brought before him in court at the very beginning of his magistracy. But this explanation of the adjournment does not, in the source document, imply the personal interest in the case which our canonical text attributes to Felix. Luke's object was rather to indicate the political motive of the delay, which lay in the difficulty of the case and the danger of a hasty solution. The private interviews with Paul of Felix and his wife Drusilla, daughter of Agrippa I, are editorial fiction, doubling the grand scene which the editor will construct later on, in which great persons, Agrippa II and his Queen Berenice, brother and sister of Drusilla, make their appearance on the stage. From what we know of the private characters of Felix and Drusilla, their qualifications as Paul's catechumens were of mediocre promise.[68]

Paul had been kept prisoner at Caesarea for two years (probably 56–58) when Felix was replaced by Porcius Festus. Hardly was Festus installed when the Sanhedrim, judging the occasion opportune for taking up the case again, renewed its plea in his court. Festus, no doubt, was unwilling to begin his tenure of office by disobliging the subjects of his administration; he yielded to the demand and soon afterwards received the delegates of Jewish authority in his official residence at Caesarea. Having heard a statement of the case, he declared himself incompetent to deal with it, on the ground that the matter in dispute was distinctly of a religious nature and of interest only to Jews; he would therefore remit the case to the judgment of the Sanhedrim. But Paul, as a Roman citizen, was not without means of escape from a decision which would deliver him to judges from whom he knew what to expect. Using his right of appeal, he invoked the jurisdiction of the emperor and demanded trial by Caesar. The appeal, legally formulated, was granted. Festus, after conferring with his

Council, gave his verdict: "thou hast appealed to Caesar; to Caesar thou shalt go" (xxv, 1–12).

It may be that the Sanhedrim had calculated that Paul would not dare formally to repudiate its jurisdiction, since, in so doing, he would place himself outside Judaism. Paul, on his side, having staked his hopes on Roman justice, had probably flattered himself that the procurator would pronounce the petition of the Sanhedrim unfounded, and order his discharge; he was a Roman citizen and his conduct was in keeping with Roman law. But the previous attitude of Felix must have caused him to reflect, and perhaps suggested to him the idea of having recourse, if the need should arise, to the higher jurisdiction that every citizen could claim. It is even possible that Festus, on deciding to send the case back to the Sanhedrim, as one with which he was incompetent to deal, himself reminded the prisoner of his right of appeal to Caesar. In any case, Paul, when the decisive moment came, seems to have had no hesitation. The choice before him being only between the sentence of death which the Sanhedrim had in store for him and the chance of a discharge offered by appealing to Caesar, he chose the Emperor's tribunal. Such was the door, so to speak, to which the Christian, escaping from Judaism, ran for safety. Did Paul indulge in illusions as to what the attitude of the imperial tribunal would be? We cannot say. Did he think that Caesar in Rome would be less accessible to Jewish influence and less inclined to consider the interests of Judaism than his procurator in Palestine? Did he even hope that Caesar, by giving him his liberty, would recognize the legality, or rather the permissibility of the Christian propaganda? Perhaps. But the contrary was to happen, insomuch that one might almost accuse the apostle of some imprudence in bringing the cause of Christianity in his own person before Caesar. But it may well be that it was but the faintest glimmer of hope that decided him to do what he did. His appeal would take him to Rome, and, if Caesar were pleased to declare him innocent, the years of his captivity would not have been wasted time.

The essential features of the proceedings are preserved in canonical Acts. But there are a few retouches and interested additions. The preliminary petition of the Sanhedrim is falsely presented as a request for a favour, and the editor has added, on his own responsibility, a plot of the Jews to kill Paul before the judgment asked for had been delivered (xxv, 3). The judicial inquiry is sketched from the source, but probably shortened, the arguments having been partly anticipated, as we have seen, in xxiv, 1–21. The decision of Festus to refer the case to the Sanhedrim which resulted in Paul appealing to Caesar is turned into a benevolent proposition, designed to oblige the Jews by the procurator, who asks Paul if he is "willing" to be judged by him at Jerusalem[69]—a false perspective of the case in which it is implied that the procurator would hold the proceedings in the presence of the Sanhedrim, whose sentence of death would be ratified by him before execution. Paul's appeal to Caesar is intelligible only on the assumption that Festus recognized the competence of the Sanhedrim to deal with the main issue; this it was that left Paul with no alternative but an appeal to Caesar. The terms of the appeal and the final sentence of Festus cannot be otherwise explained. But the editor has left his mark in what he makes Paul say about Festus being persuaded of his innocence and wanting to make his person a "present" to the Jews.[70]

The meeting of Festus with Agrippa II and the pomp and ceremony of the conference arranged for the satisfaction of this Jewish kinglet are mere editorial padding intended to provide a setting for a new speech by Paul in his own defence and a new testimony to his innocence in which the Herodian prince backs up the Roman procurator. Superficially at least this concoction is better balanced than many of the others and shows that the editor spared no pains in its composition; Paul's speech for example being constructed in the amphigoric style deemed proper in addressing royal personages. None the less the fiction taken as a whole is founded on a ludicrous improbability, the supposition, namely, that Festus had nothing to put into the report which he was bound to send to Rome along with the prisoner and hoped to get matter for the report after Paul's examination before Agrippa (xxv, 25–27).[71] It is clear that the procurator, on deciding to send Paul back to the Sanhedrim, judged that there was a real case for the Jewish tribunal and that, on the appeal intervening, it was no longer for him to furnish an account of the matter at issue, this being sufficiently furnished by the complaint of the Sanhedrim annexed to his report. But, in making Agrippa declare (xxvi, 31) that Paul would have been set at liberty if he had not appealed to Caesar,[72] the editor gives us a clear hint that Caesar in the upshot did not set him at liberty, and that he was the victim of judicial error, if not of gross injustice.

4. IMPRISONMENT AND DEATH

A few days after the session of the court into which Paul had flung his appeal to Caesar, he was remitted with other prisoners to a centurion named Julius, of the cohort Augusta, for conduct into Italy. They embarked at Caesarea in a ship of Adramyttium which made sail for the coast of Asia; Luke was with Paul;[73] Aristarchus of Thessalonica being also of the company. The Adramyttium ship not being a government vessel the companions of Paul[74] would be entered as passengers, unless they had been granted permission to go with him as his servants. Next day the ship made Sidon where Julius allowed Paul to visit the brethren in the town. Thence, after a trying voyage, they arrived at Myra in Lycia where the centurion transhipped his charges to an Alexandrian vessel about to sail for Italy. But navigation became more and more difficult, and the ship, in manœuvring to winter in Crete, at the port of Phoenix, was caught by a tempest and buffeted about the Mediterranean for fourteen days, till finally it struck a rock near the island of Malta, whence the shipwrecked company saved themselves by swimming, or on rafts hastily put together.[75]

The inhabitants of the island treated them with great humanity, and the head man of the island, Publius by name, sheltered them for three days. In Malta they were forced to remain for three months, until the return of weather favourable for navigation. The shipwreck took place towards the end of November and the departure from Malta the following March. The story of Paul bitten by a viper and receiving no hurt, and the cures operated by him on the sick of the island are within the range of possibility, but not beyond the editor's power of invention.[76]

Julius and his prisoners left Malta in another ship of Alexandria bearing the sign of the Dioscuri; three days were spent at Syracuse, one at Rhegium; after another day's sailing, anchor was dropped at Puteoli and the perilous voyage was ended. Soon they were in Rome.

The procession of Christians from Rome coming out to meet the prisoner at Appii Forum is obviously an insertion by the editor; the Forum was a day's journey from Rome in the Appian Way, and to give the captive apostle a triumphal reception at that place would have been neither easy nor well timed. So far as our information goes, the believers in Rome do not seem to have rallied round Paul during his captivity, which explains why the editor shows them so eager to meet him. The stay among the brethren at Puteoli (xxviii, 14) which ends the story of the journey, prepares the way for a display of devotion by the Christians of Rome.

The reality was more sombre. Arrived in Rome the prisoner was remitted by the centurion to the prefect of the pretorium. This person, Burrus, who held the post till the year 62, it must have been who authorized Paul, as Acts relate,[77] to take a lodging in the city, where he was to remain, with a soldier charged to guard him, until the arrival of delegates from the Sanhedrim to lay the charge against him. These conditions, we are told, continued for two years, Paul enjoying a relative liberty and unhindered in preaching his Gospel to those who came to visit him.

It is of set purpose that the editor of Acts allows no word to pass of what followed. Had the trial of Paul ended in acquittal, most assuredly he would have put it on record. The doubled scene of interviews between Paul and the Jews (xxviii, 17–28), enhanced by the final gloss[78] on the liberty given to Paul for private preaching, fictitious if anything is, constitutes the conclusion of the Book of Acts as our editor would have it. In that conclusion he gives a symbolic summary of the apologetic thesis which dominates his editing of the book: Christianity is the true Judaism, now represented by the Gentiles, because it has been rejected by the blinded Jews, and is entitled to that liberty of preaching which was not refused even to Paul in his captivity. An ideal and a theory!

One fails to see by what means or by what authority Paul, just arrived as a prisoner in Rome, was able to gather around him the leading persons of the Jewish community; and the motive of their eagerness to satisfy him is equally obscure. The speech attributed to Paul (xxviii, 17–20) is intended to show that his appeal to Caesar must not be construed as a repudiation of Judaism. The assertion which concludes it, "for the hope of Israel I am bound with this chain," in which the apostle of the Gentiles poses as the authentic representative of the Jewish faith, is the very thesis of the editor, but a thesis which Paul himself would have had some difficulty in upholding as an account of the true meaning of his apostleship. The conclusion of the second interview (xxviii, 23–28)[79] gets lost in allegorical symbolism. The editor, employing the same methods as for the fictitious session of the Sanhedrim before Lysias, represents the Jews as divided on the value of the Christian thesis, without the better disposed adhering to it more closely than the most determined of its adversaries: whereupon Paul, for the edification of posterity, hurls a text of Isaiah[80] at the wrangling group, the classical text employed in the New Testament for this purpose, in which the Eternal passes judgment on his hardened people. Israel having defaulted, the turn of the Gentiles has now come! The artifice of these stage-effects is apparent from the way in which Paul is given the air of announcing, for the first time, the rejection of the Jews for their hardness of heart; but it was important to repeat once more, as the last word, how the conversion of the pagans had directly resulted from Jewish incredulity (xxviii, 28). Thus the reader could not possibly mistake the moral of everything the canonical Book of Acts has told him. In default of believing Jews the bearers of the Gospel must needs carry it to pagans: *but the believing pagans, in virtue of their religious profession, have won the right to be counted the heirs of the promise and the only real Jews.*

The interests of history would be better served by the smallest authentic information about the issue of Paul's trial. It is certain that some time elapsed before a decision was reached, and probable that the verdict when it came was a sentence of death for the apostle and that his execution followed. To know the grounds on which the judgment was based, which we can only guess, would be knowledge of immense value to the historian. As to the delay of the trial, we may suppose that the Jewish authorities were in no hurry to get on with the prosecution and imperial justice no more hurried in terminating an affair of which, at first, it did not grasp the significance, taking it merely for a quarrel among the Jews. But this only makes us the more curious to know why, at some given moment, the case was reopened and settled. This new and final phase occurred, no doubt, at the end of the two years mentioned in Acts. If that brings us to the year 64, it follows that the occasion for suddenly taking up the trial of Paul would be that which set on foot the persecution of the Christians in Rome after the burning of the city.

But this plausible view does not seem the most probable. The somewhat abrupt conclusion of Acts has a didactic purpose: the book ends where it ought to end to serve the intentions of the editor who has foreshadowed a tragic close to the trial, but is unwilling to disclose the precise nature of the end because, by so doing, he would ruin his apologetics, while his object would be better attained by insinuating that Paul was innocent of the charge on which he was condemned, whatever that charge might be. It has been maintained by some critics, whose procedure would certainly be somewhat naïve were it not for the interested motives that often prompt it, that Paul was freed from the first accusation before the imperial tribunal, that he resumed his apostolic labours for some time afterwards, even went to Spain as he intended,[81] or, if not, returned to the East—although Acts gives us clearly to understand that he never returned—and finally came back to Rome and was put to death with Peter in 64. All of which is legend and conjecture. The two apostles were not destined to die together, but a later tradition brought them together in death, after they were dead, by way of honouring them as founders of a church which neither of them had founded, but whose prestige was enhanced by the legend of such founders. It is more probable that Paul died first, say in the year 62, and that Peter, if he died in Rome, according to an obscure tradition, not contradicted by any ancient evidence, was swept away in what is called the Neronic persecution.

The so-called Epistles of the Captivity, if written from Rome, as they probably were, contain little precise information about the two years which were beyond a doubt the last of Paul's life. Almost nothing is to be derived from the Epistles to the Colossians and to Philemon, except that Paul during the first part of his detention in Rome was full of confidence in the future: he tells Philemon to prepare a lodging for him because he is hoping soon to return to his friends. Timothy is with him acting as his scribe; Philippians (i, 1) assign him the same position. Aristarchus and Luke ("the dear physician") are there also. Tychicus who had probably been with him since his journey to Jerusalem with the collection, will carry his letter to the Colossians and visit them on his behalf. Mark, who figures in tradition as the interpreter of Peter, here turns up in the retinue of Paul: a preaching tour may soon bring him to Colossi and the brethren there are bidden to give warm welcome to this "cousin of Barnabas." The information is scanty and perhaps fragile.

In Philippians the outlook to the future is more sombre. While, on the one hand, he can say that his case has attracted much attention "throughout the pretorium"—that is, the imperial tribunal—and outside it, and that the Gospel has had some profit thereby; while, at the end of the Epistle, he seems proud to send to the faithful at Philippi salutations from "the brethren who are of Caesar's household"; while he affirms that his imprisonment "has given many of the brethren confidence in Christ," encouraging them by his presence, though a prisoner, to speak the Word without fear—yet, after all this, he has to add that other propagandists are equally zealous to stir up ill will and to increase his afflictions. Resignation touched with melancholy. Here we find him still hoping for his liberty but facing the possibility of his death. In praising Timothy, whom he will send to Philippi as soon as he can, he writes as one who feels himself all alone (ii, 19–23). Of the Roman community he says nothing. If his trial ends well he will himself come to Philippi. So he thinks no more of going to Spain; nor will he stay in this Rome, so long the object of his dreams; to the East he will return though, if we may trust the Epistle to the Romans,[82] there was no place left there to which he could carry his message (Rom. xv, 19, 23–24).

That the presence of Paul in Rome gave rise to propagandist effort in the two directions he indicates, and that the effort was crowned with success, should cause no astonishment: it explains why the number of victims in the Neronic persecution was so large. Whether Peter was among those whom he discreetly accuses of adding to his afflictions we can only conjecture. The Christian world was then a small one, but the whole of it had an interest in Paul's case. Nothing is more natural than that agents of the Gospel, considerable in number and weighty in influence, should be found active in promoting it at the time, and in the place where the least clairvoyant could see that its fortunes would be determined. That these gospellers were not all eager to come into close relations with Paul is also, given the quarrels of the past and the distress of the present, what we might expect. Needless to say the groups of believers recruited under the two types of apostleship did not constitute a single, homogeneous and centralized community. They were distinct fraternities, carrying the same label and sharing approximately the same hope. We cannot say whether the persecution, which made no distinction between the two, had the effect of uniting what remained of them or whether unity came little by little, until completely achieved at the end of the first century or the beginning of the second.

Had Paul's case been examined in Palestine its Jewish interest would have been apparent and, had the Sanhedrim been judge, what was at stake quickly understood. Paul would have been condemned as an adversary of the Law, as a debaucher of faithful Jews, as a maker of false proselytes, as the founder of a pretended Jewish sect whose root principle, the abrogation of Law, at least in all that concerned the admission of the uncircumcised and the insignificance of Law for salvation, was the very negation of Judaism. It was in these terms that the charge was brought to Rome. That it remained in this form to the end is not certain, nor even probable. The condemnation may have been obtained by a Jewish intrigue which brought into play some powerful influence at the imperial court. But it is also possible, in view of the probable date of the verdict, that the case was examined under all the rules of procedure and that the attention of the judge had been called to the true character of Christianity. In that case the question to be decided by the court would be the legality of the Christian propaganda, as the Epistle to the Philippians seems to say (i, 16), a question brought into the law courts for the first time in the trial of Paul; and it would be upon that propaganda, represented in the person of its great apostle, that sentence of death was pronounced by a Roman judge. Continuing the hypothesis, the court would understand, or at least glimpse the fact, that the new sect was not to be confounded with Judaism, since it claimed to have its place outside Jewish nationality and tradition, and that it embodied only the intolerance of the Jews, now converted into universal propaganda against the established cults and so against the Roman empire which recognized them all as more or less its own. Thus the Roman government, here acting with full knowledge of what it was about, would have declared the Christian propaganda illegal in the highest degree, and Paul by appealing to Caesar in Rome, would have brought about the official denunciation of the Christian religion in that city.

But the main interest of his career is to be sought elsewhere. Thanks to the meagre information preserved for us in the Book of Acts and completed by authentic elements in the Epistles, we are able to form some idea of the way Christianity spread itself between the years 30 and 60, from the East to the West; we see it rejected at its birth by Judaism, and yet making headway everywhere by the help of Judaism, in spite of Judaism and at the expense of Judaism. We may think of it as a train of powder winding into every part of the Roman empire where Judaism had found a footing. Most assuredly the career of Paul is a remarkable sample of this astonishing propaganda. But no more than a sample, and very far from epitomizing or representing the whole movement. Official Judaism, which supported the Sadducees side by side with the Pharisees, and tolerated the Essenes, repudiated Christianity, with violence and from the very first, as treason, as apostasy. It did so because the Christians in claiming Jesus as the Lord Christ and making him an object of worship, with salvation depending on faith in Jesus alone, insulted the Law and destroyed it. Of this new religion Paul was one of the initiators but by no means the only one, nor the first. The Christian propaganda had other agents, some known to us and many more unknown, who laboured in the pagan world under the same conditions as Paul, undeterred by the minor differences among them, all of them more than suspect in the eyes of Judaism, all destined to speedy condemnation by the imperial authority of Rome.

Chapter VI

PERSECUTION BEGINS

THE personal activities of Jesus brought him into collision with constituted Judaism as organized in Palestine under the Roman government. A like collision awaited the propaganda of Stephen in Jerusalem and the later propaganda of Peter and the two sons of Zebedee at the time of Agrippa I in the year 44. Paul in his turn had almost everywhere to undergo hostility from the rulers of the synagogues and, in many towns, an account to settle with the civil magistrates, until finally, caught between the Jewish Sanhedrim and the Roman procurator, he made his appeal to Caesar, an action on his part which brought the question of Christianity for the first time under the jurisdiction of the imperial law court. We have seen in what sense the first decision in the matter was given by that tribunal. That decision was the opening stage of a conflict, hardly foreseen at the time, which was to continue for two centuries and a half and to end in the triumph of the Christian religion. But the jurisprudence applied by the imperial tribunals to the Christian affair was not created by the trial of Paul; the fact to be noted here is that the era of what Christians are wont to style "the persecutions" properly began in the year 64. Our next task will be to define more precisely the position of Christianity under Roman law or, more strictly, under the empire as a political institution, and to ascertain the reasons which caused the empire to "persecute" the Christians. And since the empire not only "persecuted" Christianity, but attempted its suppression and extermination, it behoves us to find out why it did not succeed in either attempt.

1. WHY WERE THE CHRISTIANS PERSECUTED?

A superficial reading of the passage from Tacitus quoted on a former page (*Annals*, xv, 44) might lead us to believe that the persecution under Nero had its origin in a personal caprice of the emperor. But Tacitus is at pains to inform us that the crime alleged against the persons arrested, so far as the mass of them was concerned, was far less that of setting Rome on fire than that of "hating the human race"—an accusation hardly in legal style and vague enough to the modern mind, but charged with precise meaning to the Roman historian and involving the highest political interests of the empire. For Tacitus, "the human race" meant the population of the Mediterranean world then in subjection to Rome.

It was a world organized by the conquering power of Rome; in her drive for domination a single city, the City, had taken possession of it piece by piece. Both City and world now owed obedience to the emperor in whom the power of the City over the world was incarnate. In the sphere of religion, the City not only had gods of its own who had shared with it in the conquest of the world and to whom it paid honour, but itself was also a divine personification and, mystically speaking, a divine person- ality. Here, then, were two divinities. In one sense the Genius of Rome was the supreme divinity of the empire; beside that divinity was the emperor, the Genius of the living emperor, his imperial personality; he, in practice, was the high god, holding the world in balance. The ancient empires of the East, to which Rome had succeeded, were founded on a like conception. All the gods of the conquered peoples, like the many other gods of Rome itself, continued to function under the shadow of the two protecting deities aforesaid, attending them as helpers, so to speak, but always helping them by a dutiful obedience.

Now there was one god who managed to escape from that duty, at least in principle. This was the god of a despised people, the god of the Jews. He claimed to be the only God. This god, we know, had never been the ruler of a great kingdom, but only of a petty province, and had moreover been conquered at almost regular intervals by all the great monarchs who held successive sway in the East until the arrival of conquerors from the West, who in turn overthrew them, and that with no great effort. But, notwithstanding these humiliations, this god of the lowest of the peoples put forth a claim to be the only god in existence and his worshippers, the Jews, believed him so to be. For them there was no other god but God. Not without some impatience did Rome and her emperor tolerate this insolent caprice of a god and a people so conspicuously remarkable for their own intolerance.

No symbol of the imperial cult found its way to Jerusalem; Caligula alone, who was mad, set about the introduction of his divine image into the Jewish temple, and would have provoked the bloodiest of all the Jewish revolts had not a timely death put an end to his antics. Things went no further than the offering in the temple of a sacrifice for the emperor on whom the Jewish god was supposed to bestow a blessing, but without the slightest recognition of him as a protector. The empire, reciprocally, was willing enough to recognize this outrageous deity of the Jews, but not for a moment would it accept his claim to the exclusive homage of all the world. In the eyes of the empire at large and the emperor in person, the public proclamation by open propaganda of this deity's intention to impose himself on both of them, to the detriment of all the other existing gods, Rome and Caesar included, would be highly offensive.

Thus it came to pass that when the attempt was made to set up the Jewish god as an effectively independent deity, and when the authority of Nero was challenged by the Jews, under the leadership of men who refused to recognize on earth any master but their God, both god and people at once became the objects of pitiless repression. This was repeated under Hadrian. Rome would not leave to God even the space occupied by his temple in Jerusalem, and did not. This notwithstanding, the Jews preserved the right to worship their god in private and after their own fashion, provided they abstained from propaganda against the gods of the empire and from recruiting proselytes turned into Jews by circumcision. On these terms the Jews were able to keep their religious rule of life, and their god was tolerated as a national deity, but always watched by the police for possible offences to the imperial religion. Rome would tolerate any god who was not intolerant to Rome.

In these conditions Christianity found itself in a position delicately balanced between opposing considerations, of which the mind of that age could neither grasp the meaning nor feel the weight. Although Christians claimed to have the same god as Jews, they were not Jews and had no wish to be, while the Jews on their part repudiated them for the good reason that Christians put themselves outside the Law and its observances. Whatever might be claimed for the god, the religion was not the same. And more, as Christians were not Jews, neither were they another particular nation, side by side with the Jewish. They were only the worshippers of a highly jealous god, no less absolute in his sovereignty than the Jewish deity, having indeed only pretentions to that sovereignty, but unprovided with a nation of hereditary devotees, as were the Jews. This Christian god laid claim to the rule of the whole world, refused to be written down in the catalogue of national divinities and announced his intention to dispossess them all, without delay and without mercy. He was no abstract and remote divinity, with theoretical rights of which the time for enforcement was indeterminate; he was a present god, demanding the prompt submission of all men and the denial, equally prompt, as false and wicked of all the gods to whom the imperial power extended its recognition. In the studied and cautious language put into the mouth of Paul for his discourse before the Areopagus the editor of Acts frames the matter thus: "Passing by the times of ignorance, God now gives warning, to all men everywhere, to repent, because he has fixed the day on which he will judge the world in righteousness by the man he has appointed to be judge, whereof he has given assurance to all men by raising him from the dead."

If the invitation to repent was declined by philosophers with ironical politeness, or greeted with laughter considered permissible in the circumstances, the politicians were quite unable to see the humour of the situation, and that mainly for two reasons: first, because Christian preaching was not carried on in the calm tones affected by the Areopagus discourse; second, because popular fanaticism allowed no leisure to constituted authority for pondering the philosophical bearings of propaganda subversive of all received ideas, at enmity with all the imperial divinities and intervening, with provocative condemnation, in all the forms of worship and superstition current in the pagan world. When the missionaries of Jesus set out on their errand, their purpose was not precisely that of announcing the end of the Mosaic Law and calling for obedience to a law purely moral (they annulled the Law *de facto* without rejecting it *de jure* and were not simply pleading for moral reform); what they announced was the speedy coming of Christ on the clouds of heaven, the overthrow of Satan and his kingdom, which meant nothing less

than the complete collapse of idolatry and final end of the idolatrous empire, and the Christ in place of the emperor. So they
understood their errand and so their errand was understood by
those to whom it was addressed. We can see at a glance why
authority was disturbed, why Nero's judges put the same
construction on the case of Paul as Pilate had put on the case of
Jesus, and why public opinion in the pagan world long regarded
the Christians as atheists and horrible examples of impiety and
sacrilege. They were judged to be capable of the most abominable
crimes, and not only capable, but guilty. And the public would
have believed it even if the Jews had not made a contribution
of their own to the libel, as the apologists of the second century
accuse them of doing. But it was not upon Jewish information
that Tacitus, speaking of Jesus and the Christians, based his
epithets "disastrous superstition," "plague," "atrocity and
shame."[1]

The first collective persecution of the Christians took place
at Rome under Nero, towards the close of the year 64, very
soon after sentence had been passed on Paul. The occasion was
the fire which destroyed a great part of the imperial city.
Beginning on July 19th it continued for six days and despite the
efforts made to check it broke out again, when thought to be
under control, and lasted for three days more—an event of
ample scope to give free play to the imagination. When at last
the calamity came to an end and the first and most urgent remedies
had been applied, and the gods placated, as was fitting, by solemn
propitiations, the hunt for the guilty was taken up in earnest.
Pure chance may well have been the chief criminal, some common
accident occurring under conditions favourable to the spread of
fire. But in all such cases it is the way of the populace to seek
for causes proportioned to the magnitude of the disaster; to
account for a conflagration so monstrous incendiaries must
have been at work whose criminal capacities were out of the
ordinary. If Tacitus is to be believed, public rumour fixed on
no less a person than Nero, who thereupon sought to clear
himself by accusing the Christians: "ergo abolendo rumori Nero
subdidit reos et quaesitissimis poenis afficit *quos per flagitia
invisos vulgus christianos appellabat.*" Perhaps Nero had no need
to invent this calumny, his friends merely taking advantage of

a tale already in circulation, by way of deflecting from his person a charge which, it is permissible to think, he had not deserved.

According to Tacitus the first victims seized were some persons "who confessed." But what did they confess and under what conditions? The question will long be discussed whether they confessed to incendiary acts or merely to being Christians.[2] It may well be that the last offence was held to involve the first, the Christians being judged in advance as the worst of criminals. Remembering, moreover, the expectations and hopes by which every Christian was animated, is it not likely that many of them, as they watched the flaming city, must have thought that the end of Satan's reign was at last coming and the punishment of the wicked actually begun? To explain the accusation against them we have no need to suppose that a few were mad enough to lend a helping hand to the judgment of God.[3] But not for them was the horror, the panic, the desolation of the Roman populace; some perhaps were caught in the act of expressing their joy. Such being their general attitude, there is no need to go further in seeking the origin of a calumny which must have seemed a probable truth to those who first gave it utterance and found ready belief among the masses. It is not true, however, as Duchesne asserts (i, 64) that Tacitus allows us "to see that nobody attributed the fire to the Christians." Preferring, for his own part, the hypothesis of Nero's guilt, and insinuating it as the true explanation, Tacitus confines himself to saying that the motive of the condemnation, as it fell on the mass of the condemned, was not their supposed incendiarism but "hatred of the human race." The people, he remarks, at length took compassion on the victims "although they had deserved the extremity of punishment," the ingenuity displayed in varying the modes of execution having made it apparent that they were rather designed to satisfy the cruel instincts of him who ordered them than to meet the lawful demands of public anger: "Unde, quanquam *adversus sontes et novissima exempla meritos*, miseratio oriebatur, tanquam non utilitate publica, sed in saevitiam unius absumerenter." Thus it would appear that common opinion, fully shared by Tacitus, approved prosecution and the death penalty as justly due to the Christians, although the majority of them were not chargeable with the burning of Rome and do not seem to have been charged.

The last of the accused, like the first, were condemned as criminals under the common law without the need arising to create *ad hoc* legislation against the new religion. Tertullian himself asserts that the precedent of Nero determined the judicial position for his successors without further difficulty (*Ad Nationes*, i, 7). The correspondence of Pliny and Trajan in the year 111 does not presuppose the existence of a law directed against Christians in particular; it merely implies the point of view, a natural and spontaneous product of established institutions and customs, that the profession of Christianity was, by itself, a crime to be punished by death. No edict proscribing the Christians was issued under Nero; but on the occasion of the fire there took place at Rome a hunt for Christians which led to a great number of them being done to death. There are no grounds for thinking that a general persecution was then set on foot, but we can well believe that both then and later popular ill will in various places caused many a Christian to perish, however little the Roman magistrates, from good nature or policy, were inclined to take part in their destruction. The principle *non licet Christianos esse*, though never formally inscribed on the statute book, was in the air and governed the practice of the court whenever a Christian was put on his trial.

The multitude of martyrs who perished at Rome in the year 64 left no names behind them; for us they are anonymous. Taken by surprise, and doubtless thrown into utter confusion, the Christian community was in no shape to draw up a prompt balance sheet of its losses. Moreover, at this early date it were better to speak of Christian groups than of a single organized community. The victims, at the mercy of chance denunciation, increased in number from day to day, but there was no governing body to register their names and construct a martyrology. The Epistle of Clement to the Corinthians (5–6) speaks of these victims, but only by allusion and in terms more vague in substance, if not more general, than those used by Tacitus. In this document we find the leading place among the martyrs of 64 already assigned, it would seem, to Peter and Paul, presented as the two great founders of the Roman church, Peter, as the presumed founder of the Roman episcopate, being given precedence to Paul. If the letter of Clement was composed at Rome only some thirty years after their martyrdom it is surely matter for astonishment that the references it makes to the two apostles contain not a single informative detail as to the circumstances under which they met their death. We are inclined to think that the author knew hardly more about Peter and Paul, except the bare fact of their martyrdom, than anyone may read for himself in Acts and Second Corinthians. Although legendary tradition seems to place the death of Paul at the end of the persecution of 64, and liturgical tradition leaves us to suppose that both apostles died on the same day,4 the probability, as we have pointed out above, is that Paul perished some time before the persecution.

The fate of Peter is far more obscure than that of Paul. Of Paul we know fairly well both the time and the circumstances of his coming to Rome. Of Peter's coming to the city we know nothing. The chief argument in support of the Roman tradition that Peter came to Rome and perished there is that no other tradition and no evidence of any kind in Christian antiquity can be found to contradict it. This argument, though not absolutely decisive, is not without weight. True it is that Ephesus, during the pascal controversy, could make claim to the apostle John without meeting a protest, and Rome might well have made an equally unfounded claim to Peter without encountering opposition; but there is a difference; ancient Christian documents give the critic ground for contesting the pretension of Ephesus to John, but contain nothing to authorize an off-hand denial of the pretention of Rome to Peter. On the other hand, direct evidence as to Peter's fate is neither very old nor very precise. From the Epistle to the Romans (especially xv, 17–23) we may deduce, at least with some probability, that Peter was not then in Rome and could not have been there up to the time when the Epistle was written. We learn from the Epistle to the Galatians (ii, 11) that Peter arrived in Antioch in the year 44 or a little later;5 but the Book of Acts which records his departure from Jerusalem at that date says not a word of what happened to him afterwards. But the editor of this book, who may well have had a motive for saying nothing about Peter going to Antioch, had seemingly no motive for keeping silence about his being in Rome when Paul was there, and would presumably have mentioned it if precise information had been in his hands about a ministry carried on by Peter in Rome before the conclusion of Paul's trial.[6] We have just seen the contribution made to the subject by the letter of Clement; it amounts to a probability in favour of Peter's martyrdom in Rome. The letter of Ignatius to the Romans seems to regard Peter and Paul together as Apostles of Rome;[7] but this letter, if later than 150, adds nothing to Clement's testimony or to the more recent Dionysius of Corinth.[8] The name "Babylon" in First Peter is probably intended for Rome as the place from which the Epistle was written:[9] but the Epistle is not authentic and this trait, while proving the relative antiquity of the Roman tradition, brings us little nearer to the time in question than Clement does. The same holds true of the allusion to Peter's martyrdom in the last chapter of the fourth Gospel and in the Apocalypse of Peter.[10] The Epistle to the Hebrews (xiii, 7), if we may take it as addressed to the Roman Christians, vaguely attests the same tradition as Clement, but at an earlier date. We conclude, then, that the Roman tradition has an old, firm but rather narrow and bare foundation in traditional reminiscence. Peter had been in Rome for some time, beginning perhaps at a date just before the death of Paul, when he became engulfed in the *multitudo ingens* which Nero so cruelly put to death. The survivors of the slaughter may well have known but little of the circumstances of his death. Whether the tradition concerning the place of his burial is exact or conjectural is a question of very little import to the history of the Christian religion.[11]

2. ROMAN LAW VERSUS THE CHRISTIAN RELIGION

Roman Christianity was not entirely destroyed in the year 64 and even if it had been would not have been slow to form again, as it was formed before, by the influx of believers coming in from outside regions to carry on their propaganda and increase the number of adherents in the city, as it had done from the first. But there seems to have been no solution of continuity. The action of Nero did no more than create a temporary arrest and great disturbance in the process of its growth. Soon enough, under the Flavian Emperors, it was destined to win back its first importance. By the destruction of Jerusalem and of the temple in the year 70, Christianity lost its original centre and, we may add, its point of attachment to Judaism. The community of old believers in Jerusalem had been scattered abroad before the date of the siege and continued to exist only in a few small groups in the North of Palestine and beyond the Jordan.[12] The time was not far distant when the capital of the Roman Empire would become in fact, and then proclaim itself by right, the metropolis of the Christian world. But that great development had its own dangers.

Though fanatical Judaism had been suppressed in the year 70, but not completely extinguished—for the fire smouldered under the ashes till the time of Trajan and Hadrian—and though moderate Judaism, represented at Rome by persons in credit with the Emperors, retained its legal status, the position of Christianity in presence of Roman law was not thereby made any clearer. Speaking more exactly, it cleared up to the detriment of Christianity in proportion as the new religion became completely independent of Judaism and was recognized as independent by the Roman authorities. The Jews were not likely to countenance any confusion of the two religions, and the efforts of the Christians to acquire parity of treatment by the law were all in vain. They profited only by the favour shown to Jewish monotheism in certain circles of Roman society, and these not the least considerable.

The "foreign superstition" of which Pomponia Graecina, a Roman lady, was accused in the time of Nero (Tacitus, *Annals*, xiii, 32) and for which she was pardoned by her husband who, as head of the family, claimed the right to judge her, was probably the Christian religion. There were clearer cases under Domitian. Acilius Glabrio, consul in 91, is a probable case; that of Flavius Clemens, consul in 95, is certain.[13] According to Dio Cassius, Clemens and his wife Flavia Domitilla "were accused of atheism, an accusation which in those days made victims of many among the followers of Jewish morals." Domitian's financial policy may well have led him, not quite without intention, to confuse the Christians with the Jews, and so make the most of the *fiscus judaicus* by treating as adherents of Judaism all who adopted Jewish morals, even though uncircumcised. It should be noted, however, that what we have now to do with are the legal trials, few or many, of individuals accused of Christianity and ending in the death penalty or confiscation of goods. Clemens was executed; but this did not prevent Domitian keeping the two sons of Clemens near his person and having them educated, as his presumptive heirs, by Quintilian the rhetorician. No doubt political considerations had their part in the affair of Clemens whose uncommon "incapacity," *contemptissimae inertiae*, attested by Suetonius, may have been partly the result of his preoccupation with a mystical religion. Before that, Flavius Sabinus, father of Clemens, brother of Vespasian, and prefect of Rome under Nero, was reputed a man of very gentle disposition whom some, in his old age, had accused of weakness, though the worst to be said of him was "a man of moderation and sparing of the blood of his fellow citizens" (Tacitus, *History*, iii, 65–75). There is an affinity between the temper of this family and the spirit of the Christian religion.

An idea of the legal position of Christianity at the beginning of the second century can be derived from the correspondence between Pliny the Younger, who was legate in Bithynia in 111–112 (or 112–113), and the emperor Trajan about the procedure to be followed when Christians were on trial for the offence of their religion. We learn in the first place that this Roman magistrate, up to the time of his assuming office, had never taken part in the trials of Christians. "Cognitionibus de Christianis interfui nunquam; ideo nescio, quid et quatenus aut puniri soleat aut quaeri." All Pliny knows is that the profession of Christianity is punishable by death, but he is ignorant how the charge should be defined in judicial practice, which he had been obliged to define for himself, as best he could, according to his sense of justice, in the numerous cases when denounced Christians had been brought into his court. Neither he nor the clerks of the court knew of anything in the statute book to guide them in the course to follow in such affairs. In his answer Trajan shows that he knew no more than they did and gives no positive instructions, contenting himself with an

191

approval of the procedure discreetly recommended by Pliny in his own letter.

This letter reveals that, to begin with, certain denunciations had been brought before the court which Pliny had dealt with as follows: a threefold interrogation of the denounced persons under threat of the death penalty if the Christianity of which they were accused were not denied; execution of those who admitted the charge and persisted, unless they had the status of Roman citizens; remand to the imperial tribunal of those who had that status. It seems clear that renegades were pardoned and set free without further formality. The ground assigned by Pliny for the condemnation of the others is their obstinacy, a seemingly insufficient offence, since mere stubbornness is not itself a capital crime. All the same it was the best reason Pliny could assign for passing sentence on the Christian "Name"— setting aside the crimes attributed to the Christians by popular rumour, of which crimes he, for his part, was inclined to think them innocent. It must not be overlooked, however, that he considered himself to be legally empowered to require the accused to offer sacrifice to the gods and to the image of Caesar, and regarded an obstinate refusal as a kind of rebellion. On the other hand, he judged the religion, on which the refusal was based, to be an extraordinary superstition, but harmless enough in itself. In all of which we discern the mind of an experienced politician.

The first trials led on to others, and a multitude of denunciations came out in an unsigned document containing a long list of names. Though the charges were not in regular form, Pliny, at this further development, proceeded with greater severity than before, probably because his Council had found him too lenient in the earlier trials. Some of the persons named in the list declared they were not Christians and never had been; if these made no difficulty about invoking the gods and doing homage to their images and to the emperor's, by libation of wines and burning of incense, and finally by cursing the Christ (all flatly refused, we are told, by true Christians), their cases were dismissed. Others confessed to being Christians, but were induced to repudiate Christianity under threat of the death penalty for persisting; there were also some who said they had been Christians, but were so no longer, having given up the religion three years ago, or even twenty years ago: all these consented to perform the same acts as those who declared they had never been Christians. This notwithstanding, Pliny would not let them go scot free, but kept them prisoners pending the arrival of the emperor's instructions, doubtless because his counsellors had again advised him to hesitate before taking the apostasy of these people as proof of their innocence. Meanwhile he continued the inquisition, of which the results up to date are here passed on to Trajan.

All these renegades or apostates from Christianity emphatically affirmed that they had committed no offence or misdemeanour beyond meeting habitually on a fixed day before the dawn (*ante lucem*) for the purpose of singing together a hymn to the Christ, as to a god, and that the oath[14] they had taken as Christians, far from pledging them to commit crime of any kind, pledged them not to commit theft, brigandage, adultery, betrayal of trust or appropriation of trust-money. They alleged further that after singing their hymn, they gathered together for an innocent meal in common, and that they had discontinued even this since the legate had promulgated Trajan's decree against associations.[15] Clearly these people were regarded by Pliny as harmless enough. From the reports submitted to him he had formed an idea of their Christ identical with that of Tacitus; it was that the Christians in their meetings celebrated as a god the man who had founded their sect, and this founder he knew, as Tacitus did, under his surname of Christ.

It is to be noted from the above that one effect of the imperial edicts in Bithynia had been to change the custom of the Supper, which was no longer kept in the evening as an ordinary evening meal, but in the early morning. That it was completely suppressed is hardly probable.

A last feature to be noted in the correspondence concerns the interior economy of the congregations. To obtain fuller information on all these points Pliny caused two women employed in serving at the meetings, and having the title of "deaconess" proper to that employment, to be questioned under torture. It is clear that these women did not abjure the Christ; but the legate was able to learn nothing more from them than the renegades had already told him, unless it were the perversity and extravagance of their superstition, "*superstitiam pravam, immodicam*"—which we may understand as referring to the fanatical stubbornness of the women in their intolerant and absurd belief. The legate says nothing to indicate the existence of any priestly organization, though doubtless the Christian groups in Bithynia had their elders and deacons. We need hardly ask how Pliny finished with the obstinate deaconesses: he had them put to death in common with all the other persons denounced in the list who confessed to being Christians and did not apostatize.

He had no desire, however, to multiply these executions and his writing to the emperor was an attempt to induce him to lay down a policy of moderation. The fact plainly is that the number of people denounced was too great for prosecution to be desirable, especially if punishment had to be inflicted on the renegades who had apostatized under threat as well as on those who had abandoned Christianity of their own accord after practising it for some time; they included persons of both sexes, of all ages, of every condition, and were found in the country districts as well as in the towns. A moderated system of repression, says Pliny, had already produced good results: the congregations which had abandoned the temples of the gods, are now beginning to come back; there is better attendance at the festivals and a better sale for the sacrificial meats. Clearly the contagion has been checked, and there will be no great difficulty in recovering the deluded masses if pardon be granted them on repenting of their folly. "Visa est enim mihi res digna consultatione, maxime propter periclitantium numerum. Multi enim omnis aetatis, omnis ordinis, utriusque sexus etiam vocantur in periculum et vocabuntur. Neque civitates tantum, sed vicos etiam atque agros superstitionis istius contagio pervagata est: quae videtur sisti et corrigi posse. Certe satis constat prope jam desolata templa cœpisse celebrari, et sacra sollemnia diu intermissa repeti pastumque venire victimarum, cujus adhuc rarissimus emptor invéniebatur. Ex quo facile est opinari, quae turba hominum emendari possit, si sit pœnitentiae locus."

In all this Pliny may well have been under some illusion as to the efficacy of his tactics. But he was a philosophical magistrate, sincere and goodhearted, whose pity for the Christians was greater than his hatred of Christianity, a man who regarded persecution to the last extremity as hardly less absurd than the extremes of Christian fanaticism. So, with a pretty clear notion of what answer he would get, he decided to bring the following questions in plain terms before Trajan:

(1) Whether in the trial of Christians, account should be taken of the tender age of children who might be denounced.

(2) Whether a person who has been a Christian, but is so no longer, is not entitled to pardon.

(3) Whether the mere profession of the Christian name is a punishable offence without other proof of criminality or with only such proof as was given by common opinion of the crimes attributed to the name.[16]

These questions Pliny places at the head of his letter, the whole of which is framed in a manner likely to suggest the answers he considered suitable.

Trajan approves what Pliny has done. The problem is complicated and the particular differences make it impossible to apply a uniform rule. There must be no hunting down of Christians, as though the intention of the government were to make an end of them at a blow. When denounced and convicted they are to be punished, and about that there are to be no half measures; the punishment will be death. Christians who recant must be pardoned subject to the conditions observed by Pliny in the judgments given first. And that is all. Trajan evades the distinction Pliny had proposed between the crime of adopting the Name and the crimes connected with the Name in the opinion of the public. Pliny inclines to pardon those accused of the Name but not of the crimes: Trajan answers as though, like Tacitus, he regarded the Name and the crimes as really inseparable. But he fails to see that in letting renegades go scot free he is either pardoning criminals or contradicting himself. Of the two correspondents Pliny was the more humane and the more sagacious; Trajan was the more astute politician, his treatment of the affair revealing a mentality of mediocre good sense conformed to the popular opinion of his time. Obstinacy, in his view, is a real crime. If he understood Pliny's meaning he may have said to himself that popular opinion, after all, was not very far wrong in regarding the Christians as criminals and that these people, even if innocent of the ritual and other abominations charged against them, lived, thought and laboured in ways opposed to Roman law and order. Some political reason it must have been that induced Trajan to pass over without notice Pliny's distinction between the Name and criminality, or that referring to the age of the accused in which Pliny had shown himself inclined to confine conviction to responsible adults. (In fact women were often condemned and adolescents occasionally.) Had he not said, moreover, that a few examples would be enough to bring back the mass of Christians into the common road of fidelity to the gods? On the other hand might we not say that Trajan shows himself a man of greater moderation than Pliny by forbidding him to receive anonymous denunciations? *"Sine auctore vero propositi libelli in nullo crimine locum habere debent. Nam et pessimi exempli nec nostri saeculi est."*

We cannot but believe that both Pliny and Trajan did their best in their respective positions, but that the problem was one of those which go beyond the ordinary reach, always relative, of the human mind. How is it possible, without provoking violence and revolution, to reconcile an established social order, which seems to satisfy the demands of reason, with the consummate folly of a movement which aims at setting up a new and better order for mankind? In cases of this kind the road into the future has its course marked out not by men, but by events; and it is a road that has no ending.

The rescript of Hadrian to Minutius Fundamus (*Eusebius*, iv, 9) is on the same lines as Trajan's letter to Pliny. The emperor's instructions are that punishment is not to be inflicted on Christians in response to popular clamour; their trials are to be conducted in legal form on the strength of accusations drawn up according to the rules, the exact observance of which the judge will see to. If the accusation is unfounded, the informer is to be punished. But if the accusation is proved, if the accused confesses and declares his intention to remain a Christian, he is none the less to be sentenced and put to death.

With the measures prescribed by Trajan, Hadrian and Antoninus,[17] goodwill towards Christians had nothing to do; the real motive was regard for public order, for moderation, for sound policy. Not for a moment did the idea of protecting Christianity enter their minds; their aim was to keep it in check and repress it with the minimum of violence. So far was this from providing Christians with security, that the right to be Christians was always denied them. They were continually at the mercy of denunciation, of popular passion, of the hostility by which a magistrate, municipal or imperial, might chance to be animated.

Was there any sign of response from the Christian side to this relative appeasement? Was no effort made to mute the strings of that "hatred of the human race" which Tacitus pretends to have been proved against the martyrs of 64? It now behoves us to attempt an answer to these questions.

We search the Book of Revelation in vain for the faintest sign of mitigated hatred. This book reflects the mentality of the Christians in Asia, at least of their notables, of those whose part it was to animate and sustain the faith of the others. Not only did the author live in hourly expectation of the Second Coming; he lived also in the atmosphere of martyrdom, and dreams only of persecution and death. At the time of his writing few were being made martyrs on the earth, but a considerable number had already arrived in heaven and the immediate future was to be a time of trial for every believer still alive. The prophet comes little short of counting all the saints as martyrs and seems to believe that every true Christian will come to a violent end. He beholds in heaven a multitude of souls supplicating the Eternal to take vengeance on their persecutors. "And a white robe"—their glorified body—"was given to every one of them, and they were bidden to hold their peace a little longer until their fellow servants and their brethren had all been slain, as themselves had been" (Rev. vi, 11). In his vision of triumph, those who have been marked on earth with the seal of the living God, and now stand before God's throne and before the Lamb, are all in one class: they are "those who have come through the great tribulation and washed their robes and made them white in the blood of the Lamb" (Rev. vii, 14; xx, 4). But we have only to read attentively the letters to the seven congregations which introduce the great revelation (ii–iii) to satisfy ourselves that all the believers of that time were not quite in harmony with the grand diapason of the author's words; he bemoans and chides the lukewarm, puts it on record that fervour is declining in many quarters and foresees a time of positive defection. It would seem that Pliny's repressive action in Bithynia had produced as many renegades as martyrs, if not more. But the spirit of the Church was not in the renegades. It was incarnate in those of whom Pliny says that nothing could stir them from their outrageous superstition. These were the martyrs and their prophet was John.

John and his martyrs are not among Rome's well-wishers. They are preoccupied with the prospect of her coming overthrow. From end to end the Apocalypse is filled with the recital of calamities about to overwhelm the pagan world, persecutor of the children of God. Rome is the abominable Beast whom the Dragon has raised up against God, Christ and his faithful ones. It is Satan who makes men worship the Beast and his image, and compels all the Beast's worshippers to bear his mark. Inasmuch as the Beast is Rome he is also the Emperor of Rome; his image, which all must worship, is the image of Caesar (xiii, 16–17)—and let us not forget how Pliny compelled the renegades to burn incense in its honour. But here are the angels to proclaim the end of the empire and vengeance on idolators. One cries out: "She is fallen, she is fallen, Babylon the great, who made all nations drunk with the wine of fury and of her shamelessness" (xiv, 8). Another makes proclamation: "If anyone worships the Beast and his image and bear the Beast's mark on his forehead, or even on his hand, he too shall drink wine of fury, the fury of God, which is poured out without mixture in the cup of his wrath: he shall be tormented with fire and brimstone in the presence of the angels and of the Lamb, and the smoke of his torment shall go up for ever and ever" (xiv, 9–11). And then a word of warning to the renegades; for them, as for the idolators, eternal death is in store. Finally (xvii–xviii) our author describes with relish the punishment of the Great Harlot, before passing on to the triumph of the Christ and his saints.

We look in vain for documents of the same period inspired by a less fiery zeal for the annihilation of Rome and her empire. Unfortunately the New Testament books which evince some degree of respect for established order and constituted authority are of uncertain date. If the Epistle to the Romans were the authentic work of Paul in all its parts he could be cited as having taught the faithful in Rome to reverence the temporal powers and render them sincere obedience as instituted by God, as all authority is, for the protection of the good and the punishment of the wicked.[18] But this wise instruction is a late addition which can hardly be as early as the first century. The same must be said of the First Epistle of Peter where the same lesson is given in analogous terms (ii, 13–17) with a commentary which suggests a date near the time of Pliny. In effect the author insists not only that Christians are under strict obligation to be irreproachable in their conduct, but also that the calumnies now pursuing them make such conduct both necessary and expedient. From his own point of view he draws the same distinction as Pliny does between the "name" Christian and the crimes attached to it by common opinion. "If ye are insulted for the name of Christ, happy are ye! That any one of you should suffer as a murderer, a thief, a rogue or as guilty of sedition, must not be. But if he suffers for being a Christian, let him not be ashamed of that, but let him thank God for it. For this is the time when judgment begins in the household of God; and if it begins with us what will be the fate of those who reject his Gospel" (ii, 14–17). A day is coming, then, when punishment, as foretold by the author of Revelation, will fall on the unbelievers. Meanwhile, let the Christian govern his conduct in loyalty to the powers that be, even though they persecute him.

The First to Timothy goes further: "Before all else I lay it upon you to make supplications, prayers, intercessions, thanks-givings for all men, for kings"—meaning emperors—"and for all in authority, that we may lead a quiet and peaceful life in piety and honour, which is a good and acceptable thing in the eyes of God our Saviour, who will have all men to be saved and come to the knowledge of the truth" (ii, 1–4). Here was a believer with a mind wholly set on peace, whose hopes were centred on the conversion rather than the destruction of the Roman empire. In like manner, Clement, concluding the long prayer inserted at the end of his Epistle, calls down all the blessings of heaven on the bearers of the imperial mandate, to the end that their power may be used according to the will of God (*Corinthians* 61). We may conclude that by the age of the

Antonines the Christian mind had turned definitely towards appeasement.

Need it be added that the Gospels and Acts are in a current of feeling less embittered and more deferential to Roman authority? Pilate, when confronted by Jesus, is represented by the Gospels in an attitude identical with that of Pliny toward the Christians in his province. His goodwill for the Christ, suggested in the drawing of the scene, is intended not only to remove all suspicion of rebellion against the empire from the presumed founder of Christianity; it is introduced for the further reason that some Roman magistrates were by the time the story was told adopting a policy of moderation in dealing with the Christians, in spite of the fact that official jurisprudence, supported by popular fanaticism, required their condemnation to death. The belief, thus indicated, that moderation was on the increase, cannot have risen in the Christian mind at the time when it was under the impression of the frightful experience of the year 64, nor while Christians were suffering the hardships imposed by Domitian. It belongs to a period later than the reign of Domitian (81–96) when Roman policy had consciously and of set purpose adopted the rule of go-slow in its persecution of the Christians. The saying attributed to Jesus about tribute owed to Caesar was intended, by whoever conceived it, to put Christians on a higher plane than Jewish zealots; it may have been invented at an early date among the Jewish Christians of Palestine who had not joined the Zealots in their great revolt. But the birth of the fiction cannot be confidently dated and may be no earlier than the period when the Jerusalem ministry of Jesus was systematically arranged in the common tradition of the Synoptics.

The apologetic of Acts is constructed in the same spirit as the passages from the Epistles cited above: constituted authority—with the exception of the Jewish—is always shown as either indifferent or benevolent to the cause of Christianity, nor does the editor despair of a coming time when Christian propaganda, represented by him as ever respectful to the Roman government, will be tolerated, as Judaism actually is; while the discourse to the Areopagus goes so far as to hint that pagans, without their knowing it, may be worshipping the same God as the Christians. The apologists of the second century adopt the same conciliatory attitude, though the regime of persecution has not been abandoned either in theory or practice, and they themselves are under its threat.

3. PHILOSOPHERS INTERVENE

The popular dislike, in some respects profoundly unjust, which had fallen on the Christian religion and the strange jurisprudence which condemned Christians to death by approving suspicions which made them guilty of crimes of which they knew they were innocent, was bound to raise up apologists as soon as Christianity could produce men of sufficient capacity to put the case before the reading public and explain the extraordinary position in which Christians were placed by the joint action of common opinion and public authority. On the other side the reading public in general and the philosophers in particular began to take an interest in Christianity, but without the least sign of goodwill. Justin, the apologist of whom we shall soon have to speak, had at his elbow a Cynic philosopher named Crescens who was out for Justin's head and eventually got it; Fronto, the tutor of Marcus Aurelius, accused the Christians, in a published writing, of practising the rites of Thyestes; and Celsus was soon to come forward between 170 and 180, with an almost scientific refutation of the new religion, ending, however, by proposals for a sort of compromise with Christianity.

Of the apology presented to the emperor Hadrian by a certain Quadratus we know next to nothing. The moderate policy of the emperors evidently encouraged the Christians in efforts to gain acceptance for their claims. Quadratus, who lived in Asia, seems to have been a Christian prophet. The most remarkable feature of his apology, retained by Eusebius (iv, 3),[19] is the mention of persons raised from the dead by Jesus, of whom some were said to be still alive in the time of the apologist. As the evangelical tradition has no knowledge of these numerous resurrections, we must conclude that Quadratus was either exaggerating or that his only knowledge of the raised persons came to him in a vision. The proceeding of Quadratus had been prompted by vexations inflicted on the Christians in his part of the world.

The apology of Aristides, an Athenian philosopher, was

addressed to the emperor Antoninus[20] in the early years of his reign (before 147). The author, after presenting the neoplatonic idea of God as the Christian idea—which reminds us of the discourse to the Areopagus—gives summary refutation to the chief forms of polytheism, and then discusses Judaism, true in theology and ethics but a cult of angels;[21] finally he expounds the Christian faith and way of life. Christians, he says, acknowledge one God and one only, creator of the world, and they obey his commandments while waiting for the age to come in which they will see the Christ and receive the fulfilment of his promises. The description of Christian morals has a close affinity with the moral part of the *Didache* and with what Pliny's letter tells of the declarations made by the Christians; evidently the basis of it all is some catechism widely used in those times. But of Christology there is virtually nothing, unless we count as Christology the statement that the precepts of God are the precepts of the Christ, that Christians are willing to suffer all things for his name and their supreme hope is that of seeing him. The dominant purpose of the author is to present Christianity as a lofty religious philosophy, imposing irreproachable conduct on its adepts; this last point receiving particular attention in view of the current calumnies. The attenuated eschatology may betoken deliberate avoidance of a dangerous subject; but it may equally result from the fact that by this time expectation of the Second Coming had considerably cooled down and the attention of believers become more concentrated on the needs and duties of the present life.

It was to Antoninus also that Justin, about the year 152, addressed his *Apology*. He, too, professed to be a philosopher, "going about," as Duchesne describes him, "from city to city, dressed in his short cloak, and bearing the message of an independent thinker."[22] He was born at Neapolis in the country of the Samaritans. Never a great philosopher, he knew the different schools, notably that of the Platonists, but he was a troubled soul on whom the constancy of the Christian martyrs, of which he has been sometimes a witness, had made a deep impression. Becoming instructed in Christianity he adopted it about the year 133, probably at Ephesus, where about 135 he had a debate with the Jewish doctor Trypho. Thence he came to Rome and seems to have remained there a considerable time. He continued to wear the garb peculiar to the philosophers and to practise their manner of walking, discoursing in public on Christian doctrine and presenting it as a philosophy, or speculation of wise men, on the meaning and purpose of life, as were the other philosophies of that time, some more or less coloured by mysticism. Many writings came from his pen, not only in defence of Christians' faith against pagans, but also against gnostic heresies then swarming within the fold, and notably against Marcion. At Rome he had a public debate with Crescens, a Cynic philosopher who, like most of the philosophers of the time, was hot against the Christians. Crescens, however, knew very little about them and having the worst of it in the debate, he tried to get his adversary judicially condemned; whereupon, Justin quitted Rome, to return a little later under Marcus Aurelius. He resumed his teaching, was arrested with other Christians, tried and put to death.

With the freedom proper to the philosopher, Justin, in his *Apology*, presents his plea to Antoninus, the "pious" emperor; to his adopted sons, Marcus Aurelius, the "philosopher," and Lucius Verus, to the Senate and the entire Roman people. It is a plea "on behalf of men of every race who are hated and persecuted, himself, Justin, being one of them" (1 *Apology*, 1). Men such as those for whom he is appealing, "truly pious men and philosophers," ought not to be judged by preconceived opinion but by reality. Christians should not be condemned, except for proved crimes (if they have committed them) and not for a mere name which, by itself, proves nothing for or against those who bear it (2–4). Justin admits that some sects claiming to be Christian may not be quite irreproachable: all the more reason to make inquisition only for crimes and not to condemn a name honourably borne by the majority[23] of its bearers (5). Certainly the allegation is true that Christians worship God only and no idols, and look upon sacrifices as futile; they know very well that idolatry was the work of "evil spirits who had appeared in olden time."[24] Socrates denounced it, and the demons had him put to death as an atheist and a man of impiety; and now they are treating Christians in the same way, because the Logos, who spoke by the mouth of Socrates, "become man and named Jesus-

Christ," has revealed the truth to the barbarians. So far as these false gods are concerned the Christians are atheists; but they worship and reverence the true God, His Son Jesus-Christ, whom He has sent, and "the host of other good angels who resemble him and follow in his train."25 "When you hear it said that we await a kingdom, rightly you suppose that we mean a human kingdom; but it is of God's Kingdom that we speak, a kingdom in the life that is eternal, persuaded that God will render to every man according to his works; moreover it is the Christians' belief in this coming judgment that makes them, "of all men, the greatest lovers of peace." If all the world were penetrated by a belief so salutary, not a single wicked man would remain in existence. "In truth you seem to fear that all men will become virtuous and that nobody will be left for you to punish" (i, 11–12).

We are almost led to think that Justin takes no interest in the common eschatology, in spite of the fact that he knows the Apocalypse of John and professes millenarianism in his *Dialogue with Trypho* (81). The reason is that the *Dialogue* was intended for the edification of Christians while the *Apology* was written for pagans. Moreover, even in the Apology, the attenuation of apocalyptic eschatology is more apparent than real: in Justin's outlook the days of the Roman empire are numbered, and the best the emperors themselves can do is to make ready for the Day of Judgment (i, 68).

Justin expatiates widely on Christian ethics, citing the Gospels with a copiousness unknown in all the earlier Christian literature, and not overlooking the story of the tribute. In his commentary on that saying there is a note of pride. "Since it is our duty to render to Caesar what is Caesar's and to God what is God's, our adoration is wholly given to Him; in all other things we willingly obey you, recognizing you as kings and leaders of men and praying that in you the wisdom of reason may be one with the power of kingship" (17). For emperors must die like other men and they will be judged like other men. Dilating on that, Justin proves that men do not wholly die, appealing to necromancy, possession by spirits, oracles, the descent of Ulysses into Hades, and then caps his argument by adducing the probabilities in favour of the resurrection of the dead. As to the final destruction of the world by fire, do not the Stoics teach almost the same?

All is grist that comes to the mill of this brave apologist. What Christians tell about Jesus, he remarks, is precisely what pagans tell of the sons of Zeus, Hermes, Dionysus, Hercules, the Dioscuri and others. But all these stories are the work of demons and offer no example for human conduct. By contrast, everything is pure in Jesus; he is the veritable word and messenger of God, like Hermes; born of God, since, like Perseus, he was conceived by a virgin; resembling Dionysus in being put to death; and let us not forget his miracles, which allow of comparison with Asclepius. But in reality, the Christ alone has the special gifts which befit his name—the Son of God. The stories told of the false gods are wicked caricatures concocted in advance by bad demons, or fictions put by them into the minds of poets. Since then and until quite recently the invention of false gods has been going on: it was the demons who helped Simon Magus to get himself accepted as a god in Samaria, and has he not a statue even in Rome?[26] After him his disciple Menander fooled plenty of people at Antioch; and at this present moment there is a fellow named Marcion, of Pontus, going about everywhere proclaiming that he has a better god than the Creator of the universe.[27] The followers of these gentry are not to be confounded with true Christians. Them he goes on to defend, contrasting their well-ordered life with the debauches of the pagans, and not hesitating to mention the scandalous affair of Antinous, the favourite of Hadrian, drowned in the Nile and afterwards deified by the emperor.

Man has ever been an inventor of gods and invents them still; such at least is the opinion of Justin. But the fact emerging from this development of apology, which the modern reader will find most instructive, is that, all things considered, the mentality of a second century Christian, even an enlightened one, was not so far removed as one might think from the mentality of his pagan contemporaries; and this should help us to a better understanding of the atmosphere in which the Christian mystery, to be discussed in the next chapter, was gradually formed and of the influences contributing to its formation. The difference between Christianity and paganism is much less in theology—

than it is in mythology—and much less in metaphysics than in moral idealism.

Then comes a long dissertation on the fulfilment of Jewish prophecy in the person and history of Jesus. By the boldest of anachronisms Justin recalls how King Ptolemy had demanded the Hebrew books from Herod for the purpose of having them translated into Greek (31). From this part of the *Apology*, continued and completed in the *Dialogue with Trypho*, the most important fact to be learned is that the evangelical tradition had by this time been put into definite shape, so that the apologist could confidently and triumphantly point out the correspondence of the legend with the ancient texts, and celebrate the correspondence as a work of divine providence, ignoring the fact that the legend had, for the most part, been ingeniously drawn from those very texts by the faith of earlier Christian generations. This was not an argument to carry weight with educated pagans and has never been convincing, except for believers. Nevertheless we must take it into account if we are to understand the mystical element in the thought of second century Christianity. The extreme *naïveté* of our philosopher is seen in his daring to refer the emperors, for evidence about the birth of Jesus, to the registers of the enrolment made by Quirinius, whom he makes the first procurator in Judea (35); and for evidence about his miracles and death to official records made in the time of Pontius Pilate[28]—as though these registers and records were preserved in the archives of the empire.

To avoid the air of omitting something, the omission of which from his picture might rouse suspicion, Justin next describes the rites of Christian initiation and worship. As this part of the *Apology* deals with the new Christian mystery we shall return to it in the next chapter. Suffice it for the present to note that, according to our author, the demons, having discovered an announcement of baptism in the prophecies, at once proceeded to make rules about washings and such like purifications; the same with the eucharist which these wicked beings had imitated by setting up a similar rite in the mysteries of Mithra—the presentation of a loaf and a cup of water accompanied with certain well-known formulas. Justin seems to imply that these formulas also are not without their counterparts in the mystical language used by him in explaining the Christian rite. It does not seem to have occurred to him that some of his pagan readers might be inclined to think that it was not the pagan mysteries for which the intervention of devils was responsible, and thus derive from his analogies an idea not altogether favourable to the Christian religion.

None the less the concluding words of the *Apology* are the utterance of a sincere and courageous soul: "If that which we have submitted to your judgment seems reasonable and true, act accordingly; if you think it folly, treat it as folly, but do not condemn to death, as enemies, people who do no evil. For we forewarn you that you will not escape the judgment of God if you persist in injustice. As for ourselves, our cry will ever be 'let God's will be done.' " By way of postcript he adds the Latin copy of Hadrian's rescript to Minutius Fundanus forbidding the punishment of Christians for the profession of their faith unless they were proved guilty of offence against the law.

The so-called "Second Apology" is a sort of complementary writing published by Justin some time afterwards in which he deals with three sentences of death passed upon Christians by Urbicus, prefect of Rome. In this he addresses himself directly to public opinion and speaking to the people as brothers urges them in the name of humanity to protest against these acts of injustice, now being committed by the magistrates, under cover of the law, at Rome and throughout the Empire. He discusses three cases which have occurred in Rome. A Christian woman, tired of an intolerable husband, had finally given him notice of the *repudium*, on which the husband had denounced her as a Christian; the woman having obtained judicial delay for the preparation of her defence, the husband, by means of a centurion friend of his, caused the arrest of a certain Ptolemy who had converted the wife to Christianity; summoned by Urbicus to abjure the Christ, Ptolemy refuses and Urbicus has him put to death; a person present at the trial, named Lucius, protests against the sentence; Urbicus asks him if he is a Christian and on his answering "Yes" orders him to be led off immediately to execution; another man protests and meets the same fate (ii, 2). From all of which it is clear enough that under Antoninus the Pious, and at the seat of the imperial government, the hand of Roman justice was not asleep when Christians had to be dealt with.

Having discussed these cases, Justin, with remarkable temerity, proceeds to ridicule the "philosopher and swaggerer," whom he knows to be on the warpath against him, with the determination to bring him, Justin, to a like end (ii, 3–4). He responds with dignity to the bad jesters who ask why Christians don't kill themselves and go quickly to their God without bothering the magistrates to send them thither: God, he says, has put us in the world to do good and we confess ourselves Christians that truth may be spoken. But why, it is asked, does God let you be persecuted? The answer is—because the world has been corrupted by the doings of wicked angels and of their offspring, the demons, and because God, on account of the Christians, delays the universal catastrophe which is to sweep away for ever the wicked angels and the sinners.[29] But some will say: "Is that certain?" Justin answers: "If there were no chastisements, either there would be no God or only a God who had no interest in men; and so there would be neither good nor evil; the Logos is truth and virtue; him, and not falsehod and vice, it behoves us to follow even at the cost of our lives. As to the evil rumours current about Christians, the demons have invented them that the disciples of the divine Logos might be done to death. Oh that men will understand at last where truth is to be found!"

For the time being it was all wasted labour and the law continued its unjust chastisement of the Christians. Feeble, in many respects, as the apology we have studied may appear in our eyes, it was inspired by deep human feeling and spoke the language of reason in all sincerity. The judge—it was still Urbicus—who sentenced Justin about 165 sent an upright man, who was no fanatic, to his death. In the reign of Marcus Aurelius, other apologists, Melito of Sardis, Apollinarus of Hieropolis, Miltiades, Athenagoras, produced writings in the same sense and equally barren of immediate results. But these books were the means which turned the attention of the public to Christian literature. If the apologies cannot precisely be said to have established and propagated the faith, they began to compel adversaries to take it seriously, and some of these adversaries responded otherwise than by denunciation and sentence of death.

Celsus

The True Discourse which Celsus published against the Christians towards the end of the reign of Marcus Aurelius, perhaps in 178, contained no violent denunciation and had no resemblance to a pogrom. The attitude of Celsus is still that of one who considers Christianity a ridiculous superstition, but he knew enough about Christians to prefer their conversion to their annihilation. Here is no new edition of popular calumny, but rather appreciation of the Gospel morality. He expresses satisfaction at finding the doctrine of the Logos among the Christians; is acquainted with the sacred books which Jews and Christians have in common as well as with the books specifically Christian, the Gospels in the first place, and with other writings both of orthodox Christianity and of the gnostic sects; makes correct distinctions between these sects and the Great Church, although, from his point of view, all the forms of Christianity fall under a common reprobation.

It may be said that in this book Celsus takes a direction contrary to that of the order of proof planned by Justin, with its point of departure in Jewish prophecy. He starts off with what is, virtually, a refutation of Christianity by a Jew; that is to say, he gathers together all the objections which Jews bring against the foundation of Christian faith, namely, the Messiahship of Jesus; then, having thus deprived Christianity of its historic-theological base, he lumps the two religions together and refutes them as one, arguing, against the apologists of Judaism and Christianity alike, that the ideas of Greek religious philosophy are of superior value and greater antiquity compared with those either of Jews or Christians—a thesis not less disputable, in certain respects, than that of the Christian apologists.

Celsus applies severe criticism to the Gospel legend, especially to all that concerns the resurrection of the Christ, proving that the whole legend has been repeatedly worked over, in one Gospel after the other, in order to guard against objections which it could not overthrow. Finally, he appeals to Christians to abandon their uncompromising attitude, to accept the common religion and not to create schism in the State nor weaken it by division.[30] In the main Celsus is willing to let Christianity live, on condition of subordinating itself, in common with the ancient Eastern cults, to the imperial religion of Rome and Augustus, and of tolerating the other cults as legitimate forms of worship. Philosophically and politically, nothing seemed to him more natural, logical and necessary. But the real force of Christianity, which aimed at a goal beyond the Roman Empire, lay in its refusal to compromise. That refusal it could not abandon without being false to itself and compromising its future.

There are no signs that the writing of Celsus made any deeper impression on the Christian leaders than the apologies of Justin and the others made on the leaders either of imperial policy or of Greek thought. Christian writers contemporary with Celsus make no mention of him. By a chance encounter in the year 246 Origen came into possession of *The True Discourse* whose existence had hitherto been unknown to him; nor did he even know who Celsus was. Only through Origen's conscientious refutation of the book has it come to the knowledge of the Christian world and been preserved there. Thus did the apologists vainly attempt the instruction of the persecutors; thus did Celsus vainly attempt the enlightenment of the persecuted.

4. LATER PERSECUTION

Persecution continued. What admirers of Marcus Aurelius can help deploring that, during his reign, in the year 177, the city of Lyons was the scene of martyrdoms comparable in horror to those witnessed by Rome in 64 under Nero?[31] At the time of the Lyons martyrdoms there was a Christian congregation there and another at Vienne, both still small in number and of recent formation; their founders and a part of their converts perished in the persecution we are about to describe. Some members of the Lyons group were of Asiatic or Phrygian origin, but many were natives of the country. An old man of ninety, Pothinus, ruled the church as bishop and was assisted by the priest Irenaeus, who came from Asia.[32]

As often happened at this time it was popular passion that forced the Roman authorities to take action. The Christians were regarded with no friendly eyes by the pagan populace whose imaginations had been excited by the strange tales in circulation about what went on at the Christian meetings. In the absence of the provincial legate a large number of believers were laid hold of by a mob and, after brief interrogation by the tribune of the cohort and the town magistrates, were remanded to prison to await trial. On the return of the legate the trial began. At the outset a notable of the place, Vettius Epagathus, having announced his intention to defend the accused, was himself at once arrested as a Christian on his own confession. Various incidents marked the course of the trial and there were ten apostasies.[33] New arrests took place both at Lyons and Vienne. Some pagan slaves of Christian masters were seized and these slaves, in their terror and under prompting by the soldiers, "lyingly imputed to the Christians banquets of Thyestes, incest of Oedipus and all the things which are not to be spoken of, nor thought of, nor believed to be ever possible among human beings." This evidence created a bad impression even on people who, being related to the accused, had shown themselves less hot against them.

This made the legate and the soldiers all the more determined to get confessions under torture. Sanctus "the deacon" of Vienne, Maturus, a neophyte, Attalus of Pergamus and the young slave, Blandina, showed unshakable courage. Blandina especially astonished and exhausted the torturers, who, all day long, took their turns at her. They were amazed at the obstinate hold that life kept in that broken body. Still less could they understand the mysterious relief the sufferer found in the words she would repeat whenever they urged her to confess—"I am a Christian girl and we do nothing bad." Sanctus also was put to repeated and atrocious torture but never a word could they get out of him, save these two in latin: *"Christianus sum."* Condemned to be thrown to the beasts, the four confessors were despatched to the amphitheatre. The first to succumb were Maturus and Sanctus, after they had been scourged, dragged along by the beasts and forced on to an iron chair made red-hot. Blandina, chained to a post and offering prayers, seemed to the brethren "as one clothed with the Christ"; the beasts would not touch her. Yells from the frenzied crowd demanded the punishment of Attalus, and he had already been dragged round the amphitheatre when the legate learned that he was a Roman citizen. Thereupon Blandina and Attalus were sent back to prison. The legate, for his part, thought it best to consult the emperor. Perhaps he was disturbed by the turn the affair had taken; perhaps the evidence of the slaves against the Christians made him unwilling to take responsibility for releasing the apostates, whom he was keeping in prison. The case was identical with that which Pliny had referred to Trajan.

By the time Maturus and Sanctus came to suffer Pothinus was dead. Weakened by age and hardly breathing the old man had been carried into court amid the shouts of the infuriated mob. In presence of the judge he showed a bold front. Asked by the legate what kind of being the god of the Christians was, he answered: "If you are worthy of him you will know him." He was taken back to prison, insulted and beaten by the mob and, after lingering two days longer in the jail, breathed his last. Other confessors, younger than he, were chained in a filthy dungeon and died before receiving the final punishment in store for them. But, during the days in which the local authorities were waiting for the emperor's answer, the conscience of those who had apostasized began to trouble them. These unhappy wretches who, notwithstanding their recantation, had been kept in prison under suspicion of having previously committed the foul homicide and impurity commonly attributed to Christians, perceived that they had become objects of contempt to the pagans and of pity to their more courageous brethren. Touched by the sincere compassion of these latter, many of the apostates felt ashamed of themselves and made up their minds to withdraw their recantations.

Such was the posture of affairs when at last the answer came from the man whom modern historians are fond of calling the saint-emperor. Moved either by political considerations, or by the knowledge of the little truth there was in the tales about the crimes of the Christians, in whom he finds little to reproach beyond their obstinacy, Marcus Aurelius repeats the order formerly given by Trajan to Pliny; the renegades are to be set free; those who persist in the faith are to be put to death.

It was the time of year when deputations from the cities of Gaul were pouring into Lyons for the yearly fêtes held at the altar of Rome and Augustus; the time also of the games in the amphitheatre, and here was a supply of Christians ready for the wild beasts. The legate accordingly lost no time in rounding off the judicial business that remained to be done: all the confessors who were Roman citizens were sentenced to decapitation. There remained the apostates, whose case was not tried with that of the confessors, no doubt because sentences of release would not be pronounced in public. Those who had recovered the courage of their faith were immediately added to the group awaiting execution. None was released, says the letter which tells this dramatic story, save "the sons of perdition."[34]

During the public interrogation of the Christians there was among the audience in the court room a certain physician named Alexander, Phrygian by origin, but some years resident in Gaul, who kept encouraging the accused to be firm by making signs to that effect. The crowd, seeing what he was after, called out that it was he who was making the renegades renew their confession of the Christ, as some of them were doing. Questioned by the legate, Alexander declared himself a Christian and was sentenced to death on the spot. The very next day he made his appearance before the public in the amphitheatre along with Attalus, whose status as a Roman citizen the legate, anxious to conciliate the mob, had chosen to forget. A variety of tortures were inflicted on the two: Alexander, his mind concentrated on God, died without saying a word: Attalus, roasting on the red-hot chair, called out to the crowd as it yelled with delight on sniffing the odour of the grilling flesh, "Here is a man being cooked for the table; you seem to be fond of that diet. But we people are not cannibals, we leave that to you, nor do we harm to any man." Blandina was kept back for the last day of the show, and with her a boy of fifteen named Ponticus. The crowd present that day was debased enough below the human level to take a furious delight in the sufferings of these two children. They were heroic; Blandina, like an elder sister, speaking words of encouragement to Ponticus in the midst of their common torment. Ponticus was the first to expire. As to Blandina, the talk was that nothing could kill her. But at last, after the scourge, the wild beasts, the fiery chair had been tried in vain, they tied her up in a mat and flung her before a bull which tossed her about from side to side until, after a long time, she was dead.

213

As though the fury of man were more insatiate than the hunger of wild beasts, the mangled remains they left undevoured were denied to the survivors who would have buried them. The bodies of those who had died in prison were thrown, under supervision, to the dogs; watch was also kept over the debris of those who had perished in the amphitheatre; after six days' exposure to the public it was all raked together and burnt, that nothing might be left save the ashes. Then the ashes were thrown, amid laughter, into the Rhone, which was near-by, so that nothing at all might remain. "Now let them rise from the dead" was the comment of those who arranged this beautiful programme, and the merry jest of those who carried it out.

Here is a unique page, not, alas, in the history of the first persecutions, but in the history books, in the documentation which has preserved for us the record of them. Raise Marcus Aurelius to what height of greatness you will, there is a page in Eusebius' history that cries shame on the memory of him, illustrious as his name may otherwise be. For reasons of State Marcus Aurelius gave his sanction to the jurisprudence announced in the rescript of Trajan, sanctioned by him for the same reason.

This philosopher-king, accounted the wisest of the wise and the most humane of his time, could he not see the facts as Pliny had seen them sixty years earlier; could he not suspect that in Christianity also there was "something human" and forbid these odious and futile massacres? A girl and a boy triumphantly accuse him before the bar of posterity; their names are Blandina and Ponticus. Faced by the accusation of these innocent victims of his brutal legislation the lofty reason of the philosopher-king is overthrown and put to silence. That lofty reason of his was shortsighted; it was narrow in outlook; the prisoner of a fixed idea called common sense by the "enlightened" of those days.

Like Trajan, Hadrian and Antoninus, the mind of Marcus Aurelius was fettered to the notion of Christianity as a pestilence and a scourge, a sect of absurd but dangerous rebels, while yet he was well aware that Christians were generally innocent of the infamies charged against them by the ignorant multitude. These emperors were men of high intelligence and moderation; but they never paused to question the prejudice and bigotry on which the current notion of Christianity was founded. All they could see, and they thought it clear enough, was the contradiction offered by the new religion to the principles on which the Roman empire was, or seemed to be, established. But were these principles incapable of improvement and expansion? Had not Christianity now become a very different thing from what it was in the time of Nero, before the explosion of the Jewish war more than a hundred years before? Had not the attitude of Christians towards imperial authority changed, since the end of the first century, to an attitude of respect? Whence came the ever increasing success of the new religion? Came it not largely from the insufficiency of the others for human need? And if Christianity could draw to itself such a multitude of the disinherited, so many troubled souls, was it not because the disinherited were far too numerous in Roman society, and because the current doctrines of philosophy and official religion were too unconvincing or too hard-hearted, or too impoverished on the moral side?

It is true that the Antonines did not display towards the Christians a wanton cruelty like that of Nero, nor were they deliberate and systematic persecutors like Decius and Diocletian, though system of a kind they certainly had, with room in it for some outstanding atrocities. But this abatement was not due to any feeling for justice or to half-hearted goodwill towards Christianity. As Duchesne remarks: "it followed naturally from the contemptuous indifference of the authorities to these conflicts of sect and doctrine, their contempt arising perhaps from excessive confidence in the resisting power of philosophy and in the tendency of sects to spend their power for mischief one on another." These emperors, indeed, had good reason to count on the force of the many cults, old and new, which existed in self-ordained subordination to the imperial religion; they counted also, and knew they could count, on the force of good sense, that indefinable divinity of which philosophers are prone to consider themselves the high priests. They never asked themselves whether the no-compromise attitude in which the Christians differed from the other sects might not itself be a force—the force of a deep-seated consciousness of higher truth and a more excellent morality. In reality it was precisely that consciousness to which the tireless and charitable labours of the Christian apostolate owed their life and vigour, and which made the

215

Christian religion so rapidly contagious that it burst the dikes built against it by the "good-sense" of philosophers.

But a new "good-sense" more attractive than learned and lordly reason had been brought into being—the common sense of Christian equality; and with it came a type of virtue less harsh than the Stoic—the practical brotherhood of the Gospel. The wrangling of sects did not prevent the Christian communities inside the pale of the Church from forming compact bodies held together in close solidarity. The fact of that consciousness was apparent whenever the Christians confronted their judges in court; it was seen on every eager face among the brethren as they pressed round the prisoners at the risk of their own lives. When all was over the Christians were still there to beg for the ashes of the martyrs and give them honourable burial. Their beneficence was generous, and it was organized. Already the great congregations, like that of Rome, had their treasure chests, regularly and abundantly replenished, for ministering to the needs of the poor. After Justin has described the eucharistic service, the mystical banquet of the brethren, centre of their religious life and hearthfire of their mutual love, he goes on to say: "Those who have the means and are men of goodwill give freely, each giving as he pleased, and the collection is then laid before the president"—the bishop who presided at meetings—"who distributes it among orphans and widows, the sick and the poor from any cause, the prisoners, and travellers on their journeys"—the Christians of other congregations always received as brethren—"in short, he is the helper of every one who is in need" (1 *Apology*, 67). Under these conditions the rapid growth of the bishop's person to great consideration is easily understood. Nor need we wonder that the Friendly Society over which he presided recruited new members every day.

It remains to add that the Christianity of Justin, of Melito, or of Irenaeus, even when judged by intellect and reason, made no mean showing. In what was it inferior to the philosophy of a Plutarch, of a Celsus—nay, of Marcus Aurelius himself? Was it indeed so very different in the matter of reasonable ideas and reasoned ideology? Supreme Being, Ruling Providence, subordinate spirits, justice at the summit and sure of final vindication, and the primacy of the moral consciousness over all forms of knowledge—were not all these analogously conceived by both sides, but with more precision in Christianity and with a measure of practical achievement in daily conduct, in family life and social relationships, peculiar to itself? The good Justin was not in error when he presented Christianity as a great philosophy—a philosophy whose speech in Justin's time was the lisp of an infant, but an infant full of life and vigour and with the future in its grasp.

At the death of Marcus Aurelius the triumph of Christianity, though not due to burst upon the world till a century and a half later, was already assured, but unforeseen by the pagan world. The Christians foresaw it in faith, and were quick to note the signs of its coming as events took their course in the contemporary world. As the third century unfolded Roman paganism more and more came to resemble a vast hoarding behind which the Christian religion was gradually being built up. And so in our day it may be that Christianity in turn has become a façade behind which men are building the religion of humanity. The tree which Constantine and his Christian successors let fall, or cut down, was no longer a living thing. Thus it came to pass that Christianity, with persecution at an end, soon became master of the house. Would that it had never forgotten the lesson, taught by its own first experience, of the fundamental iniquity and ultimate futility of persecuting men for the offence of religious belief.

Chapter VII

BIRTH OF THE CHRISTIAN MYSTERY
AND OF ITS RITES

IN the preceding chapters we have seen with what rapidity the Gospel was propagated and have followed the course of a persecution that was powerless to stifle it. Behind all that, we have caught glimpses, but glimpses only, of a group life, an intense life, that gathered power in the silence and, as it were, underground, until it shook the foundations of the empire. We have already seen enough to make it clear that this life was a profound religion, and we know that the essence of it was the worship of the Lord Jesus Christ, of him who died and rose again, prince of the age to come. Our next task must be to study this worship, this cult, from the inner side and to see how it expressed its character in practice. In this chapter we shall have before us a Mystery of Salvation, figuratively presented in worship, and to some extent foreshadowed in the mystery of the Church, that strange Society of Friends which proved itself stronger than Rome and outlasted her empire. Then, in the chapter following this, we shall watch the Mystery taking form and crystallizing in a system of doctrines.

1. THE MYSTERY IN EMBRYO

The Book of Acts, in an idealized picture which has become conventional, shows us the first believers in Jesus gravitating towards the temple and publicly frequenting it every day, like other Jews, but privately breaking bread together in their own houses (ii, 42, 46). They spoke of Jesus risen from the dead and about to come again; they healed the sick in his name; they even baptized, already perhaps in the name of their Christ, those who rallied to the hope of his coming (iv, 33; v, 42). Thus, at the very beginning of the Christian religion there existed a mystical faith in Christ Jesus, a mystical bond uniting the faithful, with a ritual of membership and communion in which their unity was expressed and fortified. Before it overflowed into the pagan world, before it was officially and relentlessly repudiated by Judaism, the Jesus-sect had within it the seed of a faith and worship which soon would open the way for its growth into an independent religion.

From the very first, then, it had a faith all its own: the Master, Jesus the Nazorean, active no more on earth, was risen from the dead; he had become the Christ now at the right hand of God and ready to return with the Kingdom which he had declared would come immediately. The ardour of this faith, first kindled by Jesus himself, grew hotter in proportion as he himself became its object and its warrant, as his exaltation to heaven and glory seemed to make his coming in power to establish the Kingdom, if one may dare to say it, a thing easy to accomplish. In the atmosphere thus created by faith were born the uncriticized visions and hopes which fanned the enthusiasm of the preachers into a fire that nothing could put out.

Thus it came to pass that Jewish hopes for a new and better world, hitherto varied in form and wavering in outline, were crystallized, centralized and systematized round a personal figure, but henceforth a transcendent figure above the danger of the shipwrecks which had inevitably overtaken the wild ventures of violent Messianism. Judas the Galilean, Theudas and the Egyptian mentioned by Josephus and the Book of Acts, the fanatics of the great revolt and Barkochba left no religious sects behind them to continue their work after they had met their end. But John the Baptist, Simon Magus and Jesus were all the founders of sects which lasted on, perpetuating and exalting the founder's memory after each had suffered a violent death, which, however, in no way disconcerted his followers, but served rather to quicken their faith. A success all its own awaited Christianity. It sprang, at bottom, from the faith and vigour of the human element in the heart of that religion. Viewed from the outside, success came to it from the concatenation of causes which, to all appearance, had brought it into being: first, the tragic death of Jesus and his sudden removal from the scene had repercussions on the fortunes of his main idea which could not have happened if he had died a natural death after a long captivity; then the forcible dispersion of the hellenist believers had the effect of flinging the Gospel message into the

Mediterranean world; finally came persecution which gave the new sect a wide publicity and glorified it by the sufferings of its martyrs.

But the growth of faith in Jesus was not dependent on favourable external circumstances. Eager to magnify its Object with new dignity it soared to great heights by the sole force of its inner life. Once raised to the heavens, Jesus became immediately the Son of Man presently to come on the clouds. Up to that time it would have been a hard task for the historian to identify the Son of Man with a definable personality. But faith settled the matter: Jesus in heaven was the Son of Man making ready to come again. That the term could be applied to Jesus is proved by the fact that the application was realized; and it is not without analogies. The notion of "the Man" was easy to assimilate; a passage of the Book of Enoch applies it to Enoch himself (lxxi, 14). The application to Jesus was made early and is found fully developed in the Jewish-Christian tradition of the apocryphal Clementines. It exalted Jesus in two ways: on the one hand it made him transcendent and pre-existent; on the other it gave to his death an intelligible place in his appearance as a man on earth, of which the chief object was to prepare the way for his Great Coming as the Christ. In the Synoptic Gospels, however, the idea of the Great Coming dominates the whole presentation. There Jesus is not so much the Heavenly Man incarnate for the salvation of mortals as the Christ who is to die that he may come again in his glory. Such was the Christ of the first believers. He it was who had announced the coming Kingdom to the poor, promised pardon to repentant sinners and given his bond that the powers of God would soon be displayed on the side of the righteous. Conqueror of death, and already ruling in the heavenly places, he was about to come in his glory; "He who is Coming and we look for no other" (Matthew xi, 3) was their byword and formula in greeting the brethren. The oldest symbol of the Christian faith seems to be enshrined in the Aramean *Maranatha*—"The Lord cometh," or "Come, Lord."[1]

They spoke of him as "the Lord"[2] as an alternative to "the Son of Man." The long continued employment of the *Maranatha* formula, even in the liturgies of the Greek-speaking Christians,[3] proves the Jewish-Christian origin of "Lord" as a title applied to the Christ. In its religious and ritual sense the use of the title was evidently applied to Jesus only as risen from the dead; but it was given him immediately when the belief arose that, after dying on earth as Jesus, he had risen to heaven as the Christ. The application of the term to Jesus was unpremeditated and entirely natural but it was big with consequences as no other title could have been. The title of "Lord" had a meaning for worship, a cult meaning, not carried, at least with the same force, by the theological title "Son of Man." To Christians speaking Greek, "Lord" would unquestionably be a divine name or, more strictly, it was a name that tended to deify the figure to whom it was applied; on the one hand it placed Jesus among the divinities worshipped in the mystery cults who were familiar to pagans as mediators of salvation, subordinate to the Supreme Being; on the other hand the hellenic Christians who read the Old Testament in the Greek version found there a multitude of texts when the word "Lord" is the substitute for Jahveh,[4] the unspeakable name of God Himself and, applying these to Jesus, inevitably raised him to the level of Deity.

The first of these results—the coupling of Jesus with the mystery gods—is clearly brought out as the following passage (1 Corinthians viii, 5–6):

> For if there be many named gods,
>   be they in heaven, be they on earth,
> And as there is many a god
>   so there is many a lord,
> For us there is no God but one, the Father,
>   of whom are all things, and we for him.
> For us there is no Lord but one, Jesus Christ,
>   by whom are all things and we by him.

The paganism of that time was familiar with many lords and divine heroes and had placed Caesar among them in the first rank, even with the added attribute of Saviour. In the text cited above Jesus is not God absolutely, nor even one among many gods: he is a divine *lord*.[5] As "Lord" he is at once below the Supreme Deity and above all other created beings, possessing the maximum of godhead compatible with his nature as created, the fullness of the godhead belonging only to the uncreated Supreme.

Meditation on biblical texts led Christian thought towards the same result. Many a speculation of that early age sprang from meditation on a verse in the hundred-and-tenth Psalm:

> The Lord (Jahveh) said to my Lord (master)
> "Sit thou on my right
> While I make thine enemies
> a footstool under thy feet."

A picture, surely, of Jesus, risen from the dead and now seated by the side of God on his heavenly throne! Occasioned in the same way was the proclamation of Jesus as the Son of God, but in a sense quite other than that of the sonship which every believer could claim.

> The Lord said to me: Thou art my son;
> This day I have begotten thee.[6]

Faith went far in magnifying and exalting Jesus but, however far it might go, he remained very near to his own and in the midst of them. Stephen, as the story relates, saw him standing at the right hand of God, a vision born in the ecstacy of the first martyr; it was his answer to the high priest. But others had seen him before Stephen, or saw him afterwards. Of these visions tradition, as we said before, has retained only a few, and these typical rather than real, presented as proofs of the resurrection. What they really prove is the faith of those who had them, the faith of the first believers in the perpetual presence of their Christ. When they prayed together in their meetings, he was there; when the bread was broken at the fraternal meal which prefigured the Kingdom they waited for, he was invisibly with them at the table. Some said that they had seen him break the bread and bless it, and when others of the company, hoping to see him, saw him not, they still had the impression of his presence and felt that he was with them in spirit. According to Acts the spirit of Jesus never failed to come to the help of Paul and his companions in their difficulties, now leading them away from this plan, now guiding them to that. In very truth Jesus was a guiding genius, a guardian spirit to his own.

Quite early a particular day was consecrated to Jesus, "the Lord's Day." This was the first day of the week honoured among pagans as the day of the Sun. The day of the Sun was not consecrated to Jesus because the Christ rose on that day, but because it was the fitting day for his resurrection. In the beginning nobody knew either the day or the hour of the resurrection, for the sufficient reason that the resurrection was a matter of faith which nobody could witness as a sensible event and assign to a definite time and place. Long before the story was told of the tomb found empty on the Sunday, day but one after the passion, believers believed and preachers preached that Jesus, risen from the dead, was alive for ever with God. In a certain sense and measure the Gospel stories of the resurrection are the explanatory myth of the Christian Sunday. This at least is what the arrangement of the elements makes them: first, in all the Gospels, the discovery of the empty tomb on Sunday; then in the third and fourth, the report on Sunday of the apparitions. Sunday was also the usual day for the Christian Supper, which explains why some of the apparitions are both Sunday myths and Supper myths, jointly symbolizing the belief that the Christ was risen to heaven and yet present with his own at their common meal; for the myth of the risen Christ and the myth of the present Christ were, at bottom, one and the same. But why was the first day of the week chosen as the Lord's Day, birthday of the Christ in glory? This question remains to be answered.

We remark in the first place that the choice of a particular day could not be avoided. In the new communities, as in the first community at Jerusalem, the bond of union lay in the common meal of the brethren. It was of course impossible to maintain unbroken companionship at table; on the other hand the common meal would fail of its object unless it were held at fairly short intervals. The pattern of the week, established in Jewish custom and becoming generally adopted under the influence of the oriental cults, was bound to be followed as a matter of course needing no reflection. Once a week, then; but on which day of the week? Clearly the first day was indicated as the day most fitting for the Christians to come together, for the meal to be held in memory of Jesus and in celebration of his glory, and this, not because it followed the Jewish Sabbath or the least intention existed to link the two together, but quite simply because it was the first of the seven, the Chief Day, the day of the Sun, honoured as such, and not by pagans only. And was there not an analogy perceptible to all, and spontaneously accepted by all, between the risen Christ in his glory, and the sun in heaven and the solar gods abounding throughout the East? Need it be added that the Essenes worshipped the rising sun and that Sunday would be to them also the most honourable of the seven? Little wonder if this analogy instantly suggested itself to pagan converts as well as to Jewish converts living in pagan countries, even if they had never heard of it in Palestine.

The Christ in his glory was thought of as a Being of Light; light was the substance of his being. We need to search no further than the pages of the New Testament for proof that the object of the earliest Christian worship and prayer—the dying Stephen renders back his soul to Jesus—the Lord, the King on high invested by God with a part of his power, clothed in divine majesty and soon to come in his glory to found the Reign of God on earth—for proof that this luminous Being belonged from the first, his Jewish traits notwithstanding, to the family of the celestial gods, especially to that of the solar deities. What likeness do we see in the Christ of the Apocalypse, riding on his white horse, with his name of mystery, his eyes of flame, the sword coming out of his mouth, his flashing diadems and mantle red with blood?[7] We see the likeness of a solar deity, of Mithra as he is depicted on horseback in bas-reliefs. In that connexion a long story might be told of the Christ of the Apocalypse with his seven Churches, his seven attendant stars, his seven Spirits— he who is the Holy, he who is the True. It is the figure of an astral divinity, presiding over the heavenly spheres, like Mithra, like Attis and many another. These affinities are the natural consequence of faith's effort to see in Christ the Lord of the universe; they were felt in that effort and created by it. And so it came to pass that Jesus, prophet of the Kingdom, first becomes Messiah and rises from that to Lord of the Universe and Master of humanity. The communication to Jesus of attributes proper to the solar deities was all the easier inasmuch as they were gods of justice, gods of truth by the very fact that they were gods of light; all the easier because Jesus, identified with his own ideal of eternal justice and truth, was drawn into their company by the moral values represented as divine in their character. To Christians of the first age Jesus was the sun of justice and salvation newly risen on earth and now reigning in heaven: "the day-spring from on high which has visited us."

So the day of the Sun became the Day of the Lord, and Sunday the day of the risen Christ. How easy it was, after that, to make Sunday the day on which he rose. Once adopted as the Christian Holy Day, the justification of the usage would be complete when the Christian believed that on that day, and none other of the seven, his Lord rose from the dead. It was bound to come to that as soon as the Christians had to justify their observance of Sunday, and the more inevitably perhaps, when, under pressure of a later demand for proofs that Jesus really rose from death, the attempt was made to construct a co-ordinated story of the apparitions under a scheme of time and place. Thus, when the editor of the second Gospel would prove the resurrection by revealing the circumstances of the burial with the clinching evidence of the empty tomb, he inevitably places the discovery on the morning of the day of the sun, a little after its rising (xvi, 2). Having thus formed the picture in his imagination, belief that matters happened thus was bound to follow. The editor of the third Gospel, governed by a preconceived perspective, dates all the apparitions on the Sunday of the resurrection and places them all in Jerusalem (xxiv). The editor of the fourth carries system yet further: he notes two apparitions of the Christ to the disciples gathered in the room of the Supper with the closed doors customary at the ritual meal of the Christian communities; both apparitions take place on a Sunday, the first on the Sunday of the resurrection, the second on the Sunday following (xx, 19–29). These doubtless are intended to be reckoned the first two Sundays of the Church, made holy by visible manifestations of the Christ and indicating that all Sundays thereafter are consecrated by his invisible presence. Finally, the seer of the Apocalypse has his vision on a Sunday (i, 10).

Simultaneously with these developments, the great festival of Christian salvation, the festival of Easter, yielded to the attraction of Sunday as the day for its celebration. At the beginning this festival was held, as was natural enough, on the same day as the Jewish Passover which might fall on any day of the week, and with no difference except that it now commemorated the Christian's salvation, won for him by the death of Christ, the true pascal lamb, as the fourth Gospel teaches. The so-called quartodeciman usage, maintained by the congregations in Asia at the end of the second century and condemned by Pope Victor, was the primitive usage of all the Christian congregations and is indeed presupposed by the Gospel tradition. But the glory of the Sun's day proved irresistible, and this attraction, coupled with the growth of reaction against purely Jewish observances, soon shifted the Christian Passover to the Sunday following the Jewish celebration. Even the early Gospel of the Hebrews regards as canonical the observance of the Jewish Christians who celebrated Easter on Sunday morning after a fast lasting from the evening of Friday.[8] We are told of one great Sunday in the year when the final achievement of salvation was celebrated in the glory of the Christ rising from death to life. Thus the stories of the resurrection became simultaneously the myth of the institution of the Christian Easter and the myth of the Christian Sunday.

Let the apologist Justin bear witness. "On the day of the sun all our people come together for religious exercise, because that is the first of days, when God, having transformed darkness and matter, created the world,"—he means the spring equinox, the birthday of the world being that on which God made the light[9]—"and because, on that same day, Jesus Christ our Saviour rose from the dead. For they crucified him on the evening of Saturday, and on the morrow of Saturday, that is on the day of the Sun, he appeared to his apostles and to his disciples and gave them the teaching which we have just submitted to your judgment."[10] Here, then, is clear evidence that in Justin's time, and in the Christian circle for which he speaks, Sunday and, among them all, the great Sunday of the Passover,[11] was chosen for the joint commemoration of the resurrection of Christ, the creation of light and of the world, and the revelation of saving truth made by the Christ to his apostles. In all senses, it was the Festival of Light. In keeping with this, Christians adopted quite early, if not from the very beginning, the custom of turning to the East when engaged in prayer.[12] That this custom, explained as homage to the Christ as he rose to heaven, was borrowed from the Eastern solar cults admits of no doubt.

2. BAPTISM

In texts relatively old, baptism is presented as an "illumination" (φωτισμός) of which Jesus, needless to say, is the sun.[13] A baptismal hymn quoted in the Epistle to the Ephesians (v, 14), and more completely by Clement of Alexandria (*Protreptikos*, viii, 84), contained the following apostrophe:

> Awake, thou sleeper,
>> rise up from among the dead,
> And he who is Christ the Lord shall enlighten thee,
>> the sun of the resurrection
> Begotten before the dayspring
>> giving life by his beams.

Such were the hymns sung round candidates for initiation into the Christian mystery, but not in the earliest days of Christian religion. We have already seen how the little group of Galilean believers who, on returning to Jerusalem after the death of Jesus, announced that he was risen from the dead and coming with his kingdom—how this group baptized its recruits, as John the Baptist had done, and Jesus himself had probably done. This baptism was, before it became anything else, an act of purification, a cleansing of the whole body by immersion in water and, at the same time, a symbol of repentance, of a life changed in readiness for the Great Event expected from hour to hour. But, whether with or without first intention, it presently became the rite of admission to membership in the society of believers in Jesus and of union with Jesus himself, since it implied a profession of faith in him as the coming Messiah and as already glorified. In this way it created a kind of mystic bond between the believers and the Christ, although there was probably no thought as yet of assimilating the two, of identifying the one with the other, after the manner of the initiation rites of the pagan mystery religions which made the initiate one with his god. Its effect was that the believer belonged to Christ thenceforward and was in some way linked to him; he was baptized "in his name" and, as the name was being invoked, received the sign of Jesus-Messiah that he might be recognized as one of his own on the Day of Judgment (Acts ii, 38–41; x, 48).

Whether to disguise the fact that the rite was borrowed by the Christian sect from John's, or to emphasize the difference between the two, or because Christian baptism soon acquired a character all its own, the idea arose that it was essentially different from John's, his being only a symbol, while Christian baptism was a sacrament, a baptism of spirit charged with mystical power.[14] Strange to say, the Book of Acts gives us to understand that there were some Christians who had been baptized only in John's way (xviii, 25, 26; xix, 1–7). Apparently the intention of these texts is to represent the rite practised by the Judaizing Christians as no other than John's way of baptizing and inferior to the true baptism of the Christ. The same book, in its myth of Pentecost, has the first group of believers baptized in spirit and made, by the gift of the Spirit, into apostles of the new-born faith. By this the editor would intimate that Christian baptism carries with it a supernatural power, the infusion of a Spirit, that of God or that of Christ, who takes possession of the believer, endows him with the gift of tongues, makes him a prophet and, at times, imparts the power to work miracles.

Such a conception of baptism is what we might expect in the outburst of religious enthusiasm characteristic of the first generations and in keeping with the psycho-physiological disturbances which are frequent accompaniments of these outbursts. Johannite baptism, taken over by the earliest Christians, still closely akin to the legal washings of Judaism, was retained in its primitive sobriety by certain groups of Christians inclining the Jewish way;[15] but to the hellenizing groups, which formed the majority, it seemed a feeble rite that effected nothing and as powerless as the legal purifications were supposed, however wrongly, to have been deemed. The water in the urns at Cana, said to have been turned into wine by Jesus, tells the same tale.

The last step was to provide Christian baptism with a suitable institution-myth. For this purpose the best that could be invented was to fix the institution of spiritual baptism on the occasion of the water-baptism conferred by John on Jesus. The opening of the heavens takes place at the very moment when Jesus, coming out of the water, leaves water behind him to receive the fullness of the Spirit and be consecrated Son of God.[16] This was intended to show that Jesus was there and then revealed as the firstborn of God, the direct offspring of the Spirit, and that, like him, the faithful underwent a mystical immersion in spirit which made them also the sons of God. Surely a naïve way of revealing the original identity of Christian baptism with John's by the very means taken to mark an essential difference between the two. Later on it was deemed advisable to attribute a command to confer baptism on all new believers to Jesus himself after he was risen from the dead (Matthew xxviii, 19; Mark xvi, 16).[17]

3. The Holy Supper

As baptism was not instituted by Jesus,[18] no more, in strictness of speech, was the Holy Supper. The daily meals of the first Christian groups in Jerusalem, necessarily taken in common under the conditions in which they found themselves, quickly took on a highly distinctive mystical character. The common daily meal was already established in Jewish custom as a religious function. If there is one thing certain in the history of the birth of the Christian rites it is that the point of departure for the development of the Eucharist, "the exercise of thanksgiving," the holy supper, characteristic of the Christian religion, is to be found in the prayers, recited in common, which accompanied the meals of the Jews, in the "grace said" to God for his bountiful gift of daily food, chiefly bread and wine: "blessed be He who caused the earth to bring forth bread" and "blessed be God who created the fruit of the vine." These are the prayers clearly referred to in the mystical stories of the multiplication of loaves (Mark vi, 41; viii, 6) and of the institution of the Supper. The former stories are in themselves myths of the institution of the Christian rite, but with this difference from the latter, that the stories of the multiplied loaves refer to a communion without wine, the "breaking of bread" of which Acts also speaks (ii, 42, 46), while the stories which relate the actual institution with bread and cup, with the attached symbolism of body and blood, refer to the mystical Supper commemorative of Jesus' death and the medium of communion with the Christ who died and rose again.

It is, moreover, clear that the Supper was not, in its first stage, a sacrament in which the death of the Christ, his crucified body and his blood, were mystically represented. "The breaking of bread," the name used in Acts to designate the Supper, shows clearly enough that no special significance was at first attached to the food of which the meal consisted. The cup of wine was not in any sense a necessary part of it, and all the indications are to the effect that it was often dispensed with (later on we shall produce evidence that it was often absent even after the Supper became figuratively the death of the Christ). It is therefore with this primitive form of the Supper, in which the breaking of bread for the common meal was the essential and characteristic feature, that we must connect the story of the multiplied loaves.[19] We have already seen how the chief apparition stories are also myths of the institution of the Supper, myths, we might say, of the Risen Christ's co-presence at table, his commensality, with his disciples and believers. The disciples at Emmaus recognize him "in the breaking of bread." In the supplement to John the Risen Christ offers bread and fish to the disciples, as in the multiplication of the loaves (xxi, 13). Here the fish is itself symbolic. The meaning lies in the symbol of eating together; the material of the meal is of secondary importance.

These myths reveal the original meaning of the Supper. In the first stage the only symbolism the meaning required was that implied by common participation in the same food eaten together under the belief that the Christ-to-come was invisibly present. We can see from the *Didache* (ix, 2) how thanksgiving for the spiritual gift of salvation, and for the hope of it, presently found its way into the thanks given for the food of the body, and how the former was substituted for the latter. Here is the "Eucharist," the formula of thanksgiving, to be pronounced before the holy meal began, and first of all over the wine cup:

> We give thee thanks, O our Father,
>   for the holy vine of thy servant David,
>   which thou hast made known to us by thy servant Jesus.
> To thee be glory for ever and ever (*Didache*, ix, 2).

"The holy vine of David" is clearly the vine in Psalm lxxx, here taken mystically for the Spiritual Church, the vine of

Salvation. Follows the "Eucharist" over the broken bread (*Didache*, ix, 3, 4):

> We give thee thanks, O our Father,
> > for life and knowledge[20]
> > > which thou hast made known to us by thy servant Jesus.
> To thee be glory for ever and ever.
> As this bread was scattered on the mountains,
> > then, gathered in, became one,
> Thus may thy Church be gathered in
> > from the ends of the earth in thy Kingdom.
> For thine are glory and power,
> > by Jesus Christ, for ever and ever (ix, 3–4).

The couplet on the vine and the first couplet on the bread are counterparts respectively to the two Jewish prayers quoted above. But the gift of knowledge (gnosis) and of eternal life replace the gifts of food for the body. Moreover the Supper has now become a meal restricted to initiates in which those only may take part who have been baptized "in the name of the Lord," and it is "the holy thing which the Lord commanded not to be given to dogs" (*Didache*, ix, 5). Here then we find not only a mystical meaning but a mystical power attached to the elements, the bread and wine, of the holy spirit.

Other prayers are indicated for use at the end of the meal, which, be it noted, still has the character of an ordinary meal regarded as now finished (*Didache*, x, 1–5):

> When you have eaten enough, this shall be your thanksgiving:
> > We thank thee, Holy Father,
> > > for thy Holy name
> > > > which thou has caused to dwell in our hearts,
> > And for knowledge, faith and immortality
> > > which thou hast made known to us by thy servant Jesus.
> > To thee be glory for ever and ever!
> > Thou, Master almighty,
> > > Thou hast created all things to the honour of thy name.
> > Food and drink hast thou given for the making glad of man
> > > for which they render thee thanks;
> > But thou hast also gladdened us with food and drink of the
> > > > spirit and of eternal life
> > > by Jesus thy servant.
> > > > To thee glory for ever and ever!

Remember thou thy Church
 to deliver it from all evil
  and make it perfect in thy love;
Gather it from the four winds, make it holy
 in thy Kingdom which thou hast prepared,
For thine are glory and power for ever and ever

           (*Didache*, x, 1–5).

In this chant it would seem that natural food and drink are recalled as a reminder that Christians have higher matters for thanksgiving than that for which the Jews offered theirs. Equal prominence is given to spiritual gifts and to the Church, but with the Great Event as the background of both. For there follows immediately a mystical dialogue of the highest interest between the president and the rest of the company:

Come thou Gracious One and let the world pass away!
 Hosanna to the God of David
  Whoso is holy, let him come;
  Whoso is not, let him repent!
   Maranatha!
   Amen (*Didache*, x, 6).

In this the president announces and prays for the coming of the Gracious One, who is apparently Christ himself, announcement and prayer being uttered together in the mysterious "Maranatha"; at the same time he invites every man to search his conscience, the crowd answering with Hosanna and Amen to him who is to come, nay, who is come already. For the mystical presence of Christ in the midst of the company anticipates the parousia. At this stage the Eucharist is already a mystery; but it is the mystery of the Christian's hopes and of the unity of all believers in Christ the Spirit. Not yet has it become the mystery which continues and communicates his redeeming death; not yet have the bread and the wine become, in mystery, the body and blood of Jesus.

4. Baptism, Bread and Wine taken up into the Mystery

In First Corinthians and in all the Gospels we find the bread and the wine charged with this mystical meaning and power as the body and blood of Jesus;[21] in the Epistle to the Romans baptism has undergone an analogous transformation (vi, 1–11). This we shall consider first.

In all it has to say about the ceremonial of baptism, the *Didache* shows a marked sobriety. The moral part of the book (i–vi) is a body of instruction to be given to catechumens in preparation for receiving the baptismal sacrament. This instruction, which consists of rules of conduct only, may be relatively old, although the collection of Gospel texts which accompany the precepts seems to be an addition later than the precepts themselves. As to the ritual, there is only this simple direction: "After expounding all that"—the moral precepts just mentioned which the candidate promises to follow—"baptize in the name of the Father, Son and Holy Spirit, in running water" (vii, 1). But running water is not indispensable: "if you have no running water, baptize in other water, and, if you cannot obtain cold water, use warm"—the word baptize here understood in its proper sense as total immersion. This is made clear by what follows: "If you have neither cold water nor warm, in quantity sufficient for total immersion—pour what you have three times on the candidate's head in the name of the Father, Son and Holy Spirit." Evidently this pouring out of a little water on the head as a substitute for the immersion of the whole body shows that the water is now symbolic. But a doubt may be permitted as to whether this Trinitarian formula goes back to the beginning of the second century.

Justin appears to be the oldest witness to the Trinitarian formula to whom a date can be assigned. "Those," says he (1 *Apology*, 61), "who are persuaded of what we teach and believe it true undertake"—reminding us of the oath mentioned by Pliny—"and are instructed to pray to God and ask him, after fasting, to pardon their past sins, we praying and fasting with them."—The *Didache* (vii, 4) also enjoins the candidate to fast for one or two days before baptism, the minister of the rite and fellow-believers fasting with him.—"Afterwards the candidates are taken by us to a place where there is water, and are regenerated by the mode of regeneration by which we ourselves were born again; to wit they are then immersed in water in the name of God the Father and Master of all things, and of our Lord Jesus Christ, and of the Holy Spirit." Justin then proceeds to explain the spiritual nature of the new birth. He says that baptism is called "illumination" because the mind of the person baptized is illuminated by the doctrine he has learnt. His comment on the baptismal formula seems to turn it into a kind of symbol: The Son, he says, "is Jesus Christ who was crucified under Pontius Pilate" and the Holy Spirit he "who predicted by the prophets all that is told of Jesus."[22]

Although he never cites the fourth Gospel expressly, and is rarely inspired by it, he seems to have used it for his account of spiritual rebirth. In the discourse to Nicodemus he would read the theory of the sacrament stated thus:

> In truth, in truth, I say to thee
> Except a man be reborn of water and spirit
> he cannot enter the Kingdom of God.

In this theory of rebirth, water appears to be a principle or symbol of life rather than a purifying element. Elsewhere the fourth Gospel lays great stress on the virtue of running water as an element having eternal life and even represents the Christ as being, in his incarnation, the source of this running, life-giving water (iv, 14; vii, 37–39). It must not be forgotten that the fourth Gospel, like the others, was originally a catechism used in connexion with the rites of Christian initiation.

5. Baptism in the Epistle to the Romans

The Epistle to the Romans suggests a mystical symbolism somewhat different from the above, but one which had less influence on the subsequent course of Christian tradition (vi, 3–6):

> All we who were baptized to Christ Jesus
> to his death were we baptized.
> Thus were we buried with him
> by baptism in death
> To the end, that as Christ is raised from the dead by the
> glory of the Father
> we in like manner may walk in newness of life:
> For if we were associated to his death, by imitation,[23]
> we shall also be with him in his resurrection,

Knowing this:
> that our old man was crucified with him
>> that the body of sin might be destroyed.

What does this mean? Evidently that the baptismal immersion is a mystical burial in the water whereby the Christian is made one with Christ dead and buried, the effect being that our sinful flesh is also crucified, done to death and consigned to the grave. But, just as Christ rose glorious from death by the power of God, so the Christian emerges reborn from his baptismal immersion and comes forth from the water as one rising from his grave, mystically, inwardly and morally risen from the dead in readiness for the glory of his resurrection to immortal life. Once baptized he is a new man, dead to sin that he may live henceforth to God. We shall see later how this conception of baptism is connected with a general and balanced system of mystical gnosis in its bearing on the scheme of sin-and-redemption. In contrast to the Johannine theory in which water appears as a principle and symbol of life, it is here to be understood rather as a symbol of death, figuring the tomb of the carnal man from which the spiritual man is to emerge, but without water being the agent of the spirit's action. In this version the baptismal immersion is not a sacrament effecting the regeneration of the sinner but, if we may say so, a sacramental condition of its being effected. We get a somewhat different result, however, if we try to adjust what is said in First Corinthians (xv, 29) about baptism for the dead to the theory just summarized. So adjusted, the sacramental condition is no less indispensable and efficacious in its own way than the sacrament of baptism in the water of eternal life: baptism undergone by proxy on behalf of a person deceased is able to produce the same effect on him as it would if performed on the living man. To insist on so peculiar a feature would here, perhaps, be out of place, though it had importance in its own day. The tradition of the Church does not retain it.

Elsewhere (in 1 Corinthians x, 1–5) a parallel is set up between the Christian Sacraments and the sacraments of the Desert—the baptism of the Israelites by Moses under the cloud and in the sea, and a kind of Eucharist in the heavenly manna and the water struck from the rock. This apparently belongs to another gnosis, probably not less ancient than the former and with closer affinities to the gnosis of the fourth Gospel.

> For I would not have you ignorant,
>   brethren.
> That our fathers were all under the wet mist,
>   and that all went through the sea,
> That all were baptized to Moses
>   in the wet mist and in the sea;
> That all ate the same spiritual food
>   and all drank the same spiritual drink;
>   —For they drank of the spiritual rock[24] that
>   followed them;
>   now the rock was the Christ,—
> But that most of them pleased not God,
>   for they were destroyed in the desert.

Here is a warning that Christian sacraments will not preserve from reprobation those believers who sin as gravely as the Israelites sinned in the desert. But it would be a mistake to expect in this homiletical effort a system of sacramental theology neatly rounded off. What we here listen to are the lispings of Christian thought in its first attempts to understand the sacraments. But the movement of thought is not here towards the theory of baptism-burial as in Romans. The action of the spirit is introduced into all sacraments, even into those of the Desert, while care is taken to avoid too much magic by a warning that sacraments will not save those who offend against the Law of God. The chief interest of the passage lies in the way it links together the two sacraments of baptism and eucharist, and links them so closely that the two are carried back, in their connexion, to the Old Testament where, for our part, we should not expect to find them.

Justin gives explicit testimony that the two were thus linked together by his time (*Apology*, 65). Immediately after his bath of regeneration, the baptized person is conducted to the spot where the brethren are gathered. All then join in prayer, both for the individual baptized and for Christians in general, that their knowledge of truth may be joined to the practice of good and that eternal salvation may be theirs. "When the prayers are finished we kiss each other. Next in order, bread and a cup of water[25] are brought to him who presides among the brethren; and he, taking them, praises and glorifies the Father of all things, in the name of the Son and the Holy Spirit,[26] and delivers a long thanksgiving for all the benefits wherewith he has blessed us." Evidently the exercise of thanksgiving over the elements of the repast has become much longer since the time of the *Didache*,[27] and, equally evident, that this is not a meal that might satisfy hunger, except symbolically by the simple distribution and prompt consumption of the elements over which the prayers have been uttered. In other words we have now reached the stage when the meeting of the brethren has become wholly spiritual and nothing remains of their daily meal except the sacrament. "When the president has concluded his prayers and thanksgivings all the people answer by acclamation, saying: Amen." After which the "deacons" distribute the eucharistic elements among those present to be carried to the absent brethren (1 *Apology*, 65).

Admission to communion thus became an essential part of Christian initiation: but communion itself was no more than one part of the ritual of initiation and, for yet stronger reason, was not, even in its origin, part of the baptismal rite or an appendix to it. It was rather, in strictness of language, the rite of those who had been initiated; it was as already made Christian by his baptism that the baptized person was introduced to the sacrament. Justin himself tells us (i, 67) that the ordinary service of the Sunday Communion was performed in the same manner as that which he has just described as proper to baptism, except that it began with a more or less lengthy reading from "the Memoirs of the Apostles," that is, from the Gospels, or perhaps from the prophetical writings; the president then delivers exhortation based on the passage read; after which all rise up for prayer, eucharist (thanksgiving) and communion (*Apology*, 67). Originally the religious meal of the community, but a meal in the ordinary sense and for the ordinary purpose, the Christian Communion became a purely religious and somewhat complicated exercise, the chief liturgy of the congregations, in which the symbolic and sacramental rite of common participation in the same food remained essential and dominant.

Justin dwells at some length on the eucharist (i, 66), explaining why only those are admitted to it who have been baptized and are living conformably to the precepts of Christ, the reason being that this is no ordinary repast. "Even as Jesus Christ took flesh and blood by the Word of God, so the nutriment which sustains our flesh and our blood, blessed by the prayer of the Word, becomes flesh and blood of Jesus incarnate." By "prayer of the Word" our author understands the blessing pronounced by Jesus on the bread and the cup at the last meal he took with his disciples[28]—not the so-called formula of institution, "This is my body. This is my blood." Not till much later than Justin was the idea born which sees in these words what has been named the "form" of the eucharistic sacrament.

In his *Memoirs of the Apostles* Justin read the instructions given by the Christ with regard to the Supper. "Jesus, having taken bread, gave thanks and said 'Do this in remembrance of me. This is my body.' Having also taken the cup, he gave thanks and said 'This is my blood.' And to them alone he made distribution."—Note that Justin makes no reference to First Corinthians. Not once does he quote from the Epistles. He would seem to be unacquainted with the work of Paul, though he cannot have been wholly ignorant about him, for he knew Marcion well enough. The words which he quotes as evangelical are in approximate agreement, for the bread, to the text of canonical Luke (xxii, 19) and, for the cup, to that of Matthew (xxvi, 28).

In his *Dialogue with Trypho* (41) Justin refers to the offering of wheaten flour prescribed by the Law (in Leviticus xiv) to a purified leper, and writes as follows: "This prefigured the bread of the eucharist which Jesus Christ our Lord bade us consecrate, in memory of the passion undergone by him for the purification of men's souls from perversity, to the end that we might render thanks to God for having created for man the world and all that it contains, for having delivered us from the evil into which we had fallen and for having finally broken the principalities and powers[29] by him who came to suffer according to his will." In another place (70), commenting on Isaiah xxxiii, 16 ("bread shall be given him and his water[30] shall be sure"), Justin notes that the prophecy refers to "the bread which our Christ bade us consecrate in memory of his incarnation and of his sufferings for believers, and to the cup which he bade us consecrate in memory of his blood."

At this stage, then, the picture may be thus presented. The Christian Supper, in virtue of its institution as recorded in the Gospels, is a mystical commemoration of the death of Jesus, an exercise of thanksgiving for the redemption effected by his death, the thanks being added to those rendered to God for the gift of the created world, and a mystical participation and communion in the flesh and blood of the incarnate Word.

From a simple act of thanksgiving for an ordinary meal of bread and wine, when not of bread and water, Christian thought and practice has now arrived (*circa* 140) at a repast of which the meaning is purely religious. This has become a symbol, not very felicitous, of a unique sacrifice, an image of the Passion which saves the believer, a sacrament of communion with the dying Saviour, a communion which is the pledge of immortality. Such is the result at this stage, not arrived at all at once, but by long and complicated labour of Christian thought and as the outcome of a veritable evolution in Christian liturgy. The idea of the baptized person as made completely one with the dead Christ failed to take root in Christian tradition; but communion with the crucified Christ, by participating in the Lord's Supper, became the very centre of Christian worship. So Justin understood the matter, and this is what he found in existence, though the last step in the process cannot have been achieved long before his time.

6. THE JOHANNITE EUCHARIST

In its bearing on the tradition reputed to be apostolic the Fourth Gospel has a position all its own. The account of the last meal taken by Jesus is here the account of a developed eucharist lacking the essential words in the tradition we have just analysed (xiii, 1–17, 20, 31–xvii). With the sublimity fitting to his Person the Christ here holds the place of the presiding celebrant mentioned by Justin, but holds it as sovereign Master of the Mystery who, having himself accomplished the work of salvation, praises God that his work is done. He teaches, he prays, he offers thanks; he celebrates the banquet of divine love, of the union of the faithful in God and in the Christ who died for them; but says not a word of the bread and the wine, nor of any commemorative act. The canonical edition of the Gospel contains a double series of his instructions, xiii–xiv and xv–xvii. Both are conceived in an atmosphere purely eucharistic, and this is especially marked in the long prayer at the end of the collection (xvii), spoken by the Christ as author of salvation and first celebrant of the eucharistic mystery which shows forth his saving death:

> Holy Father, keep them in thy name,
>> those thou has given me,
>>> that they may be one as we are . . .
> I ask thee not to take them out of the world,
>> but to guard them from the Evil One . . .
> For them I sanctify myself,
>> that they also may be sanctified in truth . . .
> And the glory thou gavest to me, yea to me,
>> I gave to them,
> That they may be one
>> as we are one,
> I in them
>> and thou in me
>>> that they may be perfect in unity,
>> That the world may know
>>> that thou hast sent me
> And that thou hast loved them
>> as thou hast loved me.
> Father, those whom thou hast given me,
>> I would that where I am
>>> They too may be with me,
> That they may see my glory,
>> which thou hast given me,
> For thou hast loved me
>> before the foundation of the world.
> Righteous Father, the world has known thee not,
>> but I, I knew thee;
> And they too have known
>> that thou hast sent me.
> And to them have I made known thy name,
>> and will make it known,
> That the love wherewith thou lovest me may be
>> in them and I in them.

This utterance of sublime mysticism which we would willingly have cited in full—whence came it? Is it a vain imagination to think that one Easter Day a Christian seer, speaking in the name of the Christ, chanted it for the first time to an assembly of the faithful in one of the churches of Asia where the Christian Easter, falling on the day of the Jewish Passover, celebrated the redeeming and triumphant death of him who was the Lamb of God?

It seems certain that, in the tradition of the fourth Gospel, the institution of the Supper goes back to the miracle of the multiplied loaves (vi, 1–14). Knowing, as we do, that this miracle is, in reality, one of the oldest of the Christian supper-myths, it is not surprising that the Ephesian Gospel presents it as the symbolic institution of the Eucharist. In the first part of the discourse on the bread of life (vi, 26–51a) the symbolic bread is, in reality, Jesus himself, but not as being present mystically in the bread considered as his body. As bread is the life of the body, as manna was the life of the Israelites in the desert so Jesus, for those who believe in him, is life itself, and eternal life.

> Verily, verily, I tell you,
>> Moses gave you not
>>> the bread of heaven.
> My father is he who gives you
>> the bread of heaven,
>>> the true bread.
> For the bread of God
>> is he who comes down from heaven
>>> and gives life to the world . . .
> 'Tis I who am the bread of life,
>> who comes to me
>>> shall have no hunger;
> Who believes in me
>> shall never thirst . . .
> 'Tis I who am the living bread
>> which came down from heaven.
> If any man eats of this bread
>> he shall live for ever.

Up to this point Jesus is supposed to be explaining in what sense he is the bread of life for those who believe in him. The bread is a figure, a figure of spiritual salvation as offered and guaranteed by Jesus. But far from being a mere figure of speech, the author of this commentary on the bread of life has in mind throughout the bread of the Supper, to which he gives the mystical meaning of the *Didache*. There is a real bread of life; thanks are given for it in the Christian Supper: it is the Christ with the life that he gives to the believer. By this insistence on the reality of the bread the discourse is none the less a eucharistic utterance; but in the spirit of the *Didache*.

Now comes a sequel to this discourse, apparently a later addition (vi, 51b–58) which connects with the tradition presented by Justin as that of the apostles:

> And the bread I will give
>> 'tis my flesh
>>> for the life of the world . . .
> Verily, verily, I tell you,
> If you eat not the flesh of the Son of Man
>> nor drink his blood,
>>> you have no life in you.
> Who eats my flesh
>> and drinks my blood
>>> has eternal life . . .[31]
> For my flesh is real nourishment
>> and my blood real beverage.
> Who eats my flesh
>> and drinks my blood
>>> abides in me and I in him . . .
> 'Tis the spirit that makes alive,
>> the flesh serves for naught:
> The words I have spoken to you
>> are spirit, are life.

Here is a development presented as a commentary, or explanation given to the disciples, on the preceding passage, where the saying that bread is flesh is stated to have resulted in the amazement of the Jews (vi, 52; 59–62). It must, however, be the author of this assertion who speculates in the added passage on the mystic meaning of bread and wine as tantamount to flesh and blood.[32] According to this author flesh and blood is what they truly are, but only in a mystical or spiritual sense. What the believer eats, as he commemorates the death of Christ in the Supper, is not flesh, and what he drinks is not blood. The spirit of God and of Christ—that is the sustenance of which he partakes. A great lesson which the theologians of the age of iron no longer understand!

7. THE SUPPER IN FIRST CORINTHIANS

The same process of superimposing a religious rite on a common meal may be clearly seen in the accounts of the eucharist given in First Corinthians33 and in the Synoptic Gospels,34 with the difference that the lesson on the Supper in Corinthians seems to come from a single source while in the Gospels the introduction of the symbolic words of institution is added by a second hand. Moreover the lesson in the Epistle appears to be the older of the two, and is completed in the same Epistle by another passage (x, 1–22) in which the Supper is compared with the pagan sacrifices and given the character of a sacrificial banquet. In this passage the underlying idea is the same as that suggested by the Gospel account of the institution. This we shall consider later.

It would seem that the Corinthians, professing to carry out what their apostle had taught them, treated the Supper as an ordinary meal at which everybody ate and drank as he pleased without respecting the common bond which held them together (xi, 17–22). To make them ashamed of such abuse Paul will now recall the conditions in which the Supper was established by the Christ himself (xi, 23–25):

> I myself have from the Lord
>> that which I also passed on to you,
> That the Lord Jesus, on the night he was betrayed,
>> took bread and, having given thanks, broke it and said:
> "This is my body, which is for you;
>> do this in remembrance of me."
> Likwise also the cup, after the meal, saying:
> "This cup is the new covenant in my blood;
>> this do, as often as you drink it, in memory of me."

From this he draws the conclusion that the Supper is a solemn act commemorating the death of the Lord "till he come"; to partake of it in an unseemly manner is to eat and drink damnation; see to it, then, that everything is done in good order.

Some strange features confront us in this passage. It is strange that Paul, if he had really told all this to the Corinthians before, should here be obliged to recall it; strange that he should present it as a revelation received by him from the Lord;35 strange that a doctrine implying the theory of redemption by the blood of the

Christ, and linked artificially to the benediction of bread and wine customary at Jewish meals, should see the light in the first generation, when Christians lived in expectation of an immediate parousia. On the other hand it is significant that regard is here paid to that expectation. Evidently the vision of the institution of the Supper which Paul professes to have had is conceived in the framework of a story relating the last meal of Jesus with his disciples in which preoccupation with the Great Event was the dominant feature. Mention of it accordingly is made as follows (xi, 26):

> For as often as this bread you eat
> and this cup you drink
> You proclaim the Lord's death
> till he come.[36]

In the economy of the Supper *as a mystic rite* this reference to the parousia, made at a time when it was no longer thought of as imminent, is out of place. The mention of it is due to an old and firmly established tradition. There is ground therefore for saying that mystic commemoration of the saving death, the mystic communion with the crucified Christ, is superposed on a form of the Supper as an anticipation of the banquet of the elect in the Kingdom of God, a form clearly indicated in a saying embedded in the oldest tradition of the synoptic Gospels:

> Verily, verily, I tell you
> that I will drink no more
> of the fruit of the vine,
> Until that day
> when I drink it new
> in the Kingdom of God.

The account of the mystic Supper, in First Corinthians, belongs to the evolution of the Christian Mystery at a stage in the development of that mystery earlier than Justin, earlier even than the canonical edition of the first three Gospels but notably later than Paul and the apostolic age. It must be dated in the period when the common meal was in process of transformation into a simple liturgical act. The passage in question is a conscious attempt to further the transformation by giving it the apostolical authority of Paul. In Justin's time the transformation was fully effected; in

Marcion's time it was a thing of the recent past; so, too, in Bithynia in Pliny's time, but only just effected, the imperial orders regulating the religious fraternities having contributed to bring it about. We conclude that this lesson on the good ordering of the Supper was drawn up towards 140 in some circle where the memory of Paul was held in honour.

The mystical sense of the Supper as here understood is explained in a long passage which warns the Corinthians against taking part in the sacrificial meals of the pagans (x, 1–22); in it there occurs the following (16–17, 20–21):

> The cup of blessing, which we bless
>   is it not communion in the blood of the Christ?
> The bread which we break
>   is it not communion in the body of the Christ?
> Being all one bread, all one body are we;
>   For of the one bread all we partake . . .
> That which pagans sacrifice,
>   to demons and not to God they sacrifice it.
> Lo, I would not have you be
>   in communion with demons:
> You cannot drink the cup of the Lord
>   and the cup of demons;
> You cannot have place at the table of the Lord
>   and at the table of demons.

In this text, assimilation of the Supper to the sacrificial meal is as complete as it could be. The Christ, in his attitude to Christians who would associate with pagans in their sacrificial meals, is like a god roused to anger on seeing his altar abandoned or defiled. The eucharistic elements are assimilated to the sacrificial victims and offerings of both Israelite and pagan cults. The Christian Supper, endlessly renewed, is conceived as related to the unique sacrifice—the death of Jesus on the cross—in the same way as any sacrificial meal would be related to the immolation of the victims that furnished viands for the feast. Unnatural as this conception of the Supper was, it rested nevertheless on an analogy, mystically apprehended as a reality, between the elements of the commemorative Supper and the remains of the victims that were eaten after being offered in sacrifice to the gods. A strange position would seem to be assigned to the Christ; he is at once the divine president at the sacrificial banquet and the victim, served as meat and drink on the table. But the pagan gods, notably Dionysus and Osiris, were in the same position.

Our texts make much of the general idea of sacrificial communion which also implies the further notion of mystical communion between the victim slain and the god to whom it is offered; for, if the believer enters into communion with his god by eating the victim, the reason must be that there resides in the victim a certain mystic and divine power which acts as the medium in effecting communion between his god and him. In this respect the God of Israel, the gods of the pagans and the Christ stand on the same level: all three alike share a common table with their devotees and commune with them in the holy meal, united to them in partaking of the victim they all are eating. Although there is nothing divine in the sacrificial viands—at least so we are told (x, 19)—and nothing divine in the bread and wine of the Supper, a mystic union is nevertheless formed both in the sacrificial meals of the pagans and in the Christian Supper. But the union so formed is quite other than simple moral likemindedness between the divine beings, Jewish, pagan and Christian, on the one side, and on the other, their worshippers, be they Jews or pagans offering sacrifice, or Christians partaking of Eucharistic bread and wine. When the victim is eaten by the pagan, it is certainly not his god that he eats; neither is it the material body of the Christ that the Christian eats when he eats the bread, nor his blood that he drinks in the wine. (Let it be said in passing that this idea of communion with God by drinking the blood of a sacrificed victim was never born in the brain of a Jew.) No eating of the god's body is here, and no drinking of his blood; but a real communion of spirit is established between the god sacrificed, or sacrificed to, and those whose part in the sacrifice is to eat and drink the material of the oblation. This communion of spiritual power is in agreement with the common notion of the meaning of sacrifice, but not with the orthodox notion of Israelite sacrifice as a rendering of homage and mark of fidelity. In the texts before us it is intensely concrete and intensely alive. Not only is it a relation of reciprocal love but, more than that, a through-and-through penetration of the human by the divine in which the believer is completely possessed by the Christ-Spirit.

8. THE SYNOPTIC ACCOUNT OF THE LAST SUPPER

Many Protestant critics have maintained and many still maintain that the symbolic sayings "this is my body," "this is my blood"—at least the first of them—belong to the primitive tradition and are authentic words of Jesus, but spoken by him in a sense different from that given them by tradition and by Paul in the first instance. They contend that Jesus merely made a simple comparison between the bread broken, the wine poured out, and the fate that was awaiting him. An uncalled-for hypothesis and consequently a risky one. The sayings in question have a natural fitness to the mystical interpretation of the Supper, and to that only, and have to be teased before any meaning acceptable to reason can be got out of them—to the reason that is of those who insist on finding such a meaning.

These critics moreover overlook the hopeless incoherence in the account of the matter given in Mark (xiv, 22–25) on which Matthew and Luke are both dependent. This account is a kind of summary covering many implied meanings which the reader is supposed to understand without needing to have them mentioned. In the first rank of what is thus taken for granted and left unexpressed is the idea, which should be attributed to Paul, that the last meal taken by Jesus is the first Eucharist, the prototype on which the Christian rite is founded. In reality the Gospel account has Paul's teaching in view, and purports to be in accord with that teaching alone. But the elements of which the account is composed are not all in accordance with that. They are not homogeneous. The two types of the Supper which we have distinguished above are both represented—the ordinary meal and the mystical rite. The same occasion cannot have produced them both at a single birth, and we have therefore to look for their historical relationship. Here is the passage to be considered:

> And while they were eating,
> he, taking bread, broke it after benediction;
> He gave it to them, and said:
> "Take; this is my body."
> And taking the cup,
> after giving thanks, he gave it to them,
> and they all drank of it.

And he said to them:
    "This is my blood of the covenant,
        shed for many.
    Verily I say to you
        I will drink no more," etc.

Let us examine this. We can see at once that the words "This is my body" would be utterly unintelligible for a reader unacquainted with the Christian Eucharist. Clearly then he is supposed to be acquainted with it. He knows—not indeed what Jesus, on the hypothesis of our Protestant critics, could not have failed to say in clearing up the enigma—but what was in the mind of the evangelist and what was thought about it all in the Christian group for which the second Gospel was written. The meaning of the mysterious saying "This is my body"37 and of the mysterious saying "This is my blood" are co-ordinate to the same effect. They refer to the bruised and crucified body represented by the bread—not quite happily, the body of Jesus not having been broken in pieces—just as the wine (or water) of the cup represents the blood of Jesus (and not more happily, since the blood of Jesus was not poured out, as would have happened had he been, for example, executed by decapitation). All this would be intelligible enough to a Christian reader familiar with the developed eucharistic rite as practised in the group for which the Gospel was intended: but perfectly unintelligible on the occasion when the sayings are supposed to have been uttered. In short, it is hard to conceive or, rather, impossible to conceive why Jesus should resort to these dark sayings—for dark they then would be and there is no question of their being parable—instead of explaining in a few simple words why he was exposing himself to death. These mystic sayings have no natural sense except as referring to an established Christian sacrament, and as explaining it.

In the passage before us there is a difference in the manner of introducing the bread and the cup respectively, and it is important to note that the narrator hardly seems to have foreseen the mystic explanation of the latter. The mystic explanation of the bread is inserted at the appropriate moment when Jesus has given the broken loaf to the disciples. Coming to the cup the evangelist writes, "He gave it to them and they all drank of it" (Mark xiv, 23), whence it follows that the cup was empty when Jesus said "This is my blood"(24). There was no more *this*. Clumsy editing, one would say. Yes, and the clumsiness so flagrant that Matthew has corrected it, writing, when he comes to the cup, "Drink of it all of you, for this is my blood" (xxvi, 27, 28). But the blunder would not have been made if the words "this is my blood" had been present in the fundamental document of Mark on which the editor of canonical Mark was working. On the contrary, the formula "he gave it to them and they all drank of it" would lead on quite naturally to the sequel "I will drink no more of the fruit of the vine," etc., and this is the sequel it demands. In this sequence the implied meaning would be that Jesus himself drank of the wine-cup with the rest of the company, just as he is supposed to have shared with them in the eating of the bread. But the mystic words "this is my body," "this is my blood" are inconsistent with the supposition that Jesus himself partook of the bread and wine, which would be tantamount to saying that he was mystically nourished by his own flesh and his own blood. What could more clearly confirm the impossibility of attributing these words to Jesus in his life on earth? Mystical participation in the body and blood of the Christ becomes intelligible only when understood as referring to the spiritual Jesus, and not as referring to Jesus present in the flesh and conversing with his disciples. Moreover one need not be a master in critical science to see that the saying about the eucharistic body and blood of the Christ belongs to a wholly different current of ideas from that of the words, "I will drink no more wine," etc.

The overlaying of an earlier by a later version which is so apparent in Mark has an interest for the history of the Supper as well as for the criticism of the second Gospel. The first evangelical account of the Supper was one in which the meal was conceived as foreshadowing the banquet of the elect in the coming Kingdom, and not as a mystic and symbolical participation in the body and blood of the Christ taking place there and then. It is an old conjecture that the original story contained, in the place now occupied by "this is my body," words analogous to those spoken over the wine: "I will eat no more bread," etc., words which seem to have been preserved, with the substitution of "passover" for bread, in canonical Luke (xxii, 15–16).[38] In the original story of the Supper, Jesus was not represented as formally instituting a rite. The Supper was presented as a dutiful repetition of the last meal, in which was condensed, so to say, the memory of the many meals taken by Jesus with his disciples, together with a perpetual reminder of his death. This primitive Supper was no repetition of Jesus' death, but the recall of it in commemoration, and dominated throughout, as in the thought of Jesus himself, by an outlook towards the Great Event—in other words, an anticipation of the festival awaiting the elect in the Kingdom of heaven, accompanied by a lively sense of the invisible presence of Jesus who has died and was alive again. This type of the Supper was not confined to Jewish Christianity, but must have been the type common to both Hellenic and Jewish Christians for quite a long time. Needless to say this eschatological Supper did not suddenly give way to the mystical type outlined in First Corinthians. The approximate date would coincide with that of the modifications introduced into the Gospel books, or, let us say, the date when the Sunday Easter was substituted for the quartodeciman usage, and when the community meal ceased to be a meal and became a liturgy. This was not till after the year 70 and probably towards the end of the first century or the beginning of the second.

To sum up. We may take it as established that the eucharistic prayer in the earliest time was an outpouring of gratitude, on the occasion of a community meal, for the gift of salvation, which consisted in participation in the Kingdom of God, a gift added to the blessing of creation. Christ was thought to come in person, but invisibly, at the simple call of his faithful ones, and the meal was holy, the elements being consecrated by the prayer of thanksgiving. Then, under the general influence of the mystery cults, there was born spontaneously the idea of a mystic communion with the Christ in the elements of the Supper, a communion understood in terms of the Christ dying for the justification of men that he might rise for their glorification: the meal now becomes a wholly ritual and symbolic act around which there grows up a genuine liturgy. Finally, the idea of sacrificial communion thus introduced issues, towards the end of the second century, in causing the elements of the Supper to be regarded as an oblation which God is asked to fill with spiritual power in virtue of its assimilation to the body and blood of Jesus—as in the

Liturgy of Hippolytus. But, vastly as the Supper has grown in significance, the ritual of it still always and essentially remains an act of thanksgiving over the bread and the cup. Thus, notwithstanding the long evolution of mystic faith and theological doctrine, it still holds fast to its point of departure—the prayers of the Jew giving thanks for meat and drink.

Chapter *VIII*

EARLIEST THEORIES OF THE CHRISTIAN MYSTERY

It is obvious that the theory of the Christian mystery supported the system of its sacraments, the Christian faith which these reflect being widely different from the Jewish hope, conditioned, as it was, by the national restoration of Judaism. Much that is written in the New Testament books represents the efforts that were made, one after the other and from different angles, to equip the new religion with a balanced doctrine both in regard to the central object of the religion, the person and work of its founder, and to the form of its practice in the society of believers. To this process we now turn.

1. Theory in the Epistle to the Romans

The mystical gnosis developed in the Epistle to the Romans did not enter entire into the general current of Christian tradition, at least before Augustine, and even the influence of the Doctor of Hippo prevailed only within the Latin Church. This gnosis, however, with the additions and modifications given it in other Epistles attributed to Paul, constitutes the most complete, if not the oldest, known attempt made by Christian speculation to transform messianic faith into a theory of redemption, more or less analogous to the doctrine of pagan mysticism, but without abandoning the ground of Biblical revelation and of the Gospel message of the Kingdom of God.

In an apparently authentic part of the Epistle (iii, 27–iv, 24) Paul has proved that Gentiles were entitled to enter the Kingdom of God on condition of faith in Jesus, who became Christ by his resurrection. Abraham, he says, was justified solely by faith in the divine promise at a time when he was still uncircumcised; whence it follows that uncircumcised pagans can be saved in the same manner and on exactly the same terms as the Jews, the circumcised descendants of Abraham. Thus Gentile believers took their place, so to say, in the general scheme of Israel's hope, which was to come to fruition in the conversion of Israel itself after the Gospel has been preached to all the pagans.[1] Thus it stands in the passage before us. But the problem of salvation is resumed from quite a different point of view in the chapters which deal with the scheme of redemption. Here there is no longer question of the promises made to Abraham for his posterity, but of a plan of salvation intended by Divine Providence, from the beginning of the world, to embrace the whole of mankind, the revelation to the Jews being no more than an interlude connected with the fall of man, not the real basis of his restoration.

God, we are told, has proved his love for men in that Christ died for the redemption of the sinful human race. Here are the providential conditions under which this came about:

> As by one sole man sin entered the world,
>   and death by sin.
> And thus death passed to all men,
>   because all have sinned . . .
> As from one sole transgression
>   there followed condemnation for all,
> So from one sole deed of justice
>   there followed justification for life
> For, as by the disobedience of one sole man
>   the rest were all made sinners,
> So by the obedience of one sole man
>   the rest are made righteous.[2]

Nothing could less resemble an improvised letter than these studied declarations of which even the form is carefully balanced. But their importance lies in their matter. Two images, two men, two Adams dominate the whole of human history. The first Adam, "image of him who was to come," has by his sole transgression involved all humanity in sin and death. (A tragic interpretation of the old story of the first man being driven out of God's garden, where the Tree of Life was, for having disobeyed his Creator!)[3] The second Adam, Jesus Christ, by an act of justice, of perfect virtue, which was also an act of obedience, to wit his voluntary submission to death—the death due to all men as sinners like their father Adam, but not due to the Christ, a heavenly being by origin and nature and not descended from the first Adam—this second Adam has, by the aforesaid act of justice rendered men irreproachable before God. This, virtually, he has done for all mankind but, actually, for those who believe in him and who, through baptism, are mystically identified with him in his death and so participate in his resurrection.

The fifteenth chapter of First Corinthians is yet more explicit about the two Adams:

> Thus is it written:
> There was made the first man, Adam,
>   living soul
> The last Adam
>   lifegiving Spirit.
> But the spiritual is not first,
>   .the first is the living,
>   then the spiritual.
> The first man, being of earth, is earthy,
>   the second man is of heaven.
> As is the one earthy
>   so are the many;
> As is the one heavenly
>   so are the many,
> And as we have borne the likeness of the earthy,
>   we shall bear the likeness of the heavenly . . .
> Flesh and blood cannot inherit the Kingdom of God
>   and corruption will not inherit incorruption.

By an exigesis of extreme subtlety the two Adams are here deduced from Genesis, which is not to be wholly credited either with the Adam of perdition or with the Adam of salvation, very emphatically not with the latter. They are myth figures here adapted to Genesis and to the Gospel. The terrestrial Adam and his heavenly counterpart are the primordial Adam divided into two, the ideal prototype and its historical realization. This is the myth of Man, whence is derived the Son of Man of the Gospels, who is the pre-existing type of humanity and the destined agent in effecting his salvation. Philo[4] knew the two "men" in question, but gave priority to the celestial. Fundamentally our author has the same idea; but, taking his point of view at the historical manifestation, he puts the terrestrial man first, reducing primordial man to primacy in sin, misery and death and reserving the Celestial Man for the end of the ages.

Strange things are told us in Romans about the Law (v, 13, 20, 21):

> Until the Law
>   Sin was in the world;
> But was not counted as sin,
>   there being no law . . .
> The Law came in
>   that transgression might abound;
> But where sin abounded
>   grace abounded more,
> To the end that, as sin reigned in death,
>   so grace may reign by justice to eternal life,
>   by Jesus Christ our Lord.

The author's idea of the Mosaic Law, and indeed of law in general, could hardly have occured save to one born outside the Jewish fold, who, weighing the Law as an outsider, judged it impracticable. His view is, moreover, that man, being inclined to sin by the natural appetites of the flesh, the Law, by bringing to his notice the opportunities for sinning, would, so to say, incite him to commit the very sins it forbids. A strange mode, truly, of understanding social obligation and the reasons underlying legislation in general! Where, then, are we to look for a regulating principle and a criterion of good? Our prophet is embarrassed by no such trifles. According to him, sin, death and law are inseparably one and constitute, as it were, the Trilogy of damnation; grace, righteousness, eternal life are the Trilogy of salvation; immortality issues from righteousness, and righteousness from grace—grace granted to every man who, having faith in Jesus dead and risen from death, participates in his death and resurrection; such a believer dies to sin, lives to God, enters without effort into the way of righteousness, all under the impulse of a new spirit. All virtues are born of the spirit of grace. The logical consequence of the system would be that the believer is incapable of sin. But a formal admission of this is here avoided though it is hinted at in Romans vi, 14, and expressed in plain terms in 1 John iii, 6.

Dealing throughout with abstractions, our author believes he is dealing with realities. His conceptions are terribly ponderous, not to say mechanical, and yet not far removed from a primitive mentality. In the presence of death he is like a child seeking the key to a non-existent problem. Death, in reality, is the natural ending of every form of life on earth, and the miracle would be if man had escaped it. Death reigned before there was any sin to generate it. And what is our author's idea of sin? A fearful and monstrous abstraction, behind which, most assuredly, there is a fact only too real, but a simple fact quite otherwise explicable than by the innate corruption of the flesh and the pretended provocation of it by the law; a fact to be simply explained by human weakness in presence of the ideal born in social life, the weakness resulting from the limitations of reason, from the kind of constraint which our natural appetites impose on the reflecting will. The idea of grace is not less ponderous, nor that of redemption less artificial. Sin, the capital evil of humanity, innate in the flesh —though we are not told how—is suddenly annihilated because the Christ, having taken flesh, takes sin upon him also, but without being defiled by it, and then, by the destruction of his own flesh effects the destruction of sin in humanity at large. The idea at the back of this is not expiation, but elimination, as in most of the ancient sacrifices classed as expiatory, and notably in the scape-goat, mystically loaded with the sins of Israel, which he carries away with him into the desert. Thus the sin of the guilty human race is done away with in the body of the Man-Christ, who was himself untouched by it. Childish dreams worked up into a theological nightmare and adapted, by hook or crook, to a lofty moral conception!

To this strange system some corrections are applied by the Epistle itself (vii, 14–17):

> We know that the Law is spiritual;
> > but, as for me, I am carnal,
> > > sold to sin.5
> For what I do, I understand it not:
> > 'tis not what I would that I do,
> > > 'tis what I abhor that I do.
> Now, if what I would not is what I do
> > I acknowledge that the Law is good;
> But it is no more I who do it,
> > 'tis sin abiding in me.

Here are subtleties enough, but not without psychological meaning and moral insight. The Law, we are told, being spiritual, is so far good; but the flesh is turned towards evil, even when reason perceives the good and assents to the Law. Man now appears to be torn asunder between two tendencies, both permanent, in so much that, contrary to the system we have just examined, justification would not seem to be acquired once and for all, but to result only from a victory constantly renewed by the help of the spirit in a struggle that goes on till life ends (vii, 18–23). The conception is here more sober, more philosophic, being partly borrowed from the philosophers, and bearing marks of serious reasoning and genuine psychological experience. But we should completely deceive ourselves if we thought we could find in these theoretical views the profound and purely personal experience by which Paul was led to his faith in the Christ.

The chief author of this system had in his mind an idea of the whole world as subject, against its will, to corruption, and as sharing with believers in the Christ in the expectation of deliverance. Everything suffers violence in this lower sphere, still reigned over by evil spirits, "the princes of this world"; they it was who, according to First Corinthians (ii, 8),[6] without knowing him, "crucified the Lord of Glory." The final redemption of the suffering universe will be effected in the metamorphosis awaiting the elect. "The creation, impatiently waiting, longs for the manifestation of the Sons of God"—in their glory as they will appear in this new world; "for to vanity"—doubtless to the subordinate powers which govern it so ill—"has the whole creation been made subject, not of its own will"—having never desired such servitude—"but by the doing of Him who so subjected it"—doubtless God who appointed the evil powers to rule the visible world —"in hope that the creation also"—sharing the resurrection of humanity—"will be delivered from the bondage of corruption"— which the evil powers impose on the world chiefly through the pagan cults—"that it may attain the liberty of the glory of the children of God." And the author even speaks of the creation as "travailing" and "groaning" in company with mankind.[7]

Evidently the triumph of the elect is no longer conceived as the reign of the Christ on this earth in a Jerusalem made glorious; for the lower, material world will disappear to make room for the expansion and manifestation of the spiritual world. Nevertheless the spiritual world is not purely ideal; even the elect who will possess it are to have bodies, spiritual bodies of an ethereal substance, light, subtle and luminous (1 Corinthians xv, 35–44). As to the nature of this substance, the clearest information the writer can give us is that it will not be gross, like the matter of which the present world is composed.

So pessimistic a view of the material world might well suggest that foreign influence is here at work. It brings to mind the Persian doctrine of the world as created by the wicked Ahriman whom one day the good Ormuzd will destroy. But here the world is not the creation of a wicked god and, even if Persian influence can be detected in the idea of the world as badly governed from the beginning, that influence goes further back. The idea of "powers" which have abused the authority which God has given them over the world, and abused it both against the world and against God himself, is to be met with in Jewish apocalyptic literature of a period earlier than Christianity. But the idea appears in our texts under a stronger accent. Furthermore, the strangest of all the applications to which the idea has been put, that which presents the crucifixion of Jesus as due to the "princes of this world," is given support as sketched in the Old Testament (Zechariah xi–xiii, 8); to which the fourth Gospel gives precision by attributing the death of the Christ to one only of the princes, "the prince of this world," that is, to the grand master of the lower powers. The human agents who take part in the condemnation and execution are regarded as his tools, and as hardly responsible for what they do.

Here, then, is a profound and dauntless faith translated into the language of mythology. The author of the gnosis, of which we have just ventured an analysis, has experienced persecution, nor does he expect that persecution will soon come to an end. But, taking comfort from his belief that the elect will overcome all the difficulties and torments awaiting them, he now breaks forth into this fine outpouring of his mystical faith (Rom. viii, 28–30, 31, 35, 37–39):

> We know that, for those who love God,
> > everything converges to good,
> > > --for those called according to plan--
> Because, those whom he foresaw,
> > them he predestined to be conformed to the
> > > pattern of his Son,
> > > > that he might be the first-born of many brothers.
> Now, whom he predestined,
> > them also he called;

Whom he called;
  them also he justified
Whom he justified,
  them also he glorified.
If God is for us,
  Who will be against us?
Who will separate us from the love of the Christ?
  Tribulation, distress, persecution,
    hunger, nakedness, peril, sword? . . .
But over all that we triumph
  by him who loved us.
For I am persuaded that neither death nor life,
  nor angels, nor principalities, nor powers,
    nor height, nor depth, nor any other creature
Will avail to separate us from the love of God
  in Christ Jesus our Lord.

This powerful summary of faith can hardly have been produced before the end of the first century, or elsewhere than in a circle faithful to the memory of Paul. We are tempted to say that the author of it takes his stand on the Scriptures only as on a platform from which to take his flight above them, for his Christ is placed under the Law only that he may deliver those in bondage to the Law (Gal. iv, 4–5). Was he also born of a woman and descended from David according to the flesh? (Rom. i, 3). The Epistles answer in the affirmative, and by the fact that he was woman-born in the lineage of David he would be identified with the Jewish Messiah. But the whole system is consistent only with a real epiphany conceived as historical and incarnate in a body of flesh which, wearing the semblance of sin, must have been real also. What is said on this subject gives no ground for understanding it in the sense of Docetism, the thought of our author being everywhere entirely matter-of-fact and of the kind that could never base the redemption of mankind on a phantom show. It remains to add that the Christ he presents was, by his origin, a "power" in the same category as those who crucified him in the flesh, but, unlike them, faithful to God from the beginning.

2. THEORY IN THE EPISTLE TO THE HEBREWS

The Epistle to the Hebrews, which there is reason to think was not originally attributed to Paul, contains another synthesis, probably of somewhat later date than the foregoing, which constructs the scheme of salvation after a widely different pattern. This gnosis is developed methodically and at considerable length, and elaborately fortified with biblical quotations,[8] though in reality the gnosis is not derived from the Scriptures, but rather attached to them by a subtle exegesis. The preamble announces the general theme of the Epistle (i, 1–4):

Many times and in many ways
God, having formerly spoken
to the fathers by the prophets,
In these last of the days
has spoken to us by the Son,
Whom he appointed heir to all things,
by whom also he made the worlds,[9]
Who, being the reflection of his glory,
and expression of his substance,
Upholding all things
by his word of power,
Having effected purification from sins
sat down on the right of Majesty on high,
Becoming so much superior to the angels
that he received for his share a name more
excellent than they.

The intention of the author is to prove first that the Son, in virtue of his origin and nature as Son and reflected image of God who, by him, has built the universe, is superior to the angels— that is, to the "powers" made familiar to us in the Epistle of Paul, who are merely agents of the divine will but not mediators of salvation (i, 5–14). It is true that the Son, in his earthly mani-festation, has been only for a time the Man spoken of in the eighth Psalm whose place is below that of the angels. (The Psalm is speaking of man in general and of his eminence in the creation as only a little lower than the divine condition.)[10] The Son's place is "below the angels," that is, below that of the heavenly race, in the sense that he took flesh and blood in order that, by dying in the flesh, he might break the power of the devil, who is the lord of death and imposes it on all men. Thus the Son became man that he might deliver men from their bondage to death and lead them forth into immortality (ii, 5–18).

Greater than the angels, the Son is next shown to be greater than Moses, who was merely a servant in God's house, while the

Son is builder and head of the house. This headship belongs to the Son—and here we come to the central point of the mystery as expounded in the theory before us—because he became, by means of his death, the unique High Priest of whom Melchisedec had been the prototype. A complete gnosis is now fitted on to the name Melchisedec, a more or less mythical figure which got attached at a late date to the legend of Abraham. The hundred-and-tenth Psalm shows that quite early, perhaps long before the birth of Christianity, speculation had been active about this Melchisedec. Our theologian has his own way of exploiting the statements in Genesis (xiv, 18–20), and draws conclusions from what they do not say no less than from what they say. Melchisedec is type of the Christ by his appearance as a unique figure in history: his name means King of Righteousness, and he is called "King of Salem," that is, "King of Peace";[11] neither father, nor mother, nor genealogy is assigned to him; neither beginning nor end of his days is indicated; as priest of the Most High he is shown to be priest for ever; which tallies with the eternity of the Son of God.[12] A deduction more remarkable for courage and ingenuity than for logic. The same must be said about our author's inference that Levi, as descended from Abraham, paid tithes to Melchisedec as Abraham had done, "for he was yet in the loins of his father when Melchisedec met him." But what we have especially to note is the idea which the strange comparison of the Christ with Melchisedec is intended to make good, namely, that whereas in the gnosis of the Epistle to the Romans the rôle of the dying Jesus is that of victim only, that rôle, while still retained, is here subordinated to that of the sacrificing priest, eternal priest of humanity for ever performing his office in the presence of God. "He rose up from Judah"[13] as a star might rise, but is not said to be descended from Judah's tribe, for the Christ appeared *in history* like Melchisedec without father or mother and without human ancestry. As applied to the eternal Son of God this would have no sense, for the Son in his eternity is not without father. The Christ, then, appeared historically in the flesh, but without being born of human parentage—an idea more natural for the earthly manifestation of a being conceived as pre-existent than would be his incarnation in an embryo subject to all the changing forms of human growth.

The expiations prescribed by the Law, he continues, were only a figure; incessantly repeated as symbols, they left sin uneffaced. But Jesus has, by his death, made expiation, at one stroke and for ever, for the totality of sin. By his death he entered at once into his glory, and laid his own blood on the altar of heaven, effecting by that unique oblation an eternal redemption for sinners, the new covenant, the real covenant, by which the covenant of Sinai was set aside (ix–x, 18). By the sacrifice of the Christ, accomplished once and for ever, the sacrifices prescribed by the Law are all rendered superfluous. Simultaneously, it is by his death that Jesus attains his priesthood and his inheritance in the glory of God. "In the days of his flesh," we are told, in the days, that is, of his appearance on the earth, he had "prayed, with great outcry and weeping to Him who was able to save him from death" —to save him, that is, not by dispensing him from death, but by raising him from it alive; then, his prayer now answered, he learnt "in his passion" what obedience is; finally "having been made perfect"—that is, fully initiated into his priestly office, and fully endowed with insight into the mystery on entering his celestial dwelling place—"he became, for all who believe in him, the author of eternal salvation and a true priest after the manner of Melchisedec" (v, 7–10). There, our author declares, is the great mystery.

It may be said in passing that the prayer, the suffering and the institution of Jesus as eternal High Priest are not, as commonly supposed, to be identified precisely with the prayer of Gethsemane, the passion and resurrection, as these are told in our Gospels. They are data borrowed from the Scriptures, in particular from Psalm xxii, all the descriptive imagery of which is transposed by our author into history, especially verses 2 and 3. On the other hand the Gospel stories of the passion are largely influenced, or rather supported, by the Psalms, in particular by the twenty-second from which our Epistle draws its inspiration. Thus our author stands, in regard to the Gospel tradition, on the same ground as the author of the salvation theory in the Pauline Epistles, who is almost indifferent to the real circumstances of the life and death of Jesus, and anterior at least in point of view, if not in reality, to the definite crystallization of the prophecies into an apparently historical tradition.

Our Epistle presents Jesus as a lofty example of human perfection both in his life and death. He patiently underwent all the trials possible to human nature without sinfully yielding to them—literally "tempted in all manner of ways, according to resemblance, sin excepted" (iv, 15).[14] His death was a token of obedience to God. Moreover his death is not conceived as a doing-away of sin, but as a satisfactory oblation for it, his blood being laid by him on the altar of heaven just as the blood of the victims was brought into the sanctuary by the levitical High Priest on the day of the great expiation. This is soteriology at once moral and liturgical from which conclusions are drawn less fantastic than the theory of a righteousness that cannot be lost. Without discussing the matter, the author admits the possibility of a relapse into sin after baptism, going no further than to point out the terrible consequences of such an event. The blood of Jesus opens the door for the sinner into the sanctuary of heaven, and with such a High Priest given to men, it behoves them to keep their faith in him alive and their hope firm, to incite each other to faithfulness and good works, and not to forsake the assemblies, as some wrongly do. For, if we sin voluntarily after receiving knowledge of the truth we have nothing to expect save punishment by devouring fire, since there now remains for us no other sacrifice to expiate our sin beyond that of the Christ, the benefit of which we have already had. A formidable inference which the Church has not upheld. It suggests a date for our Epistle earlier than the Shepherd of Hermas.

Our Epistle, equally with that to the Romans insists upon faith, but understands if differently. The faith here in question is no longer an absolute trust in the mediation of Christ and in the efficacy of his sacrifice. It is the certainty of what is hoped for, the conviction of the reality of what is not seen. Its essential object is summed up in the formula: "God exists and rewards those who seek him" (xi, 1, 6). It was by faith that all the righteous were saved and all the marvels performed of which the Old Testament, and the tradition founded on it, bear record.[15] Encouraged by this cloud of witnesses let Christians confidently run the course which is opened to them, their eyes fixed on Jesus who endured the cross before sitting down at the right hand of God; let them bear with patience the trials God sends them for their good; let peace prevail between all and holiness be in every man. Jesus abides for ever, let no man be led astray by strange doctrines; the cult of the Law is out of date, our altar is in heaven, and there too is our abiding city; let us offer the sacrifice of prayer, by the Christ, to God. Let not the example of the great ones who died a glorious death be forgotten, and let obedience be paid to those who lead that they may have no cause for sorrow.

Here is morality, a morality strict and severe, but of peace and charity bound up with a gnosis of relative sobriety, and in such a way as to be a logical part of it. The gnosis, moreover, is profoundly spiritual. The author has no belief in the resurrection of the flesh; he even seems to know nothing of the imminent parousia and the reign of the elect on the earth. But, if he speaks of worship in spirit, he does not ignore baptism, the sacrament of "illumination" (vi, 1, 2), nor the Eucharist. For it is not for nothing that he exalts Melchisedec, whose only priestly action recorded in Genesis is the offering of bread and wine. There is little risk in supposing that, in the author's thought, the mystic offering of the Supper was already conceived as presented to God on the heavenly altar whereon was laid the blood of the Christ, in order that it might become, for those who took part in it, the body and blood of the Lord Jesus.[16] All that is worked out with an eye to Judaism, but from outside and afar off, and as if those whom it concerned were separated, and because in reality they had long been separated, from that religion, now regarded as a rival.

3. Theory in the Epistle to the Colossians

A gnosis analogous to the foregoing is worked out in the Epistle to the Colossians, not more in opposition to Judaism but directed, as it would seem, against a gnosis with Judaizing tendencies. Here is what we read of the Christ (i, 15–20):

> He is the image of the invisible God,
>> first-born of all creation,
> Because in him all things were made,
>> in heaven and on earth,
>>> visible and invisible;

Whether thrones, whether dominations,
    whether principalities, whether powers,
       all was made by him and for him.
Himself is before all
    and all subsists in him
And himself is the head of the body,
    of the Church.
He is the beginning,
    first-born among the dead,
That he may become in all things,
    he, first.
Because in him all the pleroma judged good to dwell,[17]
    and by him to reconcile all things to Himself
Reconciling (by the blood of his cross)
    by him, whatever is on earth,
       whatever is in heaven.

Would that the author had himself commented on his text! Would that he had told us, in particular, what he understands by "pleroma," a gnostic term, taken by him as such in his adaptation of it to his monotheistic faith and to the saving rôle of Jesus Christ! Another passage in the Epistle (ii, 8–12), which presents the same doctrine in its contrast to a false mystery, throws some light on the last citation but not enough to resolve all our difficulties:

Beware that no man capture you
    by philosophy and vain sophistry,
According to the tradition of men,
    according to the Elements of the world,[18]
       and not according to Christ.
Because in him there dwells
    all the pleroma of Divinity as body,[19]
And you are made pleroma in him,[20]
    who is the head of all principality and power,
In whom also you were circumcised
    with circumcision not of hands,
Putting off the body of flesh
    in the circumcision of the Christ,
Buried with him by baptism,
    when you were also raised with him,
By faith in the power of God
    who raised him from the dead.

It is evident that the pleroma ("plenitude"), of which the former passage told us that it had chosen Christ for its dwelling place, is the pleroma of the Godhead. But what are we to think of it when we are now told that it dwells in Christ *after the manner of body?* First we are told that the body is the Church: here we are told that baptized believers are, in Christ, made integral to the pleroma-body or, as we might say, *pleromed.* That leads to a highly comprehensive notion of the Church, but throws no light on what the pleroma consists in. Fullness of what? The question is further complicated by what is said in the first passage about a reconciliation (which an apparent gloss turns into redemption by the blood of the cross), bringing order back into both the terrestrial and celestial worlds. On this matter some light is thrown by the following (ii, 13–15):

> And you who were dead in sins
>   and the foreskin of your flesh,
> You has he made alive with himself,
>   forgiving you all your sins,
> Cancelling the clauses of the account,
>   which was against us;
> And he caused it to disappear
>   nailing it to the cross.
> Having disarmed principalities and powers
>   he put them to shame
>   triumphing over them in that condition.

The Christ has here become "chief," or head, of the principalities and powers, because he is their conqueror, having overthrown them by dying on the cross. From this it is clear that an outbreak of rebellion is conceived as having taken place in the Pleroma, in the Whole, which the principalities and powers, as members subordinate to their head,[21] form with the Christ; that the death of the Christ has reconciled men to God by effacing their sins and annulling the act which declared them sinners, doubtless the Law of Moses; that, furthermore, it has established peace in the upper world, and reconciled the principalities and powers to God by bringing them under the dominion of the Christ. The ransomed believers are made integral parts of this sublime incorporation, which is the divine Pleroma and, at the same time, the Church.

A redemption poem analogous to the foregoing is sketched in chapter xv of First Corinthians, but is there founded on the myth of the Man and the distinction between the two Adams; the resurrection also is differently conceived.[22] This, in Colossians, does not appear as the change of the body into a finer substance. In principle, the resurrection of the believer becomes real in his baptism, although his immortality remains, for the time of his present life, "hidden with the Christ in God" (iii, 3).[23] From the following passage, moreover, the definition of this gnosis appears to be aimed in opposition to a mystery-cult, more closely related than itself to Judaism, at least in external form (ii, 16–23):

> Let no man judge you about meat and drink
> about feasts, new moons, sabbaths,
> Which are shadows of things to come,
> the reality[24] being of the Christ.
> Let no one condemn you
> under pretext of humility and the right cult of angels,[25]
> Which he has seen in the initiation,[26]
> vainly puffed up by his fleshly thought,
> Unattached to the head
> by which the whole body,
> With joints and sinews provided and held up,
> increases and grows by God.
> If you are dead with Christ to the Elements[27] of the world,
> why, as though living in the world, suffer the orders
> "Take not, taste not, touch not"
> All on things destined to corruption by usage,
> a business of human laws and doctrines?
> That comes to you under the name of wisdom,
> as "right form of worship," "humility,"[28]
> "discipline of body"
> but has no value, save for fleshly satisfaction.

The terms of precision in the above passage are borrowed from the terminology of a determinate cult with its own forms of initiation and a great array of minute observances, clearly Jewish, and a worship of angels, but in which the Christ had no place. This Judaizing cult of external forms impresses our author as a materialistic religion devoted to the "Elements," στοιχεῖα, of the world. Pretending to be a philosophic gnosis it is, in fact, grossly unspiritual, and Paul is here made to oppose it with the spiritual gnosis of the Epistle. But the Paul who speaks in the Epistle (i, 23) of a Gospel entrusted to him alone and "preached to every creature under heaven (i, 23)"[29] can only have been some fervent follower of the long dead apostle, the whole Epistle being conceived, or rather adapted, some fifty years after his death, to fortify the Christians of Asia against the propaganda of a mystery-cult, possibly that of Zeus Sabazios,[30] then widely active in those regions.

4. Theory in the Epistle to the Philippians

In the Epistle to the Philippians a kind of theological enclosure within the text, unmistakably a hymn to the Christ, contains a gnosis of the same character (ii, 5–11):

> Being in the form of God
>> he judged it no lawful prize
>>> to be equal with God;
> But stripped himself
>> taking slave-form
>>> becoming human in figure;
> And, found a man in appearance,
>> he abased himself,
>>> becoming obedient even to death
>>>> (the death of the cross)
> Wherefore God thus exalted him,
>> and gave him the name
>>> above every name[31]
> So that at the name of Jesus
>> every knee should bow
>>> of beings celestial, terrestrial, infernal,
> And every tongue confess
>> that Jesus is *Lord*,
>>> to the glory of God the Father.

Pre-existing in form divine, the Christ restrains himself from usurping equality with God, as dared by the princes of this world, who cause the nations to worship them as gods. On the contrary, he threw off his celestial shape, took the form of a slave and accepted death in obedience. Here again the Christ forms part of the divine Pleroma which had been thrown into disorder by the attack certain "powers" had made on the prerogative of God, and restored to order by the Son's sacrifice of himself, all created beings, in their triple ranks of heaven, earth and hell, being subdued under him in consequence of that sacrifice. Jesus Christ is thereby proclaimed *Lord*, co-partner in the name, the power and the glory of God. All this however is but a rough outline which leaves us asking how the author would have filled in the detail of his conception. Notwithstanding the doctrinal affinity he can hardly have been the same person as the author who developed the gnosis of Colossians. The passage we have quoted is detached from its context and seems to have existed at first, independently of the Epistle into which it is incorporated, as the oracle of some Christian prophet. Colossians i, 15–20 may have a similar origin.

On the theme of the "descent" of the Christ, in which the oldest mythology finds an echo, the first Epistle of Peter has more knowledge and more to say than the Epistle to the Philippians (iii, 18–19; iv, 6):

> Christ also died once for sins,
>   that he might bring us to God,
> Put to death in the flesh
>   but made alive in spirit.
> In spirit also went he to preach
>   to the spirits who were in prison,
> Those who had been untaught in time past,
>   when the long-suffering of God waited,
>   in Noah's day when the ark was built . . .
> For this cause was the Gospel preached to the dead:
>   that they may be judged humanly in flesh,
>   but live according to God in spirit.

A persistent desire to extend salvation to the dead, especially to those drowned in the Deluge, or, one might say, to humanity at the first stage, is a curious feature of gnostic speculation. The author of First Peter seems to have formed a purely spiritual idea of the resurrection: it is as a spirit that Jesus goes to preach to the dead; he can hardly be supposed to have preached in vain; the converted dead will have risen up with him from their infernal abode, and it was doubtless in the course of his ascent to heaven that he enforced "submission on angels, powers and virtues" (iii, 22). In the Gospel of Peter, Christ on rising from the tomb is said to have already fulfilled his preaching-mission to the dead. The fourth Gospel seems to make an explicit allusion to it (v, 25, 28),[32] and perhaps it is implied in other parts of the New Testament.[33] Justin, in his reference to the matter, mentions an apocryphal text of Jeremiah which speaks of the Lord preaching to the dead.[34] Marcion has his own account of the Christ's descent into hell, but here it is with the object of liberating all those who had been damned under the Old Testament.[35]

5. GNOSIS IN THE FOURTH GOSPEL

The gnosis of the fourth Gospel is distinguished above all the others by the sublimity, balance and harmonious development of its doctrine, announced in discourses which are really hymns, and figuratively presented by means of stories constructed in symbolic language. Here is mysticism at once profound and luminous; a scheme of salvation purely spiritual and yet throbbing with life; a transcendent Christology penetrated through and through by human tenderness and a unique mode of speech which one might think had been created for the lofty use here made of it. Many have thought that the hymn to the Logos which serves as introduction to the Gospel was inserted as an afterthought; but nothing could be less certain. If there is no further question of the Logos in the body of the book, the reason is that regard for tradition restrained the writer from putting the express formula of the logos-philosophy into the mouth of the Christ. Nonetheless the preamble fits in exactly with the book as a whole and with its general doctrine, to which indeed it furnishes the key:

> In the beginning was the Logos,
> and the Logos was with God,
> and the Logos was god.[36]

Reason and spoken Word of the Eternal, the Logos was before all things, and near to God, being of God and sharing His nature, but without being God himself.

> He, at the beginning, he, was with God:
> everything was made by him,
> and without him was nothing made.[37]

The Logos, and he *alone*—this, perhaps, pointed against some gnostic fancy about the process of the "aeons"—is said to be near to God at the very beginning, because he is the creative word of Genesis, without whose power and instrumentality no created thing has come into being:

> Whatever was made alive, in him is the life of it,[38]
> and the life was the light of men.
> And the light shone into the darkness,
> and the darkness quenched it not.[39]

Life and Light: that, precisely, is the Logos, and that, precisely, as the whole Gospel will tell, is the Christ, the Son of God. He was Life and Light in the world as it subsisted in him before his epiphany, that epiphany which was made real for the particular good of humanity, and of which the Gospel will now tell. But his influence met resistance and limitation from the darkness in which it worked. This "darkness"—be it said without play on words—is the dark point of the system. It would seem to be derived from Genesis, where the darkness is a negative element opposed to the organizing work of God.[40] Here the darkness is an influence permanently at work in the world; for the "prince of this world" is clearly also the prince of darkness, to wit, Satan.[41] At this point we encounter a dualism which the Gospel does not resolve; we are not told whence comes the devil, "the father of lies."[42] He seems to personify, so to say, the whole class of "powers," elsewhere described as mismanaging the world confided to their care. As the Gospel presents him, he is the greatest of the "powers," God's enemy, a moral personification of "the darkness," a kind of Ahriman-Antichrist, whose origin, like that of the darkness, is left unexplained. Possibly "darkness" is conceived as forming the stuff of the perishable world, though the statement is not expressly made.

> That was the true light
> that sheds light on every man
> who came into the world.
> In the world he was,
> —the world made by him—
> and the world knew him not.
> To his home came he,
> and his own welcomed him not;
> But all who welcomed him,
> to them gave he power to become God's children.[43]

These are general propositions concerning the activity of the Word-light which seemingly antedate the incarnation, unless they involve it by anticipation. It will be noted that the author of the hymn makes play with the words *light, darkness, world,* understanding them alternately in a material and in a spiritual sense. The "world" is the visible universe, but it stands also for humanity as reasonable and, again, for humanity as unteachable. The precise gift which the Word-light has to confer upon men is truth and life, the truth of the knowledge of God, and the life of immortality. By the gift of these they are made sons of God, as he is:

> Born of blood or of fleshly will he was not,
> > nor of the will of man
> > > but of God was he born.[44]
> And the Logos became flesh,
> > and he dwelt among us,
> > > full of grace and truth.[45]
> Of his plenitude[46] it is that all we received
> > favour after favour,
> For the Law was given by Moses;
> > grace and truth came by Jesus Christ.[47]

Following the above comes an explanation fully in the spirit of the text: "No man has seen God at any time," not even Moses any more than the self-styled prophets of the false divinities: "the only begotten Son, who is in the bosom of the Father" (i, 18), he it is who makes him known. The invisibility of God here asserted is a principle fundamental to the Johannine theology and to the mystical gnosis on which that theology depends.[48] The Law which Moses "gave" was taught him by intermediary angels. The Logos-Christ is the only Revealer, as he is the only Saviour; none but he imparts "grace and truth," because none but he knows God in himself and is able to tell of him and explain him to his faithful believers, to his initiates. He is the exegete of God, the Master of the mystery. The operating idea is that of the unknown God, inaccessible to common intelligence but revealed in mystical initiation by a divine mediator. And there is but one true mystery. It is the Christian.

How precisely the divine sonship of the Logos stands related to its incarnation is a question not easily answered. Nevertheless it is not without purpose that the divine sonship of the believer is presented as of the same type as the sonship of Jesus Christ, the incarnate Word. The author had no intention, and felt no need, to explain the origin of the human form in which the Logos was made visible on the earth. He presents it as a real form, just as he presents as real the miracle-signs which he makes the Christ perform, while giving them a wholly spiritual signification. Meanwhile, if men of flesh and blood are born anew in spirit by a spiritual generation which has nothing to do with the union of the sexes, the fertilization of woman and the natural growth of the embryo, that is because the Word itself, by taking flesh, became the prototype of the children of God, the only begotten Son.[49] As only begotten Son of the Father, the Christ Jesus has no mother in this world, any more than he has an earthly father: the Marriage at Cana makes that clear enough. The sublime mysticism of our author, which ignores, if it does not disdain, the virgin conception, is not any more in agreement either with the idea of the incarnation of the Logos as taking place in the womb of a woman naturally fertilized or with the pre-existence of the man Jesus before the Logos-incarnation. The Logos appears in the flesh when it becomes active as the Christ. To regard such a conception as more improbable than the traditional dogma of the virgin birth would be childish from the historical point of view.

Truth to say, the Gospel itself, both discourse and narration, is in a sense another incarnation of the Logos as light and life. For it is expressly under these images of Light and Life that narrative and discourses reveal the work of the Logos-Christ. The Johannine Christ is the spiritual light of the world, and he comes to bring life eternal to men. The miracle of the man born blind confirms him in the first as principle of light; the miracle of Lazarus in the second as principle of life. Before healing the blind man Jesus declares (ix, 4–5):

Needs must I work
the works of Him who sent me
while there is day.
Comes the night
when none can work.
While I am in the world
light am I of the world.

In like manner before raising Lazarus (xi, 24–26):

> I am the resurrection and the life;
>> whoso believes in me, though he die, shall live.
> And whoso lives and believes in me
>> shall never die.

To deny the symbolic character of these miracles reveals a strange preoccupation of mind in those who make the denial. The miracles symbolize in action what Jesus expressly says in the words which introduce them.

But the Light which the Christ brings to men is no promise of access to the Kingdom of God by repentance of sin; and the Life that he gives them is not immortality on the earth at the general resurrection of the dead. Whoso believes in the Son sent from God and in his life-giving power participates at once and from then onwards in the Son's eternal life. He who believes is thereby and already among the elect; he who believes not is thereby and already damned. No Day of Judgment is needed to judge them hereafter; and the resurrection of their bodies is uncalled for (iii, 16–18; v, 24).

> So God loved the world
>> that he gave his only begotten Son,
> That whoso believes in him should not perish
>> but have life eternal.
> For God sent not the Son to the world
>> to judge the world
>>> but that the world might be saved by him.
> Whoso believes in him is not judged;
>> whoso believes not is judged already . . .
> Verily, verily, I tell you
>> that whoso hears my word
>>> and believes in Him who sent me
> Has life eternal,
>> and to judgment is not exposed
>>> but has passed from death to life.[50]

As we have already seen, the visible and material sacraments of the faith have a wholly spiritual meaning, that of an inner rebirth with participation in the eternal life of the Christ. But the Christ died, as he had lived, in the real flesh of humanity and in a state of obedience even to the death of the cross, in order that believers might live in spirit. If he appeared in flesh without being born of flesh (i, 13; iii, 5–6), it was that he might accomplish his work in his own person, the work of preaching his mystery and making a gift to men of his mortal existence.

In the canonical edition of the Gospel this doctrine, in substance too fine for the faith of the multitude, is limited and made concrete by borrowing from the older Gospel tradition and from the sacramentalism of First Corinthians, which we have already found incorporated in the tradition of the synoptic Gospels. Certain additions to the original texts of the discourses join the resurrection of the dead with the parousia of the Lord (iii, 16–18; v, 24). The supplement added to the discourse on the bread of life introduces the symbol of flesh and blood into the eucharistic Supper, the symbol which betokens mystic participation in the life of the Christ by mystic commemoration of his death (vi, 51b–58). Without exaggeration it may be said that sacramental symbolism was developed to a point where it covered the whole career of the Christ as told in the Gospels. One incident of the passion betrays it very clearly—the issue of water and blood from the side of Jesus when pierced by the soldier's lance. On this there is a comment in the first Epistle of John (v, 6–8):

> This is he who came by water and blood,
>   Jesus Christ,
> Not in water only,
>   but in water and in blood.
> And it is the spirit that bears witness,
>   because the spirit is the truth;
> For three there are that bear witness,
>   spirit, water and blood,
>   and the three make one.

This is not the gibberish it might seem to be. On the contrary, it presents the quintessence of the Christian mystery conveyed in the language of gnosis. The Son of God was made manifest on earth by water, and in water, when he came to the baptism of John; he was made manifest by blood, and in blood, when he died on the cross.[51] In both cases the Spirit bore witness; at his baptism, by descending into the Christ (i, 29–34); at his death, when the Christ "gave up" the Spirit bestowed on him (xix, 30). For the breath yielded up, mystically understood, is the Holy

Spirit set free,[52] so to say, by the death of the Christ that it may be poured out at large on believers. The three make but one because, finally, it is the Spirit who bears witness to the Christ in water and in blood, in his baptism and in his passion.

But the meaning of our passage is not yet exhausted. It must not be overlooked that, according to the evangelist, water and blood issued, and issued together, from the side of the Crucified. By this the evangelist would signify the birth of the Church, in the manner of Eve's creation as issuing from the side of Adam; in this way he shows the fountain of eternal life flowing from the side of Jesus as the Christ had announced it would—"out of his body streams of living water will flow" (vii, 38). The stream is canalized, as it were, in the sacraments of Christian initiation; the water representing baptism, sacrament of spiritual regeneration; the blood representing the eucharist, sacrament of eternal life in union with the Christ who died for men and rose from the dead. It is by means of these two sacraments that the witness, three in one, still goes on as a present fact, the Christ continuing to come by water and by blood, the Spirit continuing to bear witness to him in water and in blood. The Holy Spirit which formerly bore witness to the Christ during his earthy mission, in his baptism, and in his death, now bears witness to him continually through the medium of baptismal immersion and the eucharistic meal. Thus the Christian mystery is evenly balanced by the attachment of its two sacraments to the two extremities of the saving Christ's career, baptism and death mystically interpreted by their spiritual effects. And thus the fourth Gospel, in the correlation of its two parts, takes the form of a sublime and balanced catechism, but always, like the synoptics, a catechism of initiation into the Christian mystery.

6. Birth-Stories and the Antedating of the Epiphany

Before entering upon our study of the mystery of the Church we must needs descend for a moment from the high regions we have been exploring to mark the upsurge of a lower mysticism, of a vulgar supernaturalism and mythology, which made its appearance in Christian tradition and became no less firmly anchored there, and no less amply developed, than the metaphysical mysticism whose first forms have just been described. Ancient speculation did not confine itself to the question of the heavenly Saviour's pre-existence in eternity; it became active also, and perhaps at an earlier date, about the conditions of his birth upon the earth.

The earliest Christian generation knew that Jesus had brothers and parents, nor have the mythologues who would suppress the historical Jesus been able to get rid of these by mere conjecturing. The first groups of Jewish Christians were not nourished on transcendental speculations. Quite early, however, the idea arose that since Jesus was the Messiah, he must be son of David, and indeed was his son, since it was so written in Scripture. Doubtless those who asserted this were in no great haste to find out how it was possible; but the unbelieving Jews would not be slow to ply the believing brethren with malicious questions about the matter. It occurred to the believing party that the difficulty might be met by producing a genealogy. Two were produced, Matthew's and Luke's, which contradict and reciprocally cancel each other. Both agree in naming Joseph as the father of Jesus; but they assign different fathers to Joseph and take us back on different lines of ascent to David, one (Matthew) following the series of Kings to Jeconiah, and the other (Luke) adopting Nathan son of David, of whom the Scriptures give only the name (2 Samuel v, 14). Of such fictions the historian need take no account, except in so far as they prove the absence at the beginning of any genealogical tradition about the Davidic origin of Jesus, and reveal the general belief, in the first times, that Jesus was born, without miracle, of Joseph and Mary. For both genealogies are based on the name of Joseph as father of Jesus, and it was through Joseph that Jesus was at first thought to be of Davidic blood.[53] From this it is evident that the genealogies were invented in circles which as yet had no idea of the miraculous conception, and that the birth-legend inserted in the third Gospel was formed at first under the same conditions as the genealogies. It is true that Jesus, in this legend, is born amid miraculous circumstances, but as issue of the marriage of Joseph and Mary.

Where, when and how the idea arose of the virgin conception we can only guess. It was not in the first community of believers, nor in the very earliest time, and not without influence, at least indirect, from surrounding paganisms. Both of the birth legends represent, as they have come down to us, a somewhat complex elaboration, to which the Gospel editors have given the last touches. Matthew's legend, notwithstanding the mythological influences traceable in it, has the form of a Jewish *haggada* (anecdote) or of an haggadic collection, minutely and artificially built up on biblical texts, with formal emphasis on the connexion with scripture. From this we may conclude that this version of the legend was born in a circle of Judaizing Christianity, but of a Judaism somewhat unorthodox, in which the divine filiation of the Messiah was admitted without scruple, and pharisaic rabbinism held in suspicion. Northern Syria, between Antioch and the Euphrates, has been suggested for the birthplace not only of the legend but of the whole Gospel of Matthew.54 In those regions Judaizing Christians known as "Nazareans" were still to be found as late as the fourth century. They used an Aramean Gospel containing the birth stories of our Matthew. In Luke the stories are dominated by the spirit of traditional Judaism and conceived in connexion with a legend of John the Baptist and in dependence on it; they would seem to have originated among Jewish Christians living in northern Palestine or in southern Syria.55 The fulfilment of prophecy is hardly less implied than in Matthew's version, but is here clothed in a garment of romantic fiction.

On both sides the culminating point of the mythical legend is the miraculous conception by the operation of the Holy Spirit. Jesus is Son of God because, physiologically speaking, God is the operating cause of his generation. This is not offered in the grossly primitive sense of the old mythologies, the Greek for example, which describes the amours of Zeus and other gods, with metamorphoses appropriate to the different circumstances. Even among the pagans of that time a few pious and enlightened men were taking the matter more seriously, Plutarch holding the opinion of the Egyptians to be plausible that a woman might conceive by the approach of the Spirit of God. But this idea was not reached at a single bound from the starting point. In the ancient literature of Christianity we catch glimpses of the successive stages or, one might well say, the gropings by which the apotheosis of Jesus was realized in the faith of believers and in their catechisms.

We cannot remind ourselves too often that the point of departure for this apotheosis was the belief that Jesus had become Christ and made his entrance, so to say, into the sphere of divinity *by his resurrection*. This was the first apostolic Gospel, the Gospel of Paul and of Peter: the Son of God had been declared to be God's Son, and manifested as God's Son, *by his resurrection* (Romans i, 4). The Epiphany of the Christ, as first conceived, took place *in the resurrection itself*, and the evidence for it lay in apparitions or visions of him as risen from the dead. The earthly life of Jesus, in its relation to the post-mortem manifestation of him as the Christ, had been an indispensable preliminary but of secondary importance. His great revelations, his essential instructions were not attached to the earthly preliminary. Criticism has for some time suspected, for example, that the scene of the Transfiguration of Jesus in the Synoptics had its origin in an apparition of the Risen One. We have it so presented in the Apocalypse of Peter where it is bound up with a revelation on the end of the age, the happiness of the elect and the punishment of reprobates. It will be noted that the same perspective, but more compressed, is maintained in the preamble to Acts (i, 3–11),[56] and that quite perceptible traces of it are retained in the closing passages of Matthew (xxviii, 16–20),[57] Luke (xxiv, 44–53),[58] John (xx, 21–26; xxi, 15–19)[59] and deutero-canonical Mark (xvi, 14–20).[60] In all these cases, essential teachings, and the command to preach the Gospel everywhere, are attached to manifestations of the Risen One.

This epiphany of the Christ in his divine character has been antedated by Mark and turned into a scene of transfiguration during his earthly life. The confession of Peter prepares the way for it. Six days after Peter has recognized Jesus as Christ, Jesus appears on the mountain in heavenly glory and the voice of the Father proclaims him Son of God. The result of this antedated apotheosis—and indeed the object of it—is to place the action of Jesus in going up to Jerusalem to die there, and to place the death itself, under the banner of the Son of God, so that the witness of the apostles may rest on a wider base, and an answer be given to those who decry their witness as a story made up after the event to overcome the scandal of the cross. Note also that the same evangelist has similarly antedated the revelations of Jesus concerning the end of the world (Mark xiii), representing them as given before his death. We are entitled to say that antedating, or anticipation, has here been systematically practised. The antedating of the Transfiguration in particular, its transposition from a revelation of the Christ after his resurrection to an event in the earthly life of Jesus, once admitted as a fact, has an importance for the history of the Gospel tradition not recognized by those critics who allowed it only as a hypothesis.

A new step towards apotheosis, the more easily to be recognized because the Gospel tradition so-called seems to have held back from it for a long time, was taken by antedating the epiphany of the Son of God to the very beginning of the Galilean ministry in the baptism of Jesus by John. The Gospel of Mark is written within this framework, which dominates the tradition of all the written Gospels known to us. As the scene of the Baptism is constructed, it includes, as simultaneous, the Messianic consecration of Jesus by the Spirit, the heavenly voice which acclaims him Son of God, the institution of Christian baptism and the witness to its superiority over the baptism of the sect called after John. At those points the framework of Christian catechesis remained for a long time fixed, while keeping an open door to all the teachings given in the name of Jesus and represented as having been spoken by him before his death. The Marcan framework is easily recognized in Matthew and Luke, to which the birth chapters seem to have been added at a later date, and we have just seen that the fourth Gospel keeps within the frame of set purpose. The connexion with John the Baptist shows us the circumstances under which our frame was elaborated. It had reference to the propaganda of the sect which claimed to be derived from John, proving that Christianity was born independently of it and was pre-eminent in regard to it. Whence we may infer that the elaboration took place in a region and at a time when Christian propaganda came into competition with that of the Baptist sect. This would again bring us to the countries of Transjordania and Syria and to a time when the rivalry of the two sects was still a matter of concern to the leaders of the Christian movement.

The opening chapters of Matthew and Luke are evidence that in course of time the Marcan frame came to appear inadequate and that the attempt was made to throw back the Epiphany of the Christ to the first moment of his human existence. Always the Son of God, he had been God's Son on his assumption of humanity; the fact has been made evident in the miracle of his birth and in its accompaniment of other marvels in keeping with an event so tremendous. Such was the new theory. In the Jewish-Christian circles for which Matthew was elaborated, it seems that care was taken to give prominence to the Davidic filiation of Jesus (while giving it at the same time a symbolic turn) with the special object of barring the way to certain conclusions which might be inferred from Mark. On the one hand it might be argued that Jesus became Son of God by adoption at his baptism (this adoptionist doctrine was not ill looked on in Rome); on the other hand it might be said, with Mark as authority, that a higher power had governed Jesus from birth to death and then departed from him; or again, forcing the meaning of the epiphany, the existence of Jesus before his baptism might be suppressed altogether, as the original author of the fourth Gospel and the author of the Epistle to the Hebrews seem to have suppressed it; or, again, various forms of Docetism might be fitted into the frame, as was done by some of the gnostics and, in his time, by Marcion.[61]

To give eminence to the new conception of the epiphany, the Gospel stories made use not only of Old Testament texts but of mythical themes then current, adapting them to the texts or choosing the texts to fit in with the myths. The theme drawn upon for exploitation in both versions was that of the divine child, born in a place of no repute, whose presence is miraculously announced to shepherds;[62] though the Lucan legend, working up the theme to make Bethlehem the birthplace, has not forgotten that David was a shepherd (ii, 8-20). Matthew's legend brings in its Magi and herald-star because it belongs to a region (Persia-Babylon) where the Magi and their astrology were well known; but the star is there to connect with the Star of which Balaam, the great soothsayer, had spoken long ago as destined to come out of Jacob (Numbers xxiv, 17). The time was not far distant when the same text was applied to the impostor Messiah Bar-

Cochba, "son of the Star."[63] The theme of the divine child, or child of destiny, menaced with death by hostile powers and miraculously escaping from a massacre, is similarly exploited in Matthew, but with an eye to Moses, as prototype, and to his flight from Egypt into Midian. The construction of a myth is of all things easiest to explain; it is also true that nothing is more arbitrary nor, at bottom, more incredible than the myth itself. But the Epiphany of the Son of God had to be magnified by one means or another. Even the fourth Gospel, with all its sublime symbolism, found no better way to give lustre to the Epiphany of the incarnate Logos than to bring Jesus to the marriage at Cana for the changing of water into wine, wherein the Christ "manifests his glory" by performing a miracle borrowed from the myth and ritual of Dionysus.[64]

7. THEORY CONCERNING THE BAPTIST: THE MANDEANS

In the last two stages of our advancing exposition we have seen, at each stage, how the Christ, on the way to apotheosis, was exalted at the expense of John the Baptist. At the stage before the last the movement came into contact with John and subordinated him to itself; and again, at the stage last reached in its mythical evolution, we have seen how this same subordination was repeated, with John's legend now expanded and apparently in a manner favourable to Jesus. The same effort to subordinate John and make capital out of him is to be met with in almost every one of the passages in which our Gospels, the fourth included, have thought well to mention the Baptist. To the impartial critic the meaning of this is evident enough. It can only mean that the Christian sect, born later than the sect of John, and in some way an offshoot from it, found it also a rival in the first period; and, further, that Christianity, striving for its own pre-eminence, took pains to disguise in part the extent of its debt to the Baptist's sect, and at the same time to interpret the Baptist's rôle as a function contributing to the rôle of Jesus, making John out to be a forerunner of the Christ and conscious of himself as such—an idea which never entered the mind of John nor that of his followers. And this notwithstanding that the founders of the two sects, Jesus and John, encountered a similar fate and had the same fortune of glorious survival in the faith of their adherents. Both movements must have shared a basic belief in the imminence of the Kingdom of God, and it was evident that one essential rite of Christianity, namely baptism, was borrowed by it from the sect of John.

Some recent writers have maintained that the question of the relation between the two sects has been put on a completely new footing by the publication of the religious literatures of the Mandeans,[65] said to be survivors of John's sect, and by certain commmentaries on this literature lately put out.[66] But, however interesting the greater part of the suggested comparisons may be, they do not seem to justify the conclusions the writers would draw from them, to the effect that early Christianity and the New Testament in general depend on Johannism to a much greater extent and more directly than careful criticism of New Testament books has hitherto been able to grant. It has not been proved that the religion of the Mandeans represents original Johannism more exactly than any Christian sect of our time, or all of them taken together, represent original Christianity. Mandean religion is certainly a great gnosis, but it is an historical growth which underwent diverse influence in the course of its development and was not a great gnosis at the beginning. And this beginning may well have been much later than the birth of Christianity. No proof has been given that any one of its writings is earlier than those of the New Testament. It is certain that the general compilation of the Mandean scriptures was made in Islamic times, not under the control of a homogeneous tradition, but by borrowing from different sects and with considerable incoherence in the total result. Nothing in it betrays the least knowledge of ancient Christianity, nor even, in regard to John the Baptist, the least souvenir which could be claimed as historical and independent of the Gospels. Mandean baptism, in its ritual economy, is, rather, dependent on the baptismal liturgy of the Nestorian Church. The gnosis was a belated growth whose original point of departure may, perhaps, be the same as that of the Christian gnoses, but it has no title to a place in the genealogy of traditional Christianity. Risky—to use no stronger term—as the pretention is which would explain the literature and evolution of Christianity before Irenaeus by reference to Marcion alone, it is more risky, certainly not less, to offer the religion of the Mandeans as the true key to ancient Christianity and to the New Testament.

A position much more in need to be made good would be the following.—Christianity did not make its entry into the world and into history as a great doctrine already defined in its essential parts, but as a Great Hope, flung at large over the Mediterranean world in the name of Jesus Christ and under the covering form of Jewish monotheism. Almost immediately and for more than a century, this Hope may be seen repeating itself in the diverse mentalities of those who now in this manner, now in that, gave it favourable reception, as light is broken up by a prism into a thousand colours. A boiling ferment of doctrines, a swarming of sects, a religious chaos was produced, which would soon have broken up into scattered fragments without future, had not certain steadying forces, due to its origin, been retained throughout. To these principles of stability, more and more resolutely affirmed in the last sixty years of the second century, the institution of the Catholic Church owes its existence. But the Church before becoming an institution was an idea. We make bold to say it was also a myth, for that reason a word must be said about the myth before we study the institution.

8. Birth of the Mystery of the Church

The mystic conception of the Church was born almost simultaneously with the birth of the Christian religion. There was no need to create it; no more was needed than to take it over from Judaism, detached completely from Jewish nationalism and enlarged by adaptation to the Christian mystery. Judaism, in spite of internal divisions, less felt among the Jews of the Dispersion, was a Church. It was made a Church by common faith and hope, by the bond of confraternity which united all the synagogues one with another and with their common centre at Jerusalem, a centre at once national and religious. Judaism in its own eyes was truly "the community of God" and was proud to be.

Of this mystic community, waiting for complete accomplishment in the Kingdom of God, Christianity professed at first to be only the realization hoped for, or its beginning, or the means, the instrument by which it would be made perfect. It was thus that the new religion proclaimed itself to the Jews everywhere and to all the pagan converts to Judaism: and when Judaism finally refused to recognize the Christ, it was thus that it maintained the claim to be the true "community of God," the true Church. Christianity then declared itself "the community of God," and from that time onwards denied the claim of the Jews to the very attribute it had borrowed from them.

And so all the mystic pride of the Jews in the consciousness they had of being God's chosen people, the authentic Society of True Believers, passed over entire to the Christians. Firmly entrenched in this conviction they saw with regret, but without dismay, that they were cast out of the Jews. Paul reveals his mind on the subject quite clearly in the Epistle to the Romans: surely it was his "great sorrow and unceasing pain" to see himself separated from his brethren in Israel—or, rather, to see their blindness in presence of the Gospel. But what could he do? They were blind to the fulfilment of prophecy in the Christ; the providential scheme of salvation by faith, open equally to Jews and Gentiles, interested them not. A sad affair! But it turns out that the teachableness of the Gentiles and the unbelief of the Jews were foretold by the prophets just as those qualities are now being shown (ix–x). Soon, under the indefinite delay of the Second Coming, the salvation of the Jews lost present interest and, the question becoming speculative, the idea occurred that the Jews had providentially fallen into temporary unbelief in order to give the pagans time to rally to the cause of the Christ; the turn of the Jews would come later (xi). Until that happened, and none the less for its postponement, the hellenist Christians were the true people of God.

Organization in the mystery had not proceeded far before hellenist Christianity began to conceive itself organized as the body of the Christ. In the characteristic prayers of the *Didache* we have already encountered the idea of the Church as assimilated to the bread of the Supper made out of grain at first scattered and now brought together; thus would the Church, at present dispersed over the earth—as the Synagogue was— soon be gathered up in the Kingdom of God, united in one body, as the bread was (*Didache*, ix, 4). First Corinthians shows further how, from this point, advance was quickly made to the conception of the existing Church, no longer as a scattered society, but as one living body, the mystic body of Jesus raised from the dead. In the words "there being one only bread, one only body are we" (x, 17), we encounter the same symbolism as in the *Didache* which likens the bodies of the faithful to the Eucharistic bread; but the words which follow: "for we are all partakers of that one only bread" go beyond the *Didache* by making the one bread of which every Christian partakes, no longer the bread he eats, but the very Christ who is figured in the bread, in such way that the mystic union of all the faithful in Christ is also figured in the bread of the Supper. The rules laid down for the eucharistic meal are founded on the principle that, in order to be "the Lord's Supper" the meal must be one at which the material consumed is shared *in common*, and not one in which each participant eats and drinks what he will, so that the same bread may be Christ in *all*, and *all* one body in the Christ and by the Christ (xi, 20–21).

The theory of the mystic body is expounded at length in the instructions about spiritual gifts (*charismata*), a part of the document (xii, xiv) later than Paul but earlier than Marcion.[67] It may be taken as almost contemporary with the *Didache*, since it knows of missionaries still travelling under the name of apostles and of prophets who prophesy in meetings of the community (1 Cor. xii, 28–29; xiv, 26–33). The instructions are intended to prevent the disorder which inevitably resulted when the spiritual gifts became competitive (xii, 4–6):

> Differences of gifts there are,
>> but the Spirit is the same;
> Differences of service there are,
>> but the Lord is the same,
> Differences of working there are,
>> but God is the same,
>>> who works all in all.

If the principle is one, the effects are many. But the Church, the community, as well as the principle, must also be one. Like the human body, the Church, as the body of Christ, has many members, all necessary; these must not be jealous of each other

287

but behave as mutually interdependent, which is what they really are. The mere enumeration of spiritual functions shows that the communities were suffering from an excess of riches, and it is clear enough that a lowering of their activities had become due—apostles, doctors, wonder-workers, healers, helpers, administrators, speakers with tongues. So let every gift-bearer do his best not to annoy the others. But all this upsurge of enthusiasm was conceived as going on within the body of the Christ, and wits were taxed to prevent it upsetting the organic equilibrium.

Other formulas were used to express the mystic conception of the Church. In Second Corinthians the Corinthian community is described as "a chaste virgin" whom its apostle has espoused to the Christ (2 Cor. xi, 2). Since each community was, with the others, the Church of God, what is here said of Corinthian Christianity might be repeated of the whole. It is the application to the Christ and to the Church of an image familiar to the Hebrew prophets—the marriage of Jehovah with Israel. The author of the Epistle to the Ephesians connects the mystic notion of the Church as the spouse of the Christ with the other mystic notion of it as the Christ's body (v, 23–24). "The husband," he says, "is head of the wife, as Christ is the head of the Church, he, the saviour of the body"—meaning the body which is the Church itself. He then goes on, in his bad style (v, 23–24):

> Husbands, love your wives
> as Christ loved the Church
> And gave himself up for her to make her holy,
> purifying her in the bath of water with speech,
> To offer the Church to himself in her glory,
> having no spot, nor wrinkle, nor aught of that kind
> but holy and spotless.

Finally he quotes the text from Genesis about the union of man and woman and notes that it contains "a great mystery"— a profound secret of mystic theology—"in regard to the Christ and to the Church" (v, 32). Here our author touches the fringe of certain pagan mysteries; not does he fall far short of making the Church a transcendant personification, an *aeon*, as it is in some of the gnostic systems.

The same reflection is forced upon us by the Pastor of Hermas.

Here, however, the Church is not the eternal Jerusalem described by the seer of the Apocalypse as ready to descend upon earth, but the visible institution ready to get organized here below.[68] The Church herself is the teacher who, in the form of an aged woman, instructs Hermas in the first part of his book. She is at first shown to him seated on a great white throne and holding in her hand a book of prophecy containing threats against the pagans and a consoling promise for the righteous. A year later the same woman comes back to Hermas and this time leaves him a little book to copy in which, among other things, there is a promise of pardon, but for one occasion only, to all Christian sinners, even to apostates, who repent before the great tribulation —that is, before the approaching persecution. Hermas then learns that this woman, whom he had believed to be the Sybil, is the Church. She is old because she was created before all things, and it was by her that the world was made.

This is not a solitary instance of fantastic speculation about the Church. The ancient homily, known as the second Epistle of Clement, has the teaching that he who does the will of the Father belongs to the primal Church, to the spiritual Church, created before the sun and the moon, which is the Church of Life.[69] Now the living Church is the body of the Christ. For Scripture declares that God made man male and female (Gen. i, 27); the male is the Christ; the female is the Church, spiritual as the Christ is. The Church was revealed for our salvation, at the end of the ages, in the flesh of the Christ, showing that whosoever keeps the Church unchanged in the flesh shall receive the Holy Spirit; for the flesh is the image of the spirit, and he who changes the copy shall have no part in the original, which is spirit, and spirit is the Christ. The flesh of such an one, when united to Christ, is made capable of receiving an incorruptible life from the Spirit, and no man can express or describe the good things which God keeps for his chosen ones.

This gnosis, nonsensical farrago as it may seem, is hardly more audacious in its mode of expression than that of the Epistle to the Romans, or to the Corinthians with the thesis of the two Adams, or than that of the Epistle to the Ephesians on the Christ and the Church as a transcendant husband and wife, to say nothing of the conception in the Apocalypse of the New

Jerusalem as "the bride of the Lamb."[70] Had this line of speculation been carried much further the homily would have joined
company with gnosis in the most delirious of its expressions.
But our author checked himself and reduces his gnosis to a moral
lesson: the Church being in our flesh, as it is in the flesh of the
Christ, and we, in our very selves, being thus the flesh of the
Christ, it behoves us to guard our flesh in purity, lest we dis-
honour the Church and the Christ.

In his third vision Hermas still has the Church before him,
but this time accompanied by six young men about to construct
a building; the woman sits on a bench of ivory covered with a
white veil, and makes Hermas sit down on her left hand, because
the seats to the right are kept for the martyrs; and the young
men set about building a tower on the water with stones brought
to them by thousands of workers. The woman explains that the
tower is the Church, that is, herself; it is built on water, because
the life of the believer is saved by water—doubtless by baptism;
the six young men are the first-created angels to whom the Lord
has entrusted the government of all created beings; the countless
workers are also angels, helpers to the six; the stones, squared
and white, and fitting exactly, are the apostles, bishops, teachers
and deacons with a record of good service; the other stones
drawn up from the bottom of the water, are the martyrs—etc.
etc. At this point it becomes clear that the building of the Church
is leading up to a consideration of the end of the world. So,
when Hermas asks the woman if the end is at hand, she answers
that the tower is not yet finished, but soon will be, and that the
end will then come; meanwhile the important thing is to spread
abroad the warnings that have been received and to give heed
to them. This said, the woman addresses a severe admonition
to the faithful and especially to their leaders whom she reprimands
for their divisions (*Vision*, iii, 8–9).

In his ninth parable Hermas takes up the theme of the tower
in new detail. We now learn that the master builder, together
with the rock which serves him for a foundation and the entrance
door of the building, is the Head of the six angels, in other
words he is the Son of God, the Christ himself, who thus comes
first and not seventh in the group of higher beings; "the other
six form his retinue, on his right hand and on his left." Hermas

sees the Son of God in the fashion of "a man surrounded by glory and of colossal stature"—just as the Christ, rising from his tomb, is represented in the Gospel of Peter. Getting somewhat entangled in these speculations, the good Hermas informs us in the preamble to the parable that the Holy Spirit, who is the Son of God, and who formerly spoke to him under the figure of the Church, has since spoken to him by the Shepherd, angel of penitence (*Parable*, ix). But the Shepherd is not a simple figure. Neither is the Church which was created before all things. We may recall the feminine hypostasis of the Christ in the second Epistle of Clement, which the Church here resembles.

9. BIRTH OF THE CHURCH-CONSCIOUSNESS

The letters attributed to Ignatius of Antioch seem to have been written when the flood of gnostic heresies was at its height, and may be described as a mystic canonization of the episcopate intended to secure the cohesion of the communities and to oppose the innovators by making the episcopate into the object of a veritable cult, in which the institution of bishops is no longer merely that of a corporate body, but is tending to become a sacred hierarchy. The author gives no place to the Church-myth of Hermas and must have written later than the date of his mythology. It is not enough that a man call himself a Christian, says the letter to the Magnesians, he must *be* a Christian, and he is no Christian when he holds to any kind of union in which the bishop has no part. "Let everything be done in the concord ordained by God, the bishop presiding in the place of God, the presbyters replacing the senate of the apostles, the deacons . . . charged with the service of Jesus Christ, who was at God's right hand before the ages and was revealed at the end of them . . . just as the Lord, united to the Father, did nothing without the Father, either by himself or by his apostles, so you, likewise, do nothing by yourselves without the bishop and the presbyters . . . One only prayer, one only supplication, one only spirit, one hope in charity and innocent joy—even that is Jesus Christ, above whom there is nothing." Obedience must be rendered to the bishop: "Be in submission to the bishop, and each to the others, as Jesus Christ, according to the flesh, was in submission to the Father, and the apostles to the Father, to the Christ and to the Spirit."[71]

There is other evidence that the object of these admonitions is to avert the danger of heresy. In the letter to the Trallians (6–7) we read as follows: "I beseech you nourish yourselves on Christian food only, and abstain from every foreign plant, that is from heresy"—the word has now acquired its traditional meaning. "Its professors, to make themselves respectable, mingle Jesus Christ with their doctrine, as if they were putting deadly poison into honeyed wine . . . Protect yourselves from such people. This you will do by not getting puffed up and by keeping yourselves inseparable from Jesus Christ, from the bishop and from the precepts of the apostles. No man has a clear conscience who undertakes anything in separation from the bishop, the presbytery, and the deacons." But the practical interest evinced by this advice detracts nothing from its essentially mystic character. It serves to show how, under the menacing pressure of heresy, a vague sense of unity among Christians is now rising into a clear consciousness of that unity in which, as we know from Justin, God and the Christ are seen as present in those who have become the effectual ministers of the mystery, the chief depositories and agents of the Spirit by whom the Church has been animated from the beginning. In reality these functionaries were become the guardians of tradition, and it was a tradition of which they themselves were about to fix the form. Our author, meanwhile, proclaims them representatives of God, substitutes for the Christ, successors of the apostles; and insists far less on their doctrinal function than on their strictly pastoral and mystical rôle. He would have Christianity range itself behind the ministers of the Christian mystery, and a deaf ear turned to teachers who are working to break Christian unity by proclaiming dangerous novelties.

It is important to bear in mind that our Ignatius, who himself claims to be a bishop, and has the surname "God-possessed," is an ardent mystic, a seeker after martyrdon, of which he tells the Romans they have taught him the lesson (*Romans*, 3, 1)—a probable allusion to the Pastor of Hermas. "I write to all the Churches and send word to all of you, that I shall willingly die for God, if you do nothing to hinder it . . . Food for wild-beasts let me be, that by them I may have access to God. God's wheat am I, and the teeth of wild beasts will grind me, that I may be formed purest bread of the Christ. Give the beasts your caresses for becoming my tomb and let no fragment of my body remain that any man should have the trouble of burying it. Then shall I be truly a disciple of Jesus Christ when the world sees nothing more of my body" (*Romans*, 4). Perhaps all this is a trifle overdone and a little finer than nature; perhaps our author himself, in a situation less imaginary, would have somewhat tempered his eloquence; but there can be no doubt that his enthusiasm is sincere and that his interpretation of the consciousness of the bishop-martyr, as a eucharistic oblation to God, is superbly done.

The thought of Ignatius is saturated in eucharistic mysticism: "I have no taste for corruptible food nor for the joys of this life: I would have the bread of God, which is the flesh of Jesus Christ, descended from David, and for drink I would have his blood, which is incorruptible love" (*Romans*, 7). This refers to the heavenly and wholly spiritual eucharist; but Ignatius speaks also of the Supper: "Deceive not yourselves . . . whoso follows a schismatic shall have no part in the Kingdom of God: whoso rules himself by strange doctrines, shall not share the benefits of the passion. Have a care then to use the one only eucharist, for there is only the one flesh of Our Lord Jesus Christ, and one cup for union in his blood, one only altar, as there is but one bishop, surrounded by the presbytery and the deacons. I go back to the Gospels as to the flesh of Jesus, and to the apostles as the presbytery of the Church. Love we also the prophets, for they announced the Gospel, they put their hope in it, they waited for it, they were saved by believing in it, being in the unity of Jesus Christ" (*Philadelphians*, 3–5).

Unity—all comes back to that: Old Testament is Gospel; Gospel is Jesus Christ; Jesus Christ is God of the Christian mystery, living Spirit of the Church. But what is the Christian mystery? It is that which the bishop with his helpers the priests and the deacons administers in every Church. Two Scriptures there are not; nor two Christs; nor two eucharists; nay, rightly speaking, there are not two Scriptures. All these are one in the Christ. In practice they are all one in the bishop, representative of the Christ in the Church. And outside of this mystery—what is there? Naught but the fantasies of professors without authority, naught but the error which is all they have to offer. And God, the Christ, the Church, the truth of the Old Testament and Gospel, the mystery of salvation—where are all these to be found? Nowhere else than in their one habitation—the Christian communities closely ranked round their several bishops.

In gaining this mystic consciousness of itself, as it stood firm against the gnostic flood, common Christianity became, in very fact, the Catholic Church. Come whence they may, these impassioned letters of church-mysticism contain something quite other than the first whisperings of theological formulas destined, when their voice has grown louder, to establish or defend an abstract and subtle dogma. They speak with the full voice of vehement faith, of Christianity established in that faith, and meeting the gnostic invasion with a bold front.

Chapter IX

THE GNOSTIC CRISIS

THE great work of mystic construction which we have been studying was not suddenly brought into being. It came forth from the Gospel, but without foresight in the Gospel that it was coming. The first missionaries had barely an inkling of what it would be; it was, so to say, the spontaneous issue of their labour, brought into being by an irresistible upsurge of faith achieving a result widely different from what the faithful had hoped for. They had hoped that the Kingdom of God would come; what came was the Church.

But the Church was not formed without internal conflicts no less dangerous to its growth than the conflict with outside forces and, in the end, no less fruitful. There were three main crises. The first, hardly perceptible to us, but pregnant with consequences, was that which led to the formation at Jerusalem of the Hellenist group of believers side by side with the Hebrew. The second was that in which Judaizing opposition arose to the work done by Hellenist preachers among the pagans. But hardly were communities of Hellenist Christians established on pagan territory, than their union was threatened by the intense religious fermentation which then broke out and was constantly changing its form under the influence of the varied elements drawn into the movement. This crisis of the growing age, the third to be encountered, begun almost in apostolic times, reached its height towards the middle, and was not finally overcome before the last quarter, of the second century.

During this period the Christian mystery, whose birth and development we have sketched, was threatened with disintegration. More exactly, as the movement increased in strength it had to disengage itself from a mass of strange excrescences and parasitic growths known under the general name of gnosis. This was an ebullition, sometimes superficial or near the surface, thrown up by that deep travail of faith of which traditional Christianity was also the outcome. Rightly understood Christianity itself is a disciplined gnosis born of the same movement which produced the gnoses called heretical, and brought to its own definition in the process of condemning them. The doctrine it proclaimed was a mystical knowledge of the divine secret and of the revealed programme of salvation. Thus Christianity, in its own way, was a gnosis, and so it has always remained. Nothing could be more *gnostic*, in the special sense of the word, than the declaration attributed to the Christ in Matthew xi, 27:

> None knows the Son, save the Father;
> None knows the Father, save the Son,
> and he to whom the Son will reveal him.

But Christianity had to force a way for itself through a swarm of gnostic sects among which, had it been less sure of itself, it might easily have dissolved and perished. This process we have now to study.

I. SIMON MAGUS

The first point on which we have to remark is that Simon the Magician, a contemporary of Jesus and of the first missionaries, is presented in Christian tradition as the father of heretical gnosis. There is a sense, however, in which the gnostic crisis had its birth in Judaism long before the preaching of the Gospel, and had long been a factor in the religious syncretism which arose in the Eastern world as a result of the successive conquests of the Persians and the Greeks, and in which mysteries of salvation were flourishing elements. Writings such as the Book of Enoch and Book of Daniel may be truly described as monuments of Jewish gnosis influenced by science and mystic speculation of foreign parentage. The Jew Philo was a gnostic, if ever there was one; and the Gospel itself, born though it was from a popular current of Jewish hope, drew its first breath of life in an atmosphere of gnosis, and breathed that air more deeply as it grew up. The Christian mystery was, as it were, a rectified gnosis with the chaff and impurities sifted out, and equipped with a doctrine and sacramental mysticism all its own. The systems commonly known as gnostic are, in their relation to the Christian, parallel variations of the same movement, each with a tendency to absorb the Gospel; they are not, as they are often represented to be, the wilful and belated distortions of a Gospel to which gnosis of every kind was originally foreign. The Christian mystery, which assumed definite forms as Catholic Christianity, has never repudiated its Jewish base in the principle of absolute monotheism, where the First of Beings, the Creator of the world and the God of Israel are unconditionally identified as One. Nor has it ever cut its line of communication with the historical point from which the Gospel makes its departure in the historical manifestation of Jesus. Nor has it ever lost hold on the idea of universal salvation by the death, followed by the resurrection, of the Christ. Now this last idea, mystic through and through, and stamping Christianity as one of the mystery religions, is the creation of gnosis. Of this idea heretical gnosis took possession to sublimate it into various systems, just as it made the God of monotheism transcendent to the point where he becomes the absolute unknowable and, in the effort to spiritualize the Christ, dissolved his existence into vapour.

In representing Simon the Magician as baptized by Philip in Samaria and subsequently repudiated by Peter for attempting to buy the gift of conferring the Holy Spirit from the apostles, the legend in Acts aimed at disqualifying this founder of a rival sect, representing him as only a provisional and jealous adherent to the newly born Christianity, whom the chief of the apostles justly put to shame. This legend is not more consistent than those of a later date which show the same Simon engaged in a subsequent competition with Peter in the East, and even at Rome; but there is nothing in it to permit a distinction[1] between the leader of the sect, who figures in writers on heresy, from the magician who, according to Acts, led the Samaritans astray. The existence of Simon is not to be denied on the pretext that we know him only in legend. The fact is simply that Simon, notwithstanding that Christian tradition has made him the father of all the heresies, never was a heretic in regard to Christianity, for he never professed it. Although Justin incautiously lets himself be deceived about the worship paid to Simon in Rome it does not follow that we must reject as untrue what he says about Simon being born in such or such village of the Samaria to which he belonged, or about the doctrine held in his time by the Simonians, that is, by Samaritans. These worshipped Simon as "God above every principality, power or essence" (which should not be condemned as *a priori* improbable, seeing that Christians did as much for Jesus) with "his supreme thought" under the name Helena, made into an associated object of the cult (*Apology*, 1, 26, 56). The truth is that Celsus, twenty years later, knew of Simonians who called themselves Helenians[2] and took them for a Christian sect, the description meeting with a lively protest from Origen (*C. Celsum*, 1, 57; vi, 15). Justin had already protested against it (*Apology*, 1, 26, 6–7) but without perceiving that he had supported it by representing Simon as the father of heresy in regard to the true faith. Some analogy between the two sects there must have been in doctrine, rites and propaganda, and some kind of affinity. Otherwise the pagan opinion echoed by Celsus and the attitude of Justin would be hard to explain.

The problem of Simon is complicated with the problem of Dositheus, another Samaritan sect-founder, sometimes represented as Simon's master and sometimes as his rival.[3] He might well have been both, but the documentary evidence is not decisive. Dositheus and Simon, both Samaritans, founded sects, each his own, which long survived them. They were two Samaritan Messiahs, both deified and worshipped after their death. Dositheus claimed to be the "prophet" announced by Moses for the last days (Deuteronomy xviii, 18). Though he denied the resurrection of the dead, as not taught in the Law, his disciples proclaimed him alive after death and carried up into heaven, like Moses and Elijah before him.[4] Simon's claim to be the Messiah was made under somewhat different conditions, and with more success. He seems to have been more independent of the Law and to have professed a kind of gnosis which his followers subsequently developed. The notice about him in Acts gives two indications, the second superimposed on the first. The first tells us that he made himself out to be "some great personage" (viii, 9)— a formula applied by Acts in analogous terms to Theudas (v, 36) and referring no doubt to their Messianic pretension: this was the account he gave of himself. His following, on the other hand, are said to have proclaimed him "that Power of God which is called the great Power" (viii, 10), meaning that Simon was an incarnation on earth of the sovereign power of God. The distinction here to be noted is that the latter definition represents in brief what Simonians were saying about Simon at the time (*c.* 130) when the editor of Acts was writing. First Corinthians says of the Christ in like manner that he was "Power and Wisdom of God" (i, 24). We may conclude that incarnation of these divine attributes was an idea familiar to the first forms of gnosis.

Among the Simonians the incarnation of Wisdom was alloted to Helena, Simon's female companion: she was the Supreme Thought, mother of all things; after issuing from the abode of divinity she brought forth the angels and the angels made the visible world, but they kept their mother a prisoner in order to conceal their origin and otherwise ignored God. After various metempsychoses—the most remarkable being that in which this feminine Logos became Helen of the siege of Troy—the Great Thought turns into a prostitute in a house of resort at Tyre; there the Great Power, incarnate in Simon, finds her, buys her freedom and attaches her to himself. In this gnostic poem (which the writers on heresy, to whom we owe the account of it, did not invent, though they may have put undue emphasis on some of its fearures) the Great Power is said to have been manifested in three forms; to the Jews, as Son, in Jesus who suffered death in appearance but not in reality; to the Samaritans, as Father, in Simon himself; to other people as the Holy Spirit. Salvation among the Simonians consists in the knowledge of this mystery; the knowledge carried with it freedom from the Law, which was a work of the creator-angels, and from laws of every kind, the distinction between good and evil being a human convention.[5]—In this outline we are following Irenaeus (*Heresies*, i, 28) and Hippolytus (*Philosophoumena*, vi, 19, 20).[6]

It was not Simon who elaborated the whole of this system, and the artifice by which the authors of it would make Christianity, not to speak of other religions, into a Simonism unaware of its own true character can only be an afterthought of a time when both Christian and Simonian propaganda had long been active. It does not follow from this that Simon and Helen never existed, nor that the essential features of the system do not go back to Simon, as de Faye would have it. Would it have been so easy to make him the father of gnosis if gnosis were something to which he was wholly a stranger? The points where the two systems meet are as striking as those where they part. From what has just been said it is clear that the Simonians were aware of the meeting points and made the most of them. Frail as is the testimony of the apocryphal Clementines in regard to Simon, it is nevertheless significant that they present Dositheus and Simon as disciples of John the Baptist. In historical strictness neither Simon nor Dositheus was a successor to John, any more than Jesus was, but affinity of origin and character there must have been between all these sects which arose in the same environment and almost at the same time. Both in reality and legend the case of Simon and Dositheus is not without analogy to the case of Jesus, their relative insuccess, compared with the fortune awaiting him, being due to the limits which their origin and circumstances imposed on their propaganda. But points of difference, as we have said, are equally striking. As regards Simon, his system lacked the prestige conferred on the Christian by its lofty ethic. What he said of the Law bears indeed a strong resemblance to statements in the Epistle to the Galatians (iii, 19) and in that to the Romans (v, 13, 20; vii, 1); but the rent these Epistles tear in the theoretical idea of duty is healed by the purity of the moral feeling which inspires what they have to say. Simon's gnosis, on the other hand, was largely compatible with superstitious magic and with some degree of moral licence, and continued to be compatible with both.

2. Menander

An analogous doctrine was preached at Antioch by Menander, said to have been a disciple of Simon. He too professed to be the heaven-sent Saviour of humanity. To his disciples he promised immortality—of what kind we do not know—and conferred a baptism which gave security for it.7 Justin names Menander between Simon and Marcion, as if these three were heads of the chief sects which the pagans were in the habit of confusing, under the name Christian, with the believers of the Great Church. Simon and Menander had taught, before Marcion, that the lower world was not created by the Invisible God whose intervention had brought about the salvation of mankind.

3. Cerinthus

Of Cerinthus as a human figure we know only the name, the

approximate time of his teaching and the place where he taught. He appeared in Asia Minor towards the end of the first century. Three-quarters of a century later the opponents of the Johannine writings attributed their paternity to Cerinthus, who had been a Judaizer and a millenarian in his eschatology, while professing a Christology more or less on the pattern of the fourth Gospel. If Iraeneus is to be believed (*Heresies*, i, 26) Cerinthus taught that the Supreme Being is too far removed above the world to take an interest in its affairs; a power ignorant of the supreme God had created it, another angel having created the Law and become the god of the Jews. A power ("virtue") from the supreme God had descended upon Jesus, son of Joseph and Mary, on the day of his baptism and dwelt in him up to the moment of his passion, when it forsook him; only the human Jesus suffered death and rose from the dead. It will be noted that the descent of the "virtue" is quite expressly indicated in the Synoptics and can be found also in the fourth Gospel as finally edited. The departure of the "power" is recorded in express terms by the Gospel of Peter in the words attributed to the dying Christ: "My power, my power, thou hast forsaken me." His dualism brings Cerinthus very near to Simon. He was also a precursor of Marcion. Justin seems to have had no knowledge of Cerinthus, but the Epistle of the Apostles, an apocryphal writing of mediocre importance,[8] which seems to have come out in Asia Minor in the second half of the second century, sets out to refute him by evidence derived, as so much other evidence had been, from imaginary conversations between the risen Christ and his disciples. The author was full of good intentions, but his work is sufficient proof that gnosticism had invaded the Church. Like Valentinus he represents the Logos as born from the Ogdoad, or combination of eight Principles; as receiving his "Wisdom" from the Father before descending into the world, and as bearing witness to himself under the figure of Gabriel. The opinion has often been advanced that Cerinthus is attacked in the Johannine Epistles (i, iv, 3, ii, 7); but the passages in question, like the apparition to Thomas in the fourth Gospel, aim rather at those who denied the reality of Christ's body, the Docetists, not at Cerinthus who did not deny, as they did, that Jesus suffered death as a real man.

301

4. THE SATORNILIANS

There existed in Justin's time a sect of Satornilians whose founder, Satornil, had taught at Antioch in the reign of Trajan (*Dialogue*, 35).[9] Satornil was the offspring of Menander. According to Irenaeus he professed the existence of an unknowable God, creator of the angels and of other spiritual powers. Seven angels created man and the visible world. God, taking pity on a part of the human race, imparted to it the spark of a higher life. The creator-angels, to whom the god of the Jews belonged, are in revolt against God. To overcome them the Saviour Jesus descends from on high; he is not born on earth and is without a body of flesh; his office is to bring back to God the men who have received the spark of life. Satornil did not believe in the resurrection of the flesh; he condemned marriage and forbad the eating of anything that had life. In many respects, therefore, he was a forerunner of Marcion. Though much indebted to Simon and Menander, he, unlike them, does not set himself up as the Saviour sent from on high, but attributes that rôle to Jesus. Consequently, heretic though he be, we cannot deny him the qualification of Christian, while, from the Christian point of view, Simon and Menander qualify rather for Antichrists.

5. THE SERPENT-WORSHIPPERS

Analogous conceptions are found in other systems insufficiently known or on which we have only conflicting information, sects not named, like the foregoing, after their founders, and of which we cannot determine the origin and the localization nor the transformations they underwent in the course of a history which mostly ended in decay and oblivion. Irenaeus describes a good many of them under the general name of gnostics (*Heresies*, i, 29–31). The name Serpent-worshippers (Ophites) fits only some of them in which the serpent was made the object of a cult and given a place in their doctrine which, whether deduced or not from the story in Genesis, was co-ordinated with it. Celsus was acquainted with the Ophites whom he took for Christians, which Origen denies (*C. Celsum*, vi, 24–38). As the Simonians are in the same case, it is not necessary to suppose (with de Faye) that the Church was still tolerating the Ophites in the time of Celsus. It is a fact, however, that the Naasenians, whose name alone proclaims them a serpent-sect, attributed the rôle of Saviour to Jesus; a Naasenian hymn cited by Hippolytus (*Philos.*, v, 1, 10) makes him intercede with the Father in terms which recall something of Marduk's intercession with Ea in certain Babylonian incantations. Unsatisfactory as Hippolytus' account of them is, few ancient texts give us a better idea than these Naasenian speculations of the intense fermentation of doctrine which broke out in Christianity and around it in the second century, or of the timeliness of the barrier hastily raised by the Church to restrain it.

Origen discusses a diagram made by the Ophites which Celsus, without naming the Ophites, alleges to have been an esoteric Christian document. It resembled, as we might expect, a map of salvation which Celsus compared, not without reason to the Mithraic cosmography. It showed ten concentric circles framed in a greater circle which was the soul of the universe and named Leviathan, whose name also figures at the centre of the whole apparatus; there are seven gates to be passed guarded by seven spirits in the form of animals (lion, bull, amphibian, eagle, bear, dog, ass) with their names indicated (Ialdabaioth, Iao, Sabaoth, Astaphaios, Eloaios, Horaios) with a password for each; a transverse black line represents hell; a square space guarded by a flaming sword has to do with the Tree of Knowledge and the Tree of Life. The seven angels, enemies of the angels of light, are called archons, their chief being the demiurge, the creator, and god of the Jews who gave man the knowledge of good and evil and is himself accursed for having cursed the serpent; a sacrament called "The Seal" as Christian baptism was often called (*Apoc.*, vii, 3-8) is conferred by a "father," the candidate being "son"; this sacrament involves an anointing, since the candidate has to pronounce the words "I am anointed with the anointing of the Tree of Life." On this, Origen exclaims that the Ophites who curse the Creator also curse Jesus and cause him to be cursed by all who enter their sect—though this is not in the diagram and not true of all the Ophite sects. A preposterous doctrine in which we catch some resemblance to Marcion's system, but not necessarily derived from it.

Among the sects of which we are speaking were some which placed a female aeon besides the Ineffable Being. This was "the Mother" with whom went the successive emanations of the aeons and the successive decay of one, the organization of the lower world under a demiurge without knowledge of the Supreme God, and finally the manifestation of the aeon "Christ" in Jesus, which was to gather up the sparks of Divinity scattered about the human world and re-establish the harmony of the pleroma.[10] It would be an error to make all this depend on Marcion even if these systems are later than his. The Syrian origin of many of their speculations is betrayed by the names given to the aeons.

It would be unwise to lay too much emphasis on the extravagance of these sects, which are often working with the same materials as the old Christian writers. The question is hardly more than one of degree. The gnosis of Colossians, that of I Corinthians xv, and that of Romans iv–vi are not conspicuous for rational sobriety, and the Woman of Revelation xii has some resemblance to the Mother who figures in the systems of certain gnostic sects.

6. Basilides

Basilides was of Alexandria where he taught in the reigns of Hadrian and Antoninus (117–161). He wrote a Gospel commentary in twenty-four books entitled τὰ ἐξεγητκά. In the system of Basilides as described by Origen, the unbegotten Father, or First Principle, gave issue to Nous; from Nous came forth Logos; from Logos, Phronesis; from Phronesis, Sophia and Dynamis; from these primal beings came the "virtues," powers and angels; together they formed the population of the first heaven. There were three hundred and sixty-five heavens of which we see only the last and lowest. This is inhabited by the angels who created our world, whose head is the god of the Jews; between this god, who aimed at enslaving all peoples to his own, and the angels of the peoples to be enslaved, there broke out a conflict, to which an end was put by the intervention of Nous who, sent by the Supreme Father, took on the semblance of humanity in Jesus. At the moment of crucifixion his form changed into that of Simon of Cyrene, who died in his place. There is no reason, therefore, for paying homage to the Crucified nor for undergoing martyrdom in his name. In order to be saved it suffices to know the truth of the system taught by Basilides.

Needless to say, the Old Testament, which was the work of the demiurges, had to be rejected. A kind of magic was practised against the lower powers, certain mysterious words being recommended for the purpose, especially the word *Abraxas*, the letters of which, turned into numbers and added, equalled the number of the heavens. The human passions were substantial appendages attached to the reasonable soul, which they led into sin; evil is the punishment of sin, the martyrs themselves, even if innocent of sin in this life, suffer for sins committed in a previous existence. Reincarnation was one of Basilides' doctrines. He and his son Isidore counselled celibacy, tolerating marriage as the lesser of two evils. Faith, in the system, is a kind of substance, or hypostasis, inherent in elect souls, who thus constitute a true aristocracy both as to number and quality. The ethics of Basilides as first announced were somewhat severe; but it seems that the sect was not slow to enter upon evil courses.

7. CARPOCRAS

The sect of Carpocras, or Carpocrates, appears to be as old as that of Basilides, for there is no reason to distinguish the Carpocras who lived at Alexandria in the time of Hadrian from him whose doctrine was brought to Rome towards the year 160 by a woman named Marcellina. The case of the Carpocratians enables us to see how a certain form of gnosis could be made compatible with the most reckless immorality and furnish pretexts for the defamation of Christianity. There was, however, little enough Christianity about this sect. Epiphanus, the son of Carpocras, who died when he was seventeen, leaving behind him a book "on Righteousness," was revered as a god in the island of Cephallonia, from which his mother had come.[11] This youthful philosopher poured ridicule on the prohibition of adultery laid down in the Decalogue; the common and equal enjoyment of all things, said he, belonged to all men by divine appointment; human laws had invented the distinction between good and evil, with all kinds of private property, including the marriage bond; thus the law had created the robber and the adulterer; but community of goods and free love[12] is the law of nature. An unexpected use of Plato for achieving the downfall of Moses and the morality of the common man!

Carpocras acknowledged the unity of God, and a hierarchy of angels who had created the visible world. Human souls had also belonged to the spiritual world before they fell into matter, from which they can free themselves in all the states and actions implied in human existence by rising superior to the rules artificially established. Evidently Basilides, and Carpocras more distinctly, start off from a principle which might be called identical, save in respect of moral sense, with that which supports the theory of Justification in the Pauline Epistles, the principle, namely, that spirit and the spiritual have an eminent dignity above the Mosaic Law, and above law of any kind. But instead of making the renunciation of carnal pleasures the condition of a perfect life and a blessed eternity, the condition now lies in breaking free of the law which puts a social restraint on the lower appetites. Let sin be suppressed; but suppress it by suppressing the law which makes it sin. The satisfaction of the appetites is permitted to the wise man and even becomes, in the system of Carpocras, a positive means of his salvation, which is for that man only who has exhausted the lists of sensual pleasure in violation of every law which puts it under interdict.

As a single life would not ordinarily suffice for most men to achieve so complete a liberation, Carpocras introduced the doctrine of reincarnation to provide further opportunity for souls imperfectly liberated. Jesus, who was born and lived under ordinary human conditions, had been given as an example of the liberation which all men are called to achieve for themselves; he had triumphed over the creator-angels by breaking free from their rules and ascended to the Father from whom he came. Every man can succeed as well as he, or even better, in realizing a like liberty for himself; let him, by breaking the laws the creators have made, dissolve his partnership in their adventures. We are prepared to learn that magic had a great vogue with the Carpocratians especially as a means of combating the influence of the creators. They also offered worship to the images of the great philosophers, including an image of Jesus, of whom they professed to have a portrait made by orders of Pilate. Their morals were in keeping with their doctrine, Irenaeus declaring that he dared not believe what was told of them. Given their principles, it is permissible to suppose that their conventicles were not abodes of the purest innocence. Dregs of mysticism gone astray!

8. VALENTINUS

The influence of Plato is also to be seen in Valentinus, but his excesses were mainly of the metaphysical order and his vogue was greater than that of all the sect-leaders we have so far mentioned. Lower Egypt was his country of origin and he had studied at Alexandria, a city unique in those days for an intense fermentation of mind, of which it was a hotbed. There Valentinus had his first successes. Like other gnostics he was, in his own way, a Christian, but repressive action against heresy, so far as it existed when he began to teach his religious philosophy, had little severity, and less at Alexandria than elsewhere. He came to Rome, as Marcion did somewhat later, and there according to Irenaeus he made a long stay from the episcopate of Hyginus (139–142) to that of Anicetus (157–168). He lived there on the margin of the Christian community from which he had been excluded at a time and for reasons unknown to us with certainty. According to Tertullian he aspired to become bishop and seceded from the regular Church ("ecclesia authenticae regulae") on seeing a confessor of the faith preferred to himself. Whatever be the truth behind this statement, there can be no doubt that Valentinus, who had been educated at a time and in a society which knew nothing about the "regular" Church, came like Marcion to Rome, as the great Christian centre, for the purpose of carrying on religious propaganda. It is quite possible that his secession from the common Christianity was not made final until after he had left Rome, perhaps after the election of Anicetus, when he was in Cyprus, where he ended his days. In contrast to Marcion, Valentinus was far more a thinker and teacher than an organizer. The sect that he founded had not the wide expansion and long duration of Marcion's and was a less formidable rival of the Great Church.

The system of Valentinus was a salvation gnosis conveyed in a kind of metaphysical poem.[13] At the beginning of all things was Bythos, the unbegotten Abyss; with him was his female companion Sige, Silence.[14] When it was pleasing to Bythos, he begot of Silence another couple, Nous, the Intellect, and Aletheia, Truth; of these two were born Logos, the Thought-word and Zoe who is Life; from Logos and Zoe came forth Anthropos, primarily transcendent Man, and Ecclesia, the Church on high. This is the Eight-in-one, the Supreme Ogdoad, in which Basilides, the author of the fourth Gospel, the author of the second Epistle of Clement and even the good Hermas would all find themselves on very familiar ground. But the gnosis of Valentinus differs from theirs by being conceived in terms of the union of the sexes and its consequences; it unfolds in a series of syzygies, or conjunctions, after the manner of a mythology, and under the influence of the mythologies, which may or may not have been consciously followed. The great Babylonian poem of creation begins in like manner with a cosmogony. Apsu, the begetter of everything, and Tiamat, the sea which brings everything to birth, mingled their waters, etc. etc. The mythology of Valentinus is more realist and his gnosis more abstract, but some of his abstractions carry the mark of their origin, notably the Abyss and the Man.

The upper world does not comprise the Great Ogdoad only. Logos and Life gave birth to five couples of Aeons who become the Great Decade; in like manner Man and Church produced six couples, the Great Dodecade; Ogdoad, Decade and Dodecade make up together the Divine Pleroma—a valuable sidelight on the Epistle to the Colossians (i, 19) and on the Epistle to the Hebrews with its Aeons (i, 2; xi, 3). In the thoughts of Valentinus this "pleroma" was far from being the world of abstraction, the metaphysical dream that its terminology might lead us to think it; it is a world of ideas eternally alive, a world of mind and of transcendent realities. The genesis of the material world, which the rest of us call real, has still to be explained. For Valentinus this world was an appearance, accidental, corruptible and destined to perish. It was conceived as the result of a bad accident in the spiritual world, which happened as follows.

The last couple of the Great Dodecade are the figures of Theletos (Volition) and Sophia (Wisdom) not precisely moral wisdom, rather knowledge and skill. Sophia is seized with an uncontrollable desire to know the Supreme Father, the Abyss, who is knowable only by his Son, the Intellect (compare Matthew xi, 27; John i, 18); in this unappeasable desire she would have gone to pieces, had not Oros (the Limit) a kind of transcendent Saviour appointed by the Abyss on the outskirts of the Pleroma, prevented her dissolution. Sophia then recovers her sanity, but during her madness she had conceived, without intercourse with Theletos, an imperfect Aeon, Hacamoth, a debased copy of her mother; she was also called Wisdom, but this time by the Hebrew equivalent of the term. Hacamoth is then cast out by the Pleroma. To prevent the repetition of a similar calamity, Nous and Aletheia produce a seventh couple, Christos and Pneuma—Spirit is feminine in Semitic—who teach the others to take heed to the Limit by not attempting to know the unknowable; after which all the Aeons celebrate the return of peace, and combine to produce the thirty-third Aeon. This is the Saviour Jesus.

But the poor Hacamoth, turned out of the Abyss, has an important future awaiting her. The abortive creature was first visited in her abandonment by Christos who gave her a kind of form and consciousness. Then, realizing her fallen state, sorrow, fear and despair come over her. By a second visit, but this time by the Aeon Jesus, these passions are separated from her and used to constitute the elements of matter; matter is then explained as the congested or solidified form of the spiritual waste products thrown off by a mind in temporary distress—truly a strange procedure for explaining its origin and denying it an eternal existence. The Abyss, in the mythologies, is another name for Chaos, or unformed matter; but here it is the eternal fountain of transcendent ideas, and only on the rebound does it become the source of material existence and of the visible world! Hacamoth, however, thus relieved of her passions, continues to exist in herself as a psychic substance, and the mere sight of the angels who accompany the Saviour causes her to conceive and bring forth Spirit as a substantial entity. In this way the elements out of which the lower world is to be constructed are, if one may say so, brought together on the site in readiness for the building to begin.

The process is as follows. From her psychic substance Hacamoth extracts the demiurge who, in his turn, produces the materials and the psychic beings who together make up the visible world. Here in the lower world, the world of the demiurge, are comprised the seven heavens, the abodes of angels, but not of spirits, for the demiurge himself is not a spirit; knowing no other world than that of his own creation, the demiurge believes himself the master of the entire universe. His intention was to create man in two categories—material and psychic; but three categories exist in reality, because certain men happened to receive a germ of the spiritual substance that emanated from Hacamoth. Clement of Alexandria cites a passage[15] where the affair is explained. It tells how the demiurge and his angels, after creating man, were strangely surprised when they saw him putting forth ideas far beyond his natural condition; the reason is that the germ of spirit had fallen into him from on high and "formed in the name of the Man, he breathed in fear of the Man Above, who was in him" doubtless in virtue of the fiery particle he had received from Hacamoth; whereupon the astonished angels immediately changed their manner of working. Needless to say that from the standpoint of Valentinus' time, this third category, spiritual man, was the one predestined to become Valentinian; the psychic are the common run of Christians and the material are the non-Christians. The principle on which these distinctions are based is to be found in the New Testament. In 1 Corinthians ii, 14–iii, 3, we have the three-fold division "spiritual," "psychic," "carnal," the last two, however, seeming to form one category. The distinction between "spiritual" and "psychic" is also found in Jude 19.

It follows from the above that men of the third category have no immortality, that all those in the first are saved, since the spirit that has fallen into them cannot die; these, so to say, have only to know themselves by the Valentinian gnosis. Strictly speaking only the psychics have need of redemption. Valentinus also believes in the historical manifestation of Jesus, but his belief is strongly coloured by metaphysic and docetism. The figure of the Redeemer was material only in appearance; his humanity was psychic and spiritual. "He ate and drank in a manner all his own, without excrementation. So great was the force of his temperance that the food he ate did not corrupt within him, because he himself was not to know corruption." Clement of Alexandria, to whom we owe this citation, thoroughly approves the tenor of it.[16] The Saviour at his birth owed nothing to the Virgin Mary; the great Aeon Jesus descended upon him at his baptism and withdrew from him, along with the pneumatic element, to return to the Pleroma, when it was determined to bring him before Pilate; what was crucified, therefore, was the Saviour's psychic part in his semblance of a body; but his passion was no whit the less real on that account. The Valentinian Saviour carries with him the light of his doctrine and is the liturgical celebrant of his own mystery. Humanity will come to an end when the demiurge ceases to create; Hacamoth will be received into the Pleroma and become the spouse of the Aeon Jesus; spiritual men will be made one with the angels who accompany the Saviour; finally the demiurge along with the psychic men who have practised the law of the Gospel will be installed below the Pleroma in the place vacated by Hacamoth, and a general conflagration, in which all material men and worthless psychics will perish, will reduce the material world to nothing.[17]

Valentinus founded a school, of which ancient writers distinguish the Eastern from the Western disciples. Of the last the best known are Heracleon and Ptolemy, with whom Irenaeus joins a much less respectable person named Marcus. Among the Eastern school we hear of a certain Theodotus whom the extracts preserved by Clement of Alexandria show to have been a faithful disciple of the Master; and of the Syrian Bardesanes (154–223) whose activities fall outside our picture. If Bardesanes was at first a Valentinian he does not seem to have remained in the fold. His reputation for heresy came late and could only be retrospective after he had finished his career as an independent teacher connected with the Church at Edessa, in which Tatian was also able to keep his footing, but without leaving a much better reputation behind him. Bardesanes' writings came into bad odour when orthodoxy had become more strict than in his time.[18]

9. HERACLEON

Heracleon (c. 155–180) who seems to have been an immediate disciple of Valentinus, added some notable retouchings to his master's system.[19] Instead of a conjunction of Aeons, or syzygye, he placed the One and Only God at the summit of the Pleroma, conceiving Him after the gnostic manner under the title "Father of Truth." Similarly he makes the Logos inspire the demiurge who himself builds the visible world, the Logos thus again becoming the world-soul; he is also the Saviour of mankind and appears for the first time on earth when John the Baptist announces him. In the substance of his teaching Heracleon stands perceptibly close to the fourth Gospel, on which he wrote a commentary valued by Origen who used it in writing his own. At Capernaum, Jesus is supposed to have descended into the lowest stratum of the cosmos, which is the realm of matter; at Jerusalem he comes into the realm of the psychic.

We know from Origen how Heracleon interpreted the meeting of Jesus with the woman of Samaria. The water of Jacob's well is the symbol of "cosmic life," a life inferior and fugitive; the water that Jesus gives is eternal life, and the Samaritan woman who thirsts for it is a pneumatic; the husband whom Jesus bids her call is the mate who is waiting for her in the Pleroma; the woman has had six husbands (instead of the five of the traditional text) because six is the number for matter or evil; Mount Gerizim represents the devil and his kingdom, matter and wickedness, and the devil-worship practised by mankind before the Law was given; Jerusalem is the headquarters of the demiurge and his Jewish worship; those cults have lapsed; the spiritual worship the Father of Truth and him alone; the Father seeks for worshippers, now sunk in matter; God is spirit and spiritual souls are of one family with him, "consubstantial" with his unbegotten nature; it is to save them from their sunken condition that the Christ came down into the lowest parts of the world; redemption works by a kind of progressive illumination, beginning as an awakened feeling for the true life, which feeling is a memory of the mate which the soul possesses in the divine Pleroma. The redemption of the psychics comes about in a different manner. The woman, who is spiritual, announces salvation to her fellow Samaritans, who are psychics, and these, abandoning their former way of life, which was according to the world, come to the Saviour by faith. It is not very clear that the final result of this conversion is an immortal condition for the converted psychics.

The fate of the "Material" men (ὑλικόι) is explained in other passages. These have, for their father, the devil, whose evil nature is derived from error and ignorance; the devil cannot possess the truth and his speech is all lying; he has no liberty but only appetites; material men are his children, incapable of good and, at least in theory, doomed to perdition; in fact, a few may have all the devil's appetites without being fundamentally ὑλικόι but psychic, and therefore open to conversion.

The mitigations applied by Heracleon to the system of Valentinus bring him nearer to orthodoxy. There is no ground for supposing that this was a tactical move made by our doctor for the purpose of bringing his doctrines more into line with Christian truth. He was not without psychological insight and a true feeling for morality. No signs are betrayed in his writings of specific influence by the Pauline Epistles. This is almost as true of Valentinus—a fact to be noted in considering the history of the Epistles.

10. PTOLEMY AND MARCUS

Of Ptolemy's personal writings all that remains is his letter to Flora, probably written about 160 and preserved by Epiphanius. To judge by this specimen, Ptolemy was not a tiresome theologian, for the letter is written with some elegance and much clarity. The subject of the letter lies in the question "What is the authority of the Law of Moses?" Some—the majority of Christians—declare it wholly divine and derived from God the Father; others—probably the disciples of Marcion —make it out to be the work of the devil who created the present world. According to Ptolemy it cannot be the work of the Father because it is not perfect, and he notes that Jesus attributes permission for divorce not to God but to Moses; neither can it be the work of the devil, since it is distinctly not a bad Law, as it certainly would be if the devil, who is all darkness, were its author. It must therefore come from some intermediate being, who can be no other than the demiurge. Ptolemy shows very clearly that the Law contains elements of unequal value. In what way the devil and the demiurge come forth from a perfect God, if they do, is a question which Ptolemy promises to examine later on. As far as can be judged from the notice in Irenaeus there are no retouchings in Ptolemy's system of the essential points in Valentinus. He does however replace Bythos and Sige, as the first pair of the Ogdoad, by the Father and Grace (Charis)—which certainly improves the moral character of the First Principle.

If we may believe Iranaeus, who was a close observer of these proceedings, the gnostic Marcus was an impudent propagandist who turned the symbolism of the eucharistic mystery into magic and belonged to the class of licentious mystics or gnostics, which is certainly not the case with the two previously mentioned.

11. MARCION BRINGS THE CRISIS TO A HEAD

Though Marcion presents the mystery of salvation with greater sobriety than Valentinus, the main current of Christian thought found him not sober enough. He came from Sinope in Pontus where his father is said to have been bishop. He made a fortune in the shipping trade of those days, and his wealth seems to have helped him in his religious undertakings. Pliny's letter to Trajan has shown us that Christianity had taken firm root in the Pontus region. It is not impossible that his own father was the first to reprove Marcion for his heresies. He began his propaganda in Asia where he seems to have been opposed by Polycarp of Smyrna. About the year 140 he betook himself to Rome and joined the Roman congregation, to which he gave a large sum of money[20] after submitting a letter of explanation about his faith, which was considered satisfactory. It was probably at Rome that he completed his system, wrote his *Antitheses* and fixed the text of the *Gospel* and the *Apostolicon*. His mind, though well informed, was not of the speculative turn. He made no attempt to found a school on the outskirts of the Church nor to form small groups of initiates; he hoped rather to give the Church, and the whole Church, fixed doctrines and authorized Scriptures. Towards the year 144 the heads of the Roman congregation responded to his efforts by formal excommunication and the return of his money. After that he displayed astonishing energy in the founding of congregations on the same pattern as those which had cast him out, but on a foundation which he believed to be that of the pure Gospel. Marcion therefore was not the founder of a school. His object was to reform Christianity, we might even say, to institute it afresh. According to him Christianity had taken a wrong road from the very beginning.

For Christian communities existing up to Marcion's time Scripture meant the Jewish Bible taken over from hellenist Jews and interpreted in the Christian sense, the catechists making use in addition of a diversity of Gospel writings and, subordinate to them, of certain apostolic documents. Marcion professed to furnish the Church with the one true Scripture, exclusively devoted to the Gospel, purely Christian and containing only the revelation of Jesus. It was *one* Gospel, which he called *the* Gospel. It corresponded with the Gospel named Luke's in catholic tradition, save that it omitted the first two chapters concerning the birth of John the Baptist and of Jesus, and made short omissions and retouchings in the rest of the book. By the side of the Gospel Marcion placed his *Apostolicon*,[21] a collection of ten Epistles having the same authority and the same authenticity as the Gospel they accompanied. All of the ten were Epistles attributed to Paul; to wit, Galatians, Corinthians (both), Romans, Thessalonians (both), Laodiceans (=Ephesians), Colossians, Philippians, Philemon—the traditional collection, *minus* the three Pastorals—all with omissions and retouches similar to those in the Gospel. The sum of the matter was that Marcion, in his own way, edited known documents, for which he reserved an exclusive authority, repudiating not only all similar writings used by different communities but also, and chiefly, the entire body of Scripture which Christianity had taken over from Judaism.

The book *Antitheses* contained Marcion's own theology and the justification of his biblical canon.[22] His theology was sober enough. He professed to re-establish the teaching of Jesus in its original simplicity and paid no heed to the cosmological speculations in which most of his predecessors had indulged so freely; making no pretence to introduce a new doctrine, he would have nothing to do with the division of believers into two classes of which one was privileged in regard to the other. But, for all that, what he had to offer was a doctrine widely different from the Gospel of Jesus; it was the essential principle of gnosis reduced to its simplest expression in the absolute transcendence of spirit and the depreciation of matter, of nature as created. The strangest feature of this truly extraordinary enterprise is Marcion's belief that his system was backed by the authority of the pure Christian tradition, which did not contain it, and that it was deducible therefrom by unanswerable logic.

His point of departure for the restatement of Christianity is the Epistle to the Galatians. Professing to find there a radical opposition between Law and Gospel, he infers that the god who is the author of the one cannot be the author of the other. The character of the Old Testament was incompatible with the idea of the good and only God, father of Jesus Christ. But the Old Testament, in Marcion's view, was none the less a revelation, and he gave it credit so far as to allow that what it tells of its own god is true, the god of the Jews being, as it says, the real creator of our bad material world. He recognized also that the Old Testament foretold a Messiah, but the sort of Messiah whom the Jews were still expecting. Jesus had not been sent by the demiurge but by the Transcendent God, unknown to man till a manifestation revealed him in Jesus, and by Jesus, to the end that men might attain salvation by faith in the good God and be delivered from the bondage to which their creator had condemned them. Marcion's Christology was extremely simple. In framing it our reformer was as little embarrassed by questions of historical probability as by the objections to which his metaphysic stood exposed. The good God, having assumed in Jesus the semblance of humanity, but without taking a material body, because he owed nothing and was incapable of owing anything to the demiurge, whose domain matter was—this good God, of whom the world had no knowledge hitherto, became visible to human eyes at Capernaum ("descending" there, Luke iii, 1; iv, 31—the opening of Marcion's Gospel) in the fifteenth year of Tiberius, and then, in the course of his manifestation, first revealed the mystery of salvation and finally enacted it by the cross. Though Jesus, according to Marcion, did not die in a body of flesh, die nevertheless he did, and rose from the dead. By this death he released mankind, or at least the believing part of mankind, from every tittle of obligation to the god who had created them, the god of the Jews.

"Severe" is a term hardly strong enough to describe the

character of Marcion's moral code. He condemned marriage and allowed baptism only to the continent. He imposed various restrictions on diet, forbad the eating of flesh and abated nothing from the duty of martyrdom. His exaggerated asceticism was in harmony with the common temper of Christianity in his time, but was also logically involved in his system. Did not the human body, the flesh and all its works, proceed from the inferior god, and was it not he who had bidden mankind "increase and multiply"? Let the believer, then, who would be perfect, cut himself free of the flesh and its appetites. Marcion's sacraments were the same as those of the great Church: baptism with anointing and with the drinking of milk and honey,[23] the latter a practice not unknown in early Christian times; Eucharist with bread and water unmixed with wine, also a practice not then looked on as a shocking novelty. The inner organization of the communities was also on the usual pattern, except that ecclesiastical offices were not regarded as established in perpetuity. But this may not have been peculiar to Marcionism, seeing that the established Church-hierarchy was largely built up as a defence against Marcion.

Whether he was aware of it or not, Marcion was, in reality, more dependent on gnosis than on the Gospel, which, according to him, had been kept pure only by the apostle Paul. It was not the Gospel, nor the Epistles, nor even the revised version he had made of both to fit his doctrine, that suggested to him his theory of these two Gods, the one transcendent, unknowable and good, the other of a lower denomination, merely just and with a turn for cruelty in his justice. His religion might find satisfaction in the antithesis of the two gods, but it would not have furnished him with the antithesis had not certain gnostics taught and suggested it. But a simplified dualism closely related to monotheism was convenient ground for establishing the incompatibility of the Gospel with the Law and the essential difference between the God revealed in the one and he who had enacted the other. This was Marcion's fundamental dogma, and this it was that caused the Church to cast him out. When Justin couples Marcion with Simon Magus as an arch-heretic this is the point on which he fixes as the essence of the matter: "A certain Marcion, of Pontus, who is even now making disciples, teaches that there is a God greater than the Creator; helped by the demons he spreads his blasphemies among the whole human race, denying the Creator of the world and proclaiming another greater God who has done bigger things than he" (*Apology*, 26; cf. 58). For the same reason Justin reproaches Marcion for having a Christ other than the Son of God. Marcion's moral rigorism and his theological Docetism are regarded by Justin as points of secondary importance, in which he finds nothing to cause scandal. Nor does he find fault with Marcion for tampering with the Gospel text. Tertullian indeed insists on this, but the times had then changed and the canon of the New Testament had been fixed in the interval between him and Justin. The main object of the *Antitheses*, and the head of its offending, was to establish dualism by means of an artificial exegesis which professed to attach this dualism both to the Gospel and to the Apostolic writings.

Whether he invented his doctrine entire, or borrowed certain elements of it from one Cerdo, a Syrian, who is said to have come to Rome a little in advance of him, certain it is that Marcion in the plainest of terms affirmed the existence of two gods, and even of two First Principles. For the inferior god, though perishable, had no beginning, matter being regarded not as a third Principle but as a passive element employed by the demiurge in constructing the lower world.[24] Though Marcion does not take over the Persian dualism entire, he is distinctly nearer to it than were the Alexandrian gnostics. His valuation of the perceptible world and of human nature bears no trace of the Greek spirit. His higher God, creator of the invisible world, is not, as Ormuzd was, a god of Light, he is a god of Goodness, while his lower god, creator of the visible world, is not like Ahriman, essentially dark and evil; he is nothing worse than a god of strict justice with an inclination to harshness. The dualism of Marcion is not based on a naturalistic philosophy, but has its roots in a concrete and psychological morality. It is a dualism of which one side is summarily made to fit the Jewish religion with its Old Testament, and the other side to fit the Christian with its Gospel. Tertullian was not mistaken when he wrote: "The man of Pontus brings forward two gods; the one, our Creator, whom we cannot deny; the other his own, whom he cannot prove" (*Adv. Marcionem* 1, 2). Marcion's Christianity and his knowledge of Scripture have coloured his conception both of his God and of his anti-God, and though he has not borrowed the latter conception from the Persian Ahriman, he would never have arrived at it had he not been unconsciously under the influence of Persian dualism. Did he not teach that the visible creation would finally disappear, along with its creator, the demiurge? It remains to say that he does not seem to identify the demiurge formally with the Devil; whether or no he would give him a rôle as assistant to the demiurge is not clear.

A mind systematic rather than profound, more zealous than impassioned, more moralist than mystic, Marcion constructed, without great originality and somewhat hastily, a scheme for giving Christianity a firm basis and a definite form. In the process of constructing his scheme he availed himself of all the elements he found useful for the purpose, without claiming any other rôle for himself than that of a logically exact interpreter of the true Christian tradition. He was resisted and condemned in the name of the apostolic tradition, but his intentions were as truly traditionalist, if not more so, than were those of the men who resisted and condemned him.

The conditions under which he drew up his collection of Scriptures are perplexingly obscure. We can see clearly enough how he was brought to reject the Old Testament, like his contemporary, the Valentinian Ptolemy, and we can explain why he was concerned to provide Christians with a collection of Christian Scriptures to take the place of the Jewish Bible. What is not so clear are the reasons which determined his choice of the particular Scriptures which formed his collection and, in addition to that, the manner in which he understood his duty as their editor. However, if it would be quite foolish to credit Marcion with the idea of publishing a critically faultless text of the sources of Gospel revelation held by him to be authentic, it would seem equally wilful (having regard to the character of the man and the circumstances) to attribute to him any considerable part even in editing the texts presented by him as documents of the true faith. That supposition is the less acceptable because these texts, of which the main tenor is well enough known to us, do not expressly reproduce Marcion's doctrine. Marcion set out to link them and his system together. This he managed to do, but his system is not formally taught in the documents. How then did Marcion proceed?

It seems certain that, in the time when he was expelled from the Church in Rome (144), neither the Gospels, nor the Epistles, nor any other of the writings which compose the New Testament were in the forefront of Christian teaching. But neither were they private documents of which the congregations of believers knew nothing. The public reading of the Gospels, which we find customary in Justin's time, was practised before Marcion; and we may at least conjecture that it was the same with the Epistles, though reading from them is likely to have been less regular and less common. It follows that Marcion, in raising the Gospel and the letters of Paul to the rank of Scripture, did no more, so to say, than sublimate an established usage. The novelty of that achievement consisted solely in the exclusive authority conferred on these writings by the rejection of the Jewish Scriptures. His adoption of one Gospel only would afford no ground of complaint against him at the time when it was done, for there is no proof that four Gospels were then accepted throughout the congregations of the Great Church, all equally privileged to be read in public before assemblies of the faithful; on the contrary, it is far more probable, not only that it was not so everywhere, but that it was not so anywhere, each of the Gospels finally received everywhere having been used at first only in the circle where it originated, while the recognition of four normative Gospels, and no more, was later than the time of Marcion. When he found his Gospel in Luke it was not, therefore, a case of his deliberately picking Luke out from among four Gospels then current in the Church and choosing it, as easier than the others to bring into line with his system— for John's Gospel is much nearer to his system and Matthew would have given him no more trouble than Luke—it was not this, but a case simply of his canonizing the Gospel used in the Christian circle in which he lived, or at least in that in which he hoped to make converts, namely Rome. Luke had become the chief Gospel of the Roman Community, which at first had Mark and came to know Matthew, but used the fourth Gospel very little, though it knew that Gospel also.

As to the adaptation of Luke by Marcion for his own purpose which Tertullian half a century later describes outright as a massacre,[25] it is unlikely that it greatly scandalized Marcion's own contemporaries. In his time, variety in the versions of the Gospel caused no great concern to anybody; otherwise a single Gospel book, with a uniform text, would have reigned throughout. The truth is that Marcion would have no difficulty in accepting the Gospel writing most familiar to the Church in Rome, and the omissions he made would be the least possible. He made no capital out of the traditional and correct attribution of this Gospel to a disciple of Paul, which he did not bring forward, but simply called the book "The Gospel," as it had hitherto been called. Up to that time all evangelical books owed their credit not to the persons supposed to be their authors, but to their contents, the personal attributions not becoming important till later, when they were used as weapons against the gnostics, and especially against Marcion himself after his expulsion. Marcion's manipulations of the text seem to have consisted in the removal of whatever openly contradicted his doctrine and a few retouches of detail for the same purpose; but he made no explicit additions to give his doctrine formal support. His method was not the result of a design to insinuate his doctrine surreptitiously into the Church, for the Church had turned him out for his open profession of it; it arose from his belief in the substantial credibility of the text which he retained. Looking closely into the matter, we see that his method was not a whit more revolutionary than that of the editors of our canonical Gospels; in certain respects, indeed, it was much less innovating than theirs. Comparing the procedure of the editors of the first and third Gospels, who added the birth stories to the theme of the Gospel as they found it in Mark, with that of Marcion who left these stories out, which of the two shall we say represents the more audacious innovation?

The case of the Epistles is somewhat different. Marcion substantially contributed to raising their credit. As we lately remarked, there is reason to doubt that they were frequently read in all the congregations, as the Gospel unquestionably was, before Marcion's time. When Justin speaks of the readings that normally took place before the Sunday Communion, the books he mentions are the Prophets and the Memoirs of the Apostles (1 *Apology*, 67); but not a word does he say, in this connexion, of the apostolic writings, and he never mentions Paul; we might even say that, if Justin knew Paul, he deliberately abstains from making use of him, and how can he have failed to know him, seeing that he was so well acquainted with Marcion? But, though less regularly used for public reading, the ten epistles which Marcion appropriated had been for some time collected, and there is evidence that the collection enjoyed a large measure of credit in the Roman community and elsewhere, since First Corinthians is expressly quoted in the Epistle of Clement.[26] The relative antiquity of the collection has also good warrant in the fact that Marcion has the Epistle to the Ephesians under its original title of Epistle to the Laodiceans, along with Second Thessalonians, both of which are apocryphal. It seems, moreover, sufficiently clear that his method of dealing with the Epistles was the same as that he had applied to the Gospel: he took the collection as he found it in the Roman community and confined himself to systematically cutting and retouching it as required by his doctrine. Here again the liberties he took not only did not surpass, they did not even equal those taken by others before him in attributing to Paul letters he did not write and in interpolating those he did.

It is none the less true that Marcion founded the canon of the New Testament, the idea of which, it may confidently be said, had occurred to nobody before him. At this point the influence he exercised, both directly, and indirectly through the reaction he provoked, was momentous, and of greater moment than can be claimed, at that stage in the evolution of catholic Christianity, for any master of gnosis, Christian writer, or Church leader. If he failed to realize all that he aimed at, and if Marcionism did not become, as he intended it to become, the common faith of the Church, we know the reason. It lies in the fact that though with him the religious and moral interest took precedence of the speculative and theoretical, he underrated the vitality of Israel's monotheism and failed to see that the ethics of the Gospel were rooted in Judaism. The deepest tradition of Christianity was against him, nor did his more reasonable interpretation of Scripture make good the defects of his religious philosophy, so that, in the final result, his system of belief and of conduct came out less truly balanced than that of the Church. But, in spite of these disadvantages, Marcionism from the time of Marcion (about 145) to the end of the second century, continued to be the most formidable rival, and almost the only dangerous rival, that Catholicism had to encounter during the whole time it was in process of becoming organized into a system. Wherever Christianity had taken root, there was Marcionism beside it, challenging it by a greater simplicity of doctrine, by the plausible character of the argument against the Old Testament deity, and by the deadly earnestness of the Marcionite morality.[27]

Marcion had numerous disciples of whom the most noteworthy seems to be a certain Apelles who had sat at the master's feet in Rome and afterward corrected his doctrine at several points. While totally rejecting the Old Testament, his criticism of which was better reasoned than Marcion's, Apelles went back to a strict monotheism: there was one God only, the good God, creator of the invisible world and of the spiritual powers, or angels; the chief of these angels had created the visible world, making it an image of the invisible; the god of Israel was not this demiurge but a fiery angel—Old Testament texts supporting this will readily occur to mind—and this fiery angel was the author of evil, proved so by his clothing human souls in sinful flesh; the creator, who had tried to form the world for the glory of God, had become dissatisfied with his work and prayed the Father to send his Son to give the cosmos a better shape. In Christology, Apelles was no Docetist. His Christ took on a real body, but was not born of the flesh—"*solidum Christi corpus, sed sine nativitate*," says Tertullian (*De Carne Christi*, 6). He had borrowed the substance of his body from the stars, which were elements of the higher world. Thus truly incarnate, Jesus died a real death and rose alive. Redemption consists in cutting loose from sinful flesh and escaping from the rule of the fiery angel; the soul only is saved, and the Christ himself gave back his flesh to the elements as he ascended into heaven. In this way Marcion's logical offences were at least made less glaring. If we may believe a certain Rhodon who saw Apelles in his old age, he was no uncompromising sectary. He still denounced the prophecies of the Old Testament as false and contradictory, and stood firm on the unity of the First Principle, but he thought that "those questions were not meant to be discussed, and every man ought to rest quietly in the faith that he found real, and that all would be saved whose hope was in the Crucified, provided they were found doing good" (*Eusebius*, v, 13, 5).

At the time when Apelles was putting forward these wise propositions, towards the end of the second century, Marcionism had ceased to be a pressing and dangerous threat to the Church, though it had yet to linger on for many years to come. Irenaeus, Tertullian and Hippolytus give no special place to Marcion in the ranks of the gnostics, regarding them all, him included, as reckless dreamers who had tried in vain, or were still trying, to capture the holy Church of Jesus Christ.

Chapter X

BIRTH OF THE CATHOLIC CHURCH

How did the Church succeed in expelling from her territory this flood of multiform heresies which threatened to dissolve her unity in an endless ebullition of short-lived sects? This is the question we have now to answer. A summary answer lies in the fact that it was precisely this threat which determined the Church to fix her constitution and lay down the limits beyond which no Church membership could be. She concentrated her forces, built fortifications, based herself on the past, interpreting and defining her past against the turmoil of new theologies. Thus it came to pass that those who had caused her most disquiet, and Marcion before all others, at the same time incited her to define her doctrine, to regulate her organization and to put forth the energy which broke their efforts.

1. The Christian Prophets

We have already called attention to the important fact that the intense life of the first communities, their enthusiasm, and the popular appeal of the Christian movement had long sustained the new religion without the support of any literature having the authority of Scripture other than the Jewish Bible freely interpreted by catechesis to the exaltation of Jesus. Into this catechesis, in which the moral element was at first predominant, speculation soon began to infiltrate, but mainly at the beginning in the form of individual prophesyings, of which we have seen examples in the gnoses contained in Paul's Epistles, in the Epistle to the Hebrews, or, better, in the discourses of the Johannine Christ. These early gnoses tended to complete rather than to reform or supplant the common teaching. A check upon excessive audacity in prophetic outpourings was found in the control which these prophet-teachers could exercise on each other. First Corinthians, the *Didache* and Hermas all give instructions on this head, which were soon found inadequate, but were not without temporary effect.

325

An elementary criterion for distinguishing permissible from impermissible inspiration in a prophet is indicated in what Paul is made to say about spiritual gifts (charismata) in 1 Corinthians xii, 3:

> Also I declare to you
>> that no man, speaking by spirit of God,
>>> says: "Cursed be Jesus!"
> And that no man can say:
>> "Lord Jesus!"
>>> except by holy spirit.

Any prophet, then, who in the course of his ecstasy utters a denial of Jesus, is inspired by the demon: conversely, he who gives Jesus his rightful place by proclaiming him "Lord" can only be inspired by God. In another passage (xiv, 29–31) the regulation of the outpouring is entrusted to the prophets themselves:

> As to the prophets, let two or three be the speakers,
>> And let the rest pass judgment;
> But if revelation comes to another who is seated,
>> let the first be silent;
> For you can all prophesy one after another,
>> so that all may learn,
>>> and all be exhorted.

In the *Didache*, after the prayers to be used in common at the Supper, we find the following direction (x, 7): "Let the prophets make a thanksgiving at such length as they will." Thus the prophets, after Communion, have the right to improvise their thanksgiving without limit of time. But immediately afterwards the *Didache* forbids the reception of any preacher who teaches a doctrine contrary to the catechesis just developed in the book (xi, 1–2) which, be it remembered, is almost entirely moral and ritual, like the Christianity described in Pliny's letter to Trajan. The *Didache* knows moreover of travelling apostles and of prophets who remain at home in one place. Travelling apostles who stay more than two days, in order to get more board and lodging, or ask for money, are to be reckoned false (xi, 3–6), and this, not so much on account of their heresies, but on the moral ground that they are exploiting their hosts, though possibly heretical as well as rapacious. As to the sedentary prophets, their inspired outpourings are not to be lightly criticized, but conduct is to be the test for distinguishing the true prophet from the false. He alone is a true prophet who lives according to the Lord; who would not count him a false prophet who orders a sumptuous meal or demands money (xi, 7–12)? The prophets of old had certain eccentricities, and a few such, analogous to theirs, and "in harmony with the cosmic mystery of the Church," may be tolerated in Christian prophets, provided they do not require others to imitate them (xi, 11). A highly enigmatic concession, at least for us, and sufficiently disturbing in itself; it cannot have been maintained for long. (The ancient prophets are brought in only by way of a mitigating comparison.) The reference is to some symbolic proceedings representing "the mystery," which is, one can hardly doubt, the mystic union of the Christ and "the Church." According to Irenaeus the innocent "conjunctions" (syzygies) of Valentinus seem to have been mixed up by his disciple Marcus with certain rites of symbolic magic in which mysticism had degenerated into eroticism. What the *Didache* had in mind must have been something less abominable, perhaps a symbolic marriage between an inspired couple, which may have been real, or an affair of continency on both sides. But we can see that the author of the *Didache*, while not daring to prohibit these eccentricities, is not quite at ease in the matter.

2. DECLINE OF THE PROPHETS AND RISE OF THE ADMINISTRATORS

"True prophets" and "true doctors" who regularly contribute to the edification of the community must be adequately supported, and to this end the *Didache* lays down a sort of tithe-system (xiii) which obviously calls for a measure of administration. Accordingly we find that, besides the prophets and the doctors (teachers) with their charismatic endowments, the book knows also of functionaries elected by and for the community—overseers (bishops), ministers (deacons)—charged with the general work of organization and the right ordering of the Sunday meetings.[1] The daily conduct of these functionaries must also be worthy of the Lord; they must be honest men, disinterested, sincere and well attested; and let the congregation remember that they, too, serve it in the ministry of prophecy and teaching (xv)—an injunction probably due to an early tendency to regard them as paid employees. But it was precisely to these elected administrators, who were also in charge of the arrangements for the Eucharist, that the future belonged. We shall meet them again. At the beginning of the second century, the recognized professors of prophecy, of inspired teaching, are still in the forefront of the Christian movement and pointing the way; but already it can be dimly foreseen that if ever Christian union should be disturbed these inspired doctors are likely to be the cause of disturbance and, equally, that if union is to be maintained the work of maintaining it will be done by the elected administrators.

In this connexion the *Shepherd of Hermas* is most instructive. Hermas, too, is a prophet of the congregation like those to whom the citations from First Corinthians and the *Didache* have already introduced us. Moreover he is—if one may use the the expression—a highly conservative prophet. A contemporary of Valentinus and Marcion, with whom he doubtless came into contact at meetings of the Roman Christians, our Hermas is no purveyor of novelties and hazardous speculations; he is a doctor of the old school, altogether in the style of the *Didache*, a good man living "according to the Lord," the teacher of a morality framed on the pattern of the primitive Christian catechesis—in a word, the least gnostic of prophets. But his relation to what we have called the administration of the Church is no longer that in which we find the prophets of the *Didache*. In his Third *Vision* the Church makes him sit down on her left, with the presbyters behind him, the right being reserved for the martyrs (*Vision*, iii, 1, 8–9). He himself seems to have thought, and with good reason, that the presbyter administrators might well have been seated in front of him. But the hierarchy as he conceived it, in the order of martyrs, prophets, presbyters, was not the order destined to prevail. In fact the presbyter-bishops are already in the front rank and are not going to let even the martyrs precede them. From now on, when Hermas, in his capacity of prophet, addresses his exhortations to the community, he can have them read in public only by consent of the presbyters who preside over the Church; so he has two copies made, one for Clement (doubtless a leading presbyter) and the other for the deaconess Grapté; Clement will undertake to send the book to

outlying congregations—and so the prophet gets publicity, but
under supervision—while Grapté will use it for the instruction
of widows and orphans who are unable to attend the great
meetings and belong to the department of charitable help.[2]
It is clear, then, that while the Church in heaven still gives the
prophet Hermas precedence over the presbyters, things are
differently ordered in the Church on earth. Here the presbyters
have direct control over the prophet, insomuch that without
their authority and mediate action the revelations of Hermas
could not have seen the light either among the Christians of
Rome or elsewhere. Be it noted, these presbyters are the same
men as those who examined Marcion's doctrine and stamped it
with their disapproval. The next step to be taken, which we shall
soon see, will be that those who preside over administration
and worship will reserve to themselves the right to have their
voices heard in the assemblies, especially when prophecy is
raising a scandal.

Here, then, in Rome we find a body of presbyters who,
almost at the same time, authorize the prophecy of the Pastor
and expel Valentinus and Marcion from the community, men
whom our prophet would perhaps have treated with less severity.
What did Hermas think about this body, and what was it in
reality? According to what seems a trustworthy tradition Hermas
was own brother to the bishop Pius. But Hermas speaks only
of presbyters in general and never mentions the bishop, his
brother. In speaking of presbyters in general he betrays no
enthusiasm and seems to make no distinction between them and
the bishops whom he places side by side with the deacons.[3]
The same individuals are described indifferently as "presbyters"
and "heads of the church," or as "presbyters presiding over the
Church."[4] But however considerable these dignitaries may be,
Hermas does not hesitate to address them in pretty plain terms.
It is true that the Church is here speaking as the Pastor or Angel
of Penitence:

" 'Tis to you I speak, ye heads of the Church and occupants
of the high places. Be not like the poisoners: poisoners carry
their poison in bottles: you carry your poison and your venom
in your hearts . . . Be careful, my children, or these divisions will
be the end of you. How can you form the Lord's elect while you

yourselves are unformed? Then set about forming one another so that I, joyously presenting you to the Father, may be able to account for you to the Lord."5

From all this the fact emerges that the presbyters, so sharply taken to task by the Church, have already assumed the disciplinary control of the community. The Church and Hermas agree, not without reason, that they would be more worthy of their headship if they were less covetous of power.

It is clear that this presbyterial body already possessed considerable authority, and highly probable that it had a presiding bishop,6 whose authority was not exercised independently of his colleagues. Bishops and priests, who allowed Hermas to speak the truth about them, are not likely to have been more exacting than he in the matter of pure theology. For the good Hermas is far from being a dogmatist in that department, and looks upon heresy more in pity than in anger. He is ready to die for the Lord Christ; but his Christology is strangely indecisive; unshakably firm on the unity of God, he is totally ignorant of any Christological definition. The figurative language used in his book causes him to avoid mentioning Jesus and Christ by name. But clearly he has not the faintest idea of the Logos and its incarnation. His Son of God is far superior to the archangels, but is inconsistently presented as their leader and the first of them (*Parable*, ix, 4); elsewhere the Son seems to be identified with the Spirit (v, 2, 5, 6). In the fifth Parable, where the wanderings of his Christology are represented in a Parable of the Vine, imitated from the Gospel,7 there appears a servant named "Flesh," in whom the Son-Spirit has his abode, and whose work on the Vine has been so marvellous that the Father, agreeing with the wishes of the Son and the angels, appoints him the Son's co-heir (v, 6). But let us not jump to the conclusion that Hermas here presents his Trinity composed of Eternal Father, Son-Spirit and a God-man; for the parable is so complicated and obscure that the "servant" pre-exists in the humanity of the Son, who is also active in the Vine (v, 2, 6); from which it will be seen that the Christology of Hermas is simply amorphous and incoherent. The Roman presbyters, who were not scandalized by it, cannot have been any stricter in the definition of their own. There was however one point of doctrine on which they would allow no compromise. They expelled Marcion for attacking it. This was the unity of God.

Hermas speaks of heretics, as he speaks of the presbyters, with freedom, but without a trace of passion (ix, 22). We can see clearly that the gnostics have not led him astray. He knows them well enough and could not fail to know many of them. He finds their doctors somewhat unintelligible, presumptuous, too pleased with themselves and priding themselves on being omniscient; the higher knowledge they claim seems to him mere nonsense; on the whole he judges them more fools than knaves. Many ought to be dismissed outright—which shows that the case of Marcion was not solitary, although outstanding and the best known to us. Some have repented of their follies and been taken back into the fold; those who stick to their nonsense will be destroyed by it. This seems to have been the attitude of the presbyters themselves in the excommunications of which Hermas speaks, and it would be thus that they judged Marcion and his like; gnosis was of no account and meant nothing to them, but in doctrine they held firm by the baptismal catachism, understood in the sense of the *Didache*, as Hermas also understood it. There can be no doubt that what shocked them in Marcion was his attack on the unity of God, which they would counterattack by simply asserting against the innovator the traditional apostolic teaching of the one only God, creator of the world, and the one only Christ, Jesus the Son of God, sent by the Father to save men from their sins and to instruct them in the way of righteousness. That this tradition was an existing force is beyond question. The gnostic teachers compelled the administrators of Church discipline to exert that force with resolution against their new theologies.

It is a noteworthy fact that, except in regard to the Logos, Justin's Christology is hardly less fluid than that of Hermas. The two draw near together in the curious profession of faith in which the apologist declares that Christians believe in one only God who created the world[8] and with him worship the Son who left his Father's presence to teach true doctrine to men, having with him "the host of other good angels who resemble him, and the Spirit of Prophecy" (with which may be compared I Timothy v, 21, "I adjure thee before God, Jesus Christ and

331

the elect angels"). The Roman presbyters found Justin orthodox, and after their condemnation of Marcion, Justin pronounced his, denouncing the idea of a god superior to the creator of the world as an invention of demons. In accusing Marcion of polytheism Justin speaks as a defender of Old Testament and Gospel tradition.

3. RISE OF A SETTLED TRADITION

The watchword of the Church leaders in the campaign against gnostic heresy is found in the pastoral Epistles (1 Timothy vi, 20, 21; 2 Timothy i, 14):

> O Timothy, guard the deposit,
>> shunning impious word-play
>>> and the *antitheses* of so-called *gnosis*,
>> Professed by some,
>>> who err concerning the faith.

This couplet, the closing note of the First to Timothy, is aimed directly at Marcion and must have been written under the immediate impression of his breach with the Church or, more probably, of his attempt to change the basis of Christian teaching. "Paul," and the very Paul whom Marcion exalted to so great a height, is now heard beseeching the congregations of the faithful to "guard the deposit"—against Marcion. Against Marcion also the following profession of faith (ii, 5–6) is perhaps directed:

> God is one,
>> one also the mediator between God and men,
>>> the man Christ Jesus,
>> Who gave himself a ransom for all,
>>> as witnessed in his time.

The following hymn or prophetic oracle belongs to the same class (1 Timothy iii, 16):

> He was manifested in flesh,
>> he was justified in spirit,
>>> he was seen of angels,
> He was preached among the Gentiles,
>> he was believed in the world,
>>> he was taken up into glory.

Finally Marcion is probably included among the "lying spirits" (1 Timothy iv, 2–3):

> Who forbid to marry,
>> prescribe abstinence from foods
> which God has made to be taken with thanksgiving
>> by believers and those who know the truth.[9]

Marcion's asceticism is perhaps in the writer's mind when he advises Timothy to drink a little wine for the good of his stomach. But there is another passage (i, 4–6) where the target is not Marcion alone, but gnostics in general, with Valentinus as chief offender. Here are the instructions (1 Timothy i, 4):

> To keep clear of fables, and endless genealogies,
>> which produce wranglings,
>>> rather than divine order in faith.
> But the goal of preaching is charity,
>> coming out of pure heart, good conscience and true faith:
> Wherefrom some cut themselves off
>> in their love of empty talk,
> Setting up as doctors of law,
>> without knowing what they talk about,
>>> nor what they vouch for.[10]

These were also the views of Hermas, Polycarp and Justin. True doctrine, according to them, is a simpler affair than what these windy word-mongers have to offer; what matters above all else is life according to God.

In resisting the gnostic invasion, the defenders of the faith made continual appeal to apostolic tradition, not hesitating to represent their own denunciations of the new doctors as spoken by Paul, the "Paul," that is, of the First to Timothy (vi, 13–14):

> I charge you, before God,
>> who gives life to all,
> And before Christ Jesus,
>> who witnessed under Pontius Pilate
>>> the good confession,
> To keep intact and spotless the commandment
>> until the epiphany of Lord Jesus Christ.

The "commandment" is the apostolic catechesis and the equivalent of the "deposit" of vi, 20. The mention of Pontius

Pilate is not made for the sake of historical precision; it is a
formula taken from a hymn or rhythmical confession connected
with the ritual recitation of the passion story.

In like strain speaks the "Paul" of the Epistle to Titus (i, 9).
Let the presbyter, he says,

> Stand by the pure word according to the doctrine,
> > that he may be able to exhort in the genuine teaching,
> > and hurl back the rebels.

The context shows that the "rebels" against whom this was
directed were not pagans, nor were they, strictly speaking, Jews.
They were heretical debaters, with the turn for contentiousness
characteristic of amateurs in theology. The author says that
such people were extremely numerous in his time (Titus i, 10–11).

The author of the First to Timothy will have it that the
apostles foretold an outbreak of gnosis. The Epistle makes
Paul speak as follows (iv, 1):

> But the Spirit says expressly
> > that in the last days many will desert the faith,
> Taking up with lying spirits
> > and with doctrines of demons, etc."

It was not solely on account of their heterodoxy that the
gnostic systems are said to be the work of "demons," but also
for their mythological character, which almost turned them into
pantheons. Without making distinctions among them, these
heretics were credited with almost every conceivable vice and
crime—see the list in 2 Timothy iii, 1–9. The accusation of immorality is the daily bread of this polemic, and hardly worth
consideration, especially when formulated in general terms.

Reproducing the same diatribe against the gnostics, or
commenting on it, the spurious Jude and the spurious Peter of
the second Epistle recall, rather naïvely, that "the Lord's
Apostles" foretold "for these last times" a crop of sectaries
"who will make classifications" distinguishing two kinds of
believers, the psychic and the spiritual, "psychics themselves
without a trace of spirit"[11]—apparently another shot at Valentinus (Jude 17–19). Spurious Peter drops a hint that a little
caution will not be out of place in reading the letters of "our

dear brother Paul, in which there are certain knotty points which, to their own ruin, ignorant and unsteady souls take wrongly along with other Scriptures," namely the Old Testament and the Gospel. Who can these be but Marcion and his followers? (2 Peter iii, 15–16).

Almost contemporary with spurious Peter, we shall find Polycarp,[12] with an Epistle of John before him, attacking Marcion, as chief offender, in the following terms (Philippians 7):

"Whosoever confesses not that Jesus Christ is come in the flesh is antichrist; whosoever confesses not the witness of the cross is of the devil; whosoever twists the oracles of the Lord to suit his own desire, and denies the resurrection and the judgment is Satan's eldest son. Leave we then the futilities of that crowd and let us return to the teaching that was given us."

4. The Tradition Established

It remains only to hear Irenaeus delivering his "exposition of apostolic preaching"[13] fully assured that he is in possession of the True Faith "as traditionally taught by the elders, disciples of the apostles."[14] Immediately after him comes the *De Praescriptione Haereticorum* of Tertullian which opposes the heretics by the argument of "prescription." With that, the notion of tradition, as the Church would have it understood and as it has come down through the centuries, will be fully formed. The following passage in Chapter 19, marvellously true as a definition of Latin Christianity through the ages, gives the fundamental idea:

"Ergo non ad Scripturas provocandum est, nec in his constituendum certamen, in quibus aut nulla aut incerta victoria est, aut parum certa. Nam etsi non evaderet conlatio Scripturarum, ut utramque partem parem sisteret, ordo rerum desiderabat illud prius proponi, quod nunc solum disputandum est: quibus competat fides ipsa, cujus sint Scripturae, a quo et per quos et quando et quibus sit tradita disciplina qua fiunt Christiani. Ubi enim apparuerit esse veritatem disciplinae et fidei christianae, illic et veritas Scripturarum et expositionum et omnium traditionum Christianorum."

What Tertullian says in this passage could not have been

said as it here stands in the year 150, nor even in 180. It implies an exclusive "possession" of Scriptures, tradition and ecclesiastical authority which the church had not made good before the end of the interval between the two dates. But Tertullian's genius saw clearly the barrenness of all these disputings: saw the disadvantage the Church would suffer if she met the innovators as equals and on their own ground; saw, also, the summary procedure that was needed to put a quick end to the whole futile discussion. The one thing Tertullian did not foresee was that the system he had so clearly laid down would be turned to his own hurt, and that he would die a heretic. But the notion of "tradition," as the Church would have it understood, and as it was destined to endure through the centuries, may be counted fully born with Tertullian's assertion of the Church's prescriptive right as exclusive possessor and only competent interpreter of the sources of the faith.

This notion of tradition corresponded to a fact: the unbroken continuity of monotheistic faith, of Jewish morality taken up into the Gospel and of the worship of the Christ Jesus in the very heart of every Christian community. But, at the same time, it was and could not fail to be a somewhat fictitious assumption, an artificial but timely device of special pleading forced upon the Church by a kind of moral necessity, and onesidedly formulated in her own interest as she reacted to the pressure of a movement towards a fusion of religions on an intellectualist or pagan basis. For the idea of an absolute and unchangeable orthodoxy is in flat contradiction to the nature and history of the human mind, of human knowledge and even of Christianity itself. That which was now canonized as "the apostolic faith" was far from being the simple faith of the first believers in Jesus, nor was it that of the first apostles to the Gentile world. When Irenaeus reasons as though, between himself and the first apostles of the Christ, there was but a single generation, represented by the elders, or disciples of the apostles, he is resting upon a fiction, by then accepted, but entirely fanciful: between the second third of the first century and the time of his writing in the last third of the second, several generations of Christian believers had passed away who had not confined the expression of their belief to a repetition of the apostolic catechism. The pretended tradition, which the Church would fix for all time, was largely created in the very process of defining it. At that point in time it was nothing else than a kind of rudimentary and unformed gnosis, imperfectly coherent, in which the germ of endless disputes, nay, of heresy in many a form, lay hidden and awaiting its future development. It could not be, and never has been, anything else.

5. BIRTH OF THE CANON

We know how Marcion, cast out by the Church, had set up his own biblical canon in her face, to be used in resisting her, as need should arise. This, according to him, contained the true and authentic Gospel, the Gospel as Jesus had really preached it, which Paul alone had preserved from Jewish contamination. That is to say it contained the revelation of the good God, the true God, whereas the Jewish bible was the revelation of the Jewish god, an imperfect deity of a lower order, who was, however, the creator of the visible world, a world on the same lower level as its creator and no less imperfect than he. The idea of such a collection would never have occurred to Marcion had he not found the Church already in possession of an authorized Bible, which was judged to contain the revelation of the true God and of Christ Jesus which he, for his part, could not find there. This was the Bible of the Alexandrian Jews, in which the Church was for ever taxing her wits to find the Gospel prefigured and foretold. Marcion's acquaintance with the Jewish manner of exegesis may possibly have led him to the conclusion that this interpretation of prophecy was on the whole absolutely groundless. With these ideas in mind the arch-heretic turned to the current literature of Christianity and picked out from it the documents which he judged to give the truest account of the religion of Jesus, and then proceeded to collect them in an expurgated version in harmony with the end he had in view.

It was Marcion, then, with his belief in the unique value of the Gospel, who raised the evangelical and apostolic writings from the relative obscurity caused by the overshadowing of the ancient Scriptures, in which they had hitherto lain, more or less familiar, no doubt, to the congregation from public reading, but not yet Scripture on a footing with the books of Moses and the prophets of Israel; he it was who brought out these writings into the full light of day and endowed them with the status of Scriptures. No one doubted that they were the work of the Spirit, but, quite naturally, the prestige of the ancient Bible had hitherto outshone them. Now, if there is one thing more evident than another at this momentous juncture, it is that the Church could not effectively counter the audacity of these new theologians were it to rely solely on the existing Scriptures of Old Testament books, since these, strictly interpreted, could only be made to plead the cause of Judaism. The attack had to be met on its own ground, and this could only be done by opposing a tradition earlier to that of the innovators and by means of documents traditionally evangelical and apostolic. Certainly Marcion was under no illusion in professing that this tradition was not trustworthy. Since Irenaeus and Tertullian he is bitterly abused for rejecting or changing the apostolic writings, but neither his denial of the apostolicity of the Gospels, nor the reasons he gave for it, have been seriously discussed. When Celsus reproaches the Christians with never ceasing to make alterations in their Gospels he is perhaps only repeating something that Marcion had said after direct experience of its truth. But the cause of the Church would have been lost by admitting suspicion as to the apostolic authenticity of her texts and by making it a matter for discussion; the idea of critically examining it could not enter her mind, and did not. She boldly entrenched herself in her catechetical tradition, of which the various Gospels and the apostolic writings, or those deemed such, were also the documents; then, taking a leaf out of Marcion's book, she decided, and it would seem promptly, to canonize those of the Gospel and apostolic writings which had the usage of the congregations to recommend them or seemed likely to serve her in a situation so distressing and unforeseen.

At the time when the Church was canonizing her collection of writings she energetically went to work in assigning them to writers whose names would confer authenticity on the selected books; an assignment rather retrospective, since the question of their authenticity had been, up to that moment, of little interest. The explanations given about the New Testament books by the Canon of Muratori and the statements of Irenaeus on the origin of the Gospels are an apologia for the official collection as a whole; but already Justin had made a milder apologia for the Gospels by presenting them more discreetly under the general term "Memoirs of the Apostles," while Papias had pleaded for the ecclesiastical text of Mark and of Matthew. Both Marcion and his adversaries were eager to find assurance for texts about whose authenticity neither of them were very confident. And both sides made a virtue of necessity.

But the Church could not limit her canon as narrowly as Marcion had limited his, nor had she at the time any motive to do so. The Gospel writings to begin with were drawn up and circulated to meet the needs of the various communities, and those were selected for canonization which had been adopted for liturgical use by the most important of them. The first Gospel, as B. W. Bacon maintains, seems to have gained authority in the Syrian congregations;[15] the third held the field in Greece proper and in Rome,[16] where Mark also was in use;[17] the fourth had taken root in the congregations of Asia which were full of life at the time when the canon was made. Alexandria, at this period still a mystery to the historian, seems to have contributed nothing to the Gospel canon, although she had been fertile ground for literature of that type, but we know that she did not force the acceptance of her Gospel of the Egyptians on the canonizers and soon abandoned it herself. Perhaps she was not at first admitted to the concert of Churches, by which the Gospel canon was fixed, for Alexandria was reputed a hotbed of gnosticism, and her Gospel of the Egyptians contained more than a little of the offending article. It is possible, moreover, that the Christian groups in Alexandria were not unified early enough to speak with a single voice in the negotiations which fixed the combined canon of the Gospels and of the whole New Testament, and that this was made without consulting the Alexandrian Christians, who, however, finally accepted the decision taken by the others. It is worthy of note that when the Paschal controversy, about 180, was agitating every Christian community from Edessa to Lyons, Alexandria does not enter into direct relations with Pope Victor and sends her views on the affair, only after it was settled, to the communities in Palestine (*Eusebius*, v, 25, 23).

It is easy to explain how the three Pastoral Epistles came to be annexed to the Ten Epistles previously known as Paul's. These three letters corresponded so exactly to the needs of the hour that the correspondence cannot have been the result of chance. If not written expressly to satisfy the needs of the Church in her campaign against Marcion, they were completed and turned to such good account against him that the whole collection of thirteen Epistles may be called anti-Marcionite. We can also understand how the fourth Gospel, once accepted, would bring in the first Johannine Epistle and the two others in its train. The main difficulty of the canonists must have been that of securing acceptance, outside of Asia, for the Gospel they called John's, and first of all at Rome. Asia was its fortress. This Gospel is in keeping with the Easter usage of the Quartodecimans, which forms the background to its arrangement of the passion stories; Polycrates, with good reason, refers to this in his letter to Pope Victor (*Eusebius*, v, 24, 3); Montanism had adopted it and the Asiatic congregations made its fortune when their influence compelled the other Churches to give it recognition. Agreement on the matter was reached under the pressure of a necessity equally felt on either side and, we may be sure, not without mutual concessions and interested, perhaps concerted, adaptations of the text.[18] In establishing the canon of the four Gospels in particular there can be no doubt that a time came when the resolution was taken by all parties to establish a united front against the gnostic irruption and especially against the projects of Marcion.

Apostolicity being the quality aimed at and the order of the day, nothing came more conveniently to hand than the Acts of the Apostles, a book which had hitherto been outshone in credit by its twin brother, the third Gospel. This book of Acts was doubly to the purpose, first in its picture of Christianity as a harmless religion, loyal to the Roman empire, and then by its hostility to gnostic innovators, whom it represents Paul as denouncing in advance at Ephesus (xx, 29, 30) just as it makes him inaugurate the philosophical defence of Christianity in his speech to the Areopagus,[19] which contains the germ of Justin's apologetics— *minus* the Logos. But, notwithstanding the attractions it must have had for the canonists, the influence of this book on the evolution of Christian thought has never equalled that of the Fourth Gospel and of the Epistles attributed to Paul. Both Rome and Asia knew the first of the two Epistles called Peter's and included it in the canon as apostolic. The Apocalypse of John, declared apostolic in Asia, was received as such in Rome where, as yet, its millenarianism had raised no alarm. Justin knew and esteemed it, and the Canon of Muratori defends its reputation which had been compromised by the sudden outbreak of Montanism. But in the third century we find the catholic gnostics of Alexandria judging it unfavourably; only by the influence of the West was it saved from the discredit which overtook the Apocalypse of Peter even in Rome, where it was accepted towards the end of the second century. A strange case was that of the Epistle to the Hebrews. Although Alexandria had early attributed this Epistle to Paul; although it was read in Rome before Marcion was known there, for the Epistle of Clement puts it largely under contribution;[20] although it is cited by Tertullian as the work of Barnabas, and used by him to pour ridicule on Hermas,[21] we find nevertheless that it was not included in the canon as apostolic till the end of the fourth century. Perhaps the reason lay in the fact that Rome had begun its acquaintance with this document in full knowledge that it was not apostolic.

Whatever the truth may be about the inclusion of particular books, the fact is unquestionable that the main body of the New Testament was solidly constituted by the end of the second century. It then included the four Gospels, the Acts of the Apostles, thirteen Epistles of Paul, the first Epistle of Peter and the first Epistle of John. Needless to say this canonization of New Testament writings was not made in a day and there and then proclaimed by a council assembled *ad hoc*. But by the time of Irenaeus it appears to have been so far completed. The principle of "apostolicity" on which it was based must have been laid down at the very beginning by a kind of concert among the Churches chiefly concerned and by them made dominant. Looking closely into the matter we cannot but feel that, but for the ruling of this principle, the juxtaposition of the Fourth Gospel with the three Synoptics would not be natural in a collection intended to support the common teaching of the Church. In Rome the Fourth Gospel was long ignored and, even in the early part of the second century, Caius, a Roman presbyter, dared to launch a polemic against the Johannine writings, though this, it is true, was at a

time when Asia was in bad odour at Rome over the Easter controversy. But the testimony of Irenaeus makes it clear[22] that in
certain quarters opposition to the Fourth Gospel was lively enough
in his time and connected with the opposition to Montanism, a
movement Asiatic in origin. But, so long as these adversaries of
the Fourth Gospel accepted the first three, they were not charged
with heresy.

It must have been, then, by a formal agreement, arrived at after
full interchange of views between Rome and the Asiatic Churches,
that the principle of the fourfold or "tetramorphic" Gospel was
finally adopted. When and how cannot be stated with precision
and certitude. It was done before Irenaeus who defends the
principle with assiduity and ardour, and certainly did not invent it,
for he was in no position to lay it down for the whole Christian
Church. If a conjecture may be ventured on so nice a point, as
good a conjecture as any would be that agreement was reached at
Rome in conversations between the bishop Anicetus and Polycarp
of Smyrna. Of the reasons for Polycarp's journey to Rome
we know nothing and can only say that his great age and his
functions rule out the likelihood that he made the journey for
pleasure. Irenaeus mentions it incidentally in his letter to Victor
about the Easter controversy (*Eusebius*, v, 24 and 16). Irenaeus,
then Bishop of Lyons, who may well have known more about the
matter than he tells, relates how "the blessed Polycarp being come
to Rome under Anicetus," the two bishops "discussed between
them certain questions on which they soon came to an understanding, but avoided quarrelling on the subject" of Easter,
Polycarp being immovable in the observance he held to be
apostolic and Anicetus equally so in that which "the presbyters
before his time" had followed. Polycarp, then, did not come to
Rome to negotiate about Easter, but to examine with Anicetus
"the small differences that existed between them." The gnostic
crisis being then at its height and the Marcionite movement in
full swing, it seems probable that Polycarp came to Rome as
representing the Asiatic Churches for the purpose of concerting
common measures with Anicetus for stemming the mounting
flood of heresy. Obviously the first measure demanded by the
situation was to fix the sources from which the true evangelical
and apostolic tradition was derived. Is it not likely that among the

decisions then taken one was the determination of the number of the Gospels and perhaps also the number of Paul's Epistles? The foundation of the New Testament canon would then have been built. The rest would be completed between 160 and 180, Acts obtaining official recognition by the side of the Epistles; then, finally, the anti-montanist reaction, which threw suspicion on the Apocalypse of John, would be satisfied by excluding the Apocalypse of Peter, formerly accepted by some of the Churches, along with the Pastor of Hermas, which the Roman Church piously retained till then as an authorized prophecy.[23]

6. SHAPING OF THE APOSTOLIC CREED

A barrier of writings declared apostolic was insufficient protection against the advancing tide of innovation. Just as Marcion was using the principles of his own doctrine to interpret the Gospel and the Apostolicon, on which he professed the principles were founded, so the Church interpreted her New Testament by the principles of her catechesis, defining them with greater amplitude and precision as she reacted against the new heresies, and especially against Marcion.

As we have seen above (pp. 332 ff.) the pastoral Epistles contain the rudiments, or the echoes, of this professedly apostolic creed. So, too, Clement when he writes (1 *Clement*, 46, 6): "Have we not one (and the same) God, one Christ, one Spirit of pardon poured out on us, one (and the same) vocation in Christ?" Justin, again, seems to be paraphrasing a formula of faith when he assures the emperors that the Christians are not atheists, but believers in the true God, venerating him with "the Son who comes from him" and with the spirit of prophecy.[24] But we have no means of knowing what the precise formula was to which the paraphrase corresponds. A little further on (i, 61) Justin explains how Christians are born anew in the baptismal immersion "in the name of God, father and lord of all things, of our saviour Jesus Christ and of the Holy Spirit." These three terms of the baptismal confession can hardly be later than the year 150. They are the main features of a formulary subsequently elaborated in opposition to gnosis and concentrate what the Church was bent on regarding as the essence of "apostolic preaching."

What Irenaeus has to say (*Heresies*, i, 10) about the faith received by the Church from the apostles and their disciples affords a glimpse of the formulary in the process of shaping. It is, he says, faith

> in one only God, the Father almighty, who created heaven, earth, sea and all they contain;
>
> in one only Christ, Jesus, Son of God, made flesh for our salvation;
>
> and in the holy Spirit, who by the prophets announced the scheme of salvation, the coming, virgin birth, passion, resurrection from the dead of Christ, Jesus our Lord, his coming again in the glory of the Father, to gather all together and raise to life the whole of mankind before passing judgment on every individual.

It is to be remarked that Irenaeus in his profession of the catholic faith introduces the Gospel history of birth, passion, etc., not into his second article (faith in the Christ) but into his third (faith in the Holy Spirit) where he presents it as a *prophesied* history, precisely as Justin conceived it and as it is conceived in the Gospels themselves. It is impossible to exaggerate the significance of this feature. It shows that the modern scholar who discovers, and truly discovers, that the Gospels are histories, not of the historical Jesus, but of the accomplishment of prophecy in the Christ, is simply discovering a fact which Irenaeus seems to have known well enough. In other respects the unity of God and the unity of the Christ are affirmed against Marcion chiefly; the same is true of the incarnation, the bodily resurrection and the last judgment. Instead of giving sole prominence to the rôle of the Father in creating the world, as was done in the catechesis before Marcion challenged it, the doctrine of salvation is now brought to the front, no doubt in accord with the Epistles of Paul and with John, but also in accord with Marcion, who is here both followed and corrected.

The title of his other writing, *The Exposition of the Apostolic Preaching*, shows by its bare announcement the dominant thought of Irenaeus and the idea he had formed of the tradition as "apostolic preaching"—a preaching whose content he himself, in his time, largely contributed to defining. In this *Exposition* he recalls how "we have all received baptism for the remission of sins in the name of God the Father, in the name of Jesus Christ, son of God, incarnate, dead and raised again, and in the holy Spirit of God" (*Exposition*, 3). A little further on (6) he explains that the whole structure of the faith and the scheme of salvation rests upon the following three articles:

> God, Father, increate, invisible, creator of all things—this is the first article of our faith.
>
> And this is the second: the Word of God, Son of God, our Lord Jesus Christ, who appeared to the prophets in the form of their prophecy and according to the power of the Father's disposition; by whom were all things created; he it was who, in the fullness of time, to accomplish all things and omit nothing, was made man among men, visible and tangible, to destroy death and reveal life, and to make effective the communion and union of God and man.
>
> Third article: the holy Spirit by whose power the prophets prophesied, the fathers were instructed in the knowledge of God, the just guided in the way of righteousness; and who, in the last days, is shed forth in a new manner on the human race throughout the world, renewing mankind for God.

The article of the holy Spirit is also the article of the Church, but given a turn which avoids the condemnation of the Montanists. In his comments on the three articles, Irenaeus develops a veritable gnosis in which soteriology is adapted to cosmology and the Old Testament harmonized with the New. This gnosis, apparently derived from the Gospels and Epistles, but better balanced than the rough outlines of doctrine to be found in the canonical writings, was plainly conceived and formulated to counter the gnosis of Marcion.

We come now to the ancient Roman Creed, the date of which is still under discussion, but probably goes back to the period 150–160:[25]

> I believe in God, the Father Almighty;
> And in Christ Jesus, his only begotten Son, our Lord,
>   who was born of the holy Spirit and the Virgin Mary,
>   who under Pontius Pilate was crucified and buried;
>   the third day, he rose from the dead,
>   ascended to the heavens, sat down at God's right hand,
>   whence he will come to judge the quick and the dead;
> And in the holy Spirit, the holy Church, the remission of sins
>   and the resurrection of the flesh.

345

This, in substance, is the gnosis of Irenaeus, *minus* the Word and lacking his systematic balance, but with certain points made more precise for better correspondence with the Gospels, and always with the same emphasis on the one and only God, the creator, and on Jesus his only begotten Son, incarnate, dead and risen who will come again to judge the living and those raised from the dead. Aimed at less openly, Marcion and his gnosis are here aimed at none the less in reality.

A point on no account to be overlooked is that the term here translated "one and only," which appears in the Roman Creed, is not to be found in the old baptismal formula of Rome preserved by Hippolytus. As the second question in his profession of faith the candidate was asked: "Believest thou in Christ Jesus the Son of God begotten by Holy Spirit of the virgin Mary?"[26] In this formula the divine sonship is connected with the virgin conception, as Luke also connected it (i, 35) in the passage where the virgin conception is recorded. What the meaning of the baptismal formula really was is shown by the Liturgy of Hippolytus,[27] where a paraphrase of the Creed reappears in the Eucharistic prayers:

> We thank thee, O God, by thy dear child Jesus Christ,
>> whom in the last days thou hast sent as saviour and redeemer,
>> and angel of thy will;
>>> who is thy Word, by whom thou hast made all things;
>>> whom it pleased thee to send from heaven into a virgin's
>>> womb,
>>> and who, when conceived, became flesh and was revealed
>>> thy Son,
>>>> born of holy Spirit and a virgin, etc.[28]

Needless to say the line in the above passage concerning the Word is an addition from the personal theology of Hippolytus, a resolute defender of the Logos and of the fourth Gospel, like his master Irenaeus. But the part of the formula which presents Jesus as Son of God in virtue of his being born of God, by the instrumentality of the holy Spirit and the virgin Mary, corresponds to the baptismal formula cited immediately above which is earlier than the Roman Creed. Much older are the terms applied to Jesus, "child" of God, "angel of his will," which are nearly related to the *Didache*, while the second question of the profession looks as if its original form was only: "Believest thou in Christ Jesus, the Son of God?" The addition of "only begotten" after Son, as it is placed in the Roman Symbol, has the effect of making the sonship an eternal relation existing before the incarnation by miraculous conception. For that reason some critics hesitate to place the use of the word as far back as the second century. In any case, however, it might well have been aimed at Valentinus.

7. The Miraculous Conception

At what date the miraculous conception became an article of the faith remains a matter for conjecture. Obviously this date depends on that assigned, not precisely to the composition of the first Gospel, but to its acceptance by the Church in Rome and to the addition of the verses about the virgin conception in Luke. Not long ago some excitement was caused by a Syriac manuscript (published by W. Wright in the *Journal of Sacred Literature*, October, 1866) in which there is an account of a Council said to have been held at Rome during the reign of Hadrian in the year 119, Xystus then being bishop. At this Council the questions of the star of the Magi and of Joseph's marriage are said to have been examined. Many critics have hesitated to take this information seriously as having anything to do with the reception of the first Gospel in the Roman Church. Quite recently, however, Streeter (*The Four Gospels*, 525) and Bacon (*Studies in Matthew*, 50–59), both considerable authorities, have pronounced in favour of a connexion between the two things. They maintain that a book which, like Matthew, gave the Gospel a "beginning" other than that of Mark (see Mark i, 1) would not have been accepted in the Roman Community without further examination and testimony; but such testimony was forthcoming, and acceptance effected without much difficulty, because Ignatius of Antioch[29] had recently addressed a warm plea to Rome in favour of Matthew, highly esteemed at Antioch and by him. The second argument holds good only on the double condition of the letters of Ignatius containing the plea being authentic, and the supposed date of his martyrdom being correct, if even then. This is tantamount to saying the argument

347

is not conclusive. The first argument, which needs very cautious handling, remains to be considered.

The authority of a witness as late as that of this Syriac manuscript (fifth century), and as isolated, is not indisputable, nor are the ancient sources on which it might possibly depend (discussed at length by Bacon) and of which, by some strange chance, it would be the only echo, anything more than a matter of more or less plausible conjecture. The discussion of its intrinsic probability would be endless. There is no proof that the canon of the New Testament was drawn up at Councils properly so called, and decided book by book, and that, as Bacon contends, the Pastor of Hermas was excluded in this way from the collection.[30] Moreover, in a case like that of Matthew, the question of its formal acceptance or rejection would have been impossible in the conditions under which a Roman Council could have taken place in the year 120. A Gospel already received in some communities, as Matthew was at Antioch, and coming to the knowledge of others, was not offered to their official examiners to be promptly accepted or rejected; it merely asked for the attention of the faithful and might be long tolerated and held in esteem without entering, to the same extent as others, into the actual usage of the congregations. It is improbable that Matthew brought anything new in the way of belief to the Eastern circles where it first appeared, its compiler merely giving Gospel form to beliefs which had already taken shape. In the same way when it arrived in Rome its contents would seem to fall in with what was already known and cannot have made the impression of bringing information hitherto unheard of. So received, its credit would increase as time went on.

It is nevertheless possible that the period indicated (119–120) corresponds to a moment of great importance in the history of the Church in Rome. When Irenaeus reminds Victor that his predecessors tolerated the Easter observance of the quartodecimans without practising it themselves, he goes back by Soter and Anicetus to Pius, Hyginus and Telesphorus, and stops at Xystus as though he has now reached the point from which the Roman tradition takes its departure. It is not impossible that the Roman observance of the Sunday Easter goes no further back; but Irenaeus may also have stopped there for lack of further information. In like manner it is not impossible that our first Gospel arrived in Rome in the time of Xystus and was there received with respect but without supplanting Mark and Luke, then in use. Nor is it impossible that the growing credit of Matthew, with its birth story, soon had the effect of introducing into Luke the addition (i, 34–35) which records the virgin conception of the Christ. Finally it is not impossible that about 145–150 the miraculous conception of the Christ was introduced into the baptismal confession of faith, against Valentinus and especially against Marcion. But all these attempts to fix the date when the miraculous conception became matter of faith remain in the realm of conjecture.

8. REMAINING ARTICLES OF THE CREED

The article of the remission of sins, in the ancient Roman Symbol, seems to have a special significance. Impressed by the call of Hermas and his Pastor the Roman Church may well have established the system of public penitence for Christian sinners, as a means of defending her discipline against the many continence-sects then active, and especially against the Marcionites. The express mention of "the holy Church" aims at canonizing the traditional Church, the Great Church, the Catholic Church; at establishing it in the presence, and at the expense, of the gnostic conventicles and suspected groupings, to which this true Church will henceforth refuse all claims to truth and to holiness. It is against the gnostics also, and once more against Marcion in particular, that she affirms "the resurrection of the flesh," notwithstanding the declaration of First Corinthians "that flesh and blood cannot inherit the Kingdom of God" (xv, 50).

9. EMERGENCE OF THE EPISCOPATE AND THE CHURCH FULLY BORN

Impassioned love for the Church, and for the unity of the Church, goes back to the earliest organization of the Christian societies; beyond all question it is an inheritance from the Jewish spirit, in which the idea of a chosen people threw off its national limitations and became humanized. From the very first the community of believers in Jesus claimed to be, and was determined to remain, a spiritual homeland for the elect people of God. Spite of all divisions and, we may add, of many fallings-away, the Christian groups were kept united in the bond of their faith, of their great hope and of the fraternal practice of a truly effective charity. We have already seen how their rudimentary institutions were very naturally copied from the Synagogue. But they could not fail to undergo profound transformations of inner ordering in the course of their independent growth to maturity.

It was inevitable, even at the earliest period, that certain members would be charged with the due ordering of the meetings, chiefly of the communion supper, and with the care of the poor. The Book of Acts represents the Apostles as the first administrators of the community but soon forced to delegate the service of its material wants to seven deacons (vi, 1–6). The story is fictitious, but corresponds to one reality—that the Christian communities were organized brotherhoods from the very beginning. From the moment the groups were formed, the older men, assisted by auxiliary ministers, took the place of presidents; there were presbyters, deacons and even deaconesses. At the end of First Corinthians (xvi, 15–16) Paul mentions one Stephanas and those of his household, "first fruits of Achaia, who have taken on themselves the service of the saints," that is, the first to be converted who, ever since their conversion, have devoted themselves to the community; and he then goes on to plead that obedience should be rendered to them and to every helper who labours as they did for the common good. It would seem, then, that Stephanas and his fellow workers had already the duty of supervising as well as of serving, and were charged, as a kind of police, with the maintenance of discipline. At the end of Romans, Paul, in like manner, speaks of "the sister Phoebe," deaconess of the community at Cenchrea, who has the duty of carrying his letter, a person worthy of all respect "because she has been a help to many, including myself." With no titles or honorific badges to distinguish them from other believers, and though they had not received the indelible mark of sacramental ordination, these people were of no little con-

350

sequence in the community. It is, however, true that the ordination of elders, bishop-priests and deacons, by the laying-on of hands, is of earlier date than the editing of Acts and the pastoral Epistles, perhaps even earlier than the *Didache*.

At no period of their history did the communities allow these indispensable officers to drop out. The presence of apostles, prophets and doctors may have left them at first somewhat in the shade, but did not render them less necessary. In First Corinthians (xii, 4–5) "service" is placed below "spiritual gifts." The *Didache* gives these helpers greater honour, but still finds it necessary to urge consideration for them in the community which has elected them to office. This is no longer determined by circumstances or by their own wish to serve, as it was at the beginning.

> "Choose you bishops and deacons[31] worthy of the Lord; let them be gentle men, disinterested, sincere, well-tried. For they also exercise among you the ministry of prophets and doctors; look not upon them as of low rank, for they are entitled to respect among you along with prophets and doctors." (*Didache*, 31.)

The status of elders, as Hermas describes it, is almost the same, except that they are now acquiring greater authority and are beginning to take precedence of the prophets and the doctors.

The "overseers," or bishops, were not distinguished from the elders, or priests. The elders are also the overseers; the "ministers," or deacons, are subordinate to them. In the Pastoral Epistles three orders of administrative officers are no longer recognized, but only two, the bishop-priests and the deacons.[32] Thus each community, on becoming fairly numerous, would have a *collegium* of elders presiding over its social life, meetings for worship and works of charity; the deacons would form the executive. But though, at the outset, the elders had no teaching ministry by the side of the prophets and doctors, and though even the moral discipline of the congregation did not belong to them, the force of circumstances would, nevertheless, tend to give them a leading part, not only in discipline, but in the day to day instruction of catechumens and those already baptized. The importance of their administrative function would increase with the increase of the common resources to be managed and of the alms to be distributed, with the growing sacredness of their duties in the conduct of worship and the concurrent decline and inadequacy of inspired prophecy and itinerant preaching. The *Didache* (11, 3–5) gives us a glimpse of the latter process; the wandering apostle was now becoming a burdensome charge on the localized congregations and ill-seen by the managers of their funds.33 At Rome, in the time of Hermas, the prophet-teacher was already under the control of the presbyters, who soon set him aside altogether and themselves assumed sole charge of the day to day instruction of the congregation. The author of the Ignatian Letters speaks as though his own office were that of bishop-prophet and not as though the prophets were a separate order at the side of the bishops, priests and deacons. When Marcion tried to revive the prophets it was too late.

We can now understand why the pastoral Epistles dwell on the qualities needed in the bishop-priest and in the deacon with an insistence that seems striving to find terms strong enough. For, in reality, it is to them, not to the prophets nor to the teachers (doctors), that the "Paul" of the pastorals, through the intermediary of Timothy and Titus, commits the whole care of the congregations now menaced by a swarm of heretical doctrinaires. To Titus he writes as follows (i, 5–9):

> To this end I left thee in Crete,
>   that thou mightest complete what is unfinished,
> And appoint presbyters in every town,
>   according to the order I gave thee.
> Let each be a man above reproach,
>   the husband of one wife,34
> With believing children,
>   not suspected as ne'er-do-wells or disobedient.
> For the bishop must be irreproachable,
>   inasmuch as he is God's steward:
> Not arrogant, not hasty tempered, not given to drink,
>   not a man of blows, not avaricious,
> But a kindly host, a good man, having common sense,
>   just, pious, master of himself,
> Holding fast the sure word which accords with the doctrine,
>   so that he can exhort in holy teaching,
>   and send opponents to the right-about.

From this it becomes clear that the bishop-priest is now charged with the paternal government of the community and with the instruction of it according to "the doctrine" deemed apostolic. Obviously the office is not for new and untried hands, a point expressly made in the Epistles to Timothy (i, 3-4; v, 22; 2, ii, 2).

> Let the deacons likewise be worthy men,
>   not using words in a double sense,
> And not addicted to the wine cup,
>   not avaricious,
> Having the mystery of the faith
>   in purity of conscience
> But see to it also that they are first proved,
>   then let them serve, being without reproach;
> For those who do good service
>   win for themselves a position of honour
> And great assurance by faith in Christ Jesus.

When and how the bishop emerged from the general body of presbyters as sole president of the community, cannot be stated with precision. It is probable that from the very earliest time this body was not constituted without a head, that it had a president, but that his office did not exalt him very highly above his fellows and was not an appointment for life. It is noteworthy that Hermas, whose tradition makes him out to be the brother of the bishop Pius, predecessor of Anicetus, never mentions the bishop, and seems to have had dealings only with the presbyters in Rome. But a few years afterwards we find Anicetus sole bishop of the Roman community, just as his contemporary Polycarp was sole bishop in Smyrna. But Polycarp had then been bishop for a long time. It may well be that the monarchical type of episcopate existed in some regions earlier than in others. Polycarp himself, for example, writing to the Philippians makes no mention of any bishop at Philippi.[35] The community of Corinth, again, seems to have had no bishop at its head when the letter of Clement was addressed to it. This letter shows knowledge only of bishop-priests and of deacons, instituted by the apostles in the communities they had founded, and reappointed by election after the apostle's death. The letter does not speak of these functionaries as subject to recall at will or periodically, but as there for life.[36]

We may conclude, then, that the monarchical type of episcopate was at first instituted in certain communities, either because they were more prepared than the others for an autocratic regime, or through the pressure of personalities better endowed for leadership and ambitious to attain it. Have we not already heard the good Hermas rebuking the Roman presbyters for their love of place and power? On that road Asia may well have taken the lead of Greece proper, and especially of Rome, where perhaps there was some difficulty in centralizing the Christian groups under a single administration. It is likely enough that the gnostic peril brought this evolution to a sudden head; for while the unitary episcopate exists only in some places before the period 130–140, we find it existing everywhere after 150–160. Be it observed, moreover, that Marcion, who founded his communities on the pattern of the Great Church, recognized the distinction between episcopate, presbyterate and deaconate. These functions, however, were not perpetual in the Marcionite communities and did not form a true hierarchy. The tendency of the arch-heretic was, so to say, in the direction of democratizing church appointments, while the Church, on the other side, proceeded to fortify them more and more by an official conservation, which ended by separating the clergy from the lay believers.37 In the Church, priests and deacons became united in one body, under the rule of the bishop, to guide the Christian flock in the path of apostolic doctrine. Bishops, priests, deacons, these three, while retaining their function as ministers of charity, are now to be acknowledged as masters of the truth and hierarchs of the cult.

Meanwhile the gap which divides the Church from the heresies grows deeper and more distinct. Celsus (c. 180) clearly distinguishes the one from the other. But, more profoundly than an outsider like Celsus could feel it, the difference between orthodox and heretical was realized within the Church, which its official representatives and apologists are now declaring to be the sole guardian of the truth. Justin, who attributes pagan idolatry to wicked demons, does not hesitate to make them the authors of all the heresies from Simon Magus to Marcion (1 *Apology*, 26, 58). "There is not a doubt," Tertullian will soon be saying, "that the spirits of perversity, from whom come the heresies, were charged with the business by the devil, nor that heresies are the same as idolatry, seeing that they come from the same author and are of the same workmanship. Either they invent another God to oppose the creator"—this for Marcion—"or, if they admit only one creator they make him out to be different from what he really is. Thus every lie they tell about God is some sort of service to idols" (*De Praescriptione*, 40).

We have already heard the author of the Ignatian Letters sounding his trumpet call to the faithful to rally round the bishop. Let us listen once more to this singer of Christian unity—unity in bishops and by bishops. For he it is who may be truly said to have created the mystery of the episcopate, that mystery of which Cyprian, in the next century, was to be the worthy exponent, and which to-day would be condemned as heresy, being now replaced by the mystery of the Pope, of which our authors had not the faintest idea.

> Since love permits me not to keep silence towards you, I am eager in exhorting you to walk in step with the thought of God. For Jesus Christ, the life we can never be parted from, is the thought of God, even as bishops, established in their seats to the end of the earth, are one with the thought of Jesus Christ. Fitting it is, then, that you walk in step with the thought of the bishop, as indeed you are doing. For your venerable presbyterium is adjusted to the bishop as cords are adjusted to the lyre. Wherefore Christ is praised by the harmony of your hearts and the symphony of your love. Join you, each one, his voice to that choir, so that, with one heart and one voice, taking up in unison the key-note of God, you may sing through Jesus Christ to the Father, who will then listen to your song and recognize by your works that you are members of his Son. Good is it for you that you keep in faultless unity, for thus will you ever be united to the very God. (Ephesians 3–4.)

10. SUDDEN REVIVAL OF CHRISTIAN PROPHECY

At the moment when this admirable symphony was about to become complete, it had a narrow escape of being broken up by the discordant cries of the Christian prophets. Christian prophecy, as we have seen, was on the way to dying a natural death in the atmosphere created by the intellectualism of gnosis and the growth of the episcopate, which was fighting gnosis and growing stronger as it fought. But all of a sudden, between 160 and 170,[38] prophecy came to life again in a region which had long been accustomed to outbreaks of mystical transport. Montanus, with his women acolytes, Maximilla and Priscilla, exalted it seems by overstudy of the Johannine writings, were persuaded that a mission had been laid upon them to revive the golden days of Christian prophecy. Great was the emotional excitement in all the congregations of God, beginning from those in Asia Minor, when news spread that astounding manifestations of the Spirit were taking place in Phrygia; an excitement which became the more confused when it was learnt at the same time that the new prophets were encountering vigorous opposition, especially from the bishops, who were actively at work in refuting the prophets and were going to the length of having them exorcised as possessed of the devil.

As with other heresies, our information about Montanus and Montanism comes mainly from those who opposed them. But Montanus was not a real heretic; at least there was nothing of the gnostic about him. He and his adepts were *illuminati* who had been carried away by the Book of Revelation and expected to see the New Jerusalem descending at an exact spot, which their visions had revealed to them, between the small Phrygian towns of Pepuza and Tymon. Far from the scene of their excesses the Montanists were looked upon with favour in 177 at Lyons where Irenaeus the bishop showed them consistent goodwill. Rome hesitated long before taking sides.39 It was while affairs were in this posture that certain Asiatics, by way of turning Montanus and his followers to mockery, rejected the whole of the Johannine books. For Montanism lasted on and was getting organized round Pepuza undeterred by the persistent delay of the heavenly Jerusalem in making its appearance. Rome, under Victor, and in the first years of Zephyrinus, took no pains to be on good terms with the Asiatic bishops, and this may explain why Caius (180–235) was able with impunity to join the Asiatic adversaries of the Paraclete, the Fourth Gospel and the Apocalypse. In this Caius was also attacking Montanism.

The violence of the agitation caused by this revival of Christian prophecy was not confined to Asia Minor. Though most of the Asiatic bishops were against the movement, it got a lasting hold in Phrygia, where the headquarters of its hopes were established. But its localization in that province did not hinder its missionaries from going far into the West. Only in Africa was Montanism able to take root, and there it won over Tertullian, the greatest of the Church's apologists in that age. Great as was the effort made by Tertullian to rally the Church to Montanism, he succeeded no further than to bring about his own secession towards the year 201,[40] taking with him a small group of followers who never counted for much in African Christianity, though they managed to hold on till the time of Saint Augustine.

The historical significance of Montanism lies in the fact that here we have a rekindling of the inner fire whose light illuminated the first believers. The medium in which that fire sprang up again was doubtless favourable to such an outbreak, but the movement is best understood as a reaction of faith against gnosis, a reaction, that is, of the mystic sense against metaphysical subtleties pretending to be a philosophy of religion. It was also a movement of rigorist morality, a continence-movement proceeding from a principle different from Marcion's but not less exacting. Montanus condemned marriage by arguments which pushed to its last consequences the reasoning by which celibacy and virginity are commended to the faithful in First Corinthians (vii, 6–8, 25–34). Both in its revival of prophecy and in its rigorist morality Montanism ran counter to tendencies manifested in the Church during the second century towards a more flexible discipline, and a more solid organization, than the first age of Christianity would have found congenial. On the one hand, the Church was building herself into a fortress by submitting to the rule of a monarchical episcopate; on the other, she was adapting herself to the conditions of human society by allowing for the wants, even the weaknesses, of human nature, and by establishing a discipline of penitence for those whose courage might fail in professing their faith when threatened with death for profession, or who might commit any other sin incompatible with the principle of Christianity. Far from yielding to the Montanist movement, the episcopate was now strong enough to deprive prophecy of any part in the direction of the Christian conscience and to set up a relatively indulgent regime for the Christian sinner, but always on condition of his penitence.

The check thus given to Montanism marks the end of primitive Christianity. From that time onwards the Christian religion is the

Christian Church under the rule of bishops accounted successors of the apostles and trustees of the apostolic tradition. This Church has her Creed, of which the essential lines are now firmly drawn. She has her Scriptures, a collection of the New Testament, supported by the Old. Her worship has evolved into a Mystery of Salvation. Her whole institution is now defined sufficiently, not indeed to render future heresy impossible, but to ensure that henceforth, and century after century, the life of the Christian communities shall be ruled with sovereign right by the principle of tradition, or seem to be ruled, when the reins of government are in able hands.

So our story concludes. A religious agitation started in Palestinian Judaism by a Galilean preacher, whose aim was the Kingdom of God, and his end to be crucified as a rebel, comes to its fruit in less than two centuries as a mighty institution established throughout the Roman empire, condemned by the law, but assured of its future and equally sure of victory over the empire which persecuted it. In the whole course of this remarkable evolution nothing happened which cannot be explained by the laws that govern human life, and this may be said with confidence in spite of the obscurity resulting from the conditions under which the movement went on its way. None the less is it true that this triumph of faith, viewed in the light of religious and moral consciousness, if not a miracle, is a human marvel, in which new life was created and a work of human progress thereby accomplished. The diffusion of Judaism had prepared the ground for Christian success, but Christianity completed a victory which Judaism, though it won the first approaches, was powerless to follow up to its conclusion, and this because it had compressed an idea, broad as humanity, into the narrow form of a nationalism, in which only a few could participate. This idea Christianity held forth, under the thin covering of a religious creed, to the disinherited multitudes of the ancient world, to the multitudes without a homeland; and round it they rallied. This element of human sympathy, born in the first preaching of the Gospel and developed in primitive Christianity, this it was that carried the Catholic Church to the very forefront of history. How she has since comported herself at that eminence, in what measure she has fulfilled or not fulfilled her programme, we know. But the history of her proceedings from the end of the second century down to our time is abundantly documented. It is the pre-history of the Christian religion that we here bring to an end, a history which the cautious inquirer may reconstruct by inference, and more or less conjecturally, from testimony whose main content is, not the history, but the mystic legend of its institution.

NOTES TO INTRODUCTION

[1] *Les Livres du Nouveau Testament traduits du grec en francais avec introduction générale et notices*, 1922.

[2] A complete bibliography of the subject would fill a larger volume than this present. The list below is limited to the most important of recent works dealing with the essentials, and especially to those which the present author has used or had in view when preparing his own:

E. RENAN: *Histoire des origines du christianisme*, 1863-1881. A brilliant synthesis, needing correction to-day at many points but unequalled, at least in our literature, and never replaced.

L. DUCHESNE: *Histoire ancienne de l'Eglise*, i (1906).

B. W. BACON: *The fourth Gospel in research and debate* (1918); *The Story of the Jews and the beginnings of the Church* (1926); *Studies in Matthew* (1930).

W. BOUSSET: *Kyrios Christos* (1913, 1921).

R. BULTMANN: *Die Geschichte der synoptischen Tradition* (1921).

C. CLEMEN: *Paulus, sein Leben und Wirken* (1904); *Religionsgeschichtliche Erklärung des Neuen Testaments* (1929).

F. CUMONT: *Les religions orientales dans le paganisme romain* (1929).

M. GOGUEL: *Introduction au Nouveau Testament* (i–v, 1923 ss.); *Jésus de Nazareth* (1925); *Jean-Baptiste* (1928); *La Vie de Jésus* (1932).

C. GUIGNEBERT: *Manuel d'histoire ancienne du Christianisme* (1906); *Le Christianisme antique* (1921); *Jésus* (1933).

A. HARNACK: *Geschichte der altchristlichen Literatur* (1893, 1897, 1904); *Mission und Ausbreitung des Christentums in die drei ersten Jahrhunderten* (1906); *Beiträge zur Einleitung in das Neue Testament* (i–vi, 1906–1914).

E. HENNECKE: *Handbuch zu den neutestamentlichen Apokryphen* (1904); *Neutestamentliche Apokryphen* (1923–1924).

A. JÜLICHER: *Einleitung in das Neue Testament* (1931); *Die Gleichnisrede Jesu* (1902).

M. J. LAGRANGE: *Evangile selon saint Matthieu* (1927); *Evangile selon saint Marc* (1929); *Evangile selon saint Luc* (1921); *Evangile selon saint Jean* (1925).

H. LIETZMANN: *Handbuch zum Neuen Testament* (1926–1932); *Geschichte der alten Kirche. i. Die Anfänge* (1932).

E. LOHMEYER: *Das Urchristentum, i, 1. Johannes der Taüfer* (1932).

E. MEYER: *Ursprung und Anfänge des Christentums* (1921–1923).

E. NORDEN: *Agnostos Theos* (1913); *Die Geburt des Kindes* (1923).

R. REITZENSTEIN: *Die hellenistischen Mysterienreligionen* (1920).

A. SCHWEITZER: *Geschichte der Leben Jesu Forschung* (1913, 1926); *Geschichte der paulinischen Forschung* (1911).

B. H. STREETER: *The four Gospels* (1924); *The primitive Church* (1929).

J. WEISS: *Das Urchristentum* (1914, 1917).

J. Weiss, W. Bousset and W. Heitmuller: *Die Schriften des Neuen Testaments neu übersetzt und für die Gegenwart erklärt* (1917–1918).

J. Wellhausen: *Einleitung in die drei ersten Evangelien* (1911); *Das Evangelium Matthaei* (1914); *Das Evangelium Marci* (1909); *Das Evangelium Lucae* (1904); *Das Evangelium Johannis* (1908).

P. Wendland: *Die Urchristlichen Literaturformen* (1912).

NOTES TO CHAPTER I

1 R. Eisler's defence of the partial authenticity of supplements contained in the Sclavic version of *The Jewish War* is distinguished by great learning and subtlety. A criticism of the thesis may be found, by M. Goguel, in *Revue d'histoire et de philosophie religieuses*, March–April 1930, pp. 177–190.

2 ii, 1–16: Paul's self-defence against other missionaries, ending in a violent outburst against Jewish persecutors, in the spirit and style of Acts; iii, 2b–4, interpolation of the same character, presupposing a long experience of persecution (iii, 2a should be attached to 5: "we have sent Timothy, our brother and servant of God in the Gospel of the Christ, to know how you stand in the faith," etc.).

3 A fragment with a style all its own, making a violent breach in the moral precepts at the end of the Epistle. The apocalyptic description, which is a deliberate paraphrase of Gospel texts, stamps itself as later than the apostolic age (cf. iv, 15 and Mark ix, 1, xiii, 30; also v, 1–2 with Mark xiii, 31; Matthew xxiv, 43; Luke xii, 39).

4 The end of verse 3 seems to have been added to give the Epistle the character of instruction addressed to the universal Church. The words "and I am of Christ," in verse 12, are probably interpolated.

5 i, 17–ii, 8. "The princes of this world," in ii, 8, are not political rulers of human appointment, of whom there would be no need to inform us that they are not in God's confidence. Jesus is here called "the Lord of glory," in allusion to Psalm xxiv, 7–9. The quotation in verse 9 probably comes from some Apocrypha and must be a gloss.

6 Observe that, in vii, 10, the author appeals to the Gospel prohibition of divorce (cf. Mark x, 9), and then, in verse 12, takes it on himself to authorize the divorce of the Christian partners in a mixed marriage if the pagan partner takes the initiative. The case presented in verses 36–38, of the believing guardian of a virgin, who is given permission to marry her if he feels it necessary, does not belong to the earliest Christian age.

7 x, 12–13 looks like an editor's addition. The whole passage is a homily on the sacrament of the Supper as understood in xi, 23–26.

8 12b-14 may be another editorial addition. On the general theme cf. 1 Thessalonians ii, 1–12, Acts xx, 33–35.

9 17–18 again suspect as editorial.

10 Note that the passage forbidding women to speak in the assemblies

conflicts with what is presupposed by xi, 3–16. But xiv, 33b–35 is evidently interpolated.

11 Interpolation is betrayed not only by the higher quality of the author's aim but by the forced connexions xii, 31 and xiv, 9, which are doublets. Moreover, xiii, 13, which contradicts what has gone before, seems to have been added to the song.

12 The priority of ix is evident from the fact that, in it, the collections have not yet been made either in Macedonia or in Corinth, whereas in viii the Macedonian collection is ready and Paul has finished organizing the collection at Corinth. See Delafosse iii, 15–16.

13 The insulting invectives against the Galilean apostles (cf. 1 Corinthians 1, 2, 6, 13) are counterblasts to those which Revelation i–iii launches against Paul and his followers.

14 For the help which came from Macedonia, cf. Philippians iv, 15, 16 and Acts xviii, 2, 3 (where it appears that the money brought from Macedonia enabled Paul to give himself entirely to his preaching).

15 xi, 12b–xii, 4. If this apology is not from Paul himself, it is founded on more complete and precise information than canonical Acts. But the date assigned to the great vision in xii, 2 makes a difficulty. Paul's capital vision must have been that which converted him, which cannot have taken place about the year 40. (Can there be some influence here from Galatians ii, 1?)

16 These are dealt with by Acts xiii, 14–xiv, 23; xvi, 1–5

17 Marcion's version lacked i, 18–20, the personal visit to Peter; also the "again" in ii, 1. But this passage, which fits so ill with the context, may well be an addition.

18 v, 13–26; vi, 7–10, 12–16. It seems as though v, 1–12 should be attached to iv, 21–31, and that vi, 1–6 may be an addition; vi, 11 might rejoin the conclusion, 17–18.

19 Many critics doubt whether the salutations of xvi, 3–16 (if not also xvi, 1–2, 21–22) originally belonged to Romans, and are inclined to think them addressed to the community at Ephesus. The final doxology, xvi, 25–27, is recognized as a Marcionite addition, although the entire chapters xv–xvi were at first wanting in Marcion's *Apostolicon*.

20 To the same gnosis belongs iii, 21–26, to which iv, 15, 25 are co-ordinated. In the exposition of the gnosis vii, 7–25 seems of secondary origin.

21 i, 18–iii, 20, where the indictment of the pagans, which has a rhetoric of its own, seems to have been borrowed from a Jewish source. In ii, 14, 15 we may suspect a gloss.

22 The fragment which follows xv, 7 seems lost in this place. In the moral part, the verses in respect for established authority (xiii, 1–7) are by a later hand; 8–12 depend on the Gospel tradition. The warning against heretics, xvi, 17–20, belongs to a time when gnostic editors were at work.

23 The essential formula is Colossians i, 15–19, which should be compared with Philippians ii, 6–10.

24 Ephesus would be thought by the editors to have a better claim than Laodicea to an apostolic letter.

25 Note the quotation of the baptismal hymn in v, 14. On the other hand, it results from ii, 20; iii, 5; iv, 11 that inspired prophets still stand with apostles in the first rank.

26 ii, 6–11 is a short poem of Christian gnosis inserted by means of an artificial transition (verse 5).

27 The rules of discipline in 1 Timothy ii–iii, 13 break into the warning against false teachers, thereafter resumed, while ii, 11–15a, forbidding women to teach (parallel to 1 Corinthians xiv, 34–35), is an evident surcharge in the rules about woman's dress, etc.

28 Cf. especially 1 Clement, 36, 2; Hebrews i, 3–4.

29 In ii, 3–4 the author expresses himself in much the same terms as the author of Luke i, 1–2. Similarly in xiii, 7, where the founders of the community to which the Epistle is addressed are represented as belonging to a time long passed. Assuming that the community addressed was the Roman, the founders referred to would be Peter and Paul, here associated as we find them in Clement's Epistle.

30 We get a glimpse of Gospel tradition only in ii, 3–4; v, 7–10 is commonly regarded as a reference to the scene in Gethsemane; it refers in reality to Psalm xxii, on which the synoptic account was constructed.

31 2 Peter i. The announcement by Jesus of Peter's death (13–14), and the appeal to a great revelation on "the holy mountain," in which the apotheosis of the Christ is completed (16–19), refer to the Apocalypse of Peter, not to John xx, 18–19, nor to the Gospel stories of the transfiguration.

32 In v, 12 the author forbids oath-taking in the terms of Matthew v, 34 but without giving any sign that he is quoting a Gospel precept.

33 1 John v, 6–8 appears to be an interpolation to connect with John xix, 34–35 (water and blood, after the lance-thrust), a passage equally secondary in the fourth Gospel.

34 Note that the author proves by Psalm cx, 1 that Jesus was not the son of David (cf. Mark xiii, 35–37).

35 1 Clement, 5. The two apostles appear as legendary heroes, Peter taking precedence of Paul, as in canonical Acts.

36 The year 155, assigned by many as the date of Polycarp's martyrdom, ill accords with what we know of his coming to Rome in the time of Anicetus. It is more probable that Polycarp died under Marcus Aurelius, in 166, as Eusebius indicates. Thus the letter to the Philippians could have been written between 150 and 160.

37 Note that while Christian apocalyptic had a fixed centre in the name of Jesus, Jewish apocalyptic was always rambling loosely round the topic of the Messiah, which was not definitely crystallized round an historical name.

38 The author of the Ascension proper seems to say (ix, 14) that "the god of this world" and his auxiliaries will crucify the Son of God without recognizing him; but in that he is not dependent on 1 Corinthians ii, 8.

He also seems to say that the Christ remained on the earth for eighteen months after his resurrection, an opinion held by some of the gnostics.

39 A translation of the Greek fragment and of the Ethiopian version will be found in Henneke, *Neutestamentliche Apokryphen*, 1923, pp. 314–327.

40 The Akhmim fragment has a different order. It gives the first place to the felicity of the elect, two unnamed persons among the redeemed taking the place of Moses and Elijah as types of the promised glory.

41 An obscure passage in the Ethiopian version but better preserved in the Greek fragment (cf. James in *The Journal of Theological Studies*, April 1931, pp. 270–279).

42 This can only be the Mount of Olives. Note the same designation, "holy mountain," in 2 Peter i, 18.

43 Cf. Bacon, *Studies in Matthew*, 146.

44 The Church which Hermas sees in vision is already *old*. He took her at first to be the Sibyl (*Vision*, ii, 4); and the real Church as he knew it on earth has an experience of persecution acquired after the reign of Trajan.

45 Virtues, vices, even impressions, are freely personified by Hermas. These personifications are not, with him, simple metaphors; they belong to the old Roman animism which put a god into every phenomenon. Thus he sees the Church in the form of a respectable matron. It would be difficult to understand why his shepherd, angel of penitence, should come from Arcadia, were it not that the image has been borrowed from a non-Christian type which we encounter again in the Hermetic Poimandres, in comparison with whom the Johannine Christ is acclaimed the true shepherd.

46 I *Apology*, 66. The formula "Memoirs of the apostles" which is customary with Justin has no traditional warrant; he uses it to give distinction to this literature which he somewhat boldly assimilates to Xenophon's Memoirs about Socrates. It is not clear that Justin had the idea of a fixed canon; he appears to have made use in ordinary of the three Synoptics; also of John and perhaps of the Gospel of Peter.

47 *Heresies*, iii, 1. Note that Tatian's *Diatessaron*, about 170, is founded on the canonical Gospels and that Theophilus of Antioch, about 190, constructed a harmony of the four Gospels. The canon of four had become law at Alexandria in the time of Clement, about 200.

48 The priority of Mark results from the fact that it is to be considered as a source for Matthew and Luke. Beyond that it is impossible to assign precise dates to the stages of its revision.

49 This conclusion is wanting in the oldest manuscripts, though it is of earlier date than they. The author of it knew the three other Gospels and Acts. It has been conjectured that it replaced another conclusion either lost or suppressed. The only fact of which we can be certain is that it was intended to fill an obvious gap and bring Mark into line with the other Gospels.

50 The Meal of the Anointing (xiv, 3–9) breaks up the prelude to the arrest and betrayal and, by anticipation, doubles the last meal, where everything which concerns the Passover and the preparations for it is an interpolation in the story of an ordinary meal which took place on 13 Nisan;

of this story (where verse 24 is obviously adventitious), xiv, 23, 25 is the débris. (See my *Les Livres du N. Testament*, 273–274.)

51 Mark vi, 7–18 (Matthew x), mission of the Twelve; xii, 38–40, against the Pharisees (cf. Matthew xxiii), probably conceived in the source as the conclusion of the Jerusalem ministry.

52 Cf. B. W. Bacon, *Is Mark a Roman Gospel?* 1919, and the criticism of this book in *Revue d'histoire et littérature religieuses*, 1920, p. 627, where we read "it was perhaps for want of something better that the Roman community first accepted this Gospel text."

53 Eusebius, *History*, iv, 14, 1; v, 24, 16.

54 The collection of Logia, or discourses, was made to meet the practical needs of Christian catechesis, and there is no reason whatever to suppose that its original author was a disciple of Jesus. That hypothesis appears self-evident only to those who hold that the reason for making the collection was the desire to get a fixed and authentic version of the teaching of the Christ. But the real reason was the need to provide the catechists with an adequate repertoire of matter for their teaching.

55 The two prefaces are closely co-ordinate. On the mutilation of the preface to Acts in the editorial elaboration of that book, see my *Les Actes des Apôtres*, 133–140.

56 Duplicate of the mission of the Twelve, symbolic of the evangelization of Israel, and intended to signify the evangelization of the pagans already announced in iv, 16–30.

57 Theme resumed in Acts i, 9–11. Its connexion with the Apocalypse of Peter has been noted above, p. 37. The rôle attributed to Herod in the passion of the Christ (xxiii, 6–12) brings the third Gospel rather near to the Gospel of Peter.

58 The author effects his purpose by bringing together all the apparitions of the Risen One in a unitary perspective. There is reason to believe that the characteristic words of the mystical supper were absent in the original Luke and that the last meal was not there presented as the Passover meal. In this, its original form, the Gospel would therefore be earlier than the introduction of the Sunday Easter in the circle for which it was written, and if this circle was Roman it follows that the Gospel would be that of some Roman group which ignored or was unacquainted with the gnosis of the Epistles attributed to Paul, the harmonization of Mark and Luke having coincided with the unification of the various Roman groups.

59 In the stories of the resurrection: Luke xxiv, 12 (perhaps authentic), 24, cf. John xx, 3–10; 36–40, cf. John xx, 19–21, 27. It is probable that in Acts xii, 1–2 the original document mentioned the death of John along with that of James, conformably to Mark x, 39 and to the testimony of Papias, and that the revision of the document which brings John to the front in the first chapter suppressed the mention of his execution in deference to the Ephesian legend.

60 The hypothesis of an Aramaic original has been weightily maintained in recent times.

⁶¹ In the perspective of the first three Gospels the Galilean ministry of Jesus seems to last a few months and the Jerusalem ministry a few days; in John, the life of Jesus is crowned by a ministry of three whole years, he being regarded as forty-six when he began to teach—a symbolic trait (ii, 20). Such figures have mystical significance; but in all four Gospels chronology is only a framework for the distribution of evangelical matter.

⁶² So far as we can speak of last editions prior to canonization, when the last retouchings of all four Gospels may well have been made at the same time.

⁶³ Schmidke, *Neue Fragmente und Untersuchungen zu juden-christlicen Evangelien*, 1911, boldly contests Jerome's assertion, and even refuses him all knowledge of the Gospel in question. See on this subject Waitz in Henneke 10–32 and E. Meyer i, 261; these authors doubt only that Jerome made the double translation into Greek and Latin of which he boasts (*De viris*, 2).

⁶⁴ Waitz, 55, would attribute this citation to the Gospel of the Hebrews.

⁶⁵ Not having the context, it is impossible to say exactly what was the Easter observance of the Nazareans, except that their fast covered the whole time of the passion from the last meal to the resurrection.

⁶⁶ Waitz, 44 ff., is inclined to place it between 100 and 130, between the Synoptics and John.

⁶⁷ Collected and translated in Preuschen, *Antilegomena*, 2–3, 135–136.

⁶⁸ Salome comes on the scene and puts a question to Jesus about the end; Jesus insists on the disappearance from the perfect state of everything related to sex. Pretence of mystery on the subject.

⁶⁹ It is not certain nor even probable that it depends on the fourth Gospel in its canonical form; its spirit and composition belong rather to the pre-canonical time.

⁷⁰ Eusebius, vi, 12. Note that the bishop, without examining the book, permitted the reading of it in the community where he found it in use. On his attention being drawn afterwards to the Docetism of certain passages, he rejected it on that ground.

⁷¹ According to Clement of Alexandria, *Stromata*, vii, 17, 106. Irenaeus (*Heresies*, iii, 11, 9) says the Gospel of Truth had nothing in common with the canonical Gospels. But had he read it?

⁷² To these tendencies are attributed the suppression of all that concerns the earthly birth of the Christ, the non-paschal character of the last supper, etc. See Henneke, 74.

⁷³ It is evident that the earthly epiphany of the Christ was for a long time limited to the period between his baptism and resurrection—as in Mark, John, the Gospel of the Ebionites, Basilides, etc. The idea of miraculous conception, by itself, is mythological and does not otherwise imply encratism. It is possible that the exaltation of Mary and the infant Jesus began in gnosis. On the *Genna Marias*, mentioned by Epiphanius, 26, 2, see Henneke, 82, 83, 109.

⁷⁴ The brothers and sisters of Jesus are represented in this book as the

children of an earlier marriage of Joseph who has become quite an old man when he married Mary. Jerome transformed the brothers and sisters of Jesus into his cousins. Western tradition has followed Jerome.

75 The whole work of the Christian imagination in accounting for the origin of the religion is well summed up in the following quotation borrowed by Eusebius, ii, 1, 4, from the *Hypotyposes*, Book 7, of Clement of Alexandria: "The Lord, after his resurrection, transmitted the gnosis to James the Just, to John and to Peter; these passed it on to the other apostles; the other apostles to the seventy disciples, of whom was Barnabas"—a fragment of Jewish-Christian gnosis. The canonical books (Gospels and Acts) are concerned, on the other hand, to transform the teachings of Jesus from post-resurrection utterances into discourses pronounced by him during his mortal life. But the gnostic tradition may well be, in all respects, the older.

76 Observe that canonical Acts have collected a legend of Peter and a legend of Paul already considerably developed. The final edition of the book combines the two legends with facts having a surer basis, the whole forming an anti-gnostic synthesis—which brings us back to the preceding note. Henneke has good ground for saying (p. 140) that the question of spurious literature in primitive Christianity is still in need of investigation as a whole and fundamentally.

77 These Clementine apocrypha are, perhaps, too neglected at the present time, though the school of Bauer made much of them in the middle of the last century. We have to distinguish the *Kerygmata*, which belong to Jewish-Christian gnosis from the *Praxeis*, a work of anti-gnostic Christianity recounting the combats between Peter and Simon Magus from Caesarea to Antioch. On the highly complicated history of these Clementine romances, see Henneke, 212–215, and O. Culmann, *Le problème litteraire et historique du roman pseudo-clémentin*, 1930.

NOTES TO CHAPTER II

1 *Annals*, xv, 44: "Auctor hujus nominis Christus, Tiberio imperitante, per procuratorem Pontium Pilatum supplicio affectus erat. Repressaque in praesens, exitialis superstitio sursus erumpebat, non modo per Judaeam, originem ejus mali, sed per Urbem etiam, quo cuncta undique atrocia aut turpia confluunt celebranturque."

2 *Epistolae*, 96, 7. Christians under judicial interrogation told Pliny "quod essent soliti stato die ante lucem convenire carmenque Christo quasi deo dicere secum invicem." The *Carmen* is an alternating chant, hymn or liturgy. Pliny understands that the executed man, spoken of by Tacitus, is regarded as a god by his followers.

3 *Antiquities*, xviii, 21: Τὰ μὲν λοιπὰ πάντα γνώμῃ τῶν Φαρισαίων ὁμολογοῦσα, δυσκίνητος δὲ τοῦ ἐλευθέρου ἔρως ἐστὶν αὐτοῖς μόνον ἡγεμόνα καὶ δεσπότην τὸν θεὸν ὑπειληφόσιν.

4 From this we can see the meaning and importance of the question

about paying tribute to Caesar in the synoptic Gospels (Mark xii, 13–17 and parallels). The story was invented to prevent Christianity being confused with the Judaism of the extremists. It is by no means certain that Jesus and his first followers would have shown so much consideration for Caesar's authority. Observe that Mark puts the question into the mouths of Pharisees and Herodians, for whom the question was important.

5 The mistakes and exactions of the last procurators contributed to inflaming the religious passions of the Jews. As soon as revolution started in Jerusalem the friends of the Romans had to flee and, as the empire was then badly governed, rebellion was well organized before Vespasian was charged to suppress it.

6 Herod was not less hated than the Romans, but more skilful in exacting obedience. It was the Jews themselves and the Samaritans who demanded and obtained the deposition of Archelaus in the year 6 of our era. But the mass of the people never settled down under Roman rule to which the upper class had accommodated itself. The fire smouldered till the explosion of the year 66.

7 The date given in Luke iii, 1, if we take it as referring to the preaching of John the Baptist, is too late, although his activity as a preacher cannot have been of long duration; Simon Magus, whose date cannot be exactly given, was a contemporary of the apostolic age; Elchasai, founder of a baptist and judaizing sect in Transjordania, appeared about 100.

8 With the difference, that Simon, in the legend, was regarded as having been a disciple of John; which is not so with Elchasai. In spite of what we read in Acts viii, 9–24, it is unlikely that Simon ever found his way into Christianity, but he may have had some connexion with John or with his sect.

9 It reveals an effort to subordinate John to Jesus, by making John himself avow his subordination, or by drawing distinctions between the baptism of John and Christian baptism, but without success in disguising that the latter was borrowed from the former.

10 *Antiquities*, xviii, 9, 2. The notice finds credit because it seems to be independent of the Gospel tradition. But it may not be really independent.

11 Matthew xi, 11. But the end of verse 3: "Notwithstanding, he that is least in the kingdom of heaven is greater than he," is a Christian addition intended to make the preceding statement inoffensive. It seems, however, that to give a better balance both to the text and the thought we ought, with many church fathers and some moderns, to take this saying in a strictly comparative sense: "he that is smaller than John"—in the order of time, junior by age and manifestation, that is to say, Jesus—"is, in the kingdom of heaven, greater than he." This interpretation saves the pre-eminence of Jesus, and his importance in regard to the kingdom, without excluding John from the number of the elect. The messianic programme announced in Matthew xi, 2–6, might very well be applied, in its principal elements, by John's sectaries to John and by Christians to Jesus.

12 Mark i, 7–8 and parallels. As nobody can be either bathed or washed

in holy Spirit, it is obvious that baptism in spirit reposes on baptism in water, and the former has never existed apart from the latter.

13 Mark i, 5 speaks of the desert, the region round the Dead Sea, as the scene of the preaching and of the Jordan as the scene of the baptizing, followed by Matthew iii, 1, 5. Luke all the region round about the Jordan as the scene of the preaching. The indications of place in John i, 28 and iii, 23, though more precise, are far from being more trustworthy.

14 This baptism in running water was distinct from the legal ablutions. Holscher supposes it derived from the regions bordering on the Euphrates (Babylon) and from Mesopotamia. Renan thought the same. (*Vie de Jésus*, 103; *Les Disciples*, 462–465.)

15 Acts xviii, 24–28; xix, 1–6. From these notices we may conclude that Christian baptism was not originally understood as a baptism of spirit, as the editor of Acts would make out.

16 Matthew ii, 1, connected with Micah v, 1; 13–15, where Hosea xi, 1, which refers to Israel, is made into a prediction of the flight into Egypt; 16–18, massacre of the children, linked to Jeremiah xxxi, 15, which concerns the Captivity; 19–23, return to Judea and settlement at Nazareth linked to the prophecy "he shall be called a Nazorean," of which it is very difficult to find the origin, unless we may suppose the evangelist to be applying to the Christ, by a play of words, the saying about Samson in Judges xiii, 5, "he shall be a *nazir*"; iv, 12–16, Jesus at Capernaum, presented as fulfilment of Isaiah viii, 23–ix, 1, which refers to the Assyrian deportations.

17 The legend preserved in Luke, while contradicting that in Matthew, is better arranged, but not more consistent.

18 In Matthew (i, 1–17) Jesus descends from David through Solomon; in Luke (iii, 23–38), through Nathan. But both come to a common termination in Joseph, who was held to be the father of Jesus by the Jewish-Christian circles in which the genealogies were invented.

19 Ancient tradition was not unanimous on this point, as we may see from the anecdotes in Mark xii, 35–37 (and parallels) and from the so-called Epistle of Barnabas.

20 Cf. Holscher, 230, n. 10; 239, n. 5. Ed. Meyer ii, 423, n. 2, maintains the connexion of the name with Nazareth. On the other hand, the existence of Nazareth at the time of Jesus has been denied, but wrongly. Nazareth was then in existence and only because it existed could it be used for a forced explanation of the title Nazorean when the effort was made to efface the original connexion of Jesus and his sect with the baptist sect of which they were really the issue. There is no etymological relation between Nazareth and the Nazareans or Nazoreans, whose semitic names are written with a *tsadé*, and the nazirs, which is written with a *ʒain*. The nazirs are "men under vow" (devoted). Nazorean probably means "observer."

21 Matthew xi, 2–17 (Luke vii, 18–20, 22–25). On any interpretation the *mise en scène* and the statements attributed to the Christ reflect a polemic, courteous enough, between the sectaries of Jesus and the sectaries of John after the death of their respective leaders.

²² It was in this character that the story (Mark i, 9–11 and parallels) occupied the first place in Gospel catechizing. The story was not conceived to show that Jesus had belonged to John's sect, but to disguise it. The intention was to show forth the messianic initiation of Jesus.

²³ The dove in the story is a mythological element somewhat time-worn. Nevertheless it is not without significance that the bird of Astarte becomes the emblem of the Spirit who, in the Gospel of the Hebrews, is expressly said to be the mother of the Christ.

²⁴ This word ($\delta\upsilon\nu\dot\alpha\mu\varepsilon\iota\varsigma$) is found in the saying attributed to Herod Antipas about the miracles attributed to Jesus.

²⁵ For an analysis of the miracle stories in the synoptic tradition see Bultmann, 129–150.

²⁶ They are so represented in the Acts of the Apostles and in the Epistles, especially in those to the Corinthians. Observe also what is said in Mark xvi, 17–18.

²⁷ The journey chiefly in question is that mentioned in Mark vii, 24, 31, the itinerary of which is extremely vague. Critics since Wellhausen who suppose it to have an historical basis, by connecting Luke xiii, 31–32 with Mark 14–16, have drawn the conclusion that Jesus quitted Galilee because of the Tetrarch's threatening attitude. But, in Mark, the journey to Tyre is contrived to bring in the story of the Canaanite woman, and the return through Decapolis to provide a frame for the miracles of the deaf-mute and the second multiplication of loaves, all of them stories whose symbolic meaning will hardly be contested. On the other hand, the anecdote in Luke, which floats in air without attachment, is equally without historical consistency. It may well be that the hostility of the Tetrarch had a part in determining Jesus to make for Jerusalem; but there is nothing to prove that this motive induced Jesus to take so long a journey beyond the confines of Galilee.

²⁸ Matthew iv, 25; Luke vi, 17. The *mise en scène* which in Mark iii, 7–12 is the frame for a mass of miracles is no less artificial than the arrangement of the discourse which follows them.

²⁹ For analysis of the teaching attributed to Jesus in the synoptics see especially Bultmann, 4–129.

³⁰ In the *Encyclopedia Biblica*, ii, art. "Gospels." Goguel, *La Vie du Jésus*, is more recent.

³¹ Mark xv, 34; Matthew xxvii, 46. The saying is taken from Psalm xxii, 2. For this cry of despair Luke substitutes words of confidence borrowed from Psalm xxxi, 5, "into thy hand I commit my spirit." John substitutes "it is finished" (xix, 30).

³² Mark ii, 27. The sentence is not reproduced in the parallels perhaps because its character is rather philosophic than religious.

³³ The mention of "the brothers of the Lord" in 1 Corinthians ix, 5 and in Galatians i, 19 (James) confirms the indication in Mark vi, 3 (Matthew xiii, 55, 56) concerning the brothers, enumerated by name, and the sisters of Jesus, although the scene of the preaching at Nazareth may be constructed

to make way for the aphorism "no prophet has honour in his own country.'
Cf. Bultmann, 15, 29. Taken by itself the mention of the mother and
brothers of Jesus in Acts i, 14 would be open to suspicion.

34 Mark i, 15; Matthew iv, 17. This feature is omitted in the parallel
passage, Luke iv, 14–15; not, perhaps, without intention.

35 Granting that the reign of the Spirit began in the Christian community
after the resurrection of Jesus, Christian baptism properly so-called cannot
have been conferred before (cf. John xx, 22–23; Acts ii, 1–4, 37–38). But
that idea is forced. In John iii, 22–26 it is stated that Jesus baptized; then,
iv, 2, that he did not baptize, but that his disciples took his place in that
office; finally, vii, 39, that "as yet there was no Spirit." These statements
are contradictory, the result of theological embarrassment, the last two
apparently glosses. Weak as is the historical authority of the fourth Gospel,
it is clear that the chief author of it found nothing inconvenient in the idea
that preaching and baptism went together both with Jesus and with John.

36 *Vie de Jésus*, 312–319. Renan forces the point both in the historicity
he attributes to the texts and in the highly poetic commentary he passes
on them. But the fundamental idea may be retained. Observe that, in regard
to baptism, takes John iii, 22–23 and iv, 1 as literal history, while seeing in
iv, 2 a gloss or a scruple of the editor.

37 It should never be forgotten that an ordinary meal, especially certain
meals of primitive and ancient peoples, had a religious character. It was so
among the Jews and in particular among the Essenes.

38 Daniel vii, 13; Parables of Enoch. In the Pauline gnosis the Heavenly
Man, by contrast to the first Adam, is identical with the Son of Man of the
Gospel tradition. But this transcendental idea of the Messiah is not of
Jewish origin. The anointed of Jahveh was at first and remained, in
essentials, a man.

39 Granting the pagan origin of the notion and the influence of Chaldeo-
Iranian tradition on Jewish eschatology and apocalyptic, there is not much
room for hypothesis. The thesis of a Chaldeo-Iranian origin has been
developed by Reitzenstein. Holscher (192, n. 2) adopts it in the main; but
the history of the myth and of its evolution is still obscure. There seems
no reason to think that the myth had any influence on the preaching of
Jesus, but it is far otherwise with the apostolic tradition.

40 Reitzenstein, *Das iranische Erlösungs mysterium*, 130, maintains that
Jesus accepted and used "the Man" in an eschatological sense and with
a feeling of his own for union with God which can hardly have been
borrowed. Obscure theology, to which Holscher, *sup. cit.*, does not adhere.
This transcendent and mythical notion of "the Man" is much more easily
attributed to Jesus conceived as risen from the dead than to Jesus himself
in his lifetime. The latter hypothesis would make the primitive Gospel of
Jesus much more gnostic than it really was.

41 Josephus, *Antiquities*, xx, 5, 1; 8, 6; *War*, ii, 13, 5.

42 Implied by the editor of Acts, v, 35–39, in the words he puts into the
mouth of Gamaliel.

43 Mark xi, 11 and xiii, 1–2 has sometimes been cited to prove that Jesus and his disciples had never previously seen Jerusalem. This is transforming the little arts of the Gospel editors into facts of history.

44 Each of the two hypotheses has supporters. They are not incompatible and each can be supported by texts. But the texts are not as consistent as they would need to be to furnish support. That the preaching of Jesus had staggering success is not probable, nor that it lasted long before alarming the Tetrarch.

45 The previsions attributed to him are conceived systematically in respect to the facts foreseen, as well as to the prophecies regarded as fulfilled by his passion. Thus the agony in Gethsemane, which the fourth Gospel is at pains to suppress, localizes a scene, deduced from Psalm xxii, but originally without specification of time and place, as we find it in Hebrews v, 7–10, where it is taken directly from the Psalm and is not, as many suppose, an echo of the Gospel story.

46 Zechariah ix, 9; Genesis xlix, 11; Psalm cxviii, 25–26. If we admit the historicity of this triumphal entry into the city it would necessarily follow that Jesus deliberately set himself to fulfil the prophecy of Zechariah ix, 9. Did he, then, intend to inaugurate the Great Event on the Mount of Olives? In that case he falls into line with "the Egyptian" who according to Josephus had the same intention. But the kind of evidence on which the tradition reposes (fulfilment of supposed prophecies) gives not the slightest support to the historicity of the facts narrated.

47 The expulsion of the traders fulfils Zechariah xiv, 20; Malachi iii, 1. If Jesus and his followers had violently taken possession of the temple court, the incident would not have terminated in an academic debate as to the authority under which Jesus claimed to act; the Roman garrison would have arrested him on the spot. Compare the case of Paul in Acts xxi, 27–34.

48 The incidents recorded of the Jerusalem ministry—academic discussion on the authority of Jesus and of John, on tribute to Caesar, on the resurrection, on the David's sonship of the Messiah, and the rating of the Pharisees—were conceived independently of each other, and then linked together by artificial transitions for the purpose of filling the Jerusalem ministry with sufficient contents.

49 The opinion recently defended by R. Eisler (*Jesus Basileus*, 1930) with great erudition but feeble proofs. The additions to Josephus' *Jewish War* in the Sclavonic version, on which Eisler chiefly relies, are probably interpolations and, even if authentic, do not contain all he would draw out of them.

50 The legend of Judas is out of harmony with the legend of the Twelve to which the attempt has been made to weld it. In reality Jesus did not choose the Twelve. They were the committee to which the first community of believers entrusted the management of their affairs after the death of Jesus. Their appointment has been antedated to the time of his ministry. On the other hand, the treachery of Judas has no sense unless we suppose him to have been one of the chief disciples. In the apostolic list Judas, the

traitor, occupying the last place, is a pendant to Peter, the renegade, occupying the first place. The legend of his death in Matthew xxvii, 3–10 and Acts i, 16–20 is wholly fictitious, and the legend of his treason, founded on some texts of the Old Testament, may have no more reality than the story of Peter's denial. Cf. Bultmann, 159, 167, 171.

51 Mark xiv, 27 (Matthew xxvi, 31), where the flight of the disciples is represented as announced in Zechariah xiii, 7. John xvi, 32 is in line with Mark, but without the reference to prophecy. In Luke there is no flight of the disciples from Jerusalem; they remain there and Jesus accordingly is made only to predict the failure of their faith (xxii, 32).

52 The dramatization of the incident goes *crescendo* in Mark, Matthew, John.

53 Mark xiv, 17–21; Matthew xxvi, 21–25; Luke xxii, 31–34; John xiii, 36–38. Bultmann, 162, thinks that the sources of Luke xxii, 31–32 knew nothing of the denial ($\epsilon\pi\iota\sigma\tau\rho\dot{\epsilon}\psi\alpha\varsigma$ being an editorial insertion; but it may be understood in the active = "bringing back"). The fact is that the whole story of the denial has the look of a later addition.

54 Mark xiv, 22–24; Matthew xxvi, 26–28; Luke xxii, 19–20. In Luke the end of verse 19, after $\tau\dot{o}\ \dot{v}\pi\grave{\epsilon}\rho\ \dot{v}\mu\tilde{\omega}\nu\ \delta\iota\delta\dot{o}\mu\epsilon\nu o\nu$, and verse 20 seem to be late additions, coming from 1 Corinthians xi, 24–25 (completed by Mark xiv, 24). The reviser of Luke and Acts knew the Eucharist as a breaking of bread and it seems that in the revision of Luke he had in mind at first its eschatological meaning (the banquets of the elect in the coming Kingdom), the author of the sources being ignorant of the mystic meaning contained in 1 Corinthians. His ignorance is not surprising if the mystic meaning did not originate with Paul.

55 The elements of this older version are embedded in Mark xiv, 23, 25. The words, "Take, this is my body," seem to have been inserted in place of the original, "Verily I say unto you I will eat no more bread," etc., a formula parallel to, "I will drink no more wine," etc., in verse 25 and in Luke xxii, 15–18. In the latter mention of the Passover has been substituted for "bread," so as to make the Last Supper into a pascal feast.

56 The scene in Gethsemane has been compressed and transported in a very curious way in John xii, 27–33, when the agony appears to dissolve into an echo of the transfiguration.

57 Dramatization is obvious in the story as given in each of the Synoptics. The object is to present the Christ as master of his destiny. See *Revue d'histoire et de littérature religieuses*, 1922, p. 445.

58 This trial, in Mark and Matthew, is composed of three elements easily distinguishable: (1) the saying about the temple which Jesus boasts he could destroy and rebuild in three days, and the testimony in relation to it—a saying which embarrassed the tradition, and which, if Jesus really pronounced it, would have been brought up in evidence before Pilate as proof of messianic pretentions; the authentic version of the saying would be in Matthew xxvi, 61, in preference to Mark xiv, 58 and John ii, 19, which expressly give it an allegorical meaning; (2) the messianic declaration made

by Jesus as Son of God, a correction in advance of the condemnation of Jesus as King of the Jews and intended to account for this condemnation by the blindness of the Jewish authorities in presence of the mystic Christ, the divine Saviour; (3) finally, the scene of the outrages inflicted on the Christ (Mark xiv, 65; Matthew xxvi, 67–68), which is a fulfilment of prophecies, especially of Isaiah i, 5 and liii, 3. The last two elements are fictitious; as to the first, there is fiction at least in the setting.

59 The morning session of the Sanhedrim (Mark and Matthew), in which Luke (xx, 66 and xxiii), who omits the night session, has lodged the trial, is a duplicate of the condemnation. In the source document this was probably the meeting at which the accusers draw up the charge to be brought before Pilate. Matthew tacks on to it the legend of the repentant Judas. In all four Gospels the story of the trial by Pilate is cut in two by the incident of Barabbas, invented less for the purpose of dramatization than to transfer, from Pilate to the Jews, the responsibility for the condemnation, which is now fixed on the Jews by the most artificial of devices. In this way Pilate is made the judge in a comic opera in which the trial loses its legal form. The intervention of Pilate's wife, in Matthew, is another attempt to white-wash the procurator. Pilate is represented as unable, in law, to refuse ratification of a sentence pronounced by the Sanhedrim according to rule. Thus arranged, the editor's version of the story defies both logic and probability.

60 Annas (Hanan) had been deposed since the year 15.

61 Jesus being regarded as a political agitator, his case would be dealt with by the Roman authority and not left to be tried by the Sanhedrim.

62 It seems certain, however, that the Sanhedrim had then the right to carry out a sentence of death pronounced in a case which came within its sphere of jurisdiction.

63 Every conceivable subtlety has been employed to reconcile the time-table of the Synoptics with that of John. They cannot be reconciled. If "traditional" be taken as meaning "historical" neither of the conflicting dates is more traditional than the other. But the synoptic date is secondary to the Johannine, the chain of stories which make up the ritual drama of the passion having been originally invented to fit what may be called the Johannine hypothesis of the Christ as the pascal lamb. While it is probable that Jesus came to Jerusalem for the Passover and was crucified on one of the days of the week before the feast, it is not impossible that he came at another time of the year, and that the coincidence of the passion with the Passover was founded solely on mystical reasons, the meaning of the feast being promptly Christianized by the hellenist Christians.

64 It would be that of the first generation if it be true that the idea of the Christ as Son of Man and Son of God was accepted at once by the earliest community. So thinks Bousset (*Kyrios Christos*, 20) supporting his view, in the first place, on 1 Corinthians xv, taken as testimony of Paul. There is no reason, however, for holding that belief in Jesus, as transfigured into the Christ by his resurrection, was at once expanded into the idea of the Man-Christ pre-existent to his appearance on earth.

65 The cohort which accompanies Judas is a happy thought for enhancing the scene of the arrest. Had Jesus been arrested by a cohort of Roman soldiers the affair would have taken a very different turn.

66 This story betrays a respect for Roman authority which can hardly have existed in the ranks of Christian believers before Hellenist Christianity had become widely spread.

67 According to the dates commonly accepted for the canonical Gospels, the Gospel of Peter would have to be in dependence upon Luke. The relation of the two Gospels is probably more complex. The Herod incident in Luke has not the air of an improvised fiction, but seems rather to be the compressed version of a story parallel to that of the trial before Pilate, which had a place in the original framework of the Gospel.

68 These facts form the background, but less as memories than as themes to exploit, explain and interpret in the ritual, that is, in the mystical poem of the passion.

69 Jerome, Ep. lviii (*Latin Patrology*, xxii, col. 581): "Ab Hadriani temporibus usque ad imperium Constantini . . . in loco Resurrectionis simulacrum Jovis; in crucis rupe, statua ex marmore Veneris a gentibus posita colebatur. . . . Bethleem nunc nostram, et augustissimum orbis locum . . . lucus obumbrabat Thamuz, id est Adonidis, et in specu, ubi quondam Christus parvulus vagiit, Veneris amasius plangebatur." Places consecrated to pagan cults in Jerusalem may well have been requisitioned for consecration to the risen Christ just as the grotto at Bethlehem, consecrated to Adonis, was requisitioned for his birth.

70 John xix, 17 says that Jesus carried his cross; this to indicate the Christ's independence of mortal aid and his willing acceptance of death.

71 The aromatic wine is in Mark xv, 23; it may well have been the first form under which the fulfilment of Psalm lxix, 22 was indicated. It is from this Psalm that Matthew takes the gall, which he substitutes for the myrrh of Mark. The offering of vinegar, doubling in Mark and Matthew that of the wine mixed with spices, comes in all four Gospels as the last incident before the death of the Christ. The adventitious character of the incident is most perceptible in Mark (xv, 37), where we read that Jesus, having emitted a loud cry, breathed his last. This cry, which is inarticulate, was that mentioned in the original document; the previous citation of Psalm xxii, with all that follows from it, is a second version of the original, added by the evangelist.

72 Variations in the synoptics on the theme furnished by Psalm xxii, 7–9. Luke makes one of the robbers insult Jesus and converts the other, the incident of the good robber being substituted for all in Mark and Matthew that relates to the quotation from Psalm xxii, 2.

73 Fulfilment of Psalm xxii, 19, which John xix, 23–24 cites expressly, taking pains to distinguish, in spite of the text he is quoting, between the friendly division of the garments and the casting of lots for the robe. See my *Le quatrième Evangile*, 486.

74 We have seen above the meaning, in Mark and Matthew, of the

citation of Psalm xxii, 2 and the substitution for it by Luke and John. The latter (xix, 25–27) places the mystic testament of the Christ—the sayings or Jesus to his mother and to the beloved disciple—before the last words.

75 John suppresses this, the death of his Christ being triumphal. The prodigy seems to have been added to Mark xv, 33. Probably intended as the fulfilment of Amos viii, 9–10.

76 Also wanting in John. In the Synoptics the incident means what we read in Hebrews vi, 19–20 and x, 19–20. By the rending of the veil of his flesh the Christ enters the heavenly sanctuary, there to offer his blood, and thus open eternal life to the believer.

77 John xix, 31–37. Fulfilment of Exodus xii, 44 (Psalm xxxiv, 21) and of Zechariah xii, 10. The incident of the lance thrust may have been suggested by the last text. For the symbolic explanation connect with 1 John v, 6–7. This mystical imagery is good compensation for the centurion's profession of faith in the synoptic story and the rending of the veil. The substitution of the one symbol for the other may well have been deliberate.

NOTES TO CHAPTER III

1 The name "field of blood" is appropriate to a place of burial, but not to a cemetery "for strangers" (Matthew xxvii, 7). The idea indicated by the name is that of a burial place reserved for those who came to a bloody end in a violent or infamous death, such as suicides and executed criminals. Nothing could be more obviously artificial than the connexion of this place with "the price of blood"—the thirty pieces of silver which Judas is said to have received from the priests for betraying Jesus. The fiction contained in Matthew xxvii, 3–10, laying violent hands on certain Biblical texts (Zechariah xi, 12–13, amalgamated with Jeremiah xxxii, 6–9), has imagined a connexion between the money and the name of the place; while another fiction (Acts i, 16–20), based on other texts (Psalms lxix, 26; cix, 8), contradicts the first and connects the name with the blood of Judas, which it spills on the field bought by him with the high priests' money and where he is said, literally, to have burst. The two versions of the myth denounce each other as inventions and cancel out. "The field of blood" existed before the time of Jesus. We may conjecture that the original tradition retained some memory of a connexion between Aceldama and the crucified Jesus and that later on, when the Christ had been furnished with a befitting tomb, from which his body had miraculously disappeared to prove him risen from the dead, this connexion with Aceldama was shifted from Jesus to Judas.

2 Cf. Acts xiii, 29, and see *Le quatrième Evangile*, 496–498.

3 Matthew xxvi, 60, attributing the tomb to Joseph. Luke xxiii, 53 has "a tomb in which no man had yet been buried," followed by John who for symbolism, places the tomb in a garden.

4 Mark xv, 46; xvi, 4 insisting on the great size of the stone; Matthew xxvii, 60 does the same; Luke xxiv 2 merely mentions the presence of the stone.

5 The correspondence of this timing, in distribution, with the ritual of Adonis cannot be fortuitous.

6 John xx, 17. In the interpolated passage, 2–10, Mary of Magdala, before she yet knows that Jesus is risen, gives the information to Peter and the beloved disciple.

7 It was invented in order to conceal the real condition of the burial behind a fulfilment of prophecies.

8 These gnostic revelations are founded on instructions given by the risen Christ. So, too, are the Pauline gnosis and the Apocalypse of Peter.

9 Examples may be found in the discourses which the editor of Acts puts into the mouths of Peter and of Paul when addressing Jewish audiences. These discourses represent the apology for Christianity as presented to the Jews in the earliest Christian times.

10 John xx. The apparitions described in this chapter form the climax and bring the story to a definite end. On them the Church was founded. Chapter xxi is an addition. The Galilean apparition first described in it can by no possibility be fitted into the framework of xx. It is a parallel story, with a more limited purpose, which the author of xx, if he knew of it, decided to leave out.

11 J. Weiss, *Das Urchristentum*, 11; R. Schütz, *Apostel und Junger*, 1921, pp. 98 ff. Cf. E. Meyer, iii, 216, n. 1. But Meyer is over-hasty in deciding that a vision of Peter and study of Scripture immediately established the faith of the apostolic group; that a vision of the Twelve determined their return to Jerusalem and that Psalm cx caused them to give Jesus the title of "Lord." The requisitioning of texts did not originate this faith but followed its onward movement.

12 The word ἐκκλεσία is found again in Matthew xviii, 17, which is in the same current of tradition; but there ἐκκλεσία simply means "community."

13 Mention omitted in Matthew xxvii, 7.

14 John xxi, 15–17. The triple protestation of love, with a triple investiture in answer, seems designed to correspond with the triple denial, by way of reparation.

15 So much may be retained as historical from Acts ii, 42–46; vi, 2–3.

16 Acts iii–iv, 22. For criticism of this story see my *Les Actes des Apôtres*, 222–251. The name of John at the side of Peter is a later addition; this out of respect for the Ephesian legend and its saint. We shall see later that the same preoccupation has caused John's name to be omitted after that of James (xii, 2). In the story before us, the discourse of Peter, his arrest and appearance before the Sanhedrim appear to have been invented by the editor to fill out the picture.

17 This concludes the original story.

18 In place of these cramped conditions, which the charity of believers

could, or would, correct when they ran to extremes, the editor of Acts gives us glimpses of a fairly comfortable state of things in which pious sages live in common on a fund continually renewed, under God's blessing, by the accession of new members who bring into it all they have. Preuschen, *Die Apostelgeschichte*, 28, compares it with what we are told of Pythagoras and his disciples. But the editor is more likely to have been inspired directly by what Josephus says about the Essenes.

19 Documentation in Harnack, *Mission und Ausbreitung des Christentums*, 13, 307 ff.

20 Mark iv, 7–13, 30; cf. Matthew x. Luke ix, 1–6, 10 has the résumé of Mark's missionary discourse addressed to "the twelve apostles," and in x, 1–24 he gives the same discourse *in extenso* and makes it addressed to "seventy-two other disciples," as he found it in the source used also by Matthew. These seventy-two disciples are figures of the missionaries of the Gentiles, and the doubling is in keeping with the fiction which reserves the status of apostles to the Twelve.

21 Acts vi, 13. The elements of the text are contradictory: we are told of a legal trial before the Sanhedrim while the execution is an affair of mob violence. Many think there was no trial and that Stephen perished in a riot, stoned to death by the audience whom some discourse of his had scandalized. There is no proof whatever that the trial is a faint copy of the trial of Jesus by the high priest in the Gospels. The editor seems to have been unwilling to let Stephen be condemned on the charges brought against him before the Sanhedrim, offences against the Law of Moses. His thesis was better suited by having him massacred for reproaching the Jews for their agelong infidelity.

22 If Jesus ever uttered this saying, he did not understand it in the sense in which Stephen seems to have interpreted it.

23 Acts vii, 58, 60. All this is an interpolation in the account of the stoning.

NOTES TO CHAPTER IV

1 Cf. Heitmüller, *Zum Problem Paulus und Jesus*, Z.N.W., 1912, 320–327; Bousset, *Kyrios Christos*, 92.

2 The notice in Acts xi, 26 does not mean that the name "Christians" was bestowed on the Antioch disciples all at once, but that the pagans were not slow in so naming them. No doubt the pagans, constantly hearing the name "Christ" invoked by the new believers, took it for a proper name and thought they were calling the sect after its founder. The same would hold true of Tacitus, "Auctor hujus nominis Christus" (*Annals*, xv, 44).

3 The story about Simon in Acts viii, 5–25 is interpolated and incoherent. In certain respects Simon is the chief actor in it. But it seems that an earlier story put him in relation only with Philip from whom he wished to buy the power to work miraculous cures, which the editor of Acts turned into

a proposal to buy the Holy Spirit from Peter. In the first version Simon was denounced as a sorcerer, while in the story before us he and his sect are belittled in comparison with Christianity. The legend of Peter's relations with Simon was largely developed in later tradition and it is probable that the editor got hold of it while in process of development. It is doubtful not only whether Simon ever received Christian baptism, as the story declares, but whether he had any direct relations either with Philip or with Peter. His reputation as the father of heretical gnosis rests upon the fact that he was contemporary with the apostolic age and that his sect came into competition with nascent Christianity.

4 Acts ix, 32–35; cure of a paralytic at Lydda (on the model of the paralytic in Luke v, 18–24); raising Dorcas from the dead at Joppa (ix, 36–43, on the model of Jairus' daughter, Luke v, 21–24, 35–43, and the resurrection performed by Elijah and Elisha). These miracles are localized at Lydda and Joppa so as to bring Peter to Caesarea, the Roman political headquarters, as the right place for the conversion of a Roman centurion.

5 See *Les Mystères paiens et le Mystère Chretien*, 144–146, 153–155.

6 There seems to be no doubt as to the fact of the relationship, although we are ignorant of the circumstances in which the relations of Jesus joined the group of Galilean believers. The James who is the chief figure in the first community when Paul comes to Jerusalem for the last time (Acts xxi, 18) is the brother of Jesus and he is the identical James who, in Galatians ii, 9, is counted as a "pillar" along with Peter and John. On his first journey Paul interviewed him and Cephas at the same time; but we have seen above that Galatians i, 18–20 is probably not primitive in the Epistle. The two sons of Zebedee (John and the other James) seem to have had a rather important standing by the side of Peter; but the probability is that both of them perished in 44, while Peter had to flee from the city. James, brother of the Lord, would then become the chief person in the Jerusalem community.

7 The legend was conceived in the same spirit as the great saying which appointed Peter the keeper of the keys of the kingdom (Matthew xvi, 17–19) and, like it, must have had a Syro-Palestinian origin. But the origin cannot have been narrowly Jewish-Christian. It is in point to remember that Paul, who was never chief figure at Antioch during his life, was bound to fall still further into the background there after his death. Even in the communities of Syria and Palestine that leaned towards hellenism, legend would there tend to work in Peter's favour.

8 The tale fits in with the fiction of ix, 22–26a, where Paul is made to preach at Damascus, then has him introduced to the apostles by Barnabas, and brings him back to Tarsus, whither Barnabas goes to seek him in order to bring him to Antioch. The whole story, including the commission given to Barnabas by the Jerusalem community to go to Antioch and see what has happened there is aimed at making the Twelve the prime authors of all propaganda. It is certain that Barnabas did not remain in Jerusalem after the death of Stephen.

9 The mention of Barnabas as "Joseph called Barnabas, a Levite of Cyprus," in iv, 36–37, really belongs to xiii, 1 and is an anticipation. The former passage as a whole (36–37) is of a piece with the fictions indicated in the notes above and is highly suspect. If Barnabas was a Cypriot, it is not likely that he would have land to sell in Judea. See *Les Actes des Apôtres*, 262–265.

10 These statements express an ardent conviction which goes beyond the reality of the facts it brings to light. The disproportion between statement and fact may be explained either by Paul's visionary temperament or by the intervention of an editor who, at a later date, introduced into the Epistle a highly systematic interpretation of the facts in question.

11 Acts xi, 26 seems to reduce the common mission of Paul and Barnabas at Antioch to one full year before their journey to Jerusalem (xi, 30) and the mission in Cyprus and Lycaonia which they are said to have accomplished together. As to the journey, it took place at the date indicated (end of 43 or beginning of 44), but the motive of it was the question of the legal observances. As to the mission, it was probably not carried out in the conditions indicated but replaces the mission to Syria and Cilicia, mentioned in Galatians i, 21–24, which must have filled the greater part of the fourteen years (according to Galatians ii, 1) between Paul's conversion and his journey to Jerusalem to discuss the question of legal observances. See *Les Actes des Apôtres*, 474–476, 506.

12 Acts ix, 1–30. The story suppresses the mission-journey in Arabia (the Nabatean kingdom) mentioned in Galatians i, 17, and, in the face of all likelihood makes Paul begin preaching immediately in Damascus and in Jerusalem in contradiction to Galatians i, 17 and 22.

13 Compare 2 Corinthians xii, 14, where mention is made of a culminating vision, which is not described but may well have been, in the mind of the author, the vision which led to Paul's conversion.

14 Acts ix, 10–16: here the mission is outlined in a vision that comes to Ananias and in keeping with all that Acts will tell about Paul; Acts xxii, 1: here the mission is to the Gentiles, plainly announced in a vision Paul is said to have had in the temple at Jerusalem, after his conversion; Acts xxvi, 16–18: here the mission is laid down by Jesus himself in the original vision.

15 The fiction is not the journey into Arabia; that journey explains the intervention of the Nabatean ethnarch at Damascus (related in 2 Corinthians xi, 32–33) which determined Paul to flee the city and for which Acts ix, 23–25 substitutes a Jewish plot to kill him. See *Les Actes des Apôtres*, 414–421.

16 Cf. Acts ix, 26–30 and Galatians i, 18–20. It has been pointed out above that the editor of Acts in ix, 26–30 and xi, 22–26 manœuvres Barnabas and Paul with a view to making it appear that the foundation of the Christian groups at Antioch and elsewhere in Syria and Cilicia depend in the closest possible way on the apostles in Jerusalem, to whom in reality those foundations owed nothing at all. It will be noted that if Galatians i, 18–20 is a fiction (as it seems to be) pointing in the same direction as Acts

ix, 26–30, then the interpolator of it can have only half understood what the fiction in Acts was aimed at, for he is concerned only to subordinate Paul to Peter.

¹⁷ On this letter, of the year 41, see Seston, *L'empereur Claude et les chrétiens* in *Revue d'histoire et de philosophie religieuses*, 1931, No. 3. The letter clearly attests the attention the Roman government is paying to Jewish affairs, the fear it has of Jewish agitations which starting at one point might have repercussions through all the empire, and its intention to suppress these disturbances. But it remains possible, even probable, that Christian preaching had something to do in the movement which Claudius intends to suppress.

¹⁸ Acts vi, 9, where mention is made of Cyrenean and Alexandrian Jews among Stephen's audience.

¹⁹ The story of Mark's apostolate at Alexandria belongs to legend, and the list of the first bishops of Alexandria, like that of the Roman bishops, was made up after the event.

²⁰ What Suetonius says (*Claud.*, 25) may easily be understood in that sense, "Judaeos impulsore Chresto assidue tumultuantes Roma expulit," if we suppose that *Chrestus* stands for Christus and that Suetonius mistook the object of the agitation for the author of it. With the same event is connected what Dio Cassius tells (lx, 6, 6) of the measures taken by Claudius against the Jews in the beginning of his reign, and many connect with it the notice about Aquila in Acts xviii, 2; at the same time they adopt the year 49, indicated by Orosius (viii, 6, 15), as the date of the edict. All that is not equally consistent; we do not know on what Orosius' date is founded; the notice in Acts, an interpolation, may be a guess of the editor. That Claudius tried to expel all the Jews is improbable and action would be taken only against disturbers of the peace. If Christians were aimed at, the date must be much earlier than the Epistle to the Romans.

²¹ It would be fourteen whole years if the figure of Galatians ii, 1 has to be *added* to the three years of i, 18. But, disregarding the suspicion which falls on i, 18–20, the figure in ii, 1 seems to indicate the time elapsed since the apostle's conversion, so that we ought to *subtract* from fourteen, if not the three years, i, 18, at least the time occupied by the journey into Arabia and the stay at Damascus.

²² Text completed as indicated in note 9 above.

²³ For example, the story about the preaching at Iconium (xiv, 1–2), to which was probably attached what is said about the stoning of Paul (19–20) which the editor has transferred to Lystra.

²⁴ A tale invented to furnish a reason for the journey of Barnabas and Paul, the true object of which is given further on in xv, 1–5. Paul and Barnabas were together in Jerusalem only once and it was at the date indicated by xi, 27–30, a little before the death of Agrippa I. The prophet Agabus who figures here turns up in xxi, 10–11, an interpolated passage. Our editor was not willing that Jerusalem should have no prophets when there were so many at Antioch. For the same reason he represents Jude and

Silas as prophets in xv, 32. The famine of xi, 28 is taken from Josephus, *Antiquities*, xx, 5, 2. See *Les Acts des Apôtres*, 472, 605, 785–788.

²⁵ We have seen above how, in the editing of Acts, a common mission of Barnabas and Paul to Cyprus and Lycaonia has been substituted for their common mission to Syria–Cilicia, the former mission being placed by the editor between two journeys of Barnabas and Paul to Jerusalem (Acts xi, 30 and xv, 1–4). Of the two journeys only one took place and at the date indicated for the first; thus the substituted mission hangs in air. Other instances of one event made into two for editorial convenience will be found in the book. One might almost say that it raises this kind of amplification to the dignity of a principle. With regard to the present case see *Les Actes des Apôtres*, 474–476, 498–499, 571. Galatians (ii, 1–10) knows of only one journey of Barnabas and Paul to Jerusalem, at the date Acts assigns to the first journey, and with the object of the second.

²⁶ Acts xv, 1–2. This preamble comes from the source document and agrees in substance with Galatians ii, 1–11, if the two texts are correctly understood. See *Les Actes des Apôtres*, 565–566.

²⁷ The statement accords with the strange egotism with which, in this passage, Paul, or his interpreter, estimates his providential vocation.

²⁸ This James, brother of Jesus, is certainly intended in Galatians ii, 12; cf. i, 19. At the time of the Jerusalem meeting the other James, brother of John, was still alive and is not likely to have been a dumb member of the assembly. The preponderance of James the Lord's brother would not be established till after the disappearance of the three principal disciples of Jesus.

²⁹ Note that the theory of the double apostolate is not elsewhere formulated in the Epistle. Peter alone was the gainer by it.

³⁰ In Acts xv, 13–21 (discourse of James) and 28–29 (apostolic letter) some special observances, abstinence from blood and the flesh of strangled animals, regulation of marriage, are substituted for the collection mentioned in Galatians ii, 10. The substitution must have been deliberate, the editor having antedated the collection in the fiction of xi, 27–30, and belittled its importance.

³¹ Cf. Holscher, 199, 227 n. 2.

³² E. Meyer, iii, 420. But there is no ground to conclude with Meyer (after Acts xii, 25) that the delegates from Antioch were still in Jerusalem when James and John were executed.

³³ Acts xii, 1–2 mentions only the execution of James, but in hesitating language. Mark x, 39 leaves no doubt as to the martyrdom of both the sons of Zebedee and the text invites the conclusion that they perished under the same conditions. See *Les Actes des Apôtres*, 482–484. The martyrdom of John is suppressed out of regard for the Ephesian legend of his residence and death in Asia Minor towards the end of the first century.

³⁴ According to Acts xii, 25, John-Mark left Jerusalem, after Peter's escape, in company with Barnabas and Saul; but this because the editor wants John-Mark for the companion of the two missionaries on the apostolic

journey narrated in xiii–xiv (which never took place), and also to make him the cause of the separation between Barnabas and Paul (which was caused quite otherwise). As John-Mark was really at Antioch at the time of the separation we may believe that he had fled thither with Peter.

35 Silas, after carrying to Antioch the letter of the Jerusalem elders, left with Jude (xv, 33; 34 is an interpolation co-ordinated with 40); but he returned to Antioch since we find him there after the quarrel ready to accompany Paul into Asia Minor, as John-Mark accompanies Barnabas in Cyprus. Agrippa's persecution caused Silas also to flee to Antioch and he, too, will have come there with Peter.

36 Galatians ii, 13–14. The rating administered to Peter by Paul leads to nothing definite, but continues in the general discussion of justification by faith alone without the law. This might be counted an argument against the point of view which dominates this passage. It is difficult to understand how this point of view can have been Paul's, and no less difficult to regard the story of the conflict as a pure fiction.

37 The writer of the Epistle is unwilling to confess that Paul's reprimand had the effect of embroiling him with Barnabas and making his further stay in Antioch impossible.

38 Galatians ii, 11–14 gives good ground for believing that Paul broke with Barnabas at the same time as with Peter and for the same reason or on the same pretext. The deeper motive was the growing self-importance of Paul; the pretext or occasion would be the accommodation which Barnabas and Peter wished to make with the Judaizers.

39 Acts xii, 12. In view of the general character of the story, insistence on this detail is out of place.

40 1 Peter v, 13; testimony of John the Elder in Papias. On the gratuitously unfavourable testimony which Acts gives about John-Mark see *Les Actes des Apôtres*, 519–522.

NOTES TO CHAPTER V

1 The journey and the stay at Antioch mentioned in Acts xviii, 22 in all probability never took place. See *Les Actes des Apôtres*, 706–710.

2 As the first "we" in the edited version of Acts appears in the narrative of the stay at Troas (xvi, 10), commentators have been prompt to assume that Luke first joined Paul at this place; but some critics have supposed that he was the Macedonian of the dream who, according to our story, decided Paul to pass into Macedonia. But, if we are to determine the participation of Luke in the comings and goings of Paul and other events by the alternations of "we" with impersonal forms of speech, we must assume that the editor of Acts has made no cuttings in Luke's narrative, suppressed nothing and interpolated no fictitious incidents and discourses. Now it is certain that he has done all three. The text rather invites us to think that

he who says "we" in the Troas story had been with Paul all along. There is no risk in supposing that from their starting point at Antioch he followed Paul in his haphazard journeyings, the painful stages of which are described in terms strongly suggestive of an eye-witness. The tradition which makes Luke a Christian of Antioch may well proceed from explicit testimony of the primitive book before the editor got to work on it, and is confirmed by the fact that the original author seems well informed about Antioch affairs and to have understood the birth of Christianity from his Antioch point of view. Cf. *Les Actes des Apôtres*, 627–631.

3 Acts xvi, 1 is vaguely completed by xiv, 20–21.

4 Cf. Colossians i, 1; iv, 10–11. 2 Timothy i, 5 knows both Timothy's mother and grandmother—information which the cautious critic finds rather too complete. In Acts xxi, 20–26 the nazirate of Paul is alleged as the reason for Timothy's circumcision. But Paul, when playing his part as a Jew, could practise any Jewish observance demanded by the occasion; it was not to please the Jews that he took the vows of a *nazir*, as we shall see later on. It is hardly credible that any pagan was ever circumcized by Paul merely to please the Jews.

5 At Iconium, as well as at Antioch of Pisidia, we may to some extent supplement the vague indication of Acts xvi, 4–5 by xiv, 1–3, 19, 20, and xiii, 14, 43, 50–51—employed with discernment.

6 Pressing hard on the text of Acts we might infer that the missionaries merely traversed the country without preaching in it. This is the interpretation of the text given, perhaps without warrant, by those who construe the Epistle as addressed to the communities of Lycaonia-Pisidia which belonged to the Roman province called Galatia, but were not Galatian country. The problem of the destination of the Epistle, on which critics are divided, would be non-existent if Paul, in the course of one and the same mission, founded the communities of Lycaonia and Pisidia, and then some others in Phrygia and Galatia proper, without going as far as Ancyra and Pessinonte, the Epistle to the Galatians being finally addressed to the whole of these communities.

7 The Epistle presupposes this, and the little we know about the preaching at Iconium and Antioch of Pisidia does not contradict it.

8 Acts xvi, 9–10. The "we" appears in this passage which must have been taken without alteration from the source document; 6–8 may be regarded as a highly compressed summary. There is no reason to suppose that Luke was the Macedonian, nor that he came from Philippi.

9 Acts xvi, 22, 39–40. The edited version makes Paul's captivity last for one night marked by various prodigies, in sequence to which Paul, after getting the town magistrate to exculpate him as a Roman citizen, is said to have been set free. The earthquake and its consequences are conceived on this pattern of a theme common in religious legend (cf. Euripides, *Bacchae*, 436–441, 502–503, 606–628). There is a contradiction between the proud attitude of Paul, the humble demeanour of the magistrates, and the order to quit the place without delay. The claim to be a Roman citizen is

borrowed from Paul's trial at Jerusalem and repeated. Paul was liberated without much delay, but probably by the intervention of his friends and on their bail—a trait seemingly transposed to the story that follows (xvii, 9) —on condition of his immediate departure.

10 A story cut down and changed like the one preceding. The beginning of it comes from the source document, but the riot which drives the missionaries out of the town takes place the moment after their arrival and too soon, as it did at Philippi, this time, however, provoked by Jews, as the former was by pagans. 1 Thessalonians making no reference to any occurrence of this kind, there is reason to suspect that our editor has balanced the pagan riot which put an end to Paul's ministry at Philippi by a similar charge against the Jews of Thessalonica.

11 Acts xvii, 10–12. The notice about Berea seems to have a fictitious conclusion (13–14), which repeats what has been said about Thessalonica. The indications about Silas and Timothy (15) must have been changed by the editor; they are not in agreement with 1 Thessalonians iii, 1–2, nor even with Acts xviii, 5.

12 To be inferred from 1 Thessalonians iii, 1–2.

13 In like manner the discourse in the synagogue at Antioch of Pisidia (xiii, 16–40) is a specimen of the teaching given to a Jewish audience, and the discourse to the elders of Ephesus (xx, 10–35) a specimen of instructions to the heads of congregations.

14 xvii, 28. The line, "for in him we live and move and have our being," is also borrowed from the poem of Epimenides, entitled *Minos*, in which we also find the saying about the Cretans in Titus i, 12. (Rendel Harris, *St. Paul and Greek Literature, Woodbrooke Essays*, 7, p. 7.)

15 Though Paul did not think that Athens might be altogether neglected, we should misconstrue his mind and the mind of the first Christian generation by concluding with E. Meyer (iii, 328–9) that Athens was the chief aim of the mission, in respect of which the preachings in the Macedonian towns was no more than rapidly completed preparation, Paul's main purpose being to overthrow hellenic philosophy on the ground where it was most at home. The editor of Acts seems to have had some such notion; but to accept the famous discourse and its *mise en scène* as authentic would be placing too much confidence in his fictions.

16 1 Thessalonians iii, 1–2, 5–7 shows that Paul was afraid the group of Christians would not hold together after his departure; he avows his misgivings after being reassured by the good news which Silas and Timothy brought to him at Corinth.

17 Acts xviii, 1, 2, 3. His mission in Asia Minor seems to have been carried through in difficult material conditions. Later on Paul accepted help from Philippi. But on arriving at Corinth it would seem that he had to work for his living. It is possible also that his mishap at Athens induced him to test the ground before beginning his propaganda in the atmosphere of Corinth. In xviii, 2 the reference to the edict of Claudius is a later addition.

18 Cf. Philippians iv, 15–16, which shows that the Philippians helped

Paul in his mission at Thessalonica. It is a doubtful point whether Lydia is expressly indicated, and as Paul's wife, in iv, 3, though it has been maintained by some from ancient time.

19 The story of the Corinthian mission, like the others, is mutilated and incoherent. Besides the addition in xviii, 2 (indicated in note 17), 4 should be placed after 7 and 7 attached to the beginning of 5, reading: "But, when Silas and Timothy arrived from Macedonia, Paul took up his preaching." It is then that he leaves Aquila's house and begins to preach in the synagogue. What is said in verse 6 about his quarrel with the Jews is an addition repeating the stereotyped procedure that everywhere Paul addressed himself to the pagans only after being rejected by the Jews. Paul's difficulties began after the conversion of Crispus and the others (8); between 8 and 9 there is a gap; then mention should have been made of the difficulties which no doubt compelled Paul to leave the synagogue; the vision of 9 will then encourage him to go on with his preaching in spite of everything; but there is another gap, either before or after 11, for we expect an account of the results of his ministry and get only an indication of its length.

20 To these eighteen months we must add the time spent by Paul in Aquila's house while he waited for his auxiliaries. No account need be taken of the "many days" of verse 18, which is only a bit of stitching to make a forced connexion between the mention of Paul's departure and the Gallio incident.

21 See *Les Actes des Apôtres*, 698–699.

22 See *Les Actes des Apôtres*, 508–518.

23 Acts xviii, 18–23 is a badly constructed and largely fictitious story, indicating Syria (18) as the goal of the journey, because the editor— repeating the devices he employed on the journey of Barnabas and Paul to Jerusalem at the time of the Antioch mission—cut the last approach of Paul to the mother-community into two; the vow mentioned in the same passage (18) belongs to the last journey and we shall meet it later on. The visit of Paul to the synagogue at Ephesus is wrongly timed; like the journey to Jerusalem and to Syria it is intended to disguise the true motive which determined Paul to visit the communities he had recently founded in Galatia and Phrygia. Of set purpose the editor ignores Paul's conflicts with the Judaizing Christians, just as he will know nothing of the difficulties Paul had just encountered at Corinth, in which Apollos had been involved. See *Les Actes des Apôtres*, 703–710.

24 Acts xviii, 24–28. An incoherent and touched-up story. The restriction (25), "knowing only the baptism of John," taken rigorously, contradicts the preceding statement, "he gave exact teaching about Jesus." The restriction goes with the kind of catechizing which Aquila and Priscilla are supposed to give Apollos (26). The end of the story (28), in which the preaching of Apollos is made to consist of a prolonged refutation of the Jews, throws a veil over the voluntary or involuntary part played by Apollos in the divisions at Corinth, just as what precedes is to minimize his part at Ephesus. See *Les Actes des Apôtres*, 710–717.

25 Acts xix, 1–7. The story hangs together better than that of Apollos, doubtless because the editor has put more of his own into the latter. See *Les Actes des Apôtres*, 717–723.

26 Acts viii, 14–17. Here fiction keeps to ground level and the story may serve to throw light on that of Apollos and of the twelve disciples. See *Les Actes des Apôtres*, 368–370.

27 Cf. 2 Corinthians iii, 1, where some contempt is shown for such letters which were in common use and one would think necessary.

28 Acts xix, 8–10 is a summary of the authentic story in the source document from which the editor has cut out, as he does elsewhere, the details of Paul's success and the difficulties he encountered. To make up for this he credits Paul with a parcel of miracles which form a worthy pendant to those operated by the shadow of Peter (v, 15–16), also an invention of his own. The misadventure of the Jewish exorcist has the look of being a borrowed story adapted to the history of Paul in order to bring in somehow the edifying example given by the believers of Ephesus in burning the sorcerers' books in sequence to the former incident (18–20). See *Les Actes des Apôtres*, 752–753, 756.

29 In 1 Corinthians xv, 32 there is an allusion to fighting with beasts at Ephesus, a passage whose meaning has been much discussed and the authenticity open to discussion; in xvi, 8–9 there is mention of effectual ministry in the city, but "many adversaries." The riot described in Acts xix, 23–41 fills the place of all the difficulties and setbacks Paul had to meet at Ephesus. The passage which mentions companions of Paul (29b–31) and the allusion to companions in the speech of its local magistrate (37) having the look of surcharges, and the whole story having no real attachment to Paul's Ephesian ministry, the not improbable supposition has been made that the editor of Acts found some story of an anti-Jewish riot at Ephesus and converted it into a riot against Paul. (Hypothesis of Wellhausen, taken up in *Les Actes des Apôtres*, 752–753, 756.)

30 Acts xix, 21–22, taking account of the fact that the editor deliberately omits everything that relates to the collection for the saints at Jerusalem.

31 The editor has neutralized the significance of the collection by saying nothing about it in the situations where it played a part and by representing it as a kind of symbolic act in the fictitious story where the prophet Agabus comes in (Acts xi, 27–30). See *Les Actes des Apôtres*, 471–475.

32 E. Meyer, iii, 451, would infer from 1 Corinthians i, 12; iii, 21, where Cephas is mentioned along with Paul, that Peter also came to Corinth at this time. But we may conclude with as much probability from iii, 4–9 and iv, 6 that Apollos only followed Paul to Corinth, Peter's name being merely invoked against Paul by some of his opponents. But it remains a possibility which we may regard as little probable.

33 In this passage Paul, recalling his promise, seems anxious to keep it.

34 Acts xix, 21–22. This connects with 1 Corinthians iv, 17; xvi, 1–11 where, before announcing the coming of Timothy, he says that the col-

lection in Macedonia and Corinth is to be carried out on the lines he had laid down for Galatia.

35 Notwithstanding the somewhat cold reception Corinth had given him he had promised to return before long; later he concluded he must wait until tempers there had cooled down. Hence no doubt came the accusation of fickleness to which he replies in 2 Corinthians i, 15–20; ii, 4.

36 There seems no reason to identify this person with the incestuous man of 1 Corinthians v, 1–5, though some critics do so.

37 2 Corinthians i, 8–11, to which ii, 6 corresponds, seems to reflect such a state of mind, rather than the fear of some external danger in which Paul might have lost his life; for example, the riot described in Acts xix, 23–40 (so E. Meyer, iii, 12), in which Paul ran no danger, supposing it ever took place.

38 2 Corinthians ii, 3–4; vii, 8–12. It is this sad and severe letter which many have thought reproduced, at least in part, in 2 Corinthians x–xiii, where, rather, some fragments of it are preserved.

39 The rôle of Titus may be deduced from 2 Corinthians ii, 11–13; vii, 6–7; viii, 6, 16–17, 23, on which xii, 18 has editorial dependence. We do not know how Titus arrived in Asia at Paul's side in the nick of time to save the situation, nor how, his mission done, he disappeared from Paul's company.

40 According to 2 Corinthians xiii, 1 this was the third stay made by Paul in the city; the first, that of his mission, being much the longest; the second, certainly a short one, was that when he was checked and unable to restore order in the community; the third preceded his departure for Jerusalem and probably represents the three months which, according to Acts xx, 2–3, Paul spent "in Hellas," the editor being extremely cautious in dealing with the relations between Paul and Corinth at that time.

41 This chronology is somewhat wavering. Retaining the coincidence with Gallio's proconsulates Paul's mission to Corinth would be completed in 51 or 52, the apostle arriving at Corinth in 49 or 50, and the missions to Asia Minor and Macedonia filling the years 44–49. The mission to Ephesus cannot have been begun before 52 or 53 and ended towards 55 or 56, and Paul would then not leave Corinth for good before the spring of 56 or 57. E. Meyer (iii, 447) puts this final departure in 59; but he does this in order that he may place the death of Paul, with that of Peter, in 64, during Nero's persecution.

42 Cf. Romans xv, 26–27; xvi, 1.

43 In Acts xx, 4 Gaius is said to be "of Derbe." But the original list may have been worked over and this Gaius may be the Corinthian (mentioned in Romans xvi, 23) charged to bring the collection from Achaia. See *Les Actes des Apôtres*, 759–762.

44 The vow is antedated in xviii, 18, where the text has been retouched by the editor (see *Les Actes des Apôtres*, 704–705). This verse should be attached to xx, 16 and xxi, 23–26 as referring to the same vow. The matter in question is that of a temporary *nazirate* and a vow taken with special

reference to a pilgrimage to Jerusalem. The head was not shaved again while the vow was in force, but only on discharge from it as one of the sacrifices prescribed by the Law. The vow is antedated in the story of the fictitious journey which the editor has duplicated from the account before us. For the ordinary conditions of such vows see *Les Actes des Apôtres*, 796–798.

45 Acts xx, 5–6. The account of the sea passage is clumsily attached to the list of Paul's companions, and the "we" of the source document suddenly reappears because the editor has here picked up the thread of the original. As we know from the Epistles that Luke was not with Paul at Athens nor in the missions that followed, we may conclude that he remained at Philippi.

46 The miracle of raising Eutychus from the dead which Paul is said to have performed at Troas is on the Old Testament model, like the raising of Dorcas by Peter (ix, 36–43).

47 The editor of Acts, who says not a word about the collection, takes advantage of the stay at Miletus to lodge in this place an allocution by Paul to the elders of Ephesus on the model of a pastoral discourse to the ministers of the flock. It will be noted that the editor, whose intention is to say nothing about Paul's death, is careful to make Paul predict it (25) as a consequence of the journey he has undertaken.

48 The account of the meeting with the brethren at Tyre has, to say the least, received additions, the prophetic warning given by the brethren having a compromising likeness to what Paul himself has just said at Miletus. The seven days at Troas, the seven days at Tyre and, later on, the seven days at Puteoli (xxviii, 14) have more the look of edifying parentheses than real memoranda.

49 The conclusion of the incident (xxi, 12–14) must be nearly identical with what Luke made to follow a prediction by Philip's prophetic daughters.

50 Acts xxi, 15–16. Before the visit to James our author clumsily places a favourable reception by the brethren in general. The source document, on the contrary, represents the hospitality of Mnason as a kind of precaution against too hasty contact with the body of Judaizing Christians.

51 According to Josephus (*Antiquities*, xix, 6, 1) Agrippa I, anxious to make a show of religion, released a number of poor *nazirs* from their vows, by paying their expenses for the various sacrifices required of them by the Mosaic Law (see Numbers vi).

52 Acts xxi, 20–26. The discourse of the elders is intelligible and holds well together except for the perceptible gloss, after the words "thou seest, brother, how many thousands of Jews there are," which adds the explanation "of those who believe." Verse 22 is an artificial transition intended to make some sort of connexion between what has just been said about the disposition of believing Jews and the advice about to be given to Paul to prove his zeal for the Law before these same Jews by taking(?) a vow. The lame reference to the pseudo-apostolic decree (xv, 9) is in keeping with the false perspective.

53 From xxi, 27 it would seem that the editor thought the nazirate lasted seven days. See *Les Actes des Apôtres*, 805.

54 The brethren mentioned in xxi, 23 had certainly been under the vow for some time.

55 In the editor's thesis, all the groups of nascent Christianity, Jewish and hellenist, keep the Law, the Jewish with the rigour of the Mosaic code, the hellenist in conformity with the prohibitions supposed to apply to all the children of Noah, and not only to the descendants of Abraham. See *Les Actes des Apôtres*, 804–807.

56 Except on this supposition the sequence of the affair is not intelligible.

57 There may be an echo of the source document in xxiii, 11. But the vision is more likely to have taken place on the night following Paul's arrest. It reveals the working of Paul's mind which suddenly led him to see that he might carry his message to Rome under Roman authority. See *Les Actes des Apôtres*, 835–837.

58 The transfer of Paul to Caesarea must have followed very soon after his arrest, but the editor has deliberately thrown the circumstances into confusion. It is certain that the Jewish authorities would not lose a moment in putting forth every possible effort to get their hands on the man whom the intervention of the Roman soldiers had saved from the fury of their people. If they thought it likely that the charge of profaning the temple would fail they could still claim Paul as a religious agitator whose revolutionary activities they had the right to suppress, especially at Jerusalem. But the tribune could not hand over to them a Roman citizen whose right to be judged only in a Roman court was incontestable. Accordingly he would at once refer the case to the procurator.

59 The resumption of the story is as easy to recognize as the interpolation which breaks it up. In xxii, 23–24 we find ourselves back at the exact point where we stand in xxi, 34–35.

60 Acts xxii, 25–29. The scene is dramatized by the editor on much the same lines as his fiction of the scourging of Paul at Philippi (xvi, 35–39), which it recalls rather too vividly.

61 xxii, 30–xxiii, 10. The editor is plainly in error in making Ananias high priest in office at the time of Paul's trial. High priest in 47, he was deposed before 52.

62 For a discussion of this and the other fictions at this point, in which the naïve audacity of the editor is indulged as freely as in the story of the sitting of the Sanhedrim, see *Les Actes des Apôtres*, 838–842.

63 xxiii, 23–30. Having invented a Jewish plot against Paul our editor has now to mobilize hundreds of soldiers to escort Paul to Caesarea, but the mention of the departure by night and the halt at Antipatris may come from the source document. The report of the tribune Lysias is no less an invention than the sitting of the Sanhedrim, of which it gives an account to Felix.

64 xxiii, 31–35. The declaration of Felix to Paul (33), "I will hear thee when thy accusers are come," has no sense unless Paul himself invoked the

jurisdiction of the procurator in order to avoid falling into the hands of the Sanhedrim which claimed him.

[65] xxiv, 22–23. Two motives are alleged for the adjournment: the first, Felix knew in advance what line to take in regard to the Christian propaganda —this must come from the source document; second, that Felix wished to await the coming of Lysias—a pretext invented by the editor.

[66] xxiv, 27. The editor has thought he might add that, since Felix did not release Paul before giving up office, it was to please the Jews. The fact is that Felix left Paul's case just where it was when he was relieved of office; but during the two years of its adjournment it is quite possible that an understanding, more or less tacit, was formed between the procurator and the Sanhedrim to let the matter sleep. The Jewish authority could not have much ground for complaint so long as Paul was held prisoner and the official adjournment would seem a denial of the right Paul had claimed. For the discussion of the passage, see *Les Actes des Apôtres*, 867–870.

[67] xxiv, 22. See *Les Actes des Apôtres*, 862–863.

[68] Aged six at the death of her father in 44, Drusilla was married in 52 to the king of Emesa, Aziz, who had himself circumcised to obtain her hand; but their union was short-lived, for the procurator Felix fell in love with her at sight and succeeded in detaching her from her husband through the good offices of a friend of his, a Jewish sorcerer from Cyprus, while Drusilla made no scruple about marrying the uncircumcised Roman in her eagerness to escape from the jealousy of Berenice, her elder sister by ten years, who envied Drusilla her greater beauty (Josephus, *Antiquities*, xx, 7, 1–2). Of Felix, Tacitus writes as follows: "Per omnem saevitiam et libidinem jus regium servili ingenio exercuit."

[69] xxv, 9. The editor pretends that Festus wishes to repeat at Jerusalem the proceeding previously attributed to the tribune Lysias, that of assembling the Sanhedrim for a fuller inquiry, taking its verdict as to the guilt or innocence of the accused and getting from it a sentence which it would then be his business, as a Roman magistrate, to ratify.

[70] According to the editor's point of view, Festus understood all along that the whole affair was concerned with beliefs debated among the Jews; but the procurator, faced by the demand of the Sanhedrim, is supposed unable to refuse it, just as he will be unable to refuse ratification of its sentence, if Paul elects to be tried at Jerusalem. The case is presented in the same way as the trial of Jesus in the Gospels.

[71] The silly remark here attributed to the procurator is intended to corroborate the certificate of innocence he has just given to Paul in assuring Agrippa that Paul's activities in the affair were concerned only "with a certain Jesus, a dead man, whom Paul declared to be alive."

[72] After all, then, the examination before Agrippa provides Festus with nothing to put into his report to Caesar!

[73] "We" makes a new appearance when the sea story begins (xxvii, 1) after being in eclipse since the arrival at Jerusalem. The eclipse is partly explained by the mutilations and substitutions in the intermediate stories.

74 The only one mentioned is Aristarchus of Thessalonica; but Timothy must also have been among them.

75 The story of the sea passage has been changed only by interpolations, easily discernible, aimed at giving greater importance to Paul's rôle in this part of the story. Examples are the following: Paul's prophetic but rejected advice to winter in Crete rather than in the place called Fair Haven; reminder of this advice and announcement, in the midst of the tempest, that no lives would be lost; probably also the intervention of Paul to denounce the sailors about to desert the ship and its passengers, and the exhortation to take food (30–38). On the substantial authenticity of the story of the tempest, which has been questioned, see *Les Actes des Apôtres*, 921--922.

76 The miracle of the harmless viper and its conclusion (3–6) remind us a little too closely of the adventure at Lystra (xiv, 8–18) in the invented story of the mission which Paul and Barnabas are said to have made into Asia Minor. The marvellous cures performed by Paul are apparently introduced to provide a filling for the three months spent at Malta.

77 From xxviii, 16, which contains the last "we," the source document must have run on to the indication in verse 30 of the two years spent by Paul in the condition known as *custodia libera*.

78 xxviii, 31. Paul devoted himself to preaching the Gospel in his own house, but it was not for the purpose of enabling him to do so that the relative liberty of which he took advantage was granted him.

79 xxviii, 22–23a. But how could the Jews of Rome at this date (62) have said to Paul that they knew of Christianity only by hearing of it as a sect that was spoken against?

80 xxviii, 25b–27. The quotation from Isaiah is found again in Mark iv, 2 (Matthew xiii, 14–15; Luke viii, 10); John xii, 39–40.

81 There is no reference to this project outside the Epistle to the Romans (xv, 24), and it would seem that Paul had renounced it even before the end of his Roman captivity. But legend has not allowed the reference to it in Romans to fall into oblivion. In any case 2 Timothy iv, 16 can be understood as a first trial at which Paul was acquitted.

82 Romans xv, 19, 23–24. Paul seems to have regarded Spain as the limit of the Western world. Circumstances may have led him to consider it impossible to reach this limit, or simply to think no more about it.

NOTES TO CHAPTER VI

1 "Exitiabilis superstitio" is to be reckoned among the "atrocia aut pudenda" which flowed into Rome from all sides. Suetonius, without connecting the persecution of the Christians with the burning of Rome, writes to the same effect (*Nero*, 16): "Afflicti suppliciis Christiani, genus hominum superstitionis novae et maleficae." The secrecy of the Christian

meetings furnished a pretext for the imputation of infamous crimes; but similar imputations had previously been brought against the Jews.

2 Tacitus writes: "Igitur primum correpti qui fatebantur." The object of *fatebantur* has to be established from the context. The first reference is to the *exitiabilis superstitio* of which *Christus* is the author and the next to the multitude condemned rather for *odium generis humani*. E. Meyer (iii, 507) says that Tacitus expressly avoided being more precise because his object was to show how the prosecution of incendiaries developed, in course of the pursuit, into the prosecution of Christians in general. In reality the first Christians laid hold of were arrested as incendiaries, and those hunted down afterwards were arrested as Christians, without the establishment of any judicial distinction between the two categories. Nevertheless the text of Tacitus can only be understood naturally as meaning a confession of incendiarism by the first of the accused. But, in view of the multitude denounced, we have still to ask what these first confessions were worth. Reitzenstein, *Die hellenistischen Mysterienreligionen*, iii, 122, maintains with some probability that the inquisition was carried out by Nero's police in the interests of the emperor and that the first to be arrested were no other than the spies employed by the police for the occasion, as happened in the trial of Octavia, when a pretended accomplice appeared to confess to adultery which had not been committed.

3 A point perfectly treated by Renan, *L'Antichrist*, 154–155.

4 Clement's evocation of the Roman martyrs comes as conclusion to a long discourse on the evil deeds, discord and jealousy recorded in the Old Testament from Cain to David. The author then comes to "examples of our generation"—to be understood as meaning the Christian age, not in the chronological sense of his contemporaries—and takes the apostles to begin with: Πέτρον, ὃς διὰ ζῆλον ἄδικον οὐχ ἕνα οὐδὲ δύο, ἀλλὰ πλειόνας ὑπήνεγκεν πόνους καὶ οὕτω μαρτυρήσας ἐπορεύθη εἰς τὸν ὀφειλόμενον τόπον τῆς δόξης. διὰ ζῆλον καὶ ἔριν Παῦλος ὑπομονῆς βραϐεῖον ἔδειξεν . . . δικαιοσύνην διδάξας τον κόσμον καὶ ἐπὶ τὸ τέρμα τῆς δύσεως ἐλθὼν καὶ μαρτυρήσας ἐπὶ τῶν ἡγουμένων, οὕτως ἀπηλλάγη τοῦ κόσμου καὶ εἰς τὸν ἅγιον τόπον ἐπορεύθη . . . Τούτοις τοῖς ἀνδράσιν ὁσίως πολιτευσαμένοις συνηθροίσθη πολὺ πλῆθος ἐκλεκτῶν . . . This crowd is the *multitudo ingens* of Tacitus; but we cannot be sure that the two apostles and the crowd perished on the same occasion. We have here a retrospective view of the Roman martyrs at the time of Nero. Cf. H. Lietzmann, *Petrus und Paulus in Rome*, 228–236.

5 Cf. Acts xii, 17. We have seen above why the editor of Acts omits to mention the locality to which Peter fled.

6 Account should be taken, however, of what has been said above under the Epistle to the Philippians. Peter may have been at Rome among those of whom Paul complains that they were preaching a Gospel more or less opposed to his. The fact is that the editor of Acts, who has brought the entire Roman community to pay sympathetic homage to Paul, would have been in no mind to call attention, even if he knew of them, to the divisions,

factions and contrary currents which might exist among the Roman brethren in Nero's time. At all events it is risky to suppose with E. Meyer (iii, 508) that the "jealousy and discord," of which Clement speaks in connexion with Peter and Paul, may be interpreted as playing a part in the denunciation of Christians mutually hostile. The only precise detail known in regard to the mass of the victims concerns denunciation by pagan relatives. As to the apostles, their denunciation may well have been the work of non-Christians, without any need to make the Jews responsible.

7 *Romans*, 4. οὐχ ὡς πέτρος καὶ παῦλος διατάσσομαι ὑμῖν. This puts the letter of Ignatius on the same level as Clement and Dionysius.

8 In Eusebius, *Ecclesiastical History* ii, 25. Writing to the Romans, Dionysius said that the communities of Corinth and Rome were both taught by Peter and Paul who were equally together in martyrdom at Rome. A legendary and uncritical view of primitive history.

9 1 Peter v, 13. Mark is mentioned in this passage; also Sylvanus (12). We have seen that Colossians iv, 10 and Philemon 24 suppose Mark at Rome, but as one of Paul's followers, while John the Elder (in Papias) makes him the interpreter of Peter. All of which is uncertain enough.

10 John xx, 18–19 (a plain hint in xiii, 36). Martyrdom is clearly implied, and apparently by crucifixion, without indication of place. But, considering the late age of the testimony, we may believe that the author had Rome in mind. See *Le quatrième Evangile*, 524–525.

11 Lietzmann, 274, concludes for the authenticity of the burial places traditionally assigned to Peter and Paul.

12 Eusebius, iii, 5, 3, names Pella, beyond the Jordan, as the first place at which they stayed. It is noteworthy that the Judaizing Christians of those regions kept the name "Nazoreans."

13 Meyer, iii, 517, 554 (on the strength of Dio Cassius, 67, 14), thinks he was a Jew. But the Christian inscriptions, older than the legends Meyer sets aside, have to be reckoned with.

14 In all probability the *sacramentum* in question was the oath taken at baptism.

15 "Affirmabant autem hanc fuisse summam vel culpae suae vel erroris, quod essent soliti stato die ante lucem convenire carmenque Christo quasi deo dicere secum invicem, seque sacramento non in scelus aiiquod obstringere, sed ne furta, ne latrocinia, ne adulteria committerent, ne fidem fallerent, ne depositum appellati abnegarent."

16 "Nec mediocriter haesitavi: I Sitne aliquod discrimen aetatum, an quamlibet teneri nihil a robustioribus differant; II Detur poenitentiae venia, an ei, qui omnino Christianus fuit, desisse non prosit; III Nomen ipsum, si flagitiis careat, an flagitia cohaerentia nomini puniantur."

17 Eusebius, iv, 26 (the text quoted in iv, 13 is apocryphal).

18 Romans xiii, 1–7. A piece of padding, but introduced with a purpose.

19 This Quadratus may be the same as the person mentioned by Eusebius in iii, 37 and v, 17. As those raised from the dead are associated with those

cured of disease perhaps we should see in the multiplication of both classes a mere rhetorical flourish.

²⁰ Eusebius is mistaken in making the apology addressed to Hadrian. It has only recently been recovered and reconstructed. See R. Harris and A. Robinson, *The Apology of Aristides*, 1891, and Harnack, *Chronologie*, i, 271–273.

²¹ Cf. Colossians ii, 16–19; Acts vii, 53 (Galatians iii, 19).

²² In the *Dialogue*, 2–3, Justin himself, not, perhaps, without literary artifice, recounts the stages of his religious experience.

²³ Observe that Justin here encounters Celsus, who was acquainted with the Great Church, but views Christianity as a medley of sects affecting the same name for ever quarrelling and reproaching each other with unmentionable crimes. Origen, *Contra Celsum*, iii, 12 and v, 63.

²⁴ Justin here follows the doctrine of the Book of Enoch on the fallen angels.

²⁵ 1 *Apology*, 6. The mention of the prophetic spirit after the angels is possibly an interpolation. See Turmel, *Histoire des dogmes* (1932), 168–170.

²⁶ Justin's imagination seems to have been occupied with a dedicatory inscription to the ancient divinity Semo Sanctus. But did he find out for himself that Simon came to Rome in the time of Claudius?

²⁷ 1 *Apology*, 26, 58. In the latter passage Justin says of Marcion: "He is still teaching. . . . Many, accepting his doctrine as the only true, make a mock of us."

²⁸ 1 *Apology*, 35, 48. The supposition has been made by some that Justin had in mind the apocryphal Acts of Pilate and that he knew them. But he speaks of official and authentic Acts, which he has not seen. The references to the registers of Quirinius and to the Acts of Pilate are conceived in identical terms.

²⁹ 2 *Apology*, 5–7. Here again Justin reproduces the Book of Enoch on the fallen angels and the bad demons.

³⁰ Cf. Rougier, *Celse*, 361–429.

³¹ An authentic and contemporary account of them is contained in the letter which the Lyonnaise community addressed for the purpose to the communities of Asia and Phrygia. A copy of it was carried, with letters of the martyrs concerning the Phrygian prophets (Montanism), to the bishop of Rome by the priest Irenaeus. The story of the martyrdoms is reproduced in part in Eusebius, v, 1–4.

³² We do not know whether Pothinus also came from Asia, but the fact that the account of the trials undergone at Lyons is addressed to the communities of Asia and Phrygia points in that direction.

³³ It was thus in all the persecutions, except that the accused in 64 do not seem to have been given the choice between death and apostasy.

³⁴ The manner in which they are characterized in the letter (Eusebius, v, 1, 48) merits attention: "Those who never had a trace of faith, nor any feeling of the new marriage garment (Matthew xxii, 11–13), nor thought of the fear of God, but who by turning back brought the Way into contempt."

NOTES TO CHAPTER VII

1 The Aramean formula is retained in 1 Corinthians xvi, 22. Revelation xxii, 20 echoes it in a translation. *Mar, marana* is the Aramean equivalent of κυρίος. This may be a title of honour and a term of politeness. In Christian usage it was a messianic title, a cult name giving divine attribute to its object.

2 On the meaning and consequences of this see throughout Bousset, *Kyrios Christos*.

3 *Maranatha* still appears in the Liturgy of the *Didache. Abba* (Father) came at some time into Christian usage (Mark xiv, 36; Romans viii, 45; Galatians iv, 6). It still retains *Amen*.

4 Because, in synagogal reading, the divine name *Adonai*, "Lord," was usually read in place of Jahveh, which it was forbidden to pronounce.

5 The whole chapter forms part of an instruction on the use of the flesh of animals sacrificed to idols. The position assigned to Jesus is that of a cult-lord, but the only true Lord in that category.

6 Psalm ii, 7, quoted in Acts xiii, 32–33, where it is the equivalent of Psalm cx, 1 in the argument of Acts ii, 34–36.

7 A strange feature is borrowed from the mystery religions in Revelation xix, 16: the title "King of Kings and Lord of Lords" is not only written on the mantle of the Christ but also tattooed on his thigh.

8 Fragment of the Gospel of the Hebrews quoted by Jerome, *De viris*, 2.

9 Certain cosmogonies, the Babylonian in the first instance, naturally place the creation of the world in the spring, creation being the myth of the new year.

10 1 *Apology*, 67, 7. The concluding remark about the instructions given by the risen Christ remind us less of Luke xxiv, 44–49 and Acts i, 2 than of the Apocalypse of Peter and of some of the gnostic gospels.

11 Under these conditions it seems impossible to maintain that the Sunday Easter was only introduced at Rome in the time of Anicetus, otherwise we should have to place the editing of the Gospels after that date (157–168).

12 See Dölger, *Sol salutis*, 98 ff. Evidence in Tertullian, *Apologeticum*, 16, 9 and in Clement of Alexandria, *Stromata*, vii, 7, this last inspired by 2 Corinthians iv, 6, where the symbolism is almost Justin's.

13 Cf. Hebrews vi, 4; x, 32. In 2 Corinthians iv, 4, 6 the φωτισμός may well refer to baptismal initiation.

14 Mark i, 8, 10; Matthew iii, 11, 16; Luke iii, 16, 22; John i, 31, 34; Acts i, 5.

15 R. Reitzenstein, *Die Vorgeschichte der Christlichen Taufe*, would make Christian baptism depend on the baptism of the Mandeans. There may be a relationship between the two, but the alleged dependence is quite unproved, seeing that the Mandean sect is much later than the birth of Christianity. The only sacrament of the Mandeans was a repeated baptism which should

be compared, in its repeatable character, with that of the Elchasites. It is, moreover, established that the ritual of Mandean baptism owed much to the ritual of the Syrian Nestorians. A common origin is presumable; but to bring all back, including the Christian eucharist, to Mandean rites, is pure wilfulness.

16 See the texts cited in note 15. Belief in Jesus as the Son of God passed through the following stages. In the first stage he was consecrated God's Son and Christ by his resurrection (Romans i, 4); in the second, the consecration was thrown back to his baptism (prevailing perspective of the Synoptics); in the third, it was further thrown back to his conception. The idea of the Christ as pre-existent was bound to end in proclaiming him Son of God from all eternity.

17 The trinitarian formula in Matthew xxviii, 19 was probably added at the canonical revision and Mark xvi, 16 at the final deutero-canonical revision. In Luke xxiv, 47 baptism is implied only, as it must have originally been in the text of Matthew. John iii, 22 represents Jesus as himself baptizing. But the statement is attenuated in iv, 2 and vii, 39.

18 If Jesus baptized he did so under the same conditions as John. Some writers would have us believe that Jesus separated from John because he attached no importance to baptism. A refinement of the imagination!

19 Mark vi, 32–34 and parallels. In Mark viii, 1–9 and Matthew xv, 32–39 there is a second multiplication of loaves which is a duplicate of the first. Mark's reason for admitting the duplicate is to make the first a type of Jewish-Christian initiation and the second of hellenist-Christian. In John vi, 51–58 (discourse on the bread of life) the symbolism of flesh and blood is brought into relation with the multiplication of the loaves (5–14).

20 "Gnosis" in the text.

21 1 Corinthians xi, 2, 17–34. This is a homogeneous instruction intended to order the Supper in keeping with the mystical conception announced in 24–25 and applied in 26–34. This instruction does not depend on the Gospels nor even on the gospel tradition, except in so far as the mystic conception of the Supper, linked to the mystic conception of redemption, is inserted into a framework, previously fixed, in which the Supper is in no sense a pascal meal but prefigures the festival of the elect in the Kingdom of God. The framework in question is also presupposed in the traditional accounts of the institution in the three Synoptics.

22 The integrity of Justin's text is subject to caution. The last line about Jesus crucified and the Spirit as the author of the prophecies, and the earlier mention of the Christ and the Spirit, may have been added for conformity to traditional practices. Cf. Turmel, *Histoire des dogmes*, ii, 169–170.

23 Literally "participating (incorporated) in the symbol of his death" and not "in the image of his death" as though the author were here teaching Docetism. The baptism of the Christ, not his death, is the image.

24 The mobility of the miraculous rock in the desert is a rabbinic tradition. Philo (*Legum alleg.*, ii, 36) says that the rock is "the wisdom of God" and the manna "word of God."

25 The mention of "mingled wine" after "water" is highly suspect (ποτήριον ὕδατος καὶ κράματος). It is probable that Justin means to describe a communion with bread and water, not with bread and wine. Cf. Harnack, *Brot und Wasser, die eucharist elemente bei Justin.* On communion without wine in Christian antiquity, see Lietzmann, *Messe und Herrenmahl,* 246, 249. Tatian and the encratites, Marcion also, celebrated without wine. What has been quoted above about communion in the desert (1 Corinthians x, 1–5) may well be in accord with that practice.

26 Turmel also suspects the mention of the Spirit in this passage. See note 22.

27 But Justin shows knowledge of the rendering of thanks by the prophets which, according to *Didache,* x, 5, might be prolonged at their discretion.

28 The prayer of thanksgiving simply indicated in the Gospels. In the time of Justin the communion required only the exercise of thanksgiving over the bread and wine; the words called "the words of institution" were introduced into the liturgy at a later date. (They are artificially introduced in the liturgy of Hippolytus.)

29 The spiritual powers who ruled the visible world and without whose knowledge the coming of the Son had been effected. We have seen the place which this piece of mythology holds in diverse parts of the New Testament.

30 This confirms what has been said in note 25 of Justin's knowing the communion without wine.

31 The words, "I will raise him up at the last day," have been added to the end of verse 54.

32 For that reason probably the explanation is addressed to the disciples, not to the people who, strangers to faith, are incapable of understanding it.

33 As already said, instruction on the communion comprises 1 Corinthians xi, 2, 19–34. It is intended to authorize the mystic communion and to substitute it, as a liturgical function, for the common meal, which the primitive Supper was, and at which real abuses might occur.

34 Mark xiv, 22–25; Matthew xxvi, 26–29; Luke xxii, 14–20 (but the end of verse 19, after "given for you," and verse 20 suggest interpolation).

35 There has been much dissertation about the meaning of the preposition ἀπό (before τοῦ κυρίου in verse 23), which need not exclude intermediaries between Jesus and the author of the story. But on the hypothesis of intermediaries, as the matter concerns an act of the Christ and not a plain teaching, we should expect περί rather than ἀπό. The author places the case of the Supper among the other παραδόσεις which the Corinthians have received from him. Are all these to be transformed into Gospel traditions passed on by the Galilean apostles? Moreover, whether it be tradition or private vision, the story as here given is not in the primitive Gospel.

36 The words "till he come" are indispensable for the balance both of the phrasing and the thought. There is no ground to regard them as interpolated.

37 Because Luke xxii, 19 originally contained these words only, there is no ground for recognizing (in excluding "this is my blood") "this is my body" as an authentic saying—a metaphor employed by Jesus to indicate the fate in store for him. None of our texts has the least suspicion of this metaphor. It is highly probable that the original text of Luke referred to a supper without wine, but having the same mystic sense as the supper with bread and wine. See *L'Evangile selon Luc*, 511–512.

38 It is evident that the parallelism of the "passover," that is, the whole festival meal, with the "cup" (verses 17–18) is artificially created.

NOTES TO CHAPTER VIII

1 Romans iii, 27–iv, 24, verse 25 being the transition to the gnosis developed in the following chapters. See above, the analysis of the Epistle, p. 253.

2 Romans v, 12, 18–19. The oracular style of this gnosis attests its relatively ancient character. In 14 we read that death reigned from Adam to Moses even in those who had not sinned by imitation—$\epsilon\pi\iota\ \tau\tilde{\omega}\ \delta\mu o\iota\dot{\omega}\mu a\tau\iota$ —of Adam's sin. We might translate, "in the manner of Adam's sin." Account must be taken of this meaning of the word for the interpretation of vi, 5, $\sigma\dot{\upsilon}\mu\phi\nu\tau o\iota\ \tau\tilde{\omega}\ \delta\mu o\iota\dot{\omega}\mu a\tau\iota\ \tauo\tilde{\upsilon}\ \theta a\nu\dot{a}\tau o\upsilon\ a\dot{\upsilon}\tauo\tilde{\upsilon}$, where there is no more question of an appearance of death (Docetism) than there is here question of an appearance of sin.

3 Genesis ii, 17; iii, 19. There is nothing whatever in this ancient text, taken as it stands, to suggest that death is the natural consequence of sin. Death results from the fact that, by the will of God, man has no part of the tree of life, the fruit of which nourishes the immortals.

4 *Leg. alleg.*, i, 31; *De opif. mundi*, 134. In Philo the celestial man is the ideal, divine and absolute type of humanity indicated in Genesis i, 27; the terrestrial man is the man of history, father of the human race, to which Genesis ii, 7 would refer.

5 As a slave is sold to his master.

6 The text does not mean that a non-earthly Christ has been crucified somewhere in the clouds by the "princes of the air," but that the "princes of this world" are responsible for the passion of Jesus, just as it is attributed in the Gospels to "the powers of darkness" (Luke xxii, 53), or to the "prince of this world," the devil (John xiv, 30). There is no more reason to substitute the devil for the "princes" of 1 Corinthians and to identify him with Marcion's demiurge.

7 Romans viii, 18–27. The whole of this passage differs in style from that of the context; rather ponderous prose in which there is no parallelism; viii, 28 joins on quite naturally to 17.

8 Differing in this respect from Romans v–vi, where the gnosis may borrow Biblical language here and there but not as specific quotations;

doubtless because it is being developed on a system of its own and not as a commentary on particular texts.

9 It would be better to translate, or rather to transcribe, "by which he made even the *aeons*," but without taking this word in the full gnostic sense. The word belongs to the gnostic vocabulary, and has a meaning analogous to that of gnosis.

10 The text (Psalm viii, 6) says: "Thou hast made him but little inferior to Elohim," or "to the Elohim."

11 Hebrews vii, 1–2. "King of Righteousness" is the author's etymology of Melchisedec. The original may well have meant the god "Sedec is my King" (compare Adonizedec, "Sedec is my Lord," name of a king of Jerusalem in Joshua x, 1). Salem is understood by the author in its etymological sense. Very probably it refers to Jerusalem.

12 vii, 14. The author reasons as though Melchisedec had no real ancestors and never died. But the point of interest for us lies in the author's intention to ignore the earthly origin of Jesus.

13 ἐξ Ἰούδα ἀνατέταλκεν.

14 καθ' ὁμοιότητα helps us to understand ὁμοίωμα in Romans vi, 3–6.

15 xi, 2–40. We are even told (3) that "by faith the aeons fell into order at the word of God and the visible was not made of things that appear." This, though hardly intelligible to us, corresponds to what was said in the preamble i, 2 (see note 9 above). We would say that eternal ideas are realized in the visible world; but, to our author, the eternal ideas, as such, are just as real, if not more real, as they are when visibly externalized.

16 Cf. ix, 11–12, and the prayer *Supplices* in the Roman canon of the Mass. The Epistle to the Hebrews, which has sometimes been said to be indifferent to the Eucharist, if not to oppose it, is on the contrary full of eucharistic symbolism. We read (x, 10) that "we were sanctified by the offering" made once for all "of the body of Jesus Christ," by "the blood of the covenant" (x, 29).

17 The Peratae used the same expression—"in him all the pleroma judged good to dwell" (*Philosophoumena*, v, 2). In our next chapter the gnostics will be speaking to us again about the pleroma. The term means—God and the spiritual world as it subsists in God and forms his plenitude. The concept is founded on the idea of emanation from the source and return to it. The application of it to the Christ has never been fully and openly made by Christianity, where it has been rather compressed than developed, especially in the theology of the Latin Church. Two parallel strophes may be distinguished in the quoted passage (15–17, 18–20).

18 The conception is at once physical and theological. The στοιχεῖα are the principal parts of the cosmos and the four elements thought to constitute all bodies; but they are also the astral spirits on whom all parts of the cosmos, including humanity, were held to depend. (See Toussaint, *L'Epître de S. Paul aux Colossiens*, 137–146.)

19 The Divinity, or the divine world, being, as it were, externalized in the Christ, who is the true pleroma.

²⁰ The word πεπληρωμένοι plays with "pleroma." The literal translation would be "pleromed"—introduced into the pleroma.

²¹ We get a glimpse of what this catastrophe of the pleroma may have meant in the thought of this Christian writer; but one would like to know what the catastrophe meant—for there certainly was one—in the system which the gnosis of our Epistle opposes, while yet imitating it.

²² See above, p. 255.

²³ The meaning is that believers are parts in an invisible pleroma whose radiance is continually obstructed by the visible world in the condition to which it has come after its perversion by the "principalities" whom the Christ has conquered.

²⁴ Literally "the body." The real substance of the true mystery, which is the true salvation, is in the pleroma-Church, which is the body of the Christ.

²⁵ Unintelligible passage. Guided by verse 23 perhaps we may read verse 18 simply: ἐν ταπεινοφροσύνῃ καὶ ἐθελορησκίᾳ τῶν ἀγγέλων.

²⁶ The word ἐμβατεύων is a word of the mystery-language denoting the "first step" of initiation.

²⁷ στοιχεῖα. See note 18.

²⁸ Terms borrowed from the mystery the author is attacking.

²⁹ Prone to exaggeration as Paul was he can hardly have said that the Gospel in his time had been preached to "every creature under heaven." Cf. the spurious ending of Mark (xvi, 15), where we find the same formula.

³⁰ In some circles Jahveh Sabaoth was identified with Zeus Sabazios. On the origin of this Epistle see p. 26.

³¹ The name in question is "Lord," κύριος, a word of the Jahveh-cult. It is not the name "Jesus" which is above every name. Moreover, it is the name "Lord" that stands out in the concluding confession. The name "Jesus" corresponds to the abasement of the Christ, and "Lord" to his exaltation.

³² Verse 25 may be intended by the author in a spiritual sense and 28 a comment in terms of the common belief (see Le quatrième Evangile, 214). The descent into Hades is an old mythological theme which has undergone various transformations in the theologies. Ishtar in Babylonian mythology goes down to bring back Tammuz; the vegetation gods, who die and revive, also descend into Hades and return. Later the myth was sublimated. We have seen how the descent is treated in Philippians; there it becomes the descent of a celestial being into an inferior world. In some gnostic systems an aeon falls out of the pleroma and has to be ransomed. The descent of the Christ to the abode of the dead makes contact on one side with this old mythology.

³³ Romans x, 6, 7; Ephesians iv, 9–10 mention the descent only, without speaking of the Christ's activity among the dead. Matthew xxvii, 51–53 seems to imply the descent without definitely adopting it.

³⁴ Dialogue, 72. The Jeremiah text is quoted by Irenaeus to the same purpose, Apostolic Preaching, 78; Heresies, iv, 22. Ignatius, Magnesians, ix, 2,

says that Jesus went to raise the prophets because they had been his disciples in spirit. Hermas, *Parable*, ii, 16, has the dead evangelized by the apostles, not by the Christ.

35 On this point see Harnack, *Marcion*, 170.

36 It was early remarked that the Logos is called $\theta\varepsilon\delta\varsigma$ not $\delta\ \theta\varepsilon\delta\varsigma$. He is divine but not God absolutely.

37 To get the balance of the thought and the rhythm the words $\delta\ \gamma\acute{\varepsilon}\gamma o\nu\varepsilon\nu$ should be made part of verse 4, as many ancient witnesses do, instead of joining them to 3, where they have no reason to be.

38 Everything lives by the Logos and in the Logos. Recall the pleroma, note 17 above.

39 $\kappa\alpha\tau\acute{\varepsilon}\lambda\alpha\beta\varepsilon\nu$ can be taken in the double sense of "understand" and "contain" (or stop).

40 Genesis i, 2. The darkness floating over the Abyss is here one of the elements in the primal chaos and has nothing of the moral meaning attached to the darkness of John i, 5, where darkness is the equivalent of evil, as in the religion of Zoroaster.

41 John xii, 31; xiv, 30; xvi, 11. The "prince of this world" has the function of the "principalities" and "powers," spoken of in the Epistles; but his character is perceptibly different. He did not originally belong to the pleroma and can never have been a part of it.

42 John viii, 44. This passage defines the nature of the devil, "a homicide from the beginning," "liar and father of lies," in whom truth is not. There is no question of his initial fall: he has always been as we find him to-day. See *Le quatrième Evangile*, 299–301.

43 John i, 9–12. All the references to John the Baptist (6–8, 15) appear to have been added to the poem of the incarnate Logos: ditto the last member of verse 13. "Those who believe in his name" explains the preceding line of the poem and the plural of the verbs in verse 13 (in the traditional text) agrees with the explaining line.

44 The reading $\delta\varsigma \ldots \acute{\varepsilon}\gamma\varepsilon\nu\nu\acute{\eta}\theta\eta$ in place of $\delta\iota \ldots \acute{\varepsilon}\gamma\gamma\varepsilon\nu\acute{\eta}\theta\eta\sigma\alpha\nu$ is that of Irenaeus and Tertullian and Justin seems to read it so. This verse refers quite naturally to the birth of the Logos in time, his appearance in human form, but would come in very awkwardly if understood of the birth of believers, of which, however, the divine sonship of Jesus is the prototype. See *Le quatrième Evangile*, 101–104.

45 The word "and we saw his glory, glory like that which an only begotten son might take from his father" is an irrelevant intrusion which arrests the development of the sentence and breaks the rhythm. It is in the manner of 1 John i, 1.

46 This "plenitude" is not the pleroma of gnosis—and the point is worthy of note as marking the relations of our Gospel to religious doctrines of the time—but explains what has just been said of the Logos (verse 14) as "full of grace and truth," what is now added being the direct sequel to this assertion.

47 Many interpreters, reluctant to think that the word "grace" in this

formula can be taken in its proper sense of benefit, but with two different objects—since, according to the context (14 and 17), grace is eternal life, the objective gift of salvation—deem it possible to translate not "grace (eternal life) for grace (gift of the Law)" but "grace upon grace," that is, superabundance of salvation. But the following lines, which are explanatory, favour the first interpretation, to which the Johannine language is not repugnant. It is only in the gnosis of Paul's Epistles that the Law cannot be spoken of as a "grace," or divine favour, in the ordinary sense of the word.

48 Cf. the "invisible God" of Colossians i, 15.

49 This is the meaning of i, 13–14 even if we do not admit the reading (ὅς ἐγγενήθη) of Irenaeus and Tertullian. None the less the Son, in the body of the Gospel, is conceived to pre-exist, as Son, to his incarnation in the flesh.

50 The passages in our Gospel which speak of the resurrection of the dead in the strict sense of the formula, that of rising up after death and burial, are probably the insertions of an editor. They are v, 28–29; vi, 29, 40, 44, 54.

51 The author of the Epistle has in view specially xix, 34, water and blood issuing from the side of Jesus when pierced by the soldier's lance. Misunderstanding of the spirit of both our Gospel and the Epistle reaches its limit in those who have imagined that decomposition of the blood might have produced what looked like a flow of blood and water, or that the decomposition might have been invented to prove against Marcion that the blood of Jesus was real. See *Le quatrième Evangile*, 492.

52 Cf. vii, 39.

53 In Matthew i, 16 and Luke iii, 23 we can see editorial artifice to bring the genealogies into accord with the idea of virgin conception.

54 See Bacon, *Studies in Matthew*, 151–164.

55 Cf. Bacon, 33–35.

56 Acts i, 3–11. This preamble, artificially attached to the prologue (1–2), which has been mutilated and interpolated for that purpose, gives the impression of being a résumé or extract cut out from a more complete and developed story closely analogous if not identical with what we read in the Apocalypse of Peter.

57 The scene is analogous to that of Acts in what concerns the revelation on a mountain, but the sketching more cursory.

58 The background the same as in Acts i, 3–11 but the source document is more systematically rearranged.

59 Débris of the same traditions elaborated in another way.

60 The resemblance to Acts i, 3–11 is closer, in the more developed form of the ending of Mark made known by a fifth-century manuscript recently discovered.

61 Cf. Bacon, 148–150.

62 Bacon, 151. The theme has been studied by Gressmann and Norden.

63 Bacon, 153. The theme of the star is taken up in the Ignatian Letters

(Ephesians, 19) but not in direct relation with Matthew ii, 2, 7, 9–10, as we might hastily conclude. For the first statement made is that the birth of the Christ was unknown to "the prince of this world," and that the Lord was revealed "to the worlds" (aeons) by the star which eclipsed all other stars, destroyed magic and every bond of iniquity—which can only be understood of the Christ glorified in his resurrection.

64 See *La quatrième Evangile*, 144; Bacon, 150–151. The Feast of the Epiphany was originally Dionysiac.

65 Notably Lidzbarski, *Mandäische Liturgien*, 1920, etc.

66 The chief advocate of what may be called panmandeanism was R. Reitzenstein, *Der Vorgeschichte der christlichen Taufe*, 1929, etc.

67 On the presence of this instruction in the Marcionite collection, see Harnack, 87.

68 Hermas, *Vision*, i, 2, 4; ii, 1–3, 4.

69 2 Clement, 14, 1–2 (cf. Ephesians i, 22–23); 3–5 (cf. 1 Corinthians ii, 9).

70 Revelation xxi, 9–10. Our homilist develops the metaphor into an eternal type which, spiritual in itself, comes to sensible form in the flesh of the Christ and in his followers, who themselves are his flesh.

71 *Magnesians*, 4; 6–7 (cf. Trallians, 2–3); 13; Trallians, 6–7.

NOTES TO CHAPTER IX

1 With de Faye, *Gnostiques*, 430.

2 Origin, *C. Celsum*, v, 72. Celsus says that the Helenians took the name from their master Helenos. This must be a mistake of Celsus or of the source on which he depends.

3 Origen (*C. Celsum*, i, 57; vi, 15; *In Johannem*, xiii, 27) represents Dositheus as a Samaritan Messiah who appeared after Jesus and at the same time as Simon; in like manner Hegesippus in Eusebius, iv, 22, 5. In the apocryphal Clementines (*Homilies*, ii, 23; *Recognitions*, i, 54; ii, 8) Dositheus is said to have been a disciple of John the Baptist and to have succeeded him as leader of the sect he had founded and to have soon been supplanted by Simon.

4 This results from the testimony of Origen. See the preceding note.

5 The doctrine and the practice of the Simonians here meet the gnosis of Carpocrates, which we shall consider later on, and their Docetism constitutes an affinity to Marcion. The idea that the same divinity reveals himself, and may be worshipped under different names, is met with elsewhere.

6 Hippolytus used an addition called *Apophasis megale* which he attributed to Simon. This stands in the closest affinity to the system of Valentinus and may well not come from the Simonian sect at all.

7 Justin, 1 *Apology*, 26; Irenaeus, *Heresies*, i, 23; Eusebius, iii, 26, 1–2.

8 *Epistola Apostolorum* (ed. Schmidt, 1919).

9 Hegesippus (in Eusebius, iv, 22–27) mentions the Satornilians after the Basilideans.

10 On all these sects see de Faye, 189, 202, 349–354, 444–446.

11 See Clement of Alexandria, *Stromata*, ii, 3, 10; iii, 1, 3–4; iii, 2. Clement gives extracts from περὶ δικαιοσύνης.

12 Irenaeus, *Heresis*, i, 25.

13 On Valentinus see Irenaeus, *Heresies*, i, 1–6 and 11; *Philosophoumena*, vi, 2.

14 Ignatius, *Magnesians*, 8, 2, doubtless alludes to Sige when he says that Christ is the eternal Logos, who does *not* proceed from Silence (reading of the Greek MSS.).

15 It is not easy to find one's way through this system which has doubtless come down to us with retouchings. Inconsistence and duplication may well have existed in the original. But as there are three Saviours (Horos, Christos and the aeon Jesus) and two Wisdoms (Sophia and Hacamoth) we may suppose (invoking the résumé in Epiphanius, *Heresies*, xxxi, 4, where there seems to be only one Saviour) that the system was originally constructed on the fall of Sophia who assumed the part of Hacamoth, and on a scheme of redemption simplified to that extent (Bousset, *Gnosis*, 342). Even so the authentic quotations in Clement are enough to show that Valentinus did not construct his system with much regard to modern notions of probability.

16 *Stromata*, iii, 7, 59. Clement says elsewhere (vi, 8, 71) that Jesus was ἀπαθής. The Gospel of Peter (*Fragment*, verse 10) seems to say the same. Perhaps the Gospel of the Egyptians started this doctrine.

17 In the fragment of a homily quoted by Clement, iv, 13, 69, Valentinus addresses the initiates of his sect as follows: "You are immortal from the beginning"—that is, by nature—"you have challenged death"—in your human bodies—"that you might conquer death and that death might die in you and by you. So then, when you put the world to flight and scatter its deceitful elements without scattering the energies of your mind, you are the sovereigns of creation and masters of all perishable realities." We may see from this that Valentinus was not without eloquence nor even without philosophy. But Clement was not altogether mistaken in saying that Valentinus attributes to his "spirituals" the work of Jesus Christ himself. Between his "spiritual" mind and a stoic sage the difference is not great.

18 Cf. Burkitt, *Early Eastern Christianity* (1904), 156–192.

19 The quotations from Heracleon made by Origen in his commentary on the fourth Gospel furnish trustworthy and fairly complete information about this gnostic's doctrine. They have been collected by Brooke, *Texts and Studies*, i, 4 (1891).

20 Tertullian (*De Praescript*, 30) mentions the sum—two hundred thousand sesterces. On the letter of introduction see *Adv. Marcionem*, i, 1 and iv, 4.

21 See Harnack, *Marcion*.

22 Tertullian, *Adv. Marcionem*, i, 19: "Separatio legis et evangelii

proprium et principale opus est Marcionis, nec poterunt negare discipuli ejus quod in summo instrumento habent, quo denique initiantur et indurantur in hanc haeresim. Nam hae sunt *Antithesis* Marcionis, id est contrariae oppositiones, quae conantur discordiam evangelii cum lege committere, ut ex diversitate sententiarum utriusque instrumenti diversitatem quoque argumententur deorum."

23 Tertullian, *Adv. Marcionem*, i, 14: "Mellis et lactis societatem qua suos infantat . . . " The same usage among the Naassenes is attested by *Philosophoumena*, v, 8, and is found again in the liturgy of Hippolytus.

24 According to *Philosophoumena*, vii, 31, a certain disciple of Cerdo, named Prepon, made matter into a third principle beside the two gods.

25 *Adv. Marcionem*, iv, 2: "Ex iis commentatoribus quos habemus, Lucam videtur Marcion elegisse, quam caederet."

26 1 Clement, 47. The reference is to 1 Corinthians i, 10–12: "The epistle of the blessed Paul, the apostle, which he *first* wrote to you at the beginning of the Gospel." A little further on we find a paraphrase, without reference to the hymn of charity (xiii, 1–7). To make this hymn depend on Clement is a gross misconstruction alike of the hymn and of the Clementine letter. If Clement is in nowise inspired, for his doctrine, by the salvation gnosis contained in the Epistles, there were many others like him who wrote after the formation of the canon.

27 In the third century Marcionism was still formidable enough for Origen to be at pains to refute it. At the time of Epiphanius (*obit.*, 403) there were Marcionites in Rome, in Egypt as far as the Thebaïd, in Palestine, Arabia, Syria, Cyprus, and even in Persia. Perhaps the last adepts of the sect were absorbed into Manicheism which was closely akin to their doctrine. We may indeed consider Mani, who invoked the names of Zoroaster, Buddha and Jesus, as the last of the great gnostics. His religious doctrine had the same basis as the ancient Persian religion, later penetrated by Babylonian influence (Reitzenstein, *Das iranische Erlösungsmysterium*, 94).

NOTES TO CHAPTER X

1 This results from the close connexion between *Didache*, xv and xiv The *Didache* makes no mention of presbyters (elders)—priests—just as there is no mention of them in Philippians i, 1; in 1 Timothy iii, 2–13; in 1 Clement 42, 4; in Hermas, *Vision*, iii, 5, 1.

2 *Vision*, ii, 4, 3. The difficulty of identifying the Clement of Hermas with the author of the so-called Epistle of Clement would be insurmountable if the composition of this letter is dated in the reign of Domatian (81–96), but there would be no difficulty if the letter is not earlier than 125–135. We should then conclude that neither the Clement of the Epistle and of Hermas, nor the Hermas of *The Shepherd* were disciples of the apostles, and that there is no mention of them in the New Testament.

3 See *Vision*, iii, 5, 1, a curious passage which still takes the word

"apostle" in the wide sense of an itinerant preacher, but shows the importance attached to the presbyteral episcopate by giving it prior place to the teaching apostle and to the teaching prophet.

4 *Vision*, ii, 4, 2–3; iii, 1, 8 ("presbyters"). *Vision*, ii, 2, 6; iii, 9, 7 ("the heads of the Church")—compare Hebrews xiii, 7, 17, 24 and 1 Clement i, 3; 21, 6. *Vision*, ii, 4, 3 ("the presbyters presiding over the Church").

5 *Vision*, iii, 9, 7–10. The same persons are aimed at in *Parable*, viii, 7, 4–6, as "faithful and good men but given to jealousy about preferments and honours, and all completely in bondage to the folly of striving for the first place and for honours."

6 Recall the testimony of Justin, 1 *Apology*, 65, 67, quoted above.

7 Compare "the holy vine of David" in *Didache*, 9, 2.

8 In 1 *Apology*, 8 Justin says of the only God what Marcion was saying about the demiurge: that he extracted the world "from unformed matter." If Justin did not believe that matter was eternal, he does not seem to have asked himself whence it came.

9 In contrast to the Paul of 1 Corinthians vii, the Paul of the Pastorals recommends marriage in positive terms (cf. 1 Timothy ii, 15; v, 14; Titus ii, 4).

10 Irenaeus (*Heresies*, i, preface) and Tertullian (*De Praescriptione*), without prejudice to the authenticity of the passage, apply it to Valentinus. Tertullian applies the passage recommending marriage (1 Timothy iv, 2–3) to Marcion. Cf. 2 Timothy ii, 14; iii, 7.

11 It will be noted that the distinction between spiritual and psychic is clearly laid down in 1 Corinthians ii, 10–16. In the sequel (iii, 1–3) the psychics are said to be "carnal." We have seen above that Valentinus had three classes—pneumatics, psychics and hylics (material).

12 The private meeting of Polycarp and Marcion of which Irenaeus speaks (*Heresies*, iii, 3, 4) might have taken place at Rome. If Polycarp died in 166 he might have come to Rome about 160.

13 Title of a work of Irenaeus mentioned by Eusebius, v, 26, and preserved only in an Armenian version recently (1934) discovered.

14 *Exposition*, 3 (from the Italian translation by Faldati).

15 On this point see especially Bacon, *Studies in Matthew*, 18–23.

16 See also Bacon, 32–36.

17 See Bacon, *Is Mark a Roman Gospel?* (1919); cf. *Revue d'histoire et de littérature religieuses*, 1920, 427–430.

18 There is high probability that John xxi, 15–23 (the commission to Peter) was written in Asia for the satisfaction of the Roman community (see *Le quatrième Evangile*, 69–71). Again, in the Book of Acts the forced introduction of John's name into headlines (iii, 1, 3–4, 19; viii, 6), and the apparently forced silence kept about the martyrdom of John in xii, 2, where only the martyrdom of James is mentioned, may well have been a concession made by Rome in favour of the Ephesian legend of the beloved disciple. (See *Les Actes des Apôtres*, 55, 218–223, 227, 246, 368, 481–484.)

19 See *Les Actes des Apôtres*, 669–680, 777.

20 See especially 1 Clement, 26, 2 (Hebrews i, 3–4). It is certain that Clement uses the Epistle to the Hebrews, but he does not quote it as having canonical authority. As to his other quotations, he refers to 1 Corinthians as historical evidence and not precisely as an officially sanctioned writing.

21 *De Pudicitia*, 20: "Et utique receptior (more widely accepted) apud ecclesias epistola Barnabae illo apocrypho (forbidden for public use) Pastore moechorum."

22 *Heresies*, iii, 11, 9; *Exposition*, 99–100 (Faldati's translation, 168–9).

23 The canon of Muratori justifies the exclusion of *The Shepherd* on the grounds that the collection of prophets is complete in the Old Testament and that, not being apostolic, it cannot be admitted into the New.

24 1 *Apology*, 6.

25 Text after Lietzmann, *Symbolstudien*, xiv, in *Zeitschrift für* N.W., 1927, p. 91.

26 Πιστεύεις εἰς Χριστὸν Ἰησοῦν, τὸν υἱὸν τοῦ θεοῦ, τον γεννηθέντα διὰ πνεύματος ἁγίου ἐκ Μαρίας τῆς παρθένου.

27 Cf. Lietzmann, *art. cit.*; Hennecke, 575.

28 Καὶ υἱός σου ἀπεδείχθη ἐκ πνεύματος ἁγίου καὶ παρθένου γεννηθείς. Cf. Lietzmann, *Messe*, 158.

29 Streeter, *loc. cit.*; Bacon, 58.

30 The interpretation given by Bacon (55) of the passage in Tertullian, *De Pudicitia*, where he says that *The Shepherd* has been judged apocryphal and spurious, "ab omni concilio ecclesiarum," seems rather forced. The reference is not to a succession of set Councils, but simply to unanimous agreement.

31 The word χειροτονήσατε here translated "choose" does not necessarily imply the laying on of hands, but that meaning may be supposed.

32 1 Timothy iii, 1–13; iv, 14; v, 1, 19; 2 Timothy i, 1–6; ii, 24–26; iv, 18–20; Titus i, 5–9 (where the "presbyters" of 5 are individualized in the "bishop" of 7).

33 The Diotrephes of 3 John 9, even if he had no personal existence, is an historical type of the bishop with no liking for wandering preachers.

34 This should be taken as meaning a strict monogamy.

35 Nevertheless Philippi may have had as bishop the Valens who is said by Polycarp (*Epistle*, 11) to have made himself unworthy of his office (hypothesis of Delafosse, *Lettres de Ignace d'Antioche*, 33).

36 1 Clement, 42, 44. The language of the author of these passages is clearly not that of a man who had known the apostles and was writing only thirty years after the death of Peter and Paul.

37 Tertullian seems to have applied to the Marcionites in particular what he says of gnostics in general, *De Praescriptione*, 41.

Ante sunt perfecti catechumeni quam edocti. Ipsae mulieres haereticae quam procaces! . . . Ordinationes eorum temerariae, leves, inconstantes: nunc neophytos collocant, nunc saeculo obstrictos, nunc apostatas nostros . . . Itaque alius hodie episcopus, cras alius; hodie diaconus qui cras lector; hodie presbyter qui cras laicus: nam et laicis sacerdotalia numera injungunt.

38 In 172, according to the *Chronicle* of Eusebius; in 152, according to Hippolytus, *Heresies*, 48, 1. See the discussion of these dates in P. de Labriolle, *La Crise Montaniste*, 569. Maximilla died about 180, Montanus and Priscilla having previously disappeared. The date 172 may be a little too late; it is a question whether it originally referred to the outbreak of the movement or to some event which brought it to the attention of the communities.

39 Irenaeus and the martyrs of Lyons, without positively approving the saints of Phrygia, wished them not to be condemned. The attitude of Pope Eleutherus seems to have conformed to the views of Irenaeus. Tertullian, *Adv. Praxeam*, 1, speaks of a bishop of Rome who, on the point of giving express recognition to the Montanist prophesyings, was circumvented by the logician Praxeas, so that he suppressed the letter of approval which he had already written. It was probably round Zephyrinus (198–217) in the first years of his episcopate that Praxeas wove his plots.

40 Approximate date. The attitude of the bishop of Rome to Montanism seems to have contributed, at least indirectly, to the secession of Tertullian.

INDEX

ALFRED LOISY

THE ORIGINS OF
THE NEW TESTAMENT

(Les Origines du Nouveau Testament)

AUTHORIZED TRANSLATION FROM THE FRENCH

BY

L. P. JACKS

INTRODUCTION

THIS modest essay on the origins of the New Testament is an explanatory complement to the volume published in 1933 under the title: *La Naissance du Christianisme*—the Birth of the Christian Religion.[1] We propose to resume the examination, as a whole and with greater precision in detail, of documents born in a realm almost outside that of history and written without any care for historical truth as it is now understood. A long-established Christian tradition would exclude these documents from control by scientific and historical research, at least as to the substance of their contents, treating it as almost beyond the scope of such researches and in the main defying appreciation by their method. There are still some who would so exclude them entirely.

A preliminary question which we have not directly attacked in our former publications and which creed-bound interests tend naturally to keep alive, whether consciously or not, the question namely of the supernatural quality in the Bible, must first be probed to the bottom, in order that the rights of criticism in this field may be established without other restriction than that of the rules proper to itself. The question turns on an idea which may be taken in two senses—the idea of the supernatural—and involves a real equivocation. We are well aware that criticism is not capable of solving every problem; but neither are we ignorant that the investigations of the critic cannot have, ought not to have and, in fact, have not any limits save those of its own natural resources. No authority has the right to impose conclusions upon the critic in anything that falls within the field of his experience, the field namely of everything susceptible of methodical observation in the system of universal reality.

When the question of the supernatural has been clearly answered the field will be open for the discussion of the essential theme of this book, namely the progressive evolution of the Christian teaching, or catechesis, in all the variety of its forms. These include: (1) the Gospel or Message of Jesus and the primitive teaching about "the last things," or eschatological catechesis,

---

[1] Two earlier complements are: *Le Mandéisme et les origines Chrétiennes* (1934); and *Remarques sur la littérature épistolaire du Nouveau Testament* (1935).

as developed in Christian apocalyptic; (2) the testimony, said to be traditional, concerning the origin of the canonical Gospels; (3) study of the internal evidence afforded by these books, in respect of the Gospel according to Mark, the Gospel according to Matthew, the twin-born books to Theophilus, which afterwards became the Gospel according to Luke and the Acts of the Apostles; the Gospel according to John; (4) the contribution of the Epistle-literature to the elaboration of the primitive catechesis of the Last Things, and the testimony rendered by this literature to the preparation and the fixation of the collection known as the Canon of the New Testament.

Finally it will behove us to crown this long analysis by a general synthesis and interpretation of the conclusions to which we have been led. In this we shall see clearly how the formation of the literature, to which the name "New Testament" is given, was conditioned by the evolution of Christian propaganda and became, so to say, stabilized at the very time when the Church called catholic was constituted and declared the guardian of what it had resolved to uphold as the authentic tradition of Christianity, a tradition which it opposed to the spreading floods of *gnosis*, thenceforth to be condemned as heresy. A great achievement of humanity was here, and not a chain of miracles; an upsurge of spiritual life, but defective in its manifestations, as all things human are. But, being spiritual in origin and essence, it brought the supernatural to light in the only sense in which we of this age are able to conceive the supernatural and to regard it as playing a real part in history.

Doubtless there are some who will judge such a work to be singularly inopportune in present circumstances. The same has been said of some of the author's earlier works which were highly unwelcome to a good many people. Perhaps this book will be equally unwelcome. Whoever has enough goodwill to see in it, before all else, a rather new programme for the research that is needed in this field, and is far from being completed, will exactly discern the intention of its author. As to those who would deem it superfluous, superficial and preposterous, we shall content ourselves with supposing that they have not yet found leisure to consider the true character and infinite complexity of the subject under treatment.

6

CONTENTS

Chapter I

THE BIBLE AS SUPERNATURAL

ORTHODOX defenders of Scripture, especially its Catholic defenders, are wont to charge independent critics with lacking intuitive perception of the supernatural which, according to their accusers, shines out in the Scriptures, especially in the New Testament, thus creating a privileged position for the books sacred to Christians and clothing them with authority beyond the range of discussion. These, they say, are divine books alike by their origin and character, replete with truth for all time; records of clearly miraculous events, by which God, from the beginning of time, showed forth the salvation of humanity in signs, prepared it, and at last made it effectual.

In all this, a double meaning, an equivocation, is clearly apparent, of which both the orthodox apologist and the over-confident critic seem alike to be the victims. There are two "supernaturals." The one, which we shall designate as magical, is found existing in all religions and mythologies, as well as in fairy tales; in this kind of supernatural the Jewish and Christian Scriptures have their full share, both in their content and in the orthodox tradition which interprets them. The other, which we shall designate as moral and spiritual, is manifested by the religions of humanity in marvellous outbursts of spiritual life, more notable in some religions, less in others, but outstandingly intense in Judaism and Christianity and conferring on these two an eminent place in the moral evolution of mankind. This supernatural reality is overlooked by those extremists who can see in religion, and in its beliefs and practice, nothing more than the transmission of time-honoured and oppressive absurdities. But this supernatural, while not a miracle in the vulgar sense of the word, belongs to a higher realm than the miraculous. It is the only supernatural worthy of the name and the only kind whose real existence can be confidently affirmed. And theologians who, thinking to defend it, confuse it with miraculous magic, understand it but ill and serve it no better.

9

DIVINE AUTHORSHIP

The idea of books entirely God-made, but written in the languages of men, in the native dialects of particular peoples and in the idiom of given times, an idea widely spread in the ancient world and retained in Christian orthodoxy, is inconsistent and self-contradictory. Professional authors are relatively new-comers in the history of our race. But even if they were more ancient than they are, we can hardly imagine anything more indiscreet, not to say more flagrantly impious, than to put God among these worthies, where he has to be furnished with assistants, as though he could not dispense with them, to write down what he would say and attend to the publication of his works. Theologians tax their wits to explain how God can be, in any real sense, the author of books which he has neither written himself nor dictated word by word. Their explanation is that he *suggested* them. How do they know that? Do they really understand what they are saying?

Had they taken the pains to look into the matter, without thought of axes to be ground, they would have seen that the books themselves make not the slightest claim to the divine origin attributed to them by the theologians, but are in fact made up, in the human manner, of tradition and teaching; of rules political, social and ritual; of liturgical chants; of oracles deemed prophetic (not uncommon in the ancient world, and of which we should be hard put to it to find the fulfilment); of collections of moral precepts such as we find among all nations; and of a group of myths, clearly recognizable as such, to account for the origin of the world and of mankind. All of which has undergone an age-long process of glossing and amalgamation clearly due to human initiative, and not even to be thought of as proceeding from God's initiative in any part or stage of it. What anthropomorphism could be more naïve than that which counts the authorship of books among the attributes of God?

These remarks, it will be said, apply to the Old Testament only. They apply equally to the New. A long, slow process brought the Gospels to their present form without any sign of divine initiative at the beginning or the end or at any point between the two; at a given time they were selected, from among many, by the Church authorities and the text of their content finally determined. The same is true of the Acts of the Apostles. It is well worthy of note that the author of the third Gospel and of Acts, who wrote the prologues to Theophilus, assumes full responsibility for his work, for his method and for the object he has in view. The apostolic Epistles, authentic or not, are personal works called forth by particular occasions. Moreover a considerable part of them are forgeries, for which it would be unseemly enough to make God directly responsible. And what of the Book of Revelation—the Apocalypse of John? The best that can be said of it is that for centuries men have taxed their wits to find in it a meaning which is *not* there, for the simple reason that the meaning which *is* there was immediately contradicted by the course of events. Alas, this glowing prophecy was not fulfilled. Who can believe that it came entire from God? In short, the idea of God as author of books is a myth, if ever there was one, and a myth redolent of magic. A book written by the hand of man and filled throughout with the light of God is as inconceivable as a square circle. The books reputed all divine are simply not filled with truth from beginning to end—far from it! They contain as many errors as books of their kind, written when they were, could be made to hold.

To this notion of divine authorship, so artificial and fragile, the Church committed her future and compromised it in so doing. Persuaded that her sacred books were filled with truth for all time she has not hesitated to oppose them to the scientific movement of our age. We know what has come of that. Everyone has heard of Galileo's adventure and knows what it meant. Meanwhile the Church continues to equivocate; even on the affair of Galileo which, nevertheless, is transparently clear. She is still convinced, and would have it believed, that her sacred books contain nothing contrary to truth about the order of the universe, and that the Bible, though knowing nothing about the matter, does not contradict it, but only uses the common language of mankind which speaks of things as they seem to be. Can she really believe that by a subterfuge of this kind, which amounts to charging the Scriptures with ignorance, she is really safeguarding their divine authority? Is there any denying that the first chapters of Genesis profess to give a true account of the creation of the

11

world, the origin of humanity up to the Deluge and the genealogy of the peoples? All that is unadulterated myth, the babblings of humanity's childhood, but not unmingled with sublimity. If God is the responsible author of the story he must have been ignorant of the constitution of the universe which, on the orthodox hypothesis, he had created, and equally ignorant of the long and confused pre-history of the race which he had brought into being and established on the earth to serve him.

Not only at this starting point, but along the whole line of historical and literary criticism, the traditional doctrine is in complete collapse. To begin with, consider the question which concerns the authenticity of the documents. Since God is their author the divine guarantee covers their attribution to the particular scribes whose names they carry. What an embarrassment is thereby erected by the Pentateuch alone! The attribution of this collection to Moses is attested by Jewish tradition, but equally, it would seem, by the New Testament and by the authority of the Christ himself who, in a certain passage of the fourth Gospel (John v, 46), declares that Moses wrote concerning him. And yet it is the almost unanimous verdict of critics that the oldest sources from which the compilation is derived go no further back than the time of the Israelite monarchy, while the bulk of the cultural legislation contained in it is later than the Babylonian captivity. Not a page, one might even say not a line, can be traced to him whom the tradition of Israel and of the Christian Church regards as the founder of Jewish religion. To explain the divinity of the sources the Papal Commission of Biblical Study declared, in a memorable decree, that Moses had secretaries. The secretaries of Moses! A brilliant discovery, to be sure! But we have nothing to do with them since, if these interesting persons ever existed, we should have to admit that not a trace of their work has come down to us.

This, far from being a solitary case, is only one of the more conspicuous and significant. The case of Isaiah is also worth recalling. The book named after Isaiah as it appears in the Bible contains much besides the authentic oracles of the prophet who was contemporary with Ezechias. Notably one whole section, the last twenty-four chapters, were written, as all the evidence shows, either in presence of the conquest of Babylon by Cyrus or shortly afterwards. None the less they were reputed the work of Isaiah for the sole reason that in the process of copying the manuscript they were attached to the roll that had Isaiah's name on it. Speaking generally we may say that the oracles of the ancient prophets have been systematically completed and interpolated in the process of coming down to us. Has the veracity of God nothing to do with the false attribution of these additions to the authors of the original oracles?

The question assumes a more difficult aspect, if that be possible, when we turn to the books of the New Testament. Here all the writings have human authors who either name themselves or are expressly indicated by tradition. Everyone knows that the Church recognized and retained four Gospels respectively attributed to the apostle Matthew, to Mark (reputed a disciple of Peter), to Luke, who was a disciple of Paul, and to the apostle John. Now it is morally certain, and admitted by the majority even of moderate critics, that these attributions are, to say the least, approximative, the books not having been written all at one time by single hands nor given their present canonical form from the beginning. Many, moreover, are of the opinion that not one of the Gospels is the work of the apostolic person whose name it bears, and that the apostle John, in particular, had nothing whatever to do with writing the Gospel attributed to him. But, if God is their guarantee, his veracity demands that each of them be integrally the work of the author assigned by tradition. We shall return to these Gospels later on to find that their contents, no less than their presumed authenticity, are replete with difficulties for the apologists in question.

We have already mentioned the Acts of the Apostles, a book which, like the third Gospel, presents conditions somewhat peculiar. Alone among New Testament writings these two carry a dedication, of a well-known type in Greco-Roman antiquity. Luke was not the author of the dedications to Theophilus, the general prologue (Luke i, 1–4) forbidding us to include the author of it in the first Christian generation. Furthermore, the part of the prologue to Acts which has been preserved implies that the former book to Theophilus did not contain the birth stories and related only the *ministry* of the Christ up to the time of his death. Finally all the evidence shows that the second part

13

of the original prologue to Acts, n which the proper object of the book was stated by the original author, has been mutilated by a writer who understood that object in a different manner from the author to Theophilus and who, in consequence, had to reconstruct his book from beginning to end as, in fact, he has done. All this later writer has conserved of Luke's work is certain fragments of his memoirs of which the original author to Theophilus had made a fuller use. It follows that Luke wrote neither the third Gospel nor Acts. He wrote only certain passages of the latter book, and we are compelled to recognize at least two stages in the composition of both books. It would seem, however, that the veracity of God forbids us to observe and record such things, and obliges us to maintain that both books, in their canonical edition, are from the hand of Luke.

According to tradition Paul wrote fourteen Epistles and the veracity of God demands the belief that all are truly his. But the Epistle to the Hebrews is positively not from him; the second to Thessalonians is almost certainly apocryphal; so is the Epistle to the Ephesians; many hold that the Epistles to Timothy and to Titus, in their main contents, cannot be his. And we have already pointed out in another work[1] that there is much to be said against the full authenticity of the Epistles to the Romans, to the Corinthians, to the Galatians, to the Colossians. Here is a group of questions which the veracity of God forbids us even to raise.

As to the Catholic Epistles, there is strong reason to think that the Church deemed it necessary to include in the Canon, as pendant to Paul's Epistles, a number of others bearing the names of reputed apostolic persons other than he, notably Peter, John and the two "brothers of the Lord" James and Jude. Not one of these Epistles goes back to the first Christian age. Pseudo-James launches discreet polemic against the theory in Romans of justification by faith alone; pseudo-Jude crosses swords with the gnostics; pseudo-Peter, in the second Epistle, repeats the diatribe of pseudo-Jude and cites a collection of Paul's Epistles of which heretics are making wrong use—not as natural a proceeding as defenders of tradition would make out. For there is not a doubt that he was aiming at Marcion towards the middle of the second

---

[1] In *The Birth of the Christian Religion.*

century. Add to this that the author, at the beginning of the same Epistle, refers implicitly to the Apocalypse of Peter, composed towards the year 135; a supreme instance of false attribution, though the writing was held in credit by some of the Churches to the end of the second century. The second Epistle of Peter is a barefaced forgery. The first Epistle is not more authentic; it depends on the Pauline group and cannot be earlier than the second third of the second century. The three Epistles attributed to John were composed in the course of the same century to accompany the fourth Gospel when its claims were being pressed among the Asiatic Churches. They are no more the work of the apostle John than is the Gospel itself. But the veracity of God would give us no alternative to believing that all these apocryphal productions come from the persons whose names they bear. Need we add that the Book of Revelation is the work of a certain John who was not John the apostle?

We abstain from the cruelty of further insistence. He compromises God who makes him the author of written books.

MIRACULOUS MAGIC AS AN OPERATING CAUSE OF EVENTS

The compromising effect on traditional belief, due to confounding the supernatural with magic, is equally apparent when we consider the particular events for which magic is made responsible. We limit our remarks to a few essential points in the two Testaments.

The myth of creation in the first chapter of Genesis need not delay us for long. The creation, by the spoken word, of the different parts of the universe, childishly conceived as cut up into separate compartments, is an act of divine magic, which all the goodwill of its apologists will never succeed in bringing into harmony with the known facts of cosmic and terrestrial evolution. The wonder-story of Eden, with the creation of the first human pair and the commission of the first sin, older than the cosmic myth both in conception and structure, is also an obvious myth, a scene from the realm of enchantment where the imagination of adolescent mankind, just beginning to reflect, finds its playground. Whence comes death? is the question then asked. Imagination answers, surely death is something that need not have been; the first man and the first woman ate a strange fruit which their creator had forbidden them to eat. Among good tales here is one finely told. But nothing more.

Another such, mythological and purely pagan, is the story of the intercourse of the sons of God, the angels, with the daughters of men, of which were born the giants whose abominable conduct brought on the Deluge, a story no more worthy of belief when found in the Bible than when found in the old fables of Greece about the union of gods with mortal women, but adopted as true in both Epistles of Peter and in the Epistle of Jude.

As to the Deluge itself, it is beyond dispute that the myth was created in Lower Mesopotamia. The prototype of the Bible story has been found in the bricks of Nineveh and the priority of the Accadian text admits not the slightest doubt: another old fable which Israelite tradition has borrowed from ancient Mesopotamia and has little enough to do with the true history of mankind.

Then the Tower of Babel and the miraculous confusion of tongues, a miracle on the grand scale intended to explain the diversity of peoples, but pure fiction, explaining nothing. A genealogy of the nations which traces their descent from Adam through Noah is little more than a fantasy to smile at, whose sole historical interest lies in a crude chart, or something like it, of the peoples inhabiting the Eastern shore of the Mediterranean at the time the chart was made. Another instance of the mythological fiction to which all these prodigies are reducible.

Turning next to the origin of the Israelites we are not surprised, after what has gone before, to learn that this people also is descended from a single couple, Abraham and his wife Sarah, emigrants from Mesopotamia. Abraham and Sarah produced Isaac who had twin sons, Esau and Jacob, by his wife Rebecca, Esau or Edom, ancestor of the Idumeans; Jacob, finally called Israel, who begat of four wives twelve sons, fathers of the twelve tribes of Israel; the eleventh of these sons is sold by his brothers and carried off into Egypt where he became Pharaoh's chief-minister, in so much that on famine breaking out in Canaan, Jacob and his family migrate to the fertile lands of

Egypt, where they have various experiences; on arrival they are seventy in number; after several generations they become a great people multiplying at such a rate that the Egyptians become alarmed; the Pharaoh of the time who, we are told, knew not Joseph, gives orders to destroy all the Hebrew males as soon as born; but God, who has called Abraham out of Mesopotamia and promised the land of Canaan to his posterity, brings it to pass that the child of a certain Amram, of the tribe of Levi, is found by Pharaoh's daughter exposed in a wicker cradle on the Nile and brought up; this child is Moses; his brilliant career then follows; his flight into Midian and return into Egypt; his unloosing of plagues on Egypt by raising his magic wand which changes into a serpent; departure from Egypt of the chosen people under Moses and his brother Aaron; passage of the Red Sea which divides its waters to let the Israelites pass over and closes them again on Pharaoh's army. Then come forty years in the desert and the feeding of the people with manna and quails, and with water made by Moses to gush from the rock, ending with the departure of the host from the desert for the conquest of Canaan and the death of Moses on Mount Pisgah, whence he can see the land where Israel is to settle. Then comes the passage of the Jordan whose bed becomes dry for the march of the Israelites, and the capture of Jericho whose walls collapse at the sound of Israel's trumpets; the battle of Gibeon where Joshua makes the sun stand still that Israel may have time to complete the enemy's overthrow. After which Joshua proceeds at leisure to parcel out the conquered land among the tribes.

A splendid epic, from which, alas, history can glean hardly a particle of solid matter. Clearly enough its construction of Israel's genealogy is artificial. Peoples are not born in that way. The names, Abraham, Isaac, Jacob-Israel, certainly existed and each of these vocables must have originally corresponded to somebody or to something, but to whom, or to what, is not easily determined. Jacob, as everyone knows, won his name of Israel in a strange combat in which he got the better of God himself. His twelve sons are not simple individuals but types of heroes, divine or tribal. The patriarchal myths figure a peaceful occupation of Canaan and these are doubled, so to say, by myths of a conquest which, taken as they stand, are hardly less imaginative than the former. The adventures of Joseph make a noble story linking the two series of myths together, but nothing of it can be retained by the historian. That relations existed of old between the tribes and Egypt is beyond doubt, but what is here narrated of them never happened. It is to be noted that the legend cannot even give the name of the Pharaoh who exalted Joseph and welcomed his family, and is equally ignorant of the name of the Pharaoh who turned oppressor. Commentators are still cudgelling their brains to discover these names; they may continue to cudgel them to the end of the world but will never find what they seek. The Moses legend is a counterpart to the myth of the oppression and miraculous flight, which the different sources of the Pentateuch have adorned with prodigies enough and to spare. The least uncertain point of the Moses legend is its attachment to the sanctuary of Kadesh. If Moses ever existed it was at Kadesh that he gave out the law, near to the fountain of Judgment, and manipulated the casting of lots (*urim* and *thummim*) which seems to have traditionally belonged to Levi. The Book of the Covenant was not his work, but belongs to the time of the monarchy; neither was Deuteronomy which dates from the reign of Josias, if not from the first years of the captivity; nor the legislation known as Levitical which is less ancient than Deuteronomy. And not only is the authorship of these books none of his; it is improbable that he had any part in the migration of the tribes towards the land of Canaan. This movement had a character very different from that of a conquest achieved by one sweeping stroke. When exactly it began we cannot say and it was not completed before the establishment of the monarchy. Various movements of penetration have to be distinguished; one, from the South by the tribes of Judah, Simeon and Levi, of which that of Judah alone succeeded, the tribes of Simeon and Levi becoming exhausted in the course of it, while another thrust, by the Northern tribes, was made to the East and, in course of time, with more success. It is possible that Joshua played a leading part in the early battles, and that is all we can claim to know about him. Few persons nowadays can seriously believe that he caused the sun to stand still over Gibeon, which some chronicler inferred from what he read in a collection of heroic songs, the *Jashar* (Joshua x, 13). This chronicler, whether understanding or misunderstanding what he read, was clearly the dupe of his gift as a story-teller.[1]

Of the other Old Testament miracles we pause but for a moment over that of Jonah shut up for three days and three nights in the belly of a great fish, and while there even composing a hymn to the glory of the Lord. To question the historicity of this splendid story is doubtless impermissible, but belief in it is not easy. From the historical point of view it has the same guarantees as the adventures of Puss-in-boots or of Hop-o'-my-thumb.

We hasten on to the New Testament which is hardly less penetrated by magic than the Old. On the very threshold we meet an undeniable proof in the stories of the miraculous birth. Two genealogies confront us: the first in Matthew (i, 1–17) comes down from Abraham to Jesus; the second in Luke (iii, 23–38) goes up from Jesus to Adam. (As to the latter we have only to think for a moment on the degree of impossibility involved, in a genealogy of any individual belonging to the human race, which takes its departure from the origin of that race itself. For that reason alone the bare idea of such a list of ancestors belongs unquestionably to the realm of magic.) In the generations covered by both lists they disagree, and will never agree in spite of all the forced and ridiculous conjectures of their interpreters. Moreover—and this is the chief point to be noted—it is clear to all who open their eyes that they were invented to show that Jesus was descended from David through his father Joseph, the last name on the list. This, their original aim, is completely upset

---

[1] It seems probable that the original citation ended with the distich given in verse 12:

> Sun stand thou still over Gibeon
> And thou, Moon, over the valley of Ajalon,

the object of the apostrophe being different from what the writer of *Joshua* takes it to be. In the Greek version of 1 Kings viii, 53 we find a similar citation, with the reference, which seems to have alone preserved the complete text, as spoken by Solomon about the Temple. Reconstructed from the Greek text their meaning would be:

> "Jehovah has fixed the Sun's place in the heavens;
>   He bade the Sun take his stand beyond the darkness;
> I have built thee a house for thy habitation
>   In which thou shalt dwell month by month."

This refers to the passage of the sun through the signs of the Zodiac and is borrowed from a creation-poem. It was easy in the time when *Joshua* was written to make the sun stand still. Cf. *Iliad*, ii, 411; *Odyssey*, xxiii, 243.

by the introduction of the idea of the virgin conception at a later stage in the development of the story.

That is not all. The two stories, in their main features, have independent origins. That in the third Gospel seems to be a counterpart to a legend of John the Baptist, to which it has been joined on. It presents the parents of Jesus, already espoused, in their home in Nazareth when the angel Gabriel appeared on the scene—and need we say that the proceedings of angels do not impress the modern historian as very solidly guaranteed? Gabriel informs Mary, whose fiancé Joseph is said to belong to the house of David, that she will give birth to a son who will be the Messiah; as guarantee that the promise will be fulfilled he cites the case of Elisabeth whose miraculous pregnancy may well serve for testimony. Here comes a surcharge on the original text in the two verses which announce the virgin conception (Luke i, 34–35). Passing over the marvels which immediately follow and adorn the story, we come to the circumstance which brings Joseph and Mary from their home in Nazareth to Bethlehem, the city of David, in order that Jesus may be born there—the census for taxation ordered by Quirinius. Now the census of Quirinius did not take place before the year 6 of our era, and we are told that the whole affair happened in the time of Herod who died four years before our era began; whence results a difference of at least ten years between the birth of Jesus and the census of Quirinius. To this our hagiographer has paid no heed, and the exegetes labour in vain to put the matter right. We have no heart to dwell on the intervention of angels on the memorable birth-night to guide the shepherds to the cradle. Eight days afterwards the child is circumcised, at the end of forty taken to Jerusalem to be ransomed as a first-born; the aged Simeon prophesies concerning him; the venerable Anna likewise, and the parents return quietly to their home town of Nazareth. The legend is a work of art, and of next to no value as a record of historical happenings.

Luke's story, moreover, flatly contradicts the legend in Matthew, which is no less artificially constructed and no better founded than the other. In this Gospel the home of Joseph and Mary is not Nazareth, but Bethlehem, where they are living as an espoused couple, and it is at Bethlehem that the miraculous conception takes place, an angel explaining the matter to Joseph and quieting the misgivings which such an announcement could hardly fail to arouse. All this happens, so the hagiographer informs us, as the fulfilment of an oracle in Isaiah vii, 14, on which he puts a forced meaning—a point we shall not dwell upon, since a meaning, more or less forced, is put on all the Old Testament texts alleged to have their fulfilment in the New, a proceeding well in keeping with supernatural magic by forcing into texts meanings not naturally theirs. After this the legend becomes solemn and tragic: astrologers (Magi) arrive from the East at Jerusalem to adore the King of the Jews about to be born there —they have seen the rising of his star. Disturbed by the news Herod assembles his wise men who declare that the Messiah must be born in Bethlehem, for so, they say, the prophet Micah has foretold. The astrologers accordingly take the road to Bethlehem, Herod requesting them to return to Jerusalem to report. The star reappears, and guides them to the house where the child is laid; they enter, adore, offer their gifts, and, a premonitory dream warning them not to see Herod again, they return to their country by a different road. Another angel commands Joseph to fly into Egypt with the child and his mother, to escape from Herod's inquisition. So to Egypt they depart, thereby accomplishing an oracle of Hosea (xi, 1)—which refers to the Israelite people. Follows the massacre of children in Bethlehem and the region round about, according to a prophecy of Jeremiah (xxxi, 15)—forced like the others into the service. At last the cruel Herod dies; an angel bids Joseph return to Judea, to Bethlehem; but this he dares not do and betakes himself instead to Galilee, to Nazareth, thereby fulfilling a saying of prophecy concerning the Christ: "he shall be called a Nazarene." But the exegetes have been unable to discover where the prophecy is to be found.

The important point to note is that Matthew's legend is incompatible with Luke's from beginning to end: the two are equally full of marvels and magic; but neither is inwardly consistent and the two cancel each other out. In their mythology and magic they belong to the history of the growth of belief and throw not a ray of light on the historical origin of Jesus.

Supernaturalism of the same type, a mixture of magic and mythology, colours the main body of the Gospel narrative to a lesser degree, but it is far from being absent. Moreover it is clear from the outset that the account of the public career of Jesus, from his baptism by John to his death and entry into immortal life, though having a certain resemblance in all the four Gospels, is understood by the fourth, as to its principal features, in a sense quite different from that given to it by the first three.

In the first three, a figure, to all seeming that of a human being, presents himself for John's baptism and receives it under miraculous conditions, in which he is invested with the Messianic dignity of the Holy Spirit. This Spirit is henceforth to possess him, having first appointed him Son of God. Setting aside the secondary variants in the three Gospels this scene clearly represents the consecration of Jesus as Messiah and is at the same time the prototype of Christian baptism, in other words it is the first and principal stage in the formation of the myth of the Christ and of the institution of baptism. Though Jesus was probably baptized by John it was not under these conditions. In this we see that the synoptic account does not begin as an historical record of Jesus the teacher. It begins as doctrinal instruction, as a catechesis, by presenting a doctrine to the Christian initiate. All that follows up to the end is in keeping with the beginning.

As we shall later study in detail the growth of the Gospel catechesis, we confine attention for the present to its general features. It is certain that all the materials of the Gospel catechesis, various and ill-ordered as they are, are intended to show that the teaching was wonder-working. Jesus is the Messiah announced by the miracle of his baptism. To this point of view everything is systematically adjusted. The aim is the instruction of Christians, not at presenting the real course of Jesus' ministry which, for all who have eyes to see, consisted in the announcement of the imminent Kingdom of God; in this the rôle of miracle-worker can have had but a very small place. The number of miracles of which a *detailed* description is given is not considerable, and it is worthy of note that whenever a miracle is described in detail the meaning of it lies in the saving work accomplished by Jesus; its mystic significance as a work of salvation always outweighs the importance of the material facts. With regard to these latter the Gospel narratives are completely indifferent, witness the facility with which different evangelists change the setting, modifying at will the order and connection of events and circumstances, and not hesitating, by way of making the proof more convincing, to introduce what we may call *editorial* miracles to heighten the *mise en scène* or to make a discourse more impressive. Offensive as such proceedings may be to modern standards, they are valuable to the critic by revealing the ground on which the Gospel stories are constructed, the ground namely of doctrinal teaching and pious legend, and not the ground of history. We shall enter later into fuller detail; note only, as typical examples, the *bloc* of miracles which Jesus, in Mark iii, 10–12, performs, before proceeding to the mission of the apostles; the miraculous cure of the two blind men (ix, 27–33) in which Matthew doubles the cure of Bartimeus at Jericho, and the cure of the deaf mute brought in at the same point (ix, 32–34), both to provide ground for the answer Jesus will presently give to John's messengers; in like manner the raising of the young man at Nain (Luke vii, 11–17), which a reviser of the third Gospel improvises for the same purpose and on the same occasion, to say nothing of the miscellaneous collection of miraculous cures which he inserts so oddly (vii, 21) in the middle of the dialogue between Jesus and the messengers. By these proceedings the evangelists themselves invite us to rate such miracles at their proper worth. They are piled up to satiety and without more scruple than if they were metaphors.

The second part of the synoptic catechism, introduced by Peter's confession at Caesarea Philippi, has a perspective leading up to its dominating feature in the saving death of Jesus, which he is represented as predicting on various occasions for the instruction of his disciples. Fundamentally this part of the catechism is intended to explain the mystery of the Communion Supper along with that of the Christian Easter, celebrated on Sunday. We know that the observation of Easter on this particular day of the week was adopted by the majority of the Churches, beginning with the Roman Church, in the course of the second century. Needless to say it was not the primitive custom. It is certain that the earliest believers were in the habit of celebrating their Passover on the movable day when the Jews celebrated theirs, and it was only when the idea of a distinctively Christian method of salvation had been elaborated that it was deemed expedient to separate from Jewish practice by celebrating on a fixed day, as the culminating point of the divine epiphany and saving work of Jesus. This was his resurrection, and Sunday, which had already become the Lord's Day, that is the day consecrated to the immortal Christ, was obviously the day on which the resurrection must be supposed to have taken place. Here again we are on doctrinal ground, the ground even of gnosis and mystery, not on that of history or attested fact.

But even at this point the Gospel narratives are far from reflecting a consistent and homogeneous tradition. The stories of the Passion and of the Resurrection are loaded with other matter and full of incoherencies. In Mark the last meal of Jesus, which was not a paschal meal in the earliest version of it, has been doubled in the story of the Anointing (xiv, 3–9), the intention apparently being to arrange a kind of holy week, in which the institution of the Supper was commemorated on Thursday evening, when Jesus himself was said to have celebrated the Passover; the Passion would then be assigned to Friday. Passing over the flagrant impossibility of Jesus being arrested and tried by the Sanhedrin on the holy night of the Passover, we find that he remains in the tomb for the whole of the Sabbath (Saturday) and is raised up just before the dawn on Sunday morning. Such is the underlying myth which supports the ritual commemoration on Sunday.

We know how the authentic version of Mark ends abruptly with the discovery of the empty tomb by the women who flee in panic without telling any man of the miracle they have seen. At a yet older stage in the formation of the Gospel it would seem to have concluded with the centurion's confession of faith (xv, 39), the moment of Jesus' death being considered as also the moment of his resurrection to glory and immortal life. But this simple conception of his resurrection, which was certainly held by the first believers, was presently deemed insufficient. The discovery of the empty tomb was then imagined to provide a material proof, the resurrection being now conceived under the idea that the dead body of Jesus must have been re-animated and delivered up *from a tomb* in which it had been immured for some time. This materialized conception of the matter is pursued in the other Gospels to the point of extravagance and in self-contradictory forms, the material body of Jesus being endowed with the immaterial quality of spirit, while the Christ is represented (in Luke and Acts) even as taking part in the meals of the disciples. In addition to this self-contradiction, Luke flatly contradicts the stories in Matthew and Mark who place the first apparition of the risen Jesus in Galilee. From all this the conclusion follows that what we have here is not a historical tradition of a factual resurrection which, after all, is not an observable fact of the physical order, but an assertion of faith. The stories of imagined apparitions are, for the most part, apologetic constructions for buttressing belief by clothing it in material form. Whence it follows in this crucial case, as in that of miracles in general, that the only history we can glean from stories of supernatural magic is the history of belief.

THE CHRIST OF THE FOURTH GOSPEL

The primary difference between the point of view of the fourth Gospel and that of the Synopsis is that the Christ it presents is not a human being raised above humanity by a Spirit emanating from God, but a divine being *from the outset*, a hypostasis, an original emanation, the transcendent Son, the Logos of God. This Son or Logos is made manifest in the flesh that he may gather believers, who, by true faith in him whom God has sent, will themselves become God's children. The Son has neither father nor mother in this world. Nevertheless, in his earthly manifestation, he appears as the member of a family, is reputed son of Joseph and has a mother and brothers. But the book, *in the form in which it has come down to us*, seems to attribute to the Christ an existence completely human, assigning him a real birth followed by an integral human life up to the age of thirty after which his ministry, as divine revealer of a mystery, begins and lasts for about three years. Not only is this in violent and consciously intended contradiction to the Synopsis but is an addition and a contradiction to the fundamental idea of the fourth Gospel itself, the idea namely of a divine incarnation for the manifestation and fulfilment of human salvation, the said manifestation having no need to pass through preparatory stages while concealed under a developing human envelope.

25

It remains to add that, while the Johannine Christ is presented as revealing and instituting the religion of spirit, he fulfils that function exclusively by means of two revealing images, light and life, which after all are sensible symbols, and by "signs" which are not merely symbols but miracles, prodigies effected by supernatural magic, intensified in narration to enhance the spiritual lesson, which, on its side, tends to compromise the material reality of the facts in the story. But their material reality is none the less intended by the narrator. Thus: the Christ is the Light of the world; proof, the miraculous cure of the man born blind: the Christ is resurrection and life; proof, the raising of Lazarus after four days in the grave. Both these marvels are presented as factually occurring, and as leading up to the spiritual dénouement. The same method is applied in the presentation of the other miracles.

The stories of the Passion and of the Resurrection are constructed on a like principle. Although they have been retouched to soften their profound and significant difference from the synoptic presentation, the Johannine stories of these events were originally written and still remain, under all that has been added, in harmony with the primitive Easter observance, known as quartodeciman, the Christ being deemed to have died on the 14 Nizan, on the day and at the very hour when the paschal lamb was sacrificed. The contradiction of the Synoptics on this essential cannot be resolved. Nor could the conflict as to the two observances, which went on during the second century.

The divergence shows that both dates are commemorative. Neither can pretend to indicate the chronological place of the Passion. They are ritual conventions, not history. Both being symbolic, and the one no more historical than the other, the historian is under no obligation to choose between them. They are mutually destructive.

Note further, on account of its importance, the incident of the lance-thrust. This incident, though secondary, fictitious and a late insertion into the story, is full of meaning. Not only is it presented as the fulfilment of two prophecies, but the water and blood that flow from the pierced side of Jesus are figures of the sacraments of Christian initiation, baptism and the Supper, and of the double witness of the Spirit, emitted in the last breath of the

Crucified. To find in the natural decomposition of blood an explanation of a miracle and symbol so finely conceived, as some would do, is an exercise of ingenuity in which only a blind exegesis could indulge itself (John xix, 30–37; cf. vii, 37–39; 1 John v, 6–8).

The Johannine stories of the resurrection, which have been worked over in successive revisions of the Gospel, are incoherent and self-contradictory. They are out of harmony with the underlying principle of the Gospel itself, according to which the Christ returns to his eternal life, which had been interrupted, as it were, by his temporal incarnation, with the last utterance of his expiring breath. Incoherently with this spiritual conception, tradition introduced a proof of material resurrection by proclaiming the discovery of the empty tomb. Incoherently again, the Christ, entering through closed doors as an *immaterial* spirit, proceeds to show the disciples his *material* body scarred by the nails and the lance, and the scene is repeated a second time to convince the sceptical Thomas. Here is miraculous magic enough: but there is more to come. A supplementary chapter (xxi) is given up to an apparition in Galilee, doubtless derived from the oldest tradition of the post-resurrection visions, in which the risen Jesus mingles for a time in the daily life of his followers. But the end of the story shows that the whole episode has been introduced for the purpose of creating some sort of link between the glorious memory of Peter, head-shepherd of the Christ's sheep, with that of the beloved disciple of Jesus whom the churches of Asia venerated as their supposed founder, the true and truthful author of the Gospel in which these great marvels are reported. But the Johannine Gospel, like the others, is so full of such marvels, and in a sense fuller of fiction than they, that we cannot bind the historian to accept all these operations of miraculous magic, as real events irrefragably attested. They are constructed for a purpose.

THE TRUE SUPERNATURAL

It would be idle to press further our proof of the presence in the Bible, even in the New Testament, and in the Gospels, of a supernatural magic unthinkable by contemporary intelligence. In the supernatural so understood we have here no part or lot, for

27

the plain reason that it is untrue, that it crumbles to pieces, save so far as it is held together by the ignorance of the believing masses, and by the wilful blindness of the theologians who refuse to see what is before them; nor can the suspicion be avoided that these theologians sometimes play a part which ranges them with opportunists, apologetic politicians, exegetical strategists, rather than with those who really and personally believe in this false supernaturalism, which they seem determined to impose as a perpetual burden on the religious mind. We beg to tell them, and to say it once for all, that their pretensions are preposterous and their assumption of infallibility an unpermitted revolt against exact knowledge. In the measure to which they condemn themselves to follow their principle they deprive their works of all claim to scientific value.

Let those who seek edification in such proceedings find the edification they seek. Our own task is to establish the real position of the biblical problem in our time, and to show the place that remains for the true supernatural when the false supernatural of magic and myth has been dismissed.

The problem before us is that of ascertaining, without exaggeration and without reticence, the true place of Christianity in the scale of religious values, taking full account of the development in our time of the natural sciences, of our knowledge of the universe, of anthropology, of human palaeontology, of historical and pre-historical archaeology, of general history and the philosophy of history, and of the knowledge of man himself. With an urgency which no words can fully express we invite the theologians of all the Christian confessions, and believers of every religion in the world, to ponder the infinite perspectives which now open before us on all sides and in presence of which all the cosmogonies, all the mythologies, nay, all the theologies bequeathed to us by antiquity vanish like the dreams of childhood.

Consider the immensity of the universe and the harmony of its laws as now revealed to us; the mystery of infinite worlds moving eternally on their way in the unfathomable depths of space; consider the mystery of the atom, of the infinitely little, each one a world and yet hardly perceptible to our senses, enshrining in itself the mystery of the great universe, as it confronts us in the life of every star and of all the stars in their totality. In the presence of that what becomes of all the ancient mythologies, including the biblical? In strictness of speech they come to nothing. To be sure, the mystery of the universe does not suppress the mystery of God, but intensifies it beyond measure and shifts it to regions where all the old definitions of God vanish like bursting bubbles. The idea of a completed and simultaneous creation of all things—what now becomes of that? What madman in our days would dare to write down the age of the universe in arithmetical figures? In the ages when the religions of the world were born and their sacred books indited, barely a suspicion had arisen of the mystery of the universe and the mystery of God as they now confront us. An important fact in itself and in its consequences.

That is not all. There is another mystery equally ignored by all the religions in their sacred books, the mystery of man. On this, as on the other, all they have to offer is fable, the work of the imagination. Into the slow and painful ascent of man as he rose from the animal condition to a growing consciousness of his humanity, our vision now begins to penetrate, even to the countless millenniums of his pre-history; even on the origins of history a new light now begins everywhere to fall, and chiefly on the ancient history of the neighbouring East where the religion of Israel and the Christian religion had their birth. Of this mystery, gradually disclosing itself to our astonished gaze, the Bible, in truth, knows next to nothing. Israel and its God, who became the Christian God, are late comers into human history and into that of the Eastern Mediterranean; their sacred legend is relatively recent, and, being a legend, cannot be fitted in with the history, as now reconstructed, of the second millennium before the Christian era and with that of the two or three preceding millenia. Still less can it be fitted with the incalculable millenia before history began, of which the legend knows nothing whatever. In regard to the remote past of the human race, and to the mysterious past of the universe, the legend hangs in air without connection. It is no more a final revelation of the mystery of man than of the mystery, unknown to it, of the universe, but goes on its way without a suspicion of where the human mystery lies.

In the relations to both these mysteries the biblical legend is the work of that fable-making faculty whose activities M. Bergson has lately described with so much perspicacity, though without sufficiently insisting on the fact that fable-making is not dead, but is still at work in all religions, and even plays a part, up to a certain point, in the construction of all the philosophic systems.

Need we add that Judaism and Christianity, originally as limited in their outlook towards the future as in their consideration of the past, cannot be accepted as a revelation, and a perpetually valid and sufficient rule, of that religious and moral ideal towards which humanity has never ceased to press forward through all its many illusions and fallings away? The messianic expectations in which Christianity had its birth were, so to say, a short-term revolution of limited range alike in the world and the social order. Here again we encounter an element of that false supernaturalism from which neither Judaism nor Christianity felt any need to shake itself free, although neither religion could grow, or even hold its own, without progressively enlarging the scope of its aspirations and hopes, as in fact they were constrained to do.

Contemplate these stupendous facts. Are they not enough, is not their certitude sufficiently established, to justify the impartial observer, who is also a man of goodwill, but intent on the truth before and above all else, in asserting that the religious phenomenon of Judaism and Christianity is not an absolutely unique and incomparable fact of history, nor a primordial fact of history, nor a fact fully realized in history, needing nothing to be added, till our race, after an indefinite future, comes to its end? May he not affirm that here is no revelation for all time given to humanity in its cradle, fully complete at the outset and never since then falling short of its plentitude, destined, in virtue of its initial force, to guide humanity to the end of its evolution, an end which none can foresee and is undisclosed by the revelation itself? Be it said, quite simply, that Judaism and Christianity, taken together, are not the revelation they have professed to be, but an outstanding manifestation of religion, probably the most remarkable humanity has produced.

Deeply considered, the real economy of the universe, of which we now begin to get glimpses, is more marvellous than all the old cosmogonies; and the real history of man is a revelation of wonders greater than all the mythical schemes of salvation.

Does this imply that religion must now be imagined as having no future on our planet? By no means. What has perished for ever is the dominance, in the concept of religion, of the false supernatural. In a sense, the Christian ideal has never been more necessary, never more immediately applicable, than it is to the movement of civilization in our time. What then is the Christian ideal? It is expressed in the notion of the reign of justice, realized or realizable by the law of love, the noblest ideal our minds are capable of grasping, but presented in the Gospel, thanks to its eschatological form, in Utopian colours and to be realized by magic. It is expressed again in the notion of inward peace, product of faith in the profound value of the regenerated soul, of spiritual life under the law of justice and love, a notion found in the writings attributed to Paul, but there presented in a form not less mythical than in the heretical gnoses. Lastly it finds expression in the vision of a universal society of believers, the true Catholic Church, the common fatherland of souls, united in the practice of justice under the law of love, the confident conviction and clear consciousness that they are being born to a higher life through the working of this sublime law; of all which traditional catholicism, with an imposed orthodoxy, a ruling hierarchy and a papacy blindly imperialist, while professing to be a true representation, is but a caricature.

The essence of Christianity may be found in this ideal, unrealized though it has been at any period of Christian history; nay, it is the essence of the religion of humanity, advancing to perfection, with ever increasing promise, in a future to which no limit can be assigned. But to look for a clear conception or express formulation of it in the New Testament would be the most childish of anachronisms. We find it there only in germ, embedded in supernatural magic. But the germ was alive; there was already in it a large measure of spiritual life, that is, of the true supernatural, which must either grow and expand in the individual soul and in society, or humanity will perish.

Just as the Christianity of old, in adapting its message to the conditions of the Mediterranean world, impressed itself on that age by bringing to it a human ideal far superior to that of the pagan religions and the speculations of Greek wisdom, so it behoves the followers of the gleam in our time, to free Christianity from traditional fetters, to enlarge it to the dimensions of the rightful aspirations and needs of civilization, to raise speculation to the height of true science in all its findings, welcoming the light from whatsoever quarter it may come. Above all the travail of humanity, in the midst of which we are living, let the children of the light proclaim on high the divine principle of love, of devoted love, to the end that a religion may arise, crown of the Christian religion and of every other, all taken up into one, and concentrated on the perfecting of humanity in the life of the spirit, that is, in communion with God.

Chapter II

THE ESCHATOLOGICAL CATECHESIS

CHRISTIANITY was not founded on a revelation contained in a book peculiar to itself; nor, in strictness of speech, on the Jewish Bible, though this was its only sacred book when the Christian message was first proclaimed, and so remained for a long time, even after it had begun to produce its own religious literature. Nor was its departure taken from any abstract dogma or lofty mysticism. It rested on a popular and uncriticized belief which Jesus embraced with all the ardour of an unquestioning faith, and with a perfect trust in the God who watched over Israel and guided the destinies of all mankind. The central affirmation of this faith, the theme of it, was the imminent coming of the Reign of God. The same theme, enhanced by faith in Jesus, now raised from the dead and waiting to return in glory as the Christ, was also the central affirmation of the preaching we call apostolic, and it was carried further in the literature of Christian apocalyptic, more or less expanded and enriched with additions, some even foreign.

THE FIRST CATECHISM

As far as we can judge in the extreme poverty of documentary evidence bearing on the point, a poverty far greater than has hitherto been generally admitted, the message of Jesus, so far as it consisted in teaching, was of the greatest simplicity imaginable. It was summed up in the formula "Repent! for the Reign of God is at hand." John, surnamed the Baptizer, had proclaimed the same message before Jesus took it up. Neither John nor Jesus was the founder of a school; nor was John a hair-splitting theologian, nor a man profoundly versed in the Scriptures. He was a prophet by intensity of conviction, the prophet of a single oracle, and Jesus, after him, lifted up his voice in the self-same trumpet-call.

It is true that John, as his surname indicates, was a prophet with a rite. This rite was baptism, which was no common ablution, nor a substitute for the purifications prescribed by the Law, but a total immersion, understood as a sacrament of repentance, a token of moral cleansing and a passport into the Kingdom of God. This rite, to which we can hardly doubt that Jesus submitted, was taken up and continued by Christianity, Jesus himself having conformed to it. By the Christians, as by John, baptism was originally practised in close connection with the announcement that the Kingdom was at hand.

Like John again, Jesus, during the short time his ministry seems to have lasted, was given a surname the meaning of which, though less clear than the surname carried by John, must be closely analogous if not almost identical. As John was called *the Baptizer*, so Jesus was called *the Nazorean.* "Nazoreans" was also the name of his followers, called so after him (cf. Acts xxiv, 5). It was a sect-name. It was not as originating from Nazareth that he acquired the name. On the contrary, it was because he was a Nazorean and recognized as such that the supposition grew up later of his Nazareth origin, with the afterthought, probably conscious, of causing the real meaning of the name to be forgotten. Now the orthography of this word excludes as impossible the sense of "consecrated" or "under a vow" (the *nazir* of Jewish tradition; cf. p. 21) and points distinctly to that of "observer of a rite" (*nôtzer*), the rite "observed" being unquestionably that practised by John and his disciples, to wit, baptism. There is certainly no disparagement of Christianity in recognizing that its followers were a baptist sect at the birth of the religion, for that is what they really were and what Christians have remained ever since.

The Reign of God announced by John and Jesus implies that a judgment will be held at the outset, a severe judgment of God. In that we see an unmistakable feature of the prophetic tradition. The general judgment is, as it were, the preliminary condition and natural introduction of the divine government. Hence it is that the exhortation to repent precedes the announcement of the Kingdom; hence it is that baptism, the sacrament of cleansing, is the mystic certificate of innocence wherewith to face the Judge. All that holds together well and demands no great effort of mind to understand. For us, no doubt, the idea of a judgment of all mankind is not quite the simple idea that it was for those who first announced it; but that need not detain us. The great difficulty that criticism has to overcome in these matters lies in the way our creed-bound exegetes have of twisting or overlooking facts which are not in harmony with their own religious feelings, and in the way more independent minds fail to grasp the true nature of these facts when they offend their sense of what is reasonable—habits intelligible enough but difficult to cope with.

As examples, take the following. To that age the idea of the Kingdom of God was just as simple as the idea of a general judgment, but no more capable of becoming realized in the conditions imagined for it by those who announced its immediate coming. What were these conditions? As the dead were to be judged along with the living, a general resurrection of all the dead must naturally precede the general judgment—a condition which a moment's reflection will show to be quite unrealizable at any point of history: none the less the idea was accepted without the need to criticize it being felt either by the prophet or by his audience. Then again, the wicked were to be separated from the righteous, excluded from the Kingdom and punished as they deserved—a thing clearly impossible in the normal current of human life on our planet. Along with this, the righteous dead who have been raised and the righteous who are still living will enjoy happiness without alloy in the land promised to Abraham, Isaac and Jacob. Who that knows anything of the natural conditions of human life can imagine the establishment of such a society? But our prophets, John and Jesus, were unconcerned with natural conditions, and their faith, in consequence, was entirely untouched by the crowding objections which assail the modern mind in the presence of these ideas. This, however, affords no reason for changing the thought of Jesus by distilling his simple hope of the Kingdom into some fine essence more intelligible to our age, or seemingly so.

Another condition attached to this reign of justice and happiness was its *immediate* realization: it was *at hand*. This condition was self-evident: it was impossible to conceive that a miracle so great and so ardently desired would be indefinitely postponed. God was coming, and God is not a lingerer. So, too, with the urgent call to sinners—repent, and lose not a moment about it, for the Judge is at the very doors! To say that all that is unbelievable is to say nothing to the purpose, for the fact is that it was believed, and believed with a faith which had no turn for the

35

critical discussion of its object; nor was it believable otherwise. And so firmly was it believed that the contradiction it continued to receive from the course of events availed but very slowly to damp the ardour of the faith and that, even to-day, in Christian communions most emancipated from tradition, the outlook is more or less still dominated by the vision, far off, of the Great Event.

It seems, then, that no essential difference is to be remarked between the teaching of Jesus and the teaching of John. The deliberate subordination of John to Jesus, more or less plainly avowed, in which the Gospel teaching would place him, does not belong to history. It seems certain also that the distinction made between the two baptisms, which represents the baptism of John as simple baptism in water and the Christian rite as baptism in spirit, was imagined in Christian tradition long after both prophets had perished, with the object of marking the difference of the two sects and of enhancing the value of the Christian sacrament. It may be affirmed without the least hesitation that John could never have professed, nor even conceived, the subordination assigned him by the evangelists. That being so, it must not be taken for granted that John, the herald of the Great Judgment, announced himself at the same time as the precursor of the Messiah.

A comparative estimate of the two masters, formulated after their disappearance and inserted into the Gospel catechesis, invites us to suppose that there existed between them a difference of temper and attitude. It runs (Matthew xi, 18–19; Luke vii, 33–34):

> John came neither eating nor drinking,
>   and they say: "he has a demon."
> The Son of Man came eating and drinking,
>   and they say: "a glutton and wine drinker,
>   friend of publicans and sinners."

It would seem that, essentially, both played the same part, John with a more decided turn to asceticism and Jesus with a more liberal address and a gentler way with sinners. None the less it is said, in another passage (Mark xi, 30–32), that the baptism of John was "from heaven," and the Jewish authorities are severely blamed for not having sought it while publicans and harlots were eager to be baptized (Matthew xxi, 31–32; cf. Luke vii, 29–30).

It is obvious that so simple a faith did not need elaborate explanation. But one point it specially behoves us to note, because so many deliberately shut their eyes to it: the faith proclaimed by the two prophets *was subversive of established authority and, in essence, revolutionary.* The Kingdom of God was no metaphor; it was a real Kingdom and excluded that of Caesar. Hence the speedy coming of God to reign on earth meant also the speedy overthrow of Roman power, at least in Judea, and the disappearance of the petty Herodian prince who reigned in Galilee. True, neither John nor Jesus advocated armed revolt against the rulers of this world; but this made little difference in view of the essential fact that both prophets announced their immediate destruction. Is it likely that the authorities would regard the popularity of such teaching as politically harmless? The point is of importance as showing that the preaching careers of John and of Jesus could not be, and were not, of long duration. We are bound to regard them as soon suppressed, even though our texts do not give us clear statements to that effect.

In all this are we laying down too narrow a base to support the Christian religion? Are we not overlooking some sublime element that would justify the eager reception accorded the message by a significant portion of so religious a nation as the Jews? Must it not be that Jesus reveals a religion destined to become universal and to last for ever?

All these questions are unanswerable because, in the reality of the matter, they have no existence. This is not the place to show that the Gospel of Jesus and the Christianity that came after it are, in reality, a single movement, outstanding among all others, produced by that mysterious force which operates through all religions and urges humanity forward on the highway of spiritual progress. That we hold to be proved, because it is a fact of history. The question whether the Gospel of Jesus, as we have just described it, is too narrow and fragile a base for the many forms of Christianity which have issued from it in the course of ages, and are still issuing, affords no matter for discussion. When something has happened and is a fact, the question of its possibility no longer exists.

Some of our Christologists take too much upon themselves when they imagine they can explain the origin of Christianity by giving Jesus the honour of having formally taught the essence of their own religion. No essence of religion expressible in abstract forms was proclaimed by Jesus. He spoke to his fellow countrymen of things in which they were interested and in language they could understand. Our doctors of divinity are unaware that they are constructing a Christ in their own image, nor do they perceive that such a Christ, if he had lived in the time of Pontius Pilate would not have found two men to follow him nor one to be his enemy. Learned discourse on the methodology of New Testament criticism is as irrelevant to our present business as are the special pleadings for supernatural magic, or the baseless conjectures of those who deny the historicity of Jesus.

The sole point we have here to make good lies in the question whether the Gospel of Jesus, as we describe it, accounts for the response, somewhat limited, that his preaching evoked in his lifetime, and whether that Gospel presents itself naturally and intelligibly as the initiating cause of the Christian movement. Here there is no difficulty, since we know that Jesus preached the imminence of the Kingdom, and that disciples survived him who integrated their new faith in him as the Christ risen from the dead with their former faith in the speedy coming of the Kingdom as announced by him.

The idea of the Reign of God was widely spread in the region where, and at the time when, Jesus appeared on the scene: this explains why he was able to gather disciples around him. The idea was not the property of learned men or theologians; still less of politicians. It was the form of a popular faith, and a faith intense enough to provoke outbreaks of violence. Judas the Galilean who made himself notorious at the time when Quirinius carried out his census was a frenzied devotee of the Kingdom, his principle being that the people of Israel had not, and ought never to have, other Master upon earth than God. This was also the principle of the fanatical instigators of the war which led to the ruin of the Temple of Jerusalem in the year 70, and the same war-cry inspires the revolt of the Messiah Barkochba in the time of Hadrian, which completed the ruin of Jewish nationalism. Between these furious zealots and prophets of the

Kingdom such as John and Jesus there was only one difference, but a difference that went to the root of the matter. The zealots believed that they were able, and under the duty, to promote the Coming of God by force of arms: John and Jesus left the fulfilment of God's promise entirely to God. The faith was the same, but with John the Baptist and Jesus the Nazorean it has a colour of spirituality lacking to the others. On the one side as on the other there was the same confidence in the speedy annihilation of Roman rule.

If that be considered, it is not only evident but cannot fail to be evident, that the Gospel of Jesus was not conceived by himself under the form of absolute religion destined to become the universal religion of humanity *in saecula saeculorum*. Never did he propose to institute a religion; he announced that the great hope of Israel's religion was on the point of fulfilment. Never did he dream of sending out propaganda all over the world; he said that the Reign of God was about to be set up in Judea. Never did he behold the long centuries of the world's history stretching away into the future; for him, history, the story of man's wandering from God, would come to an end immediately with God's arrival on the scene. The speculations of modern Christologists who fancy they are discovering the essence of Christianity were foreign to Jesus. Most assuredly he was neither a Roman Catholic, nor an orthodox Protestant nor a liberal Protestant of any denomination: in all that his share was nothing and could not be anything, for he was a man of his time. Had he possessed the faintest conception of what was in store for humanity in the centuries to come, his message of the coming Kingdom would have been impossible and, needless to say, he would not have risked his life proclaiming it.

Christian believers in all the Confessions are naturally loath to admit that the Christ, the object of men's faith and worship, can have been in some degree the victim of illusion. This, from the earliest times, they have never been willing to recognize, and that is precisely why the original Gospel message has been progressively changed, diluted and doctored, a process which still goes on in the efforts of contemporary interpreters to palliate the reality by any means available, taxing their wits to foist upon the Christ their own notions of his work. But Jesus was rather the victim of his human environment than of an illusion peculiar to himself, his illusion, such as it was, being one widely shared by his countrymen and in his time. In itself it was a generous illusion and helpful in raising humanity from its low estate. And what more would you have to the glory of him who lived for the illusion and died for it? But was there no germ of life beneath it? Doubtless there was, and who denies it save those who would substitute for his illusion an abstraction out of their own workshop or their own illusion of some mechanism falsely named supernatural?

THE GOSPEL STORY NO PART OF THE EARLIEST CHRISTIAN TEACHING

That the death of Jesus was not the end of his life is proved by the fact that he lived on afterwards. In history proper his life covers space of the smallest: but he has lived on outside history or, if you will, above it. It is a frequent saying that Christianity was born in history. The assertion is true, though often understood in a sense far beyond what historical testimony is available to warrant. But nothing could be more incontestable as an historical fact than the appearance of Jesus in the time of the Emperor Tiberius and the procurator Pontius Pilate. In point of fact, our sure knowledge of the circumstances in which he finished his message and met his death amounts almost to nothing; nor is our knowledge greater of the process which brought his first disciples to believe in his resurrection and to proclaim it abroad. As to the Gospel, or message of Jesus, which we have just explained, it was conceived almost outside human history, and as its *terminus ad quem*. He who preached it and they who accepted it had no suspicion that it would be told as a story for the edification of generations to come. For that reason there has never been a history of it in the proper sense of the word; and there never will be. Still less are we able to find any sure historical tradition concerning the resurrection of Jesus and his exaltation as the Christ to come. These were matters of faith; in no sense or degree were they facts attested by the historical records of external proof; faith called unto faith in proclaiming them. Had the mentality of the disciples been of the kind that believes only on material proof, they would have had nothing to believe. For those proofs did not exist when their belief was born; they were only imagined later on to meet objections by the story of a miraculous resurrection of the material body, operated by magic. The first believers had no conception of any such phenomenon.

Paul's Summary of the Primitive Teaching

Here are the terms in which Paul sums up his own catechesis (Romans x, 9–10).

> If you confess with your mouth that Jesus is Lord and believe in your heart that God has raised him from the dead, you will be saved. For by the heart we believe to gain righteousness and by the mouth we confess to gain salvation.

What is the "salvation" here spoken of? Simply admission to the Kingdom of God which the Lord Jesus is about to bring in. From this we see that the teaching, which we may regard as the primitive catechesis, announced the speedy coming of the Kingdom, as did the gospel of Jesus. Like that gospel it demanded repentance for sin and it practised baptism as a guarantee that sin was remitted. Beyond that it presented the risen Jesus as *Lord*, exalted in his immortality to the right hand of God. This profession of faith was all gathered up as it were in one word, *Maranatha*—"the Lord comes," is on the point of coming (cf. 1 Corinthians xvi, 22). From First Corinthians (i, 12–15) it results quite clearly that the above profession of faith in Romans, in which the earliest catechetical teaching was summarized, was the profession required of catechumens at baptism, early administered in the name of Jesus Christ. And since Paul thus baptized in the name of Jesus Christ we may well believe that the practice was started by the missionaries of Antioch, who had come to the decision, before Paul, to receive pagans to baptism without imposing circumcision.

The custom of conferring baptism in the name of Jesus Christ was doubtless not universal at the very beginning. It is quite possible that the earliest group of disciples in Jerusalem continued to confer it after the manner of John, accompanied with a profession of faith in Jesus risen from the dead; and it would be the same with some propagandists outside Judea. This would explain the case of Apollos who had been touched by the faith in his native country of Alexandria and who, while well informed of the things concerning Jesus, was ignorant of other baptism than that of John (Acts xviii, 24–25), the statement which follows (xix, 1–7) about the disciples who knew only the baptism of John, and whom Paul baptized in the name of the Lord Jesus, probably referring to converts made by Apollos, though what then follows about the Holy Spirit coming upon them and their speaking with tongues is obviously the writer's embroidery. It is conceivable that the Antioch missionaries, including Paul, made use in their catechetical teachings of an express formula containing the principle of salvation for all men by faith in the Christ as risen from the dead, nothing else being required and the necessity of legal observances thereby repudiated. In that they would be repeating, with John the Baptist, that descent from Abraham according to the flesh availed nothing, and that God could raise up posterity to Abraham from the stones on the highway (Matthew iii, 9)—a posterity according to spirit, to faith.

On this point let us hear the testimony of Paul, an unimpeachable witness, in his letter to the Romans (iv, 13, 16):

> The promise made to Abraham and his posterity that they should inherit the world did not come to him through the Law but through the righteousness of faith. . . . It is through faith, that it may be through grace, so as to guarantee the promise for the whole of posterity, and not only to that part of it which comes by way of the Law, but to that which comes through Abraham's faith, for he is the father of us all.

This passage demands the most thorough consideration; it is an authentic expression of the Christian faith in the earliest period of its diffusion in the Roman world. A promise was given by God to Abraham as a man of faith and to his faithful posterity. The faithful posterity in question are those who are now persuaded that God has raised Lord Jesus from the dead. Now the resurrection of Jesus guarantees the promise to Abraham that he and his posterity are to be "heirs of the world." But the heritage of the world is not a blessed eternity in heaven: it is the happiness of the faithful, made righteous by their faith, *on this earth* under the Reign of God—the Kingdom. The saying "my Kingdom is not of this world" (John xviii, 36) was not attributed to the Christ by Paul.

There is therefore no difficulty in obtaining a clear idea of Christian catechetical teaching in its primitive form. The career and ministry of Jesus had no place in it; the coming of the Great Kingdom dominated the outlook; Jesus, raised from death as Christ the Lord, was about to bring it in; let every man prepare for it by repenting of his sins, of which baptism will give him remission. A catechesis at once moral and eschatological.

While the first form of the catechesis is thus clearly defined, documentary evidence is defective as to the detail of its evolution to the form which followed. It seems, however, that a considerable time elapsed before it included any record of the personal action and teaching of Jesus in the course of his mortal life. We have two proofs of this; first, in the book known as *The Teaching of the Apostles*, the *Didache* (*circa* 100); and second, in an indication furnished by the Epistle to the Hebrews (110–130) concerning the common form of Christian instruction at the time and in the circle to which the book belongs. We consider them in turn.

Evidence from the "Didache" and the Epistle to the Hebrews

The *Didache* in the form in which it has come down to us contains elements of relatively late date, for example, the formula of baptism "in the name of the Father, the Son and the Holy Spirit" and the text of the Lord's Prayer, which has been taken from Matthew's Gospel, but in its original substance and general tendency it represents a type of catechesis current in certain Christian churches of the East, probably the Syrian, between the years 100 to 130. The gist of the moral instruction preliminary to baptism consists in the doctrine of the "two ways," in which a Jewish book of morals is adapted to Christianity; following this are summary rules for baptism and the communion supper, and the whole is crowned by monitions appropriate to the coming of the Lord. So here again we have a type of Christian catechetical teaching still dominated by the expectation of the Second Coming and marked by a complete absence of any reference to the earthly life of Jesus and any defined notion of Christology.

The Epistle to the Hebrews sets out to teach a Christological gnosis which it sharply distinguishes from the teaching common to all Christians, 'that is, from the theme of the baptismal catechesis, as follows (Hebrews vi, 1–2):

> Leaving behind us the elementary theme of the Christ, let us raise our minds to the perfect theme (that of gnostic initiation) instead of laying the foundation over again, which foundation is repentance from dead works, faith in God, the doctrine of baptisms, imposition of hands, the resurrection of the dead and eternal judgment.

These last are what the author a little earlier has described (v, 12) as "the rudiments of divine revelation." The indication is the more significant inasmuch as this author desires above all to recommend his gnosis and, by way of contrast, incidentally calls to mind the common catechesis in which he sees the rudiment only of saving truth. To repeat this rudiment would be useless, he says, in the case of those who have gravely violated the moral rules laid down in it, since no further relief or remission of sin is available after baptism (vi, 4–7):

> For it is impossible that those who, once illuminated, have tasted the heavenly gift, participated in the Holy Spirit, tasted the good word of God and the power of the world to come, and then fallen—it is impossible that these people be renewed unto repentance a second time, since they crucify the Son of God, so far as the Son of God is in them, and put him to public shame. For the land that absorbs the rain that often falls upon it, shares the blessing of God, but that which produces thorns and thistles is condemned and under a curse (Genesis iii, 17); its end is to be burnt.

This commentary completely explains the object of the common catechesis as practised in the author's time, and shows that it had received by then some additions to the first form described above. "The elementary theme of the Christ," "the rudiments of divine revelation" are now called "illumination," though they mostly consist of moral and eschatological instruction; the moral instruction teaches the virtues to be practised, the sins and vices to be avoided, what of the past has to be deplored and what must be repented of before receiving the baptism which purifies the penitent. Express mention is made of faith in God, which shows that Christian propaganda is now being addressed either to recruits who come direct from polytheism or even to those tainted by heresies, which now (110–130) had wandered far from the true faith in regard to the Godhead. What the author means by the "doctrine of baptisms" is somewhat obscure. Does the plural indicate a complication of the ritual? Clearly the rite is less simple than in the time of Paul, the chief new elements being revealed in what the writer says about "imposition of hands," "the heavenly gift" and "participation in the Holy Spirit." Moreover, since "doctrine" is the writer's theme, we are invited to suppose that he is here discriminating among the baptismal rites then practised with a view to defining the normal type of the sacrament. "The imposition of hands" and "participation in the Holy Spirit" are certainly connected, and constitute a rite that goes with baptismal immersion, but is distinct from it. In "the heavenly gift" and "the power of the world to come" we can hardly fail to detect a mystic interpretation of the Supper. "The good word of God" is the divine guarantee of salvation, which the whole of this conveys. It is to be noted that there is a complete absence of any special reference to Christology, though the whole may be regarded as "the elementary theme of the Christ," a theme, however, which, elementary though it be, remains as it was in the earlier form and has its climax in the resurrection from the dead and the judgment to come. But the mystical sense of the Christ's death is not absent, since the Christian sinner is said to crucify the Christ anew "so far as the Christ is in him." But this last statement is probably the author's commentary.

To what extent and in what manner did teaching deemed to be that of Jesus in his earthly life enter into this catechesis? We cannot say. In one passage (ii, 1–14) the author alludes to the preaching of Jesus, and traces, so to speak, an apostolic chain from the Gospel onwards. After describing the superiority of the Christ over the angels he concludes as follows:

> We must therefore pay the more attention to what we have heard, for fear that we perish. For if the word spoken by angels (the revelation of the Old Testament and especially of the Law) held good, and all transgressions and disobedience received due punishment, how shall we escape if we neglect so great a salvation which, proclaimed at the beginning by the Lord, was confirmed to us by those who heard him, God acting with them by signs, prodigies, divine miracles and distributions of Spirit according to his will?

From this we learn that the author knows, or thinks, that salvation was first announced by Jesus himself, but there is nothing to indicate whether, in his understanding of the matter, the announcement includes much more than the promise of the Reign of God. On the other hand it is overwhelmingly clear that the earliest age of Christianity is seen by him as far off and enveloped in the mists of legend. He himself does not belong to the age called apostolic but is distant from it by more than one generation. Moreover his conception of the passion and the resurrection is not that of the Gospel story. For him the resurrection means the entry of the Christ on his immortal life. In like manner, while he is quite firm in asserting the real existence of Jesus and his rôle as the announcer of the Gospel, there is not the slightest ground for maintaining that he makes what we now call the Gospel tradition any part whatsoever either of the elementary Christian teaching of which he summarizes the content, or of the gnosis which he develops in his Epistle.

As to the Passion of the Christ, what is said about it in the Epistle has no direct relation to the Gospel story. The theme proper of the Epistle, the gnosis it sets out to develop, is the priesthood of Jesus, and it is in connection with this that we read as follows (v, 7–10):

> He who, in his days of the flesh, having offered to Him who was able to save him from death prayer and supplication, with strong crying and tears, and being answered in his anguish, learnt, though a Son, obedience by the things he suffered and who, made perfect (initiated by death into his high priesthood), became, for those who obey him, the author of eternal salvation, having been proclaimed by God high priest after the order of Melchizedek.

This passage, taken as a whole, relates to the mystic gnosis of the Epistle, but has a relation to it also in the detail of the prayer that was answered. For this allusion does not refer, in reality, to the prayer which the Synoptics place in Gethsemane on the eve of the Passion, nor to the cries or prayers which the same Gospels attribute to Jesus on the cross. The author views the whole redemptive action of the Christ, from his humiliation in suffering to his final exaltation, as prefigured in Psalm xxii, which is also the source from which the evangelists have drawn the scene in Gethsemane and the cry of Calvary. Our author therefore is not referring to the tradition called evangelical, nor does he depend upon it. He is making use, for the dramatization of his mystery, of the same texts which, in the Synoptics, we find converted into narrative.

TEACHINGS OF THE RISEN CHRIST RECEIVED IN VISION

That sayings attributed to the *Lord* Jesus were introduced into the primitive catechesis of the Last Things, while it was still the only form of teaching extant, is not an impossibility; but there is a probability, amounting almost to certainty, that a goodly part of the teachings collected in the canonical Gospels, even those incorporated in the public preaching of Jesus, began as teachings of the Risen Christ, of Christ the Spirit, believed to have been received by his organs, the Christian prophets.

The apparition of the Risen Christ in Matthew xxviii, 16–20, together with the discourse there attributed to Jesus, was privately accorded to the eleven disciples, but contains nevertheless the formal institution of the apostolate to all nations, we might even say the institution of the Church, and the promise of the continued presence of the immortal Christ "until the consummation of the age," that is, of the then present age of the world. Here we must recall that these eleven "disciples," or the Twelve, were never in reality apostles to all nations, nor strictly speaking apostles at all (see *The Birth of the Christian Religion*, 137–140). This conclusion of Matthew, therefore, cannot be earlier than a date well advanced in the second century. In the teaching it attributes to the Risen Christ it echoes a relatively old tradition of which we have many other witnesses.

The deuterocanonical ending of Mark (xvi, 9–20) belongs to the same class. A little later, as finally revised, than the ending of Matthew, it is conceived in the same spirit, and contains an instruction to the Eleven to employ the time before the Second Coming in "preaching the Gospel to every creature," with an assurance that abounding miracles would reward their faith. Matthew and the Epistle to the Hebrews present the same legendary conception of the primitive apostolate. In the same way the fourth Gospel represents the apostolic mission as instituted, with power to forgive sins, by the Christ after his resurrection (xx, 21–23).

In the supplement to this Gospel (xxi) the miraculous draught of fishes is a symbolic representation of the apostolate to the whole world, and Peter, whose martyrdom is predicted, is appointed shepherd of the entire Christian flock. Here we have the débris of a wider tradition, evoked at this point to further the entry of the Johannine version of the Gospel into the current of the catechetical teaching then become common.

But the most explicit testimony to the post-resurrection character of this later catechesis is to be found, as to certain aspects, in the Third Gospel and the Book of Acts. In the Gospel (xxiv, 13–53) it is the Risen Christ who makes clear, first to the disciples at Emmaus, and then to all the disciples assembled, that what has happened to Jesus was announced in the ancient Scriptures. (From this we may infer that the practice of building the Gospel narrative on Old Testament prophecies was believed to derive from instructions given to that effect by the Risen Christ.) It is also the Risen Christ who sends them out "to preach repentance and the forgiveness of sins to every nation, beginning at Jerusalem." The same theme is resumed in the opening of Acts (i, 1–12), unquestionably by the same editor of the original document, but in an expanded setting. Here the time of the Christ's manifestation to his followers after his rising from the dead is enlarged to forty days. (This time-scheme, designed to fit in with the story of Pentecost, is an accessory contrivance, like the whole development of the theme. What we find in it replaces the second part of the original prologue, suppressed by the editor along with everything the writer to Theophilus had to say about the circumstances in which the disciples became convinced that Jesus was risen.) The Risen One, we are told, speaks to his followers about the Reign of God. The disciples ask him whether he is about to re-establish the Kingdom of Israel here and now, and are told in reply that the Day of this restoration is God's secret, and that the disciples of Jesus, while waiting for his return, must serve him as witnesses "in Jerusalem, in all Judea, in Samaria and to the ends of the earth." (This is the actual order of Acts, but with different indications from those of the analogous statement in the source exploited by the editor.) Thereupon Jesus is carried up to heaven in a cloud, and two angels inform the disciples that he will return in like array. In conclusion we learn that the scene took place on the Mount of Olives. A point to be kept in mind, not only because the place is messianic, but because we shall find it again in the Apocalypse of Peter, which seems to have had the same setting as the source document made use of by the editor of Acts in summarizing it into the passage before us, the whole forming a revelation of the Last Things ending in the exaltation of Jesus Christ in heaven.

Evidence of the Apocalypse of John

We turn to the Book of Revelation, the Apocalypse of John. This, as we can recognize at the outset, is not merely an instruction of the Risen Christ; it is a complete book addressed by Jesus to the faithful, with one of his prophets for intermediary. The case is not solitary but assuredly one of the most considerable. Here we find the immortal Christ delivering his oracles more than sixty years after his resurrection, and it is a noteworthy fact that, in this long prophecy of the Last Things, the Christ recalls neither the preaching nor the miracles attributed to him in the Gospel. His teaching here is purely eschatological. But his eschatology shows signs of erudition; it is almost an eschatological textbook.

Certain parts of this compendium have a meaning which awakes curiosity to the uttermost: to begin with, the letters addressed to the seven churches which introduce the great revelation. Why did the immortal Christ dictate these letters to his amanuensis? It was not the amanuensis, assuredly, who began the practice of corresponding with churches. Clearly he is here adopting a method practised by writers who, in those times, were in the habit of inditing letters to churches or, more exactly, the method practised by one writer in particular, whose Epistles were then making a stir in that part of Asia where the Apocalypse saw the light. The letters to the seven churches make a violent attack on Paul's Epistles and on those who uphold them. It may be said without paradox that the seven letters to the Asiatic churches would never have been written if Paul's Epistles had not existed before them. The entire book is an affirmation and defence of eschatology; but the author would not have been so absolute in his assertion that the end was at hand, nor so vehement against Paul and his literature, had he not felt that eschatology was already menaced. It was menaced by the gnostic movement then taking shape and by the gnosis, or the gnoses, which were beginning to find their way into the Epistles. And there was a further menace from the delay of the Second Coming, which menace, as time went on, became ever more deeply felt and disquieting; it was the void created by this delay that he set himself to fill by his series of plagues adjusted in order. These, at bottom, are all variations on a single theme, dominated by the outlook to the predicted end, which seemed to be ever fading into the distance.

But the prophet himself is not exempt from gnosis. Independently of his borrowings from astral mythology, which he makes perhaps unknowingly, since he found them already made in his source, notably the myth of the heavenly woman and her son carried up to heaven as soon as born that he may escape from the dragon (xii, 1–6), and independently of this, the symbolic name "the Lamb," under which the Christ is usually designated in the body of the book, show him familiar with the Christian symbol of the Christ as the paschal victim. He is therefore nearer than he thinks to the Pauline gnosis which he condemns in the prelude to his great vision. We might even suppose that he had been initiated into the sublime gnoses of the fourth Gospel since, in one passage (xix, 13), he mentions incidentally that the name of the triumphing Christ is "the Word of God." But this must have been added later in order to create a link between the Apocalypse and the Gospel, at the time when it was decided to attribute the two books to the same author—the apostle John.

For this attribution to the apostle the author himself is not responsible. An important feature characteristic of the Christian prophecy now before us is its complete authenticity, in the sense that the author never makes claim to any other status than that which he assumes in presenting his revelation to the churches. This status is indicated thrice over in the following passages. First the title of the book (i, 1–2):

> Revelation of Jesus Christ,
>   which God gave him,
> To reveal to his servants
>   What must soon happen,
> And made clear by a messenger, his angel,
>   to his servant John,

> Who attests it as the word of God,
>> and the witness of Jesus Christ,
>> Even all that he has seen.

Next, in the address (i, 4–6):

> John,
>> to the seven churches in Asia
>> Grace to you and peace, etc.

Next, in the introduction (i, 9–11):

> I, John, your brother and companion
>> in the tribulation, the Kingdom and the waiting for Jesus,
> Was in the isle called Patmos
>> for the word of God
>> and the testimony of Jesus.
> I was in the spirit, on the Lord's Day,
>> and I heard behind me a great voice,
>> as of a trumpet, which said:
> What thou seest, write in a book,
>> and send it to the seven churches,
>> to Ephesus and to Smyrna, etc.

On his own showing the author is a simple believer named John, an ordinary prophet of the churches in Asia to which he addresses himself, with special attachment to Ephesus, just as the good Hermas, a little later, was an ordinary prophet of the church in Rome; for the time being he is confined to the island of Patmos and there he has his vision. He makes no pretence to be an immediate disciple of Jesus, still less to be one of the Twelve. He knows of the Twelve in the legend which has made them "apostles of the Lamb," and their names are graven on the foundation stones of the wall of the eternal Jerusalem (xxi, 14). He has no suspicion that one day, and soon, he will be counted as one of those Twelve. Thus the Apocalypse is, in itself, an authentic book, nay, an honest book, and the more valuable for that reason as throwing light on our present subject. For it proves beyond gainsaying that Christian prophets continued for a long time to deliver oracles in the name of the immortal Christ, and did so without evoking the teachings which Jesus is supposed to have given before his death.

Unfortunately it remains to be added that our Apocalypse, with its honest writer, was very soon promoted to apostolic dignity by the conscious and interested fraud of others. That, too, is a fact and one which helps us to understand the practice of authors who, unlike John, wrote Apocalypses purporting to contain teachings of the Risen Christ, under false names deliberately assumed. That was the case with the Apocalypse of Peter, to which we now proceed.

Evidence from the Apocalypse of Peter

As this Apocalypse did not succeed in finding its way into the Canon (or rather in remaining there) nobody in our time finds it worth while to defend its authenticity as the work of Peter. But the document is none the less important for the student, since it reveals the same preoccupation as the Apocalypse of John, that, namely, of satisfying and reassuring those who were anxiously waiting for the Second Coming. This it does by explaining the delay as in the order of providential designs, and, further, by making use of events already happened or of legends already formed in the author's time.

There can be no question that the Apocalypse of Peter, like the other writings falsely attributed to this apostle, the two epistles to begin with (both of which succeeded in getting into the Canon and remaining there), was published in Peter's honour, with the object of enhancing his personality, already become legendary, and for the consecration of the legend. But the intention was, also, to carry on the tradition of teachings given by the Risen Christ, by that time well established. What makes this eschatological compilation of peculiar interest is that, in addition to precise information about the legend of Peter, it contains considerable elements which the Gospels antedate and transpose to the earthly ministry of Jesus.

Elsewhere we have made a detailed analysis of this Apocalypse (see *The Birth of the Christian Religion*, pp. 35–39). Here we note the following points:

(1) Dependent on the Apocalypse, composed about the year 135, are, with high probability, the first Epistle of Peter and, with certainty, the second Epistle, which, moreover, is not earlier than 170.

(2) In all it professes to predict about the martyrdom of Peter, the Apocalypse does not depend on the fourth Gospel (xxi, 18–19,

and previously in terms more veiled, xiii, 36), but the Gospel rather depends on the Apocalypse or on the legendary tradition on which the Apocalypse depends.

(3) A similar relation exists between the Apocalypse and what may be read in the last chapter of Luke and the first of Acts, concerning the teachings of the Risen Christ, his instructions about the end of the world and his ascension into heaven (see above, p. 48); that is to say, in the writings named after Luke the view of these things is analogous to that of the Apocalypse, though less balanced and somewhat incoherent, so that here also these writings, if not dependent on the Apocalypse itself, depend on a document analogous or identical with its source.

(4) Lastly, the Apocalypse, which might seem to have transformed the scene of the Transfiguration in the Synoptics into the story of the ascent into heaven, on the contrary presents that story in its proper place and original setting. From which the presumption clearly follows that the discourses on the Last Things in the Synoptics and the parable of the barren fig-tree in Luke (xiii, 6–9), were first conceived as teachings of the Risen Christ.

Taking it all in all, the so-called Apocalypse of Peter is a dramatization suggested by the primitive eschatological catechesis which we may regard as summed up in the declaration attributed to Peter in his discourse after Pentecost (Acts ii, 36):

> Let all the house of Israel know of a surety that
> this Jesus whom ye crucified God has made
> Lord and Christ.

The Ethiopian version of the Apocalypse, it is true, contains certain features which might have led us to suppose that it depends on the Gospel story of the Transfiguration. But Second Peter took the leading feature from the Apocalypse, the voice from on high (2 Peter i, 17): "This is my beloved Son in whom I am well pleased." What is improbable, and must result from a surcharge on the original, is that the author should have written the words we first read in the Ethiopian version after the description of the happiness of the elect:

> "I rejoiced, I believed and took confidence, and I understood the
> words that are written in the book of my Lord Jesus Christ. And I

said to him: 'Desirest thou that I build here three tents, one for thee, one for Moses, one for Elijah?' Then he answered me in anger: 'Satan is making war on thee, he troubles thy thought. There is only one tent, etc.' "

All that, beginning with the inept reference to Gospel literature, is a paraphrase of the synoptic story of the Transfiguration and of the rebuke undergone by Peter, in Mark and Matthew, after the messianic confession. But the whole passage has all the marks of an interpolation, the original text of the Apocalypse resuming its course in the words which follow: "And suddenly there came a voice from heaven, etc." That granted, the conclusion remains, as was conjectured long ago, that the transfiguration scene in the Synoptics is an antedating to the earthly life of Jesus of what, in the eschatological teaching, was the assumption of the Christ into heaven before the eyes of the disciples on the Mount of Olives. But this has a much wider bearing than has been commonly supposed.

The antedating of this scene was done deliberately with the object of transposing a passing vision of the Christ's glory into his career on earth, and of putting the messianic stamp on that part of the Gospel story which is consecrated to the death of Jesus. This part begins with Peter's confession at Caesarea Philippi, equally antedated from the story of the Transfiguration and co-ordinated with it, but so arranged that Peter appears in it to his disadvantage, understanding nothing (at least in Mark, but with a contradiction in Matthew) of the mystery of salvation, of the death that is necessary and of the glory of which he has been given a glimpse. In reality, Peter did not confess Jesus as the Christ until he had acquired his faith in the resurrection. Moreover, the anticipation betrays itself in the prohibition which forbids the disciples to proclaim Jesus as the Christ before his death, and in the command to the witnesses of the Transfiguration to keep silence about it until Jesus has risen from the dead. All that is profoundly significant. And there is more to the same effect.

Other Evidence of Antedating

Another instance of antedating is to be found in the story of the baptism of Jesus (Mark i, 11; Matthew iii, 17; Luke iii, 22), in which the heavenly voice utters the same words. The object of this is, again, to put the messianic stamp on what was for long the Gospel catechesis—the activity of Jesus from the baptism of John until his death and assumption into heaven (Mark: cf. *supra* p. 23; Acts i, 1–2, except for the surcharge which introduces the interpolated verses that follow).

The stories of the miraculous birth in Matthew and Luke are anticipations of a different order from the preceding. But it may be said, without falling too far into paradox, that what is offered as the Gospel tradition has no proper base of its own, the Gospel catechesis being, for the main part, an antedating and duplication of the Last Things—the primitive eschatological catechesis. It remains for us to see under what conditions this transposition was carried out.[1] Needless to add that the fourth Gospel, the latest of the canonicals, is conceived from beginning to end as the story of a divine epiphany. It is obvious that these conclusions must find their confirmation in our coming discussion and analysis of the Gospel catechesis, to which we shall proceed in due course.

[1] On the antedatings here mentioned see Bacon, *Studies in Matthew* (1930), 145–164.

Chapter III

THE EVIDENCE OF TRADITION CONCERNING THE GOSPELS

WE shall presently describe the birth and growth of the evangelical teaching, or catechesis, as far as it is possible to do so, that is, by means of near and reasonable conjecture. But before proceeding to this it is necessary to examine thoroughly the external evidence, known as the evidence of tradition, concerning the documents which contain the catechesis, that is, the Gospels. Of the external evidence at our disposal the most striking is that which Irenaeus attributes, in regard to the fourth Gospel, to the "Elders" who had known John. This evidence about the fourth Gospel, as we shall see, is bound up, in the utmost possible closeness, with the sayings of Papias about the Gospels of Mark and Matthew, making a unity of the two testimonies; there is nothing of equal antiquity concerning the Gospel of Luke. The result is, that if the united testimony of Irenaeus and Papias should turn out to be worthless, no resource, or nearly none, will be left to the historian of the pretended tradition save that of a conscientious analysis of the *internal* evidence in the texts themselves. In addition we shall find that the Gospel of Luke and the Book of Acts contain an attestation about themselves the meaning and bearing of which will need to be disengaged.

IRENAEUS

To begin with, let us see how Irenaeus commends the fourth Gospel to honour among Christians. In *Heresies* (ii, 22, 5), speaking of the gnostics, he writes of them as follows:

> Under pretext that "the year of the Lord's favour," of which the prophet speaks (Isaiah lxi, 2), support their chimera, they pretend that the Lord preached only for one year, and that he died in the twelfth month of that year.

Irenaeus would here seem to be charging only gnostics with error. In reality, he is attacking the common perspective of the first three Gospels, where the events and teaching of Jesus' ministry are assembled in a way which gives them the appearance of occupying a short time, ending with the Passover which brought him to Jerusalem, where he met his death. The third Gospel, in fact, specifies the providential year as the fifteenth of Tiberius (Luke iii, 1), and is at pains to give in full the text of Isaiah, relating to this "year of grace," in the discourse attributed to Jesus by which he inaugurated his public preaching at Nazareth, "where he had been brought up." It would seem, then, that the opinion of the gnostics had been originally professed, and that publicly, by Jesus himself.

Let us now see how Irenaeus accommodated the statement in Luke to the chronology which he claims to be that of the fourth Gospel:

> They suppress the period in the Lord's life which was the most important and the most honourable, that of his complete maturity when his teaching won for him universal respect. How can he have had disciples if he had not taught? And how can he have taught if he had not reached the age of a master?

Strange reasoning; especially when we remember that, in the view of his Person taken by the fourth Gospel, the Incarnate Logos, the Son of God had no need to graduate, before he could speak with authority. But this is a case of propping up a thesis, in which the interest to be defended determines the quality of the argument brought forward to support it.

> For at the time he presented himself for baptism, he had not yet reached the age of thirty, and was only entering on his thirtieth year.

This at least is how Irenaeus understands the somewhat confused statement in Luke iii, 23. But immediately following there is a notice in the text which contradicts the sense of the whole passage and can only be a clumsy interpolation:

> Beginning from his baptism he preached for one year only and died at the end of his thirtieth year, still young and before attaining a ripe age.

If this sentence be authentic it can only be an "indignant exclamation" of Irenaeus against the holders of an opinion judged by him to be preposterous. More probably it is, as Turmel maintains,[1] the work of an interpolator who "shamelessly makes

---

[1] *Histoire des Dogmes*, i, 319, note 1.

nonsense of the thought of Irenaeus." In any case the most careless of critics would hardly make Irenaeus say, in the quoted sentence, that the Elders support the opinion which the same Elders and Irenaeus have vigorously combated in the whole course of the argument. But he proceeds:

> Now thirty years is the age of youth which, as all men agree, continues to forty years. Between forty and fifty begins the age of maturity, at which our Lord gave his teaching, as the (fourth) Gospel attests; and all the Elders who in Asia were in contact with John, the disciple of the Lord, declare that they hold that from John, who remained with them to the time of Trajan.

We shall presently see how the fourth Gospel corroborates the testimony of the Elders. The Elders had good ground for knowing the corroboration and we can make a shrewd guess as to why they knew it. From what follows it results that this "John, disciple of the Lord" was also an apostle. The designation is somewhat loose, but tends to support the opinion now called traditional, namely, that the fourth Gospel is of apostolic origin. As it was then well known that the Gospel in question had but lately come into being, pains were taken to put on record that John had lived to a great old age—"till the time of Trajan" (98–117). These Elders who had conversed with John would have heard him in the early years of the second century. If we go by the Johannine chronology, this John would have been much younger than Jesus, but even so he would have been of a ripe old age at the beginning of the second century. In addition, those who drew up the appendix to the fourth Gospel (xxi) have also been at pains to inform us that "the brethren believed he would not die" (23), and have not failed to add that it was this disciple, so old, so unusually old, who wrote the Gospel and that they knew, yes, *they* knew, that his witness was true (24). All of which very plainly comes from the same workshop and serves the same cause.

Unfortunately for their efforts, John, the son of Zebedee, never set foot in Asia and cannot have died of old age, having perished, along with his brother James, at the hand of Agrippa I, in the year 44, long before the idea occurred to anybody of making him the author of the Apocalypse or of the fourth Gospel. The Gospel of Mark (x, 37–40) is here an unimpeachable authority. It represents the two brothers, John and James, asking Jesus to give them the two chief seats by his side in the Kingdom:

> And Jesus said to them: "Ye know not what ye ask. Are ye able to drink the cup I have to drink or to be baptized with the baptism where-with I must be baptized?" They said to him: "We are able." But Jesus said to them: "The cup that I have to drink ye shall drink, and with the baptism wherewith I have to be baptized, ye shall be baptized. As to sitting on my right hand and my left, that is not mine to give: it is for those for whom it has been prepared."

This scene was conceived independently of the Ephesian legend about John and long before it gained credit in the churches. Whoever described it (whether he invented it or not matters little) knew or believed he knew for a certainty that John and James had suffered martyrdom, probably on the same occasion. James was put to death by order of Agrippa I in the spring of 44, and the clumsiness of the formula used by the editor of the Acts in recording the matter (xii, 2) gives ground for thinking that the execution of John, mentioned in the source document before that of James, was afterwards suppressed out of consideration for the Ephesus legend which by that time had become estab-lished. A jealous care for this legend is perceptible in other passages in Acts and even in the third Gospel, from which the above story of Mark (x, 35–40) has been deliberately omitted. The critic has other grounds for affirming as a certainty that neither the Apocalypse nor the fourth Gospel is the work of John the son of Zebedee and one of Jesus' first disciples. But, though fictitious, the testimony of the "Elders who had known John" gives abundant food for thought.

Irenaeus continues:

> But some of them saw not only John but other apostles, and heard the same things from them, attesting a similar story.

So we are to believe that all the apostles met together in Asia. Polycrates of Ephesus in his letter to Pope Victor mentions only Philip, and mistakes him for another, for the Philip of whom he speaks was he whom Acts presents as one of the Seven, a com-panion of Stephen. Irenaeus amplifies the evidence. Finally he returns to the argument furnished by the fourth Gospel concerning the age of the Christ:

> Moreover the Jews themselves who then disputed with the Lord Jesus Christ make the matter clear. When the Lord told them that their father Abraham had desired to see his day, they answered him: "Thou art not yet fifty years old and thou hast seen Abraham!" (John viii, 56–57). Now this saying has no sense except as addressed to one who was over forty, is not yet fifty, but not far short of it.

Nothing could be clearer, and Irenaeus might have strengthened his case by quoting another passage of the Gospel connected with the foregoing. After the expulsion of the traders from the Temple the Jews say to Jesus (John ii, 18–22):

> "What sign showest thou, that thou hast done this thing?" And he answered them and said: "Destroy this temple and in three days I will raise it up." The Jews then said: "Forty-six years was this temple in building, and thou, wilt thou raise it up in three days?" But he, he spoke of the temple of his body. When therefore he was raised from the dead his disciples remembered that he had said this, and they believed the Scripture, and the word that Jesus has spoken.

All the elements of this picture are taken from the Synopsis, but with a different marking of time and place, and with nothing new except the interpretation. The variation "destroy this temple" renders inoffensive, and full of mystic meaning, the saying brought up in evidence against Jesus at the trial which ended in his condemnation: "I will destroy this temple and rebuild it in three days." In that form of the saying would lie the proof of his messianic pretension. Here the same pretension is implied, but with a totally different meaning. The temple, we are plainly told, is now the body of the Christ; the Jews are challenged to destroy it by putting him to death, and Jesus undertakes to restore it by raising it from the dead. But this conversation does not belong to the realm of historical fact; it is a mystic vision, a kind of enigma, to which the key is not to be found in anything we can learn from history about the building of the Temple. Commentators, therefore, walk blindly into a trap when they attempt, as many have done, to explain the forty-six years by connecting them, as the old interpreters did, with the time occupied by the building of Solomon's Temple, or with its reconstruction by Zerubbabel, while many of the moderns, with a candour wholly scientific, imagine they have found the key in the reconstruction begun by Herod in the year of Rome 734–5 (29–19 B.C.) and finished about 63–64. The forty-six years would bring us to 27–28 of our era. Is not that a marvellous coincidence? But more marvellous still than the pretended coincidence is that our learned exegetes, speculating on this conversation as though it had really taken place in the circumstances indicated, should have overlooked the fact that the redactors of the fourth Gospel, who between 125 and 135 arranged the story, were little concerned with Herod and his temple building, and the further fact that, while they found the forty-six years somewhere, it was certainly not in personal recollections, of which they had none, nor in Josephus, whom they had not consulted, but in some passage of Scripture which they had opportunely dug out to serve as base for their chronological arrangement of the age of Jesus—the passage which the disciples are said to have believed later. This text exists: it is the passage in Daniel (ix, 24–27) where the angel discourses about the seventy week-years which are to elapse before the messianic age. The seven weeks which pseudo-Daniel sets apart in this prophecy were to be understood as covering the temple of Zerubbabel and the age of the Christ, and the half-week, which is distinguished from them, as referring to the duration of his ministry. In this way Jesus would be about fifty years old when he died (John viii, 57) and exactly *forty-six* when, shortly after the beginning of his ministry, he drove the traffickers out of the Temple. This explanation of the forty-six years was given long ago by the author of the treatise *de Montibus Sina et Sion*, a treatise preserved among the works of St. Cyprian (*edition*, Hartel, iii, 108). This is the only explanation that fits the mystical character of the story. So explained, we are not surprised on reading (ii, 22) that the disciples did not understand the mystery until after the resurrection, and that then "they believed the Scripture and the word that Jesus had spoken," having by that time perceived the meaning of Daniel's prediction and of the Christ's declaration about the temple destroyed by the Jews and raised again after three days. All that balances perfectly, if we place ourselves outside history, as the authors of the story did, and inside the realm of mythical fiction.

It follows that Irenaeus, and the Elders before him "who had known John," were not deceived in saying that their assertions concerning the Christ's age were authorized by the Gospel; they are indeed to be found there either logically implied or plainly announced. It appears, moreover, that this edifying concert of "Elders" and Gospel cannot have been fortuitous, the nature of the case making that impossible, and that both the construction of the testimony of the Elders who had seen not only John but other apostles, and the introduction into the Gospel of the passages where we read indications of the Christ's age, are, at all points, the work of one and the same group. Who were these persons? They were the very men who edited the Gospel and first presented it to the Christian public, and at the same time constructed the testimony of the "Elders who had seen John and other apostles." Gospel and testimony are the offspring of one and the same fiction, of which the object was to guarantee the apostolic origin of the book, so as to assure its acceptance by the churches. In the end the fiction took hold, and it is no exaggeration to say that modern criticism has not escaped from its grip, though it seldom has the hardihood to maintain that Jesus at the time of his death was approaching his fiftieth year.

Be it noted, however, that when we here speak of the Gospel we have in mind the book as it was first presented to the churches of Asia, without prejudging the greater part of the elements which entered into the composition. Some of these elements are later than this first publication, having been added to procure the acceptance of the book, alongside the Synoptics, by the whole body of Christian churches, and not only by those of Asia. In the other direction, the first version of the book embraced elements of older date than itself. But these considerations belong to the history of what is commonly called evangelical tradition, for which we prefer the exacter name of evangelical catechesis. Our task has been to examine the so-called traditional witness to the fourth Gospel, and our conclusion is that no such witness exists, what claims to be such being in truth a colossal fiction, one of the most noteworthy in the entire history of the New Testament and one of the easiest to verify (cf. *Remarques*, 172, n. 1).

The common opinion has hitherto been that the testimony of Papias of Hierapolis in the name of John the Elder concerning the Gospels of Mark and Matthew has no connection with the testimony of the Elders, who claimed to have known John, in regard to the fourth Gospel. We have just seen that the latter testimony was aimed at the Synopsis or, more exactly, against all Gospels of the synoptic type with the object of assuring a greater, if not an exclusive, authority to the Johannine type. Now it may well be that the sayings of Papias are, in their origin and primary intention, co-ordinated with the pleading in favour of John, in which case we shall be led to attach no more historical weight to them than we have found due to the Elders who claimed John's authority. Let us see, then, how the matter stands with these sayings of Papias, on which there has been endless dissertation among exegetes, but perhaps without perception of their real significance.

Papias wrote in five books an *Explanation of the sentences of the Lord* which has not been preserved. Eusebius calls attention to it in his *Ecclesiastical History* (iii, 39), gives some extracts and at the end reproduces "the tradition which Papias has passed down to us concerning Mark who wrote the Gospel." It is therefore a fragment taken out of the context that Eusebius offers to the consideration of his readers. It runs as follows:

> And the Elder said this: "Mark, having become Peter's interpreter, wrote accurately, but not in order, all that he remembered, of the sayings and doings of the Lord. For he had not heard the Lord nor been of his company, but later, as I have said (he accompanied) Peter. Peter gave the teaching, as the need arose, but without arranging the sayings of the Lord in their order, so that Mark was not mistaken in thus writing down certain things as he remembered them; for his only care was to omit nothing of what he had heard and to insert nothing false."

Such, then, is what Papias has to tell us about Mark. And here is what he says about Matthew:

> "Matthew made a collection of sentences in the Hebrew tongue, but everyone translated them as he could."

It is to be noted that, in another passage quoted earlier, Papias says that he had questioned those who had seen Andrew, Peter,

Philip, Thomas, James, John, Matthew, and was also informed of what was said by "John the Elder and Aristion, disciples of the Lord." Clearly then he distinguishes two Johns, the Apostle and the Elder, as Eusebius remarks. In addition Eusebius affirms that Papias has been in direct contact with John the Elder and with Aristion, though this is not deducible from the texts he quotes. In any case the distinction between the two Johns is important, and for Papias it is John the Elder alone who came into Asia. Thus it is clear that "the Elders who had known John" have passed off John the Elder as the Apostle John.

A further point of importance is that Papias is *paraphrasing* the sayings of John the Elder about Mark. Plainly it is he who explains and excuses what John the Elder denounces in Mark's lack of order. But the Mark of Papias is a legendary figure, as John the Elder's Mark already was: he is the Mark of the first Epistle of Peter (v, 13)—which is not authentic—whom this Epistle, in all probability, would discreetly commend as an evangelist for the good reason that the Gospel of Mark had been in existence for some time when the Epistle was written. The information furnished about him by the Elders and by Papias may well be less dependable and go back less far into the past than is commonly believed, since it belongs to the same family, as we shall presently perceive more clearly, with the information about the fourth Gospel furnished by the Elders who had known John, the value of which we have already assessed. The praise of Mark's accuracy comes only from Papias, who was in no position to verify it, but whose intention was to paraphrase the assertion of the Elder in a manner favourable to Mark. All that we have to examine is this assertion; the intentions of those who formulated it in the name of the Elder may well have been less disingenuous than those of Papias.

About the notice concerning Matthew interpreters are divided, some maintaining that it comes from the Elder, others that Papias alone is responsible for it. The latter opinion is improbable. On his own responsibility the good Papias would never have depreciated the Gospel of Matthew (which he certainly knew) as this notice does. There is no doubt that he failed to catch what the Elder's assertion was aiming at and so reproduced it without commentary. But the two statements about Mark and

Matthew run parallel, and aim, together, at putting a measure of disqualification on two Gospels, widely used by the churches, in comparison with another Gospel, doubtless regarded by their author as superior to the other two.

Nor have we to search far to find the Gospel more unquestionably apostolic, better ordered than Mark and more reliable than the translations of Matthew. This incomparable Gospel is assuredly the fourth, said to come from an immediate disciple of Jesus; the Gospel with the admirable chronology, whose merits are praised by the Elders who had known John, and which, moreover, reproduces the Lord's discourses as the beloved disciple of the Christ had heard and collected them, that disciple of whom the Elders themselves emphatically attest that his "witness is true" (John xxi, 24; xix, 35). The conclusion is that the sayings of the Elder about the Gospels of Mark and Matthew, transmitted to us by Papias, and the sayings of the Elders, piously preserved by Irenaeus, about the fourth Gospel, the duration of the Christ's earthly life of fifty years and the length of his ministry, issue from one and the same source.

With all this before us there is no need to engage in controversy on secondary points, for example whether the Gospel of Mark, to which the Elders and Papias refer, was identical with that of Christian tradition; or whether the "sentences" or "oracles" of Matthew are a source only of the first Gospel, that from which the discourses of the Christ have been taken and which may really come from the apostle Matthew. What imports before all else is the value of the evidence as such, and this, being nothing at all, discussion of these details is superfluous. As to Mark, the reference is certainly to our second Gospel, but from what we are told about it nothing can be deduced as to the stage to which the drafting of it had arrived in the time of John the Elder (that is, at the time of those who put words in his mouth) or in the time of Papias. The judgment before us refers to the Gospel as a whole, an erroneous judgment as we shall presently see, but which, even if it held together, would not permit us to prejudge the re-arrangements, retouches and additions undergone by Mark from the time of its first drafting to the time when the fixing of the canon of the four Gospels determined also the fixation of their text.

As to the notice about Matthew, it also certainly points to our first Gospel, and not to one of its sources. Neither the Elder nor Papias had any acquaintance with the theory, formulated by modern critics, of the two sources of Matthew—Mark and the *Logia*. If they speak in particular of the Lord's discourses, it is because these discourses formed, in their eyes, the distinctive matter of the Gospel, apart from what it had in common with Mark. What their purpose required them to say about them is what they tell us, namely, that they were first given out in the Aramean language, of which we have only the untrustworthy translations into Greek. As to the stories in Matthew, neither the Elder nor Papias was concerned to know whether they came from Mark or from another source; but these stories shared in the defect attributed to Mark, which is also represented as originally a translation of information which must have been received in Aramean from Peter. These testimonies taken as a whole are marked, by their very character, as insusceptible of the discussion proper to documentation truly traditional and historical. Their evidence is tendentious, constructed for a purpose and non-historical.

That this is the real character of the evidence results from the way in which it is presented, which rules out the possibility of assigning it a very early date. It treats the Gospels as catechism, and this is important, since the catechism in question, the manual of Christian initiation, is presented as a narrative of the earthly career of the Christ up to the climax of his death and resurrection. They tell the story of a divine epiphany, which forms an introduction to the mystery of salvation. Without a doubt the Gospels are precisely such a catechesis and not a history of Jesus. But neither can there be any doubt that this conception and form of catechesis are not primitive in any sense, since the original instruction of converts at the so-called apostolic age was essentially moral and eschatological, and so remained for a considerable time afterwards. Now the evidence we have been considering reveals a complete and radical transformation of the original catechesis, which has become, at the date of the evidence, not only *the* Gospel or evangelical message, but is now fixed in written Gospels, of which there are already a goodly number. Plainly Mark and Matthew are supposed to be earlier than John, which is now being put forward to supplant them. This carries us far, very far, from Gospel origins. Nor do our witnesses show signs of having even a suspicion of the evolution which produced the books whose merits they discuss and whose comparative values they assess.

Considered from this point of view, the information they profess to give us is amazingly puerile. In the notice relating to Mark it is implied that Peter was a kind of universal missionary, which he never was, except in a legend of late origin. But this active missionary, who would seem to have made the round of the known world (he is supposed to have come to Rome, as the two Epistles of Peter make out), could probably express himself only in Aramean, no small drawback for an apostle to the world at large, even were his ministry limited to the Jews dispersed about the world, as our texts in no wise indicate that it was. Peter, so the evidence runs, not knowing Greek, would teach his hearers in Aramean; but he had Mark for interpreter; what he taught his hearers was what Mark the interpreter has reproduced in his Greek Gospel; and Mark, though accurate, has put no more order into his book than Peter put into his preaching. Let us attend carefully to what this is meant to convey. Certainly it does not mean that Peter, in his preaching, would sometimes place the passion of the Christ before his baptism; what it is intended to convey, and to convey nothing else, is that Peter's catechizing, reproduced by Mark, does not give a correct picture of the Christ's career. And that is why we are to think that Mark is not the best catechism for the initiation of Christians; the true catechism, and the only true, is that of John. This, for a wilfully contrived anachronism, is cleverly done; but it was contrived at the moment when the Gospel ascribed to John was a newcomer in process of being introduced to the Christian public, while the Gospel attributed to Mark was an old-timer, possessed and used by many churches. Moreover, as our coming analysis will soon show, the Gospel of Mark is very far from being a translation of apostolic teaching, Peter's or another's.

The Gospel of Matthew, whatever else it may be, was not translated from Aramean any more than that of Mark was. It was imagined to be so because, just as the apostle Peter spoke in Aramean, so the apostle Matthew must have written in the same language. The difference was that Matthew, unlike Peter, had no disciple to act as his translator into Greek; the first-comers undertook the operation without further credentials. To risk this statement the authors of it had no need to be acquainted with the different versions of the first Gospel. The idea of translation had suggested itself spontaneously and was found useful for disqualifying Matthew, as well as Mark, in favour of the Johannine Gospel. The only historical fact to be got out of the statement is that the first Gospel was known to the churches of Asia, and attributed to the apostle Matthew, at the time the statement was made. That this or that element in Mark or in Matthew was first written in Aramean is probable enough; but that is not the question now before us. The same may be said about the sources of the fourth Gospel.

The fiction on which all this evidence rests is concerned with the Gospel of John. It implies that Gospels of the synoptic type were in existence and held in credit, and we can name two of them without hesitation—Mark and Matthew, reserving the case of Luke for the time being. The two Gospels are discreetly denounced as not having known the real duration of the earthly life of Jesus and of his public ministry, or at least for not rendering them correctly. Moreover, it is certain that the Elders did not fix the duration in question in accordance with any historical tradition, but were moved only by considerations of theological fitness according to a typology constructed for a purpose, in which the concept of a Christ purely divine was combined with that of a teaching Christ, a Christ come to earth and in the flesh, to live for a time among men and teach them the secrets of God in a mystery. This framework for the life and activity of the incarnate Logos, presented as though it were historical, is manifestly the work of a gnosis which the Gospel has incorporated into itself. It follows that the elaboration of the Gospel, as such, is, in large measure, the work of the very persons who invented the fiction by which they commend it as superior to the others already in use. Thus the Johannine Gospel is proclaimed by its own showing to be later than the Gospels of synoptic type, in comparison with which its champions exalted its value as a Gospel book, a catechism transcendently exact; the one, therefore, to be preferred above all the rest.

The name John guarantees nothing, for the apostle John is out of the question; nor is there ground for supposing that John the Elder played any part in the fiction which takes him as its point of departure. Speaking strictly, "John" is no more than a date or a label affixed to the monumental fraud which commended the fourth Gospel to the high consideration of the Christian churches. Fundamentally, John the Elder has as little to do with the fourth Gospel as with the Apocalypse. His person and his name, deliberately identified with the person and name of the apostle John, were exploited by those whom we may politely describe as the author-editors of the Johannine library.

But what dates are to be assigned to the birth and evolution of the Gospel catechesis? For the moment, when our concern is less with the catechesis itself than with the external evidences regarding it, we note that the work of John the Elder in the churches of Asia was finished about the year 110. A point is made of telling us that he died at a great age, having lived to the time of Trajan; and this may be true. At the other end of the chain of evidence is Papias. We cannot state precisely the age in which Papias wrote his *Explanation of the Lord's sayings*, seeing that this excellent but rather limited man (according to Eusebius who had read the book) was somewhat behind his times. But he must have written long before Irenaeus. If he wrote after the outbreak of Marcionism we can hardly suppose that so great an explosion of heresy would have left him untouched. Let us then suppose that he wrote about 140. The launching of the Johannine group of books was not much earlier than this date. But it is improbable that Papias had personally known John the Elder; he merely repeats what has been told him. There is nothing, therefore, to prevent us placing the first publication of the Johannine Gospel, and the attribution of the Apocalypse to the same author as the Gospel, towards the years 130–135. The way in which the Gospel was offered to the churches proves that Mark and Matthew were known previously, not indeed in the rigorously fixed form of the canon, but with their traditional attributions. Matthew therefore would be earlier than 130, and Mark, on whom Matthew certainly depends for the framework of his story, would go still further back. Thus the existence of these two Gospel catechisms, with attributions of authorship either apostolic or equivalently so, is almost certainly guaranteed by the first third of the second century.

Since these attributions of authorship are false, there are no signs to carry us further back. It is noteworthy that so late as 140 Basilides was putting out a Gospel under the name of Glaucias a disciple of Peter—probably following the example of Mark—and that Valentinus who, about the same time, perhaps a little earlier and before Marcion, had published his, set his "Gospel of the Truth" under the authority of Theodas, a supposed disciple of Paul. It is possible, even probable, that some first drafts of the Gospel catechesis, with no author's name attached, may have existed before the year 100; but it must be confessed that we know nothing about them.

The conclusions to which we have come will not be accepted by scholars who defend the authenticity of the letter of Ignatius of Antioch, who place the letter of Polycarp to the Philippians about 110, carrying back the letter of Clement to the Corinthians to 95 and the Epistle to the Hebrews to about 80. We have given elsewhere[1] the weighty reasons which tell against that opinion. The letters named after Ignatius of Antioch are, in their first form, apocryphal; they are the work of the Marcionist bishop, probably named Theophorus, who wrote about the year 170; they were interpolated in the catholic interest about 200, and the Epistle of Polycarp to the Philippians, written about 150–160, was interpolated to give them weight. The letter of Clement of Rome to the Corinthians is by the Clement named in the Shepherd of Hermas (*Vision*, iii) about 130–140, and we have already seen the date of the Epistle to the Hebrews. The values and the dates commonly assigned to these documents are highly convenient for building up an apologetic system. We have abandoned them because they seemed to us, on examination, to be wholly false and incompatible with the real evolution of primitive Christianity.

THE THIRD GOSPEL

The reader will probably be asking why, in the preceding discussion, no mention has been made of the writings ascribed

[1] *Remarques sur la Littérature Epistolaire du Nouveau Testament*, 103–105, 113, 147–169.

to Luke, namely the third Gospel and the Acts of the Apostles. The answer is that our witnesses, the Elders and Papias, say nothing about them. Beginning with Irenaeus, ecclesiastical authors proclaim with one voice that both books are the work of Luke, a disciple of Paul, the Gospel of Luke having the same relation with Paul as that of Mark with Peter. But when Irenaeus affirms (*Heresies*, i, 1, 1) that "Luke, the companion of Paul, put into a book the Gospel preached by him," the assertion is as groundless and false as the Elders' presentation of Mark as a translation into Greek of Peter's teaching. Before Irenaeus, Justin seems to have counted Luke among the "Memoirs of the Apostles"; and before Justin there was Marcion whose Gospel was regarded by Irenaeus, Tertullian, and other writers who knew it, as a mutilated Luke.

In Marcion, it was simply "*the* Gospel" without the addition of an author's name. The book of *Antitheses*, in which Marcion explained his system and justified his biblical canon, not having been preserved, we are ignorant how Marcion understood the relation of his own Gospel book to that which the great Church guarded under the name of Luke. It is in the highest degree improbable, not to put it more strongly, that the Church received a Gospel hitherto unknown to it from the hand of Marcion,[1] and equally probable, on the contrary, that, among the various types of catechesis current in the great Church, Marcion would choose for his own use that one among them which he judged to have the best credentials, lacking only adaptation to his doctrine; it was, indeed, a moral necessity of his situation that he should do so. On the other hand we should probably be wrong in thinking that Marcion found the Gospel of Luke exactly in the form in which the canonical version preserved it, and that this version contains no line added to it after Marcion's time. But it cannot be admitted for a moment that Marcion is responsible for having, in any sense, created the Christian catechesis and that the whole Gospel literature proceeds, in any way, from him. It is impossible to make Mark depend on Marcion, for it is Luke, in Marcion's version, as in the others, which depends on Mark. To be sure, Marcion complicates the problem of the

[1] Thesis of P. L. Couchond in *The Hibbert Journal*, January 1936, pp. 265–277; *Is Marcion's Gospel one of the Synoptics?* refuted by the author of the present book in the same Review, April 1936, pp. 378–387, *Marcion's Gospel*.

Gospel catechesis, but he does not suppress it. Nor is it easy to see how, from this anonymous book, there could have arisen the twin books, the Gospel according to Luke and the Acts of the Apostles, together with the prefaces connecting the one with the other. In reading the Marcionite Gospel, so far as known to us, it is easy to see how Marcion has, so to say, rubbed down pre-existing Gospel materials to prevent them contradicting his doctrine; but he does not invent them. Moreover, the total invention of such a book, in the conditions in which he is supposed to have achieved it, is quite inconceivable. We conclude that Marcion was not the founder of Gospel catechesis. He took it up at a given point in its development in a given type, that of the third Gospel, which, in the part common to the two writings, was not very different from the canonical text.

The opening of Marcion's Gospel shows that his most drastic cuts were made at the beginning. It opens as follows with a combination of Luke iii, 1a, and iv, 31–32:

> The fifteenth year of Tiberius, in the time of Pilate, Jesus descended at Capernaum and taught in the Synagogue. And they were all astonished at his doctrine for he spoke with authority.

The cure of the demoniac (iv, 33–35) immediately follows; then, considerably contracted, comes the previous scene of the preaching at Nazareth, with the conclusion (iv, 28–30) fully retained; next, the story resumes its thread from Capernaum (iv, 40–43); next, the calling of the four chief disciples and the miraculous draught of fishes. All that compared with our Luke gives the impression of abridgment and arbitrary re-arrangement. From the omissions at the beginning of chapter iii we gather that Marcion decided not to preserve the baptism by John, the genealogy and the temptation in the wilderness. As to the omitted stories of the miraculous birth, it is impossible to say whether Marcion omitted them deliberately or whether the copy he had before him did not contain them. But what he has preserved shows that Marcion was working on a text already in existence as he did, in another book, with Paul's Epistles.

One would give much to know why Papias had nothing to say about the third Gospel. But had he nothing to say? If we begin by supposing that he must have known it we shall have to conclude either that he said nothing or that Eusebius thought his remarks about it might be neglected as of no interest. But these are not precisely the terms in which the question ought to be faced. What most concerns us to know is why the "Elders" who knew John did not bring the third Gospel under a condemnation similar to that which they passed on Mark and Matthew. For it is evident that, if they had passed any such judgment on Luke, Papias would not have failed to reproduce it, nor Eusebius to call attention to it. From which we may infer that the patrons of the fourth Gospel refrained from judging Luke. Was it that they did not know it, because the Gospel according to Luke had no circulation among their Asiatic churches? Or, on the contrary, did they know the Gospel and prudently keep silence about it because it was held in honour among their people at the time when they were laying plans to make their pretended Gospel of John prevail over the others?

Since they knew Mark and Matthew it is hardly probable that they knew nothing of Luke, whose original area of diffusion seems to have been Rome and Greece proper, besides some points of contact with the Syrian Orient implied by the birth-legend and the Book of Acts. We know, moreover, that the Gospel named after John was not the oldest Gospel catechism; "the Elders who had known John" make that clear enough. In their time, as we have shown, the catechism had become *evangelical*, in the sense that it was understood as being, naturally and necessarily, a presentation of the doings and teachings which had characterized the messianic career of Jesus, these doings and teachings forming henceforward the authentic manual for instructing the Christian initiate. Under these conditions is there any serious objection to the conjecture that the Gospel called Luke's was the very Gospel most widely authorized in the Asiatic churches before the introduction of the Gospel named after John? If this hypothesis be admitted we can understand why our worthy Elders did not risk an open attack on the text in use, among their churches, for initiation into the Christian cult.

There is, indeed, one serious objection that can be brought against the above hypothesis. It is that Luke contradicts the Easter usage adopted, at least to the end of the second century, by the Asiatic churches. These churches celebrated Easter on the variable day of the week when the Jews celebrated the Passover, while Luke, in its canonical form, like Mark and Matthew, authorizes celebration on Sunday only. To resolve this difficulty we must briefly examine the exact position revealed, by the prologues to Theophilus (Luke i, 1–4, and Acts i, 1–2), as the position of the third Gospel in the evolution of evangelical catechesis.

Later on we shall undertake a more thorough discussion of the writings ascribed to Luke, but the two prologues to Theophilus interest us, at this point, as witnesses to the history of the Christian catechesis, because they permit us to determine the character, the purpose and the age of the first book to Theophilus, which tradition made later into the Gospel according to Luke. Now what does the first prologue tell us (Luke i, 1–4)? It tells us that "many having undertaken to compose a narrative of the acts accomplished (among believers) according as they have been handed down by those who were from the beginning witnesses of the word, it has seemed good (to the author, after serious and long observation of the matter) to write in continuous sequence (the matter needed) for the sound instruction of the catechumen."

The man who wrote this did not belong, and was far from belonging, to the very first age of Christianity. Gospels have been written before his; Mark certainly and others probably, such as the primitive form of Matthew, or various versions of the original eschatological teaching which might have been considered as narratives of the first origin of Christianity (such as the Apocalypse of Peter). The writer, like many in our own day, has no suspicion that the primitive teaching was an exclusively *eschatological* catechesis; he thinks that it has always been *evangelical*, and a story told by the first witnesses of Jesus. Papias and the "Elders who had known John" thought the same; our author cannot be much earlier than they. Let us place him, without hesitation, at the beginning of the second century, and with no insistence on the first years of it. At length he has decided that he, too, will write "exactly and in order," late as it is! This is not a man of the first Christian generation, nor even of the second; we need not hesitate to place him in the third or the fourth; therefore, he is not Luke.

Whoever he was, and for us he is anonymous, he decided, when he came to write the prologue to the second book, to follow good usage by summarizing what he had put into the first. Let us listen to what he says and reflect on it:

> I composed the first book, to Theophilus, about all that Jesus did and taught from the beginning (of his ministry), until the day when he was carried up (to God).

What follows after the first part of the prologue to Acts (i, 1–2) is merely a clumsy surcharge intended to bring in, by hook or crook, the long interpolation substituted for the second part of the prologue, in which the original author states what he proposes to put into this, his second book, destined to become later the Acts of the Apostles. Enough that we know what he purposed to present in his first book, namely, "the doings and sayings" which had given its character to the messianic ministry of Jesus. Note that our author uses terms similar to those of Papias; but note further, and especially, that the stories of the miraculous birth are not included in his summary description of the content of his Gospel, but rather excluded. No doubt there were many other differences between the first book addressed to Theophilus and the canonical Gospel of Luke. Whence it follows that Marcion, before he came to Rome, and while still in his own country of Asia Minor, may have known a version of Luke from which the birth-stories were absent.

And we have to remark also, and in the first place, that, as we shall later prove, the story of the Last Supper in the canonical edition of Luke is evidently founded on an original version in which the last meal was not the Passover meal, and that this original has been altered after the event, and additions made to it so as to bring the story into line with the observance of Easter on Sunday only.

The internal evolution of our author's first book to Theophilus would, then, lead us to conclude that, in its original form, it corresponded with the usage of the quartodecimans as preached in the Asiatic churches. The same may be said with equal truth of Mark, in which it is generally agreed to recognize the presence of an ancient Roman Gospel. Thus we see that the evolution of the Gospel catechesis is linked with the general evolution of

Christian belief as was also, from the first, the substitution of the Gospel catechesis for the eschatological. All this, taken together, was a unitary movement, the reality of which is not to be contested, but which we must avoid the mistake of over-simplifying. And all this we offer as prelude to our investigation of the Gospel catechesis in the Gospel books. It is possible, indeed rather probable, that the churches of Asia, before accepting the Gospel named after John as their regular manual of Christian initiation, had made use of another Gospel in harmony with their quartodeciman celebration of Easter and that this Gospel was a pre-canonical form of Luke. Certain points of contact between the third Gospel and the fourth would thus be explained, but this is not the place to discuss the matter. We have now to analyse the books representing the Gospel catechesis, in detail and with all possible precision.

Chapter IV

ANALYSIS OF THE GOSPEL CATECHESIS

THE GOSPEL ACCORDING TO MARK

THE catechesis we have called evangelical, though officially certified by names deemed to be apostolic, does not go back to the earliest age of Christianity and is far from such antiquity. First and foremost it is a *catechesis*. True it is that the majority of modern critics, in our time, obstinately regard it as a collection of memories, more or less authentic, of the life of Jesus. It is, however, nothing else than a manual of Christian initiation, as the eschatological catechesis was before it, but with this difference, that whereas the latter presented the *risen* Christ, glorious with God and on the point of coming to set up the Great Kingdom, the evangelical catechesis presents the Christ, the Kingdom and the Good News in quite another light. In the eschatological teaching the epiphany of the Messiah has yet to come; in the gospel teaching this epiphany is antedated, and considered as already effected in and by the earthly life of its hero; this earthly epiphany, coming to its climax in the death and resurrection of Jesus, is what the evangelical catechesis now offers. This anticipation corresponds to a general move forward in belief, to the need of defending the faith, and to the transformation of the primitive Gospel into a mystery of salvation incorporated, so to say, with the present life.

Under the light of these observations we now venture upon an analysis of the four evangelical books, beginning with that which all probabilities indicate as the oldest, that is, the Gospel according to Mark.

THE FIRST PHASE OF THE MARCAN CATECHESIS

An unprejudiced reader of our second Gospel could not fail to recognize that it contains, beneath a certain superficial unity, a conglomerate of incoherent materials which ill disguise the additions made to an original form or the transformations it has undergone, and this in cases where the material is of most im-

77

portance. We may, without much difficulty, distinguish two parts in the Gospel; one may be called the baptismal catechesis, in which the epiphany of the Christ is begun in the baptism of Jesus by John; the second, which may be called the catechesis of the Communion Supper, or of the saving death, may be said to open with the confession of Peter and to be completed on the discovery of the empty tomb, offered as material proof that Jesus rose from the dead. It is obvious that here we must confine ourselves to pointing out the features that are most striking and the contradictions most evident.

First of all, that the epiphany of the Christ, and the catechesis, are strictly confined to his *public* life. Accordingly, the messianic consecration of Jesus is effected, or seems to be, by his baptism, or on the occasion of it. The presentation of John the Baptist (Mark i, 1–8) serves as the needed preamble to this baptism, a preamble embarrassed by the fact that the covering prophecy, quoted as coming entirely from Isaiah (xl, 3) comes, as to its first part, from Malachi (iii, 1), thereby betraying the overlapping text from Malachi as a surcharge. The account of John the Baptist is obviously intended to present him as a forerunner subordinate to the Christ, and his baptism as an empty sacrament, prelude to Christian baptism in the Holy Spirit—a distinction imagined after the event and ill concealing the original identity of the two rites. Moreover, Matthew (iii, 7–12) and Luke (iii, 7–9; 16–18) having here a more extended text, original in relation to Mark, the presumption is that Mark depends on their source; in other words, that the account of John the Baptist is a later addition in Mark's catechesis. In like manner the story of the temptation in the wilderness gives the impression of being a shorter account original in relation to Matthew (iv, 1–11; cf. Luke iv, 1–13). All the features in this picture of Jesus presented as Messiah at his baptism betray the antedating of the messianic consecration, which the earlier eschatological catechesis reserved for the *risen* Jesus. At this stage of the catechesis it is at his *baptism* that God says to him: "Thou art my beloved son; in thee I am well pleased" and not, as in the Apocalypse of Peter, after his resurrection (cf. *supra*, p. 52).

Looking closely into the matter, it is perfectly natural that, in the early rudiments of the Gospel catechesis, Jesus should be represented as making his first appearance at the moment when his public ministry began, and that afterwards the feeling should arise that this was also the right moment to explain the initial relations between John and Jesus, between John's baptism and Christian baptism by interpreting John's providential mission as preliminary to the higher messianic mission of Jesus. Moreover, the descent of the Spirit into Jesus seems to be understood, not as a simple operation of the Spirit, but as the realization of an immanence of the Spirit which, in Jesus, was itself his higher being, the very person, we might say, of the Son of Man, of Christ the Saviour. The description of the descent as "like a dove" marks the perceptible individuality of this Spirit.

Next in order comes the calling of the first disciples (i, 16–20) whom Jesus is deemed to have intended for apostles. Another anticipation. We shall have many occasions to remark that the apostolate was originally understood as instituted by Jesus when risen from the dead, and in place of its institution after his death we shall find the myth of the miraculous draught of fishes during his lifetime.

Mark appears to be specially interested in the thaumaturgic activity of Jesus, and chiefly with the cure of the demoniacs, whose evil spirits recognize the messianic quality of their exorcist. It is no part of our purpose to discuss these cases from the pathologist's point of view, nor their relation to the real history of the Galilean prophet, a history which the documents withhold from our grasp and which it is not their object to narrate. Whoso will may believe that Jesus cured many of these madmen, exorcising their evil spirits, who loudly proclaimed him the Messiah, in spite of the constant injunction laid on them to keep silence, lest he should be recognized. The systematic intention of these stories is quite clear. In Mark i, 24 the man with an unclean spirit says to Jesus: "What is there in common between us and thee, Jesus of Nazareth? Thou art come to destroy us! I know who thou art, the Holy One from God." The cures of the demoniacs are offered as proofs of Jesus' supernatural powers, confessed by the demons themselves. The fourth Gospel, as we know, drops the argument and omits all these demoniac-cures. The importance attached to them by the Synoptic catechesis is all the more significant. Note that the cure of the Capernaum demoniac (i, 23–

26, 27*b*) is superimposed on the scene of the preaching in the synagogue (i, 21–22, 27*a*, 28) and belongs, therefore, to a secondary layer of editorial deposits (as also i, 34*b* and the last words of 39). Thus we may conclude that this earliest form of Gospel catechesis was not completed *currente calamo* by a single author. On the contrary it was a long time on the anvil.

To commentators in search of its historical explanation much embarrassment has been caused, more or less everywhere, by the *silence* which Jesus enjoined on the cured demoniacs, on the sick whom he healed (i, 32–34), on individual witnesses of his miracles and sometimes on his disciples, a silence which the Gospel editors declare to have been actually kept in regard to some of the events they have just recorded. But the explanation is quite easy, not indeed by any circumstances attending the ministry of Jesus, but by those of the Gospel catechesis in the process of its formation. Our Gospel catechesis was first drawn up with an eye to the eschatological catechesis, already in being, in which Jesus was exalted to Messiahship when he ascended to God, and not till then. From the moment his epiphany as Messiah was thrown back into his public ministry on earth an explanation became necessary of these marvellous novelties, now heard of for the first time as belonging to the activity of the Christ *before* his saving death. The silence repeatedly enjoined on these occasions was the explanation, naïve enough, but indispensable, of why they had not been heard of before.

It is not surprising, then, that Jesus has to withdraw himself from the crowds of sick folk flowing into Capernaum. He resolves to preach elsewhere, his mission being essentially that of a teacher (i, 35–39). This is required because moral instruction must have its place in the catechesis under elaboration. Hence the place assigned to it beside the miracles.

The healing of the leper (i, 40–45) takes place in a setting of Jewish legalism and under injunction to keep silent; the story, as arranged by its editor, is clearly that of the day at Capernaum told over again in another form, and with the same deep significance—the ministry of salvation brought by the Christ to the Jews.

There follows a series of anecdotes in which Jesus is shown in conflict with the Pharisees, a conflict whose real background consists of certain later points of friction with Jewish legalism, and belongs to a time when the Christian sect was already separated from the main stock of Judaism. The paralytic of Capernaum is the first case (ii, 1–12), editorially constructed as a miracle of healing, on which has been grafted a declaration addressed by Jesus to the Pharisees concerning the power "of the Son of Man to forgive sins on the earth" (ii, 5*b*–10). In Mark's Gospel the Son of Man is identified with the Christ of mystery, who by his death has paid the penalty of human sin; a conception which corresponds to an important stage in the growth of the Gospel catechesis, though perhaps not the earliest.

The second case is the association of Jesus with publicans and sinners (ii, 15–17); these are they who need salvation; it justifies the mission to the Gentiles. The third is the question of fasting (ii, 18–22); the answer of Jesus inclines to allegory; his disciples will have their fast-days in commemoration of his death (19–20) —a touch which dates the invention of the incident. The following sentences present Jewish legalism as outworn, another mark indicating an origin long after the age called apostolic. The fourth case presents two anecdotes about the Sabbath aimed at rabbinical casuistry; the first is the story of the ears of corn, in which the disciples are defended by the example of David and by the rational aphorism: "The Sabbath was made for man," etc., capped by the saying not in line with the preceding: "So that the Son of Man is Lord even of the Sabbath," meaning that the Christ of mystery can dispense his followers from a sabbatical observance. The second sabbath-story presents a miraculous cure (iii, 1–6) justified by the right and duty of everyone to do good at all times. Our catechesis is here attacking official Judaism on the highest ground. But note how this whole *bloc* of stories is concluded (iii, 6): the Pharisees take counsel with the Herodians how they might destroy Jesus. All the cases we have been considering are grouped from a point of view which looks back on the death of the Christ as a past event. In its first stage the Gospel catechesis did not place them as far away from that termination as they are in the passages now before us.

In the chapters that follow we find a good deal of matter that is, in truth, little more than padding. First come two short scenes, of which one presents the beneficent activity of the

Christ (iii, 7–12) and the other the choice of the Twelve (13–19).
In the actual arrangement of the stories, the first seems to prepare
the way for the dispute about the exorcisms here placed after the
intervening choice of the apostles. Matthew and Luke use it as
preamble to the great discourse which appears in Matthew as the
Sermon on the Mount. Obviously a piece of no historic significance which the Gospel draughtsmen could insert wherever they
found it convenient. The choice of the Twelve, which is represented as taking place "on the mountain," was not made at the
very beginning, as here depicted. The Twelve, who we are here
told were chosen as apostles at the side of Christ during his lifetime, were not so elected even after his death. They were the
leaders of the first believing group in Jerusalem, and were only
transformed into apostles by a later legend which at first opposed
them to Paul and put them above him. In other parts of Mark's
Gospel we shall find their importance deliberately belittled.
Whence the presumption that the two short scenes now in
question are additions of later date to the catechesis named after
Mark.

The dispute about the exorcisms makes an unnatural breach in
the story of the attempt by the family of Jesus to bring him back
into the house (iii, 20–21 and 31–35). The disputants are nascent
Christianity and Jewish doctrine, and their dispute turns on the
probative value of Christian exorcisms. If the move made by the
family be taken as historical, it reflects no honour on his kindred,
whom Jesus himself is made to repudiate on the spot. The story
may be taken as relatively an old one. But may it not be intended
as a figure of the Jewish attitude towards Jesus, who has found
outside official Judaism a new family in his faithful believers?
None the less this group of sayings, motived by ill-will, has been
carefully put together. As it has no attachments to what precedes
or follows it must have been placed where it is for amplification
of the narrative.

A point of difficulty not to be passed over in silence is the
mention of sin against the Spirit, which is said to be the only sin
that is unforgivable (iii, 28–30). This declaration is in keeping
with a particular conception of the Spirit, and of its rôle in the
Church, of which no explanation is given in our texts. Although
the editors of Mark have tried to integrate it with the dispute

about exorcism, its presence there is adventitious. Luke (xii, 10) gives it as an isolated saying among others concerning the action of the Spirit. Matthew (xii, 31–32) attaches it, like Mark, to the dispute about exorcism, but gives it rather different form, identical, in the main, with the reading in Luke. While Mark distinguishes blasphemy against the Spirit, alone punishable, from blasphemy in general, Matthew and Luke declare "a word against the Son of Man" to be a pardonable offence, in contrast to blasphemy against the Spirit, for which there is no pardon. There is no proof of any kind that Mark's reading is primitive in relation to Matthew's and Luke's, of which it is rather a deliberate attenuation. What we need to know is how the difference between blasphemy against the Son of Man and blasphemy against the Spirit can have been conceived. There is no reason to have recourse to Montanism for the explanation of this singular feature. It was in opposition to the "spiritual men" of gnostic theory that the Church declared itself the depository and dispenser of the Spirit (cf. Acts viii, 18–24), and sin against the Spirit is committed by him who denies the Church that privilege. The saying thus fits in with the notion of the Spirit as replacing the Christ in the guidance of the Church. We must therefore regard it as an element of secondary origin and a relatively late addition to the Synoptic catechesis (cf. *supra*, p. 44).

Another conglomerate, of which the elements are more or less erratic, consists of parabolic discourses (iv, 1–34). Here the drafting seems to have passed through several stages. A first edition had assembled certain parables as a specimen of Jesus' teaching, that of the Sower and that of the Seed, with a preamble and appropriate conclusion (iv, 1–9; 21–29, 33). A second has inserted, after the parable of the Sower, an aside addressed by Jesus to the disciples in explanation of the parable (iv, 10, 13–20) and perhaps the parable of the Mustard Seed and other sentences (iv, 21–25; 30–32), taken from the collection of Jesus' oracles which must be assumed as a common source of the three Synoptics. Between the demand for explanation and the commentary on the Sower, a final edition has lodged a reflection on the object of parables in general, which is said to be that of causing the blindness of the Jews predicted by Isaiah (vi, 9–10), while it is "given" to the disciples alone to "understand the mystery of the

Kingdom of God." This mystical interpretation of the parables, along with "the mystery" in which we are to look for their inner meaning, is a belated final touch. The parabolic mode of utterance, which was common among the rabbis of the time, has nothing in it to cause blindness, and the parable of the Sower is to be commended for the ease with which it can be applied to the results of Gospel preaching. But it is in regard to the mystery of salvation by the death of the Christ that parables are deemed to have become a cause of blindness "to them that are without"— meaning, no doubt, the Jews in particular and unbelievers in general. In other passages of Mark we find that the Galilean disciples themselves are not immune to this blindness. Perhaps that is the reason why the request for explanation (iv, 10) is so strangely attributed to the people who were about Jesus "with the disciples."

The discourse in parables is followed by four miracles, appeasement of the tempest (iv, 35–41), cure of the madman at Gerasa (v, 1–20), raising of Jairus' daughter and cure of the woman with an issue of blood (v, 21–43). These form a group the members of which are apparently bound together, though the group as a whole stands isolated in the compilation. The stories are full of life, but of life given to them by the faith and imagination of the narrator rather than by the precision of real memories or by intimate connection between the parts of the action. That they are not, in some degree, legendary reproductions of incidents that really happened cannot be rigorously demonstrated; still less can it be disproved that they are largely constructed, according to pre-existing types, to the glory of the Christ; the first of them giving pre-eminence to power over the elements presented under the figure of his rôle as Saviour, and especially his presence with the Church in the days to come; the second, power over the demons and their master, in conditions which symbolize the conversion of the pagans; while the third, in its double recording (cleansing of a woman affected with perpetual impurity and raising of a dead girl to life), presents the Saviour's rôle which, by faith, procures both pardon and immortality for mankind.

It cannot be said that this symbolism is a gratuitous supposition on our part. For the evangelist and for his first readers the chief interest of these stories lay precisely in the symbolism.

There, too, is the only reasonable explanation and the only possible justification of two indisputable facts which force themselves upon us in spite of ourselves: the extreme poverty of the evangelical legend in narratives considered as such, and the not less extreme incoherence, together with the artificial and arbitrary character of the literary construction. The two things that mattered most to the success of the catechesis in the attainment of its object were moral instruction and the education of faith. With this end in view the evangelists were able to find, or to put into their more or less fictitious narratives, the depth of meaning which they had discovered or introduced with the parables. No complicated method is needed to understand it, and it can be proved without endless research.

The four miracles are followed by a series of incidents still worse adjusted each to other than their predecessors. First comes the fruitless preaching of Jesus "in his own country" (vi, 1–6), a repetition in some respects of his preaching at Capernaum (i, 21–22; 27a–28), but here turned so as to figure the failure of Christian propaganda among the Jews; it probably contains nothing to guarantee historical tradition except the indications about the family of Jesus. The mission of the apostles (vi, 7–13) duplicates that previously mentioned (iii, 13–15), but in the present context, with an abridgment of the discourse which Matthew and Luke (x, 1–16) give *in extenso*, it figures Christian propaganda among the Gentiles. The story of John the Baptist's death (vi, 17–29) is legendary throughout. Introduced most unnaturally by statements put into the mouth of Antipas (vi, 15–16, an enlargement of viii, 28) and violently wedged in between the mission of the Twelve and their return, it might seem to be wholly without purpose. But, for the Gospel editor who inserts such a passage, the object in view would be, not to record the death of John as a matter of interest belonging to the narrative, but to hint that his burial was the end of him, a rather summary way of disowning any relation of Jesus and Christianity with John and the sect which survived him.

The first multiplication of loaves, for which the return of the disciples prepares the ground, is a symbolic miracle if ever there was one, and we are repeatedly told that the disciples understood nothing of its meaning (vi, 52; viii, 21). It represents the oldest myth of the institution of the Christian communion meal, not yet arrived at the eucharistic theory in which the saving death of the Christ was mystically signified in breaking the bread-body and distributing the wine-blood of Jesus, but at the earlier stage when the Father was praised for the life and knowledge which "he has made known by his servant" Jesus, as in the *Didache* (ix, 2 and x, 2).

Welded on, as best might be, to what goes before, comes the miracle of walking on the water. The symbolism is analogous to that of the calmed tempest (iv, 35–41) which it duplicates, the construction showing influence from the first stories of so-called tradition about apparitions of Jesus after his resurrection. In that respect it antedates material which belonged originally to the eschatological catechesis, images of the invisible presence of the Christ among the faithful as they waited for his second coming.

The next passage, relating to the coming of Jesus to Gennasar, or Gennesareth (vi, 53–56), is a transition piece, an interlude loaded with miracle, which betrays the editorial hand but has no significance peculiar to itself. It forms a natural introduction to the anecdote of the Syro-phenician woman (vii, 24–30) from which it is cut off by the dispute about the washing of hands. This dispute is a fragment of anti-Jewish polemic for which this was probably thought to be the best place. Like the discourse in parables, it is built up on some sayings attributed to the Christ (vii, 9–12; 14–15), the last of them imparting moral instruction in terms rather gross. This has been overlaid with a gloss (vii, 3–4), a prophetic quotation (6–8) and an admonitory explanation, the whole tending to make Jesus proclaim the futility of Jewish prohibitions and scruples about food.

The miracle of a cure operated at a distance, in response to the mother's prayer, on a girl possessed by a devil, the mother being a woman of the country and said to be Syro-phenician, forms a counterpart to the story of the Roman centurion in the other two Synoptics (Matthew viii, 5–13; Luke vii, 1–10) and signifies in like manner that nations never visited by Jesus, as the Jews have been visited, will be saved by him. The cure of the deaf-mute in the country of the Decapolis is a miracle operated for symbolic reasons in pagan territory, which are also the reasons for the utterly unintelligible itinerary which the narrative makes Jesus follow between the two miracles of multiplied loaves. This cure of the deaf-mute, peculiar to Mark, is counterpart to that of the blind man at Bethsaida (viii, 22–26), the two being cut out on the same model. Both must be attributed to an editor of Mark who may have freely exploited some deposit of written or oral tradition, or may himself have constructed the two stories with a view to the lesson to be drawn from them, on the lines of other Gospel narratives or of the practice commonly followed by exorcist-healers in those times.

No argument is needed to prove that the second miracle of multiplication is a duplicate of the first. It may have been imagined to figure the initiation of the Gentiles into the Christian mystery; or it may be that another version of the first miracle has been utilized for that purpose. At all events it is not by chance that in the first multiplication twelve baskets full of fragments are left over, twelve being the cypher for Israel, and corresponding to the Twelve who first governed the community of Aramean-speaking believers in Jerusalem, while in the second miracle there are seven baskets, the cypher for the Gentiles, corresponding to the Seven presiding over the group of hellenist believers whose dispersion after the death of Stephen set on foot the propagation of the Gospel outside Palestine and among the pagans. It is noteworthy that the second multiplication does not occur in the third Gospel, and that the stories are omitted which Mark has lodged between the first and the confession of Peter: whence we may infer that this long section of Mark (vi, 45 to viii, 26) belongs to a late stage in the development of our Gospel.

As though to explain and justify the future reprobation of the mass of the Jews the evangelist has introduced, after a second multiplication of loaves, a sentence about the Pharisees asking for signs, in which Jesus refuses the sign demanded (viii, 11–12). This trait comes from a source known to Matthew (xii, 38–40; cf. xvi, 4) and to Luke (xi, 29–30). But in the source the sign mentioned is the sign of Jonah. Did our evangelist reflect that the sign of Jonah, that is the sign of the resurrection, did not take place for the Jews? It is more probable that the sign of Jonah, which was made much of at the first, soon became embarrassing with its three days and three nights, which could not be fitted into the liturgical framework adopted by most churches in the second century for commemoration of the Passion and the Resurrection. The liturgical framework being interpreted as a chronology in which Jesus rose the third day after his death it was difficult to see how he could have spent three days and three nights in the tomb, like Jonah in the belly of the fish.

Thinking it appropriate to follow this up by a reflexion of his own, on the first disciples' lack of understanding in presence of the mystery of salvation, our editor attaches it to a saying about the leaven of the Pharisees, which the collection of *logia* places in another context (cf. Luke xii, 1*b*), his object being to make Jesus unsuccessfully hint to the disciples that the two multiplications signify the inexhaustible gift of salvation: whereas the disciples were thinking only of food to put into their mouths. As an historical record it is of no value. But the indication it gives of ill-will towards the Galilean disciples is important and should be kept in mind.

The cure of the blind man at Bethsaida (viii, 22–26) has also a symbolic value, but falls into another current. It serves as introduction to Peter's confession and seems intended to figure the progressive education of the first disciples, their adhesion to the messianic faith and the origin of the Jewish-Christian community. If we refer to the third Gospel, where Peter's confession follows on immediately after the multiplication of loaves (Luke ix, 10–21), it would seem that the version of Mark which the writer to Theophilus has reproduced presented the two events in the same close succession, and localized both the miracle and the confession at Bethsaida. A complete misunderstanding of the character and origin of our documents is shown by those critics who explain the relation between Mark and Luke, in this part of the two Gospels, by supposing that Luke was making use of an accidentally mutilated copy of Mark. Is it, then, so natural that Mark, in its earliest form, had the multiplication of loaves and the calming of the tempest, etc., twice over? In these matters the simplest hypotheses are not always the best. To be sure, canonical Mark is a very slender document; nevertheless it shows no lack of duplications, re-shapings, overlays and editorial superfluities.

With the confession of Peter (viii, 27–30) we enter on the second part of the Gospel catechesis, the cycle of the Last Supper, and encounter at the outset an almost certain antedating of an element fundamental in the eschatological catechesis, namely Peter's faith in Jesus-Messiah, in Jesus-Christ. No account need be taken of the preamble (viii, 27–28) which has already served to introduce the legend of John the Baptist (vi, 14–16). The essential element is the messianic confession of Simon: "Thou art the Christ." As in all similar cases, the imposition of silence on the disciples (viii, 30) is a sure sign that material of post-resurrection origin is being thrown back into the record of Jesus' ministry on earth. Whatever the historical preparation may have been for Peter's faith in Jesus as the Christ, his first *affirmation* of that faith was not made until, in his belief, Jesus was already risen as the Christ. That granted, we may be sure that the natural sequel, and probably the original sequel, to Peter's confession is to be found in the declaration of Jesus (ix, 1), with all restriction removed, "Those who are here shall see the coming of God's kingdom," intimating that the Great Event is at hand. Attached to this is the disciples' question about the preliminary coming of Elijah, with the answer given by Jesus (ix, 11–13): "Elijah indeed is already come, and they have done to him what they would, as it is written of him," to be understood of the ministry of John conceived as preliminary, not to the earthly ministry of Jesus, but to the advent of Jesus-Messiah in the Kingdom of God. The insertions in the text between these two eschatological utterances belong to the development of the Gospel catechesis. Let us now consider these in turn.

The first insertion (viii, 31–38) opens with the first announcement of the passion and resurrection of the Son of Man, and we are told that the announcement was made publicly, in contrast to what just before has been indicated concerning the Messiahship of Jesus. Now the Son of Man is constantly, in our Gospel, the Messiah who redeems mankind from sin by his saving *death*; he is the Christ of the salvation-mystery as presented in the gnosis of the Epistle to the Romans. There follows, on the announcement, a vigorous protest from Peter, who has understood nothing of the mystery's economy, with the yet more vigorous reprimand of Jesus: "Get thee gone, Satan!" etc. (viii, 31–33). This episode, plainly to Peter's discredit, falls into the current of mystical gnosis and is in line with the invectives launched in the Pauline Epistle against the old disciples, reputed apostles and treated as Judaizers. After this comes a general call to renunciation as a normal condition of salvation (viii, 34–38); this is a gloss of the evangelist on sayings taken from the collection of *logia*, an oracle of some Christian prophet speaking in the name of Jesus (cf. x, 38–39; 32–33). Taken by themselves these sayings in the *logia* already implied the obligation laid upon the believer to become united mystically and morally with the risen Christ, if he would be recognized by Jesus when he came in his glory.

The second insertion (ix, 2–10) is the miracle of the Transfiguration, an antedating of the exaltation of Jesus as the Christ, of his assumption into glory, as taught in the eschatological catechesis. Here the final exaltation is reduced to a provisory miracle, prelude to the final glory. The antedating is again betrayed by the charge to keep silence, which we are told was kept by the three witnesses of the miracle. These witnesses were chosen with a purpose in view; because this abbreviated miracle could not be conveniently presented as a public spectacle, and also because it was designed to exhibit the three disciples as witnesses who did not understand what they saw, aiming especially at Peter, who is credited with the absurd notion of domiciling Jesus, Moses and Elijah on the mountain by building three tents for them to live in (cf. *supra*, pp. 53-4).

The miracle of the epileptic (ix, 17–29), artificially co-ordinated with the miracle of the Transfiguration, is a common case of exorcism, but strongly dramatized, with a view to emphasizing the power of true faith, in presence of the mighty and beneficent Christ, the incredulity of the Jews and the impotence of the disciples. The mention of a journey *incognito* across Galilee serves to bring in a second prediction of the Passion (ix, 31–32), presented as not understood by the disciples, and for the same reason.

There follows a series of lessons the interconnection of which is not easily grasped; they must have been taken from the collection of *logia*, and compose a catechesis mainly ethical, which the

Gospel editors have framed in their usual manner. First comes the lesson of apostolic service, conceived as having been pro-voked by the preposterous claims of the disciples—another point not intended to enhance their glory—and combined with instruction on the obligation to receive the least of the Christ's people, and the advantage that follows from receiving him as one who is the Christ himself and God in the Christ (ix, 36–37). Next, the saying: "Who is not against us is with us," strange counterpart to "who is not with me is against me" in the collec-tion of *logia* (Matthew xii, 30; Luke xi, 23) here brought in as conclusion to the anecdote about the unqualified exorcist (ix, 38–40), together with the saying about the cup of water given in the name of the Christ (ix, 41; cf. Matthew x, 42)—the whole permeated by the spirit of mystical gnosis. Next, propositions about scandal and the punishment in store for him who causes it (ix, 42), and on scandal already experienced, which must not continue, on pain of Gehenna. Finally, the metaphor of the savourless salt with the appropriate lesson (ix, 49–50).

From this example, one of many others, we are able to see that the Gospel editors proceeded in their work as if the sayings they utilized were teachings whose sense was not very clearly defined, and whose connections of time and place in the life of Jesus could be laid down at will, for the simple reason that nothing whatever was known about the matter. We have already remarked how they operated in the same way with the facts adorning their narratives. By these proceedings they were able to construct and fill out a legend, astonishingly poor in real memories, into the artless mosaic before us, whose incoherence is ill-dis-guised by the manifold devices of the editors to provide it with a containing frame.

The itinerary of the journey to Judea is vague enough, and the editor, in search of matter to garnish it, found to hand the ques-tion of divorce (x, 1–12), the saying about children, with whose simplicity men should accept the announcement of the Kingdom (x, 13–16), and the case of the rich young man (x, 17–22), into which are brought the sayings about the difficulty of salvation for the rich (x, 23–27) and the reward in store for those who have left all for Christ (x, 28–31). The reprobation of divorce is a characteristic feature of early Christianity. We are given the biblical ground for condemning divorce (x, 2–9), the origin of which has still to be explained. The biblical argument is some fragment of controversy on the subject; the reprobation is taken from the collection of *logia* (cf. Matthew v, 32; Luke xvi, 18); the setting is artificial (cf. 1 Corinthians vii, 10, where the reprobation seems derived from Christian mysticism). The story of the children is the original version in relation to the version which doubles it in ix, 36, but seems to have been conceived to enforce the duty of receiving the announcement of the Kingdom with unquestioning simplicity.

Though not otherwise dated or localized, the anecdote of the rich young man is more circumstantial, but, in spite of this, is tybical rather than historical. Even the saying: "Why callest thou me good? None is good save God" is a mystic subtilty rather than a living trait; the command to follow Jesus seems to carry, not a literal sense, but the moral sense of initiation into the Christ and entry into the community of the believers, while the reflections on the difficulty of salvation for the rich are made to fit in with corresponding features in the narrative. Entirely second-hand and artificial is the promise of double reward, in this world and the next, to those who have followed Jesus, that is, to believers (x, 28–31). The source, derived perhaps from the eschatological catechesis, probably contained the promise of thrones to the twelve disciples, as arranged in the tradition which glorified them (Matthew xix, 28; cf. Luke xxii, 30): the outlook toward the messianic triumph has been replaced by the promise of reward for renunciation and by a clear and detailed prophecy of the Passion (x, 33–34).

Judging by the preamble to it (x, 32) and by the context of it (x, 32–34) this prediction seems intended to introduce the Jerusalem cycle of the Gospel legend; taken as a whole and in connection with what follows (the request of James and John and the lesson of service, 35–45), it would seem to be constructed on the idea of the messianic triumph, as we have just seen, but so as to push it back in order to mark the conditions to be fulfilled before the Great Event. After the two earlier prophecies of the Passion, the point made prominent is the lack of understanding on the part of the disciples, especially on Peter's. Here this lack of understanding is fixed upon James and John, and figured by their claim to the two highest thrones on the right and left of the Christ. Jesus answers by announcing their coming martyrdom and throwing back upon God the distribution of places in the Kingdom; after which he turns to the disciples in a body and gives them the lesson of service, of which all are supposed to be in need, supporting it with the authority of his own example: "The Son of Man is come to serve and to give his life as a ransom for many." Both the pretensions of the disciples and the lesson of service have been anticipated in the preceding cycle (ix, 33–35). This repetition and expansion of a lesson already given is yet another witness to the poverty of the tradition. As we have just seen, the lesson of service corresponds to the mystical conception of salvation by the death of the Christ and to the age when the Christian community was organized. Its insertion into the legend of Jesus is, therefore, artificially contrived.

The miracle at Jericho (x, 46–52) is presented under the same conditions as the chief miracles in Galilee. It is a symbol and figure of salvation, of the light given to faith. It is fittingly placed at the threshold of the great mystery and may have been originally conceived as a fulfilment of prophecy (Isaiah xxxv, 5). The story is otherwise isolated, and the narrator has not thought of making it contribute to the coming outburst of enthusiasm on the Mount of Olives. All the incidents in the Passion cycle of the Gospel are presented as independent one of another, the reason being that they are not a sequence of memories but are deduced, more or less, from biblical texts.

Clearly, also, the messianic triumph on the Mount of Olives (xi, 1–10) has been constructed on certain Old Testament texts (cf. Zechariah ix, 9; Psalm cxviii, 26; Genesis xlix, 11). The localization of the incident is in like manner related to a text in prophecy (Zechariah xiv, 4). Have we not already seen the Mount of Olives chosen for the messianic exaltation (*supra*, p. 54)? The invention of the preliminaries in Mark is a masterpiece of childlike invention (xi, 1–6).

In what follows an artificial time-order is constructed to serve as frame for the events narrated and the teachings recorded. This time-order may well be in direct relation with the ritual commemoration of the events described, which are presented in their

93

mystical meaning and value, and not in the order of their real historical sequence, so far as they can be said to belong to that order at all.

The cursing of the fig tree (xi, 12–14) and its effect (xi, 20–21), separated the one from the other, sit awkwardly astride on the expulsion of the traders, an independent story, conceived as a fulfilment of prophecy (Malachi iii, 1; Zechariah xiv, 21), like the messianic triumph, with which it is logically co-ordinate. The miracle of the fig tree is a symbolic act, conceived in the same spirit as the parable of the fig tree (Luke xiii, 6–9), if not constructed upon it, to represent the Christ's futile visit to Israel and placed, with that intention, in connection with the arrival of Jesus in the temple. But, with a view to amplifying the teaching of Jesus in Jerusalem, this fiction is joined by the editors to the lesson of faith (xi, 22–23), taken from the collection of *logia* (cf. Matthew xvii, 20), which they have exploited in the story of the epileptic (ix, 23–24; *supra*, p. 90). To this are added some words on the certainty of an answer to prayer and on the need to pardon one's neighbour in order to obtain pardon from God (xi, 24–26; cf. Matthew vii, 11; xviii, 19; Luke xi, 5–13; xviii, 1–8).

By an editorial combination the question of the priests (xi, 27–33) seems to be related to the expulsion of the traders, as the latter is more or less attached to the messianic triumph (xi, 12–14 makes a place for the cursing of the fig tree before the expulsion of the traders, while xi, 18–19 is a general remark originally conceived as the conclusion of the Jerusalem stories). In answer to the priests' demand for the authority on which he claimed to act, Jesus is made to pose an embarrassing question about the baptism of John. To discuss its historical probability would be wasted time; it bears witness to the link which originally existed between Christianity and the sect founded by John, to the advantage which Christian apologetic sought to derive from it and to the purely rabbinical subtilty of the argument when first started. Originally the incident must have figured among the sayings about John the Baptist, of which the main body is preserved in Matthew xi, 2–19 and Luke vii, 19–35.

The natural conclusion of this story would be the retreat of the questioners (xii, 12: "And leaving him they departed"), who

94

thereupon send some of the Pharisees to trap him over the question of tribute. Between the anecdote and this conclusion someone has intercalated the parable of the Wicked Husbandmen (xii, 1–11), a short apocalypse which turns on the fall of Jerusalem, the evangelization of the pagans and of the assumption of Jesus into glory; a fragment of apologetic in the style of the discourses attributed in Acts to the first Christian preachers, and even ending with the usual quotation of the apologists (Psalm cxviii, 22–23). This must be the work of some Christian prophet, utilized at first as the conclusion of the Jerusalem ministry (note the correspondence of xii, 12a with xiv, 1–2) before being replaced for that purpose by the great apocalyptic discourse (xiii).

The question and answer about tribute to Caesar is intended to prove that the Christ was not a rebel against Roman authority. It was composed to prevent the Christians being classed with the Jewish Zealots, in revolt against the empire. No such question arose for Jesus and the believers of the first generation; but, when hopes of the Second Coming began to waver, the timeliness of thus defining the principle involved is not hard to understand.

Just as the question about tribute was conceived, for the setting of the scene, as posed by the Pharisees in league with the Herodians, so the question about the resurrection (xii, 14–27) is raised by the Saduccees, people "who say there is no resurrection," but here presented in a body, whereas in the preceding case the precaution had been taken of bringing to the front only "*some* of the Pharisees and Herodians." The intention evidently was to show Jesus in conflict at close quarters with the principal Jewish sects. And yet no two things could belong to regions further apart than this question and that of the tribute, since the point raised about the resurrection is treated as a dispute of the schools, while the greater part of the passage, both question and answer, might have been borrowed, just as it stands, from Jewish scholastic. Nevertheless there are two elements in Jesus' answer: a direct argument drawn from the actual conditions in the Kingdom of God, and an argument derived from a mystical and spiritual conception of immortality, which is the more remarkable in this passage by reason of its incompatibility with the vulgar notion of the resurrection retained in the *corpus* of the anecdote, and which we shall presently see applied to the Christ himself.

Immediately following comes the Great Precept of love to God and man, brought in, like its predecessors, without natural connection. Taking the anecdote literally we should conclude that this principle, in which many in our time have gone out of their way to find the essence of the Gospel, was not announced by Jesus until he had to answer an academical question posed for him by a scribe who wished to test the soundness of his judgment. Comparing Mark's account of the incident with Luke xii, 25–28, it seems that the story was first constructed without any indication of place, and that the questioner himself found the good answer to his question, Jesus merely praising him for answering so well. This the tradition of Mark has transposed to the Jerusalem ministry, and it is evident that the canonical version of the Gospel has been arranged so as to put the first announcement of the great commandments in the mouth of Jesus. At least it is clear that the Gospel editors were not thinking about "the essence of Christianity."

The whole group of these arguments is wound up by the saying: "No man dared to ask him any more questions." The perspective is conventional; for, between the announcement of the Kingdom and Jewish authority, there was nothing to debate in matters of casuistry, morals or even chronology. But our Gospel goes further. It exhibits Jesus as taking the offensive and publicly raising the problem of the Christ (xii, 35–37). The scribes say that the Christ is the son of David; but are not the scribes under deception, seeing that David himself, in a text inspired by God (Psalm cx, 1), addressed him as his Lord? Tradition has here picked up, probably without understanding, some story born in Christian circles in which the authority of Scripture was invoked to get rid of the Messiah's Davidic descent, and profession made that the Lord Christ had no need of descent from an earthly king, if indeed he was humanly descended at all. So, once more, what we have before us is an anticipation, in which Jesus himself is made to bring to light the text which Christian tradition soon pitched upon as meaning that he was Lord Christ, not by filiation to David, but became so by resurrection from the dead.

The tradition of Mark has borrowed from the collection of *logia* an abridgment of invectives against the Pharisees (xii, 38–40) just as it borrowed from the same source an abridgment of the discourse on the apostolic mission (this collection seems originally to have consisted in the main of moral precepts and of anti-Jewish polemic, in keeping with the eschatological catechesis). If, in these cases, more was not taken from the source, the reason is that Mark's tradition makes no pretence to replace it, but rather indicates it by way of reference.

The story of the widow and her gift of two farthings (xii, 41–44) comes we know not whence. This story, which is of mediocre import, was probably constructed on a theme previously known, and inserted here for the simple reason that the compiler was in search of something more to say. It attaches to nothing in the context, and has no analogy with the other incidents grouped together as appropriate to the Jerusalem ministry.

Finally comes the great apocalyptic discourse (xiii) of which a detailed analysis would here be superfluous. Critics freely admit that it is based on a short Jewish apocalypse earlier than the capture of Jerusalem and the destruction of the Temple by Titus in 70: we may even assume that it goes back to the time of Caligula. This Jewish apocalypse, adopted by the Christians, has been filled out at various points, as much to enrich its moral significance as to show that Jesus himself had revealed to his disciples that many things must happen before the Great Event, by him announced as near at hand. Needless to say the apocalypse in its Christian form is later than the year 70, and that it was not elaborated all at once; the three Synoptics give it in three different versions. All three attach the main prophecy to a special prediction about the destruction of the Temple (Mark xiii, 1–2; cf. Matthew xxiv, 1–2, Luke xxi, 5–6). But Mark's tradition has a significant peculiarity in that it makes Jesus address the discourse in private, as a secret, to the four leading disciples—a proof that the Gospel catechesis at first knew nothing of the discourse as forming part of Jesus' teaching at Jerusalem. It is yet another fragment of the eschatological catechesis antedated in the evangelical.

The summary impression left by the above analyses is to the following effect. While the legend of the Galilean ministry, critically speaking, is extremely thin and artificially constructed, the story of the Jerusalem ministry, in spite of all these readjustments and additions, is even thinner and more artificial. Of the latter legend almost nothing is matter of fact save the very point which tradition has done its utmost to disguise, namely that Jesus came to Jerusalem as the herald of the Great Event, fully confident that he would succeed, through the intervention of God, in rooting out the rule of the foreigner and all the abuses rampant in Israel. This is what he expected. What met him was the wooden stake of crucifixion, unaccompanied by the extraordinary actions, discussions and discourses recorded in the story before us.

They waste their labour who search in the realm of historical reality for the solution of a problem that belongs to the realm of mystical speculation and religious myth-making. Such is the problem presented to exegetes by the contradiction between the Gospels as to the day on which Jesus suffered the death-penalty. According to the fourth Gospel it was the very day on which the Jews sacrificed the paschal lamb: according to the first three it was the next day, Jesus having eaten the Passover with his disciples on the day before (cf. *supra*, pp. 23–24). Critical exegetes up to now have been slow to recognize that this disagreement has nothing to do with the true day on which the Passion took place as an historical event, a day unknown to both sides, but corresponds to two divergent Easter observances between which the Christian churches were divided in the second century, those of Asia, which kept Easter on the same day as that on which the Jews kept the Passover, and the other, which celebrated theirs on the following Sunday, the fourth Gospel being in line with the Asiatic usage, called quartodeciman, while the Synoptics were in line with the celebration on Sunday. It is intelligible, on general grounds, that the first Christians should keep Easter on the same day as that on which the Jews kept the Passover. It is also intelligible that very soon they began to find in their Easter festival a sense peculiar to Christianity, in which the Jewish commemoration, at the Passover, of Israel's liberation gave place to commemorating the gift of salvation by Jesus Christ. Thus, for the churches of Asia, Easter celebrated the saving and triumphant death of the Lamb, the Lamb-Christ, the Lamb of God. Neverthe-less the custom established itself elsewhere, and gradually spread, of transferring the Passion, now become the Christian Easter, to the Sunday, the Lord's day, the day of the *risen* Christ, adopted as the day of *resurrection* on which the work of salvation came to its crowning point, rather than on the day of *death*, the commemora-tion of which was now attached to the preceding Friday, while the institution of the eucharist, now become a mystic symbol of the saving death, remained attached to the last meal of Jesus, understood as the paschal meal. Thus the Gospel catechesis, in its two forms, canonized the quartodeciman observance on the one side and the Sunday observance on the other. On neither side was there any concern to fix the historical day on which Jesus suffered. We do not even know the precise year of the Passion; little wonder then that we are ignorant of the day. But let us first consider how Passion Week is presented in Mark.

The Passion in Mark

According to our Gospel (xiv, 1–2) two days before "the Passover and the feast of Unleavened Bread"—this, in the language of Mark and Matthew, might mean the previous day, that is, 13 Nizan, but including in it what would be for us the evening of 12th—"the high priests and scribes" decided to make an end of Jesus, but to avoid arresting him during the festival, which might have provoked a tumult among the people. The matter in hand, then, was to get the affair over before 14 Nizan, the day of the feast. This preamble, which seems of ancient date in its present place, does not agree with what follows. It naturally introduces, and should be followed by, the plot hatched between the high priests and Judas for the secret arrest of Jesus (xiv, 10–11). But between the two there has been intercalated the scene of anointing at Bethany (3–9), lodged precisely in the place occupied by the last meal of Jesus—the evening on which 13 Nizan began. The writer having delayed this last meal in order to identify it with the Jewish Passover—the evening on which 14 Nizan began—has put another meal in place of that originally indicated as the last; but, just as he introduces into the last meal the symbolism of the saving death along with the institution of the mystic Supper, so he introduces it into his duplicate of the last, making use perhaps of some story in which a sinful woman pours ointment on Jesus (cf. Luke vii, 36–50). The inventor of the scene in Mark was no admirer of the disciples who are here represented as railing at the woman for wasting her money, while Jesus has to explain to them the mystic sense of what she has done. It is interesting to note that the statements of Jesus about "the Gospel preached throughout the whole world" presupposes that the Gospel catechesis, to which the writer assigns a place in the scene just constructed, has already taken a constituted form.

Follows the bargain struck between the high priests and Judas for the betrayal of Jesus (xiv, 10–11). The question may well be asked whether the rôle assigned to Judas is not fictitious from beginning to end, a symbol of Judaism as the villain of the piece. The truth is, as we shall see, that the Judas-legend underwent continuous enlargement in Christian tradition, and that Judas (if he ever existed) cannot have been one of the Twelve, since the college of the Twelve was not instituted by Jesus. He is also an embarrassment in the legend of the Twelve, which was first formed with no knowledge of Judas. We have already called attention (*supra*, p. 92) to the saying about "the twelve thrones" reserved in the Kingdom for Jesus' companions (Matthew xix, 28): are we then to suppose that Judas was to occupy one of them? A traitor being needed for the elaboration of the drama, imagination invented the rôle of Judas and biblical texts were duly found to give authority to the legend.

The story of the last meal comes between the traitor's compact and the arrest of Jesus (xiv, 12–31). The preliminary story (12–17) of the finding of the guest chamber is a writer's fiction equally artless and cut to the same pattern as that of the tied colt which introduces the messianic triumph on the Mount of Olives (xi, 1–6). It was deemed appropriate to make Jesus, as the meal proceeded, announce the coming treachery of which he was to be the victim, the circumstances and form of the prediction showing that the writer had in mind the text of Psalm xli, 9 (expressly quoted in John xiii, 18), while the threat aimed at the traitor suggests that the evangelist was already acquainted with some sombre legend about Judas, such as that in Matthew xxvii, 3–8 and Acts i, 16–19.

The essential point of the meal lies in its mystical relation with the Christian Supper, of which it is the prototype. But two different conceptions of the Supper are present in the story, one superimposed on the other. According to the earlier conception it was imagined that Jesus, in the course of this his last meal, which was not the paschal meal, after pronouncing the customary benediction on the bread and the cup, announced to the disciples that their next meal together would be in the Kingdom of God (xiv, 25). In this type the Supper was understood as anticipating the fellowship of the elect with the Christ in his Kingdom, an anticipation in which memory of Jesus' death and resurrection is implied only. Upon this primitive and eschatological meaning of the Supper, already figured in the miracle of the multiplied loaves, the editing hand has grafted (xiv, 22–24) the conception of the mystic Supper, according to which the bread becomes symbolically the body of the Christ, and the wine his blood, the Supper being now understood as a rite of holy communion with Jesus, redeemer of mankind by his death, as announced in I Corinthians xi, 23–25. Note that, in this conception, the Christ is the paschal lamb of the Christians, and that this was not the precise point of departure for fixing Easter on Sunday. This in passing; what we have here to point out is the editorial artifice of the superposition. The artifice is clearly perceptible in Mark (xiv, 23–25):

> And taking the cup, after giving thanks, he gave it to them, and they all drank of it. And he said to them: "This is my blood of the covenant, shed for many. Verily I say unto you, I will drink no more of the product of the vine until that day when I shall drink it new in the Kingdom of God."

When the disciples had drunk the wine, the time was past for saying "this is my blood," which is here made to follow the drinking. The natural sequence after "they all drank of it" is "I will drink of it no more," etc. This was the order in the basis-story: it spoke *only* of the bread that he would eat no more and of the wine that he would drink no more till they ate and drank together in the Kingdom of God. The institution of the mystic Supper ("this is my blood," etc.) is a highly distinct afterthought in the development of the Gospel catechesis.

The meal over, the company withdraws to the Mount of

Olives, and Jesus announces the defection of all the disciples conformably to the prophecy in Zechariah xiii, 7, a prediction of early date in the tradition, as is also the discovery of the suitable text. But what follows (xiv, 28): "But after my resurrection I will go before you into Galilee" is a palpable surcharge to bring in the discovery of the emptied tomb, a fiction whose adventitious and later character is thus plainly indicated. Another prediction is that of Peter's denial (xiv, 29–31). It is obvious that the denial, if it really happened (or even if it did not), and the defection or flight of the disciples must have formed part of the tradition before it was deemed advisable to make the Christ predict them. But, in view of the ill-will to the original Galilean disciples, and especially to Peter, which characterizes one of the currents in Mark, it is permissible, in the one case as in the other, not only to suspect, but to affirm, that even the story of the denial has been invented at all points in the tradition of Mark, although it seems to have been retouched on the last revision which attenuated Peter's cowardice by his repentance (xiv, 72). After all, the blow hits Peter no harder than the story of his protest at the first prediction of the Passion, or that of his obstinate slumber during the threefold prayer in Gethsemane, in which the offence is also thrice repeated. Indeed, the whole scene in Gethsemane, the agony of the Christ in the Olive Garden, seems, when probed to its base, to rest entirely on Psalm xxii (cf. Hebrews v, 7, a witness independent of our Gospels, but not pointing to the scene in Gethsemane; cf. p. 46). In the Gospel before us the whole story (xiv, 32–42) is given a turn which brings out the stupidity of the three leading disciples in presence of the mystery of the redeeming death. At the last moment (xiv, 42) another prediction, that of his coming arrest to follow the betrayal of Judas, is attributed to Jesus.

A rabble, recruited by the Sanhedrim in the middle of the night and guided by the traitor, now lays hands on Jesus after brief resistance by the disciples, in which a servant of the high priest has an ear cut off, the evangelist giving prominence to the kiss of Judas, the sign agreed between him and his following, and to Jesus' declaration that all has been providentially arranged (xiv, 24–50)—the dramatic presentation of an event of which the real conditions are unknown to us. Then comes the conclusion, which is primitive in relation to the rest: the disciples take to flight in a body, abandoning Jesus to his fate; which contradicts what is to be told us a little later on about Peter's proceedings and his denial.

A trait peculiar to our Gospel which the others have not retained, doubtless thinking it insignificant, is the incident of a certain young follower in the crowd who fled naked, leaving in the hands of his assailants the cloth that covered him (51–52). Certain exegetes believe that this unknown and mysterious youth can be identified with Mark in person. Far more probably the incident is intended to fulfil a line of prophecy, "the courageous among the mighty shall flee away naked in that day" (Amos ii, 16). It has been said that such an application would be forced. Doubtless it would, but it is no less likely for that reason. Can any application of prophecy be found hereabouts which is not forced?

The crucifixion of Jesus is explicable on one ground only: he was sentenced to death and executed by the Roman authority as a sower of sedition against itself, and simply so. The efforts of the traditional legend have been concentrated on transferring responsibility for his death to the Jews, and on doing this in such a way as to make it appear that the death sentence was extorted from Pilate, or imposed upon him, while he, for his part, acknowledged the perfect innocence of the accused. In pursuit of this purpose a sentence by the Sanhedrim was imagined, and condemnation pronounced on the ground that Jesus laid claim to be Son of God, that is, to the divine character which belonged to him in the faith which accepted the Christian mystery. In this there is a double anachronism: first, in view of the fact that the Sanhedrim, in the time of the procurators, had retained full powers over the Palestinian Jews, except in matters political; and, second, that Jesus, as all four evangelists are compelled to admit, was condemned to death by Pilate on political ground as "King of the Jews," that is, to use equivalent terms, as a messianic agitator laying claim to some kind of royalty in Israel subversive of the imperial government. Historically the case of Jesus is intelligible only if we admit from the outset that he was sentenced to death by Pilate alone, acting as representative of Roman authority. Need we repeat once more that our texts are in no way concerned with history in the strict sense of the term? Their object is catechetical and, in a minor degree, apologetic.

The fictitious account of the trial before the Sanhedrim (xiv, 55–65) is oddly entangled with Peter's denial (53–72) of which a beginning is made in 53–54 and the rest of the story, given in 66–72. But, of the two stories, that of the denial is the added one. The trial scene is constructed of three elements easily distinguished: first, the evidence of the witnesses (55–59) which agrees with the saying about the temple, which Jesus was accused of boasting he would destroy and rebuild in three days, a saying which seems to have caused considerable embarrassment in Christian tradition and which, if really spoken, may have been brought up in evidence before Pilate as proof of messianic pretensions; second, the declaration of Jesus affirming his character as Son of God (60–64), brought in at that point to correct the impression given by the condemnation of the pretended King of the Jews, and to account for this condemnation by the blind fanaticism of the Jewish authorities in the presence of the Christ of mystery, divine saviour of mankind; lastly, the scenes of outrage (65) introduced for the accomplishment of prophecy, especially Isaiah l, 6; liii, 3 (Septuagint). Peter's denial, in Mark's account of it, is complicated by a *double* cock-crow. We get a glimpse of a simpler story behind it in which the crowing of the cock was not a narrative detail, but an indication that it was the third hour of the night (according to Roman usage) when the triple denial was finished (cf. xiii, 35).

The morning session of the Sanhedrim, held before Jesus is led away to Pilate's court (xv, 1), now duplicates the nocturnal session at which he was condemned. Originally, in the tradition of the second Gospel, this may have been the meeting at which the accusers concerted the charge to be brought before Pilate. In the trial before the procurator nothing has real consistence save the charge—that of pretending to messianic royalty. Our Gospel (xv, 2–5) places the interrogation of the accused before the accusation, in presence of which Jesus keeps silence, as he had done before the witnesses of Caiaphas, and for the same reason— the fulfilment of Isaiah liii, 7. Pilate's astonishment at his attitude is made to prepare the incident of Barabbas (6–15). Whatever may be the source of this fiction, which defies all probability, the aim of it is to relieve Pilate's responsibility, while establishing the innocence of Jesus. Only at the last moment does the procurator concede the order for execution which he is represented in like manner as not being able to refuse in law, the verdict of the Sanhedrim having been given according to rule.[1] Before handing Jesus over to the Jews, Pilate has him scourged, after which there follows a scene of mockery in the pretorium, of comic royalty, probably in imitation of the ancient carnivals which ended in the execution, sometimes pretended and sometimes real, of the carnival king. But here probabilities are all against the reality of a scene which is conceived in a fulfilment of a prophecy (Isaiah liii, 3–7) prefiguring the glory awaiting Jesus as celestial King (cf. Hebrews ii, 9).

Finally the soldiers, after divesting Jesus of his mock purple, give him back his own clothes and lead him off to crucifixion (xv, 20); to carry the cross, they lay hold of a bystander, Simon, a Cyrenian, "father of Alexander and Rufus" (21). So precise a detail in a story otherwise lacking in signs of clear memory, is somewhat surprising. The precision may be affected, like the name of Jairus in the resurrection miracle or that of Bar-Timaeus at Jericho. But the detail was not invented to signify that the believer must carry the cross as he follows Jesus, since it is not under compulsion, as here, that the cross must be carried: the object was rather to spare Jesus the humiliation of carrying it. The sad procession goes on its way and finally comes to a halt at a place called Golgotha, that is, Calvary (xv, 22), which was probably the usual place for execution by this method.

It seems likely that, in the story at the base of all this, mention of crucifixion (24a) followed immediately on the arrival at Golgotha, and that what is said further on about the inscription on the cross (26) followed the fixation of the body. The incidents of the aromatic wine (23) and the division of the garments (24b) mark the fulfilment of prophecies; the indication of the hour (25) belongs to the writer's systematic time-scheme which proceeds to divide the day of the Passion into four parts, the judgment of Pilate taking place in the first quarter and the fixing to the cross in the second—details connected with the ritual commemoration

---

[1] The situation in which Pilate is thus placed is not without analogy to that of certain Roman magistrates who, *in the time of the Antonines*, found themselves compelled to sentence Christians to death against their own conscience.

rather than memories. The offering of aromatic wine may be the first form under which the fulfilment of Psalm lxix, 21 was represented: "They gave me gall for meat and vinegar to slake my thirst"; while the refusal by Jesus was possibly suggested by verse 22 of the same Psalm. The clothes of the executed criminal were the perquisite of his executioners, but the evangelists mention it only as marking the fulfilment of Psalm xxii, 18. The inscription bearing the charge is a detail of Roman usage; it is mentioned by the evangelists in order that the cross may have above it the idea of messianic royalty, and they have worded it accordingly. "The King of the Jews" is the simple wording of our Gospel. The two thieves crucified with Jesus (27) are mentioned to signify the fulfilment of Isaiah liii, 12, expressly cited in the common text of Mark, though not in the oldest manuscripts. The incident was suggested by the text. The passers-by who wag their heads in derision come from Psalm xxii, 7; the insults of the Sanhedrim, who we might think had moved in a body to Golgotha (31–32), adding themselves to those of the crowd (they seem to be a late addition) are aimed at the Christ of faith, Saviour and Son of God (cf. Psalm xxii, 8; Matthew xxvii, 43); while the reproaches of the two thieves (32) are a climax to the ignominy, and complete the fulfilment of the Psalm (xxii, 7).

Dense darkness envelops the scene and lasts for three hours, from the sixth to the ninth. The darkness is an addition in Mark's version; it comes from Amos viii, 9–10 (connect with the trait mentioned above, p. 103). At the ninth hour Jesus cries with a loud voice in Aramean: "My God, my God, why hast thou abandoned me?" Such a cry of distress, say some of our modern critics, perhaps a little innocently, no one would ever have dared to put into the mouth of Jesus had he not really uttered it. They are the first words of Psalm xxii, which may be said to have guided the whole construction of the Passion, and it is natural enough that the idea of putting the first words of the Psalm on the lips of the dying Christ should occur at once to the evangelists, not indeed as attributing to him any feeling of despair (!) but the better to bring out the full realization of the Psalm, both in the incidents of the Passion and in the mind of the Christ. The appeal to God (Eli) provokes a paltry jest from a bystander about the name Elias, followed by the offering of vinegar (another fulfilment of Psalm lxix, 21 *supra cit.*; cf. Psalm xxii, 16). Then Jesus, after emitting a great cry, breathes his last (37). In the fundamental document this cry, which is inarticulate but of superhuman violence, was the only cry mentioned, the quotation of Psalm xxii and what followed it being added in the course of the Gospels formation. At the moment of death the temple veil is rent from top to bottom and the centurion on guard cries out: "This man was the Son of God." The rending of the veil has the meaning of Hebrews vi, 19–20; x, 19–20. It signifies the rupture of the "veil which was his visible flesh" and the liberation of the Christ for his entry into the heavenly sanctuary, there to make oblation of his blood and open the way for believers into Eternal Life.

The centurion's profession of faith is the evangelist's; the witness also which the Gentiles render to Christ the divine. At the beginning, and for some time afterwards, this must have been the conclusion of the Gospel legend. Admirable conclusion and of high significance when rightly understood! It means that the Christ, freed from his earthly covering of flesh, enters immediately into the glory of his eternal life. His resurrection is spiritual; it coincides with the moment of death; death and resurrection may be commemorated simultaneously: the glorious death that saves mankind, the last sigh of Jesus and the exaltation of the Lamb; the three coincident. And this, clearly understood, will help us greatly to put the right value on the next stage of the Gospel revision.

What we now go on to read (xv, 40–xvi, 8) corresponds, in general, to the later concept of a material resurrection of the body verified the third day after the death of Christ. It would seem that there were present on Calvary certain women, their existence unsuspected hitherto, who had ministered to Jesus in Galilee and followed him to Jerusalem; we are told their names (xv, 40–41).[1] According to our Gospel these women it was who established the fact of the resurrection. But in order that a material resurrection may take place a tomb must be indicated and suitable conditions provided. Legend has provided them.

So it happened that a certain Joseph of Arimathaea, a new-

[1] The rôle assigned to these women in the service of the Christ and his companions is that of the widows who, in the earliest times. ministered to the wants of the Christian communities.

comer on the scene and as unexpected as the women, a distinguished member of the Sanhedrim who awaited the Kingdom of God and was for that reason interested in the fate of Jesus, though we are not told that he was his disciple—that this Joseph had the courage to beg permission from Pilate to bury the remains of the crucified. Before granting it, Pilate sends for a centurión and gets assurance that Jesus is really dead. This is to rule out the theory that the body had been carried away, a question disputed between Jews and Christians, neither of whom knew anything of what had really happened. The permission granted, Joseph purchases a winding sheet, which must be a new one for the Christ, wraps the body in it and lays it in a sepulchral cave, the evangelist forgetting to tell us how the cave came to be at Joseph's disposal. The tomb is said to have been hewn out of a rock, doubtless in reference to prophecy (Isaiah xxii, 16; xxxiii, 16); the great stone closing the entrance is to enhance the coming miracle. Finally the Galilean women, who have been brought to Calvary for the purpose, take note of the exact spot in the cave where the body has been laid. And all that takes place in the last minutes of "the preparation," that is, at the moment when Friday's sun is setting and the Sabbath about to begin (xv, 42–47).

In this way the story is given a form which makes Jesus remain in the tomb for the entire length of the Sabbath day, *plus* the first hours of the following night. As he will leave the tomb on Sunday morning, the theft of the body could hardly be effected without violation of the Sabbath, of which the disciples are supposed incapable. Moreover the chief advantage of the arrangement is that it assigns the resurrection to the Day of the Sun, the Lord's Day, the Day of the Risen Christ, chosen as necessarily the Day of Resurrection. It is with this aim in view that the crucifixion is fixed on Friday, the Sabbath offering all the advantages needed for the duration of the period in the tomb, alike for apologetic, as we have just seen, and for symbolism, the repose of the Sabbath day providing a fitting conception of the kind of interval that death would cause in the existence of the Christ. Nevertheless the time arrangement is somewhat mechanical, though this accords with the materialized conception of the resurrection it is intended to serve. We may add incidentally that a relation exists between this ritual and symbolical time-scheme and the arrangement of the fêtes of Adonis, which comprised a first day of feasting for the marriage of Adonis, followed by his death, then a day of mourning and, on the third day, the mystical fête of the resurrection. This relation cannot be fortuitous, since the text in Hosea (vi, 2–3) which was held to announce the resurrection of Jesus, seems to contain an allusion to the fêtes of Adonis.[1]

The Sabbath ended, three women, Mary of Magdala, Mary the mother of James, and Salome, buy spices to embalm the dead body, and, Sunday morning come, arrive at the tomb just after the sun has risen. We are to suppose that Jesus had risen from the tomb as the sun rose, for the great stone is rolled to one side, the tomb is empty and a man in white, that is an angel, tells the women that Jesus the Nazarene[2] is risen and bids them inform the disciples and Peter to go into Galilee, where they will find him, as he foretold (xiv, 28; *supra*, p. 34). The frightened women then take to flight and "say nothing to any man."

So ends the authentic text of the Gospel named after Mark. The discovery of the empty tomb is held to be guaranteed by the experience of these women whom fear has prevented from speaking of it. The Gospel editor, a simple and well-intentioned man, says no more, the reason being that he is conscious of stating a fact, a pretended fact, of which nobody has heard until he here discloses it. Moreover he knew well enough that, according to a tradition from which he had not the least intention of departing, the disciples' faith in the resurrection was formed in Galilee. And, further, he probably felt himself incapable of relating the later manifestations of the risen Christ, or thought he might abstain from doing so. We may well believe that his powers of invention had already been exercised to a point which made him think it advisable to call a halt. The silence he attributes to the women is to be explained in the same way as are the injunctions to say nothing imposed on all the anticipations of Jesus' Messiahship during his earthly career.

The evangelist did not suspect that his story would soon be

[1] Cf. Glotz, *Les fêtes d'Adonis sous Ptolémée*, ii, in *Revue des Etudes grecques*, xxxiii, 12, April–June, 1920.
[2] A form substituted for "Nazorean" to mean more surely "from Nazareth"; cf. *supra*, p. 34.

judged unsatisfactory. But, before that feeling arose, other revisions of the Gospel catechesis had supplanted his in the usage
of the churches. The conclusion known as deuterocanonical, the
addition of which was deemed necessary, served simply to put
his Gospel more or less in accord, for the Christian reader, with
the other forms of the catechesis. Some of our exegetes discourse
learnedly about the lost end of Mark—one of the problems for
which no solution can be found for the simple reason that they
have no real existence. We have already said a word (p. 69)
about the approximate date of Mark.

Chapter V

ANALYSIS OF THE GOSPEL CATECHESIS

(*continued*)

THE GOSPEL ACCORDING TO MATTHEW

THE other witnesses to the Gospel catechesis must now be examined. The Gospel named after Matthew, in view of its close dependence on Mark, will be taken first; the writings ascribed to Luke and the Gospel named after John, which require special examination, will be considered later.

MARK FOLLOWED BY MATTHEW

The sketch of the legend of Jesus Christ as presented by Mark is meagre enough; but, meagre as it is, the Gospels rest upon it, especially Matthew, and Luke also, while John, who would correct it, has no other. In this we have conclusive proof of the initial poverty of what we are wont to call the Gospel tradition. In Mark it consists more of invention and of compiler's arrangement than of tradition in the strict sense. The same is true of the others, and of Matthew in the first place, which has, moreover, even more distinctly than Mark, the character of a compilation. The evidence is unmistakable that the latest revision of Mark has been absorbed, almost entire, into Matthew, though not without a partial dislocation of the material; numerous discourses, largely common to Matthew and Luke, have been inserted; and just as the construction of Mark reveals a long process of editorial operations, so the collection or collections of these discourses are progressively constructed compilations, while some of the discourses embodied in the compilation are themselves compiled. From this and from what our previous study of the Gospel catechesis and our analysis of Mark have taught us, we may safely conclude that the elements of moral instruction, with which the discourses in Matthew are almost exclusively occupied, represent, in their totality, the moral part of the eschatological catechesis, both in the elements which were simply borrowed from Jewish tradition and in those which, at first, were directly attributed to the *risen* Christ.

Before proceeding to relate the public ministry of Jesus, for which our Gospel borrows the sketchy frame given it by Mark, it presents a kind of pre-history, parallel to what we read in Luke, but so completely different as to leave no sign that the two disparate but equally fictitious stories are closely related by dependence on a common source, though we may say that they answered the same demand of the Christian consciousness. In our Gospel this pre-history comprises a genealogy of Jesus, his miraculous conception and early infancy (i–ii). Having next described the preliminaries of the Gospel preaching (iii–iv, 22) parallel to Mark (i, 1–20), the writer announces the two-fold activity he attributes to Jesus, the chief object of most of the book: "to preach the Gospel of the Kingdom and to heal all manner of disease and all manner of sickness among the peoples." We find, accordingly, all through the book, that the teaching function takes precedence of the healing activity, each main section beginning with a great discourse, or compilation of sayings, followed by a series of narrated events. These sections are as follows:

(1) The discourse known as the Sermon on the Mount (v–vii), a veritable summary of the Christian Law expressly confronted with the Jewish Law, followed by ten miracles (viii–ix, 26) freely selected from those which Mark recounts before the death of John the Baptist. (2) The discourse on the apostolic mission (ix, 35–x) which brings in a succession of precepts intermixed with some fragments of Mark omitted from the preceding selection. (3) The discourse in parables (xiii, 1–52), dominating the rest of the Galilean ministry (xiii, 53–xvii) in which the directing hand follows the order laid down in Mark. (4) A less extensive discourse (xviii) but important for the evangelist as bearing on the organization of the churches; this introduces the departure from Judea and the stories of the Jerusalem ministry (xxi–xxii). (5) The discourse against the Pharisees (xxiii) and the great apocalyptic discourse (xxiv–xxv), which close the preaching of Jesus and bring on the stories of the Passion and of the resurrection (xxvi–xxviii). In all probability the distribution of this book of initiation to the mystery of the Christ into five

sections—it may equally be called the book of the Christian Law —was conceived with an eye to the five books of the Jewish Law. In virtue of the influences it has undergone and the preoccupations it reveals, the Gospel according to Matthew can be described as Jewish Christian. Beyond doubt it is of Syrian origin; but it does not seem to be of great antiquity.

Genealogy and Birth Story

The Christian catechesis, at the beginning, knew very little about the life of Jesus prior to his public preaching; it knew, in fact, next to nothing. When curiosity arose as to these antecedents it led, not to investigation of the real facts of his earlier life—it was probably too late to make useful inquiries into that— but to imagination of what ought to have happened. The early stories in Matthew, no less than those in Luke, are adhesions to the main body of the Gospel of which they constitute the preamble, and the part whose mythical character is most obvious; they are fables built up on biblical texts in fulfilment of prophecies. Their character as fabulous is easiest to verify in Matthew because most of the texts in the writer's mind are expressly cited. The material of the stories may have been partly borrowed, consciously or not, from ancient mythologies of Eastern origin, and then worked up with an eye to Old Testament texts deemed to be prophetic.

The material begins (i, 1–17) with a genealogical list from Abraham to Joseph. Of Joseph we are told, not without some embarrassment,[1] that he was only the putative father of Jesus, espoused to the Virgin Mary, of whom was born Jesus. Evidently the evangelist found ready to his hand a list at first constructed to show how Jesus, through his father Joseph, was the authentic descendant of the patriarch Abraham, father of the faithful, recipient of the divine promises, and of King David from whom the Scriptures declared—or so it was believed—the Messiah was to issue. To prove the genealogy entirely fictitious would be

---

[1] Embarrassment is shown by the variation in the ancient readings, notably by the reading of the Syrian *Codex Sinaiticus*: "Jacob begat Joseph; Joseph, to whom the Virgin Mary was betrothed, begat Jesus who is called Christ." It is vain to contend that this cannot be true reading when compared with the equally awkward reading of the canonical version: "Joseph, espoused to Mary, of whom was born Jesus," etc., which deprives the genealogy of all meaning. The true reading, *pre-evangelical*, is surely: "Joseph begat Jesus, called Christ."

waste of argument; it is even doubly so; first, because its fundamental datum, the biblical point of departure, the patriarchal
legend namely, does not hold together and, second, because the
dates corresponding to the monarchy and to the later times are
inexact or simply imagined. Three series, of fourteen names
each, were aimed at, which ought to give a total of forty-two
ancestors from Abraham to Joseph (or to Mary); actually there
are only forty, since that was the number wanted; doubtless then
David must be counted twice over as last of the first series and
first of the second, and the same with Josiah, chosen for no
reason, as last of the second and first of the third. A mystical
number-play intended to show that Jesus was the Messiah
promised to Israel.

The symbolic fiction of the genealogy was in currency before
the stories of the miraculous birth, no less fabulous and symbolic, were elaborated. The two fictions were co-ordinated.
First comes the story of the virgin conception (i, 18–25) forming
a commentary on the prophecy in Isaiah (vii, 14) with the names
of Joseph and Mary, furnished by tradition as the parents of
Jesus. In the Septuagint translation[1] Isaiah speaks of a virgin
who would conceive; this our story understands of a virgin who
would conceive without intercourse with a man; which is not
what the text in Isaiah was intended to convey. Mary is presented
as betrothed to Joseph and impregnate by the action of the Holy
Spirit, that is, by God himself. This causes perplexity to Joseph
who, observing Mary's condition, plans to repudiate her privately;
whereupon an angel intervenes in a dream and informs Joseph of
the miracle, Mary's husband thus becoming the guarantor of his
wife's virginity. This artless fable, though modelled on the text
in Isaiah, may have been invented as an answer to some sally of
Jewish wit about the virgin conception of Jesus—for example,
the slanderous legend preserved in rabbinic tradition—at the time
when the idea of it first saw the light among Christian circles in
the East. The text in Isaiah would not have sufficed, by itself, to
produce the belief; this was suggested quite simply by ancient
mythology. The story as it originally stood in Luke, also

[1] Moreover it is not certain that the word virgin (*parthenos*) which appears in the
original translation is equivalent of the Hebrew *alma*. It may have been substituted by a
Christian hand for the more exact translation "young woman" (*neanis*). The detail is
unimportant for our subject.

founded on the text, had nothing to say about the virgin conception.

Our evangelist, believing that he had warrant in the prophet Micah (v, 2) for the birth of the Messiah at Bethlehem, supposes it to have been the home of Joseph and Mary. He gives no account of the actual birth of Jesus but illustrates it by a fantastic tale. As became a Son of God, Jesus had his star, and certain wise men from the East who were expecting the appearance of the star, because Balaam, one of their ancestors, had predicted it (Numbers xxiv, 17), set out to pay homage to the newly born King of the Jews. Arrived at Jerusalem, they inform Herod of the place where his birth is due to happen; this causes a great commotion; the learned men are summoned to council; yes, Bethlehem is the place, for Micah has said it. To Bethlehem the magi accordingly go, and there the star reappears to show them the house where the Christ is laid; they enter, adore and present their gifts, as announced in Psalm lxxii, 10–15 and Isaiah lx, 6. The lore of fairyland has no tale more marvellous.

The life of the infant Christ is now to be threatened by the wicked Herod. We are told that the magi, warned by a dream, did not return to Jerusalem to report as the King had ordered, while Joseph, on his part equally warned by a heavenly messenger in a dream, took flight into Egypt with the mother and child. But the tyrant, in his rage, makes a futile slaughter of all the children in Bethlehem and the neighbouring region, and succeeds only in procuring the fulfilment of an oracle of Jeremiah (xxxi, 15) concerning the sorrows of Rachel (ii, 13–18). The text in Jeremiah refers to certain events of the Captivity; the legend was conceived independently of the text and is, in the last analysis, the myth of the divine child, a solar deity, whom the dragon of darkness would devour at his birth. We find this myth again in the Apocalypse (xii) applied to the Son of the Heavenly Virgin, the Christ, and almost in its native form. The Gospel transports the myth from heaven to earth, where it has no more reality than in heaven.

The sojourn in Egypt was suggested by historical types (Abraham and Moses) and our evangelist has the hardihood to apply to the infant Christ a text of Hosea (xi, 1) which refers to the Jewish people. His next task was to manage the coming of the

holy family into Galilee, where tradition located the manifestation of Jesus. So, on the death of Herod, another angel comes in
a dream to Joseph with the order to return. But Bethlehem of
Judea is too dangerous for a place of abode, since a son of Herod,
Archelaus, is now reigning in that province. A new dream,
accordingly, guides them towards Galilee—our evangelist being
apparently unaware that another son of Herod (Antipas) is
reigning there—and Joseph settles down at Nazareth, thereby
fulfilling the saying of prophets: "He shall be called a Nazorean."
Which of the prophets said this, and where it is to be found, the
commentators have had some difficulty in discovering. The
name "Nazorean" is intended by the evangelist to mean "belonging to Nazareth." But mention of Nazareth is made nowhere in
the Old Testament. The pretended prophecy rests on a play
of words, and probably refers to what is said in the Book of
Judges (xiii, 5) about Samson and the "nazir." We have seen
above (p. 34) what seems to have been the original meaning of
"Nazorean."

The whole of this birth legend thus resolves itself, on analysis,
into a phantasmagory of myth and symbol. But let us never
forget that what was always held to be the main theme of the
Gospel was the doctrine of salvation, and not the legend by
which it was conveyed. This remark covers our whole study of
the evangelical legend.

The Baptism and Temptation

The baptism of John, the baptism of Jesus and the temptation
in the desert serve as introduction, in Matthew as in Mark, to the
main theme of the catechesis, to which they are preliminary. A
transition of the most artificial kind, and inaccurate into the
bargain, here attaches the account of John to the birth stories—
"in those days" (iii, 1). It was not at the time of the Christ's
birth, and probably not for many years afterwards, that John
appeared on the banks of the Jordan. For the account it gives of
John (iii, 1–12) our Gospel made use of Mark and of the source
from which Mark borrowed what he chose to take from the
discourse there tatributed to John. The account has been arranged so as to allow for the usual introduction by a prophecy
(Isaiah xl, 3). The writer is also mistaken in making John address

his allocution "to the Pharisees and Sadducees," for it was not among them but from the common people that John gathered his following. The discourse is edited from the Christian point of view which subordinates John to Jesus. And a difficulty is created by what is said about baptism "in holy Spirit and fire." At the end of the discourse (iii, 12) the fire is that of eternal punishment, which is hardly to be associated with the Spirit in the baptismal formula. It would seem that in the common source of the three Synoptics there was no mention of baptism with the Spirit but only of baptism with fire; that Mark, in substituting Spirit for fire, in that part of the discourse to which he gives a Christian turn, has radically changed the meaning of the statement attributed to John; that Matthew and Luke have followed Mark by combining his reading with that of the source-document, and by taking "fire" as here the symbolic accompaniment of baptism (recall the "tongues of fire" in the miracle of Pentecost); and, finally, that the document behind it all originated in the Baptist's sect and that, in it, John was represented as the precursor of God (rather than of Messiah) in the coming judgment. "Fire," in the two passages where it is mentioned, would thus refer to the fire of judgment and punishment. It remains to add that John, having adopted the rôle of Elijah, would clothe himself accordingly, or be said to do so.

It has already been pointed out that the baptism of Jesus by John in the Gospel catechesis is the institution of Christian baptism mythically presented and the antedating of his messianic consecration when risen from the dead. The editors of our Gospel, in which Jesus is born of the Spirit and so consecrated Messiah at the moment of his conception, were therefore bound to explain in some way why Jesus wished to be baptized by John, and for this purpose an imaginary interplay of dialogue is introduced between John, who would refuse to baptize him by whom he, John, ought rather to be baptized, and Jesus, who overcomes the reluctance of his precursor by alleging the obligation on both of them to fulfil "all righteousness." Thus the baptism of Jesus acquires for all believers the authority of a great example, while remaining, as before and always, the moment of Messiah's epiphany, clearly signified by the descent of the Spirit and the voice of the Father proclaiming his well-beloved Son (iii, 13–17).

The story of the baptism, though mythical, has some historical foundation in the relations of the Christian sect and, at first, of Jesus himself, with John the Baptist. In distinction from this, the story of the temptation is purely mythical. It reflects speculations which arose in early Christianity about the great trial through which Jesus passed in order to prove his obedience to God. Originally the great ordeal lay in the death he voluntarily accepted; it is shown forth in advance, as we have already seen and shall see again, in the agony of Gethsemane connected with the imminent reality of the redeemer's death. The scene of the temptation in the desert is another anticipation, but bears a different sense. It is here the personal trial of the Messiah as such, led by the Spirit itself into the wilderness, there to be assaulted by the prince of this world, "Satan" in Matthew, "the devil" in Luke, who appears in the story to have earthly royalty in the present age, and all its splendour, at his sovereign disposition, or thinks that he has. Two myths seem to be combined in the Christian version: that of the man of God retiring into the desert for initiation before entering on his providential mission, and that of the combat between God's agent and the Power of Evil, who tries to give him a fall or to win him over to his own service. Without entering into minute details of exegesis we may observe that the three assaults, or passages of arms, are, to judge by the blows exchanged, theological contests in which the weapons are biblical texts, as in rabbinical arguments, and that the first two temptations solicit Jesus to work miracles of supernatural magic, by turning stones into bread to satisfy his hunger, or by flinging himself from a pinnacle of the temple to prove that God is with him—miracles which, in themselves, are not so very different from those attributed to Jesus in the Gospels, but with a different significance; and, lastly, that the third solicitation, that of obtaining the kingdoms of this world by an act of homage to its prince, has a distinctly moral character—the betrayal of God to the advantage of Satan in order to usurp the power of divine authority which God alone can confer on his agent. In other words, the Christ cannot, ought not and will not be a conjurer as, for example, Simon Magus is said to be, nor a spurious Lord, invested by Satan with authority falsely called divine such as are the Roman empire and its emperor, Rome's Caesar, the

Beast of the Apocalypse, whom we are not surprised to find linked in the myth before us with Simon the Magician. The whole picture has a profound meaning which can hardly have been put into form before the years 120–130. It may be added that the vague outline of the scene in which the action is set attests the mythical character of the subject. The mountain, for example, from which all the kingdoms of the world can be viewed, is not to be found on any map.

Jesus Begins to Preach

Mark brings Jesus directly from the desert to the Sea of Galilee by way of the Jordan (i, 14–15); Matthew, on the other hand (iv, 12–13), supposes that Jesus, having learnt of John's imprisonment (effected during the sojourn in the desert), withdrew from Judea to Nazareth and afterwards made his way to Capernaum, to the land of Zebulun and Naphtali, because a prophecy of Isaiah (viii, 22–ix, 1) required him so to do. There is no need to linger over the situation beyond saying that it is in the manner of our evangelist, who has a turn for situations which he thinks prophetic. Arrived at the lake-side Jesus begins to preach, saying: "Repent, for the reign of Heaven is at hand." Matthew constantly uses the phrase "the reign (or kingdom) of Heaven" in passages when the other Synoptics say "the reign of God." The two phrases are synonymous; but Matthew conforms to the rabbinical usage which employs the word "Heaven" in order to avoid naming God. Whether the evangelist chose the word on his own account or found it in the source, or sources, from which he took the discourses of the Lord, the point is interesting as attesting a relation between our Gospel and the Jewish Christianity of Palestinian Syria.

In the calling of the first four disciples (iv, 18–22) Matthew follows Mark exactly (i, 16–20). But immediately afterwards, omitting the preaching scene at Capernaum, he constructs his introduction to the Discourse on the Mountain (iv, 23–v, 2), where he reproduces Mark's setting of the omitted scene (i, 28, 39; iii, 7–8, 10–13) of the preaching at Capernaum, and of the calling of the Twelve, stories not preserved by the editors of Matthew. It is another illustration of the truth that what our

Gospels are concerned with is the symbolic presentation of their topics while unconcerned with their historical accuracy.

The Discourse on the Mountain

The common source of the Sermon or Discourse on the Mountain (v, 3–viii), which has its parallel in Luke (vi, 20–49), where it takes place in a plain, seems to have contained the Beatitudes (Luke vi, 20–23) as an isolated exordium; the antithetical comparison of the Law and the Gospel (the principal theme of Matthew v, 17–48); the comparison (Luke vi, 43–45) of the good and the evil tree; the warning to those who give Jesus lip-service without observing his precepts (Matthew vii, 21–23); the parable of the two houses (Matthew vii, 24–49) illustrating the contrast of the diligent and the negligent hearer of his word. This shows that, already in the source, the Discourse was a compilation of detached sayings, a discourse, therefore, never delivered. None the less it has a preamble suggesting delivery, which Mark himself has used for another occasion, the calling of the Twelve, and in which we find again the gathering of crowds, numerous cures and even the mountain, which has nothing to do with the matter in hand.

Originally the Beatitudes (v, 3–12) were four in number (as in Luke vi, 20–23), eschatological in meaning and reflecting the situation of persecuted believers. They are the outpouring of some Christian prophet, selected as a kind of exordium for the discourse before us. Either our evangelist, or the version he has chosen for reproduction, has given the Beatitudes a moral turn by paraphrases and by addition, making the real poor into "the poor in spirit," the hungry into "those who hunger for righteousness," and adding to them "the gentle," "the merciful," "the pure in heart" and "the peacemakers." Before coming to the parallel between Law and Gospel he inserts the similes of "salt" (v, 13) and "the lamp" (v, 14–16), applying them to the disciples and pointing to the Good Example (cf. Mark ix, 49–50; iv, 21; Luke xiv, 34–35; xi, 33).

The long instruction on the relations of Gospel and Law (v, 17–48) is addressed to Christian communities already formed outside Judaism. The moral sayings of which it is composed were originally independent, but the work of bringing it to its present

form as a collection must have been earlier than the compilation of our first Gospel. The dominant idea, expressed in the
preamble (v, 17–18) was that the Law subsists as an integral
element, but completed, in the Gospel; the idea of a spiritual and
moral realization of the Law, more perfect than the literal fulfilment of prescriptions by the Pharisees, is superimposed upon it
(v, 17, 20). The antithetic presentation of the two moralities is
not carried through without considered design in the arrangement. The first example (v, 21–22) opposes the Mosaic prohibition of murder to the Christian prohibition of anger and insult;
but, while the Law forbids murder, that is not with a view to
permitting or commending outrageous language. Before passing
to the second antithesis the writer inserts two counsels of practical wisdom; the first, on reconciliation (v, 23–24) which alludes
to the temple cult, is, in all probability, a precept of Jewish
morality; the other, on the drawbacks of litigation (v, 25–26) is
a counsel of common prudence, awkwardly applied, by suggestion, to the question of salvation. Such various proceedings make
it plain that we are here in the presence of a compilation of moral
precepts, not of an ethical treatise logically constructed, still less
of a discourse continuously spoken.

The second antithesis, which bears on adultery and evil
desires, is more forced than the first, since evil desires are forbidden by the Law no less than by the Gospel, which shows this
play of antitheses to be an exercise in academic debate, as malevo-
lent as it is uncalled-for. To the second antithesis the Gospel
editors have judged it opportune to annex an injunction against
yielding to the involuntary suggestion of the senses in general,
which Mark had found in a collection of sayings on "causing to
stumble" (ix, 42–48).

The third antithesis (v, 31–32) brings out the Christian
reprobation of divorce which the Law allows: it is derivative
in relation to Mark x, 2–9. An exception is introduced into
the prohibition by Matthew: "save in case of fornication,"
which upsets the balance of the antithesis and weakens its
effect.

The fourth antithesis (v, 33–37) is directed against oath-taking
which the Law allows while forbidding perjury. The entire piece,
a discussion in rabbinical casuistry, may well be a personal con-

tribution of the compiler who drew up this whole series of oppositions.

In the fifth antithesis (v, 38–42) a subtle contrast is drawn between the legal rule of an eye for an eye and the teaching of long-suffering and renunciation, a lesson which must originally have stood alone.

The same applies to the sixth antithesis (v, 43–47) in which the lesson on loving enemies is opposed, quite improperly, to the legal precept "thou shalt love thy neighbour" interpreted as though it meant "thou shalt hate thy enemy," which the Law says nowhere, and which the evangelist has no right to make it say. Thus we are bound to conclude that the famous parallel between Law and Gospel, which dominates the Discourse on the Mountain, is far from deserving the admiration bestowed upon it by commentators.

Complete in itself and composed in very accurate rhythm, the teaching of the three works of piety, almsgiving and fasting (vi, 1–6, 16–18), which is found only in Matthew, has been introduced into the Discourse by an editorial combination. This lesson, also, is addressed to Christians already separated from Judaism, whose essential practice it preserves, while forbidding practice after the manner of the "hypocrites," by which no doubt we are to understand the Pharisees, who are supposed to do these works less to please God than to win applause from men. In the second paragraph, relating to prayer, the Gospel editors have thought it fitting to introduce the Lord's Prayer with a didactic preamble (vi, 7–8) and a complementary lesson on the need to pardon men their offences if we wish to be ourselves pardoned by God (vi, 14–15). Luke (xi, 1–4) gives the same prayer in a shorter form and in a different connection, from which it would seem that the prayer itself, of which the core is Jewish, was not worded at first in the traditional form as given in Matthew. While it goes back to the earliest times of Christianity, there is no certainty that it was enjoined by Jesus himself.

The special lessons which now follow (vi, 19–30) are found dispersed in Luke but are here gathered together by Matthew to give more body to the Discourse: treasures to be amassed in heaven, not on earth (vi, 19–21; Luke xii, 33–34), a saying in harmony with the spirit of the earliest Christian community and doubtless also with that of Jesus, but possibly borrowed from Jewish wisdom; simile of the eye, light of the body (vi, 22–23; Luke xi, 34–36), a *dictum* of uncertain application with a slight rabbinical flavour, which somehow found its way into Christian tradition; impossibility of serving two masters, God and money, at the same time (vi, 24; Luke xvi, 13), another proverb of which the moral application may not have been confined to Christians; exhortation against worry about food and raiment, because God provides them (vi, 25–33; Luke xii, 22–31), a lesson on the same note and probably of the same origin as the preceding but with a more distinctively Christian tone; lastly, a saying against anxiety for the morrow, a counsel of common wisdom, to which the evangelist has added a clause ("for the morrow will be anxious for itself") which corrects and slightly contradicts the care-free attitude enjoined by the Gospel.

It is likely that, in the common source of Matthew and Luke, the injunction against judging others (vii, 1–5; Luke vi, 37–38, 41–42) followed the lesson on loving one's enemy (v, 44–48; Luke vi, 35–36): a precept of social discipline, rather than of charity, which must have come from Jewish wisdom. The caution against giving holy things to dogs (vii, 6), peculiar to Matthew, is also in the style of a Jewish proverb which Christian tradition found adaptable to its own use and capable of many different applications. The lesson about prayer (vii, 7–11; Luke xi, 9–13) was probably placed in the source next to the Lord's Prayer. In the first revision of the Discourse the command to do unto others as we would be done by, an ancient precept of Jewish morality, must have come between the lesson on loving one's enemy and the caution against judging. The comparison of the two ways (vii, 13–14), familiar in Jewish morality, is an importation into the Discourse, here combined by the Gospel editors with that of the two gates (cf. Luke xiii, 23–24). The warning against false prophets has no sense except as concerning Christian communities already formed. It makes the transition to the figure of the tree and its fruits (vii, 15–20; Luke vi, 43–45), a proverb of easy moral application, placed in the source after the lesson against judging. The declaration as to who will be admitted into the Kingdom of God is composed of two elements: one on the true disciple (vii, 21), a duplicate of that on the true parents (xii, 50), and the other a menace against false disciples (vii, 22–23; Luke xiii, 26–27) who are here false Christian teachers; the whole of it must have been first announced to the community in the name of Jesus. The final comparison of the two houses (vii, 24–27; Luke vi, 47–49) was constructed on a given theme to wind up the Discourse. What we read afterwards about the impression made on the crowd (vii, 28–29) is simply transposed from Mark i, 22.

Taking the Discourse as presented in the canonical version we have before us a treatise on Christian perfection, compiled by the evangelist for the edification of the Churches.

The Ten Miracles supporting the Discourse

To start the series of ten miracles in which Jesus now proceeded to manifest his healing power, the story of the leper (viii, 1–4) has been borrowed from Mark (i, 40–44). In the common source of Matthew and Luke, the Discourse on the Mountain was followed immediately by the story of the centurion (viii, 5–11), as in Luke vii, 1–10: conformably to its symbolic meaning, the saying about the elect who will come from the East and the West has been inserted into it (cf. Luke xiii, 28–29). Thus, while the healed leper represents the elect of Israel, the centurion with his sick servant stands for the elect of the Gentiles. By a free use of editorial discretion the cure of Simon's mother-in-law (viii, 14–15) is next brought in from Mark i, 29–31, along with the numerous miracles of healing which Mark declares were performed on the evening of the same day; in all these our evangelist discovers a fulfilment of prophecy (Isaiah liii, 4). Here he breaks the sequence of stories in Mark, and has Jesus embark on the Sea of Galilee in order to bring on the miracle of the calmed tempest (viii, 18, 23–27; Mark iv, 35–41) and the cure of the demoniacs at Gadara. But before the first of these miracles, he is minded to insert the answers of Jesus to two persons who wished to "follow" him, not in his coming passage of the lake, but as disciples (viii, 19–22; cf. Luke ix, 57–60). Notwithstanding the localization of the two episodes, these doubtless borrowed from the collection of *logia*, the scene hangs in air, nor is it easy to grasp firmly the meaning of the answers attributed to Jesus. At Gadara (instead of Gerasa) Matthew introduces two demoniacs who make in concert the same demonstration as Mark's one demoniac in the synagogue at Capernaum (Mark i, 23–27)—to the great perplexity of commentators. But our evangelist is concerned to retain only the essential features of the miracle, while compensating for his omission of Mark's demoniac at Capernaum by having two at Gadara. (One might suspect him of not being altogether serious in his miracle stories; but the truth is that he is somewhat indifferent to matters of fact.) After this come the cure of the paralytic (ix, 2–7), with the preliminaries of the miracle, as in Mark ii, 1–12, cut down; the calling of the publican (ix, 9; Mark ii, 14), with the saying about associating with sinners (ix, 10–13; Mark ii, 15–17) and the explanation about fasting (ix, 14–17; Mark ii, 18–22). Here the publican, instead of being named Levi, as in Mark, is called Matthew, which has the effect of bringing him into the apostolic college. The conjecture is not too risky that the change of name is connected with the attribution of the Gospel to Matthew, which is not the better guaranteed on that account, the whole being fiction with a purpose (in the apostolic list of x, 2–4 care is taken to accentuate the identification: Matthew the *publican*). The series is concluded by the cure of the woman with the issue of blood and the resurrection of the daughter of Jairus (ix, 18–26) perceptibly abridged from Mark v, 22–43; the cure of two blind men (ix, 27–30), duplicate of the two we shall meet at Jericho (xx, 30–34); and finally by the cure of the deaf-mute demoniac (ix, 32–34), duplicate of the incident (xii, 22–24) which later on will give rise to the dispute about exorcism. The last two miracles may be classed as purely of editorial origin, invented by the evangelist himself to fill up his gallery of prodigies.

Mission of the Twelve

Our Gospel does not relate the calling of the Twelve but presupposes it by inserting, probably from Mark (iii, 13–19), the list of their names in the preamble of the discourse concerning their mission. This preamble (ix, 35–x, 4) draws inspiration from the earlier preamble to the Discourse on the Mountain (iv, 23–v, 2) and also from Mark (vi, 7–13, 30–34), which relate the mission with the preliminaries to the first multiplication of loaves, and are the source of the figure of sheep without a shepherd, associated with the remark about the fewness of the harvest-men. The remark seems to have served, in the common source of the three Scriptures, as exordium to the discourse, and like the discourse itself corresponds, not to the situation of Jesus when preaching in Galilee, but to the time of the first efforts to propagate the Christian religion. If the prohibition to go to the Samaritans and the pagans belongs to the original version, the discourse would be clearly revealed as the work of a Judaizing writer contemporary with the first missions to non-Jews and opposed to them. The missionaries are to operate as exorcists and healers of disease, and they are to announce that the Kingdom of Heaven is at hand (x, 7–8; Luke x, 19; cf. Mark vi, 7; Luke ix, 1–2). The order to carry no money or provisions reflects the conditions of the mission to the Jews. What is said about the house in which the missionary is to lodge, and the care that must be taken not to change it, belongs to a time when the propaganda was carried on, not in public, but privately, to individuals and from house to house. The gesture to be made to mark the reprobation of an inhospitable town is purely Jewish. Woe to the town which repulses the messenger of the Gospel (x, 15; Luke x, 12)! What is said about the likelihood that the apostles will not have gone the round of the Israelite cities before the arrival of the Son of Man (x, 23) was possibly attached, in the source, to these last considerations. The warning: "I send you forth as sheep in the midst of wolves" (x, 16) must originally have introduced the practical instructions, as in Luke x, 3. The conduct prescribed for those who have to confront judges applies to believers of all types and is a later addition to the mission-discourse (cf. Luke xii, 11–12; Mark xiii, 9–13; Luke xxi, 12–17): this feature is later than the trial of Paul and Nero's persecution. Here the evangelist, his mind preoccupied with the persecution, remembers the saying "the disciple is not above his master" and works it into his theme (x, 24–25; cf. Luke vi, 40; John xiii, 16; xv, 20). The next saying, on courageous profession of faith (x, 26–33), was at first an independent lesson (cf. Luke xii, 2–9) in which three elements are to be distinguished: the proverb "nothing is hidden that will not be revealed," with its somewhat forced application to the matter of the Gospel (x, 26–27); the exhortation to fear nothing, since God watches over his own (x, 28–31);

the statement about the witness the Christ will bear before his Father to those who have confessed him before men (x, 32–33). All this is intelligible only as referring to the situation of Christians in the time of the first persecutions. Not more in keeping with the earliest age is what we read about the divisions in families caused by Christian preaching (x, 21; cf. Luke xii, 51–53). The same is true of the call to renunciation (x, 37–39; cf. Luke xiv, 26–27) utilized by Mark (viii, 34–35) as a rectifying complement to Peter's confession; and again of the promise to those who receive the Christ's envoys (x, 40–42; cf. Mark ix, 41; Luke x, 16), a promise here paraphrased into the peroration of the discourse. Putting all this together, what could show more plainly that the discourse was never delivered? What we have before us is a short dissertation on the Christian apostolate composed of elements differing in age and diverse in spirit. It is noteworthy also that "when Jesus had made an end of commanding his disciples" it is not they who go out to preach but Jesus himself who is represented as doing so (xi, 1). The Twelve were never apostles.

Jesus and John the Baptist

Just as in Mark (vi, 14–29), so in Matthew (xi, 2–19) the question of John the Baptist follows after the mission of the Twelve, but with a different sequel, introducing certain fragments from the collection of sayings, thus gathered together in the source, in which John's name makes an appearance. In these passages the earliest Christianity defines its attitude, as well as its apology, with reference to the Baptist sect, from which it was derived, and the statements found in them appear to belong to a layer of catechetical tradition older than the myth of Jesus' baptism by John. The setting of the scene is artificial. John is represented as having heard of Jesus and as sending from his prison to ask him if he is "he who cometh"; Jesus, in answer, unfolds a kind of messianic programme largely founded on texts in Isaiah (xxxv, 5–6) which, it is supposed, John must admit and which Jesus has already fulfilled (xi, 2–3; cf. Luke vii, 18–19, 22–23). It is obvious that the miracles previously recounted in our Gospel have a point to point correspondence with those mentioned in Jesus' answer, and nothing could be more compromising either to the authenticity of the answer or the historicity of the miracles. At least it is evident that the last two of the ten miracles (the two blind men and the deaf-mute) are invented to support the answer as given. In the same way, the finest of Mark's miracles, reproduced in Matthew and Luke, may have been conceived to fit the same programme, though Mark does not mention it. A second fragment (xi, 7–11) is framed in terms so lyrical in praise of John that we may suspect them borrowed from the Baptist's sect; but the text from Malachi (iii, 1), in which the rôle of the Baptist is defined, has been given a Christian turn so as to make John appear as herald of the Christ and not of God only, and the praises accorded to John are cancelled out by the final remark: "But his junior in the Kingdom of Heaven," that is, Jesus "is greater than he." Finally, the relation of John to the Kingdom is defined in terms which suppose the Baptist dead and the Christian Church founded long ago (xi, 12–15; cf. Luke xvi, 16).

In the concluding sentence (xi, 16–19; Luke vii, 31–35) application is made of a popular saying to denounce the incredulity of the Jewish people equally deaf to both God's envoys, John and Jesus. To this our Gospel attaches the invective against the Galilean towns (xi, 20–24; Luke x, 13–15), adapted in the source to the mission-discourse, along with the exclamation of thanksgiving (xi, 25–30; Luke x, 21–22) which in the source was connected with the return of the apostles. Both invective and thanksgiving are oracles of Christian prophets speaking in the name of the immortal Christ and, for the thanksgiving, in the spirit of mystical gnosis.

Jesus in Conflict with the Pharisees

After these instructions the evangelist has decided to exhibit Jesus as a target for the hostility of the Pharisees, who reproach him for allowing his disciples to break the Sabbath and for not observing it himself (xii, 1–14), maliciously attribute the success of his exorcisms to Beelzebub, the prince of the devils (xii, 22–27), and invite him to prove his mission by signs (xii, 38–42). The two sabbath stories are taken from Mark (ii, 23–iii, 6, with the significant omission of ii, 27, "the sabbath was made for man," etc.), and are completed, the one by an argument drawn from the priests' service in the temple and by a quotation from Hosea (vi, 6 already utilized in ix, 13); the other by a comparison (the sheep fallen into a pit) borrowed from the same repertoire as the other arguments directed against the Pharisaic sabbath practice (cf. Luke xiii, 15; xiv, 5). Next, after abridging Mark's indications about the afflux of multitudes and the numerous cures operated by Jesus (which he had already copied for his introduction of the Discourse on the Mountain), our editor has judged it opportune to emphasize the command to the cured persons to keep silence (xii, 16–17), by exhibiting it as the fulfilment of an oracle in Isaiah (xlii, 1–4; xli, 9).

The dispute about the exorcisms (xii, 22–37) comes from Mark (iii, 22–30) and the collection of *logia* (cf. Luke xi, 14–15, 17–23); having been used elsewhere (ix, 32–34 the cure-story which brought on the dispute), the evangelist here adds blindness to the deafness[1] of the demoniac (xii, 22; Luke xi, 14). In the collection of discourses, the two comparisons of the kingdom divided against itself and of the armed man (Mark iii, 23–27) are followed by the saying: "Who is not with me is against me," etc. (xii, 30);[2] these comparisons the evangelist has found already separated by the argument about the Jewish exorcisms (xii, 27–28; cf. Mark iii, 23–27); after the saying about blasphemy against the Spirit (*supra*, p. 79), he has inserted the comparison of the tree and its fruit (already utilized vii, 16–20) and of the treasure within (xii, 34–35; Luke vi, 45), both lessons of common wisdom here adapted to a Christian moral theme, and he has added to them a rider of his own (xii, 36–37); he has transposed the remark about relapse into demoniacal possession after exorcism, and placed it after the answer to those who asked for a sign (xii, 43–45; Luke xi, 24–26) in order that he may interpret it as aimed at the incredulity of the Jews and as a forecast of their destiny. By this interpretation he neutralizes an experience which attests the futility of the results obtained by exorcism and which, in consequence, cannot be attributed to Jesus or to Christian exorcists.

To the Jews who "ask for signs"—that is for miracles giving better proof of a divine mission than that of simple cures—Christian tradition here answers that the only sign the Christ will

---

[1] M. Loisy's translation of κωφός.
[2] In contradiction to Mark ix, 40 and Luke ix, 50, where we read "who is not against me is with me."

give is the miracle of Jonah repeated in his own resurrection (Jonah ii, 1–2), and by denouncing the unbelievers whom the example of the Ninevites and of the Queen of Sheba will confound on the day of judgment (xii, 41–42; Luke xi, 31–32). The saying of the Christ about his true mother and brethren (xii, 46–50) is then brought in from Mark iii, 31–35, but with omission of the motive assigned by Mark for the action of the family, namely their belief that he was out of his mind (Mark iii, 21). The correspondence between the experience of Jonah and the case of Jesus buried and risen from the dead must have been evoked in tradition before the ritual commemoration of the Christ's death and resurrection was attached in common usage to Friday and the following Sunday, with which time-scheme three days and nights of Jonah's experience are incompatible (cf. *supra*, p. 87), and must have made the comparison compromising and best neglected. In all this it is plain enough that our evangelist editors, if not themselves the inventors of much they tell of the Christ's doings and sayings, freely act on their own initiative in the arrangement and interpretation of the materials they employ.

DISCOURSE IN PARABLES

The transition to the discourse in parables (xiii, 1–32) is made by a clumsy formula which might lead us to think that this discourse was delivered on the same day as the preceding instructions. In what follows our evangelist reproduces Mark for the setting of the scene (xiii, 1–2; Mark, iv, 1); for the declaration concerning the aim of parables (xiii, 10–15; Mark iv, 10–13), but bringing forward into it the *dictum* "To him that hath shall be given," etc., otherwise placed by Mark (iv, 25), understood of Christians and Jews, expressly citing the prophecy of Isaiah (vi, 9–10) by which Mark was inspired; then inserting a saying (xiii, 16–17) about the advantage enjoyed by believers in the Christ over believers in the Old Covenant, which in the collection of *logia* was in close proximity to the mission discourse (as in Luke x, 23–24); and, finally, following Mark in his explanation of the sower (xiii, 18–23; Mark iv, 14–20). For the parable of the seed (Mark iv, 26–29) our evangelist substitutes that of the tares (xiii, 24–30), which he has freely developed, if not composed entire, in view of the interpretation he intends to give of it a little further on (xiii, 36–43). To the parable of the mustard seed he adds that of the leaven, borrowed from the collection of discourses which has the same application as the mustard seed. He introduced the concluding words of Mark (iv, 33–34) and illustrates them by a biblical quotation (Psalm lxxviii, 2) in which he imagines he can see a prophecy of Jesus' parables. Amplifying, so to say, Mark's statement (iv, 34) about the Christ's explanations of his parables, given to the disciples in particular, he brings in a commentary on the tares (xiii, 36–43) and then the similes, more or less allegorical, of the hidden treasure (44), of the pearl (45–46), of the net (47–50)—a paraphrase of mystical terms already familiar to Christians, rather than similes. Finally, to wind up the discourse, he puts in the parable of the master of the house, figure of the Christian teacher, who can bring out of his coffers things old and new (51–52). It is to be noted that the parable of the tares refers to the recruiting of members by the Christian communities, intimating that the elimination of the unworthy should be postponed to the final judgment.

Next follows the preaching of Jesus at Nazareth (xiii, 53–58), the evangelist here anticipating the stories which Mark places between the discourse in parables and this anecdote, in which he softens down certain features. After that come the sayings of Herod, considerably abridged, about the Christ (xiv, 1–2; Mark vi, 14–16), the story of John's death (xiv, 3–12; Mark vi, 17–29), the mission of the apostles (Mark vi, 7–13) having been mentioned at an earlier stage. The effect of the transpositions thus effected is that the departure of Jesus for the first multiplication of loaves is occasioned by the death of John; instead of the Twelve coming back to their master after their mission, as in Mark vi, 30, it is now the disciples of John who come to announce his death to Jesus—an indication not without meaning.

Light retouchings are discernible in the story of the multiplied loaves (xiv, 13–21; Mark vi, 31–44). Mark's story of the miraculous walking across the sea (xiv, 22–33; Mark vi, 45–52) is repeated, but adorned with a symbolic episode; that of Peter also walking on the sea to join company with the Christ, a great marvel which, like the main body of the story, must have originally belonged to the resurrection cycle (cf. John xxi, 7). Our evangelist corrects Mark's conclusion by substituting a profession of messianic faith (xiv, 33) for what he says about the blindness of the disciples in presence of a prodigy (Mark vi, 51–52).

He emphasizes the miracles operated in the land of Gennesaret (xiv, 34–36; Mark vi, 53–56); he shortens and retouches the dispute about the washing of hands (xv, 1–20; Mark vii, 1–23) while forcing into it the saying about blind leaders of the blind, to be understood as foretelling the downfall of Pharisaic Judaism. The anecdote of the Canaanite woman (xv, 21–28; Mark vii, 24–30) is somewhat more developed so as to bring out more clearly that the personal ministry of Jesus was confined to Israel. Having spoken twice already of deaf-mutes our author turns Mark's story (vii, 31–37) of another deaf man of the Decapolis into a generalized picture of manifold cures (xv, 29–31). For this story, as for the preceding, he corrects Mark's geography, so as to keep Jesus out of pagan territory.

In the second story of multiplied loaves (xv, 32–39) he follows Mark (viii, 1–9)—without notable variation. The mention of Jonah in the refusal of a sign (xvi, 1–4) recalls the first version (xii, 38–40) of the twice-told incident, which here returns in the form given it by Mark. The strange development that follows about the blindness of the disciples in regard to the leaven of the Pharisees and the leaven of bread has, in like manner, been copied from Mark (viii, 14–21), but Mark's conclusion is here given a turn to make it appear that the disciples understood the lesson that Jesus would have them learn (xvi, 12). As to the blind man at Bethsaida (Mark viii, 22–26), he is clearly a double of the blind man of Jericho, in whom we have already encountered him, antedated in a colourless miracle (ix, 27–31; *supra*, p. 125).

In its account of Peter's confession our Gospel has arranged a kind of verbal antithesis between the Son of Man (xvi, 13) and the Son of God (xvi, 16) which seems to foreshadow the distinction between the two natures of the Christ. But his chief alteration of Mark's account (viii, 27–30) is the insertion of the celebrated address to Peter (xvi, 17–19). "Blessed art thou, Simon son of Jonas," etc., a saying which can only be ascribed to the immortal Christ, and goes far beyond the primitive form of the confession in Mark. There cannot be a doubt that this saying was conceived in the East, in some circle devoted to the memory of Peter, head of the apostles and head of the Church, to counter the claim of the mystical Paul in the Epistles.

For the instructions which follow the Confession (xvi, 20–28)—in which our evangelist seems to be unconscious that Peter's protests against Jesus' announcement of his coming death and resurrection, and the crushing reprimand administered to him (xvi, 22–23) are in flat contradiction with the solemn praise of him as prince of the apostles—for these instructions and for the story of the Transfiguration (xvii, 1–13) Matthew copied Mark almost word for word, adding only a short explanation about Elijah, in regard to which the disciples are credited with intelligence, in substitution for Mark's indication to the contrary a little further back (ix, 10). The incident of the epileptic (xvii, 14–21) is a perceptible abridgment of Mark (ix, 14–29). The lesson on faith forms the epilogue, for the disciples only (xvii, 19–20; Mark ix, 23; Luke xvii, 6). After the second prophecy of the Passion (xvii, 22–23) the disciples are represented as sorrowing instead of not understanding, as in Mark ix, 30–32 and Luke ix, 45. Peculiar to Matthew is the anecdote of the money and the fish (xvii, 24–27) in which an old story is utilized; it answers a question of moment to the Jewish-Christian Churches, even after the destruction of the temple, which question Jesus was supposed to have solved. Contrary to what he is made to say later about tribute to Caesar (xxii, 15–22), he here seems to deny obligation to pay.

The confusion of Mark (ix, 33–50) in his arrangements of the lessons which follow the second prophecy of the Passion is somewhat straightened out and retouched. Instead of disputing as to who among themselves is the greatest (Mark ix, 34) the disciples now ask who is greatest in the Kingdom of Heaven, and Jesus answers by enjoining a childlike spirit, humility and the service of humble believers (xviii, 1–5; Mark ix, 36–37; x, 15). The incident of the stranger whom the disciples had found casting out devils is omitted, together with the saying "he that is not against us is for us." In the warning against "causing to stumble" our Gospel completes Mark from the collection of discourses and arranges a combination, as ingenious as unconvincing, to bring the parable of the lost sheep into his theme (xviii, 12–14; Luke xv, 4–7).

It seems that, in the collection of the discourses, the teaching of forgiveness followed the warning against causing the "little ones to stumble" (xviii, 15–22; Luke xvii, 1–4), and for that reason Matthew gives it in the place of the exhortation to be at peace among themselves (Mark ix, 50). But within it he intercalates a rudimentary scheme of church discipline which enjoins a triple admonition of sinners and excommunication of him who refuses to hear the voice of the community, and includes the power to bind and loose, and the presence of the Christ at the meetings for prayer. Matthew is alone in daring to put oracles expressly concerning "the Church" into the mouth of Jesus (xvi, 18 and xviii, 7). All these were, originally, oracles of the immortal Christ. The parable of the wicked servant and its moral (xviii, 23–35) naturally follow the teaching of forgiveness, but Luke's tradition seems to have been ignorant of this parable.

For his account of the journey into Judea and the preaching at Jerusalem our evangelist follows Mark with the addition of various sayings and parables. In the preamble (xix, 1–2) he substitutes a number of unspecified cures for the unspecified teaching mentioned by Mark (x, 1). In the dispute with the Pharisees over divorce he is careful to introduce the exception for adultery as he did in the Discourse on the Mountain (v, 32) and he adds a lesson, in the mystical style, on continence and voluntary castration (xix, 10–12) in line with the earliest Christian ruling on celibacy and virginity (cf. 1 Corinthians vii, 25–26). The story of the blessing of children (xix, 13–15) is lightened, relatively to Mark x, 16, of matter which would have made it a repetition of the story already told (xviii, 1–5).

In the anecdote of the rich young man (xix, 16–22) the evangelist has clumsily corrected the question as it stands in Mark x, 17 ("Good Master, what shall I do . . . ?") into "Master what good thing shall I do?" and changed the answer ("Why callest thou me good?") into "Why askest thou me about the good?" in order to avoid making Jesus refuse the attribute of goodness which belongs to God. In what is said about the difficulty of salvation for the rich (xix, 16–26) he conforms to Mark. But to Peter's question about the future of the disciples (Mark x, 28)

Jesus first answers (xix, 28–29) by the promise of twelve thrones, which must come from the collection of *logia* and which Mark seems to have omitted deliberately, so as not to have it apply to the Galilean disciples (cf. *supra*, p. 92). The teaching on retribution (xix, 29–30) is completed by the parable of the labourers in the vineyard (xx, 1–16), a theme adopted by Christian tradition and applied to the universality of salvation, but not in very clear agreement with the *dictum* at the head of the parable about the first becoming the last, evangelically interpreted as meaning the reversal of conditions in the Kingdom of Heaven, rather than the bringing of all conditions to an equality.

Jesus in Jerusalem

The confused perspective, obvious in Mark (x, 32–34), before the third prophecy of the coming Passion, is effaced in Matthew's version (xx, 17–19), but the evangelist makes Jesus expressly specify the mode of his death as crucifixion. In order to avoid attributing to the son of Zebedee pretensions disapproved by Jesus, as Mark does (x, 35–45), he brings forward their mother to demand for them the first two thrones in the Kingdom of Heaven (xx, 20–28). We have already seen that he has two blind men at Jericho to compensate for his omission of Mark's blind man at Bethsaida (Mark viii, 22–26). In describing the triumph of the Christ on the Mount of Olives (xxi, 1–9; Mark xi, 1–10) he is at pains to cite Zechariah (ix, 9) and even brings *two* asses on the scene, wrongly thinking that two are mentioned by the prophet. He makes the demonstration last all the way to Jerusalem in order to describe the commotion in the city on the arrival of Jesus (xxi, 10–11). Probably knowing Mark's source he suppresses the interval placed by him (Mark xi, 11) between the Christ's first visit to the temple and the expulsion of the traders. He has also thought well to fuse into one briefer story the two separated fragments on the withered fig-tree in Mark xi, 12–14 and 20–25. After the expulsion of the traders he introduces a collection of miraculous cures, with a new messianic acclamation in fulfilment of prophecy (Psalm viii, 2) and to the confusion of the high priests and doctors of the Law (xxi, 14–16).

Profiting by the mention of John the Baptist in Jesus' answers

to the priests' question about his authority, the evangelist inserts
the parable of the two sons before that of the wicked husbandmen (xxi, 33–46; Mark xii, 1–12), applying the former to the
leaders of Judaism, who had not believed in John, and to the
sinners, who had (xxi, 32; Luke vii, 29–30). This application, at
first independent of the parable, and fitting rather badly to it,
is intended to assimilate the case of John to that of Jesus in
presence of Jewish incredulity (cf. xi, 16–19). Both the parable
itself and its direct application have the look of being a retrospective assessment, and a justification, of the results obtained by
Jesus and by Christian preaching after him in the attempt to
convert the Jews. After the parable place is found for that of the
marriage feast, borrowed from the collection of discourses
(xxii, 1–10; Luke xiv, 16–24), but here enriched with a second
conclusion not found in Luke—that of the man who had no
wedding garment (xxii, 11–14). This supplement is aimed at bad
Christians (cf. the parable of the tares, xiii, 24–30, 36–43); but
the *corpus* of the parable is probably based on a theme borrowed
from Jewish tradition, and here applied allegorically to questions
that arose in the early recruiting of converts.

Of a purely editorial kind are the modifications of Mark in the
story of the tribute (xxii, 15–22; Mark xii, 13–17), of the polemic
with the Sadducees about the resurrection (xxii, 23–33; Mark xii,
18–27), of the question about the great commandment (xxii,
34–40; Mark xii, 28–34), of the relation of the Messiah to David
(xxii, 41–46; Mark xii, 35–37). But the question about the great
commandment is regarded as being raised by the Pharisees with
a sinister motive, and nothing has been retained of the praise
accorded by Jesus to the questioner (Mark xii, 34; cf. Luke x,
25–28). In our Gospel the Pharisees are nothing else than an
active source of perdition and the implacable enemies of Jesus.
They personify refractory Judaism in its hostility to Christian
propaganda.

In the discourse against the Pharisees the indictment of Judaism
is carried on throughout from the point of a Christianity already
separated from Judaism, and is unintelligible if taken otherwise.
We have before us the oracle of a Christian prophet aimed at the
people and the city held to have crucified Jesus. The original
discourse, imitated from the ancient prophets, contained seven

comminatory reproaches,[1] and seems to have been at first presented as the last pronounced in public by the Christ. In Matthew it opens, as an ordinary instruction, with a kind of Judaizing preamble denouncing the hypocrisy of the Pharisees, whose teachings are to be followed, but not their example (xxiii, 2–3). The first two invectives (as in Luke xi, 43–46) are spread out by Matthew into a series of reproaches (xxiii, 4–7) the last of which, their love of being called "master," has been added to make way for a lesson addressed to Christians, who must recognize no master on earth save the Christ, nor claim any dominating power one over another (xxiii, 8–12). To compensate for the two maledictions thus transformed the evangelist inserts two others: the first against the proselytizing activities of the Pharisees, as intemperate in zeal as disastrous in effect (xxiii, 15); the second against their casuistry in the matter of oath-taking (xxiii, 16–22; cf. v, 34–37). Thus the prophet's invective becomes a complete indictment of rabbinic Judaism, which was still powerful and active after the fall of Jerusalem.

Omitting the story of the widow with two mites (Mark xii, 41–44) as of mediocre importance, especially in this place, the great apocalyptic discourse immediately follows. Jesus begins by predicting the ruin of the temple (xxiv, 1–2; Mark xiii, 1–2); then, removing to the Mount of Olives, he addresses to the Twelve (xxiv, 3), and not, as in Mark, to the four leading disciples (Mark xiii, 3–4), his great revelation of the Last Things. Here we find all that Mark has (xiii, 5–37) with the addition of inserted supplements mostly taken from the collection of *logia*: fragments (xxiv, 23–28; perhaps also 36) more abundant than in Mark, of the discourse which Luke reports separately in another connection (Luke xvii, 20–37) and which were intended, in the earliest version, to abate the feverish expectation of the Second Coming; simile of the night-robber (xxiv, 43–44; Luke xii, 39–40), representing an apocalyptic belief of early Christianity rather than a personal teaching of Jesus; parable of the two servants (xxiv, 45–51; Luke xii, 41–48), bearing on the expecta-

---

[1] As follows: (1) Luke xi, 46; Matthew xxiii, 4. (2) Luke xi, 43; Matthew xxiii, 6. (3) Matthew xxiii, 13; Luke xi, 52. (4) Matthew xxiii, 25–26; Luke xi, 39–40. (5) Matthew xxiii, 26–28; Luke xi, 44. (6) Matthew xxiii, 29–31; Luke xi, 47–48, culminating in (7) the prediction of ruin, Matthew xxiii, 32, 34–39; Luke xi, 49–50; xiii, 34–35— probably a citation from a Jewish apocalypse.

tion of the parousia in the same way as the preceding figure; parable of the ten virgins (xxv, 1–13; cf. Luke xii, 35–36; xiii, 25–27), constructed in Christian tradition as an allegory on the theme of Christ the husband of the Church (cf. 2 Corinthians xi, 2) and bearing on the delay of the parousia in order to bring out the need of positive preparation for the Great Event; parable of the talents (xxv, 14–30; Luke xix, 11–27), a common theme superficially Christianized and adapted, in Christian tradition, to the question of eternal rewards (note in xxv, 29 the insertion of a *dictum* already recorded in xiii, 12); finally the description of the Great Judgment, a piece peculiar to our Gospel, apparently taken from Jewish eschatology and given a Christian turn (xxv, 31–46).

THE PASSION AND THE RESURRECTION

The stories of the Passion and the Resurrection are transcribed from Mark with variants mostly of little importance. Remark, however, that the date indicated by Mark (xiv, 1) is placed by Matthew in the mouth of Jesus and turned into a prophecy of the coming Passion (xxvi, 1–2). Certain characteristic additions have been introduced: the mention by name of the high priest taken from a good source; the thirty pieces of silver given to Judas, to conform with Zechariah xi, 12, and preparing the way for the legend, to come later, of the traitor's death; the designation of him by name during the last meal (xxvi, 25), a detail intended to bring out the clairvoyance of Jesus, but at the expense of probability; the rebuke to the disciple who draws his sword in the Garden of Gethsemane (xxvi, 52–54), from which it appears that Jesus suffers himself to be captured in order to fulfil the Scriptures; the repentance of Judas who returns the thirty pieces to the priests, commits suicide and buys a field, afterwards called "the field of blood" and made into a cemetery for strangers, thereby fulfilling a prophecy in Jeremiah;[1] the message sent by Pilate's wife to the procurator sitting in court, a romantic fiction

---

[1] The strangest element in this fiction is not, perhaps, the astonishing liberty of the interpretation given to the prophetic text, in which a passage in Zechariah (xi, 12–13) is combined with a statement in Jeremiah (xxxii, 6–9), but the indication of the burying-place called Aceldama, of which the name itself, to which the Judas legend has been violently adapted, would seem to imply its use as the common place of burial for suicides and executed criminals, that is, very probably, the place where the dead body of Jesus was disposed of.

intended to bring out the witness to Jesus' innocence borne by highly placed Romans; Pilate washing his hands in order, by a symbolic gesture, to throw back on the Jews a responsibility they hasten to accept (xxvii, 24–25), another fiction which is held to discharge Pilate of the death sentence passed on Jesus, and makes the murderers of the Christ invoke the punishment in store for them; the substitution, again for the fulfilment of prophecy (Psalm lxix, 21), of gall for myrrh in the wine offered to Jesus on arriving at Calvary (xxvii, 34); a supplement to this, taken from Psalm xxii, 7–8, in the insults cried by the chief priests to Jesus on the cross (xxvii, 43); the earthquake, the opening of tombs, the rising of the dead at the very moment when Jesus breathes his last (xxvii, 51–53), miracles easily imagined, but in which the evangelist himself becomes somewhat embarrassed, since he feels constrained to add (53) that the dead did not come forth from their opened tombs till after the Christ had risen from his. But the fact is that this resurrection of the dead was at first conceived in keeping with the original conception of the Christ's resurrection to immortality as taking place, not after death and two days' burial in a tomb, but immediately, at the very instant when he emitted his last breath, the conception of the resurrection found in the Epistle to the Hebrews.

Mark's account of the burial and resurrection of Jesus is filled out by Matthew with the following supplements:

The military guard at the tomb deputed by Pilate at the demand of the chief priests and Pharisees to prevent the theft of the dead body by the disciples (xxvii, 62–66), an apologetic fiction (substituted for Pilate's inquiry of the centurion in Mark xv, 44) the intention of which will appear in its completion further on; the earthquake in the night of the resurrection; the angel descending from heaven among the guard, rolling away the great stone under their eyes, seating himself on the stone and addressing the women on their arrival (xxviii, 2–7), a fiction which xxvii, 62–66 seems to require for completion (and substituted for Mark xvi, 3–5); the apparition of the Christ to the women (xxviii, 9–10) represented as having the duty laid on them to inform the disciples, instead of keeping silence as in Mark xvi, 8; the bargain struck between the chief priests and the guard to deny the resurrection of Jesus and say that the disciples stole the dead body while the sentinels were asleep (xxviii, 11–15), a fiction of late origin invented to answer the theory of Jewish polemists arguing against the first fiction of the empty tomb; finally the scene of the great apparition to the Eleven on the mountain in Galilee (xxviii, 16–20), a scene invented to fill the serious gap which the conclusion of Mark, as it then was, seemed to present, and where our evangelist read no more than what we find there to-day in the oldest manuscripts. Assuredly this scene is admirably drawn and betokens a better and higher inspiration than the invention of a guard at the tomb. Noteworthy is the interpolation into it of the baptismal formula "in the name of the Father, the Son and the Holy Spirit," which was not in use before the second half of the second century. Here is a profession of faith in the immortal Christ and in his watch over the church. The outlook towards the Second Coming has now grown dim; the apostolic legend is fully formed, and the Galilean disciples, who were never apostles, here stand forth as endowed by Jesus with power to convert the world.

The Gospel named after Matthew has great interest for the historian, but his interest is not due to positive information he finds there concerning the life and death of the historical Jesus. What he finds is the gospel legend simplified and developed by the same means which created the first form of it; these were meditation on the ancient Jewish Scripture and imagination in the service of apologetic. Most important among the contents of the first Gospel is the mass of teachings attributed to Jesus, of which the second Gospel offers only a very small part. There, again, what Matthew gives us and Luke, in the main, repeats after him, is something wholly different from a collection of discourses really delivered. But, in Matthew as in Luke, we get a glimpse, between the lines, of the labour by means of which tradition, as it furnished the Christ with a legend, furnished him also with a teaching. Legend and teaching, largely antedated from the eschatological catechesis, were far less the expression of memories about the historical Jesus than of faith aroused by him and founded on him, of a morality practised in his spirit by the earliest Christian communities, and of his mystical presence in the Christian cult. The approximate date of this compilation has been already indicated (p. 69).

Chapter VI

ANALYSIS OF WRITINGS ATTRIBUTED TO LUKE

PERHAPS a day will come when enlightened criticism, on the sole evidence of the prologues which stand at the head of the third Gospel and of Acts, will decide that the author who there addresses himself to Theophilus, and those who arranged the canonical edition of his work, must both be ranked in the same category as the apologists of the second century, who pleaded the cause of Christianity before the Antonines, and that he and they doubtless lived in that age. But as the force of this evidence has not yet got home in current exegesis, we shall now subject these prologues to a new examination and afterwards proceed to analyse the writings they introduce, with a view to ascertaining the true character of the two books.

THE PROLOGUES

Like Justin (*circa* 140), who would impress educated pagans with the importance of the evangelical writings by calling them "Memoirs of the Apostles," so the author of the two books to Theophilus which became, in their canonical edition, the Gospel according to Luke and the Acts of the Apostles, had furnished his bipartite narrative with a double dedication modelled on those which were customary in his time. Who the Theophilus was, to whom this homage is offered, we do not know. He may have been a Christian or a notable catechumen really named Theophilus; or so named rather in adulation or for prudential reasons; or, again, he may be only a typical person representative of what, at this time, was the aristocracy of the Christian religion. Nor do we know any better who was the author of the dedicatory prologues. But tradition, having need of an apostolic name to give authority to the two books, naturally pitched upon Luke, the stories in Acts about the mission of Paul being founded on the notes or journal of one of Paul's companions, whom there is every reason to identify with the physician Lukas mentioned in the Epistles. Nevertheless it is clear that neither the two books in their totality, nor even the prologues, can be attributed to a writer of apostolic time and, consequently, not to Luke. The latter point is important inasmuch as, by examination of the prologues alone, we gain a sufficiently sure base-line for our analysis of the books they introduce.

The prologue to the Gospel introduces the entire work as the original author conceived it. The wording is as follows (Luke i, 1–4):

> Forasmuch as many having undertaken to compose a narrative of the matters established among ourselves, as they transmitted them to us, who from the beginning were witnesses and ministers of the word, I also, who for a long time past have followed everything with care, deemed it a good thing that I should write an orderly account for thee, excellent Theophilus, that thou mayest perceive the certainty of the truths wherein thou hast been taught.

No small difficulty confronts the critics who would have us believe that the person here speaking is Luke, and make out that he wrote his two books before the year 70. Their difficulty will be to explain how, by that time, many writers had already produced an account of the origins of Christianity or even of the career of Jesus. Yet the writer makes it clearly understood that the literary work on which he now embarks is of a kind largely cultivated before his time; and he must have known its products better than we do. A writer who uses language such as this cannot have written before the second century when Christian literature had got into its stride, and by Christian literature we here understand the production of gnosis in every variety that paid homage to Jesus as the Saviour of mankind. The fact that our author is at pains to announce that his work will carry every guarantee shows clearly that he knew of others which, in his view, could make no such claim. What he, for his part, has written, is an account of things established among believers. The "things" in question are also "facts"; but not naked facts; not the raw material of which a chronicle is made; they are facts full of meaning and, we may venture to say, full of faith; they are saving facts; which means exactly, for us, the sacred legend of the origins of Christianity. When our author speaks of "matters established among *ourselves*" he does so because he has the sense of tradition, and because the Christianity of his own day is in line of continuous descent from the age called apostolic. But he lets us see, clearly enough, that the apostolic age is already far behind him.

All this author and his contemporaries could do, and all they did, for the purpose they had in view, was to collect information coming down, when traced to its source, from those who "from the beginning were witnesses (of the 'facts') and afterwards ministers of the word"—the "beginning" in question being understood as the beginning of *the* Gospel, the teaching and salutary work of Jesus. Here the meaning of the "facts" (or "the things") is allowed to slide into that of "the word," because the facts have by this time become the matter of the teaching. Moreover, as the witnessing ministers in question can be no other than the "disciples" whom Christian tradition made into "apostles," we must understand the writer's meaning to be that the men who had been in Jesus' company and eye-witnesses of his beneficent activity, afterwards became "ministers" of the evangelical message which celebrated and perpetuated his saving work. So our author understands the matter. But this mode of understanding it cannot possibly be that of a contemporary with the apostles, but is precisely the point of view found in the Epistle to the Hebrews (ii, 3–4) where mention is made of "a salvation which, having been first proclaimed by the Lord, was confirmed to us his hearers, God joining in their witness by signs and prodigies, by manifold miracles and by distribution of the Spirit according to his will." This is a summary, systematic and idealized, of the beginnings of evangelical and apostolic preaching, a view taken of an object seen far off in the past. We have said already, but cannot too often repeat, that the Galilean disciples were never missionaries, to the world, of faith in Jesus. It was not they who founded the hellenic-Christian Church. Nor were they ever the guarantors of the gospel legend.

Our author "for a long time past" has attentively "followed," not the course of a history of which he has not been a witness, but the *documents* of a tradition he sets out to interpret, the documents, that is, of a legend elaborated before his time even in regard to the so-called apostolic age, though he may well have had very precise information at his disposal for that part of his work which refers to Paul. What he claims to do is to present a well ordered and continuous exposition, conformable to a certain type of received doctrine; briefly, a safe compendium for the believer of what for us is the gospel catechesis, or legend, and the legend of the apostles.

Such was the conception which the writer to Theophilus set out to realize. But his work has not been transmitted to us as it was conceived and realized by him. The prologue to Acts has been added to and mutilated in a way which makes it perfectly clear, before examining the two books in detail, that both the evangelical legend in the third Gospel and the apostolic legend in Acts, as written by our original author, have been re-written and overlaid with secondary work in their canonical version. First, then, let us consider this prologue. Here it is (Acts i, 1–3) in the form given it in the manuscripts commonly judged the best (the Alexandrian text):

> I composed the first book, O Theophilus, on all that Jesus, from the beginning, did and taught, until the day when, *having given command to the apostles, whom he had chosen by the Holy Spirit,* he was taken away. *They also it was to whom he presented himself alive after his passion by many proofs,* etc.

In the recension known as the Western (notably the manuscript *Codex Bezae*) the same text runs as follows:

> I composed the first book, O Theophilus, on all that Jesus, from the beginning, did and taught, until the day when he was taken away, *having given command to the apostles whom he had chosen by the Holy Spirit, and to whom he gave orders to preach the Gospel. They also it was to whom he presented himself,* etc.

It would serve no purpose to discuss the variants in the witnesses to the two texts. What here merits attention is the part common to both versions, which alone is authentic:

> I composed the first book, O Theophilus, on all that Jesus, from the beginning, did and taught, until the day when he was taken away.

We might also translate "until the day when he was assumed." For the reference is not to an *ascension*, or visible passage to the skies, as in the scene described a little later in our version of Acts, but to the *assumption* by the Christ of his heavenly life. This is the proper term which the writer to Theophilus had already used when, to mark the solemnity of Jesus' departure for Jerusalem, he wrote (Luke ix, 51): "Now it came to pass that when the days of his *assumption* were being fulfilled, he stedfastly set his face to go to Jerusalem." The "assumption" is the instant passage of Jesus to God at the moment of his death, as understood in Hebrews x, 12 (cf. *supra*, p. 139).

In the lines quoted above, the writer to Theophilus took up again the thread of his former book. The prudent exegesis of the credal professions may twist his words in all possible ways to get the desired meaning out of them, but it will never succeed in making him say that his first book contained the birth-stories now to be read at the opening of the third Gospel. Quite clearly they imply the contrary and it would be superfluous to argue the point.

It is no less evident that the first part of the prologue to Acts, recalling the object of the former book, necessitates a second part, fellow to the first, in which the object of the second book (Acts) will be described with equal precision. This part has disappeared. It has disappeared because a reviser of the second book, the same reviser who introduced the birth-stories into the first, has suppressed it in order that he may replace it by the infelicitous accretion attached so awkwardly to the part of the original prologue which he has preserved—the accretion italicized above. Both in the Alexandrian and in the Western version this violent surcharge and deliberate interpolation announce themselves as such by the clumsy way in which they are tacked on to the original. What this reviser is aiming at is to bring on, by hook or crook, the account he is about to give of the forty days which the risen Jesus is to spend with his disciples and the instruction he is then to leave with them. We have not to go far to find the reviser's motive for the substitution. The second part of the original prologue had to be suppressed because what it said differed from what he wanted it to say, perhaps announcing certain events on which he intended to keep silence, or excluding fiction which it would suit him to insert. There is not a doubt that the original writer to Theophilus understood the posthumous life of the Christ, and the awakening of the disciples' faith in his resurrection, in a manner quite different from our reviser's presentation. But the point on which attention should be fixed at the moment is the character of the interpolation and its bearing on the character of Acts as a whole. The interpolation is not, as some have tried to make out, a phenomenon limited to the first page of the book; it is the first step in a process of editorial rearrangement and reconstruction which extends, in all probability, to the very end of the book. And the hand which has thus recast the second book to Theophilus has also been at work on the first.

Proof of this is furnished by the first words of the interpolation: "having given command to the *apostles* whom he had *chosen* by the Holy Spirit." Here we have an indisputable reference to the calling of the Twelve in Luke vi, 12–16. There we learn that Jesus, after a night of prayer on the mountain (we are not told its name), "summoned his disciples and *chose* twelve from among them, whom he named *apostles*." Then follows the list of the twelve, which we find reproduced (with the omission of Judas) at the opening of Acts (i, 13). Can we doubt that the hand which wrote all this in Acts is the hand of him who described the choice of the Twelve in the Gospel, and there gave them the name of apostles in readiness for the mission he now gives them in Acts? Once more we have to remind the reader that the Twelve were never apostles even in the proper meaning of the word, least of all in the outstanding and exclusive sense given to that vocable by the writer who recast the two books to Theophilus. The Twelve were the members of the directing committee charged with ordering the affairs of the group of Hebrew believers whom they had recruited by privately conducted propaganda in Jerusalem (cf. *The Birth of the Christian Religion*, 109–112). There is not the least evidence that they were ever itinerant preachers, and never did they regard themselves as commanded to evangelize the world. But, after the lapse of a considerable time, when the need arose to combat the claims of the party which was proclaiming the apostolic pre-eminence of Paul, whose writings it was guarding and amplifying, certain circles of Eastern believers were at pains to exhibit the Twelve as the only true apostles, as the true founders of the Church and the guarantors of tradition, and as instituted for that eminence by the Christ himself. In this picture Peter assumes the rôle of chief while Paul is subordinated to these great apostles who, all things considered, are, in that capacity, nothing more than a figment erected into a tradition (cf. *supra*, p. 140). This fiction our editor introduces at the outset of his work because, while it is the first word of his interpolations, it will also be the last word of the interpolated book.

The sequel has other surprises in reserve. First comes information unique in the New Testament, except for a kind of summary indication at the conclusion of the third Gospel. For forty days after his death Jesus is represented as living almost continuously with his disciples "speaking of the Kingdom of God," that is, of the Kingdom about to come—a point not without significance. (It is remarkable that the interpolator of this surprising news has nothing to say of the resurrection on the third day, nor, seemingly, of the two special apparitions related in the third Gospel.) The truth of the matter is that he boldly introduces, at the very beginning of Acts, certain data taken from the eschatological catechesis and closely connected with the Apocalypse of Peter, the forty days terminating with the ascension of the Christ into heaven, localized on the Mount of Olives, as in that apocryphal book. But we are now to see that the instructions here attributed to the Christ are not uniform, and that the eschatological data are broken into by intrusions of mystical theology.

The writer shows Jesus as sharing a common life with his disciples for a *continuous* period, that is, as one not yet risen from earth to heaven, for there is no suggestion of many visions and apparitions that came and went at intervals. He spends the time instructing them about the Reign or Kingdom of God; in other words, about the conditions of the Great Event. "And living with them"—which might also be translated "eating with them," perhaps a reference to the breaking of bread—"he charged them not to go away from Jerusalem but to wait there for the promise of the Father which (he said) you heard from me." According to the words that precede, "the promise of the Father" can only mean the promise of the Great Event; according to the words that follow, something quite different is in question—and brought in most unhappily—namely, the promise of baptism in the Holy Spirit, the miracle of Pentecost, or at least that part of the miracle which concerns the gift of the Spirit: "For John baptized with water but ye shall be baptized in the Spirit a few days hence" (i, 5). To this the "apostles" react as though they had heard only what Jesus had said about the Kingdom (i, 6): "Whereupon they came together and asked him, saying: 'Is it at this time that thou art about to restore the Kingdom to Israel?'" Jesus answers the question in the sense in which it is asked, but refuses to indicate a date (i, 7): "And he said to them, 'It is not for you to know the times and the moments, which the Father has fixed by his authority'": after which the text again runs off the track towards the Holy Spirit (i, 8): "But ye shall receive power, the Holy Spirit coming upon you." Falling again into the general perspective the discourse concludes with the words: "And ye shall be my witnesses at Jerusalem, in all Judea and Samaria and to the end of the earth."

We are on safe ground in thinking (with Turmel, *Histoires des dogmes*, ii, 160–162) that everything in this passage which concerns the Spirit is an afterthought inserted into the context. Note that the same phenomenon occurs at the end of the third Gospel (xxiv, 49*b*) where the promise of the Spirit is surcharged on the instructions of the Christ concerning the fulfilment of the prophecies and preaching the Gospel to all nations. The eschatological teaching is crowned by the story of the Ascension. This is conceived throughout with an outlook towards the Great Event (i, 9–11) and comes to its point at the end when two angels impressively inform the witnesses of the miracle that Jesus will descend from the heavens in like manner as he has ascended into them. Be it remembered that the same story of the Ascension, with some intentional variations, was placed by the same hand at the end of the third Gospel (xxiv, 50–53). May it not be that all this eschatological scenery was called up by way of answer to certain people who had a spiritual conception of the Christ's immortality, and that the writer to Theophilus was, or seemed to be, on that side?

ANALYSIS OF THE THIRD GOSPEL

The third Gospel does not betray a well marked-out plan. After the birth-stories, an accretion on the first book to Theophilus, we may distinguish, in the body of the book, a first section (iii–ix, 50) for which Mark has furnished the setting and the greater part of the matter, all concerning the Galilean ministry; a second (ix, 51–xix, 27) apparently narrating the journey from Galilee into Judea, but into which the revisers of the text have lodged almost everything that is not borrowed from Mark; a third section (xix, 28–xxi) founded entirely on Mark and covering the Jerusalem ministry; finally the stories of the Passion and the Resurrection (xxii–xxiv), of which a considerable part comes from the last editors. Note, however, that the last three sections might be understood as one continuous part, dominated by the outlook towards the death of Jesus, and be counted together as the second part of the book.

The birth-stories are in complete disaccord with Matthew's though more consistent in themselves. The element of marvel is more restrained; they strike a softer note and affect a greater precision of detail. But, just as the gospel legend made a point of annexing John the Baptist to Jesus, as introducing him to his ministry, so here an analogous relation is set up between the Baptist's birth and the Christ's, the one, so to say, preparing the way for the other and enhancing its significance, while the whole is imitated from Old Testament stories of miraculous births with a view to showing that Jesus came into the world under conditions familiar to the most faithful type of Judaism, and not only under the conditions marked out by the prophets.

It would seem, however, that Christian tradition has here taken over and duplicated a legend about John conceived in the Baptists' sect. The first scene (i, 5–25) shows the annunciation of John, who is coming to do what is written of Elijah by the prophet Malachi (iii, 1; iv, 6), with the stage-accessories imitated from the births of Isaac, Samson and Samuel. The second (i, 26–56) gives the annunciation of Jesus and the visit of Mary to Elisabeth; Mary, whom the first Christian version of the legend seems to have attached to the race of Aaron, is at Nazareth, and is cousin to Elisabeth. During her betrothal to Joseph who, on his side, is of the race of David, she receives assurance from the angel Gabriel that she will become the mother of the Messiah. The conversation between the virgin and the angel about the miraculous conception is a surcharge made at the last Christian revision. In the earliest arrangement the story (as otherwise attested by an old Latin manuscript) went on at once to Mary's acceptance of the angel's announcement (i, 38) in contrast to the doubt of Zacharias (i, 18) in the first scene, the case of Elisabeth being cited by the angel (i, 36) as a miraculous guarantee that the child about to be born from the coming marriage of Mary with Joseph would be of messianic dignity; in this way the original version found fulfilment of the prophecies relating to the birth of Messiah (including Isaiah vii, 14). This also explains the visit of Mary, now *enceinte*, to Elisabeth, who holds the same relation to Mary as John to Jesus. To complete the balance, the canticle (*Magnificat*, i, 46–55), imitated from Hannah's song (1 Samuel ii, 1–10), and probably added in revision, was at first attributed to Elisabeth, making a counterpart to the canticle of Zacharias in the following scene.

The third scene presents the birth of John (i, 57–80) in close correspondence to his annunciation, the song of Zacharias (*Benedictus*, i, 68–79) being added, like that of Elisabeth. The two songs, imitated from the Old Testament, seem to have existed at first independently of the legend into which they are here incorporated, the *Magnificat* being adapted to it by the addition of a single line (i, 48) in keeping with Elisabeth's condition, and the *Benedictus* by the passage relating to John (i, 76–77).

The fourth scene represents the birth of Jesus at Bethlehem and his presentation in the temple. To get Jesus born at Bethlehem the Christian editor of the book to Theophilus conceived the unfortunate idea of bringing his parents thither to satisfy the census taken by Quirinius, mentioned by Josephus, which took place ten years after the death of Herod (cf. *supra*, p. 20). The scene is set to recall the memory of David, the shepherd ancestor (cf. Psalm lxxviii, 70–71); the intervention of the angelic host and their song (ii, 13–14) is a reviser's addition, as is the remark about Mary (ii, 19); conformably to the Law Jesus is circumcised eight days after birth (ii, 21); on the fortieth day a legal sacrifice, which the narrator seems to confuse with the ransom of the first-born, takes place for the purification of Mary, equally prescribed by the Law (ii, 22–24); two venerable saints, an aged man and an aged woman, salute the infant Christ with prophetic voices (ii, 25–38); here again the story of Simeon is an intromission by the editorial hand, and the same is true of the passage concerning Mary (ii, 34–35). The primitive conclusion of the story is in ii, 33, placed at first after 38. Note the candour with which the author of the primitive story uses the words "his father and his mother."

The anecdote of Jesus at the age of twelve is intended to cover the open gap between the birth-stories and those of the Galilean ministry. Here Jesus assumes the attitude of Son of God, to the great astonishment of his two parents, showing that this story of the child-prodigy was introduced into the Jesus-legend without regard to the miraculous conception. (In ii, 51 the line about Mary's memories has all the look of a postscript.)

Whether the synchronism which stands at the head of the stories relating the ministry of Jesus represents a traditional datum, and, if so, in what measure, cannot be stated with certainty. Only the chief indication, the fifteenth year of Tiberius, is primitive and must originally have referred to the *epiphany* of Jesus, and not to his birth; but the accumulation of time-indications is editorial and probably borrowed from Josephus. The mention of Annas who held the high priesthood from the year 6 to the year 15 is an error, shared, it is important to note, by the third Gospel with the fourth. Joseph, named Caiaphas, was high-priest from 18 to 36. If Jesus was born before the death of Herod, he would be at least thirty-two years old when he began to preach. But these chronological combinations are most uncertain.

The stories of John's preaching, Jesus' baptism and the temptation in the desert (iii, 2–22; iv, 1–13) are built up, like Matthew's, on Mark and the collection of *logia*; in the notice about John (iii, 2–6) the quotation from Isaiah (xl, 3–5) has been extended; the Baptist's teaching, addressed to "the multitudes" (iii, 7–9; Matthew iii, 7–12), is followed by special injunctions given, at their separate request, to the multitudes, the publicans and the soldiers (iii, 10–14)—a free amplification by the editing hand; from the same hand comes the setting in which we find the declaration of John about his mission as forerunner and the distinction of the two baptisms (iii, 16–17); and, similarly, the notice about John's arrest, here antedated, because the editor will avoid reproducing the long story about John's death in Mark vi, 17–29.

The account of the baptism (iii, 21–22) is somewhat abridged from Mark (i, 9–11) but so as to bring into relief the miraculous circumstances of the event, presenting it as a prototype of the baptismal ceremonies in Christian communities. To this a genealogy of the Christ is mechanically attached bringing on a statement as to the age of Jesus at the beginning of his ministry. This genealogy, like Matthew's, was at first intended to establish the Davidic descent of Jesus as a son of Joseph—shown by the clumsy invention "as was believed" in iii, 23—and diverges from Matthew's in a way which betrays them both as artifacts. The constructor of the genealogy going back to Adam "who was the son of God," merely aimed at being complete(!); but the editor of the Gospel had in mind the universality of salvation for the human race.

In the story of the temptation (iv, 1–13), Mark (i, 12–13) is combined with Matthew's source (iv, 1–11), and the order of the last two temptations is reversed because, the first temptation having taken place in the desert, that of the earthly Kingdoms was located between the desert and Jerusalem, and Jesus better placed after the third for bringing him back into Galilee—thereby straightening out the perspective.

For the account of Jesus' entry on his Galilean ministry it is doubtful whether we have to do either with the writer to Theophilus or with an imaginary proto-Luke. The redaction has created a striking scene, like that of Pentecost in the beginning of Acts; Mark's mention of the return to Galilee is there amplified (iv, 14–15) but his summary (i, 14) of the teaching attributed to Jesus is omitted as insignificant; then, after mentioning a successful preaching tour of the synagogues, the Christ is brought to Nazareth, a scene transferred from Mark vi, 1–6 and worked up into a large picture symbolic of the reprobation of the Jews to the profit of the Gentiles (iv, 16–30; for the setting of the scene cf. Acts xiii, 14–16). Various enrichments are here added to Mark's brief narrative; first, a citation from Isaiah lxi, 1–2; lviii, 6) containing the messianic programme (parallel to that of vii, 22 and Matthew xi, 5 but of a more spiritual character) and also the preacher's theme; then a popular saying: "physician heal thyself" with rather forced application to Jesus for failing to repeat at Nazareth the miracles he had performed at Capernaum; this followed up by a commentary attached to the proverb "None is prophet in his own country," illustrated by the widow of Sarepta and Naaman the Syrian, and made to refer to the entry of the Gentiles into salvation (iv, 25–29); lastly, the miraculous escape of Jesus (iv, 28–30), figure of the Christ's triumph over his murderers and of Christianity over persecution.

In order to recover the broken thread of Mark's narrative Jesus is now brought back from Nazareth to the Lake of Tiberias, but first halted at Capernaum. This has the effect of postponing the calling of the disciples till after the events which it precedes in Mark—the preaching in the synagogue and the cure of the demoniac, the cure of Peter's mother-in-law, the miracles of the evening, the secret departure of Jesus and his preaching in the villages of the neighbourhood (iv, 31–44; Mark i, 21–39). The calling of the first four disciples, which contains little of Mark's account, borrows the scene-setting from the Discourse in Parables (Mark iv, 1). By incorporating the miraculous draught of fishes (cf. John xxi, 2–13) the story becomes, like the preaching at Nazareth, largely symbolic, the myth of the institution of the Christian apostolate, which was originally attached to the manifestations of the risen Christ. But our editor, who will localize these manifestations in Jerusalem, has transposed the miraculous draught to the story of the vocation. Of the myth of Peter, as chief apostle of the immortal Christ, there is here more than a bare hint.

The story of the leper (v, 12–14) brings us back to Mark (i, 40–45; Matthew viii, 1–4) and we continue to follow him with that of the paralytic (v, 18–26; Mark ii, 1–12; Matthew ix, 1–8), the calling of Levi and the remarks on associating with sinners, the question of fasting, and the sabbath stories (v, 27–vi, 11; Mark ii, 13–iii, 6; Matthew ix, 9–xii, 14). Next in order the choice of the apostles (vi, 12–16; Mark iii, 13–19; cf. Matthew x, 2–4), in which we have already recognized the hand of the interpolator who mutilated the prologue to Acts, is made to precede the preaching and the miracles by the lake-side (Mark iii, 7–12; cf. Matthew iv, 23–v, 1). This scene, set in a plain, serves as introduction to the Discourse which, in Matthew, is delivered on the mountain.

While Matthew has amplified the Discourse on the mountain, furnished him by the common source, by teachings taken from elsewhere, the redaction of Luke, which has also made some additions, seems to have been more inclined, on the whole, to retrench. Beyond a doubt it has preserved the primitive form of the Beatitudes (vi, 20–23; cf. Matthew v, 3–12). But the artificial counterpart of Maledictions (vi, 24–26) must have been added, the instructions about the love of enemies being very awkwardly placed immediately afterwards (vi, 27–36; Matthew v, 38–48). The antithetic parallel between Gospel and Law, elaborated in Matthew, was out of harmony with the editor's apologetic thesis of the fundamental identity of Judaism and Christianity, which dominates the canonical version of Luke and Acts; the precept of charity, therefore, is all that has been retained of it. Inserted into the lesson on judging and fraternal correction we find the figure of the blind leader of the blind (vi, 39; Matthew xv, 14) and of the master and disciple (vi, 40; Matthew x, 24–25), both of which the source seems to have placed in a different context, as in Matthew. The figure of the trees, valued according to their fruits (vi, 43–45), has been preserved more exactly than in Matthew (vii, 15–20; xii, 33–35), but the warning to those who trust unduly in their personal relations with the Christ has been cut down in order to give the greater part of it in another place (vi, 46; xiii, 26–27; Matthew vii, 21–23). The Discourse ends, as in Matthew, with the simile of the two houses.

Next comes the cure of the centurion's servant at Capernaum (vii, 1–10), a story probably taken from the common source. The intervention of the centurion's friends, who represent believing Gentiles, is to accentuate the symbolism by showing Jesus as not entering into direct relations with the pagan suppliant. The raising of the widow's son (vii, 11–17) is an editorial insertion placed at this point to justify the answer Jesus is about to give to John's messengers. The message of John, the answer of Jesus and the sayings about the Baptist (vii, 18–35) come from the common source. Before giving Jesus' answer the redaction has intercalated a collection of miracles which Jesus performs there and then. (We may recall that this is a practice common to all the evangelists.) The reflection on the relation of John to the coming of the Kingdom in Matthew xi, 12–13 is reserved for another context (xvi, 16) and its place taken by the remark on the respective attitudes of Pharisees and sinners towards John (vii, 29–30; Matthew xxi, 31–32).

The story of the sinful woman (vii, 36–50), framed in with the parable of the two debtors, is peculiar to the redaction of Luke. The inspiration of it comes from the story of the anointing in Mark (xiv, 3–9), with some influence from that of the adulterous woman (John viii, 3–11), or from some account of a woman sinner appended to what Mark tells of Jesus' relations with publicans (Mark ii, 15–17). The adjustment of the parable to the anecdote, brought about by a passage to fill the gap (vii, 44–46), is unsuccessful, the logic of the matter leading to the conclusion, not "her many sins are forgiven, because she loves much," but "she loves much, because her many sins are forgiven." The mention of the women who followed Jesus (viii, 1–3) is inserted with a view to the rôle assigned to them in the discovery of the empty tomb (xxiii, 55–xxiv, 12). Needless to say the names attributed to the women, co-ordinated with the story of the one who was a sinner, have no better historical guarantee than the story itself.

A forced transition introduces the Discourse in Parables (viii, 4–18) which contains the following, taken from Mark (iv, 2–25) with slight abridgment and compression: the sower; the request of the disciples for explanation; the double answer of Jesus; but not the last two parables, the seed (Mark iv, 26–27) being omitted and the mustard seed (Mark iv, 30–32) reserved for another context. Omitted also is Mark's conclusion (iv, 33–34), and replaced by the saying about the true mother and brethren (viii, 19–21, dropping Mark iii, 21 and abridging iii, 31–35; Matthew xii, 46–50).

By another forced transition we come again into the current of Mark (viii, 22–25). Repeated after that Gospel are the following: calming of the tempest; exorcism of devils from the demoniac of Gerasa; cure of the woman with the issue of blood and raising the daughter of Jairus; the mission of the Twelve; talk of the people round Herod about John the Baptist; then, dropping John's death (Mark vi, 17–29), the first miracle of multiplied loaves, which here has no second, is brought on forthwith and followed immediately by the confession of Peter (viii, 22–ix, 17; Mark iv, 35–vi, 44).

A long section of Mark (vi, 45–viii, 26; Matthew xiv, 22–xvi, 12) is thus omitted. Of secondary origin in Mark, this section may have been unknown to the writer who addresses Theophilus.

The editor of his work must have known it, since he uses some of its indications elsewhere, but was not inclined to reproduce the whole, either to avoid using some of it twice over or because some parts of it would have ill-accorded with his apologetic aims. None the less, the confession of Peter (ix, 18–21) comes in without natural connection and hangs in air, as though a gap has been left or a cut made after the miracle of multiplied loaves (cf. *supra*, p. 88).

The account of Peter's confession follows Mark viii, 27–30, but we miss the rebuke administered by Jesus to Peter between the first announcement of the Passion and the lesson of renunciation, together with the saying about the near parousia (ix, 23–27; Mark viii, 34–ix, 1). The Christ's fiery reprimand to Peter (Mark viii, 32–33) has also disappeared. Whether deliberate or not, the omission is significant.

The story of the Transfiguration (ix, 28–36) is lightly retouched, but there is no trace of the statements which follow in Mark ix, 9–13 and Matthew xvii, 9–13, mention being made only of the silence kept by the disciples regarding the miracle. The cure of the epileptic (ix, 37–42) is abridged from Mark but without the conclusion (Mark ix, 28–29; cf. Matthew, xvii, 19–20). The second announcement of the Passion is introduced by a general statement about the incognito which Jesus was resolved to keep henceforth in Galilee, the form of which contradicts that of Mark (ix, 21; Mark viii, 30). Without mentioning his return to Capernaum, note is made of the disciples disputing about the first place (ix, 46–48; Mark ix, 33–37), and of the stranger exorcist "who followeth not us" (ix, 49–50; Mark ix, 38–40). Then Mark is suddenly left aside, the editor showing elsewhere (xiv, 34–35) that he knew his concluding sentences (Mark ix, 49–50).

Mark abandoned and other Sources drawn on

Before returning to the guidance of Mark our editor now proceeds to fill in his story of Jesus' journey from Galilee to Judea with a miscellaneous collection of anecdotes and sayings, which he probably found in his source unfurnished with any indications of time or place, and each originally constructed independently of the others. A chain of connected memories is the last thing they can possibly be.

The solemn formula with which the writer to Theophilus introduced the departure of Jesus for Jerusalem (ix, 51): "As the appointed time drew near for him to be caught up" to heaven (cf. Acts i, 1; *supra*, p. 144) is submerged under an ill-conceived story in which James and John, the two "sons of thunder" (Mark iii, 17), demand the destruction, by lightning, of the Samaritan village which has refused to receive them (ix, 52–56); a fiction invented by the editor, and of importance as figuring the evangelization of the pagans, like the journey into Samaria, which Jesus never made (cf. Matthew x, 5–6). Attached to this anecdote are three answers which Jesus is made to give to people who wished to "follow" him. The first two (ix, 57–60) are found also in Matthew (viii, 19–22); the third (ix, 61–62), like the second, is a popular saying or proverb adapted to the Christian theme of salvation.

The first two answers, in the source, stood in close proximity with the discourse on the apostolic mission, here reported (x, 1–16) as addressed, not to the Twelve, who have had already Mark's abridgment of it (ix, 1–5), but to seventy-two disciples, invented for the occasion, as symbolizing, both by their numbers and the part assigned to them, the evangelization of all the then known peoples of the world. The body of these instructions seems to follow the source more closely than Matthew does (x, 7–16). The invective against the Galilean towns, otherwise placed by Matthew (x, 13–16; Matthew xi, 21–24), has been inserted before the conclusion of the discourse (x, 16; Matthew xi, 1): we may infer from it that Galilee, in the earliest time, was not, in any degree, a centre of Christian propaganda. The success of the seventy-two, and the comments passed on it by Jesus, have no more historical reality than the mission itself, but they have the same symbolic character. In the prayer of thanksgiving (x, 21–22; Matthew xi, 25–26) the last strophe in Matthew's version (xi, 28–30), "come unto me all ye that labour," etc., is replaced by words of congratulation to the disciples on seeing the accomplishment of ancient prophecies (x, 23–24; cf. Matthew xiii, 16–17). By this substitution the editor's apologetic is better served than by the declaration in Matthew, where the cult of Jesus appears as the life and soul of Christianity.

By an editorial device, perceptible both by the awkwardness

of the transition (x, 25) and the embarrassment of the conclusion (x, 37), the parable of the Samaritan is tacked on to the question about the great commandment (x, 25–28). It is the Samaritan who has determined the placing both of the introductory anecdote and the parable which follows (cf. *supra*, p. 96). By itself, the parable should rather be placed in Jerusalem; but, in order to be in keeping with the theme already begun, a Samaritan has been substituted, as a type of charity, for a simple Israelite. The story of the two sisters has likewise been conceived or arranged for symbolism, Martha representing Judaism, or Jewish Christianity, and Mary the Gentile believer.

In the teaching on prayer (xi, 1–4), the Lord's Prayer lacks some of the petitions present in Matthew's version (vi, 9–13); but the pre-canonical reading of the first petition: "May the Holy Spirit come upon us and let it purify us" (confirmed by xi, 13 and apparently Marcion's reading) belongs to a baptismal liturgy not of the first age, in which the bestowal of the Spirit is given particular prominence (cf. *supra*, pp. 36 and 147). Still on the theme of prayer, the parable of the importunate friend next follows, a tale of no moral significance and probably borrowed from a rabbinical tradition. Then come sayings and comparisons relating to the answering of prayer (xi, 9–13 where 12 is the editor's addition), probably derived from the collection of *logia* (cf. Matthew vii, 7–11).

The editor has his own way of combining the dispute about exorcism (xi, 14–15, 17–20; Matthew xii, 22–30, 43–45; Mark iii, 22–27) with the refusal of a sign from heaven (xi, 16, 29–32; Matthew xii, 38–41) which followed in the source. Omitting the sentence about blasphemy against the Holy Spirit, which he keeps for another place, he inserts or constructs a duplicate of the saying about the true mother and brethren (xi, 27–28) previously lodged in viii, 19–21, and places it between the separated parts of the present arrangement. In referring to the sign of Jonah he is careful to avoid the compromising precision of the three days and three nights. The simile of the lamp (xi, 33; already used viii, 16, after Mark) here comes back from the collection of *logia*, linked with that of the eye, light of the body, the evangelist becoming somewhat entangled in a wordy paraphrase (xi, 34–36; Matthew vi, 22–23).

Nothing could be more arbitrary than his conversion of Jesus' lightning invective against the Pharisees (Matthew xxiii, 1–36) into table talk at a dinner party (xi, 37–54). In order to give these terrible threats the appearance of conversation, he cuts them into two series, the first against the Pharisees in general (xi, 39–44), the second against the scribes (xi, 46–52); one part of the citation (49–51) which, in the source, was the peroration of the discourse against the Pharisees (cf. Matthew xxiii, 33–39) is here, as it were, deprived of its sting by inserting it between the second and the third of the woes denounced upon the scribes, while the first threat (Matthew xxiii, 25–26) is watered down into an exordium for what follows. In xi, 52–54 he constructs a transition of vague generalities to the next conglomerate of teachings.

This consists of fragments seemingly drawn haphazard from Mark and the collection of *logia*, and bound together by little tricks of editing. The fragments are as follows:

On the leaven of the Pharisees (xii, 1; Mark viii, 15; Matthew xvi, 6) with the editor's gloss; exhortation to proclaim the Gospel boldly (xii, 2–9; Matthew x, 26–33 in the Mission Discourse); on blasphemy against the Holy Spirit (xii, 10; Matthew xii, 32; Mark iii, 28–29; cf. *supra*, p. 83); promise of the Spirit's help for disciples summoned before Jewish or pagan tribunals (xii, 11–12; Mark xiii, 9–11; Matthew x, 19–20); parable of the rich fool (xii, 16–21), a tale of no originality but easily convertible to the evangelist's aims, with his own introduction (xii, 13–15); warning against preoccupation with things of earth (xii, 22–31; Matthew vi, 25–34); on treasure in heaven (xii, 31–34; Matthew vi, 20–21); on vigilance in expectation of the Judgment (xii, 35–36, an allegory akin to the parable of the virgins, Matthew xxv, 1–13) with the simile of the night-robber (xii, 39–40; Matthew xxiv, 43–44); comparison of the good and the wicked servant (xii, 41–46, but not so well balanced as in Matthew xxiv, 45–51) with a gloss (xii, 47–48) which seems to be inspired by the parable of the talents (Matthew xxv, 14–30); divisions in families produced by the Gospel (xii, 51–53 with an artificial transition 49–50; Matthew x, 34–36); signs of the times not understood by unbelievers (xii, 54–56; cf. Matthew xvi, 2–3); finally, brought in by purely mechanical joining (xii, 57), the figure of the man who exposes himself to condemnation and imprisonment unless he speedily come to terms with his adversary (xii, 58–59; Matthew v, 25–26).

The same preoccupation with the coming end of the world is apparent in the passage which follows (xiii, 1–5) about the slaughtered Galileans and the men of Siloam killed by the falling tower—incidents understood as foreshadowing the ruin in store for the Jewish people. The same preoccupation, again, in the parable of the fig tree (xiii, 6–9), an allegory related on the one hand to the mission of Jesus and, on the other, corresponding in meaning to the cursing of the barren fig tree in Mark xi, 12–14, 20. All the above, in this paragraph and the preceding, must derive, in the last resort, from the eschatological catechesis.

A sabbath story follows (xiii, 10–13), in which, if we read in the light of the context, the cure of the crippled woman may signify the salvation of the Gentiles. The parables of the mustard seed and of the leaven (xiii, 18–21; Matthew xiii, 31–33; Mark iv, 30–32) have been suggested, in their substance, by the rapid progress of Christianity in the Roman world. Then comes an ill-tied parcel containing the following miscellany: allegory of the narrow gate (xiii, 22–24; Matthew vii, 13–14); a sentence inspired by the parable of the virgins (xiii, 25; cf. Matthew xxv, 11–12); a caution to those who think that their personal relations with Jesus will secure them on the Day of Judgment, in which we may perceive the oracle of some Christian prophet against unbelieving Jews (xiii, 26–27); a saying about the elect coming from the four quarters of the world to replace the children of Abraham (xiii, 28–29; Matthew viii, 11–12), another oracle belonging to a time when the evangelization of the pagans, begun in spite of the Jews, was making headway; connected with this, the saying about the first becoming last and the last first (xiii, 30; Matthew xix, 30). The response of Jesus to the threat that Herod Antipas would fain kill him (a threat which has no historical basis, but is imitated from Amos vii, 10–17), contains a repetition (33), in other words, of what has been said just before, perhaps a gloss on the editor himself: it brings on the lament over Jerusalem (xiii, 34–35) which he has detached from the discourse against the Pharisees (Matthew xxiii, 37–39), not daring to mention it in table talk (*supra*, p. 159). All this, again, must be largely borrowed from the teaching of the Last Things, the eschatological catechesis.

Another incoherent conglomerate: a sabbath story (xiv, 1–6) sketched round an argument (xiv, 3) with no symbolic background; advice about behaviour when invited to a feast (xiv, 7–11) turned at the end into allegory (repeated after the parable of Pharisee and publican, xviii, 14; Matthew xxiii, 12); advice to invite only the unfortunate (xiv, 12–14), derived from the parable that follows in harmony with the ideal extolled in Acts; parable of the great supper (xiv, 15–24) allegorized (while keeping closer to the source than Matthew xxii, 2–10) to signify the salvation of the disinherited, as well as the pagans, in preference to conceited Jews; the lesson of renunciation (xiv, 25–27, this time taken from the collection of *logia* (Matthew x, 37–38; Mark viii, 34–35); similes of the man who would build a tower and the king who would go to war, adapted, but not well, to the lesson of renunciation (xiv, 28–33); finally, the simile of the salt (xiv, 34). All these pieces, which are of very diverse origin, serve the purpose of the evangelist for what they are worth. To discuss the reality of the facts or the authenticity of the sayings would be wasted time and labour. Save for the editor's preoccupations they have no consistency.

The three parables of divine forgiveness, the lost sheep (xv, 3–7), the lost drachma (xv, 8–10, less felicitous and possibly modelled on the preceding), the prodigal son (xv, 11–32) are turned, by the setting of the scene (xv, 1–2), into a defence of Jesus against an attack of the Pharisees. The last of the three combines the theme of the lost son found again with certain features imitated from a fine oriental tale preserved in the Acts of Thomas;[1] towards the end it develops into an allegory of the jealous attitude attributed to the Jews in regard to pagan converts.

The parables of the unfaithful steward (xvi, 1–8) and of the rich man and Lazarus are constructed throughout as a direct attack on the Pharisees. The first is a completely immoral story which some good people have tried to utilize by fitting it with edifying applications which hardly fulfil the requirements of a

---

[1] The story is given in full in the author's *Le Mandéism et les origines chrétiennes*, 126–127. It has points of strong resemblance to the parable of the prodigal son. Burkitt (*Early Eastern Christianity*, 1904) thinks it may be attributed to Bardesanes.

rigorous logic. Following this come a remark on the lack of intelligence among believers in making sure of their eternal welfare (xvi, 8*b*); advice to make friends in heaven by giving money to the poor (xvi, 9); advice to merit spiritual good by a faithful use of temporal riches (xvi, 10–12) and the impossibility of serving God and money (xvi, 13).

The remark on the ill-will of the greedy Pharisees and Jesus' reply (xvi, 14–15; cf. xviii, 9–14) are a literary device for introducing another parcel of sayings, which are not inserted in their proper place: on John and the Kingdom of God (xvi, 16; Matthew xi, 12–13); on the perpetuity of the Law (xvi, 17; Matthew v, 18), doubtless to be taken in a spiritual or typological sense; against divorce (xvi, 18; Matthew v, 31–32); the whole group tending to support the theory of the Gospel as the real fulfilment of the Law, to which the conclusion of the succeeding parable of the rich man and Lazarus is also related (xvi, 19–31).

The main body of this parable (19–26) is the adaptation of a well-worn theme concerning the eternal happiness of the poor and the eternal torment of the rich, but the appendix (27–31) brings out the hardening and reprobation of the Jews incapable of seeing prophecy fulfilled in the Christ. Nor should we dismiss too lightly the question whether the author of the parable may have had in view the resurrection of Lazarus described in the fourth Gospel as a miracle thrown away on the Jews (John xi, 1–46). On that hypothesis, however, we should have to admit that our parable contains a rather free criticism of the Johannine story and that the writing of it cannot be dated very early.

Yet another conglomerate: warning against causing the little ones to stumble (xvii, 1–2; Matthew xviii, 6–7); command to forgive (xvii, 3–4; Matthew xviii, 21–22); the power of faith (xvii, 5–6; Mark xi, 22–23; Matthew xvii, 20; xxi, 21); service of a master and service of God (xvii, 7–10); then, an expansion of Mark i, 40–45, the story of the ten lepers, where the action of the one who "was a Samaritan" puts the Jews to shame.

At the next stage, the editor, after a preamble of the usual type for starting point, brings in an apocalyptic discourse (xvii, 22–37) which Mark has also utilized (xiii, 21) and Matthew more fully (xxiv, 27–28, 37–41). The preamble (xvii, 20–21), a pure literary device, seems intended to replace what Mark says (xiii, 32; cf.

Acts i, 6–7) about the ignorance of the Christ regarding the day of the Second Coming. As to the assertion that "the Kingdom of God is in the midst of you" there is no reason to search, as is the wont of confessional apologetic, for the idea of an inward and individual realization of the divine Kingdom. What probably the evangelist had in mind was the preliminary reality of it in the Christian community (cf. xiii, 18–21); moreover the discourse contradicts the preamble. The parable of the widow and the judge (xviii, 1–5), a story with the same ethical quality as the importunate friend, co-ordinates this discourse with an eschatological application (xviii, 6–8). The parable of the Pharisee and the publican (xviii, 9–14) is conceived in accordance with the evangelical idea of the Pharisee as the type of incredulity and pride and of the publican as humble and believing; it becomes, in application, a prophetic threat to Judaism.

Return to Mark

We come back again to Mark with the story of the babes brought that "he should touch them" (xviii, 15–17; Mark x, 13–16; Matthew xix, 13–15), after which there follow in succession the story of the rich young man and the lessons attached to it (xviii, 18–30; Mark x, 17–30); the final announcement of the Passion (xviii, 31–33; Mark x, 32–34; Matthew xx, 17–19), dropping the greater part of Mark's preamble (x, 32) and the request of the sons of Zebedee for the two best places in glory (Mark x, 35–40). Owing to the latter omission the healing of the blind man at Jericho comes in immediately after the announcement of the Passion (xviii, 35–43). A further difference is that the blind man is healed before Jesus enters the town and not, as in Mark, when he leaves it, thus reserving Jericho as locality for the incident of Zacchaeus; the blind man standing for converts to Jewish Christianity, and Zacchaeus, the double of Levi the publican, for converts to hellenic Christianity, the future course of the Gospel thus falling into the outlook towards the parousia, with which the parable of the talents is supposed to be concerned.

The parable of the talents in the version before us (xix, 11–27), presents a complete transformation of the theme of retribution, as in Matthew's version xxv, 14–30, into an apocalyptic allegory. Nothing could be more tendentious than the preamble which announces this, or than the glosses which effect it. Highly significant, however, are the words of the preamble: "They supposed that the Kingdom of God was immediately to appear." The saying is not easily explained as a conjecture of the evangelist; but to know whence it is derived would be valuable information. In any case it may long have been matter of common memory among the Christians of Palestine and Syria that the first believers expected the coming of Messiah to take place at Jerusalem. The story which follows of the Christ's passing triumph on the Mount of Olives was certainly conceived as a foreshadowing of this final victory (cf. *supra*, p. 93).

Though abridged from Mark (xi, 1–10), the messianic demonstration on the Mount of Olives (xix, 28–38) is enriched by two incidents: protest of the Pharisees against the disciples' acclamations and Jesus' reply (xix, 39–40; cf. Matthew xxi, 15–16), and the prophetic lament of the Christ weeping over Jerusalem (xix, 41–44). It is no matter of chance that this last fragment replaces the symbolic story of the blasted fig tree in Mark. It is followed by a very brief account of the expulsion of the traders from the temple (xix, 45–46; Mark xi, 15–17).

A general statement (xix, 47–48) to be taken up and completed later (xxi, 37–38) replaces Mark's more detailed account of Jesus' comings and goings between Jerusalem and Bethany. Mark is followed in the discussion with the priests about Jesus' authority; in the parable of the murderous vinedressers; in the Sadducees' question about the resurrection; in the saying about the Christ as David's Lord; in the concise warning to the Pharisees (xx, 45–47) and in the widow with two mites (xxi, 1–4; Mark xii, 41–44).

The long apocalyptic discourse (xxi, 5–36) comes also from Mark (xiii, 1–37) with the difference that here the discourse is delivered in public. Some details are retouched: omission of the saying that the Son himself knows not the day of the Great Event (Mark xiii, 32) and complete recasting of the peroration. The final notice, about Jesus' daily habit and the pressure of the crowds to hear him preach, give the finishing touch to the setting of the scene. This notice (xxi, 37–38) seems to have some dependence on the story of the woman taken in adultery, which has disappeared from the synoptic tradition and got inserted, as an interpolation, into the fourth Gospel. It cannot be by mere chance that the wording of it corresponds so closely with the introduction to that story (John vii, 53–viii, 1–2).

The Lucan Story of the Passion

In the story of the Passion the plot of the Jewish magistrates to do away with Jesus and Judas' betrayal of him come together (xxii, 1–6; cf. Mark xiv, 1–2, 10; Matthew xxvi, 1–5, 14–16) as they must have been presented in proto-Mark. The story of the anointing (Mark xiv, 3–9), which the canonical version of Luke anticipates in that of the sinful woman (*supra*, p. 155), must have been unknown by the writer to Theophilus (proto-Luke). The preparations for the paschal meal, in the canonical version, are copied from Mark xiv, 12–16. In the account of the Supper the two elements of the story, the one superimposed on the other, dimly discernible in Mark (xiv 22–25), are clearer in the common text of Luke (xxii, 14–20). But, comparing the variants of the text in the oldest manuscripts, it seems that the second element (the words "given for you" at the end of verse 19 and again in verse 20) is almost entirely interpolated. It is even probable that in proto-Luke—the writing to Theophilus—the last meal was not the paschal meal, but type of the primitive form of the Supper, with the eschatological outlook to the Kingdom, in which Jesus was represented as eating bread and drinking wine with his followers for the last time under the existing conditions of the world, "this Passover" in verses 15 and 16 being a later substitution for "this bread."

Attached to the primitive, or eschatological, account of the Supper, and only explicable as so attached, comes the disciples' dispute about primacy, which brings on the lesson of service, and is combined with the promise of thrones and the intimation of future banquets together in the Kingdom (xxii, 24–30; cf. Mark ix, 34–35; x, 42–45; Matthew xx, 25–28; xix, 28). The apostrophe to Simon is intended to be a promise of his absolute indefectibility in the faith (verse 32 should be translated "and thou, *gathering them together*, strengthen thy brethren") and a prevision of Peter's eminent part as the initiator of faith in Jesus risen from the dead. With this the announcement of his coming denial (xxii, 33–34; Mark xiv, 29–31), and the denial itself, are in contradiction, and stand out clearly as postscripts of the editing hand. To the same source must be attributed the commands addressed to the disciples in prevision of the dangers awaiting them (xxii, 35–38), and introduced as testimony to the Christ's foreknowledge.

The scene in Gethsemane (xxii, 39–46) is more simply constructed than in the canonical version of Mark (xiv, 26, 32–42). Probably founded on proto-Mark, it lacks the hostile thrust at the three principal disciples, surcharged in the canonical version (Mark xiv, 33–34, 37–41). The passage relating the appearance of the angel and the sweat of blood (xxii, 43–44) is omitted in certain manuscripts; whether authentic or not in our Gospel, it represents a secondary development in the formation of the story. The account of the arrest (xxii, 47–53) corrects certain traits in Mark (xiv, 43–49) and introduces, before the speech of Jesus to those who have come to arrest him, a small miracle— restoration of his ear to the high-priest's servant (xxii, 50–51). Not a word is said about the flight of the disciples, the editor having decided to keep them in Jerusalem.

The nocturnal sitting of the Sanhedrim (Mark xiv, 53–64) is omitted, perhaps because the writer to Theophilus had found no trace of it in proto-Mark. To fill the remainder of the night of the arrest the editor has spread out Peter's triple denial (xxii, 54–62; Mark xiv, 53–54, 66–72; Matthew xxvi, 57–68, 69–75; cf. John xviii, 15–18, 25–27), to which he has given a dramatic touch by the presence of Jesus, who awakes the culprit's memory and penitence by a look. The scene of derision in the high-priest's house has also been lifted from Mark (xiv, 65) and in like manner the details of the morning meeting of the Sanhedrim (xxii, 66–71; cf. Mark xv, 1) have been transposed from the nocturnal séance in Mark xiv, 60–64. All these borrowings go to prove the indigence and instability of the tradition. We must not forget, however, that fragments of the original version by the writer to Theophilus may have been suppressed, as they have been in the sequel, the Book of Acts.

In the account of the trial before Pilate the influence of proto-Mark may perhaps be discerned in the fact that the accusation by the Sanhedrim is made to precede the interrogation by Pilate (xxiii, 1–3, 13–25; Mark xv, 1–15; Matthew xxvii, 2, 11–18, 20–25). But immediately after Jesus' avowal that he is King of the Jews, our editor puts a declaration of his innocence into Pilate's mouth. This, at bottom, is an editorial contrivance indispensable for effecting a transition to the appearance before Herod, that complete superfluity, borrowed perhaps from some Gospel then recent, in which responsibility for the Christ's condemnation and death was boldly transferred from Pilate to Herod, as it is in the apocryphal Gospel of Peter. We again pick up the thread of Mark with the incident of Barabbas, round which are grouped repeated assertions of Jesus' innocence (xxiii, 18–25; Mark xv, 6–15; Matthew xxvii, 15-18, 20–26). The incident has the appearance of being another editorial addition (xxiii, 22 repeats 15 which again repeats 4), the idea being that Pilate was compelled to pass sentence of death on Jesus merely to satisfy the hatred of the Jews.

Our Gospel's account of the execution conforms to Mark's in the following: carrying of the cross by Simon of Cyrene; crucifixion between two robbers; division of the garments; mockery by the Jewish magistrates; presentation of vinegar, turned into an act of derision on the part of the soldiers; inscription on the cross; admiring outcry of the centurion, but with a significant attenuation of the formula from "this was the Son of God" to "this was a righteous man."

Turning now to the differences, we recognize the spirit and hand of the editor in many additions: prophetic allocution of Jesus to the women of Jerusalem on the road to Calvary (xxiii, 27–31); prayer of the Crucified for his executioners (xxiii, 34; cf. Stephen's prayer, Acts vii, 60); insults by one of the robbers, prayer of the good robber and Jesus' answer which show Jesus and the robber believing that they will pass at death, not into the tomb, nor into Hades, but "into Paradise" (xxiii, 39–43; cf. xvi, 22–23, the case of Lazarus and Dives carried at death, the one into the bosom of Abraham, and the other into hell); prayer of trustful abandonment to God uttered by Jesus with his dying breath (the words of Psalm xxxi, 5, substituted, as more edifying, for Psalm xxii, 1 in Mark xv, 34); multitude of witnesses present at the death scene and their mourning afterwards, suggested, like the lamentation of the women in xxiii, 27, by a passage in Zechariah (xii, 10–14). A pathetic picture of Jesus' death painted by pious imagination.

Mark's citation of Psalm xxii, 1 in Aramean was eliminated in favour of Psalm xxxi, 5, not because it seemed a cry of despair (for its origin was well known), but because it ran a risk of being imperfectly understood, while for most readers, the Aramean words and the sorry jest they provoked from the soldiers would have no interest. But the chief reason for the change lay in the danger that the words might be taken in the sense of a gnostic doctrine which Mark was thought to favour, the doctrine, namely, that the "aeon" Christ descended on Jesus at his baptism and returned to heaven the moment he expired. This dangerous meaning is contained in the version of the cry given by the Gospel of Peter "My Force, My Force, thou hast left me!"

The author's detention of the disciples in Jerusalem has various consequences. (Observe that every trace of the writer to Theophilus is lost from the moment that Jesus breathes his last.) Our evangelist brings "all his acquaintance" to Calvary together with the Galilean women (without their names, these having been given previously, viii, 2–3): the presence of the women is in conformity with Mark (xv, 40), who is closely followed for the story of the burial by Joseph of Arimathaea; for the rôle of the women as witnesses of the interment; for the discovery of the empty tomb on Sunday morning (xxiii, 50–xxiv, 3; Mark xv, 42–xvi, 7; Matthew xxvii, 57–xxviii, 7). At this point we encounter a piece of verbal jugglery: instead of going on with Mark (xvi, 7) to the coming apparitions of Jesus in Galilee, two angels (cf. Acts i, 10) remind the women of predictions made by him *in Galilee* of his passion and resurrection (xxiv, 6–7); the women then pass on the message to the disciples, who refuse to believe a word of it (xxiv, 8–11; cf. Mark xvi, 8, where the women say "nothing to any man").

The passage describing Peter's visit to the tomb is lacking in several manuscripts, but allusion to the matter of it seems to be made later on (xxiv, 24). If it is authentic the last revision of our Gospel has been influenced by the fourth (cf. John xx, 3–10). We are ignorant of the traditions or sources from which our evangelist has constructed his apparitions of the risen Christ; doubtless he has put a good deal of his own into the stories. The apparition to the two disciples of Emmaus, in which he places in the mouth of Jesus his own (the evangelist's) system of

Christian demonstration by the Scriptures, is finely conceived as an ideal and symbolic story. Nevertheless the conclusion (xxiv, 33–34): "They found the Eleven . . . who said 'the Lord indeed is risen and hath appeared unto Simon,' " is wholly unintelligible. To balance the story, the Emmaus disciples ought to say to the others: "the Lord indeed is risen and hath appeared unto *us*." Has the passage suffered accidental damage? Or may it be that Simon's name has been brought into it to do justice to Peter's vision (cf. 1 Corinthians xv, 5)?

The story of the apparition to all the disciples which ends with Jesus' ascension into heaven (xxiv, 36–53) is lacking in unity; the incidents are crowded together, they are without connection between themselves and the perspective in which they are placed is of the vaguest. The same theme is resumed at the beginning of Acts with complementary precisions, and certainly by the same editor, or editors. Instead of taking the two accounts as contradictory, on the ground that the Gospel seems to have deliberately placed the Ascension on the night which followed the morning of the Resurrection while Acts put an interval of forty days between the two, the signs rather indicate that we should interpret the one text by the other, the two having been conceived as reciprocal complements and belonging to the same series of fictions. Slight touches in the Gospel narrative suggest interpolation. The ancient authorities which omit Peter's visit to the tomb (xxiv, 12) omit also "Peace be unto you" (36) and further on (40) "when he had said this, he showed them his feet and his hands," two passages which again indicate the influence of John. Finally in the last verses there are two doubtful readings: "he was carried up into heaven" (51) and "when they had worshipped him" (52). In the last two cases omission may have been deliberate to avoid seeming contradiction of the story in Acts with its interval of forty days. We may recall that here, as in the parallel story of Acts, the promise of the Spirit is a postscript (*supra*, p. 147).

The Gospel known as Luke's, in the form in which it has come down to us, is a compilation analogous to that of Matthew. In it we find the first book to Theophilus not only augmented by the birth-legends but substantially remodelled and completed, and the same operations have been carried out on the second book in the Acts of the Apostles. The question of dates is one question for the two writings both in their original and their canonical forms. Enough has been said to entitle us to affirm that the author of the original books to Theophilus wrote in the early years of the second century, at a time when the Christian community in Rome had not entirely rallied to the observance of the Sunday Easter. The subsequent edition presupposes the Sunday observance as completely adopted. Apart from this and supporting it, the dependence of Marcion on the third Gospel (*supra*, p. 71) leads to the conclusion that the traditional text of the Gospel was fixed a little before 140, save perhaps for slight retouchings.

THE SECOND BOOK TO THEOPHILUS CONVERTED INTO THE BOOK OF ACTS

Our analysis of the opening of Acts went no further than the story of the Ascension (i, 9–11). Appended to this story there follow, rather confusedly (12–14), the indication of the disciples' return to Jerusalem, the list of the eleven apostles, which could not be worse fitted to its context, recalling Luke vi, 13–16, where the editorial handiwork has been already noted (p. 146), and mention of the persons who, with the "apostles," are represented as constituting the first group of believers. The particular mention of the women, of the mother and brothers of Jesus, reveals the editing hand. It is that of the editor whose interest in Mary appears in the birth-stories. Mother and brothers now appear as witnesses to the tradition—a bold touch.

Notwithstanding the clumsy insertion into Peter's discourse of a legend about the end of Judas (i, 18–19; cf. Matthew xxvii, 3–10) the account of the choosing of the twelfth apostle (i, 15–26) is all of one piece with, and reflects the chief editor's notions about, the object and meaning of the apostolic witness and its depositaries. The legend of the choice of Matthias and the legend of Judas are directly and avowedly related, making up, in their combination, a single edifying fabrication.

After this artificial introduction come, first, the inauguration of the Christian religion by the miracle of Pentecost, and then, in a double series (iii–iv, 31; and v, 17–42) the conflicts of the apostles with the Jewish authorities in Jerusalem and, in the space between the two passages, a picture of the interior life of the new community and of its progress, helped on by miracles (iv, 32–v, 16). The story is pure invention throughout, but not all of one piece. Peter's discourse is in two parts. The first part, concerning "the gift of tongues" (ii, 14*b*–21 where the outpourings of glossology are confused with the power to speak in different languages), turns on the descent of the Spirit following up certain adventitious elements in the description of the event (ii, 3–4, 6*b*–11, 13). The second part (ii, 22–32, 34–36; ii, 33 and 38*b*, a little further on, being surcharged to keep contact with the first part) corresponds with the fundamental elements of the description. It is obvious that this doubling both in the story and in Peter's discourse is related to a phenomenon we have already observed in the story of the Ascension (*supra*, p. 148). It does not follow that the second editor had the idea of baptism as a purely spiritual act; for it will appear, from other cases where the same interpolator intervenes, that the gift of the Spirit joins on to, and is sacramentally completed by the baptismal immersion in water, which John the Baptist is supposed to have administered to the apostles. Was not this also the case with the typical baptism—that of Jesus?

The scene of Pentecost taken as a whole foreshadows the evangelization of the world, and for that reason is placed as introduction to the story of apostolic preaching, just as the scene of Jesus at Nazareth (Luke iv, 16–30) has been transposed to the opening of the Christ's preaching and arranged as betokening the ulterior fortunes of the Gospel. The conversion in mass of more than three thousand persons(!) follows this fine miracle and solemn discourse and, like miracle and discourse, has no historical foundation. What we go on to read (ii, 42) about the conduct of the converts, their attendance on the apostles' preaching, their coming together to break bread and falling to prayer, may be inspired by the source, but in this place is only edifying padding, as is also the conclusion of the chapter (ii, 43–47) which repeats what has just been said twice (i, 14; ii, 42) and duplicates what will be said further on (iv, 32–35) about the common use of material goods in the apostolic community.

The cure of the paralytic was, in reality, the first public incident to draw attention to the presence in Jerusalem of people who claimed to be followers of Jesus the Nazorean (iii, 1–10). The original account of it has been overlaid in various ways: first by the mention of John at the side of Peter (the surcharge is especially clear in iii, 4, "Peter fixing his eye upon him, *with John*"; the motive for this emphasis of John will appear later on), then by an amplification (8–10) which completely upsets the story; and by a solemn oration of Peter (12–26) substituted for the explanation which the circumstances called for, and which the resumption of the narrative in iv, 1 ("as they talked with the crowd, the priests arrived") supposed to have been actually given. The mention of the Sadducees at this point is intended to indicate that the bitterest form of Jewish opposition to Christianity came from the heresy which denied the common hope of Israel. Now follows a series of fabrications: the arrest of Peter leading on to the appearance of the two offenders before the Sanhedrim next day (iv, 3); the conversion of five thousand men by Peter's oration—particularly outrageous; the scene of the great assembly of persons in authority to consider the matter (5–6); the question (7) then put by the court to the accused which the writer to Theophilus had made the temple police previously address to Peter; and Peter's answer, here paraphrased into a profession of faith, the supposed presence of the cured man in court plainly revealing the hand of its inventor. (It was in the temple and on the spot that Peter, in answer to the police, replied that the paralytic had just been cured by the name of Jesus the Nazorean.) No less fictitious is the sequel to the story; the secret session of the Sanhedrim after clearing the court and the ridiculous embarrassment of the assembly, in which, however, a single echo of the source document may be detected: "they recognized"— i.e. the police recognized on Peter's answering their question "that (he and his companions) had been in the company of Jesus." The bold reply of Peter (and John) is a late insertion, but the natural conclusion of the incident, as the source reported it, seems to be preserved in the threats to which the police confined themselves, not daring to do more than threaten in presence of a crowd which sided with Peter (iv, 21–22). The scene that follows, with the prayer, into which a prophetic quotation (Psalm ii, 1–2) is painfully introduced, and with a little Pentecost for conclusion (iv, 23–31) is an editorial creation from beginning to end.

Of the succeeding *bloc* of stories (iv, 32–v, 16) hardly anything can be retained as historical. Glosses abound in what we are told about the community of goods among the believers (iv, 32–35, at least, is the editor's paraphrase); the same in the notice about Barnabas in which his name, Levitical status and place of origin are all we can retain, the rest being the first step in the process of falsification applied later on to the considerable part played by this great man in the foundation of hellenic Christianity. Whatever may be the source of it, the hair-raising story of Ananias and Sapphira is another invention intended to exalt the prestige of apostolic and ecclesiastical authority. As to the countless miracles performed by the apostles, and especially by Peter (v, 12–16), the only morsel of the tale which a prudent reader can accept as veridical is the mention of the place (the Porch of Solomon) where the believers were accustomed to gather amid the mingled caution and admiration of the lookers-on—signs which show clearly that there was no *public* preaching—with a few words in v, 12*b*–14 about the recruits gained by private propaganda.

Again, the writer gives rein to his imagination in a succession of tales which rather repeat the form of those already told or anticipate others to be developed later on. In v, 17, instead of "and rising up, the high priest," etc., the reading should probably be "Annas the high priest" as in iv, 6 (cf. Luke iii, 2). The imprisonment of all the apostles, v, 17–18, matches that of Peter and John in iv, 3; their miraculous deliverance, v, 19–21, is on the same model as that of Peter's in xii, 6–11; the meeting of the Sanhedrim, v, 27–29, is a replica of iv, 7–12; the secret meeting v, 34–40 a replica of iv, 15–17. The intervention of Gamaliel prepares for the part he will be called upon to play in the legend of Paul, xxii, 3. (The reference to the enrolment, v, 37, betrays the author of Luke ii, 1–3, but the affair of Judas the Galilean and of Theudas, in Gamaliel's speech, 35–39, have been placed in their wrong order by some copyist.) Gamaliel's speech is the high light of the picture and is intended to show what, in the author's opinion, should be the attitude of Jewish authorities to the Christian movement.

The account of the hellenist believers and of the beginning of propaganda to the Gentiles is in four sections: Stephen and the Seven (vi–vii); the dispersion of the group (i.e. of hellenist believers), the exploits of Philip and the conversion of Paul (viii–ix, 31); the apostolic journey and the conversion of Cornelius (ix, 32–xi, 18); the foundation of the Antioch community and the first journey of Barnabas and Paul to Jerusalem (xi, 19–30; xii, 25) with the intercalated account of the persecution under Agrippa I (xii, 1–24).

Stephen and the Seven

The list of the Seven belongs to the same class as the list of the Twelve and is neither more nor less authentic. But the Seven never were deacons acting under the Twelve as edited Acts would have it believed (vi, 1–6); they were the head-men of the *Greek-speaking* group of believers which soon got separated from the original Hebrew group which spoke in Aramean. The statement about the progress of the word (vi, 7) probably replaces the more prosaic information by the writer to Theophilus concerning the activities of the *Greek-speaking* group; the accession of a *few* priests is not impossible. The information about Stephen (vi, 8–15) comes in part from the original work, if not from Luke himself; but instead of loading him with miracles (8) the original would probably note that he was the first to announce *publicly* that Jesus was the Messiah, in the synagogues of the Greek-speaking Jews in Jerusalem. What the suborned witnesses and the popular voice are made to say (vi, 11–12) is a replica and anticipation of what immediately follows (13–14) about his accusation before the Sanhedrim. The base document seems to have described a legal trial by that body; mention of the prisoner's ecstasy (15) comes from the source, perhaps also the high priest's question (vii, 1); but the immediate sequel to this, in the source, was the ecstasist's answer to the question: "I see the heavens open," etc., in vii, 56. Stephen's long speech (vii, 2–53) is an interpolation by the editor between the question and the answer, intended to introduce the reader to the conception of the Jews as the guilty nation before God, proved so by a long history of perpetual infidelity to Divine revelation, guilt which they have now brought to a head in the treatment meted out to Jesus. Except for the words: "they stopped their ears" (vii, 57, where the outcries and popular tumult are an addition) the editor must have suppressed everything in the source which indicated that the death sentence was passed and carried out strictly according to Jewish law. The source stated simply that Stephen was stoned outside the city (58); but the editor, having forced into this passage a reference to the young man Saul, repeats the lapidation (59), and in a like manner having already given (from the source), Stephen's dying words in 59, he has to give him others in 60. The phrase about Saul being a consenting party is to bring on the next topic, that of Saul in the rôle of persecutor.

As imagined by our editor the persecution of believers was indiscriminate, and Saul the chief agent in conducting it (viii, 1, 3; 2, referring to Stephen's burial, is an insertion; 3 seems better placed before ix, 1). The story of Philip's apostolic exploits in Samaria is awkwardly lodged in that of the persecution, the frame of which is wholly fictitious. The only believers who had to flee from Jerusalem were the chief members of the *Greek-speaking* group. In representing the persecution as indiscriminate and as including both groups, Hebrew and Hellenist, the writer would hide the division which existed between them and avoid giving the hellenists the credit, which was really theirs, of carrying the Gospel beyond Judea. By this falsification he becomes involved in all sorts of contradiction. First he represents the entire body of believers, Hebrew and Greek, taking to flight and dispersed "except the apostles" (viii, 1); next, we have Saul entering all their houses when they were no longer there, and haling them to prison. The description of Philip's apostolic work in Samaria (viii, 5–6) is a commonplace of the type in which the editor is wont to indulge his fancy and, whatever it may mean, must clearly be attributed to him.

Exploits of Philip: Simon Magus and the Ethiopian Eunuch

The story of Simon Magus (viii, 9–24) is not all of one piece. There is a first story which represents Simon as amazing the Samaritans by his sorceries (viii, 9–11); amazed in turn by Philip's miracles, he proposes to buy from him the power to do as much. But this conclusion is submerged in another tale (viii,

14–25). The apostles at Jerusalem, informed of what is going on in Samaria, are minded to have Peter and John on the spot, and send them off (the mention of John is here, too, a late postscript as in iii, 1, 3–4, 11). They confer the Holy Spirit on Philip's converts, and it is for having tried to buy the power to do this that Simon gets a cutting reprimand from Peter (viii, 20–23). This proves the existence, at the time it was written, and in some rudimentary form, of the legend which told of a conflict between Peter and Simon the Magician; the writer would here tell how the conflict began. Moreover we here see the Church, through our editor as spokesman putting forth its claim, against the gnostics, to a monopoly of the Spirit (cf. p. 83) and expressing the claim by a special rite, appended to baptism but distinct from it, the rite which confers the Spirit by imposition of hands.

The tale of the Ethiopian Eunuch converted by Philip on the road to Gaza leaves nothing to be desired for naïveté and extravagance (viii, 26–40). The building up of the story on a text from Isaiah (liii, 7–8) repeats the procedure by which nearly all the discourses in Acts are made up, the whole being apparently conceived as the fulfilment of prophecy (Isaiah lvi, 3–7; Psalm lxviii, 31). It is here of little importance whether the tale was invented by the editor or found by him ready made.

Saul—Persecutor and Convert

The legend of Saul, persecutor and convert, now follows (ix, 1–30); the theme of his conversion is treated thrice over (ix, 1–19; xxii, 3–21; xxvi, 4–18) with variations which seem to betray, not the use of different sources, but the extreme licence which the editor allowed himself in exploiting the matter. This legendary tale reposes on information obtained from the Epistles: "Saul, who is Paul" is converted near Damascus in consequence of a vision, after persecuting the believers in Jesus; this upon an erroneous supposition for, at the time in question, the only believers were in Jerusalem, and it is in that city that he should have played the part of persecutor before betaking himself to Damascus, where the vision overcomes him for Jesus. As to the first part of the story, the commission to persecute given to Saul by the high priest is, in the conditions indicated (ix, 1–3), quite inconceivable; the dramatic picture that follows of Saul blinded by the luminous vision is just as unbalanced; the third tale, of Paul's initiation to Christianity by Ananias, under the guidance of two visions, one for the initiator and the other for the candidate (ix, 10–19a), is modelled on a well-known type to be met with, for example, in the Mysteries of Isis. Pure invention of the editor is Paul's ministry in the synagogues of Damascus (ix, 19b–22), while the circumstances of his flight (ix, 23–25) are partly by the same hand—the plot of the Jews—and partly borrowed from 2 Corinthians xi, 32–33, or from the tradition behind that passage. The impression produced on the Jerusalem believers by Paul's arrival, the intervention of Barnabas, Paul's preaching at Jerusalem, his departure for Caesarea and Tarsus after a new plot against him by the Jews—all these belong to the same class as the foregoing. But it suits the editor's purpose to represent Paul as hurrying away to meet the old apostles and to be associated with their ministry in the holy city—in flat contradiction to Galatians i, 15–17, 21–24.

Fictions about Peter

A stock phrase on the prosperous condition of the churches in Palestine (ix, 31), which at the time in question were not in existence, serves to introduce a number of tales about Peter: two miracles, that of Lydda, imitated from the cure of the paralytic in Luke v, 18–25 and a duplicate of the cure previously performed by Peter himself in the temple (iii, 1–16), and the resurrection of Dorcas at Joppa, imitated from the raising of Jairus' daughter in Luke viii, 41, 42; 49–56, and from the resurrections effected by Elijah and Elisha; next, after localizing these miracles in places that would bring Peter on the way to Caesarea as the right place for the conversion of a Roman officer, comes the conversion of Cornelius, with the usual apparatus of preliminary visions (x, 1–23), the meeting and reciprocal explanations (x, 23–33), Peter's discourse (x, 34–43) making him the announcer, before anybody else, of the principle of universal salvation, and the baptism of Cornelius, all to make it appear that this same Peter was the first to accept a pagan convert without compelling him to be circumcised (x, 44–48). The same motive inspires the apology for his conduct which Peter goes on to offer to "those who were of the circumcision" in Jerusalem (xi, 1–18). All this our editor places before coming to the foundation of the Church in Antioch, by way of putting Peter above Paul and of reserving to Peter the initiative as apostle to the Gentiles.

Foundation of the Church in Antioch

The account of this foundation (xi, 19–26) and of the alms immediately sent to Jerusalem by the new community (xi, 27–30; xii, 25) now follows, but is awkwardly mixed with the story of the persecution by Agrippa I and the death of the persecutor (xii, 1–2, 20–24). The first lines (xi, 19–21) come from the source-document and are continuous with those already given in viii, 1, 4 about the propaganda carried on by the dispersed hellenists after the death of Stephen. But the representation of Barnabas as sent to Antioch by the mother-church in Jerusalem (xi, 22–24) is the writer's fiction, another fragment from the source (xiii, 1) making it clear that Barnabas was one of the fugitives who carried the Gospel to Antioch and were the first to receive pagans into the fold without compelling them to be circumcised: the same motive which inspired the fiction of Peter converting Cornelius here turns Barnabas into a delegate from the Jerusalem believers while the reappearance of Paul (xi, 25–26) is all part of the same scheme. The statement in xi, 26b that "the disciples were called Christians first in Antioch" certainly comes from the source.

The next fabrication concerns the prophets who come to Antioch from Jerusalem announcing an approaching famine, in consequence of which the faithful at Antioch make a collection and send it to Jerusalem by the hands of Paul and Barnabas (xi, 27–30). These Jerusalem prophets are replicas of those whom the source-document will presently indicate as already in Antioch (xiii, 1). In like manner the journey of Paul and Barnabas to Jerusalem with the collection in their hands is substituted for that which they made, at the indicated date, for the different purpose of discussing the legal observances. Finally, the collection here mentioned has been substituted for the assessment demanded of the missionaries to the outside world at the Jerusalem meeting over the legal observances (cf. Galatians ii, 10). The famine has been taken by the editor from Josephus (*Antiquities*, xx, 5, 2).

The persecution organized by Agrippa I was doubtless connected with the policy of Claudius to suppress Jewish agitators. The account of it here given comes in the main from the source; but it is probable that the writer to Theophilus recorded in this passage the execution of John as well as of James, the editor sparing John to avoid contradicting the Ephesian legend of his survival, which may also be the reason for the omission from canonical Luke of the incident in Mark x, 35–40 when Jesus predicts the martyrdom of John (cf. *supra*, p. 59). The miracle which procured escape for Peter (xii, 3–19) has the unmistakable look of an invention, but our inventor has avoided mentioning the locality to which Peter betook himself in his flight from Jerusalem (xii, 17) saying only: "he went away to another place." The supposition is irresistible that Peter found his way to Antioch and that the editor avoided mentioning it because he was determined to keep silence about the conflict there between Peter and Paul. But the composer of Acts knew the legend of Simon Magus (*supra*, p. 176) and this creates a possibility that the "other place" so mysteriously designated was meant to be Rome. But did Peter ever find his way to that city?

What became of Peter after his Flight?

The fate of Peter is understood in this passage according to some tale of which the import is not easily measured. At first sight there seems no ground for maintaining that Peter was put to death, along with James and John, in the persecution ordered by Agrippa I. But was not John brought to life again in legend, and did not the composer of Acts intentionally omit the mention of his death and let him live on? May not the same proceeding have been adopted for Peter? Is it entirely natural that the composer of Acts has not a word to say about him after the meeting at Jerusalem? True it is that the Epistle to the Galatians takes him to Antioch after this meeting and shows him there in conflict with Paul (Galatians ii, 11–21). But the story of this conflict is all of a piece with the false account given in the same Epistle (ii, 1–10) of the meeting in Jerusalem. Peter, James and John, who appear there as the "apostles" they never were, and as "pillars," are, in that capacity, figures of legend. May it not be that the story of the Antioch conflict is the first form of the "tradition" which represented Simon Peter and Simon Magus in deadly strife? The matter is shrouded in a little mystery for which an explanation has yet to be found.[1]

The account of Agrippa's death (xii, 20–23), though very different from that given by Josephus (*Antiquities*, xix, 8, 2), cannot be altogether independent of it. Barnabas and Paul, returning to Antioch, are said to take John-Mark along with them, the compiler's reason being that he will need him there later on to explain the separation of Barnabas and Paul (xv, 37–40).

Confused Account of Paul's Journeys

Having made into two the one and only journey to Jerusalem which Barnabas and Paul ever took in company, the compiler is minded to fill the void between them by a great mission which cannot be other than fictitious. Other evidence makes it certain that the debate on the legal observances with the Jerusalem believers was not the sequel to the mission about to be described but to that jointly conceived by Barnabas and Paul in Syria and Cilicia (cf. xv, 23; Galatians i, 21; ii, 1, 9). As to the mission intercalated by the compiler (xiii, 4–xiv), it is clearly made up by combining into one the independent missions undertaken, *after the separation of the two apostles*, by Barnabas into Cyprus (xv, 39) and by Paul into Lycaonia, Pisidia and Galatia (xvi, 1–6). The fragment from the source-document standing at the head of these stories (xiii, 1–2), taken in itself, represents the Antioch congregation as under the teaching of five prophet-instructors, of whom Barnabas is first and Paul last—doubtless because he joined the community after the others. Originally the names of Barnabas and Paul were followed by a short personal note about them—this, changed in form, has been used at an earlier stage. The Spirit commands that these two of the five prophet-teachers are to be appointed for special service, that is, for preaching the Gospel, as their whole-time and continuous occupation, on the spot in Antioch and in the surrounding country (Syria and Cilicia, anticipated in xi, 26). A line of surcharge (xiii, 3) indicating that they were immediately "sent away" adapts the original statement to the story that follows of their felicitous joint mission to Cyprus–Pisidia–Lycaonia.

[1] See the articles "Simon Magus" and "Simon Peter," by P. W. Schmiedel, in the *Encyclopedia Biblica*, vol. iv. *Translator's note.*

It would be wasted labour to discuss the stories about the mission to Cyprus (xiii, 4–12), Sergius Paulus and the two sorcerers, Bar-Jesus and Elymas. They are wholly fictitious. The words "Saul who is Paul" (xiii, 9) must have belonged originally to the enumeration of the five Antioch prophets in the fragment from the source (xiii, 1). Leaving Cyprus, the two missionaries are supposed to make for Perga in Pamphylia, where Paul leads off with a discourse in the synagogue (xiii, 16–41). Observe that from now onwards Paul is brought to the front while Barnabas' name is little more than a *pro forma* insertion—a peculiarity easily explained when we remember that this joint mission never took place. None the less the story of it may contain elements belonging to the mission which Paul, later on, undertook by himself in these .countries, and which, in the place assigned to it in Acts, is reduced to little more than a bare itinerary. The preaching scene at Antioch of Pisidia (xiii, 14–15) follows a conventional type (cf. Luke iv, 16–17). The first part of Paul's discourse (xiii, 16–25) is a résumé copy of Stephen's speech; the second (26–41) a variant of Peter's to the Jews in Jerusalem; the whole constructed to convey an idea of Paul's preaching to Jews. Not less artificial is the account of the second Sabbath (42–52). Vague terms are used for the story of Iconium (xiv, 1–7). The miracle at Lystra (xiv, 8–10), modelled on the cure of the temple paralytic in iii, 1–10, brings on, not quite naturally, the mistake of the people of Lystra who conclude that the missionaries are gods (we are in the land of Philemon and Baucis) while the protest of the apostles is a prelude to Paul's coming discourse on the Areopagus. The stoning of Paul by the Jews, here unnaturally brought in (xiv, 19–20), may come from the source-document, where it belonged to Paul's passage through Iconium (cf. xiv, 5; 2 Corinthians xi, 25). All that follows (20–28) is pious padding. In order to bring his travellers back to their starting point at Antioch the compiler returns them through all the towns from which they have just been driven out. Finally, having got them back to Antioch, he makes them say, with a view to introducing the affair of the legal observances, next to follow, that "God had opened a door of faith to the Gentiles"— as if the Antioch community to whom this information was imparted were not itself partly composed of uncircumcised pagans.

The story of the commotion about legal observances (xv, 1–29) opens with a passage from the source-document to Theophilus. Some brethren, come down from Jerusalem, have been making trouble in the Antioch community by putting it abroad that the Law is obligatory on converts from paganism and, in consequence of the disturbance, Barnabas and Paul are delegated to go into the matter with the elders at Jerusalem (xv, 1–2). But fiction immediately breaks out in the triumphant journey through Phoenicia and Samaria and in the scene-setting of the apostolic conference (3–5); in Peter's discourse (7–11) in which the Cornelius affair is called up; in James' discourse in which approval is given to Peter's thesis, with a reminder of certain prohibitions obligatory on pagans in any case. These prohibitions were in force in some of the churches, but the reminder about them in the letter (23–29) addressed to believers in Syria and Cilicia is there a surcharge (28, doubling 25). The message, as reported in the source-document, was sent "by the elders and the brethren," "the apostles" has been added in a surcharge— a point that deserves consideration. In the message as reported by the source the Judaizing agitators were disavowed, the Jerusalem brethren delegating two of their members to carry the letter to the brethren in Antioch and the neighbourhood (in 26 the praise bestowed on Barnabas and Paul should be replaced by that given to the message-bearers, Silas and Judas, in 22). The conclusion of the story (30–33, 35) may come from the source, except the remark about Silas and Judas, "they too being prophets" (32) which connects with the fiction in xi, 27–30 (*supra*, p. 178). The same is true of 34, inserted by the compiler to make a fit with 40.

Exit Peter: Paul now Occupies the Stage

From this point onwards the Book of Acts is exclusively given up to narrating Paul's missions and captivity; for the writer is deliberately silent about his death. The story of the separation of Paul and Barnabas (xv, 36–41), has been imagined to hide the real cause of strife between Paul and the other missionaries, the isolation in which Paul afterwards found himself and the difficulty of his relations with other propagandists and with the Jerusalem elders. Having anticipated the evangelization of the towns in Lycaonia and Pisidia (xiv, 28) the compiler has now nothing new to tell about them (xv, 36–xvi, 10); he stops at Lystra only for the story of Timothy's circumcision, perhaps invented to compensate and neutralize what is said about Titus in Galatians ii, 1–3. What we read about Paul promulgating apostolic decrees in the churches of Lycaonia is a superfluity added for edification. The source-document has furnished the compiler with the itinerary followed by Paul and his companions (Silas and probably Luke himself) from his departure in Phrygia to his arrival in Troas, but Luke's notes of the journey must be greatly abridged.

The circumstances of the departure for Neapolis, of the arrival at Philippi and of the way in which the preaching began there, are all trustworthy indications lifted from the source-document, but only a few echoes from the source are to be heard in the romance constructed by the compiler to crown the mission at Philippi. The incident of the pythoness, "the maid with the spirit of divination," exorcised by Paul (xvi, 16–19) contradicts the charge brought before the magistrates (20–21) which comes from the source, as do also the popular excitement and the flagellation and imprisonment of the accused (22–23); but the earthquake and the wonders to follow can be nothing but an invention added by the editor; similarly, the pardon Paul is made to procure from the magistrates. The truth of the matter must have been that Paul and Silas, under security given by their friends (a detail which seems to have been shifted into the succeeding story, xvii, 9), were set free on condition of their quitting the city without a moment's delay.

The story of the mission at Thessalonica (xvii, 1–9) must be a greatly shortened and altered version of the source-document. The account of how the preaching began in the synagogue conforms to probability, but the Jewish riot which compels the preachers to flee seems to be a shortened repetition of the riot at Philippi. The notice about Berea (10–13), copied from that about Thessalonica, is no less doubtful, especially in its conclusion (14–15 is not an agreement with 1 Thessalonians iii, 1–2, nor even with Acts xviii, 5).

It is a question whether anyth'ng of the source-document survives in the account of Paul's visit to Athens (xvii, 16–34).

His discourse to the Areopagus is the work of the compiler philosophizing in the style of the second century apologists for Christianity a verse from Aratus (28) replacing the quotations from prophecy which adorn the other discourses in Acts. The rest of the story (16–21, 32–34) does little more than provide a frame for his allocution. But the mention of the small number of converts and of two proper names (34) may come from the source.

At the end of the Corinthian ministry (xviii, 1–16), and as a postscript to the account of it, we encounter another Jewish riot which brings Paul into court before the proconsul Gallio (12–17), the object being to make this high magistrate of Rome proclaim that theological disputes between Christians and Jews have no interest for Roman authority and are matters for the disputants to settle between themselves. The wholly concocted story about Sergius Paulus already encountered (xiii, 7, 12) warns us to be careful when Roman officials are brought into the tale. But if there is anything of historical value in the Gallio story, the date of the proconsulate, 51–52, would merit retention.

The true story of the Corinthian mission has not come through without additions and retouches: the mention of the edict of Claudius against the Jews is added to the notice of Aquila and Priscilla (xviii, 2); so, too, what is said at first about Paul's preaching in the synagogue (4). According to the story in the source, Paul, arriving unaccompanied at Corinth after leaving Athens, worked at his trade in Aquila's house (1–3) until the arrival of Silas and Timothy; when "the word took hold on him" (5 which should follow 3). The uproar among the Jews (6) is another contribution, of the familiar type, from the editor's stock-in-trade. Paul, thus inspired, moves from Aquila's house to that of Justus Titius (7) in order to have easier access to the synagogue. After recording the conversion of Crispus, and a great number of other Corinthians, the source went on to describe the serious difficulties that then arose for Paul and of the encouragement he received from a consoling vision (9–10). The account of his difficulties has been dropped, and one has the impression of another gap between the consoling vision and the indication of the time spent by Paul preaching at Corinth (11).

The stories preliminary to that of the mission at Ephesus are remarkable for a confusion which cannot be accidental. From the very outset, Paul's coming pilgrimage to Jerusalem is vexatiously mixed up with the visit he made to the Galatian churches on his departure from Corinth (xviii, 18–23); the mention of his departure (18) is surcharged with a phrase connecting it with the Gallio affair; Syria is noted as the end of the journey (cf. xx, 3), because the compiler's plan is to bring Paul to Jerusalem between the mission to Corinth and that to Ephesus, and for this purpose he splits Paul's last approach to the Jerusalem brethren into two journeys. Thus we are told of a "vow" taken by Paul, a circumstance in keeping with the pilgrimage; but this vow is precisely the "nazirate" which belongs to the last journey to Jerusalem and comes up in xxi, 23–24, 26. In like manner the visit of Paul to the synagogues (19–23a) is an awkward addition to the source. The intention of it all is to hide the true reason why Paul made no stay in Ephesus, namely, that he was in haste to visit the churches of Galatia and Phrygia in order to counter the Judaizing propaganda which had begun in those regions.

The account of Apollos (24–28) may have been taken from Luke's memoirs, but has been touched up by the editor: the restriction "knowing only the baptism of John" (25), and the completion of his Christian education provided by Aquila and Priscilla are not to be strictly taken. It is the compiler again who would have us believe that this man's service to the Corinthian church consisted in his bold and continual refutation of the Jews (28). His aim in all this is to throw a veil over the rôle of Apollos as Christian preacher at Ephesus itself, and the involuntary part he found himself playing in the subsequent divisions at Corinth. The twelve Ephesian disciples whom Paul is said to have baptized (xix, 1–7) are the converts of Apollos, their number probably reduced, whom the editor presents, along with their master, as adepts of an inferior Christianity and recipients of an unspiritual baptism: save as being, in some measure, historical, the case is parallel to the pure fiction of the converts baptized by Philip in Samaria (cf. p. 176) who had not yet received the Holy Spirit.

All that now remains of the authentic story of Paul's Ephesian ministry, which has been mutilated like all the others, is contained in a few lines (xix, 8–10), from which all details are omitted of the success obtained and the difficulties encountered. We are informed instead of cures operated by garments which had touched Paul's body (11–12), matching those of the same compiler's invention, operated by Peter's shadow (v, 15–16), and of Jewish demon-quellers who, on attempting to drive out a demon in the name of Jesus, are turned upon by the demoniac and soundly beaten up—an anecdote picked up from somewhere and made to adorn the history of Paul. Finally we learn of the tremendous impression made by this incident on the believers, who hastened to burn the books of magic in their possession (17–20); another fiction for the edification of Christian readers. Alas for our loss of the record left by the writer to Theophilus, deliberately emptied of its historical substance and the void filled up with this pitiful stuff!

Continued Manipulation of the Source

The last part of Acts is no more solid in construction than the parts preceding it. Paul at the end of his Ephesian ministry planned to revisit Macedonia and Achaia before proceeding to Jerusalem and from thence to Rome (xix, 21). In order to facilitate the accomplishment of this design he sends two of his companions, Timothy and Erastus (22) to prepare the way in Macedonia. So much comes from the source; but the fact is disguised that the business in hand was to gather a collection for Paul to carry to Jerusalem; a veil is thrown over the fearful dangers encountered by Paul in Ephesus and on the incidents which hindered the fulfilment of his plan, notably the divisions which arose in the community at Corinth, the measures that Paul had to take in consequence and the way in which these obstacles were finally overcome. In place of all that, the compiler tells a story of a riot that broke out against Paul in Ephesus (23–40) in which the lines concerning Paul and his friends (29–31, from "having seized Gaius," and 37) are clearly additions made to the story of an anti-Jewish riot which the compiler has here twisted to his own purpose. What we are told of Paul's departure for Macedonia and Hellas is insignificant (xx, 1–3: the compiler avoids the mention of Corinth). But "the three months" which the compiler assigns to his stay in Hellas probably marked, in the source, the time he spent in Corinth before his departure for Jerusalem. The list given of his travelling companions doubtless includes most of the delegates appointed to carry the collection for the "saints" in Jerusalem; but the list is given too early since Tychicus and Trophimus, the Ephesian delegates, were not to join the party till its later arrival at Miletus.

The itinerary comes from the source-document but has been cut up by editorial insertions. The resurrection of Eutychus by Paul at Troas (xx, 7–12) is to match the resurrection of Dorcas by Peter (ix, 36–42). The compiler has used the halt at Miletus to furnish Paul with an oration (18–35) as a model of the pastoral instruction to be given to the church-leaders. The true reason for the halt was that Paul had to avoid Ephesus and that Miletus was the appointed rendezvous where he was awaiting the bearers of the collection from the Asiatic churches. It is noteworthy that the compiler who, as we shall see, will avoid recording the death of Paul, is here careful to make him give a premonitory hint of it in the course of his speech and to say that he will never visit Asia again (25). The source account has evidently been loaded with new matter in the story of the meeting with the brethren at Tyre: the prophetic warning given to Paul (xxi, 4; cf. xx, 23) hangs in air, while the scene of farewell (xxi, 5–6) repeats that of Miletus, just described (xx, 36–38). In the account of the halt at Caesarea, in the house of Philip, the mention of his four prophetically-gifted daughters would naturally be followed by some prediction on their part, but none is forthcoming. Instead of it the compiler has substituted a prediction by Agabus (10–11) whom he has already exploited in an exactly parallel fiction (xi, 28), bringing him from Jerusalem expressly for the purpose. But the conclusion of the incident (12–14), which comes from the source, seems to indicate that Paul's answer followed a prediction given by Philip's prophetic daughters.

Equally derived from the source are the details of the departure from Caesarea (xxi, 15, except the first words "after these days," co-ordinated with xxi, 10); the arrival at Jerusalem and the lodging with Mnason of Cyprus; probably also the visit to James on the day following their arrival; but the compiler has awkwardly inserted a favourable reception by the brethren before the visit to James. In the account of this visit we look in vain for any mention of the collection which was certainly presented and accepted on that occasion. All we are told is that

Paul gave the story of his mission and that the elders praised God for the results (19–20). That done, the elders address Paul in a speech (20–25) which the compiler has done his best to make unintelligible. Paul is informed that thousands and thousands of *believing* Jews are persuaded that he is everywhere turning Jews away from the Law; in order to reassure them he has only to join himself to four brethren who are undergoing a *naẕirate* and pay the expenses due on the fulfilment of their vow; as to the Gentile believers, the duties incumbent on them have been already regulated (a lame reference to xv, 28–29). Let those make sense of this rigmarole who can. What is wrong with it all is clear enough. There were no "thousands and thousands" of Judaizing Christians in Jerusalem and all that is needed is to efface the word "believing." The people exasperated by Paul were the Jews in general, and there can have been no question of reassuring *them*, but only of escaping from their wrath. To effect this Paul, who is himself under the nazirate vow (recall that the compiler has anticipated the vow in xviii, 18), is to join the four brethren who are under the same conditions and in this way will have a good chance of not being observed (the reference to xv, 28–29 is obviously by the hand which interpolated the apostolic letter).

It was a wise precaution, but it failed of its purpose. The proceedings of Paul, the character of the riot that arose in the temple when his presence there was discovered, the intervention of the military tribune and of the Roman soldiers (xxi, 26–34) are taken from the source, which is remarkably precise in these details. But, at the point when Paul is about to be taken into the barracks of Antonia, the compiler perpetrates a manifest interpolation, which stands out among all the others for its audacity. He exhibits Paul as delivering a speech to the Jewish people on his merits as a Pharisee, his conversion and vocation, in order that the Jews may appear, on this solemn occasion, as opposed to the salvation of the Gentiles (21–22). The way in which Paul is made to claim his rights as a Roman citizen (24–29) repeats the earlier and fictitious scene in xvi, 35–40 (*supra*, p. 176). There is no doubt that Paul had to make good his status as a Roman citizen, but he did so to escape the vengeance of the Jewish authorities and get his case adjudicated by the procurator.

The meeting of the Sanhedrim, convoked by the procurator to inform him on the case (xxii, 30–xxiii, 10), is fabrication from beginning to end. The compiler would have it believed that the Pharisees were in accord with the Christians in regard to the messianic hope. An element from the source-document probably remains in the account of Paul's vision (xxiii, 11) which ought to have been reported as belonging to the night which followed his arrest, indicating the turmoil of his mind after his capture, and how he was led to base his hope on ever getting to Rome on an appeal to Roman authority. In order to hide Paul's determination to have recourse to Roman authority the compiler imagines a Jewish plot to kill the prisoner, which a nephew of Paul, also invented for the occasion, reveals to the tribune; the consequence being that this officer decides to get Paul out of the way by transferring him to Caesarea (12–22). The general circumstances of his removal from Jerusalem to Caesarea must have been indicated in the source, but the compiler has magnified the size of the military escort (23–24) and himself composed the tribune's report to Lysias, which has no more reality than the meeting of the Sanhedrim to which it refers (25–30). The journey to Caesarea and the delivery of the prisoner to the procurator Felix are from the source (32 is an adjustment to the magnified size of the escort).

The development of the legal proceedings has been deliberately obscured by the compiler. In the scene-setting for the judicial investigation presided over by Felix the naming of the high priest is an error: Ananias was not high priest in Felix' time (xxiv, 1; same error xxiii, 2). The speech of the advocate Tertullus (2–9) and Paul's reply (10–21) are in the compiler's manner. The impression is given that the case was thoroughly investigated, whereas the question then at issue was that of competence to try it. Some influence from the source may be detected in what Paul says about the time elapsed since his arrival in Jerusalem (11) and in the veiled reference to the collection (17). Felix, "knowing all about" Christian propaganda, adjourns the decision (22), though the time for resuming the investigation, "when Lysias shall come," is probably editorial. The measures ordered in regard to the prisoner (23) come from the source. Paul's conversation with Felix and his wife Drusilla (24–26) is a forerunner of the grand affair constructed later on for Agrippa II and Berenice (xxv, 13–xxvi, 32). The intention ascribed to Felix of placating the Jews by not releasing Paul before handing over his powers to Festus (27*b*) has the look of another editorial touch.

The subsequent narration of the resumption of the affair on the arrival of Festus (xxv, 1–5); the sitting of the court (6–8, doubtless a shortened account); the decision of Festus (9); the appeal to Caesar and the granting of the appeal by the procurator (10–12), so far as the substance is concerned, come from the source. The editor has turned the demand of the Sanhedrim for delivery of the prisoner to its jurisdiction into one asking for a "favour" and inserted a Jewish plot (3). By no possibility could Festus remit Paul to the Sanhedrim as an act of benevolence. The very terms of the final sentence make it clear that appeal to the imperial tribunal was the only means left to Paul for saving his life (10–12). It is the compiler who represents Festus as, on the one hand, persuaded of Paul's innocence and, on the other, willing to make a present of his person to the Jews, who would certainly have put him to death. The dialogue between Festus and Agrippa and the story of the meeting organized for the satisfaction of this petty Jewish king are a long piece of editorial padding, though there are signs that it is not by the same hand as the general run of earlier fictions. It is made to rest upon an absurd supposition, namely that Festus had nothing to put into his official report and hoped to get material from the meeting (26). What the compiler is aiming at in all this is to accumulate proofs of Paul's innocence and so discredit in advance the condemnation passed on Paul in Rome, of which when he comes to it, he will say not a word.

The narrative of the journey from Caesarea to Rome (xxvii, 1–xxviii, 16) seems to have been changed only by additions mostly intended to raise Paul's importance. These are easily detected: prophetic warning, unheeded, to winter in Crete instead of at the place called Fair Haven; recall of this warning in the midst of the tempest and prophecy of safety for the ship's company; denunciation of the sailors who would abandon the ship and leave the passengers to perish in it; encouragement by word and example to take food (xxvii, 9–36, "While waiting for day," 33, runs on in the source with "they lightened the ship," 38; 37

should come after 44). In the account of the stay in Malta and of the end of the journey we may suspect the little miracle of Paul and the viper, the cures performed on the Governor and other inhabitants of the island, the stay of seven days at Puteoli, and especially the story of the whole Roman community coming as far as the Appian Forum and Three Taverns to present themselves to Paul (xxviii, 15).

The last "we" of the source-document occurs in the notice of Paul's arrival in Rome and of the permission extended to him to remain in his own lodgings under the continual guard of a soldier (16). This was probably followed in the source by mention (30) of the two years spent by Paul under these conditions to which the compiler has added a gloss (31) to bring out the liberty then enjoyed by the apostle to preach in his own dwelling. The scene, twice repeated, of his interviews with the Jews of Rome (17–28; 29 is a gloss repeating 24–25) stands out among all the other fictions as most clearly the compiler's work. Taken together with the final gloss in 31 it constitutes the conclusion of the book as conceived by the final editor, and symbolically sums up the apologetic thesis he aimed at making good: that Christianity is the true Judaism and, the Jews having rejected it, its true representatives are now the Gentiles; that being so, it has right to the liberty which Roman law allows to the Jewish cult.

Significant Silence of Acts as to the Fate of Paul

We know not, and probably will never know, at what point the writer of the second book to Theophilus brought his story to a close. But there is no denying that the canonical Book of Acts came into being long after the death of Paul; whence it follows that the silence of the compiler regarding it is voluntary and deliberate. He says nothing about it because what he knew and might have said would not have been easily reconciled with his apologetic aims. It may be objected that he could not hide a fact of this kind if it had already happened. The answer is that from one end of the book to the other he is busy in omitting from the facts he knew all those of which he did not wish to speak, and in falsifying at will the shape of those which it suited him to record or which he found it impossible to pass by in silence.

The interest of his apologetic was not the only consideration which governed his proceeding. He is quick to seize any opportunity to leave the way open for the currency of certain legends to which it would have been imprudent to give overt support. After all, his silence about the death of Peter is every whit as surprising as his silence about the death of Paul. We have seen what he leaves us at liberty to infer when, coming to Peter's flight from Jerusalem, he tells us mysteriously that the chief of the Twelve departed "to another place." The document known as the Canon of Muratori may possibly throw some light on the silence of Acts regarding the death of the two apostles. The author of this text observes quite innocently that Luke—whom he supposes to be the author of Acts—"has left aside the passion of Peter and the departure of Paul for Spain," which probably means, "and the passion of Paul after his journey to Spain." This is the Roman legend as completely formed at the end of the second century, which was already in existence, though less sure of itself, when Acts was shaped and elaborated about 130–140. To reproduce the legend at that date was more than the compiler of Acts dared to do; but still less was he disposed to put it out of the question. We may recall how careful he is in the third Gospel and in Acts to avoid contradicting the Ephesian legend about the apostle John.

But then, it will be said, is not the third Gospel, whatever may be said of the others, a book of history along with its sequel the Acts of the Apostles? No: both are for catechetical edification, and we have said enough to prove it. But does not the silence of Acts, explained as above, become an argument against Peter ever coming to Rome? It is quite possible, and we have already hinted that there is need for a new inquiry into the matter (cf. *supra*, p.179).

Chapter VII

THE GOSPEL ACCORDING TO JOHN

WE have already unmasked the audacious literary fiction by means of which the Gospel called John's was introduced to the Asiatic churches among which it was first published and presented as embodying the only perfect type of Gospel catechesis. Such a mode of presenting the book makes it clear that the intention of its authors was not to complete the synoptic catechesis but to supplant it outright, in which, however, this new catechesis did not succeed. It is equally certain that the Johannine Gospel owed much, in its first form, to the Synoptics, and that in order, at a later stage and in regions outside that of its origin, to render it acceptable along with them, various additions were made to it with a view to bringing it more into line with the books in opposition to which it was at first brought out, and giving it a greater resemblance to them. The first publication can hardly have been effected before 135–140; the additions and retouches on synoptic lines will have been introduced soon afterwards when Asiatic Christianity was uniting with that of other churches to make common front against the flood of gnosticism and especially against Marcion. It is none the less true that the fourth Gospel is, essentially, a gnostic document, although its structure-form proclaims it a Christian catechism: moreover it has absorbed a number of gnostic pieces, rhythmic utterances of mystic teaching, originally composed outside the Gospel framework and incorporated with it by methods to be indicated presently, just as the Synoptics have incorporated many a fragment of the earlier eschatological teaching. The result is that the Johannine catechesis is hardly less complex than the synoptic. We cannot claim to untie all its knots. At least let us see what patient analysis of the book will reveal.

Taking it as traditionally constructed we can distinguish in it two principal parts: first, the Epiphany of the Christ, as Logos or incarnate Son of God, in his public ministry (i–xi); second, the preliminaries, teachings and circumstances of his death and resurrection (xii–xxi).

THE PROLOGUE: FIRST PHASE

Dissertation on the prologue to John, its origin, integrity and relation to the body of the book, has been going on for a long time and in many quarters. Here we confine ourselves to a positive statement of what seems to us most probable. Taken as tradition presents it (i, 1–18) the prologue is not a part of the Gospel in the sense of a preface summarizing its theme, but a deeply thought out explanation of what is to follow, and this explanation, thrown into the form of a theological poem, may originally have existed independently of the book to which it is now attached. This prologue, moreover, in the canonical presentation of it, has been glossed and surcharged, as the Gospel itself has also been in every one of its parts.

The first strophe declares the origin, creative activity and life-giving manifestation of the divine Logos (1–5; in 3–4 the logical and rhythmical balance of the strophe requires the cutting of the lines thus: "And without him nothing has come into being. What has come into being, in him was life. And the life," etc.). Our prologue thus announces itself at the outset as, in substance, a piece of high gnosis, and a poem exactly rhythmical in form. But what now follows immediately is not in perfect keeping with this sublime beginning. At this point, and again later on, the sequence is broken by reference to John the Baptist, two interpolations, each striking a false note in the context and dislocating its primitive structure (6–8, 15–16). The object of these intrusions is clearly that of conforming our Gospel to the synoptic tradition freely interpreted in the sense of the Johannine gnosis. But it would be grave error to suppose, as some have done, that the prologue was originally concerned with John the Baptist himself. Whatever may have been said, the Mandean texts furnish not the slightest support to such a conjecture.[1]

It is in concrete terms that the author of the poem describes the manifestation of the divine Logos, made flesh that he may gather around him the children of God, these regenerated by the grace and truth which Jesus Christ procures for his own, as Moses procured Law for the Jews. But the gloss which brings John the Baptist into the poem is not solitary; others have been practised. The line "to those who believe in his name"

[1] See *Le Mandéism et les origines chrétiennes* (27–46, 148–155).

(12c) is an explanation co-ordinate to what follows in the traditional text, *"they* who *are* not born of blood," etc. At first sight one sees no need to say that the children of God are not made such by human generation: but the primitive reading is that known to Irenaeus and Tertullian: "He who was born not of blood, nor of the will of the flesh (nor of the will of man) but of God," the words "nor of the will of a man" having been added to emphasize the miraculous conception of the Christ, the original text simply stating that the Christ was born of God, because the Logos had taken flesh to himself by a mode with which natural generation had nothing whatever to do (cf. Jesus' reply to Mary, ii, 4 and Hebrews vii, 3). After (i, 14): "And the Word was made flesh and dwelt among us" the next words should be "full of grace and truth" continuing with 16–17, and dropping "we beheld his glory, as of the only begotten son from the Father," the last a heavy handed and prosaic gloss. Finally, the verse (i, 18): "No man has seen the Father," etc., is a theological gloss intended to explain how the Word-Son, as the sole master of the mystery and the exegete of God, is able to bring grace and truth into the world.

Restored to its original form the primitive poem would read as follows:[1]

> Au commencement était le Logos,
>> et le Logos était près de Dieu,
>> et le Logos était dieu.
> Il était au commencement près de Dieu:
>> tout par lui s'est fait,
>> et sans lui ne s'est fait rien.
> Ce qui s'est fait en lui fut vie,
>> et la vie était la lumière des hommes;
> Et la lumière dans les ténèbres luit,
>> et les ténèbres ne l'ont point saisie. [   ]
>
> La lumière vraie,
>> qui éclaire tout homme
>> est venue dans le monde,
> Dans le monde Il fut,
>> le monde (qui) par lui a été fait,
>> et le monde ne le connut pas.

[1] As translation would destroy the rhythm of the poem as here restored by M. Loisy, his version is presented in the original. The empty brackets indicate the points at which the poem has been glossed or interpolated. *Translator's note.*

Chez lui il est venu,
    et les siens ne le reçurent pas;
Mais, tous ceux qui l'ont reçu,
    il leur a donné pouvoir de devenir enfants de Dieu. [   ]

Lui qui, non des sangs,
    ni du vouloir de la chair, [   ]
    mais de Dieu est né.
Le Logos est devenu chair
    et il a habité parmi nous, [   ]
    plein de grâce et de vérité. [   ]
(Et) de sa plénitude tous nous avons reçu,
    grâce pour grâce,
Parce que la Loi par Moïse a été donnée,
    la grâce et la vérité par Jésus-Christ sont arrivées. [   ]

John the Baptist has been surreptitiously introduced into the prologue by way of preparing for his express testimony to the Christ. This testimony is distributed over two major scenes (i, 19–28, 29–36) which are again subdivided into smaller. The opening scene presents, first, the question of the priests; then, the question of the Pharisees: the second contains, in the first half, John's direct and express witness to "the Lamb of God," whose precursor he declares himself to be; in the second he claims to have seen the Spirit descending upon him who baptizes in the Spirit. "The Lamb" must have been consciously borrowed from the Apocalypse; in the final phase of the Gospel we shall find the mystical relation of the Christ to the paschal lamb clearly indicated. The utmost care is taken to avoid the statement that Jesus was baptized by John, and the general outlines of the scene, in spite of apparent precision in a few details, are wavering and uncertain. The indication of the locality where John was then operating as "Bethany beyond Jordan" has the look of affectation on the part of the narrator. He seems to have known all the places he mentions, but it would be imprudent to conclude that there is any historical warrant for localizing the Baptist at Bethany. Many a marvel which never took place is localized by our narrator quite as minutely as is the incident before us.

Editorial artifice is not less apparent in representing the first disciples of Jesus as sent to him by John; but the transition to the stories (35–37) is unnatural and the indication of the return to Galilee (43) is out of place. The disciples are called up on four occasions (35–39, 40–42, 43, 44–51), all four first conceived as preliminary to the coming manifestation of the Christ in Galilee. The anonymous disciple of the first vocation, discreetly associated with Andrew, and won to the faith before Peter, is probably he who later on will be marked out as "the disciple whom Jesus loved" (xiii, 23). Peter, when his turn comes, is nevertheless allowed a certain prominence, this being the occasion on which Simon receives his surname, but without any indication of its mystic meaning. The Philip, here honoured by a call confined to himself alone (43), is probably the Philip of whom Asiatic Christianity retained some memory. Nathanael, who receives a fuller notice than any of the others, is a person unknown to the synoptic tradition.

Were these stories taken as historical, or even as pretending to be so, they would leave the reader with a hopelessly confused impression. Andrew and his unnamed companion are represented as believing, on the assurance of John the Baptist, that Jesus is "the Lamb of God"; but Andrew's statement to his brother Simon is: "We have found the Messiah" (41) and Philip, speaking in the same sense, says to Nathanael (45): "we have found him of whom Moses in the Law, and the prophets, did write; he is Jesus, son of Joseph, of Nazareth." And Jesus himself, when his gift of second sight has caused Nathanael to recognize him as "Son of God, the King of Israel," declares that he is "Son of Man" (51): "Verily, verily I say unto you, ye shall see the heavens open and the angels of God ascending and descending on the Son of Man" —an assertion not clearly made good in the sequel to the stories. Certainly the writer does not wish it to be understood that Jesus was the real son of Joseph, nor that Nazareth was his real birthplace. He merely accepts the synoptic interpretation of the word "Nazorean." The true definition of the Christ lies in his qualification as Son of God in the transcendent sense established by the prologue; all the rest is intended to convey that the Christ and the Son of Man of the Synoptics are identified with this Son of God.

The sons of Zebedee seem to have been forgotten in our Gospel's account of the calling of the disciples, whence it follows that the anonymous disciple, probably the well-beloved, is not, so far as that goes, identified with the apostle John. On the whole our compiler has not troubled himself to be complete in his account of the vocations, for he seems to suppose, from now on, that Jesus has around him the group of Twelve.

The Miracle at Cana: the First "Sign"

All we have read up to this point is preparation for the epiphany of the Christ, which begins in the miracle at Cana. To the commentators who know exactly where Cana is to be found on the map we would say: enough if we localize it as the place where Jesus first "revealed his glory," so that, from that moment, "his disciples believed in him." The epiphany apparently takes place in a domestic circle; there is a marriage at Cana: the mother of Jesus is there; Jesus arrives with his disciples; they are invited to the feast; but there is no more wine. Jesus orders six urns, placed there for Jewish purification, to be filled with water; the water is changed into wine; and this is the first "sign" given by Jesus. Observe that the miracle is a "sign"; for it is precisely in this that it differs from the same prodigy when performed in the sanctuaries of Dionysus, from which our author has borrowed it. What does the sign signify? The general meaning is that the economy of the Law with its rules of outward purification must now give way to the life-giving economy of faith in the immortal Christ, as symbolized in the Christian sacrament.

Let us pause to consider the feature of this "sign" which, from the earliest time till now, has most disconcerted the commentators. When Jesus and his disciples have taken their places among the guests the wine has given out; the supply for the marriage is exhausted. Jesus' mother then says to him, "there is no more wine." Jesus replies, "Woman, what is there (in common) between me and thee? My hour is not yet come." His mother says to the servants, "do whatever he tells you." Whereupon Jesus orders the urns to be filled and the miracle is effected. What can we make of this? Taken one by one as they stand the statements are incoherent and make up an unintelligible phantasmagory. But not so when we consider the profound meaning of the whole presentation. The mother of Jesus is not mentioned by her proper name; but the person designated is Mary who is, apparently, Jesus' mother, just as Joseph has been previously named as, apparently, his father (i, 45). But this mother stands also for the Judaism which waited for the Kingdom of God, and it is in that character that she is made to declare "there is no more wine." Jesus begins by answering that between him and his putative mother there is nothing in common, because there is nothing earthly in his origin; his hour, which has not yet come, is the hour of his death, on which salvation depends. None the less, he does, there and then, what he has been implicitly asked to do, giving the lesson in the form of a symbol.

Second Sign: Expulsion of the Traders from the Temple

The second "sign" worked by Jesus is the expulsion of the traders from the Temple (ii, 13–17). But before coming to it we are told (12) that Jesus went down to Capernaum, he, his mother, his brothers and disciples. This is the first mention of his brothers, which we might have expected at an earlier stage; but we are beginning to understand that our evangelist is engaged upon something very different from biography. At Capernaum their stay has but a few days' duration because "the Passover of the Jews is at hand" and Jesus will seize the opportunity to manifest himself in Jerusalem. The idea is that the Christ will not preach in Galilee till after he has preached in Jerusalem and in Judea. He is taken to Capernaum only for the purpose of doing a measure of justice to the synoptic tradition (especially Matthew iv, 13), and at the same time arranging a transition to the narrative that follows. From now onwards it is apparent that our gospel editor takes the line of restricting the ministry in Galilee that he may enlarge a ministry in Jerusalem and Judea, which is almost entirely ignored by the synoptic catechesis.

As the author has previously used the expression "the purifications *of the Jews*," so now he speaks of "the Passover *of the Jews*." The reason is that his readers are Gentile Christians unacquainted with Jewish customs, and that he himself looks upon Judaism from the outside as one who himself is not a Jew. Moreover the object of Jesus in coming to Jerusalem at the time of the Feast is, not so much to take part in it, as there and then to "manifest his glory." As the synoptic tradition sees in the expulsion of the traders the first act of the messianic ministry in Jerusalem, so our evangelist attaches it to Jesus' first stay in the holy city. But he interprets it after his own manner, not merely as an act of authority, but as a "sign."

Without pausing over details in the description of the occurrence, let us fix attention on the passage most characteristic both of the spirit of our Gospel and of its chronology (ii, 18–22, already quoted and discussed, p. 60).

The question here ascribed to "the Jews" after the expulsion of the traders is the question which, in the Synoptics, is put to Jesus by the elders of the Sanhedrim (Mark xi, 27–28; Matthew xxi, 23–24; Luke xx, 1–2) combined with the demand for a sign in the same Gospels (Matthew xii, 38; cf. Mark viii, 11; Luke xi, 16). In the Christ's reply as here given a sign is actually offered, but one that would have been wholly unintelligble to his audience, as indeed it has remained for many commentators. This reply is, in effect, an enigmatic combination of Jesus' answer to the demand for a sign in Matthew (xii, 39–40) with the saying of the Christ about the temple, brought up against him in the synoptic account of the trial before Caiaphas (Matthew xxvi, 61; Mark xiv, 58). But here there is a difference in the phrasing. Instead of "I will destroy this temple," he now says "destroy it," as though challenging the Jews to destroy it themselves. For the temple of which he now speaks is his own body. His answer is thus equivalent to the refusal of a sign for the present and, for the future, to the sign of Jonah in the sense given to it by Matthew (*loc. cit.*). To discuss the verisimilitude of the reply would clearly be quite superfluous, and equally so to discuss, from that point of view, what the Jews answer about the forty-six years occupied by the construction of the temple. In the final analysis, what the writer would here convey is his conception of the age of the Christ, forty-six years when he expelled the traders, forty-nine (completed) when he died, so that his jubilee year would be that of his entry on the immortal glory awaiting him on his resurrection (cf. *supra*, p. 61). The disciples themselves are described as unable to find the key to this symbolic riddle till after the resurrection of the Christ (22). We are, then, in presence of a second "sign" parallel to the "sign" of Cana. Like the first, it figures the renewal of the Covenant, substituting Grace for Law, and brought about by the death and resurrection of the incarnate Son of God. Let who will believe that what is here narrated really happened.

The remark on the numerous conversions which Jesus made on this occasion in Jerusalem and on the little value he attached to them, because he knew what was in man (23–25), must be understood as referring to inadequate faith or, rather, to a lower and Judaizing type of faith. This was probably aimed originally at vulgar Messianism and the notion of the Kingdom of God as purely terrestrial and eschatological. So understood the remark links on to the case of Nicodemus and brings on the discourse supposed to have been addressed to him.

Nicodemus

The case of Nicodemus (iii, 1–12) is imagined in order to provide an apparently historical frame for the teaching about spiritual regeneration which the Son, sent from God to save the world and not to judge it, procures for the believer by baptism (5–6, 8, 11–13, 16–18). We find accordingly that this teaching contains an implied criticism of the common eschatology, even that of the Johannine apocalypse. The opening part has been broken by interruptions in accordance with the narrative framework, which almost have the effect of transforming this didactic poem into a dialogue between Jesus and Nicodemus (7, 9–10, 14–15). We shall encounter other applications of the same technique, by means of which interlocutors with Jesus are made to commit blunders, or speak beside the point, in order to bring out the sequent instruction. Nicodemus is a development of the questioner in the Synoptics who asks Jesus what he must do to "inherit eternal life." In the Synoptics Jesus answers the question by laying down the moral conditions for admission to the Kingdom of God; here, the Kingdom is an inward possession of the believer, realized in the Church, to which the believer is initiated by a symbolic act effecting the spiritual regeneration of the individual performing it, and in keeping with the faith in him which the Son, come from God, claims for himself. This lesson on regeneration by water and the Spirit is the first explanation of the spiritual Gospel and comes in most aptly.

We find the lesson completed by a second witness borne by John the Baptist (iii, 26–36); it is the work of an editor, constructed by transposing elements taken from the Synoptics (Matthew xi, 2–19; Luke vii, 18–35). The setting of the scene (22–26),

in spite of its geographical precisions, is wholly fanciful. But let
the fact be noted that the writer finds it quite in order to represent both Jesus and John as baptizing simultaneously and at no
great distance the one from the other. (An unconvincing attempt
to put this right is made later on (iv, 2) where we are told that
Jesus did not baptize, but only his disciples.) An altercation
arising about the matter between John's disciples and *a Jew* (a
correction which makes nonsense; the original text was *Jesus*),
the disciples come to John to inform him of the proceedings of a
rival Baptizer, which they seem to regard as disloyal to him:
whereupon John explains himself, recalling his former witness and
proclaiming the transcendent superiority of Jesus (note in 28 the
figure of the bridegroom and the best man at the wedding, echo
of Mark ii, 19–20; Matthew ix, 15; Luke v, 34–35). John's discourse has the same look of planned construction, and of superposition, as the story introducing it.

The Woman of Samaria

From now onwards reference to John is incidental only
(v, 33, 36; x, 40–41). Nevertheless the theme of water and the
Spirit is not abandoned, but is taken up again in the story of the
Samaritan woman, where it will be completed by the theme of
the harvest (iv, 5–42). An artificial junction links this episode to
the Baptist's testimony (1–4); but the narrative, taken as a whole,
is not all of one piece. It looks as if an original story in which
Jesus and the woman were the only speakers had been subsequently enlarged by the passages which refer to the disciples
(iv, 8, 27, 31, 33, 37–38); there are signs also that, in order to
harmonize with the present context, the primitive itinerary
which made Jesus pass through Samaria on his way from Galilee
to Judea, has been turned round and the whole episode antedated.
The setting of the scene is constructed with the same technique
which set the scene for Nicodemus, and the conversation proceeds
by fits and starts, as these are prompted by the irrelevant replies
of the woman to Jesus' remarks. The main purpose is to develop
the mystic theme of living water, the gift of the Spirit, which is
also the gift of immortality, and, at the same time, to bring out the
insignificance of the common eschatology in presence of this
mysterious truth: "God is Spirit and it is in Spirit and truth that

worshippers must adore him" (24). What is said about the harvest (35–38) is an allegorical paraphrase of a synoptic saying (Matthew ix, 37–38; Luke x, 2) combined with the Sower of the parable; those who "have laboured" are Jesus and the apostolic generation; the reapers are the evangelist's contemporaries. Needless to say, the conversion of the Samaritans and of the Samaritan woman is no fact of history but a symbol of the Gentiles converted to the Christian mystery.

A New Series of "Signs"

After the first miracle at Cana Jesus returns to Jerusalem and appears there as master of the Temple; after the second (revival of the royal officer's son) he returns to the holy city to show himself master of the Sabbath. The first cycle of miracles and discourses concerns the superiority of Christianity, religion of Spirit, over Judaism, religion of ineffectual symbols; the second cycle, which includes the cure of the royal officer's son, the cure of the paralytic at Bethesda and the multiplication of the loaves, together with discourses interpreting the last two (v, 19–46; vi, 22–71), will reveal Jesus as the active principle and sustaining food of the true life. But first it is necessary to bring Jesus from Samaria into Galilee.

This change of place is an editorial device, the departure being explained by the saying: "prophet has no honour in his own country," which comes from the Synoptics (Mark vi, 4; Matthew xiii, 57; Luke iv, 24). But here it receives a particular application which many commentators are slow to observe. Jesus has just been recognized as "Saviour of the World" (42) by the Samaritans; but it is not in the order of Providence that the glory of the Son of God, though revealed in the course of his earthly existence, should be recognized before his death by all men on Israelite territory, the exception of Samaria not destroying the rule.

The new series of "signs" begins at Cana, where Jesus, operating at a distance, cures the royal officer's son (46–54), a transposition to Cana of the synoptic cure of the centurion's son (Matthew viii, 5–13) or servant (Luke vii, 1–10) at Capernaum. Instead of directly prefiguring the conversion of the Gentiles, as in Matthew and Luke, the story here becomes a lesson in the true kind of faith, that which believes on the strength of the uttered word, the characteristic faith of mystical Christianity which ought to characterize the Gentile church, in contrast to the kind which demands miracles.

After curing the officer's son, Jesus leaves Cana and comes to Jerusalem where he cures a paralytic on the Sabbath day (v, 1–18). By this miracle an opening is made for a description of the life-giving work which the Father has sent his Son into the world to accomplish (19–30). While invoking the witness borne to him by the Father, Jesus reproaches the Jews for not hearkening to what John has said of him and for paying no heed to what Moses has written (31–47). All of it is legendary fiction, and cannot indeed be anything else. The evangelist has two reasons for allotting so large a place to the Judean mission; on the one hand, he is working a polemical theme against the Jews objecting that Jerusalem is the true place of the prophets and of the Messiah's epiphany; on the other, he partly dispossesses Capernaum in favour of Cana in order that Jesus may not appear to have preached only in one little corner of Galilee.

The text does not give the name of the feast for which Jesus "went up to Jerusalem," but calls it "the feast of the Jews," their feast *par excellence*, which can only have been the Passover. Irenaeus says that this Passover is the second of three he has counted in the public life of the Christ (*Heresies*, ii, 22, 4), and would hardly have been more positive if he had actually read the word "Passover" in the passage before us; perhaps that is what he did read. The chronological scheme of our Gospel involves a total duration for Jesus' ministry, or epiphany, of three and a half years, the messianic number (cf. *supra*, p. 60). This is why three Passovers are indicated before that which coincides with his death: the first follows the first miracle at Cana (ii, 13); we are now at the second; the third will be mentioned in connection with the multiplication of the loaves (vi, 4). The history of the text shows that, in order to bring John into line with the Synoptics on this point, attempts were made to suppress both the second Passover and the third. It is, however, true that the Johannine chronology is imaginary and symbolic; but so is everything that it encloses. The paralytic miraculously cured at the Pool of Bethesda is the paralytic of Capernaum symbolically interpreted (cf. Mark ii, 9, 11; Matthew ix, 5, 6; Luke v, 22–24) and combined with the synoptic Sabbath story (Mark iii, 1–5; Matthew xii, 9–13; Luke vi, 6–11).

Discourses following the "Signs"

The attitude of the Jews in presence of this violation of the Sabbath corresponds to the conclusion of the Sabbath stories in the first three Gospels (Mark iii, 6; Matthew xii, 14) but with an addition, entirely Johannine in conception (v, 16–18), linked on to the declaration of Jesus about the everlasting joint action of his Father and himself: "for this cause the Jews sought the more to kill him, because he not only brake the Sabbath, but also said that his father was God, making himself equal with God." This brings on the first instruction concerning the working of God, with the Son working in conjunction. To this discourse a few additions have been made for the purpose of somehow adjusting a mystical theory of salvation to the popular conception of the Last Things, which the theory contradicts by suppressing it (v, 22; 28–30, referring to a material resurrection, opening of tombs, etc., are in contradiction with the texts which represent the resurrection as purely spiritual).

The second discourse (31–47), in which the witness of John and of the Scriptures is evoked against the Jews, seems to be entirely of secondary authorship. But it is possible that the passage: "I am come in the name of my Father and you receive me not; if another comes in his own name, him you will receive" is aimed at the false Messiah Barkochba. In the sayings attached to the Feast of Tabernacles (vii) there are some which relate to the cure (v) of the paralytic (vii, 20–24, or rather 15–24, since 25 is exactly in sequence to 14). A transposition has obviously taken place in the text. The fact is that while the fourth Gospel, at one stage of its compilation, was constructed on an orderly plan, there has been considerable dislocation of the plan in subsequent redaction.

The sixth chapter is dominated throughout by the idea of the Christ as bread of life; the multiplication of loaves (1–14) is the symbol of it; the miracle of Jesus walking on the sea (16–21) is an aid to its comprehension; the four discourses that follow (22–40, 41–51, 52–59, 66–71) explain it more fully. The different impressions produced on the Jews by each of these discourses represents the Jewish attitude towards the mystery of salvation, in contrast to the Christian. The general effect is to bring the mystery to summary form in the doctrine of the living and life-giving bread and in the corresponding sacrament.

The Bread of Life

The setting for the multiplication of the loaves is copied from the Synoptics (Matthew xiv, 15; cf. Mark vi, 33) but combined with the scene of the Discourse on the Mountain in Matthew, the miracle itself being constructed so as to symbolize the new faith and the mystery of salvation. The reason for saying "the Passover of the Jews was at hand" is that the multiplication of the loaves, already a figure of the eucharist in the synoptic account, is going to be presented in the same way in the coming discourse on the bread of life, and that a reminder of the Passover is a fitting introduction to the eucharistic symbolism about to be presented. Fundamentally, this is the place at which our Gospel places the institution of the Supper, the eucharist being considered throughout by the evangelist as a mystery which ought not to be offered to his readers in the direct terms used in First Corinthians (xi) and in the Synoptics.

The story of the miracle is also borrowed from the Synoptics but with a few added touches to adapt it to the Johannine conceptions; notable is the personal intervention of Philip and Andrew, whom we know already in the vocation stories (i, 40, 43), and in a conclusion all its own. The crowd, impressed by the miracle, conclude that Jesus is the Messiah and are about to carry him off and make him King: but Jesus gives their enthusiasm no countenance and withdraws out of their reach. In this both Jewish Messianism and the common eschatology of the Christians are implicitly condemned.

In the miracle of the Christ walking on the water we find the same free and symbolic adaptation of what the Synopsis has to tell (Matthew xiv, 22–27, 32–33; Mark vi, 45–52). The lesson is that the immortal Christ will never abandon his own, all appearances to the contrary notwithstanding.

By an obviously forced transition the crowd, which had been the witness and beneficiary of the multiplied loaves, is brought back to Jesus, on the following day, to hear his discourse on the bread of life (vi, 22–58). In its original form the discourse is a didactic poem, like the discourse to Nicodemus, and quite as easy to reconstruct if we eliminate the interplay of dialogue, which breaks the poem at several points (28–31, 34, 41–42, 51a–52), and omit a special instruction on predestination which someone has tried to incorporate into the main discourse, an interpolation made in order to affirm the resurrection of the dead (end of verses 39, 40, 44). Moreover it is clear enough that the last strophe of the poem (to be extracted from 53–58, dropping "I will raise him up at the last day" in 54 and 58b) has been added to introduce the sacramental system taken by the synoptic tradition from First Corinthians (xi, 24–25), the symbolism, namely, of the bread-body and the wine-blood of the Christ.

Like the end of the discussion, the end of the story which frames it (59–71) is also editorial work. The intentions behind it are various; to soften down the hardest sayings of the discourse, in the last strophe, by an explanation which emphasizes their spiritual character (61, 63);[1] to create the opportunity for Peter's confession, imitated from the Synoptics but with a Johannine interpolation (Matthew xvi, 16; Mark viii, 29; Luke ix, 20), and to make room for the first denunciation of the traitor Judas (64–65, 70). The whole is intended to bring out the blindness of the Jews and of certain Judaizing Christians in presence of the mystery just explained. Even Judas is not, as some would have us think, an individual traitor on whom the apostle John vents his spite. He personifies the Jews' hatred of Jesus and of Christianity.

SECOND PHASE

The scene for the second phase of the Christ's combat with the Jewish enemy is laid exclusively in Jerusalem and covers the last year of Jesus' ministry. The events and discourses of chapter vi having been dated with reference to the Passover at the beginning of this final year, those which fill the five chapters to follow, and end at the great Passover coincident with the Passion, fall into two groups attached for their placing to two intermediate festivals, that of Tabernacles and that of the Dedication. De-

---

[1] Verse 62, asserting the bodily ascension of the "Son of Man" is a gloss.

pendent on the first are some polemic discourses and the cure of the man born blind, with the discourse that follows it (x, 1–21), the whole dominated by the idea of the Christ as light of the world. The second group marks the definite breach between the Christ and the Jews (x, 22–42). Before the last Easter will come the raising of Lazarus, symbol of the Christ-life and greatest "sign" of all.

The preamble (vii, 1–13) introducing this second series of doings and teachings is deeply confused. Jesus abstains from going about in Judea because the Jews are resolved to kill him and confines himself to Galilee; the Feast of Tabernacles coming round, his brothers, who however do not believe in him, urge him to go to Jerusalem and reveal himself there as what he pretends to be; Jesus refuses, alleging that his hour is not yet come; his brothers then depart for the Feast; he follows them *incognito*; goes up to the temple in the midst of the solemnities and begins to teach. The opening of the preamble is based on the cure of the paralytic at the Pool of Bethesda (cf. v, 16–18), but the dialogue with the brothers, parallel to the remarks exchanged between Jesus and his mother at Cana, suggests that Jesus is about to show himself at Jerusalem for the first time. His brothers, moreover, personify incredulous Judaism. Instead of vainly speculating on the meaning of it all, we are content to remark once more that our Gospel must have been worked over more than once before assuming its final form. Let it be remembered also that the first words of the preaching attributed to Jesus in vii, 15–24 need to be placed at the end of the story of the paralytic in v.

The preamble analysed in the last paragraph introduces the discussion, which is placed further on (vii, 25–36), concerning the origin of Jesus, where an answer is given to an objection from the Jews. Their objection is that everybody knows where Jesus comes from, whereas, when Messiah shall appear, nobody will know his place of origin. Jesus answers that the Jews are under a great illusion in thinking they know that he comes from Nazareth and is the son of Joseph; he alone knows whence he came and who sent him. (A certain kind of critical benevolence must be applied to the matter if we are to overlook the plain contradiction of the birth stories in Matthew and Luke conveyed by these statements.) Duplicates are not wanting in these chapters (vii and viii): for example, the discussion on the presumed origin of the Christ, the Jews maintaining that he was not to come from Galilee but from Bethlehem in Judea and would belong to the race of David (vii, 40–52), which takes us over the same ground as vii, 26–38 and implicitly repeats the contradiction of the birth stories in the Synoptics; and, again, the repetition of the attempts to take Jesus prisoner, and each time with no success (vii, 30, 44; viii, 20, 59). Found anywhere else than in a book we are accustomed to venerate, and is truly worthy of veneration in many parts of it, these wranglings about the origin of the Christ would impress us as a rather tiresome academic exercise. They are the echoes of ancient controversies between Christians and Jews.

An editorial hand has inserted into the text a passage (vii, 37–39) which it is important to note, not only on account of its correspondence with another insertion into the story of the Passion (xix, 31–37), but also because it is seldom rightly understood. The passage should read as follows:

> Now on the last, the great day of the feast, Jesus stood forth, and cried, saying:
>
>> If any man is athirst, let him come to me,
>>   and let him drink, him who believes in me,
>> According as Scripture has spoken,
>>   *Rivers of living water shall flow out of his belly.*

In applying this quotation (Zechariah xiii, 1; xiv, 8) to the believer, the writer introduces a gross and incongruous image. And the more incongruous inasmuch as Jesus alone, and not the believer, can be thought of as the source of the water of life. The writer is referring to the water that burst from the side of Jesus at the stroke of the soldier's lance, and accordingly takes pains to tell us (39) that the living water is the Spirit, to be given to believers when Jesus has entered into his glory.[1]

Another interpolation which has no connection whatever with the evolution of the written Gospel is the section known as the story of the woman taken in adultery. It belongs to the late history of the Greek text and falls outside the scope of our present

---

[1] For the full discussion of this passage, which has many important bearings, see *Le Quatrième Evangile*, 270–273.

THE ORIGINS OF THE NEW TESTAMENT

inquiry. Deliberately banished from the synoptic tradition, of which the story is a lost fragment, it has got itself, by the strangest of accidents, here tacked on to the Johannine Gospel (vii, 53–viii, 11).[1]

Immediately following this intrusion, Jesus' controversy with the Pharisees resumes its broken course. He now answers the last objections raised in vii, 41, 52, although, if strict regard be paid to the everchanging *mise en scène*, it would seem that he cannot have heard them. After declaring himself "the light of the world," he defies his adversaries, telling them that he alone knows whence he comes and whither he goes, while they know nothing of either. By this he means that he comes from God and returns to God. Declarations of this kind afford a sure starting point for determining the conditions of his epiphany as the Christ, both as to its opening and its close; it will be seen that they exclude both an earthly existence before epiphany and a corporeal resurrection after death. Needless to say his auditors understood not a word of it (viii, 12–29).

Close attention should be paid to the following (viii, 28–29):

> When ye have lifted up the Son of Man,
> then shall ye know what I am,
> And that of myself I do nothing,
> but even as the Father has taught me,
> so speak I;
> And he who sent me is with me;
> He forsakes me not,
> because what is pleasing to him, that do I.

This seems to be an intentional contradiction of the saying —a quotation from Psalm xxii, 1—which Mark (xv, 34) makes into the dying outcry of Jesus, and which might easily be misunderstood (cf. *supra*, p. 168). Whence we may infer that the passage is a late development in the text.

In the final phase of this dispute (viii, 20–59) a discourse on Jesus' Father, who is God, and the Jews' father, who is the Devil (viii, 26, 38, 42–47, 54–55), seems to have been broken up by the compiler and the interstices filled with an unrelated argument about Abraham (30–37, 39–41, 48–53, 56–58). In connection with Abraham comes the indication about the age of Jesus (57):

[1] See *op. cit.*, 278–286.

"Thou art not yet fifty years old, and thou hast seen Abraham!" (An ancient variant reads: "Abraham has seen thee.") The fact is not without significance that this indication of Jesus' age is found in an editor's addition and not in a fundamental document.

The Light of the World

On leaving the temple, where the Jews had tried to stone him, Jesus reveals himself as "light of the world" by curing a man born blind, a "sign" which brings out the spiritual blindness of the Jews (ix). The interrogation of the man's parents is possibly interpolated into the original story of the miracle (ix, 18–23). A man *born* blind makes a suitable figure of humanity ignorant of the blessings of revelation, but the Johannine story aims primarily at intensifying the cure of blind men localized by the Synoptics in Galilee and at Jericho; moreover this evangelist times the miracle on a Sabbath day. The Pharisees, spiritually blind, as usual represent Judaism in its unbelief of the Christian gospel. But the last lines "for judgment I came into this world," etc., are the compiler's addition. There has been nothing to raise the question of "judgment" in the proper sense of the word; but in any case the Christ, as we have already been told, did *not* come "to judge the world, but to save it" (iii, 17–18).

The Good Shepherd

The poem of the Good Shepherd (x, 1–18) must at first have existed independently and without connection with the story of the blind man. Verse 6, to the effect that the audience did not understand what Jesus was saying, is a compiler's invention together with verse 7, which takes up the broken thread of the poem: other additions are the lines about the Christ as the Door (9: the original must have been: "I am the *shepherd* of the sheep"); and the verses on the sheep outside the fold who must be brought into the flock (16). The question has often been raised as to the identity of the false shepherds who came "before" Jesus and are here stigmatized as "thieves and brigands" (8). Is the reference to Moses and the Prophets? If so, would it here be said "that the sheep heeded them not at all"? Nothing is gained by the omission, found in certain texts, of the words "before me"; that only leaves the assertion vaguer than before and does nothing to

211

answer the question. The Jewish teachers, then; or the false Messiahs? More probably the reference is to the spiritual powers which have hitherto taken part in governing human affairs but have not succeeded in seducing the children of God. And is there no connection with the mystical shepherd—allegory in Zechariah xi, 4–17; xiii, 7–9? The question remains. A piece of narrative is added (19–21) to complete the framework intended to link these events and discourses with the Feast of Tabernacles.

Three months afterwards comes the Feast of Dedication, and Jesus is in the midst of the solemnities. After defining once more his rôle of saviour of all predestined to salvation he is again threatened with stoning (22–31). He explains why he has the right to call himself the Son of God, and then evades further persecution by retiring beyond Jordan (40–42). What we are told as occurring at the Feast of Dedication forms the conclusion of the controversies that have gone before: the preamble (22–24) is certainly the compiler's work, and Jesus' words about the sheep who give heed to his voice and will never perish seem to have been originally the last strophe of the allegorical poem of the Good Shepherd (x, 25; starting from "the works that I do" but without "I and the Father are one," (30) added to make transition to the attempt at stoning).

The argument by which Jesus is made to justify his claim to divinity is the compiler's argument. Its defence of the saying "I and the Father are one" is remarkable rather for subtilty than for exactitude (31–39). It ends in another attempt of the Jews upon Jesus' person and by another escape from their clutches (39).

The account of Jesus' retreat into Perea (40–42) may be part of the frame within which the story of the resurrection of Lazarus was originally enclosed, but it has been glossed by the lines which refer to John and to the numerous conversions effected by Jesus. These believers beyond the river are another figure, after their kind, of the diffusion of the Gospel beyond the borders of Israel. When the writer of this passage makes the Jews say "John gave no sign," it is because he found no miracle of John's described in the Synoptics. But he has overlooked the passage where we are told that the tetrarch Antipas, on hearing about the miracles of Jesus, immediately made the comment: "Here is John risen from the dead," which leaves no doubt that miracles analogous to those of Jesus were attributed to John. It would indeed be surprising if it were not so.

The Raising of Lazarus

And now, at last, the greatest of all the miracles recorded in the Gospels, the resurrection of Lazarus, supreme revelation of the Christ who is life (xi, 1–14), encounters the full intensity of Jewish unbelief and brings on the final catastrophe. The high priests and the Pharisees—such, according to our Gospel, is the composition of the Sanhedrim—resolve to put Jesus to death as the only way to prevent the conversion of the people; and Jesus, whose hour is not yet come, goes into hiding, awaiting the time of the Passover, the hour decreed by Providence as the termination of his existence on earth (xi, 1–57).

It need hardly be said that this distinctively Johannine "sign" is charged with the maximum of symbolic meaning, attained by concentrating and intensifying the resurrection of Jairus' daughter and of the young man at Nain (Mark v, 35–42; Luke vii, 11–17). Our Lazarus has a resemblance to Simon the Leper (Mark xiv, 3); but we have already seen (*supra*, p.162) that the Lazarus of Luke's parable (xvi, 19–31) is rather dependent upon him. The two sisters in Luke (Martha and Mary, x, 38–42) are turned by the compiler into sisters of Lazarus; Mary, as a further improvement, is substituted for the sinful woman of Luke (vii, 37–38) and for the woman of the anointing in Mark and Matthew. But these combinations, which have sorely taxed the ingenuity of commentators, were not all effected at a single stroke. At the very outset (xi, 1–2) the text is visibly glossed by the notice about the sisters, whose rôle in the story is largely superadded to the original.

The original version seems to have contained the message of "the sister" announcing the sickness of Lazarus (xi, 3); Jesus' comment on the sickness (4); the announcement that he would go to Judea, with the disciples' objection and the Christ's reply (7–10); the dialogue between Jesus and "the dead man's sister" (21–27), Jesus having arrived not four days after the interment, but at the moment when the funeral was just over; Jesus weeping with the other mourners (33, omitting his indignant groan); the visit to the tomb and the order to remove the stone (34–39, again omitting the repeated indignation and Martha's remark about the condition of the corpse); the removal of the stone; Jesus' prayer and the resurrection of the dead man (41–44). The later additions aggrandize the miracle, but give it the mechanical turn characteristic of supernatural magic.

The essence of the matter lies, not in the miracle as such, but in the truth it offers to belief, truth which the miracle is intended to drive home and make good. Nothing else really counts. The work of raising a dead body to life is but the guarantee of a work with importance of another and higher kind, the universal and final work of raising humanity to life in the Spirit. The resurrection of Lazarus, as it was originally conceived, was not intended either to announce or prefigure the bodily revival of all the dead, but as symbolic testimony to the *spiritual* resurrection, the eternal life of all who believe. Observe that not a word is said as to what became of Lazarus after he was loosed from his grave clothes and "let go" (44). The reason is, that in this miracle, as indeed in many another already encountered, the reader is invited to carry his vision beyond earthly contingencies and find in higher truth the conclusion of which the story itself seems to stop short. And what is the conclusion here? It is that whosoever believes in Jesus is in present possession of eternal life; he has escaped from a house of death to which he will never return; he is "let go" for unceasing advance, in light and life, to God, heaven and everlasting glory; and humanity, regenerated in like manner by the ever-living Christ, and so made the true Jerusalem of earth, begins to mingle with that eternal Jerusalem into which it will be wholly merged at the end.

Sequel to the Great Miracle

What we read of the effect of the miracle and the information laid before the Pharisees (46) may come from the source (omitting "which came to Mary" in 45), together with the notice of the Pharisees laying plans to put Jesus to death (53). But the deliberations of the Sanhedrim and the unwitting prophecy of Caiaphas (47–52) are editorial supplements. So, too, are the words "high priest for that year" which suppose that the Jewish high-priesthood was an annual office, like that of the Asiatic bishops, and involves an error about the conditions under which Caiaphas held the pontificate (cf. *supra*, p. 151). The retreat of the Christ to the town called Ephraim (?) and the conversations of the Jews waiting for his arrival at the Passover duplicate his previous retreat into Perea after curing the man born blind (x, 40–41), and the remarks of the Jews who waited for him at the Feast of Tabernacles. It would seem that the source-account placed a very short interval between the resurrection of Lazarus and the Passover, and that it kept Jesus at Bethany, because the Passover was approaching and his hour at hand.

The anointing in the house at Bethany is a symbolic prelude to the death of the Christ (xii, 1–8); the triumphal entry into Jerusalem (9–19) prefigures the glorious issue of his departure from the visible world; his last discourses forecast its results—the conversion of the Gentiles (20–36) and the reprobation of the Jews (37–50). The accounts of the anointing and of the triumph are fragments of the synoptic tradition, here transposed and turned in the Johannine sense by the same hand which added its supplements to the raising of Lazarus. Mark (xiv, 1; cf. Matthew xxvi, 2) places the anointing two days before the Passover; this writer says "six days before," doubtless for some symbolic reason; the sixth evening before the Passover would be that of the Sabbath before the Passion in correspondence with the Sabbath of interment, the triumphal entry next day (9 Nizan) thus anticipating the triumphal resurrection of the following Sunday. The accusation of theft lodged against Judas (4–6) replaces the betrayal for money in the Synoptics; when the hour comes for Jesus to suffer himself to be arrested, there is no bargain between the Jewish priests and the traitor, as in the Synoptics, but Satan informs them by the mouth of Judas where they can find and capture him. The qualification of Judas as a robber indicates the length to which the writer is willing to go in utilizing the synoptic tradition about him; but his putting Judas in charge of the alms-bag, in analogy with a practice of the early Christian communities, must surely be an anachronism. Notwithstanding the efforts made to bring the messianic triumph somehow into sequence with the raising of Lazarus, it is doubtful whether this piece of the synoptic catechesis (the triumph) belonged to the original economy of our Gospel.

Of secondary authorship also is the discourse in the temple

which Jesus is made to deliver about the Greeks, or Gentiles, who ask to see him (20–36). Noteworthy features are the artificiality of the preamble, in which Philip and Andrew again appear, and the curious transposition into the middle of the discourse (27–30) of a sublime equivalent for the synoptic scene in Gethsemane. In this equivalent the Christ's prayer is transformed from the synoptic version, in which he prays to be saved from the fate awaiting him, into a distinct refusal so to pray; instead of so praying he calls upon God to glorify his name. This better befits the Johannine conception of the Christ. After that, in place of the consoling angel in Luke (xxii, 43), comes a voice from heaven echoing the voices of the baptism and the transfiguration in the Synoptics. This miraculous interlude is not for the encouragement of the Christ, who is above all such needs, nor for the crowd who are pictured as not understanding it, but for the education of the Christian reader. The last discourse to the Jews is symbolic throughout. It is followed by a last disappearance of Jesus into hiding (36). In manner like to his disappearance, the light of the Gospel, offered to the Jews, will pass away from them into Gentile possession. Such is the design of Providence, and the Jews are powerless to hinder it.

A yet later and, if possible, a more unreal addition is the afterthought conclusion of the Jerusalem ministry (37–50), in which the compiler makes Jesus deliver a new discourse (44–50), after the Christ has been finally withdrawn from his incredulous audience. This discourse (to which 24–25, 31–32, 35–36 in the previous discourse seem originally to have belonged) may have been found ready-made and here utilized by the same editor who applies the text from Isaiah (vi, 9–10) to the reprobation of the Jews at the moment when the Christ's ministry among them comes to an end (39–41). The same use of this text is made by the Synoptics in connection with parables (Mark iv, 12; Matthew xiii, 14–15; Luke viii, 10) and the compiler of Acts gives it the same application at the end of his book (xxviii, 26–27. For the quotation in xii, 38 of Isaiah liii, 1, cf. Romans x, 16).

So ends the Johannine account of Jesus' ministry. Everything in it is governed by symbolism which all the circumstances are constructed to suit without regard to the consistency of the narrative. The discourses, moreover, are surcharged with repetitions revealing the anti-Jewish bias which so often inspires the editorial elaboration of the source. The original miracle stories all betoken the spiritual work of Jesus which the original discourses proceed to explain. The editors, elaborating the original, have striven to show that the Jews understood nothing of the mystery of salvation and the spirituality of the Gospel: accordingly they kill a Messiah whose greatness is beyond them, and whom the death they inflict upon him renders back to the eternal glory whence he came, and so makes him the saviour of the world.

THE CYCLE OF THE PASSION

The second part of our Gospel presents the Christ's rôle of Saviour, the conditions in which he is to exercise it and those which he laid down as the foundation of the Christian community. The conversations at the last supper reveal to the disciples how salvation is ordered and the glory to come, together with the law of love by which they are bound for ever to the immortal Christ. This law is first illustrated by washing the disciple's feet (xiii, 1–17); it is there expressly promulgated (31–35) and placed between two predictions; the first declaring the treachery of Judas and pointing out the beloved disciple (23–26); the second announcing Peter's denial (36–38). The Christ proceeds to exhort his faithful ones, promising them a place in his Father's house, assuring them of his continued presence, even of his and the Father's immanence in them (xiv, 1–14, 18–24, 27–28). In the midst of it all he breaks in with a double promise of the Holy Spirit which the Father, in his name, will send them (15–17, 25–26). The preamble to the washing of feet (xiii, 1–3) appears to have been retouched and surcharged. What is this supper, "after" which the washing takes place? The original author probably gave at this point an account of the last meal; this has been suppressed, because a second writer, under the influence of the Synoptics, had introduced it already (xii, 1–8) in the story of the anointing. Doubless the original account, which we are bound to believe underlies all this, seemed too unorthodox to be retained. The washing of feet, so ill-placed that its character as a surcharge càn hardly be mistaken,[1] must belong to an intermediate account into which interpolations have later been introduced, this version being related by its principle idea and the subtilty of its symbolism to those parts of the first Johannine Epistle which speak of purification from sin by the blood of the Christ (1 John ii, 2; iii, 5; iv). Thus the washing of feet, in its character as memorial of the Christ as a servant, living and dying with those who were his own, must have been substituted in an earlier version for the symbolic distribution of bread and wine, that is, for the eucharistic symbols. For that reason the washing is said to be a repetitive completion of the essential purification realized once for all in baptism (6–10).

There are details in the story which would be quite unintelligible if we failed to take account of the profound meaning which attaches to the scene as it is described, not only as a whole, but in the details also. In reality the "service" which the Christ is rendering to his own is that of *his death*, of which the eucharistic love-feast is a figure; and for that reason Peter's opposition to the act which Jesus would perform (6–7) is the equivalent of the attitude assigned him by the Synoptics at the first announcement of the Passion (Mark viii, 32–33; Matthew xvi, 22–23). In like manner the reply of Jesus, "if I wash thee not, thou hast no part in me," is a defiance of all probability unless we understand the symbolism of it. Is Peter, then, to be damned because he has refused to have his feet washed by Jesus? The words refer directly to the Christian mysteries, baptism and the eucharist, both regarded as necessary for salvation, both inseparable from the unique symbol of life-giving water and from the unique idea of salvation procured by Jesus in the death by which he became alive for ever. There is no question here of overcoming the personal repugnance of Peter to having his feet washed by Jesus. The matter in hand is to combat the Jewish Messianism in the words attributed to Peter, which imply that he would not have Jesus lower himself to the service of a life-giving death; to which Jesus replies that by this service the sanctifying rites which

---

[1] Normally ablutions of this kind took place *before* the meal. But from the moment that the washing was made into an eucharistic symbol, it had to be presented as a pendant to the meal or, better, *after* it. Some manuscripts read "a meal taking place," others "a meal *having taken* place"; the first reading, seemingly a correction to avoid contradicting what follows in xiii, 21–30 where the meal is still in progress.

unite the Christian to the source of life are guaranteed as permanently efficacious. Already, in earlier passages of our Gospel,
baptism and the eucharist have been proclaimed as necessary to
salvation (vi, 53); so far is the Johannine Christ from being
indifferent to these sacred and efficacious symbols. His interest
in them is entirely natural. He is himself, by the definition given
of him, a kind of living and ever-active sacrament and, along with
this, a Master of Mystery and a God to be worshipped.

The following sayings, attributed to Jesus either during the
meal or after it, and all of high mystic significance, may be considered as coming from the fundamental account:

xiii, 31–32, God is about to glorify his Son; xiv, 1–3, the
Son goes to prepare for his own a place near the Father; 6–7,
he himself is way, truth and life; whoso knows him knows the
Father and has seen him; 10–13 (after "the words which I speak
unto you") his works are the Father's works and whoso believes
in him will do the same, and yet greater works, because the Son
goes to the Father and will do all that is asked of him; 19–21,
23–24, soon the world will see the Son no more, but those who
love him and keep his commandments will see him; the Father
and the Son will make their abode in them, for the word of the
Son is that of the Father.

These instructions are, at the outset, twice interrupted by
compilers' additions regarding the treachery of Judas in xiii,
10–11 (after the words "and you are clean") and in 18–19. It
might seem that the betrayal is here brought in for the purpose
only of maintaining the atmosphere of darkness and death which
envelops the last meal of the Christ with those who loved him;
that may be so, but the writer will not lose the opportunity to
recall that Jesus knew all that was in store for him; moreover
the felony of Judas had been foretold in prophecy, and Jesus
must cite the Scripture which announces it (Psalm xli, 9). Of
secondary origin also are the sentences (xiii, 12–17, 20) borrowed
from the synoptic tradition (cf. Matthew x, 24, 40; Luke vi, 40),
the connection of which with the mystic example of the washing
is not very obvious, to say nothing of their connection with the
predictions of Judas' treachery.

An editor of our Gospel, perhaps the last, has given a Johannine
turn to the direct announcement of the betrayal (xiii, 21–30),

in which the Christ is made to reveal the traitor's identity to the beloved disciple; a somewhat childish piece of imagination, notwithstanding the symbolism in the "sop" (mouthful) given by Jesus to Judas (26–27). This is the first occasion on which the beloved disciple is brought into prominence, and it is in his honour that our editor exploits the denunciation of the traitor in the Synoptics (cf. Mark xiv, 19; Matthew xxvi, 22; Luke xxii, 23). In the perspective of the story the disciple in question can only be one of the Twelve, but his anonymity has the immediate effect of suggesting that he is a symbolic figure, type of the true disciple, even though his introducer intended him to be identified with an historical person to whom the composition of the Gospel might thereafter be attributed. The place assigned him at the Christ's side makes not only a relation of personal friendship with Jesus, but complete partnership of the well-beloved in the spiritual riches which are to overflow mankind from the breast of Jesus (cf. vii, 38; *supra*, p. 209). It is to this disciple that Peter turns to find out who is to be the traitor, and it should be noted that an analogous relation, in which the beloved disciple takes the lead, exists between the two every time they appear on the scene in company (xviii, 16; xx, 4–8; and again xxi, 7, 20–22)—a plain indication of the superiority claimed by the Johannine to the common apostolic tradition. The incident of the sop given to Judas must be secondary in relation to the preamble. In the preamble (xiii, 2), the devil has already entered into Judas before the meal began; here he is delivered to Satan after eating the sop, which he eats to his damnation (cf. 1 Corinthians xi, 29; Luke xxii, 3).

The exhortation to mutual love, conceived in the spirit and style of the first Johannine Epistle (cf. 1 John ii, 7–10; iii, 23) is a surcharge on the announcement of Peter's denial, which has already been borrowed from the synoptic tradition as it stands in Mark, Matthew and Luke. One feature not derived from that source is the veiled allusion to the later martyrdom of Peter, in the symbolic words "thou shalt follow me afterwards." This mysterious prediction, we must add, is far from being an indication that the passage which contains it is either primitive or of high antiquity.

The mystic allocution flows on from xiii into xiv, unmindful of the inserted conversation between Peter and Jesus. Similarly intercalated into its continuation are the following:

The naïve question by Thomas about the locality to which Jesus says he is about to go (4–5); the no less naïve demand of Philip, "show us the Father," and the words in which Jesus expresses his astonishment (8–10*a*); the promise of another Helper, the Spirit of Truth (15–17, 25–26); and the question of Jude (22).

The Spirit appears in our Gospel mainly as the continuator of the revelation inaugurated by the Christ, and its action is partly merged into that of the Christian sacrament. Thus, in a sense, the Spirit is a substitute for Jesus. We may recall at this point that in the Acts of the Apostles the reign of the Spirit is brought in by the miracle of Pentecost which takes place ten days after the Ascension. In the mind of the Gospel editor there can have been no thought of a *human* substitute, Marcion, Montanus or any other, since it is expressly stated that the Helper will "be with you for ever" (xiv, 16). In any case the discourses, in their original form, rule out the possibility of a substitute for the immortal Christ, who abides continuously in those who love him (cf. 1 John ii, 1 where the Christ is himself the Paraclete, the Helper). Finally, it is evident that the reflections (27–31) which follow the reiterated promise of the Paraclete, and end with the words "Arise let us go hence," were imagined by the compiler of the preceding instruction with a view to proceeding immediately with the story of the Passion. But another compilation, three chapters in extent (xv–xvii), has been inserted between this point and the opening of the Passion story (xviii, 1).

Last Instructions of the Christ

No introduction is arranged for this new collection, the reader apparently being invited to take it as the continuation of the preceding discourse. The subjects treated in it are, moreover, the same as those in its predecessor, as follows:

Allegory of the vine (xv, 1–10) urging the disciples to remain united in the Christ, the source of eternal life, and direct exhortation to abide in the love of Jesus (11–17). Condemnation of a world gone astray which will hate the disciples as it has hated their Master (18–25 and perhaps xvi, 1–4). New promises concerning the Spirit which will support the disciples in persecution and condemn the world (26–27; xvi, 5–16). New announcement of persecutions to come, but the sorrow of the persecuted will be changed into joy, and the Christ himself will visit his own (xvi, 16–24). All this Jesus has spoken in plain terms, because he is about to depart; let the faithful, in the hour of persecution, be at peace in him (25–33). Finally the Christ, to crown his exhortations, offers to his Father a long prayer that all believers, present and to come, may be preserved in mystic union with himself (xvii).

Like those that precede them these last instructions of the Christ are presented as though he were giving them to his disciples while still among them but with death immediately before him; in reality they are addressed, by the immortal Christ, to his Church. But though in a manner complementary to what has gone before, they are not all to be regarded, either separately or together, as pieces of secondary composition.

The allegory of the vine, with the exhortation attached to it (xv, 1–17), may be considered as a primitive document self-contained and independent of the compilation in which it now finds a place. The allegory has an orderly development in the style of the prophets (cf. Isaiah v, 1–7; Jeremiah ii, 21; Ezechiel xv, 1–6; Psalm lxxx, 8–16). The suggestion of it comes from passages in the Synoptics where mention is made of the vine and its fruit, chiefly from what is said about wine in their account of the eucharistic institution (Mark xiv, 25; Matthew xxvi, 29; Luke xxii, 18). The first words, then, are enough to show that this new course of instruction has the same close connection with the eucharist as the two preceding chapters, always linked to the eucharist, as they are, by the conception of that highest form of love which is willing to die for the sake of the beloved. Considered from another point of view, the allegory of the vine which, in some parts, makes a fellow to that of the Good Shepherd (x, 1–18), is the less well-balanced of the two, the author pressing hard on disparate images, that of the gardener who tends the vine and that of the necessity for the branch to remain united to the main stem. As supporting the application made of them to the Christ and to the disciples, the two images are ill-matched.

While love is the relation between the Christ and his own,

the world, on its side, is characterized by the hate it bears to both of them. The theme has already been indicated in vii, 7; cf. 1 John iii, 13–16 where the hatred-theme is also treated in connection with the love-theme. But here the brief discourse on the world as the enemy (18–25) comes in awkwardly. Its secondary character appears in its making a back reference (20) to a statement, lacking in originality, already made in the text (xiii, 16).

In like manner, the new dissertation on the "Helper" (the Paraclete) is of feebler inspiration (xv, 26–xvi, 15). What is said there about the judgment to be passed on the world (xvi, 8–11) is a confused rigmarole which recalls the least impressive passages in the first Johannine Epistle. One interesting statement, however, stands out from the rest: "the Paraclete shall declare unto you the things that are to come." To what else can this refer than to the Johannine Apocalypse? If that be admitted, the inference will follow that all the passages about the Helper were added by the compilers of the Johannine collection of books, and that these additions were made at the time when they were engaged in the attempt to obtain acceptance, under the same apostolic name, of the Apocalypse, the fourth Gospel and the three Epistles. Another important point to be noted is the saying in xvi, 4: "these things I said not unto you at the beginning *because I was with you.*" These words sound strangely as coming from the Christ. Without intending to do so the author has given away the secret that the speaker has long quitted this world and that, while seemingly addressing his first disciples, he is really speaking to the Church of the second century.

The final Consolation (xvi, 20–24, 26–28, 32–33), given in view of the coming persecutions, was possibly at first an independent composition. A preamble has here been constructed for it (16–19) which might be understood as referring to the Christ's resurrection, his apparition and even his second coming; but the Consolation to which it leads on has a different theme; it is a hymn of the mystic union, spiritual and perpetual, with the everliving Christ, a hymn of his return in that sense. An interruption by the disciples has been introduced into the Consolation itself (29–31, to which 25 is co-ordinate). Intercalated in also the remark on the parabolic, i.e. allegorical and symbolic, character of the teaching in all these discourses. But the disciples' interruption has been inserted by an editor who wished to emphasize their lack of intelligence and to give a character of formal prophecy to the allusion made in the discourse to their abandonment of Jesus in the Passion (32).

Let it be noted that, on this point, the Synoptics in their canonical form, do not say so much, and that the Johannine account of the Passion gives it flat contradiction. With this the Gospel of Peter, which probably depends on John, is in agreement, and the version very possibly retains a primitive datum. Contrasting with the disciples' abandonment of their Master comes the saying: "but I am not left alone, because my Father is with me" which we have already encountered (viii, 16, 29). It has the same bearing here as before (*supra*, p. 210).

"In the world ye shall have suffering; but be of good cheer; I have vanquished the world." So the Consolation ends, in language which expresses confidence in victory to come; but the voice which speaks is, before all else, that of the Christ in glory, the Christ of the Eucharist, imparting courage to Christians everywhere. In the very act of dying, the Christ, now in glory, overthrew the world and the prince who ruled it (cf. xii, 31). Those who love him and whom he loves, his own, will conquer the world in their turn, nor will they fall into the hand of its prince when they, too, come to die.

The final prayer of the Christ (xvii) is not only the crowning utterance to the lessons taught, but the eucharistic keynote of the Last Supper, conceived as the first Love Feast (Agape). We may regard it as the first act of solemn thanksgiving, the first eucharist, a supreme utterance of Christian charity appropriate to the occasion. Jesus begins by asking that he may be glorified, because his work is done (1–8). Then he commends his loved ones, whom he is leaving in the world, to the care of the Father (9–19). Finally he prays that God, the Christ and the loved ones may all be one in love (20–26). His prayer is a lyric, constructed rhythmically and with balance of the parts.[1] Although apparently uttered in particular circumstances, it may, originally, have had no place in a Gospel story. We may take it as a type of eucharistic prayer, placed in the mouth of Jesus as master of the mystery;

[1] For the prayer with which the hymn concludes, as restored by M. Loisy, see Appendix to this chapter. Translator's note.

perhaps the oracle of some Christian prophet first recited to the community at the Easter celebration, not as the common thanksgiving but as the prophet's own. The same may be true of other passages in our Gospel, especially of the discourses after the Supper, of which the analysis is now concluded.

Two small additions may be detected in the final prayer: the profession of faith in verse 3, impersonal both in form and tone, out of keeping with the context and with nothing in it specifically Johannine; and verse 12 "except the son of perdition, that the Scripture might be fulfilled" evidently added to correspond with xiii, 18, 21–30, but equally out of place with the foregoing.

THE JOHANNINE ACCOUNT OF THE PASSION

The arrangement of the Passion and the Resurrection stories in our Gospel has, to all appearance, an almost systematic ordering; the Christ is now returning to his Father; he goes by the way of death; he arrives by resurrection. The scenes of his arrest; of his appearance before the high-priest, with Peter's denial of him; of Pilate passing judgment; of the crucifixion; of the burial; of the resurrection—all these follow in an order and develop in a manner that furnishes a worthy conclusion to the revelation of glory, which has pursued its course from the beginning of the book. But the story is far from being all of one piece.

It may be said that the Johannine Christ himself controls the conditions of his arrest. He dispatches Judas on his errand, commanding him to do quickly what he has to do (xiii, 27). When the hour strikes, he repairs with his disciples to the place where the traitor will come to take him, a garden beyond Kedron (xviii, 1; note that the name Gethsemane is omitted). Judas, on his side, calls up the Roman cohort and the tribune in garrison at the tower of Antonia, and with them the service-men of the Sanhedrim; this last to enhance the importance of the scene about to be enacted; for we may be very sure that if the armed forces of the procurator took any part in the affair there would have been no need either of the temple police or of Judas himself; nor would Jesus have been taken before the high-priest. When the force arrives at the garden, Jesus advances to meet it, demands its business, and receiving the answer that they are looking for Jesus the Nazorean, speaks a word that throws them all backward to the ground. Then he gives himself up, ordering his captors to let his companions go.

Introduced into a scene of such dignity, the sword-stroke that cut off the ear of the high-priest's servant is clearly out of place and keeping. But the compiler who mentions the incident knows that the servant was called Malchus; that his right ear was the one cut off; that the disciple who struck the blow was no other than Peter, and that Jesus rebuked him: "return thy sword to the sheath. The cup my Father has given me, shall I not drink it?" (10–11). This, surely, is the cup of Gethsemane which Jesus in the Synoptics prays the Father to remove from him. Peter's sword-stroke takes the place of the protest he raises in Mark (viii, 32) and Matthew (xvi, 22) at the first announcement of the Passion; and the rebuke he now receives is the Johannine equivalent of the terrible apostrophe: "get thee gone, Satan." From instances such as this, of which there are many in our Gospel, we may learn how to interpret its dependence on the Synoptics, and judge at the same time in what kind of relation to theirs is the treatment of Peter's prestige by the editors of John. Here, as in Mark, Peter is the man to whom the mystery of salvation is at first wholly unintelligible, and who, in his ill informed zeal, would prevent its realization. Of the remaining traits in the story of the arrest, the omission of Judas' kiss is not less significant than these additions.

The story continues (xviii, 12): "Then the cohort, the tribune and the Jews' servants laid hold of Jesus and led him to Annas." This follows on naturally after the order given by the Christ to leave his disciples at liberty,[1] and marks as a secondary addition the intervening incident of Peter's outbreak and the severed ear. But the account of Jesus before the high-priest is loaded with postscripts to a degree which has baffled interpreters from the first; even the textual history of the passage shows that it has been revised again and again, in the vain attempt to find a satisfactory reading, and the same is true of like attempts made by modern critics. The confusion arises from the fact that the primitive account knew of only one high-priest, Annas (Hanan); it knew nothing of Caiaphas as concerned in the matter, and, equally,

---

[1] xviii, 9 is a lame reference to xvii, 12.

nothing of Peter's denial. Caiaphas has been joined to Annas to make some sort of agreement with Matthew xxvi, 57, when it is to Caiaphas and not, as here, to Annas that his captors take Jesus; this is done by making him son-in-law to Annas, on the ground that several sons of Annas had become high-priests and that Caiaphas was presumably one of the family. His antecedents are also recalled (xviii, 13a–14; cf. xi, 49–50; *supra*, p. 214).

Peter's denial, imported from the Synoptics, we find divided into two parts (xviii, 15–18; 25–27) for the editorial convenience of finding a rôle for a certain unnamed disciple who is said to have been an acquaintance of the high-priest's, and can be no other than the well-beloved. This disciple introduces Peter to the high-priest's court, where he has the unpleasant surprise of encountering a kinsman of the Malchus whose ear he had cut off. All these precisions reveal the compiler of our Gospel as a man of lively invention. It is abundantly clear that in the original account not one of his disciples followed Jesus after his arrest (xviii, 8; xvi, 32).

The author of the foundation-story who knew Christianity as the religion of a sect, reduces the whole trial before the high-priest to an enquiry about Jesus' disciples and teaching (19). Jesus answers that he has always spoken openly to the world, either in the synagogues (Galilee)[1] or in the temple (Jerusalem); let the question of his teaching be asked of those who heard it. (In reality the author is replying to the Jews and pagans of his own age, who alleged that Jesus had preached only in a lost corner of Palestine and converted a few ignorant Galileans.) At this answer one of the court officials, judging it an impertinence, strikes Jesus with his hand: this is all that the author chooses to retain of the ignominious scene described in the Synoptics (Mark xiv, 65; Matthew xxvi, 67–68; Luke xxii, 63–65). Jesus answers with great dignity (23), so great indeed that the answer would be too solemn for so mean an insult were it not that the insulter stands for the unbelieving Jews, murderers of the Christ and persecutors of his followers. Thereupon the inquiry closes, and Jesus is taken away from the quarters of the high-priest (Annas in the original story, Caiaphas in the altered text) to Pilate's praetorium.

[1] It is, however, the fact that only one case of this is reported in our Gospel (vi, 59).

The author is careful to note that this happened on the morning of the day in the evening of which the paschal lamb was sacrificed. This timing is more important to him than the imagined consequence in the development of the scene. For it results from the date indicated that Jesus died on the day and at the hour of the paschal sacrifice; in this way our Gospel represents the Christ's passion as confirming the Easter usage of the quartodecimans. This, for him, was the essential matter; but it leads him on to imagine that the Jews must have abstained from entering the praetorium from fear of contracting legal impurity (28); nevertheless he makes Jesus go in. The tribunal is in front of the palace, a kind of open space where a crowd of Jews awaits the result of the proceedings inside, an unnatural arrangement constructed with the object of introducing a private conversation between Pilate and his prisoner, when Jesus will utter some lofty sayings which the writer will not allow him to utter in the presence of Jews. In consequence of this arrangement, the judgment scene falls into two parts, as Pilate goes away from the Jews, who are outside the building, to Jesus, who is inside, and then comes back from Jesus to the Jews.

The trial now proceeds as follows. First, the procurator receives the accusation which "the Jews" (the Jewish magistrates) refuse to withdraw and deal with themselves, on the ground (29–31) that they have no right to pronounce sentence of death (which was true at the time the evangelist was writing, but not in the time of Jesus). This happened, remarks the author (32), in order that Jesus might be *crucified*, as he had predicted,[1] crucifixion being a punishment which Roman authority alone could inflict. Pilate then goes inside to interrogate the accused who, on receiving the blunt question "art thou the King of the Jews?" makes the mystic answer that his "kingdom is not of this world" and is not defended by armed force; he is King "that he may bear witness to the truth." These sublime declarations are beyond Pilate's comprehension, but he concludes that there can be no harm in a king of truth, and accordingly goes back to the Jews to inform them that he finds no crime in the prisoner (38). At this the Jews break out into protest, declaring that the accused falls under the stroke of the Law for

[1] iii, 14; viii, 28; xii, 32–33.

saying he is the Son of God (this is the charge of blasphemy, which in the synoptic account,[1] is ground of condemnation by the Sanhedrim; but here "Son of God" is taken in the Johannine sense). Troubled by this, Pilate now goes back to Jesus and asks him whence he comes. No answer. Pilate insists and impresses on the prisoner that he has power to release him or to put him to death on the cross; Jesus replies that he would have no such power had not Providence conferred it upon him; so much the heavier is the guilt of Satan who has prompted Judas and the Jews to deliver him to Roman justice (xix, 7–11). Reassured on that side, Pilate makes a new effort to get the accusation withdrawn, only to meet with fresh protest from the Jews, who cry out that a pretender to kingship is Caesar's enemy, thus returning to the political charge with which they had begun. This brings Pilate to the end of his resistance. Yielding to the necessity of the situation (needless to scrutinize his psychology) he has Jesus brought out and makes him sit down on the judgment seat. The right translation here is "made him sit down," as the Gospel of Peter and Justin (*Apology*, 35) both understand it. If we suppose that Pilate himself sat down, the common translation, the whole scene loses the significance intended by the evangelist, who imagines it as the presentation of a king to his subjects only to be rejected instead of acclaimed. This is the meaning of Pilate's announcement to the Jews "behold your King!", of the clamour that immediately breaks out for the crucifixion of the man offered them, and of the declaration that they will have no king but Caesar. Faced with this blind obstinacy Pilate, we are to suppose, is now powerless to refuse sentence of death, and has no alternative but to hand Jesus over to them for crucifixion (13–16). It is the doing of the Jews, then, that the King of Truth is condemned to death as the King of Israel.

The picture before us, remote as it is from all reality, even from verisimilitude, is nevertheless grand in conception and in the profound irony with which, from the height of a sublime mysticism, the Jews are exhibited. To conform with the Synoptics there have been wedged into it the incident of Barabbas (xviii, 39–40) and the mockery in the praetorium (xix, 1–3), the latter symbolically dramatized and corrected as the presentation of

---

[1] Mark xiv, 61–64; Matthew xxvi, 63–66; Luke xxii, 66–70.

"the man" (4–6). But this added presentation repeats in advance the presentation of "the King" (14) and greatly diminishes its effect. Note how, at the end of xix, 6, we are back at the point where we left off at the end of xviii, 38. Note also that in xviii, 40 the Jews are made to "cry out *again*" though our Gospel has not mentioned any previous cry. This is a slip of the interpolator: by inadvertence he here follows Mark xv, 13, whereas for the whole of the Barabbas incident he has been following Luke xxiii, 16–19.

The Crucifixion

Having obtained the sentence they demanded the Jews lead the condemned to the place of punishment, Jesus himself carrying his cross (16*b*–17; in contradiction to Luke xxiii, 26). The sequel, however, shows clearly (23) that the execution is carried out by Roman soldiers, Pilate himself controlling the details (19–22). The contradiction of the Synoptics on the point of Simon of Cyrene carrying the cross is deliberate, the set purpose of the evangelist being to bring out the Christ's free and sovereign control in the preliminaries of his death and in death itself. Perhaps also there was an intention to combat certain gnostics who, like Basilides, maintained that Simon was crucified in the Christ's place. They bring Jesus "to a place called the Skull, Golgotha in the Hebrew"—the synoptic designation—"where they crucified him, and two others with him, one on either side, and Jesus in the midst" (18). The author refrains from saying that these two companions were thieves; this by way of suppressing the suggestion of infamy.

The inscription on the cross gives occasion to a symbolic incident (19–22): despite the opposition of the chief priests, Pilate maintains the wording of it, "Jesus the Nazorean, the King of the Jews." Thus Jesus keeps his Kingship and Christhood, let Jewish incredulity protest as it will. The three languages betoken the universal sovereignty of the Son of God.

In the incidents that follow, up to the original conclusion of the book (xx, 30–31), it is not easy to distinguish what belongs to the fundamental document from the secondary additions. What we are told about the division of the garments may be secondary: it is the forced interpretation of a prophetic text (Psalm xxii, 18) the fulfilment of which had to be marked, the "garments" and the "vesture" meaning the same object. Doubt-less more was intended than to mark the fulfilment of a prophecy, the robe without seam suggesting an allegory in which some of the Fathers recognized the Church. Such a symbolism, however, is not in the same current as that of the "signs" encountered at an earlier stage, such as those of the man born blind and the raising of Lazarus.

The latter symbolism returns in the incident that follows, the words spoken by the Christ to his mother and the beloved disciple (25–27). As this incident concerns only the mother and the disciple, it may be assumed that the other women whose names are given (25) have been added to achieve some sort of agreement with the Synoptics. Here again, as in the story of Cana (ii, 4), Jesus addresses his mother as "Woman"; but this time he does not repudiate her. The meaning of the incident seems to be that converted Jews must accept hellenic Christianity as the legitimate offspring of the old Covenant, while the same Christianity, on its side, must regard as its mother the Jewish-Christian Church with its Old Testament tradition.

The last incident preceding the death of the Christ is the offer of vinegar; it marks a simple fulfilment of the prophecy in Psalm lxix, 21. But a touch of symbolism is not wanting, for the vinegar is offered with a bunch of hyssop, in allusion to the paschal ritual (Exodus xii, 22) which prescribed the use of hyssop to splash the house-doors with the blood of the lamb. The sym-bolism is somewhat far-fetched. Its presentation as a fulfilment of Scripture has the look of being a surcharge. The beginning of the verse (28a) is in contradiction with the end of it, which brings in another Scripture still to be fulfilled. We should read as follows: "Jesus, knowing that all was accomplished"—his rôle com-pletely finished according to providential designs, whether ex-pressed in Scripture or not—"in order that the Scripture might be fulfilled, said, I thirst." The natural sequel to "knowing that all was now accomplished" comes after the presentation and reception of the vinegar (30): "he said, it is finished. And bending down his head, he poured out the spirit."

This peaceful and willing death is the Johannine substitute for the scene in the first two Gospels, in which a great cry escapes from Jesus at the moment when he expires (Mark xv, 37; Matthew xxvii, 50). It figures the gift of the spirit which Jesus, with bent head, breathes forth in his last breath on the beloved group gathered round the foot of the cross; they symbolize his Church. The death of the Johannine Christ provides no scene of agony, ignominy and darkness, for it is nothing else than the resurrection of Jesus to his glorious and blessed eternity; his death and his resurrection are coincident. We must bear that in mind if we are to understand the meaning attached to Easter by the quartodeciman Christians of Asia.

Their Easter, coinciding with the Jewish Passover, might fall on any one of the seven days of the week, but it is a fact to be noted that up to this point our Gospel had not told us on which day the Christ's death took place. We are now going to be told, and to see how the Johannine Easter was made to fit in, by one means or another, to the synoptic framework in which Easter is celebrated on Sunday. The very first incident to follow the death of Jesus in the Johannine account informs us that Jesus died on the evening of a Friday and that he had to be buried before the Sabbath of next day. In its basic form the passage (xix, 31–37) informing us of the finishing blow administered to the victims and the prompt removal of the three bodies for common burial (31) is quite independent of the Synoptics and may well represent an important tradition, inasmuch as this tradition would contradict not only the stories of the Christ's burial in the Synoptics but those which, under synoptic influence, are now to follow in the Gospel before us. But, in the traditional form in which it comes down to us, there are features in the paragraph which class it among the latest additions to be found in our Gospel; these are, first, the symbolism of the water and the blood betokening the Christian sacraments, and, second, the calling up of a text from Exodus (xii, 46), "not a bone of his body shall be broken," which symbolically identifies the Christ with the paschal lamb, and another from Zechariah (xii, 10), surcharged upon the former, and made to predict the lance-thrust of the Roman soldier. The passage referring to the incident in the first Johannine Epistle (1 John v, 6–7) is also an interpolation in that Epistle, but stands there as the authorized interpretation of the Gospel passage now before us, the two possibly coming from the same writer. According to this interpretation we are to understand the Spirit which John the Baptist saw descending on Jesus and which Jesus, with his last breath, poured out upon his own, as connected with water and blood, the water of baptism and the blood of Calvary figured in the Eucharist, the two together bearing one inseparable witness to the immortal Christ.

There is something more in the passage as it has come down to us. The Gospel compilers attest the prodigy on the testimony of the beloved disciple who was present when Jesus died. But who are the compilers who allege this testimony? They are the same persons as those who would have it believed that the Apocalypse, the Gospel and the three Epistles are all the work of one author, and that author the apostle John (cf. xxi, 24). We may conclude that the scene in our Gospel, the witness of the beloved disciple and the attribution of the book to the apostle John are integral parts in a single fiction of late invention.

Burial, Resurrection and Apparitions

The story of the burial by Joseph of Arimathea is borrowed from the synoptic tradition. To him has been added Nicodemus who brings with him a great weight of spices to furnish the Christ with a princely embalmment. (The compiler forgets that the utmost haste was necessary to get the body buried before the Sabbath began, and that an embalmment on this scale would be a very lengthy operation.) Needless to say the "garden" in which the sepulchre is situated has a mystic meaning: it is the new garden of God where the Church, the new Eve, will be drawn from the side of the new Adam; the new sepulchre and the spices belong to the same current. But it may well be doubted whether the author of the Gospel in its original form, who understood everything in a spiritual sense, and the resurrection most emphatically so, was concerned to this extent with the dead body of Jesus, or that he is responsible for the stories in our present fourth Gospel which turn the resurrection into a miracle of the physical order, attested by material proofs.

To find a clear path through the events described in chapter xx is no easy task. The descriptions show signs of successive retouchings, and elements belonging to the fundamental document are but dimly discernible. Three apparitions of the Christ follow without a break; the first to Mary of Magdala (1–18) on the morning of the resurrection; the second to the assembled disciples on the evening of the same day (19–23); the third, again to the disciples, now including the sceptical Thomas, on the Sunday following (24–29).

The first apparition is surcharged with the news carried by Mary to Peter and the beloved disciple (1–2, after the words "she saw the stone had been turned aside from the sepulchre"); by the visit of the two disciples to the tomb, where it becomes clear that this addition, as well as the foregoing, has been imagined to the greater glory of the beloved disciple, who must be the first to believe in the resurrection of Jesus, contrary to what the primitive tradition tells of Peter; finally, by the appearance of angels to Mary (11–14, after "as she wept, she stooped")—this to make agreement with the synoptic introduction of angels, but a meaningless repetition of the apparition of Jesus himself. In this, the message to the disciples entrusted to Mary has a solemn dignity: she is charged to inform the "brethren" that Jesus has reascended to God. But the attempt to determine exactly the original meaning of this first apparition is a vain one. The story of it must have been modified profoundly, doubtless because it differed too obviously from the other Gospels.[1]

Brief as it is, the account of the second apparition has been overlaid at several points. In the general arrangement it resembles the account in the third Gospel (Luke xxiv, 36–40, 45–49). We are inclined to think that, to the original creator of the scene, this was the one and only sensible apparition of Jesus after his resurrection, expressed in the simple statement that, the disciples being assembled and the doors closed, Jesus appeared in their midst and said: "Peace be unto you." Immediately after there is a surcharge, intended to prepare the way for the coming apparition to Thomas, of which that story, when it comes later, has no knowledge—"and saying this, he showed them his hands and his side" (xx, 20a), the reference to the soldier's lance-thrust probably due to the compiler who has inserted that episode in the story of the Passion. As though there were nothing surprising in the apparition, the only sentiment attributed to the disciples is that of joy (20b). After which Jesus repeats his salutation and

---

[1] On the ancient writers who substitute the mother of Jesus for the Magdalene, see *Le quatrième Evangile*, 504.

gives them their mission (21; cf. xvii, 18 and Matthew xxviii, 19–20). Although the repeated salutation (21) may be a surcharge, added to prevent the discourse of Jesus being only the announcement of a mission, it is probable that the words which follow, about the power to remit sins, also come from the original author, omitting those which refer to the insufflation of the Spirit.

The third apparition (24–29), made for convincing Thomas, is an appendix to the second, and due to some reviser who was concerned to demonstrate the reality of the Christ's bodily resurrection; the remarks of Thomas, "if I see not the mark of the nails," etc., makes that clear enough. Nevertheless the moral of the story is to the effect that normal faith has no need of such proofs. It is possible that the anecdote was added to combat Docetism, but what it directly contradicts is the doctrine of the original evangelist, which taught the spiritual immortality of the Christ, but not the material resurrection of his dead body. It remains to note that this third apparition is conceived by the author as definitely the last to occur. After the words "blessed are they who, not having seen, believe" any further apparition stories would be worse than superfluous.

The concluding lines (30–31), concerning the object of the book, come from the writer whom we may call the first editor of the Gospel. They give no sign that he wished to be regarded as an apostolic person. Moreover he bids farewell to his readers with the unmistakable air of having finished his work and completed the mystic instruction of the Christian. After this the chapter that follows is clearly marked as an accretion, of which the effect is to derange the primitive economy of the whole book.

The Supplementary Apparition

This supplementary chapter has the threefold object of relating an apparition of the risen Christ to Peter and six of the disciples by the Lake of Tiberias (xxi, 1–14); the rehabilitation, by a triple profession of love, of Simon-Peter to whom the Christ confides the care of his sheep (15–17); predictions of Jesus about the martyrdom of Peter and the future of the beloved disciple (20–23), an editorial invention, relatively late, and connected with the attribution of the Gospel to this disciple in the epilogue (24–25).

To the same editor belong, without counting retouches and the arrangement of the material he is working on, the formula of introduction (1); the rôle of the beloved disciple in the miraculous draught, where the disciple is before Peter in recognizing Jesus (7); the statement about the number of fish and the resistance of the net, symbolic touches in the editor's usual vein; finally the number in the series assigned to the apparition (14). The whole is composed of borrowings from the synoptic tradition of apparitions in Galilee, and from the third Gospel. The general intention of it all is, beyond doubt, to make the Johannine Gospel acceptable in the churches at large, the prominence given to Peter being certain to win the approval in particular of the church in Rome. But the conglomerate of material here collected from various sources is as far as possible from holding together. It breaks up on analysis into the following borrowed elements: the miraculous draught of fishes, which is a myth of the institution of Christian propaganda, anticipated in Luke v, 1–11 (the introduction just here of this, the primordial, meaning of the miracle, is somewhat strange); the incident of Peter plunging from the boat into the sea in order to be with Jesus again, which recalls a similar incident in Matthew (xiv, 25–33, the antedating of a resurrection story); the meal of bread and fish, recalling the miraculous multiplication of the loaves (vi, 5–13), the meal with the pilgrims of Emmaus, and especially the peculiar feature of the broiled fish in the apparition to all the disciples recorded by the same Gospel (Luke xxiv, 41–43).

The solemn colloquy of the Christ with Peter (15–17), in which the primacy of the apostle is consecrated, has been consciously moulded into an equivalent of what we read in Matthew xvi, 17–19, which it imitates even to the form, and in Luke xxii, 32, though it was at first conceived independently of this Gospel. It is a safe conjecture that the prediction of Peter's martyrdom (18–19, echoing xiii, 36) was worded with an eye on the Apocalypse of Peter (*supra*, p. 53). All this, for better or worse, and for worse rather than better, is crowded into the same perspective.

The last sayings about the beloved disciple (20–23) are of the feeblest invention, but are intended to prepare the way for the conclusion of the chapter (24–25), which is also to be the conclusion of the book. The object aimed at is to present the Elder,

John the Old, a well-known figure long resident in Asia, as author of the Gospel and to convey a hint—no more than a hint is given—that he is the same person as the apostle John, son of Zebedee. Who are the "we" who guarantee his testimony (24)? They are "the Elders" who had known this John and brought out under his name the collection of Johannine books. We thus see that this supplement to the Gospel, intended to make it acceptable to all the Churches, was also intended to give it apostolic authority and value.

Such, then, is the sublime but inconsistent book whose destiny it was to dominate Christian theology and to fix its form. How did it originate?

Towards the end of the first century or the beginning of the second there lived a mystic prophet, a master of gnosis rather than an apostle of the faith, from whom came forth the hymns and symbolic visions on which the fourth Gospel is founded. A little later, towards 135–140, his sublime meditations were collected and framed in a Gospel story, to be used as a manual of initiation into the Christian faith, like other books of similar form already in circulation among the churches. The chronological framework was probably fixed at the same time and a part of the borrowings made from the synoptic tradition. At this stage and in this form the book had no auther's name attached to it and its diffusion was limited, or nearly so, to the province of Asia. Some fifteen or twenty years later, towards 150–160, the Marcionite heresy having broken out, this Asiatic book was amended, completed and more or less worked over, not only by the addition of chapter xxi, but by other retouches and additions in the main body; it was then boldly presented as the work of an apostle. But everything was welcome that gave satisfaction to faith, and the result just described was accepted by those whose will-to-believe found the truth in it. Thus it came to pass that, when the Montanist controversy broke out, the adversaries of these pretended writings of the apostle John found nobody to listen to them. When later, towards 190, the great controversy arose about the keeping of Easter, the Roman Church failed to perceive, or pretended not to perceive that, while the Synoptics supported the ritual tradition of Rome and of most other Christian churches, the fourth Gospel supported the different tradition followed by the churches of Asia.

APPENDIX

The concluding Prayer in Chapter xvii.[1]

Holy Father, keep them in thy name,
   those thou hast given me,
      that they may be one as we are . . .
I ask thee not to take them out of the world,
   but to guard them from the Evil One . . .
For them I sanctify myself,
   that they also may be sanctified in truth . . .
And the glory thou gavest to me, yea to me,
   I gave to them,
That they may be one
   as we are one,
I in them
   and thou in me
      that they may be perfect in unity,
   That the world may know
      that thou hast sent me
   And that thou hast loved them
      as thou hast loved me.
Father, those whom thou hast given me,
   I would that where I am
      They too may be with me,
   That they may see my glory,
      which thou hast given me,
   For thou hast loved me
      before the foundation of the world.
Righteous Father, the world has known thee not,
   but I, I knew thee;
And they too have known
   that thou hast sent me.
And to them have I made known thy name,
   and will make it known,
That the love wherewith thou lovest me may be
   in them and I in them.

[1] See *The Birth of the Christian Religion*, p. 241. (Appended here by the translator.)

Chapter VIII

THE EPISTLES AND THE CATECHESIS

WE have already seen how the epistolary method of instruction was employed in the early times of Christianity as a complement to the catechesis properly so called. This service was rendered in various ways; sometimes by genuinely authentic letters; sometimes by recourse to literary fiction, which might consist in amplifying the apostolic letters by interpolations, as happened to certain letters of Paul, or in publishing apocryphal letters under apostolic names, as in the case of those put out under the names of Peter, John, James and Jude, as well as of some ascribed to Paul. These letters, whether authentic or not, are samples of Christian teaching in the earliest times. As we follow the evolution of the catechesis we shall find that this epistolary literature reveals three stages, or forms, of its teaching. At its point of departure it is eschatological, concerned, that is, with the coming Kingdom; at the second stage it becomes penetrated by gnosis and begins introducing gnostic themes into both the eschatological and the evangelical teaching; finally, when gnosticism has got out of hand and is producing a flood of heresies, it turns against them, becomes anti-gnostic, and gives the catechesis a turn in that direction.

THE FIRST STAGE—ESCHATOLOGICAL

When Paul set out as an independent missionary, about the year 44–45, he went about the world founding church after church, without fixing his abode anywhere, except when imprisonment immobilized him. In such conditions epistolary relations were the only means by which control could be maintained between the churches and their founder; without them these newly formed communities would have run the risk of dissolution. External difficulties attended the propaganda and internal difficulties were almost inevitable; in addition to which the very peculiar situation of Paul in regard to the other missionaries gave rise to a campaign of abuse against which he had to defend himself. It is a probability as near as possible to certainty that not all his writings have come down to us; and the same is true of the letters written under somewhat different conditions by the other missionaries, by Barnabas for example, which are irrecoverably lost. The surviving letters and notes of Paul are not correspondence of the ordinary kind; they are all concerned more or less with his apostolic labours, and their interest for us lies precisely in that.

1 *Thessalonians*

The oldest of these letters subsists in the first Epistle to the Thessalonians.[1] The Christian group at Thessalonica had been recruited by Paul, accompanied by Silas and Timothy, in 48–49, and the letter was written from Corinth about 50–51. It is addressed in the name of Paul and his two auxiliaries "to the community of Thessalonica (which is) in God and the Lord Jesus Christ (i, 1)." But the writer, or dictater, of the letter is evidently Paul himself. The believing group forms a spiritual unity, an *ecclesia*, in God and in Christ. The beginning of the letter (i, 2–10) contains praises which may seem exaggerated, but are really encouragement. The point to be retained is the important indication it gives of the object of the Christian catechesis at this stage:

> People tell of you what a reception you gave us, and how you were converted from idols to God, to serve the God who is living and true, and to await the coming from heaven of his Son, whom he raised from the dead, Jesus, who saves us from the approaching wrath.

Paul seems to have wished greatly to revisit his converts that he might assure himself of their perseverance; but he can do no more than send Timothy from Athens. Timothy on returning finds him at Corinth and gives a most favourable report on his mission, at which Paul is greatly consoled; so let them continue to advance on the good way (ii, 17–iii, 2a, 5b–13). The passage ends thus:

> The Lord make you to grow and abound in love among yourselves and towards all men, as ours towards you, to strengthen your hearts, (rendering them) irreproachable in holiness at the coming of our Lord Jesus with all his saints.

[1] For a critical analysis of this document see our *Remarques sur la litétrature épistolaire du Nouveau Testament* (1935), pp. 85–89.

The dominating feature in the apostle's outlook is, clearly, the Coming. This it is which gives added urgency to the moral precepts, first and foremost to those concerned with conjugal chastity (iv, 2–8):

> For you know what teaching we gave you in the Lord Jesus; that you abstain from unchastity: that each of you learns to possess his own vessel in sanctity and honour, not with passionate lust, *like Gentiles who know not God* (Psalm lxxix, 6); not to deceive his brother nor do him injury in his own affair, because the Lord is the avenger of all that, as we told you and proved before . . . It follows that he who pays no heed to this, it is not to man he pays no heed, but to God.

This has nothing to do with commercial relations; "his own vessel" is his wife, and the affair by which he may receive injury is adultery. This advice on sexual morality, which touches the heart of the existing situation, should be compared with the studied casuistry of 1 Corinthians vii, where the same matter is dealt with. The same may be said of the counsels that follow (iv, 9–12) on the practice of fraternal love to all men, with this application:

> Make it a point of honour to lead quiet lives, to do manual work, as we advised you to do, and to deal honourably with those outside, that you may be dependent on nobody. The Great Event will come as a surprise for everybody, but those who conform to these counsels have nothing to be afraid of. Till the Coming there will be no time for sitting with arms crossed, gazing at the sky (iv, 11, 12; v, 2, 4, 6).

Corinthians

The letters to the Corinthians are, in one respect, of less importance to our present inquiry; they deal less with the Christian catechesis and more with the divisions that arose in the community, the difficulties Paul had to face and the means he took to overcome them. The first letter, written about the year 55, when Paul was on the point of leaving Ephesus, was occasioned by divisions that had recently broken out and which the apostle believed he could allay by his message and by sending Timothy. In the letter he entitles himself as "called to be an apostle of Christ Jesus by the will of God," perhaps because his standing as an apostle was being challenged. In writing to Thessa-

lonica he had claimed no title. The faithful at Corinth, like those
at Thessalonica are "waiting for the manifestation of our Lord
Jesus Christ," that is, for his second coming in his "day"—the
day when the Kingdom of God will appear. But, while there is
agreement in this matter, there are divisions in another:

> I beseech you, brethren, in the name of our Lord Jesus Christ, that
> you all make the same profession, and that there be no divisions among
> you, but that you be all united in the same feeling and the same think-
> ing. For it has been reported to me of you, my brethren, by Chloe's
> people, that there are disputes among you. I mean this: one of you
> says "I am Paul's man"; another, "I am for Apollos"; another, "I am
> for Cephas." Is Christ then divided? was it Paul who was crucified for
> you? or was Paul the name in which you were baptized?

We have already seen in what circumstances Apollos won his
position among the Corinthians (*supra*, p. 185). If there was also
a party for Cephas, it had not been created by Peter's presence in
Corinth, but by people who had doubtless come from Syria with
the story that the only genuine apostles were those of the Jerusalem communion. Paul has sent Timothy to Corinth to restore
order. Moreover he will soon come himself and, if need be, will
apply the rod to those who think too highly of themselves (iv,
17–21). He has heard of a horrible scandal; there is among them
a man "living with his father's wife; let this incestuous person
be expelled from the community" (v, 1–2, 6–7a). As to the
collection for the saints at Jerusalem, they must arrange the
matter as Paul has already done in Galatia, so that he may find
the money ready when he arrives from Macedonia, and if the
amount is important he will take their delegates with him
to Jerusalem after himself spending some time among them
(xvi, 1–9).

In the Second to Corinthians two short letters are embedded
which concern this collection, both lodged in the very middle of
the Epistle, and it may be said in passing that they are enough to
prove it a relatively late compilation; for, plainly, they were not
written at the same time. Moreover each letter has its own
subject clearly defined and was probably at first written without
connection with any other message; finally, the place they
occupy shows that they were originally attached to the group of
chapters i–vii and later, in order to simplify the transcriber's

work and get more reading substance, the group x–xiii was attached to the group i–ix, the two being apparently addressed to the same destination. The older of the letters (ix) has inadvertently been placed second.

In the older letter Paul encourages the Corinthians by saying that he has held them up as a model to the Macedonians. "In experiencing this service of yours" the saints at Jerusalem "will praise God for the submission which led you to confess the Gospel of the Christ and for the generosity of your contribution to them and to all" (ix, 13). The collection does, in fact, prove that a real fraternity was established between these young Christian communities and, further, that the "saints" of the motherchurch were held by them in respect. The second letter (viii, omitting the mystic gloss of verse 9) states that the collection in Macedonia is now completed and that the Macedonians have shown themselves generous givers; let the Corinthians, then, whose goodwill was expressed when the affair began, lose no time in giving a fitting completion to this fraternal and beneficent work, and let them respond to the efforts of Titus and of the other brethren who are gone with him to Corinth to see the business through.

Titus had first visited Corinth as peacemaker to the quarrelsome community and been successful. "You won his heart," wrote Paul (vii, 15) in a letter earlier than this second note about the collection "and the more completely when he called to mind how teachable you all were, and how you received him with fear and trembling." The fact of the matter is that Titus played the rôle of mediator, not only between Paul and the Corinthians, but also between Paul and the Jerusalem elders, and that his interest in the collection for their necessities was not unconnected with his mediating work in regard to them.

Perhaps a reminder will here be in place as to who these "saints" were and how it came to pass that they were poor. They were the men of the primitive faith, the original believers, the dauntless heroes of the Great Hope, abiding in Jerusalem and there expecting the coming of the Christ on the clouds with the Kingdom of God in his train. They were poor because they were wholly preoccupied in expectation, in waiting and waiting always. Paul himself would never have thought of bidding them, as he wrote to the Thessalonians, to work for their living and be a charge to nobody.

The First to the Corinthians has told us that there were divisions in the community. Some elements of a second letter, sad and severe in tone, written after Paul had made an attempt at Corinth to allay the mischief, which had only further inflamed it, are preserved in chapters x–xiii of our Second Epistle (x, 1*a*, *c*, 2*a*, 9–11):[1]

> I, Paul, who am humble when present with you, am bold when away from you, beg you that when I come I may not have to be bold, that I may not seem to be frightening you with letters. For his letters, they say, are severe and strong, but his bodily presence is weak and his speech of no account. Let him who says that, ponder thus: that as I speak in my letters when absent, so I will act when I come to you.

Paul goes on to defend himself against lack of sincerity in his dealings with the Corinthians. The only fault they could find with him is that of having asked them for nothing and of living among them on help sent him from Macedonia: this charge, if charge it be, he will continue to incur (xi, 6*b*–12*a*; xii, 13–15). The reproach of trickery recurs further on (xii, 16) but his reply to it has been suppressed (we need not ask why) and replaced by a reference to the collection (17–18). The author of the substitution, to whom the whole completion is also due, here makes Paul refer to what is written in our chapter ix, without perceiving that he commits an anachronism, the present letter being earlier than that which deals with the mission of Titus. Paul is now ready to come to Corinth for the third time, but fears that he will find there the same controversies and quarrels as before, and that he will have to groan over many who have been sinning of late and have not repented in the least of the unchastity, shamelessness and debauchery they have engaged in (evidently something quite different from the case of incest referred to in the first letter). He repeats that when he comes he will not mince matters, and warns his correspondents of what they may expect, in the hope that it will save him from having to go to extremes (xii, 19–xiii, 2, 10*a*). Taken realistically this evidence helps us to understand the moral situation, which seems to have improved later, though

---

[1] See *Remarques*, 54–57.

much less through Paul's message than by the subsequent intervention of Titus.

The letter of reconciliation, the third written by Paul to the Corinthians, may be extracted from the first *bloc* of the compilation (i–vii). It was written in the name of Paul and Timothy (i, 1–2). The apostle begins by describing the extreme despondency he has experienced in Asia—impossible for us to say whether it was due to some external peril or to the grief which had overwhelmed him at the thought of the condition in which he had found and left the Corinth group. But God had been pleased to deliver him from that affliction. If he has not kept the promise he made to the Corinthians to visit them again, the reason is that he was unwilling to be twice among them in a state of distress; now he is pleased with what they have decided about the man who had offended; but he waited impatiently at Troas for the return of Titus whom he had sent to Corinth on his behalf; passing through Macedonia he met Titus who told him the happy result of his mission, the sorrow of the Corinthians and their zeal for their apostle. "I rejoice," he concludes, "that in all things I can rely on you." The message is deeply impressive, though many of its details are dark to us (i, 8–11, 15–20, 23; ii, 1–13; vii, 6–16). But at least it enables us to recognize the authentic accent of Paul when it is his own voice that speaks to us. But if we are helped thereby to understand the personality of the catechist, we have to look elsewhere for the light on his catechism.

Galatians

On this point, the Epistle to the Galatians, of which the first version goes back to 55–56, will give us a little information. At least we may learn from it something of Paul's method in defending his doctrine and practice against the Judaizing emissaries who had more or less got the upper hand among his Galatian converts. He broaches the matter as follows (i, 6–7):

> I am astonished that you so quickly desert him who called you by grace, for another Gospel, which is no Gospel at all; I refer to the people who are upsetting you and trying to overthrow the Gospel of the Christ.

The people to whom he refers retain the promise of the Kingdom and profess that Jesus is the Christ, but they disturb the conscience of the believers by changing the real conditions under which the promise of the Kingdom was given. And here are the conditions (iii, 6–9, 11, 14*a*, 15–18, 19*b*):

> *Abraham believed in God, and that was counted to him as righteousness* (Genesis xv, 6). Understand, then, that men of faith are the very sons of Abraham. Scripture, foreseeing that God would deem the Gentiles righteous in virtue of their faith, predicted it to Abraham: *in thee shall all the Gentiles be blessed* (Genesis xviii, 18). So then, men of faith are blessed along with faithful Abraham[1] [   ]. That no man is deemed righteous before God by the Law is evident, *since the righteous shall live by faith* (Habakkuk ii, 4). Now the Law is not based on faith, but *who does that, by that shall he live* (Leviticus xviii, 5) [   ] so that the blessing comes at last to the Gentiles. But then, I speak in terms of human affairs: it is ever the rule that nobody treats a man's will as of no account or makes additions to it. Now it was to Abraham that the promises were made and to his posterity. God did not say to *posterities* in the plural, but to his *posterity* (Genesis xii, 7; xxii, 18) which is the Christ. Now I say this: a disposition previously ratified by God cannot be invalidated by the Law which came four hundred years later, so as to cancel the promise. For if the heritage depend on the Law it ceases to depend on the promise. Now it was in promise that God made a gift of the heritage to Abraham, until the *posterity* should arrive which the promise was concerned with[   ]. For you are all one in Christ Jesus. But if you are in Christ then are you the posterity of Abraham, heirs in virtue of the promise.

After recalling the circumstances in which he had evangelized the Galatians and saying how much he wished he were with them to enlighten them (iv, 11–20), he resumes his theme as follows (iv, 21–23, 28–31):

> Tell me, you that want to be under the Law, pay you no attention to the Law? For it is written (Genesis xvi, 15; xxi, 2, 9) that Abraham had two sons, one by a bond and the other by a free woman; but the son of the bond was born according to the flesh, but the son of the free in virtue of the promise [   ]. Now you, brethren are, like Isaac, children of the promise. But just as then the one born of flesh persecuted the other born according to Spirit, so it is to-day. But what says the Scripture? *Drive away the oondwoman and her son; for the son of the bond shall not inherit with the son of the free* (Genesis xxi, 10). Therefore, brethren, we are not children of the bond woman but of the free woman.

---

[1] The empty brackets to indicate that an interpolated passage is being omitted.

Then follows an exhortation to forsake error and return to rightmindedness.

Resumption of the Theme in the Epistle to the Romans and extraction from it of the Primitive Message

The theme is resumed, but with better logical order, in Paul's letter to the Christians in Rome, written at the beginning of the year 56, at the moment when the apostle was making his arrangements to leave Corinth for Jerusalem, whence he intended to journey to Rome. Note that the letter to the Thessalonians is addressed to "the community of the Thessalonians which is in God," etc.; those to the Corinthians "to the community of God which is at Corinth"; that to the Galatians "to the communities of Galatia"; whereas the letter to the Romans is destined "for all the beloved of God in Rome" (i, 7). Doubtless there were several Christian groups in Rome, which, without being rivals, were not yet united into a single church. In the preamble (i, 8–17) Paul states his intention and defines the theme which he desires his letter to make good:

> So, as much as in me is, I am anxious to preach the Gospel to you who are in Rome; for I am not ashamed of the Gospel. For it is the power of God for the salvation of every believer, to the Jew first, but also to the Greek. For God's righteousness is revealed in it by faith and for faith, as it is written, *whoso is righteous by faith*, shall live (Habakkuk, ii, 4).

And here is how he makes this thesis good (iii, 28–iv, 14, 16–24; iii, 27 adjusts the argument to the interpolated context; cf. ii, 17).

> We hold that a man is made completely righteous by faith without any works of the Law. Is God the God only of the Jews? Is he not also God of the Gentiles! To be sure he is God of the Gentiles, for there is only one God, who will make the circumcised righteous by faith and the uncircumcised by means of it. Are we then abolishing the Law by faith? Not in the least. We are giving the Law a firm basis.
>
> What, then, was it that Abraham, our ancestor according to the flesh, discovered for himself? For if Abraham became righteous by doing the works of the Law, he had something to be proud of, but not before God. For what says the Scripture? *Abraham had faith in God and that was imputed to him for righteousness* (Genesis xv, 6). Now the wages of a workman are not considered as a favour but as his due,

247

while to him who does no works, but has faith in him who makes the ungodly righteous, his faith is imputed to him for righteousness. In like manner David describes the blessedness of the man whom God counts as righteous without works on his part. [Here follows the citation of Psalm xxxii, 1–2.]

Was this blessedness promised to the circumcised, or to the uncircumcised as well? Again I say: *His faith was imputed to Abraham for righteousness.* How then was it imputed? To Abraham as a circumcised man? No, but when he was still uncircumcised. And he afterwards received the sign of circumcision as seal of the righteousness of faith, a righteousness won by him in his uncircumcised condition, to the end that he might be the father of the uncircumcised believers, to whom righteousness would be imputed in like manner, and father also to the circumcised, who follow in the steps of our father Abraham's faith.

The promise made to Abraham that he should inherit the world does not hold in virtue of the Law, but in virtue of the righteousness of faith. For if the followers of the Law are the heirs, their faith is of no account, and the promise given to it comes to nothing [   ]. That is why faith is the one thing that matters, so that all proceeds by favour, and the promise made secure for all posterity, not only for that which follows the Law but for that which is in the faith of Abraham, who is the father of us all, even as it is written *I have made thee father of many nations*—all this in the presence of God who makes the dead alive and calls the non-existent into being, and in whom he had faith. From his despair of posterity he passed to hoping in faith that he would become the father of *many nations*, even as God assured him, *thy offspring shall be numberless* (Genesis xiii, 16). He knew that his body was virtually dead, for he was nearly a hundred years old, and that Sarah's womb was also dead, but that did not weaken his faith in God's promise. On the contrary his faith asserted itself the more, and he was fully convinced that God was able to give him the promised posterity. And that is why it was *imputed to him for righteousness.* Now the words "imputed to him" were not written for him alone, but for us as well, according as we have faith in him who raised Jesus from the dead.

The subtilty of the argument is entirely in the Rabbinic style. But what becomes of Israel in all this? Is not Israel after all God's chosen people? Paul has his answer to the objection, and in the answer he explains the economy of salvation (ix, 1–5a, 6–13, 30–x, 21; xv, 8–12):

I speak the truth in Christ, I lie not; my conscience bearing me witness in the Holy Spirit that my sadness is great and my heartache incessant: I could wish myself under the curse of Christ for the sake of my brothers, my kinsmen in the flesh who are Israelites; theirs is the sonship, the glory, the tables of Law, the rite of worship and the promises; of them is the Christ an issue according to the flesh [   ].

Now it is not possible for the word of God to become obsolete. For Israel is not the totality of Israel's descendants; all are not children who are descended from Abraham. No; it is *through Isaac that thy posterity shall be reckoned* (Genesis xxi, 12). I mean that all children of the flesh are not children of God; only the children of the promise are counted as posterity. . . .

The case of Rebecca's twin sons is then cited. Although both were Isaac's offspring it is yet written of them: "Jacob have I loved, but Esau have I hated" (Malachi i, 2–3). Comment is as follows:

What shall we say then? We say that the Gentiles, who were aiming at righteousness, attained it, the righteousness that comes of faith; whereas Israel, who were aiming at a law of righteousness, failed to reach that law. And why? Because they sought it, not by the way of faith, but by conduct, and ran into the stone that makes men stumble, according as it is written. [Here follows citation of Isaiah viii, 14; xxviii, 16. The letter continues (x, 1).]

Brethren, my heart's desire and my prayer to God are for their salvation. I can bear witness to their zeal for God; but not a zeal enlightened by knowledge; for, in their ignorance of the righteousness of God, they failed to submit to it and sought rather to establish their own. For the end of the Law is the Christ, that everyone who believes in him may thereby become righteous. For Moses wrote of the righteousness which comes by the Law, *whoso practises that, by that shall he live* (Leviticus xviii, 5); but the righteousness which comes of faith speaks differently (Deuteronomy xxx, 12–14): *Say not in your heart: Who will go up to heaven?*—to bring the Christ down—or: *Who will go down into the abyss?*—to bring the Christ up from among the dead. No, what faith-righteousness says is this (Deuteronomy xxx, 14): *very close to thee is the word in thy mouth and in thy heart*—meaning the word "faith" which we preach. Mouth and heart mark you. For if you confess with your mouth that Jesus is Lord, and believe in your heart that God has raised him from the dead, saved you shall be. For with the heart we believe to be made righteous, and with the mouth we confess to be saved. For the Scripture says (Isaiah xxviii, 16): *Whosoever believes in him shall never be put to confusion.* There is no difference here between Jew and Greek, seeing that all have one and the same Lord, who is full of bounty to them that call on him, *for everyone who calls on him shall be saved* (Joel ii, 32). But how shall they call on a Lord in whom they have no belief? And how believe in a Lord of whom they have never heard? And how shall they hear of him without a preacher? And how shall we preach him unless we are called?—even as Isaiah writes (lii, 7): *how beautiful are the feet of him who brings good tidings.* But not all have yielded to the Gospel, even as Isaiah says (liii, 1): *Lord, who has believed our report?* So then, faith comes from preaching, and preaching by the word of the Christ. But, say I, have they not heard it? Yes, they have: *their voice has gone all over the earth and their words to the end of the world* (Psalm xix, 4). Then, I ask, have they not understood? Moses was the first to say it: *I will make you jealous of a nation that is no nation; I will provoke your pity for a nation with no understanding* (Deuteronomy xxxii, 21). Then Isaiah boldly says: *I have been found by those who did not seek me; I have revealed myself to those who question me not* (lxv, 1). And to Israel he cries: *I have held out my hands all day long to a disobedient and contradictory people* (lxv, 2).

Now I tell you [continuing with xv, 8] that the Christ has been ready to serve the circumcision by showing them God's veracity in confirming the promises made to the patriarchs and that the Gentiles glorify God by his mercy, according as it is written (Psalm xviii, 49): *Therefore I will exalt thee among the Gentiles and sing praises to thy Name.* And again he says (Deuteronomy xxxii, 43): *Rejoice, ye Gentiles, with his People.* And again (Psalm cxvii, 1): *Praise the Lord, all ye Gentiles, and let all peoples extol him.* And Isaiah once more (xi, 10): *there shall be a shoot of Jesse springing forth to rule the Gentiles: in him shall the Gentiles hope.*

At this point the fundamental thesis of the letter written by Paul to the Roman Christians comes to its natural close. The letter is no skeleton outline, but a complete exposition, well balanced and well developed, of what Paul, in the given circumstances, had to say to these Christians. The complementary matter, added by other hands to the original document, is entirely superfluous. Least of all does it need the juxtaposition[1] of a gnosis, which contradicts it at every point of its structure, nor the emollient paraphrases which try to make the gnosis fit in with the primitive teaching here revealed by Paul; nor the violent outbreak against pagans and Jewish sectaries in the opening chapters (i, 18–iii, 26); nor the moral counsels (xii–xv, 7) which are wholly foreign to its theme. We have now to examine the original conclusion of the document (xv, 14–xvi, 16, 19*a*, 20–24).

Paul declares himself persuaded that the recipients of his letter have no need of his exhortations; but, as minister of the Christ among the Gentiles, he simply desires to fortify their good dis-

---

[1] We say "juxtaposition" in opposition to certain expositors who, without taking the trouble to probe the matter, make it a case of *fusion*—the fusion of two doctrines.

positions. The truth is that the results of his ministry have been such as to justify him in a certain boldness before God and in a measure of pride in the Christ Jesus. Has he not carried the preaching of the Gospel, starting from Jerusalem, throughout the entire circuit of the Eastern Mediterranean—the statement is somewhat summary, but this was not the moment for entering into detail—and has he not done this while holding to it, "as a point of honour, to preach the Gospel only in places where the Christ's name was unknown, so as not to build on another man's foundation"? All the same, he would have come to Rome long ago, had he not been prevented. These statements should not be taken too literally; none the less there is one thing that may be deduced from them for a certainty: while the Christians of Rome were in considerable numbers, it is clear that they had not been recruited there by renowned propagandists of the new faith, nor by any one of them. They had drifted into the imperial city from various quarters, and such propaganda as they could carry on would be a private affair among individuals. Hence Paul could look upon Rome as new ground. So his intention is to establish himself in Rome for some time with a view to going later into Spain, doubtless with the idea of carrying his message to the furthest point of Western civilization. We should be in error in supposing this to mean that he thought it his mission to convert the then known world. He meant simply that he hoped to carry the name of the Christ, and the announcement that the Kingdom was at hand, to the furthest point he could reach—a simple programme joined with a great simplicity of outlook. The teaching we have just considered fits in with it perfectly.

He goes on to say that before visiting Rome, he must go to Jerusalem to deliver a collection gathered up from the believers in Macedonia and Achaia, and he asks his friends in Rome to help him with their prayers that "he may not fall into the hands of Jewish unbelievers" and that his "service for Jerusalem may prove acceptable to the saints there." Of the two conditions only the second seems to have been fulfilled.

There has been much discussion on the long list of salutations at the end of the Epistle, some critics holding, gratuitously enough, that Paul cannot have had so many personal acquaintances in Rome, and supposing, still more gratuitously, that the list refers to believers in Ephesus: as if, with Ephesus in view, Paul would not have had to salute a formed community, instead of the listed individuals such as he here cites by name. The personal salutations are satisfactorily explained as addressed to believers who belonged to groups scattered over a wide region. The conclusion of the list implies that these persons had now found their way to Rome. This conclusion should be reconstructed as follows (xvi, 16, 19a, 20–23):

> Salute each other with a holy kiss. All the churches of the Christ salute you [   ]. For your obedience has come to the knowledge of all [   ]. The God of peace will soon crush Satan under your feet, etc.

Why all the churches should salute certain Ephesian believers by the mouth of Paul is by no means clear, but that Paul should pass on to the Roman Christians the greetings of all the churches he had founded in the East is intelligible enough. Moreover what is said about the common knowledge of their obedience to faith in the Christ is in keeping with what Paul has written in the preamble of his letter (i, 8): "your faith is celebrated throughout the world." The praise bestowed by the two passages clearly concerns the same persons.

We conclude that Paul's original letter to the Romans is an unimpeachable document from which we may learn with certainty the precise form of the eschatological catechesis—the primitive teaching of the End of the World. In substance it was as follows:

> *Jesus, risen from the dead as Christ and Lord, is at God's right hand; to him and to those who believe in him belongs the "heritage of the world"; he will establish the Kingdom of God over the whole earth and annihilate the powers which have so long made it the Kingdom of Satan.*

SECOND STAGE IN THE EVOLUTION OF THE CATECHESIS

The transformation of the primitive catechesis of the Kingdom, which we have just considered, into the evangelical catechesis of salvation, followed in the steps of the transformation which changed the Christ of the imminent Coming into a divine redeemer, whose terrestrial career, a mystic epiphany more or less substituted for his lately expected epiphany on the clouds, was so conceived as to make him author of the mystery of salvation. The catechesis of Mark, the catecheses of Matthew and Luke, the catechesis of John show, in that order, the advancing steps of the transformation. But, just as it is impossible to assign a precise date to each new element, as revisers introduced it into the catechesis represented by the four canonical Gospels, so it is equally impossible to fix the dates of those gnostic and anti-gnostic elements which were interpolated into the Epistles named after Paul and into the other Epistles of the New Testament canon.

On what principles these added elements are to be distinguished from the original matter, and their significance explained, may be gathered from our former work *Remarques sur la littérature épistolaire du Nouveau Testament* (1935). In the present book, therefore, it would be superfluous to demonstrate at length what we have proved in its predecessor, namely, that if Paul be the author of the teaching we have just studied, so far as it is developed in the Epistle to the Romans, it is impossible that he be, at the same time, the author of the gnostic system interpolated between the broken fragments of that teaching, and flatly contradicting it while pretending to give it a firmer standing. Had the two expositions been lodged in the same brain they would have been fused into one, instead of appearing, as they do, at cross purposes and dislocating the Epistle. That is a psychologic and literary fact against which sentiment and theology are powerless. Let the official apologists of Catholicism repeat *ad libitum* their charge, if they can do so with straight faces, that we have misunderstood the intimate harmony of the Great Apostle's thought and are incapable of placing ourselves at its centre, since we lack the faith that was Paul's. We, on our part, know that these are words without meaning. We know also at what centre these champions of authenticity have taken *their* stand. It is the centre of accepted convention and of orders received from the Pontifical Commission on Biblical Study.

The Superadded Gnosis, not Paul's, in the Epistle to the Romans

We now proceed to examine the gnosis in Romans, taking account of variations and additions made to it in Galatians and Corinthians. The gnoses in Philippians, Colossians, Ephesians and Hebrews demand separate consideration as presented under different conditions.

In the gnosis of Romans, Israel and Abraham drop out of view, nor is the theme any longer concerned with the promises made to them, nor with the Christ who is to come, nor with faith in the Christ risen from the dead as the sole condition of admission to the approaching Kingdom of God. It is now a question of the *whole human race*, in bondage from its beginnings to sin and death, which the Christ, descended straight from heaven, has ransomed by his own death, and is now ready to share his divine immortality with all those who mystically unite themselves to his death and resurrection in the rites of Christian initiation. The essentials of this gnosis have nothing to do with promises contained in the Scriptures; they are concerned with the revelation of the mystery hidden in God till now revealed, which mystery, when occasion demands it, is expressly distinguished from the eschatological catechesis with its foundation in Scripture. Moreover, the two catecheses present marked differences of style as well as of subject-matter. While the eschatological thesis is developed almost in the language of every day, and as though the author were augmentatively conversing with his readers, not as a philosopher, but as a rabbi making good his case with a grand array of subtly interpreted Scripture texts—while this is the way of Paul's catechesis, the gnostic theme on the other hand, with its point of departure in the biblical myth of the first sin, takes form as a system of doctrine, a theory of moral philosophy with a certain measure of logical appeal. In this presentation the argument does not need a Scripture text to support each step of its advance, but bids for acceptance on its own merits in a way which suggests that the system was originally constructed independently of the Epistle into which it has been inserted. Needless to say that with this difference of subject and style there goes a different vocabulary. This will be obvious at once to anyone who will take the pains to compare the two.

Here, to begin with, is the preamble to the gnosis very cleverly inserted before the development of Paul's eschatological theme (iii, 21–24, where it will be noted 21 seems to have been first written to make sequences with i, 16–18, the whole of i, 19–iii, 20 being added later):

But the righteousness of God has now been revealed without the Law [   ]. It is a divine righteousness; but all men can win it by believing in Jesus Christ. For there is no distinction among men in this respect, since all men have sinned and fallen short of the divine glory. This righteousness is bestowed on men as a free gift of grace, thanks to the redemption effected by the Christ Jesus, whom God appointed propitiatory victim [   ] to demonstrate his righteousness, after passing over sins committed under his forbearance, and in view of the revelation of his righteousness due to come in this present time and to make it plain that he is, himself, righteous and that he deems every man who has faith in Jesus to be a righteous man.

The making of men righteous by their faith (justification of faith) is still the theme; but it is neither the righteousness, nor the faith that we encountered before. In this new presentation righteousness means liberation from the sin which has ruled the world since Adam, while faith is unwavering confidence in the redemption effected by the death of the Christ in his quality of propitiatory victim for the whole of mankind. The thesis recurs further on in passages now separated but originally forming a single *bloc*—v, 1–8, 10–vii, 6; viii, 1–9a, 10, 12–13, 23b–25, 28–35, 37–39; iv, 25 makes a forced transition.

We are first told that our hope is grounded on the fact that, while we were yet sinners, God revealed his love for us, the Christ dying on our behalf; reconciled to God by the death of his Son we too are rendered immortal by communion in the death and resurrection of the Son whom God has raised from death. This has providentially come to pass, and the way of it is as follows:

> The explanation is that sin came into the world by one man, and death by sin, and that thus all men were doomed to death because all have sinned. For there was sin in the world before the Law was given, but it was not reckoned as sin because there was as yet no Law. But death had dominion from Adam to Moses, even on those who had not sinned after the manner of Adam's transgression, and Adam is a figure of him who was to come.

In this statement there are some enormous absurdities which neither philosophers nor historians need spend time in discussing. Let us rather take up the doctrine of the two Adams, the two heads of the human race—the man, Adam the sinner who stands as the antitype of the other man, Adam the Saviour Jesus Christ.

First Corinthians (xv, 21–22, 45–47) will tell us that, of the two men, "the first is terrestrial, the second celestial"; the first, "living animal"; the second, "life-giving Spirit." The exposition goes on:

> But it is not the case that the trespass committed and the grace bestowed are in equal measure; for while all other men die in consequence of one man's trespass, the grace of God and the free gift by the grace of the one man [   ] Jesus Christ, overflowed in far greater measure to all those others. Nor is the effect on them of this free gift on an equality with the effect which followed the sin of the first sinner. For while the judgment on the one sin was a sentence of condemnation, the free gift after many sins is a sentence of acquittal. For while by one man's sin, death reigned over all mankind through him alone, all who receive the abundant gift of grace and righteousness shall reign in life by that One who is Jesus-Christ—which is a far greater thing. Go to, then: as all mankind was condemned for a single act of sin, so, by a single righteous act, justification for life became available to all. For, as by the disobedience of one man all the other men in the world were made sinners, so by the obedience of One, they are all made righteous. The Law was introduced in order that sin might abound; but where sin abounded grace abounded still more, so that, just as sin formerly reigned by death, grace now reigned by righteousness to eternal life by Jesus Christ our Lord.

If anyone choose to believe that this wholly abstract, scholastic and false conception of the Law was imagined and professed by a man who had long lived in obedience to the Law, we shall not pause to argue with him. The writer continues:

> What are we to infer from this? Shall we remain in sin that grace may abound? . . . Have you forgotten that all of us have been baptized into Christ and, in that, are baptized into his *death*. This means that we have been buried with him by baptism unto death, so that, just as Christ was raised from death by the glory of the Father, we also are to walk in newness of life. For, if we are associated in his death by this symbol, we are equally associated in his resurrection, knowing, as we do, that our old man has been crucified with him, that the sinful body might be destroyed. . . .

In the same sense the Epistle to the Galatians understands the Christian as a "new creation" (vi, 15); the Second to Corinthians has a like conception (v, 17). The writer proceeds:

> Thus there is no condemnation now for those who are in Christ Jesus, for the law of spirit of life in Christ Jesus has delivered thee from the law of sin and death. For God [   ] having sent his own

Son in the semblance of sinful flesh, and because of sin, has condemned sin in the flesh, so that the righteousness of the Law is fulfilled in us who walk not according to flesh but according to spirit. . . .

For I reckon that the sufferings of the present time are not to be compared with the glory due to be revealed in us. For the eager creation longs for the manifestation of the sons of God. For futility has been imposed on the creation, not of its own will, but by the will of him who imposed it, with the hope that the creation itself, as well as ourselves, will be delivered from slavery to corruption, that it too may share the liberty of the glory of the children of God. For we know that the whole creation is united in suffering and cries of pain till now; and not the creation only but [   ] we ourselves inwardly cry with pain as we wait for filiation, for deliverance from our body; for it is in hope that we are saved. . . .

But we know that to those who love God everything converges to good, to those called according to plan, because those whom he foresaw, them he predestined to be conformed to the image of his Son, that he might be first born among many brothers. Now, whom he predestined, them also he called. Whom he called, them also he deemed righteous, whom he deemed righteous them also he glorified. What, then, shall we say to that? If God is for us, who will be against us? . . . Who shall separate us from the love of Christ? For I am persuaded that neither life nor death, nor angels, nor principalities, nor present, nor future, nor powers, nor any other created thing can separate us from the love of God which is in Christ Jesus, our Lord.

A noble theory, conceived by an impassioned soul. And something more. We have here a gnosis sketched in grand outline, but an outline that needs to be filled. For the part played by the Law is strangely lowered. Opposed to the triad Law—sin—death stands the triad grace—righteousness—immortality. What can the Law be, then, but the auxiliary of sin? Moreover, one sacrament only is thrown into relief—baptism. But palliations are introduced, notably the short dissertation on the inner conflict that arises between the consciousness of duty and the carnal lusts; by this the opposition between the Law and grace, shifted from the ground of abstract theology to the ground of moral philosophy, becomes the opposition of natural desire and spirit, the Law itself becoming "the oldness of the letter" which gives place to "the newness of spirit."

The Gnosis Developed in Second Corinthians

The same point of view, in which the Law regains a significant and positive rôle in the scheme of salvation, is resumed

257

and developed at length by the author of certain mystical passages in Second Corinthians (ii, 14–vi, 13). In the extracts we propose to give from this Epistle, Paul the mystic, who is effaced behind his subject in Romans, advances into the foreground:

> Our ability comes from God, who himself has made us able ministers of the new covenant, not of the letter, but of the spirit. For the letter kills, but the spirit makes alive.

The letter is the Law, and the letter kills if we remain confined within it; rightly understood, then, the ministry of the Law is here, in Second Corinthians, a ministry of death, as we find it in Romans. None the less the Law can lead on to the spiritual gnosis, to the true Gospel of the Christ, playing the part of "pedagogue" (Galatians iii, 21–25). We take up the sequence of our text (2 Corinthians iii, 7):

> Now if the ministry of death, in letters graven on stones, shone with such splendour that the children of Israel could not look on Moses' face on account of the passing splendour of it, how much more glorious will be the ministration of the spirit! For if the ministration was glorious when it condemned to death, the ministration which justifies vastly excels it in splendour. Indeed the former splendour was no splendour at all compared with this higher. For, if that which was passing away shone with splendour, how much more glorious shall that shine which will never pass away.
>
> Having such a hope in me, I use no disguises; I am not like Moses, who veiled his face that the children of Israel might not see the passing splendour on it. Ah, but their intelligence was blinded; for, indeed, to this very day the same veil hangs unlifted over the reading out of the Old Covenant, for the Christ alone can take it away; yes, to this very day, when Moses is read, the veil falls on their hearts. *But the veil is lifted from the moment they turn to the Lord* (Exodus xxxiv, 34).

The author repeats himself a little, unless the phrases headed by the words "to this very day" are textual variants. But, whichever hypothesis we prefer, the meaning remains the same. We may well ask whether the recruits Paul had gathered in Corinth would have understood a single word of these subtleties. It is true that here the Mosaic revelation counts for something as having a figurative sense; but to what a distance are we now come from Paul's eschatology with its climax in the second coming of the Lord! However, a great advance has been made by admitting the co-ordination of the two Covenants, of which the gnosis in the Epistle to the Romans gives no sign. But here is the conclusion of our passage:

> Now the Lord is the spirit, and where the spirit of the Lord is, there is liberty. And all of us, with faces uncovered, reflecting the splendour of the Lord, are ourselves transformed into the same image from one splendour to another, the splendour that comes from the Lord, from the spirit.

Ancient Scripture, then, is a figurative enigma, in which the gnostic Christian may read his participation in the splendour of the Christ-Spirit. A kind of mystic vision in which the initiate into a Mystery finally sees himself clothed with the splendour of his God.

The ministry of him whose mission it is to proclaim such a Gospel is unique:

> By manifestation of the truth I commend myself to every man's conscience before God. And what if my Gospel is veiled? Veiled it may be, but only among the lost, there where the god of this age has blinded the minds of the unbelieving, that they see not the light of the Gospel of the splendour of the Christ, who is the image of God.

"The god of this age" is the chief archon who presides, with such indifferent success, over the destiny of our world and the present age (compare "the princes of this age" in 1 Corinthians ii, 8; "the prince of this world" in John xii, 31; xiv, 30; xvi, 11). He may be Satan, but certainly not Marcion's demiurge. As to "the lost" and "the unbelieving," they are not unbelievers in the general doctrines of theology, but those whom the mystic Paul regards as the adversaries of his own doctrine, and whom he treats as Judaizers.

> It is not myself that I preach, but Christ Jesus and myself your servant for Jesus.

Following this (iv, 7–15) comes a dithyrambic eulogy of the special apostolate claimed by this mystic Paul, who has also much to say about himself in the Epistle to the Galatians (see our *Remarques sur la littérature épistolaire*, 33–45, 50–57). We do not propose to repeat here what we have said in that work about the inconceivable pretensions there put forward by the mystic Paul, nor to discuss again the accusations brought by this Paul, Paul only in name, against his straw-made Judaizers, the question seeming to us sufficiently elucidated in the former discussion. To proceed:

> Though my outward man is wearing out, my inner man is renewing itself from day to day; for my light affliction of the moment is preparing me for a plenitude of eternal splendour beyond all conceiving, my gaze being turned not to things visible, but to things invisible; for the visible pass away, but the invisible are for eternity. Indeed know I well that, if the earthly tent I dwell in were to melt away, I have a home from God, a house not made with hands, eternal, in the heavens. . . . Being, then, of good heart, and knowing that while at home in the body I am an exile from the Lord—for I walk by faith in him, not by sight of him—I have no fears, and would rather be an exile from the body and at home with the Lord.

The purely spiritual idea of the resurrection contained in this passage is unmistakable and needs no insistence. How near it brings us to the Song of Love in 1 Corinthians xiii! But how far it takes us from the eschatological catechesis of the real Paul!

> Love of the Christ holds me, my conviction being this: that One having died on behalf of all, all are then dead; and he died for all, that the living should live no more for themselves, but for him who died on their behalf and rose from death. The result is that from henceforth I, for my part, know no man according to the flesh. Even had I known the Christ according to the flesh, I would not now know him in that way. To tell the truth, if any one is in the Christ, he is a new creature; old things have passed away; see, they have become new!

We can hardly hide from ourselves that this mystic notion of salvation was conceived with the eschatological catechesis in mind, perhaps even with an eye to the evangelical catechesis, as the Synopsis presents it in substance. Nor can we fail to see that, on this theory, the Christ of flesh in his human life counts for very little, or even for nothing at all, in comparison with the Christ-Spirit in his immortality. That the intention of it all is to depreciate the Christ of the so-called Judaizers, that is the Christ of the common tradition, is almost equally evident. But what prevailed in the long run was not this uncompromising mysticism. The author goes on:

> But all this comes from God, who has reconciled me to himself through the Christ and given me the ministry of reconciliation. Because God was in the Christ, reconciling the world to

himself, not holding men guilty of their transgressions, and im-
planting in men the message of reconciliation. So, then, I am an
ambassador for the Christ, as if God were preaching with my
voice. Be reconciled to God! On behalf of Christ I so entreat you!
Him who knew not sin, he made to be sin on our behalf, that we
poor men may become God's own righteousness in him.   Following his leading in all that, I thus exhort you not to receive the
grace of God in vain.

Here we come back into the current of the mystic doctrine
already encountered in the Epistle to the Romans, but with a
marked difference in the emphasis now laid on the unique rôle
attributed to Paul in the economy of salvation, in which he is
represented as the accredited ambassador of God to the human
race. A purely theoretic conception, if ever there was one, and
formed at a great distance from the first Christian age; the more
plainly so as the system of gnosis here presented is visibly of
later date than even the gnosis in Romans, of which, in certain
respects, it offers an attenuation.

The Eucharist Finds its Place in the Mystery

In all we have had under review no sign has appeared that the
eucharistic Supper had any place in the mystery of salvation.
Perhaps its place was not defined as early as that of baptism.
Or is it not more likely that it was held secret? Does not the
fourth Gospel strictly avoid speaking of it in direct language,
and is there not a like reserve in the Epistle to the Hebrews? We
find it, however, in certain secondary parts of the gnosis presented in First Corinthians; and first of all in the account of the
normal course of the Supper (xi, 17, 20–34. See *Remarques*,
60–64):

> For I myself have had it passed on to me from the Lord, and have
> passed it on to you, that the Lord Jesus, in the night when he was
> betrayed, took bread and, after thanksgiving, broke it and said: "This
> is my body, which is given for you. Do this in remembrance of
> me." Likewise, after the meal, the cup, saying: "This cup is the new
> Covenant in my blood. Do this, whenever you shall drink it, in
> remembrance of me." For every time you eat this bread and drink
> this cup you proclaim the death of the Lord, until the time when he
> comes.

The first point to be noticed in the above passage is that the author has the evangelical catechesis in mind and that he intends his mystic doctrine of the Supper to be set in a frame which by this time had become traditional, that, namely, of the early eschatological view of the Supper, which conceived it as a memorial meal symbolic of the Christ to come, and as a fore-taste of the banquet of the elect in the Kingdom of God. In this way the meaning of the concluding formula, "you proclaim the death of the Lord, till the time when he comes," is explained. In like manner we can understand the double meaning involved in the mode of presentation, which exhibits the author as having received from the Lord himself a "tradition" either ignored or forgotten by the Corinthians. He presents the Supper as a tradition, which it really was from its origin, and at the same time fixes the meaning he desires it to have as a mystery, while affecting merely to recall it. Doubtless he found both the bread and the cup, with another commentary, in the story he is here exploiting, and the mention of the Great Coming, is also taken from that source. There is ground for saying, then, that by a kind of compromise between later gnosis and primitive eschatology he has introduced his mystic interpretation of Jesus' last meal into the earlier frame of the eschatological view of the Supper. It follows that this compromise is less ancient than the gnosis we have just considered. It seems, however, to be earlier than Marcion; and the testimony of Justin, who found this very compromise introduced into the synoptic Gospels, attests its relative antiquity (compare our analysis of the story in Mark, *supra*, p. 100).

Another fragment of First Corinthians is presented under similar conditions—the instruction on eating meat sacrificed to idols (x, 1–22), in which the sacraments of Christian initiation are both mentioned. The author appeals to the sacraments of the desert as a type of the Christian sacraments. The chief interest for us of this curious passage lies in its making of baptism and the eucharist the two parts of one sacrament, so connected that they can be found combined in the Old Testament, which is the last place in the world where one would expect to find them; for the rest, the homiletical character of the passage is made obvious in the moral lesson it is chiefly intended to convey. The comparison would also suggest a form of the sacrament in which water was used instead of wine; but we have discussed that elsewhere (see *The Birth of the Christian Religion*, p. 238, and *Remarques*, 65, n. 2). Let us rather consider the relations which the passage institutes between the Christian Supper and the pagan sacrifice:

> The cup of blessing which we bless, is not that communion in the blood of the Christ? The bread which we break, is not that communion in the body of the Christ? Because, though we are many, there is only one bread, only one body; for we all partake of the one bread.

This communion with the Christ is pronounced incompatible with participation in the sacrifices of the pagan religions, even though the meat offered to idols is only meat and the idols themselves nothing at all. But, behind the meat which is only meat and the idol which is nothing, there are the demons, and they are to be reckoned with:

> What the pagans sacrifice, to the demons they sacrifice it and not to God; and I would not have you in communion with demons. You cannot drink the cup of the Lord and the cup of demons; you cannot share the Lord's table and the demons' table. What! shall we provoke the Lord to jealousy? Are we stronger than he?

The Christian has communion with his Lord in the Supper because the Supper mystically realizes the death of Jesus and brings it into spiritual operation. In this we get a clear perception of the idea which the Christian mystery formed of its Christ and see, at the same time, the fundamental affinity between the Christian and the pagan mysteries in their conception of eternal salvation. Another passage of the same Epistle (viii, 4–6) on the question of idol-meat puts the matter beyond all doubt:

> About the eating of idol-meats, we know that no idol exists in the world and that there is no God but ours. There may be so-called gods either in heaven or on earth, but, for us, there is only one God, the Father, the source of everything and for whom we exist, and our Lord, Jesus Christ by whom all exists and we exist.

So, then, there is only one God and one Lord, but the universe harbours lesser powers, more or less dangerous, against whose influence we need to protect ourselves. The fundamental ideas of this Christian gnosis are not far removed from those of pagan mysticism current at the same time.

The Christological Gnosis in Philippians, Colossians and Hebrews

More precise definition of the Christological gnosis is to be found in the short poem picked up by the Epistle to the Philippians (ii, 6–11); in the Epistle to the Colossians (i, 15–20) and in the Epistle to the Hebrews (i, 1–4). On this we confine ourselves to summarizing the conclusions reached in our *Remarques*.

The poem inserted into the gnostic-moral part of Philippians (see *Remarques*, 91–95) is the oracle of some Christian prophet, a Christian gnosis earlier than its context in the Epistle, certainly earlier than the gnosis in Hebrews, but probably not earlier than the mystic gnosis of the great Epistles. It conveys the following information.

There existed a being in godlike form, not God himself but a sharer in the divine splendour and under the orders of the Deity. Merit is ascribed to him for not affecting equality with God— which implies that other beings of the same order had the insolence to put themselves forward as gods and to get themselves worshipped as such. The being in question put off his godlike form to take human form and, in that form, to submit to death in obedience to God; in recompense for that obedience he has been elevated to God's right hand, where he is worshipped as *Lord* and carries that name. Behind this profession of faith in one only God, and in the kind of shared divinity bestowed on Jesus, there lies a cosmology, a world-economy, a doctrine of salvation, consisting in the restoration of the cosmic and human economy which has been thrown into disorder by the backsliding of mankind and by the fall or failure in duty of certain powers. This background of the poem is purely gnostic. We see it only in glimpses; enough to conjecture its general form but not to reconstitute in all its parts.

A christological poem has been similarly inserted into the Epistle to the Colossians. This, too, is the oracle of a Christian prophet inserted as an afterthought into the Epistle, which is in no sense whatever the work of Paul (see *Remarques*, 95–101). The cosmogony is different from that in Philippians, and there is another conception of the divine mediator, a deeper gnosis and probably of later date. Here he is the image of God, living and active, in whom and by whom (so says the second strophe of the poem) the universal balance is to be restored after an overthrow of which we are not told the circumstances. The soteriology is less clearly outlined than in the poem of Philippians. Nevertheless it is made clear that "the first born of all creation" has now become "the first born of the dead"; he has become so by making himself man, undergoing death as man, and by rising from the dead as the first born of the risen: by the power of this saving death the divine order, "the Pleroma," which has been shattered, will be restored. We are told in the body of the Epistle (ii, 14–15) that the Christ has "brought us all to life with him, having wiped out the writing against us (the Law), with the clauses that condemned us; he has taken them away by nailing them to the cross; having despoiled the Principalities and the Powers, he has put them to shame, triumphing over them by his own might." The "Pleroma" is a gnostic term which should be taken here in the sense given it by the gnosis, that is, as the totality of all divine emanations and creations. The restoration of this Pleroma in the Christ implies reconciliation with God. As to the "body" of this divine redeemer, we are told further on (ii, 9) that "the entire Pleroma of Divinity resides *bodily* (that is, in the manner of body) in the Christ; thus the "body" and "the Church" are not confined to the believing part of humanity and to the church on earth, but comprise the body of the now balanced universe and the Church whose members are worlds, as the author of the Epistle to the Ephesians (i, 19–23) also understands them. With this meaning we are told (Colossians ii, 10) that the faithful are "pleromed"[1] in the Christ. All that is pure gnosis, if gnosis is to be found anywhere; but not the same gnosis as that of the poem in Philippians. As regards the diversity of gnoses which have found their way into the Epistles, the writer of the present book is altogether innocent; he is not their inventor; he merely endeavours to understand them, but without attributing them, in spite of their manifest diversity, to Paul as the sole author of them all.

---

[1] "Complete in him" (A.V.); "made full" (R.V.); "reach your full life" (Moffatt); *pleromés* in the French. *Translator's note.*

The Christ-gnosis in Hebrews

Another gnostic definition of the Christ is given in the Epistle to the Hebrews. This gnosis is more deeply studied than the preceding and the author takes greater pains to exhibit the Christian revelation as the consummation of those which God made "to the fathers by the prophets." But here also the Son is an image, an imprint of Divinity, an agent in creation by whom God made "the worlds." The text says "the aeons," which are neither "the age" nor "the worlds," but the series of existences in their harmonious hierarchy and time-order (cf. xi, 3). The author insists that the Son of God is higher than the angels in name, status and nature, the reason for his insistence being that he knows of people who class, or seem to class, the pre-existent Christ in one category with the celestial spirits called angels; is not that pretty much the case with the good Hermas? And might we not, with no great difficulty, interpret the christological poem of Philippians in the same sense? For the rest, the body of the Epistle is mainly occupied in explaining how "purification from sin" is effected, the Son of God having come to earth in order to accomplish, by his death and the offering of his blood, an act of priestly expiation, of which Melchizedek of old was the type.

The author understands the statement about Melchizedek (Genesis xiv, 17–20) in a way of his own (see *Remarques*, 108–109). The Christ, besides being the true "king of justice" and the true "king of peace," is an eternal priest after the order of Melchizedek. He has come into the world to accomplish a priestly and redeeming work; he is "without father" and "without mother"; therefore "without genealogy" and so "without beginning of days," for he pre-existed his earthly manifestation; nor has his life an ending, because his death began his immortality without any waiting in the tomb, or rising of his body, for he entered the heavenly sanctuary at once and for all "through the veil, that is, through his flesh" (x, 20). Thus he would have us understand the miracle of the rent veil in the synoptic tradition of Mark, Matthew and Luke. This again is gnosis, embroidered on a groundwork of Biblical texts, but genuine gnosis, though linked with the revelations of the Old Covenant.

Moreover, the author himself is at pains to inform us that we are in the realm of gnosis, and the point merits consideration (v, 11–vi, 2). The doctrine he expounds belongs, he says, to the order of "perfection," that is, of gnostic initiation, and this he distinguishes from what he calls "the elementary theme of the Christ," meaning the common catechesis of his time and place. This catechesis, as we have already shown (p. 43), was still almost entirely eschatological in its teaching.

The comparison of his readers to little children, whose normal nourishment was the milk of this elementary doctrine, shows that he knew the analogous remark of the mystic "Paul" who in First Corinthians (iii, 1–3) employs this same comparison, informing his readers that, because they are incapable of receiving it, he has withheld from them the wisdom which, in the self-same context, he nevertheless expounds for their instruction. In both cases the contradiction arises in the same way. It comes from the fact that the primitive catechesis, under the lapse of time and the evolution of ideas, had come to seem more or less obsolete and that pains were being taken by new teachers to comment and correct it in the light of a teaching with another character. So strange a perspective allows no other explanation, though many commentators, even critics, are still loth to perceive it.

The Gnosis in the First Epistle of Timothy and the First of Peter

The short Christological creed, rhythmically formulated, in 1 Timothy iii, 16 must here be mentioned: it is perceptibly older than its context (see *Remarques* 118–119):

> He was manifested in the flesh,
> he was vindicated in the spirit;
> He was seen by the angels,
> he was preached among the Gentiles;
> He was believed on in the world,
> he was taken up into glory.

This poem has the same character as those in the Epistles to the Philippians, Colossians and Hebrews, and the same spiritual idea of the resurrection, by which the Christ is "vindicated," the glory of his immortality making good the ignominy of his death.

The First Epistle of Peter is inspired by an analogous doctrine, but the author adds to it on his own responsibility a descent into hell, in which the mystic gnosis is coloured by a touch of pagan mythology (iii, 18–22; iv, 6; see *Remarques*, 120–131). Both gnosis and style begin to show signs of decay; both are derivative in their relation to most of the gnoses previously considered.

The romance of the descent into hell is borrowed from the Book of Enoch and mediately from old Eastern mythologies. The "spirits that were in prison" are the fallen angels who, mating with women, produced the giants and provoked the punishment of the Deluge. To these fallen spirits the Christ-Spirit goes with the good news; they are the first to submit to the immortal Christ, the other celestial powers being conquered by his ascent into heaven, as these others are by his descent into hell. The preaching of the Gospel to the general mass of the dead was accomplished by the Christ himself on the occasion of his instructing the fallen angels. Thus all who lived on earth before the coming of the Christ have had their chance of salvation; condemned to death as "men of the flesh" and as punishment for their sins, the grace of God has enabled them to live again in spiritual glory. It would seem, then, that this author knew only of a spiritual resurrection, whether for the Christ himself or for the human believer.

Moral Teaching in the Epistles

All our Epistles are more or less weighted with moral teaching. The earlier Gospel catechesis had its own, as the preaching of Jesus had, and that from the very first. *"Repent*, for the Kingdom of God is at hand" is an urgent appeal for a change of life. But it will be more in keeping with our present purpose to point out briefly how the interest taken by the mystic teaching of the Epistles in the moralization of life extends progressively over wider fields in proportion as excitement about the Second Coming passed into decline, and even, with many, to the point of extinction. Hence the insistence with which the moral renewal, implied in the spiritual and mystic rebirth of the believer, is brought to the front; hence, too, the production of short codes of religious morality, clearly such, for the individual, for the family and for social relationships. The last chapters of the Epistle to the Romans are thus occupied (xii–xv, 7), in which we may note especially the surcharge, out of relation to its context, recommending obedience to established powers, because they come from God (xiii, 1–7)—certainly this proclamation of the divine origin of the imperial powers does not belong to the first Christian age (see *Remarques*, 30–31). Some parts of First Corinthians are short treatises on moral discipline, or even of casuistry, such as the instructions about marriage and virginity (vii). The teaching on spiritual gifts (charismata), which concern the right ordering of Christian assemblies (xii, xiv) appears under like conditions, but with this striking difference, that the interpolation in its midst of the Song of Love (xiii) is on an infinitely higher level than the disciplinary matter which the singer of it had before him and into which he or somebody else thought the hymn might be fittingly inserted (see *Remarques*, 69–74). The instructions on the control of "speaking with tongues" (glossolaly) may be placed side by side with the queer little dissertation on the veiling of women (xi, 5–16) while praying or prophesying, and we may recall the more recent interpolations which forbid them to speak at all (xiv, 34*a*–35; cf. 1 Timothy ii, 8–15).

The Epistle to the Galatians contains instruction in mystic morality conceived in the same spirit as the distinctively gnostic passages (v, 13–26; vi, 7–10, 12–16). The Epistle to the Colossians, taken, as a whole, is a moralizing gnosis, but it includes special precepts for wives, husbands, children, fathers, slaves and masters. The Epistle to the Ephesians is in the same case, except that it waters down the moralities of Colossians. Finally, the First of Peter is a mystico-moral homily with special applications; respect for established authority (probably imitated from Romans xiii, 1–7); advice to slaves, wives, husbands, and encouragement to martyrs. In the last we are told that to suffer for the name of Christ and as a good Christian is a thing of little moment, provided one has not to suffer for crime of the common order (iv, 12–19). But the counsels which the author addresses to the leaders of the Christian flock, where the Christ is characterized as the chief shepherd, place him in the time of the Pastoral Epistles, although, unlike them, he makes no allusion to the gnostic peril.

DELAY OF THE SECOND COMING: ANXIETY AND APPEASEMENT

Would Christianity have survived if it had not been supported by faith in the imminent coming of God's Kingdom and the parousia of the Lord Jesus? The question is idle in view of what happened. There is no doubt that the minds of thoughtful Christians were early preoccupied, as was natural, with the delay of the Lord's Second Coming. Reasons for the delay were found; but the fact is that, in the end, such reasons ceased to be sought for, because, without dismissing the Christian hope in its primitive form, it became modified and softened down in a way to render the delay no longer tormenting. But that was the work of long centuries which lie outside the scope of the present history. What does lie within our scope is to show how the expectation of the Second Coming was soon reduced, from its first fever-heat, by faith in the invisible presence and help, here and now, of the immortal Christ. Moreover, a consciousness more intimate and more profoundly mystical was soon grafted on to this. It was the consciousness of everlasting union, begun in the present life, with the Christ of the mystery. The sensitive consciousness of Christ's life in his Church and in each soul that belonged to him had the effect, in the end, of virtually neutralizing the anxious expectancy in which the first believers waited for the resurrection of the dead and the coming of the Kingdom, but without destroying belief in either.

The Second Epistle to the Thessalonians gives the impression of a real disquietude about the matter. The chief object of this Epistle is the short dissertation (ii, 1–12) on the delay of the Lord's arrival and the manifestation of a person whom we may call Antichrist, though in reality he was a false Jewish Messiah, probably Barkochba (see *Remarques*, 89–91). The delay in the fulfilment of prophecy was to be of brief duration and the Lord would arrive in the very near future. But although the prophecy remained unfulfilled this apocryphal Epistle was not compromised on that account: Marcion himself kept a place for it in his collection, and that very shortly after it appeared. It should not be overlooked that the author, who seems to have been a man full of common sense, gives his readers some excellent advice on the necessity of daily work, imitated from an authentic part of the First Epistle (iv, 11, 12). We may conclude, then, that while faith was apt to grow anxious about the Second Coming, there was no great difficulty in reassuring it, even at this early date.

A broader explanation of the delay is offered in a secondary fragment of the Epistle to the Romans (xi) where the question is discussed whether the reprobation of the Jews is final or temporary. Their reprobation is declared to be provisional, the hardening of the Israelite majority having been providentially arranged to give time for the accession of the pagans. That achieved, Israel will be reconciled and the resurrection of the dead, the Great Event, will follow. And here the author of the explanation breaks out in admiration of the "depth" of the divine wisdom. Note the perceptible intercalation of the same idea in the synoptic apocalypse (Mark xiii, 10; Matthew xxiv, 14 where it is added "and then will come the end"; Luke xxi, 24 touching "the times of the Gentiles" represents a different idea).

The conflict, more or less open, between the mystical conception of salvation and the teaching on the coming End is clearly portrayed in the gnostic Epistles attributed to Paul, where eschatological Christianity is directly attacked as Judaizing error; on the other side, the letters of the Christ to the Seven Churches in the Book of Revelation denounce the disciples of the gnostic Paul as false Christians and a danger to the true faith (see *Remarques*, 141–146). The conflict ended in a compromise, but not till after much wrangling.

The substitution of mystical Christianity for its eschatological predecessor might be described as discreetly effected by the mystical "Paul" of the Epistles and the author of Hebrews; but the change was not effected in the faith of the churches as the two writers conceived it. The First Epistle of Peter would belong to the same category, except that the author is not fully conscious of his gnosticism. Nevertheless certain exaggerated forms of the gnosis, so outrageous that they had to be treated as heretical, had the effect of producing some reaction to the eschatological cause. The place of some of the Epistles in the evolution of this conflict and its final solution is not otherwise easily determined.

The Epistle of James is a strange specimen of moral teaching combined with the minimum, not of gnosis only, but of eschatology. The author devotes a free, but not violent criticism to the theory of salvation by faith without works, which he refutes by exegetical means similar to that employed by Paul in constructing the doctrine. There is nothing to show that he was referring to the other, the mystical, theory of salvation to be found in the Epistle to the Romans as it has come down to us. While he was not ignorant in the matter, his incomprehension of it is such as to be equivalent to radical hostility. What is most interesting in his case is the cavalier way in which he criticizes the doctrine, as though it were a mischievous opinion of no great importance, the mere mention of which was enough to condemn it. In the history of Christian literature this Epistle belongs to the precanonical age of the New Testament when the writings attributed to Paul were not considered as in any sense authoritative, or worthy to be placed on the same level as the Scriptures of the Old Covenant.

The Pastoral Epistles to Timothy and to Peter

The three Epistles known as Pastoral have all the same object —the institution of a system of government which will put the churches in a posture for effective resistance to the attacks of dangerous innovators.

To understand this effort of resistance it will be helpful to go back at this point to a passage in Acts (xx, 18–35) which has the same object; we refer to the discourse which Paul is supposed to have addressed to the elders of Ephesus whom he had summoned to Miletus apparently to receive his final instructions, and which commentators have described as a model of pastoral theology. And indeed, the discourse, though apocryphal, is an outstandingly fine piece of its kind and for us highly instructive, since it was composed in full view of the gnostic crisis in the second quarter of the second century, and in the same spirit as our three Pastoral Epistles. The Apostle begins by recalling his own devoted activity, more or less in imitation of the gnostic "Paul." He foresees the fate in store for him at the end of his journey to Jerusalem and declares himself ready to sacrifice his life. Here are his admonitions:

> Take heed to yourselves and to all the flock in which the holy Spirit has made you bishops to feed the Lord's church, which he has purchased with his blood.

This carries us forward to a time much later than Paul's meeting with the elders who came to bring him a collection made in Asia for the Jerusalem saints. The churches have their appointed heads, elders or supervisors, priests or bishops, placed by God's will and the Christ's in authority over the flock now threatened by destructive propaganda:

> I know well that after my departure grievous wolves will come, not sparing the flock, and that even from among yourselves men will arise with perverse speech in their mouths, to draw away disciples after them. Therefore watch, remembering that for three years, night and day, I ceased not to exhort every one with tears. . . .

He concludes by recalling the virtues in which he has set them an example. Who were the heretics here aimed at in particular? Gnostics, surely, in the second quarter of the second century. But which? And where was this discourse composed? If in Asia, who would be the heretics whom the author describes as rising up "even from among yourselves" of the Asiatic churches? And of these who was more dangerous between 130 and 140 than Marcion? At all events we here come into contact with the very theme with which the writers of pseudo-apostolic letters, and the Pastorals in the first place, were continually occupied about the same time.

Our three Pastoral Epistles are so closely related that a common origin is quite possible and, were their literary composition homogeneous, their date would be easily determined. A glance at the conclusion of the First to Timothy (vi, 20–21), where the *Antitheses* of Marcion are aimed at under their proper name, would be enough to settle the matter. Moreover, Marcion knew only ten Epistles of Paul's; had the Pastorals in 140 figured in the collection of the Apostle's letters Marcion would certainly have retained them. But the first draft of the Epistles may be contemporary with the outburst of Marcionism.

Having made elsewhere a detailed analysis of these documents (*Remarques*, 114–126) we shall here confine ourselves to two points in the First to Timothy: the instruction to pray for persons in authority and for the emperor in particular (ii, 1–3) and, yet more important, the regulations laid down for the choice of bishops and deacons (iii, 1–6).

The episcopal function is regarded as of great importance (iii, 1–7). The qualities enumerated in detail as requisite for the office are, in one part, such as would be demanded in a high functionary of the temporal order. This gives a clue to the date, and the fact that the bishop is spoken of in the singular is to the same effect. To be sure, he is not expressly distinguished from the priest (elder), but it is pretty plain that, while the episcopate is not yet fully monarchical, it is nearly so. And the rules laid down are not solely for the man to be elected; they are equally for his electors. The same is true of what is said about deacons, who are mentioned in the plural, since their number is to be proportioned to the size and the needs of the church. The deacons, or "ministers" (iii, 8–13), whose business is concerned with external order and material needs, must possess qualities analogous to those demanded in a bishop. Care is taken to specify the virtues needed in their wives, and it is obvious that these same virtues are indispensable, and for stronger reasons, in the wife of the bishop. There is also a discipline for widows of whom a certain number, wisely selected, are well fitted to serve the community (v, 3, 5–7, 15; it would seem that v, 4, 8–14, 16 is a complementary surcharge).

The advice given to Timothy presumably implies that he is a kind of archbishop presiding over the organization of all the churches (iii, 14–15; iv, 6; v, 1–2; vi, 3–5, 8–14, 16). Note how in these instructions, which belong to the first draft of the letter, the obligation is stressed to guard the words of faith and good doctrine, to turn a deaf ear to "impious fables and old wives' tales" and to reprove the man "who teaches a strange doctrine and is not devoted to the wholesome words of our Lord Jesus Christ; conceited sect-makers who delight in vain arguments and see in religion a means of making money." (He would be indeed a bold man who maintained that such a sample of gnosis came from Paul.) Have done with novelties; there is a fixed deposit; a doctrine of faith; an orthodoxy; so we must have a rule of faith, a discipline for conduct, and there must be men in authority to compel the observance of what is prescribed. There is no getting away from the fact that the spiritual atmosphere of all this is wholly different from that of the oldest Epistles. Nascent orthodoxy, indeed, is already summed up in a profession of faith (ii, 5–6; v, 21). The brevity of v, 21 is highly significant: "I adjure thee before God, Christ Jesus and the elect angels"—note this trinity—"to obey the rules without prejudice, doing nothing in partiality." With this goes violent denunciation of indiscipline, gnostic or otherwise. The denunciation, however, is made here in terms too general to permit our identifying the persons aimed at.

A more precise denunciation, but surely of later date, is that which some reviser has joined on to the short Christological poem quoted above ("he was manifest in the flesh," etc. (iv, 1–5), see p. 267). The denunciation is given as a revelation of the Spirit (iv, 1). The formula of introduction, "the Spirit says," may strike us at first as strange, but is unquestionably in the same class as that found in the Apocalypse (ii, 7, 11, 17, 29; iii, 6, 13, 22): "He that has an ear let him hear what the Spirit says to the churches." The Spirit and the Christ are two names for the same (cf. 2 Thessalonians ii, 2 and especially 2 Corinthians iii, 17). The Christian prophets, as they uttered their oracles at the bidding of the Spirit, were speaking in the name of the immortal Christ. Now there can be no doubt that in the passage before us the Spirit is aiming at Marcion and his adepts, who prohibited marriage and abstained from certain foods precisely as here described, while they attributed the creation of the visible world, not to the supreme God, but to an inferior deity. The text before us thus falls into line with the explicit denunciation of Marcion's *Antitheses* at the end of the Epistle (vi, 20–21). To the same chronological level (*circa* 140) belongs the advice to Timothy to drink a little wine (v, 23). But the interest of him who gives the advice is not really in the condition of Timothy's "stomach." This is his way of implicitly condemning the abstinence of the encratites, and in particular of Marcion, who would not allow the use of wine even for the Holy Supper.

The same remarks apply to the solemn adjuration addressed to Timothy towards the end of the Epistle (vi, 13–16). This has the sound of a formal profession of faith; and that indeed is what it is. The commandment to be guarded is the "deposit" spoken of in the concluding injunction (vi, 20–21; *supra*, p. 273). The deposit is a "precept," that is, the Christ's teaching as deposited in the Gospel books. In like manner, the "good confession" of the martyred Christ is an echo of the Gospels; but they are not the source from which the mention of Pontius Pilate has been taken; that comes from a profession of Christian faith already officially adopted. Nevertheless, the background of this creed is the Gospel scheme of the Passion, and it is significant that the final utterance, on the invisible God, whom no man has seen or can see, is closely related to the fourth Gospel (John i, 18; vi, 46; cf. Matthew xi, 27). This suggests the question whether the Pastorals are also of Asiatic origin. The question is reasonable. But what we have to be clear about, first and foremost, is that this profession of faith, in which the eschatological and the Gospel catecheses seem to meet, is anti-Marcionite in its essential aim. It is against Marcion that the author so impressively affirms the identity of the one eternal God, master of all things, with God, the creator of the world and Father of Jesus Christ. We are here in the full current of the anti-Marcionite reaction between 150 and 170.

The Second to Timothy gives less space than the First to questions of Church discipline, but while affecting to enter into personal details (discussed in *Remarques*, 122–125) it presents Paul as the type which Timothy—that is, the leading churchman —must make his model (cf. Acts xx, 18–35, *supra*, p. 272). The apostle, represented as a prisoner in Rome, orders Timothy, who is at Ephesus, to come to him, and at the same time gives him instructions which, if they were authentically Paul's, would have been no more needed and no more appropriate than those of the first Epistle. It is worth noting that the author seems to be acquainted with the Book of Acts in its traditional form, iii, 11 being apparently a reference to the fictitious stories in Acts xiii– xiv, 20 (cf. *supra*, p. 181); further, that he combats an advanced form of gnosis and that, in some secondary additions, the Epistle expressly repudiates it, and Marcion in particular.

Paul is represented as rejoicing in the memory of Timothy's affection for him and in the sincerity of his faith; let him revive the gift of God which he received by the imposition of Paul's hands (in 1 Timothy iv, 14 Timothy has been ordained by the Elders; but the difference is not of essential import and the two indications are compatible). Let him be strong and unashamed of his captive master, nor discouraged from bearing testimony to the Gospel, which Paul, spite of his sufferings, continues to preach in full confidence; let him guard the instructions received from the apostle, that "good deposit"; let him pass on the teaching he has kept to safe men, and fight on like a good soldier of the Christ. If we wish to reign with the Christ, we must die with him and for him, as Paul himself has died: this is the doctrine to be preached, paying no heed to disputes that lead to nothing, silly questionings and arguings, but always using gentleness in dealing with the enemies, if perchance God will bring them to conversion and grant them escape from the snares of the demon. Timothy knows what Paul has suffered; all who would live in the Christ are thus persecuted, while the impostors go from bad to worse, "seducers and seduced." So let Timothy preach on like a brave man; yes, even though the time be come when men are running after teachers who pander to their passions. As for Paul, he has had his day, finished his course, kept the faith, and he knows that God has a crown ready for him; and it will soon be his. All this makes a homogeneous whole, in which the modernists of that day were duly branded, but not without an effort to bring them over to the true faith.

Emphasis should be laid on the injunction to Timothy to avoid the "impious babblings" of those who declare that the resurrection has already taken place (ii, 16–18). The surcharged passage ii, 19–26 (which joins on to 14–15) may be aimed at the Marcionites. The attack on the seducers of women (iii, 6–9) is directed against the licentious gnostic sects, such as that of Marcos, the disciple of Valentinus. The praise of the ancient Scriptures (iii, 15–16), a sudden intrusion in the context, is also a counterblow at the gnostics who rejected the Old Testament, and to Marcion as the chief of them.

The Epistle to Titus

The Epistle to Titus seems to be founded on the false supposition that Titus was a disciple of Paul on the same level as Timothy. So far as we can judge from the authentic text he was nothing of the kind (see *Remarques*, 125–126). Equally in substance as in form the Epistle to Titus has a closer resemblance to the First to Timothy than to the Second, and might even be considered a duplicate of the First; just as Paul is supposed to have left Timothy at Ephesus in the quality of chief bishop, so he is made to leave Titus in Crete to carry out the organization of the churches founded in that island. In all the towns Titus is to institute "elders" (priests) as bishops (i, 5–9); the bishop is to possess such and such qualities, substantially as in the First to Timothy (iii, 1–4), with more insistence laid on the need for his being a master in doctrine. For there seem to have been in Crete many circumcised heretics fond of Jewish fables; but the quoted saying of Epimenides on the vices of the Cretans is a mere literary ornament and gives no clue to the sectaries the author has in mind (i, 10–16). They are certainly the same persons who, towards the end of the letter, are said to busy themselves with "fools' questions, genealogies, disputes about the Law." Perhaps Crete is not the region where they were really to be found. It is not impossible that certain heirs of the Pauline tradition kept up the strife against Paul's adversaries, representatives of common Christianity, and treated them as Judaizers. While not impossible it is not very probable, and the artificiality of the whole composition makes it useless to search for precise applications.

Titus is to preach sound doctrine and to give specified counsels, some to old men, some to old women, some to young people, some to slaves (ii, 1–11). The series is parallel to that found in other Epistles notably in 1 Timothy. This must have been the common theme of catechism (cf. 1 Peter ii, 13–iii, 7).

The grace of God has appeared to men that they may follow the laws of the good life, in expectation of the manifestation in splendour of our great God and Saviour Jesus Christ. Here we have the identification of the Christ with God which is also to be met with in both Epistles to Timothy. This, as we have remarked elsewhere, is not a feature of Marcionism but of modalism (see *Remarques*, 116).

In giving this teaching Titus is to speak with authority and to enforce respect for his office (cf. 1 Timothy iv, 12). He will command obedience to magistrates (cf. 1 Timothy ii, 1–2; Romans xiii, 1–7; 1 Peter ii, 13–14); he will enjoin the practice of benevolence to all men and bid Christians remember that they were formerly as mad as other people, until God in his pity was pleased to save them by the bath of regeneration (passage about the effusion of the Spirit, iii, 6–7, seems to have been added); let every man, then, apply himself to good works and keep away from vain disputes; let the man who foments faction by those means be thrust out, if he fails to mend his ways after due warning (iii, 11). All this makes a kind of summary of the more diffuse synthesis, or compilation, represented by 1 Timothy; it has a studied conciseness and lays greater emphasis on the exclusion of incorrigible modernists; it is also free from surcharges directly aimed at the Marcionites.

The first draft of the Pastorals seems to have been anti-gnostic but not expressly anti-Marcionite; the canonized edition is formally anti-gnostic with some new matter added directly against Marcion; thus we may infer that the first draft was earlier than the explosion of Marcionism and the canonical later. Books of this kind were the more eagerly received by the Church into her apostolic collection at a time when she was setting up the New Testament as a barrier against the inundation of gnosis; they openly condemned the gnostic heresies, and represented the first effort to stem the flood in the name of a tradition deemed to be apostolic, embodied and guarded by bishops regularly appointed to rule the churches. Henceforth the function of teaching is to be in the hands of these bishops, and the prophets are no longer to have a place at their side. In 1 Timothy i, 18 and iv, 14 there are indications that the prophets took part in what we might call Timothy's episcopal consecration; but once consecrated, the rôle of teacher is the bishop's exclusive privilege. The formula "The Spirit says," in 1 Timothy iv, 1 (*supra*, p. 275) is a conventional cliché introducing an oracle deemed to be traditional.

The Epistle of Jude

With an apostolic title, and an opening and conclusion appropriate to a letter, the Epistle of Jude is, in the body of it, an anti-gnostic fulmination, or rather a fragment of diatribe set in the frame of an Epistle. The title-address (1–2), visibly marking a distinction from that given to the Epistle of James (i, 1) presents the author as one of those whom the Gospel calls "brothers" of Jesus (Mark vi, 3; Matthew xiii, 55). But, as James modestly calls himself "servant of God and of the Lord Jesus Christ," so Jude not less modestly calls himself "servant of Jesus Christ and brother of James." The doxology (24–25) which serves as colophon, shows some signs of modalism, resembling the preamble in that respect. In this intervening space (3–23) we find a series of object lessons; first, of the Israelites rescued from Egypt, of whom large numbers were destroyed for their unbelief; next, of the disloyal angels, who deserted their posts and are now in prison (these are the imprisoned angels, to whom the Christ preached in hell, mentioned in 1 Peter iii, 19–20; see *supra*, p. 267); finally, the men of Sodom and Gomorrah whom God exterminated for their filthiness. The sectaries whom the author is denouncing have revived all these abominations, although the example of the archangel Michael when he disputed with the Devil over the body of Moses ought to teach them better manners towards the Celestial Powers (this refers to an incident related in the apocryphal book called *Assumption of Moses*). These impious scoundrels repeat the crimes of others who stand accused—Cain, Balaam, Korah, of whom Enoch wrote; and a quotation follows which can be found at the beginning of the Book of Enoch (Ethiopean version). The false teachers are finally characterized as drivelling critics, pompous orators and flatterers with an eye to the main chance.

> As to you, beloved, remember the words of prediction spoken by the apostles of our Lord Jesus Christ, which told you: "At the end of the time mockers will appear who go the way of their impious lusts." These are they who make schism, psychics, not having the spirit, etc. (17–19).

We note, but without lingering on the point, the equivocal phrasing peculiar to this outlook, phrasing which always recurs in parallel cases, for example, in 2 Peter iii, 2–3. Here, plainly, the innovators aimed at boast of being "spiritual" (which they are not) and treat as "psychics" (which they are themselves) the common run of Christians. Compare what the mystic "Paul" is made to say, in 1 Corinthians iii, 1–4, about "spirituals" and "carnals."

In spite of its quotations from apocryphal books, which for us constitutes its originality, there is no disguising the fact that this diatribe against gnosis is a feeble composition, and as violent as feeble. Nevertheless, the author, so far as we can understand him, enjoins his readers at the end to save those who are perishing while avoiding defilement by too close contact. What makes the composition an apostolic letter is nothing more than the address in the preamble and the doxology of the colophon. As the Second of Peter is inspired by the diatribe which forms the *corpus* of the composition, and derives nothing from its epistolary form, it is possible that pseudo-Peter did not know it as an Epistle, but knew and used only the document, afterwards furnished with a framework of epistolary form at the beginning and the end. Hypothetically therefore we may place the diatribe between the years 130 and 140, and its conversion into the pretended Epistle of Jude about 150.

The Second Epistle of Peter

Pseudo-Peter has made full use of Jude's diatribe, but has omitted his quotations from apocryphal books, which perhaps were beginning to come under suspicion in pseudo-Peter's circle. While the Second of Peter already depends for its central part (ii) on the diatribe which constitutes the substance of Jude, its first part (i, 3–21), in which he exalts the testimony of the prince of the apostles, is as clearly dependent on the apocalypse of Peter—the capital point for the understanding of this falsely attributed Epistle (see *Remarques*, 131–137). The third part (iii) is the author's direct refutation of the gnostic sect which was pouring mockery on the delay of the Second Coming. Peter's pretension to the universal apostolate is announced in the superscription (i, 1–2) which has the strong look of a form in regular use.

An easy transition introduces the second part of the Epistle (ii). As there were false prophets in olden time, so now there will arise, among "believers," false teachers who pervert the truth. This is followed by a denunciation of gnostics in general, especially those with immoral tendencies, all in better logical order than the corresponding part of Jude. There is no mention of the unbelieving Jews, so ill-placed in Jude at the head of his list of reprobates: after recalling the disloyal angels, the people drowned in the Deluge are next brought in, as they must have been in the source (cf. 1 Peter iii, 19–20; iv, 6); what follows is a paraphrase of this common source. For himself, when not following his source, the writer is much preoccupied by jests that are being made in certain quarters about the delay of the parousia (iii, 1–13). The pain he has taken to keep his instruction in line with the

First to Peter is significant, notwithstanding the difference in dates between the two. Some of the surcharges in the first Epistle, such as iii, 19–20; iv, 6, can hardly be much earlier than the Second. Our author answers the mockers as best he can; the world, he remarks, has already perished by water in Noah's flood, and the present world is going to perish by fire. God, in his pity, is delaying the event in order that all of us may have time to repent; but a thousand years are to him as but one day. Nevertheless, the day of the Lord will come like a thief (cf. 1 Thessalonians v, 2; Matthew xxiv, 43–44; Luke xii, 39–40). In that day the heavens will disappear in roaring flame; the elements will become white hot and melt and the whole earth with everything in it will be consumed to ashes.

With this prospect before him let every man keep himself unspotted and undefiled, making the most of the respite (iii, 14–18) "as our dear brother Paul, according to the wisdom given him has also written to you," etc. The warranty here given by Peter to Paul provides the critic with a valuable clue. It is clear that, by the time these words were written, Peter and Paul, in spite of what the Epistles make the latter say, had become definitely reconciled in the current tradition concerning them: and, further, that Paul's Epistles were held to be Scripture, though certain heretics, with Marcion certainly in the first rank, were strangely perverting them. This could not have been written before the year 170. But one would gladly know what Epistles the writer had in view. Was it the original collection of ten? Or that of thirteen; or that of fourteen, with Hebrews included? This last is possible, if the writer were of Alexandria.

The Three Epistles of John

The three Epistles named after John keep more or less closely to the Fourth Gospel, and it is not surprising that the satellites present the critic with the same problems as the parent orb. Not that their origin presents even the shadow of doubt; all three come from the same workshop, if the term may be used, as the Gospel, not so much completing as convoying it, and helping to promote its diffusion and its credit. The first Epistle especially, which has the form not of a letter but of a homily, and is not all of one piece, seems to have been compiled in the closest possible connection with the Gospel book. The fact that certain passages are written in regular rhythm has given rise to the conjecture that the formless instructions are the paraphrase of a didactic poem analogous to the chief discourses in the fourth Gospel. But there is no other proof of the hypothesis.

A solemn prologue, in heavy-handed imitation of the prologue to the Gospel, reveals the general intention of the book (i, 1–4):

> That which was from the beginning, that which we have heard, that which we have seen with our eyes, that which we have gazed upon and our hands have touched concerning the Word of life (life has been manifested, and we have seen, we testify and declare unto you the eternal life that was with the Father and has been revealed to us); that, I say, which we have seen and heard we announce unto you, to the end that you may have communion with us; verily our communion is with the Father and with his Son, Jesus Christ. And this we write that your joy may be complete.

This opening is enough to give the character of the whole: a watery paraphrase of the ideas which form the base of the Gospel, tiresome in its repetitions—life, light, love, union with God and in God. We leave the matter there and proceed to point out some notable peculiarities of the compilation. We read (ii, 1b–2):

> If anyone sin, he has a *defender* with the Father, Jesus Christ the righteous. He is, himself, propitiation for our sins, but not for ours alone; for the sins also of the whole world.

When those words were written the fourth Gospel had not yet spoken of *"another* Defender, the Spirit of the Truth," the *Paraclete*, who would fill the place of the Christ, now gone back to God, in helping the faithful (John xiv, 16–17; xv, 26; xvi, 13; cf. *supra*, p. 221–223).

The author knows the Apocalypse and on two occasions speaks of the Antichrist, but for the purpose of explaining—very freely it must be confessed—that Antichrist is already come in the person of divers heretical teachers. On the first occasion these heretics are denounced for denying that Jesus is the Christ (ii, 18–22). On the second occasion we are told that the spirits must be proved, "because many false prophets are come into the

THE ORIGINS OF THE NEW TESTAMENT

world"; and the test is this: "every spirit that confesses Jesus
Christ come in the flesh is of God," and whosoever does not
confess Jesus "is of Antichrist, of whom you have heard say that
he is coming and who now is already in the world." This second
denunciation aims at Docetism and, very probably, at Marcion.
In the first case the author—if he weighed his words, which is
not certain—is not thinking of the Docetists but of people who
distingush the heavenly *aeon*, which was the Christ, from the man
Jesus; this would be the error attributed by tradition to Cerinthus
who maintained that the *aeon* Christ was united only for a time
with the man Jesus, a doctrine which might be adjusted with a
little forcing to the Gospel catechesis of Mark. Whatever be their
precise application the two denunciations presuppose an outbreak
of gnostic heresies in the Asiatic circles to which the Epistle
belongs, the probability being that the two denunciations are not
concerned with the same heresy, since they are not by the same
writer. We shall presently see, moreover, that the second Epistle
is in line with the second denunciation, which would thus be the
later of the two.

Towards the end of the Epistle we come upon a remarkable
surcharge clearly aimed at Docetism, the relation of which to a
surcharge to the same effect in the fourth Gospel cannot be
fortuitous. The author is in course of proving that whosoever
believes in Jesus and obeys the law of love is born of God and is,
by his faith, victorious over the world (v, 1–5). The faith in
question is based on the witness that God has rendered to his
Son, the witness being that God has given us the eternal life
which is in his Son (v, 9–12). At this point the author, intentionally picking up the original conclusion of the Fourth Gospel
(John xx, 31), proceeds to write: "I have written this to you that
you may know you have eternal life, you who believe in the name
of the Son of God." But some reviser of the Epistle, before
introducing the testimony thus rendered by God to his Son, has
thought fit to insert the following gloss (v, 6–7. Verse 5 is a late
interpolation, which does not here concern us) about the Christ
and the witness rendered to him.

> This is he who comes by water and by blood, Jesus Christ,
>   not with water only,
>   but with water and with blood;

284

And he who bears witness is the Spirit
  because the Spirit is the truth.
So there are three that bear witness;
  Spirit, water, blood;
  and the three make one.

We have already pointed out the relation between this parenthesis and the incident of the lance-thrust in the story of the Passion (pp. 209, 232), and the inference to be drawn from that relation for the common history of the Gospel and the Epistles.

The two short Epistles that follow have more resemblance to letters; but they were never addressed to anybody. Both are explicitly attributed to the Elder, that is to the person whom the fourth Gospel invests with authority as the beloved disciple and the author of the Gospel itself.

The first is written for a church whom it names Lady Elect. Her children are bidden to practise charity and be on their guard against seducers who, denying that Jesus is come in the flesh, are Antichrist and people not to be received into houses nor saluted in the street (4–11). This discloses the purpose of our short letter—to support the denunciation of Docetic gnosis in the first Epistle.

The third letter is supposedly written to a believer in the church to which the former was addressed. This time the object is to commend the travelling brethren who carry the good doctrine— i.e. the Johannine writings—to the care of friends, and to discredit the church leaders who, like the conceited Diotrephes, refuse to receive the Elder and his books. The reference is to the bishops who would have nothing to do with the new fourth Gospel and drove out its supporters.

To sum up. The Epistles called after John contain religious and moral doctrine co-ordinated to that of the fourth Gospel, denunciation of certain gnostic heresies, and highly forced reasons for accepting the testimony supposed to guarantee the apostolic character of those doctrines and of the writings that contain them. The two short Epistles and the canonical edition of the first go back to the neighbourhood of 150–160 and the first version of the first Epistle to 135–140.

Chapter IX

CONCLUSIONS

WHAT we now proceed to gather up is not a heap of certitudes, but a sheaf of hypotheses which we endeavour to bind together, according to their degree of probability or verisimilitude, in order that we may reconstruct the history of which we directly see the outcome only. The outcome is that, towards the end of the second century, there existed a collection of writings called the New Testament, in use among the congregations of the Church called catholic, and sharply distinguished from the sects which had broken off from it, or formed on its frontiers, this collection being placed side by side with another which the said Church had inherited from Judaism and called Scriptures of the Old Testament. It must be added, however, that the Church's collection of the Old Testament was not completely identical with the official Scriptures of Judaism, for it included certain writings, or fragments of writings, held in honour among the hellenizing Jews of Egypt. Nor was the New Testament collection identically the same in all the churches of the Mediterranean world. There was general agreement on the four Gospels, the Acts of the Apostles, thirteen Epistles of Paul (the Epistle to the Hebrews attributed to Paul in the East was not recognized as apostolic in the West), the First of Peter and the First of John. But the Epistles of James and of Jude, the Second of Peter and the two short Johannine Epistles were not universally accepted, and the Apocalypse of John was long under discredit, in the East, after the beginning of the third century. Indeed there was a group, attacked by Irenaeus, which rejected all the writings attributed to John as apocryphal, and this opposition was active in Rome about the year 200. On the other hand, writings, such as the Epistle of Clement to the Corinthians and the Pastor of Hermas, were long read as public lessons in many of the churches.

As to the origins of the New Testament writings and to their collection, they are, as we have seen, very imperfectly documented. Only by faith can the four Gospels, the Acts of the Apostles, Paul's Epistles, the catholic Epistles and the Book of

Revelation be accepted as apostolic and integrally authentic. The verdict of criticism is otherwise (cf. *supra*, p. 10).

THE PROPHET JESUS AND HIS ORACLE

Jesus, who lived in the time of Tiberius, when Pontius Pilatus was procurator of Judea, was not formally recognized as Messiah or Christ till after his death, when his disciples proclaimed him as the immortal Christ at the right hand of God, whence he would presently come to establish on the earth, more precisely at Jerusalem, that Reign of God whose speedy arrival he had himself announced in his lifetime. The historical existence of Jesus is postulated and implied throughout the entire history of the Christian religion. That is why we abstain from proving it. Such a proof is no business of ours, save in so far as the history of the New Testament origins depends on him who was historically, if not the founder of the Christian religion, at least the initiator of the Christian movement. Moreover the hypotheses of the mythologues, who have recently denied that Jesus ever existed, do not require refutation, seeing that they are all built on air, no positive proof being forthcoming that the particular myths ever existed which, according to these conjectures, are the foundation of the Christian religion. And even if this were the time for criticism of such theories, this is not the place for it.

Our sole business, in our present undertaking, is to determine, by reference to the New Testament literature, what the conditions were under which this human life was lived, a life on which, from the historical point of view, our information is most imperfect; and that for a double reason; first, because the Gospels never were and never pretended to be historical documents for the earthly life of Jesus, but were manuals, in short books, of instruction in the cult of the Lord Jesus Christ; and, second, because these books, which were not otherwise concerned in gathering exact information about Jesus, are later by three-quarters of a century to the time when Jesus, after a very brief period of teaching in Galilee and Jerusalem, ending in his death by crucifixion under sentence of Pontius Pilatus, was proclaimed as alive for ever with God and in readiness to come with God's Kingdom. Nor does the rest of the New Testament tell us any more of the matter than do the Gospels, since all these writings presuppose the faith as already acquired and give no direct information as to how the faith first came into being. One thing, however, is clearly evident: the name of Jesus and the speedy arrival of God's Kingdom were indissolubly bound together from the furthest point to which Christian memory went back. That is very far from being a fact of no account. But it does not inform us how Jesus himself brought into being the faith of which he soon became the object.

That the time when Jesus made his appearance in history, and faith in Jesus-Messiah was born, was a time of great religious and national excitement is another indisputable fact. The Jewish rising in the year 66 which ended in the fall of Jerusalem and the destruction of the temple in the year 70, was, in all strictness, a messianic movement, founded on the essential principle of the Jewish national hope, to wit, that Israel owed obedience to one master only, to God, the establishment of whose Kingdom would involve the complete overthrow of foreign rule. So far as we are able to judge, the Galilean prophet Jesus whom his contemporaries called Jesus the Nazorean[1] was possessed by the same idea. According to him, the arrival of the Great Kingdom, the rule of justice and salvation, was on the point of realization; God would erect it on the ruins of the idolatrous government, and repentance was the necessary preparation for that sweeping revolution. A certain John, named the Baptizer, of whom it would seem that Jesus was originally a disciple, had proclaimed the same message before him, baptismal immersion being the sacrament of repentance, of purification and of the right to be admitted to God's Kingdom. From the very beginning Christianity was the religion of a baptist sect, for Jesus himself had not only received baptism after John's manner but sanctioned it in that form. Those who would make out that Jesus repudiated John's baptism are breaking a perceptible link between Jesus and the religious conditions of his time; and such links are rare.

So far as Jesus can be said, in strictness of speech, to have *taught*, the speedy arrival of God in his Kingdom was the substance of his teaching. Unlike the Zealots, who advocated armed

---

[1] A personal qualification, with no mythological significance, *Nazorean* being, so far as we can ascertain, a sect-name which could be applied to individuals.

revolution,[1] Jesus expected that the liberation of his people would be the work of God alone, the firm simplicity of his faith saving him from the fanatical blindness of the hot-heads who imagined that by armed revolt against Rome they would come to the help of God, or force his hand. Nevertheless it was the same faith as theirs that rendered him blind to the inevitable danger of his advance on Jerusalem, where he was certain to find himself immediately confronted with the power whose destruction he was announcing, at least by implication.

It may be affirmed with the minimum risk of error that he was the prophet of a single oracle only, as John the Baptist seems to have been before him. That he speculated at length on the part reserved for him in the coming Kingdom is improbable; nevertheless the place assigned him by his disciples after his death rather suggests that he did not expect that his rôle in it would be that of an ordinary participant. That his public activity included the part of a healing exorcist is rendered highly probable by the fact that his disciples played the same part after him; indeed the character of a man of God could hardly be conceived, in his time and place, without including that function. When, further, we have admitted the profound and humanely moral character of his message as the dominating feature of its form and nature, we have said all that the historian is able to say about his activity without overpassing the limits of safety.

The above statement is made only as justifying the following conclusion, which concerns the proper subject of our study: Jesus was a prophet rather than a teacher of doctrine; he did not regard himself as the founder of a new religion; something of his prophetic and humane spirit survived in the sect which claimed him as its head; but he has left on the literature of the New Testament only a faint impression of his personality and the memory of his death. His cult-legend is widely different from a direct and faithful image reflected in a mirror.

Jesus was dead, and almost immediately the belief arose among his followers that he was the Messiah about to return. Their faith in his message of the swiftly coming Kingdom did not change its ground to the extent to which the Gospel stories might

[1] Though the name of a Zealot figures in the list of the Twelve (cf. Luke vi, 15; Acts i, 13. Note also that *zealot* is the exact translation of the epithet *Canaanite* applied to the same disciple in Mark iii, 18 and Matthew x, 4).

lead us to suppose; they are stories of much too late invention, and too systematically worked out to represent the travail in the soul of his followers when Jesus' fate overtook him. In the Gospel stories they are presented as receiving material proofs of his resurrection, proofs never received, for they were impossible, and would have been superfluous in any case, because they are without appeal to a mentality such as theirs was at the time. For them, Jesus was not raised from the dead in the gross, almost brutal, manner in which tradition told the story at a later date. Jesus had passed on to God *at death* in full possession of his selfhood—so said the spirit that was in them. To the fate of his dead body they gave not a thought and asked not a question about it. Him whom God had sent was now with the God who sent him; there he was, alive and glorious at God's right hand, and thence, in life and glory, as the Christ, he would soon be coming to establish the Reign of God upon the earth. Such was their faith; but it was born without a literature, for not a line had yet been written about it in any Christian book.

It would be a mistake to expect from the New Testament authentic information about the catastrophe which ended the earthly life of Jesus, or about the new direction into which his disciples' faith was turned by the catastrophe, though we know very well who was the chief agent in giving it that turn. He was Simon, called Peter. But the third Gospel seems to have retained some traces of the state of mind in which Jesus and his following of Galilean enthusiasts brought the proclamation of the Kingdom to Jerusalem at the stage immediately *before* the catastrophe fell.

We read in that Gospel that Jesus, after the halt at Jericho, delivered a parable "because he was near to Jerusalem" and because *"they all believed* that the Kingdom of God was on the point of appearing" (Luke xix, 11). This was not a feature imagined after the event, and to be immediately refuted in the sequel. It is a datum of genuine tradition which the evangelist could not wholly eliminate, but which he only thought he would correct by fitting on to it the parable of the talents (12–27), which has no relation to it whatever, though touches added to give it a relation throw a little light on the mentality of Jesus and on the Christian mentality at the time when the Gospel legend was beginning to take shape. These touches are the following: "A man of noble birth went away into a far country to be made a king and to return"—meaning that Jesus, already dead, has gone to heaven to receive messianic royalty. (All that follows about the money distributed among the prince's officers would be out of keeping with the opening were it not that the Christ is conceived as already appointed the judge of mankind as well as Messiah.) But the final touch (27) corresponds with the opening: "As to these my enemies, who would not that I rule over them, bring them hither and slay them in my presence." Such is the crime which has brought destruction on the Jewish people; him whom God had made Christ in heaven, him whose speedy coming the Christian preachers are announcing, they had refused to recognize. In this way the parable furnishes a sketch, rudimentary enough, of the primitive faith, although it was not put into writing till after the year 70, if not till after 135.

Equally illuminating is the saying, about which Christian tradition became so confused, "I will destroy this temple and rebuild it in three days"—attenuated in Matthew (xxvi, 61) "I *can* destroy," etc.; corrected in Mark (xiv, 58) "I will destroy this temple *made with hands*, and in three days build another *not made with hands*"; while Acts (vi, 14) make it appear as a charge against Stephen. This may well have been really alleged against Jesus in the trial before Pilate, as a proof of messianic pretensions. If so, it would indicate a highly exalted state of mind in him who pronounced it, combined with a reforming zeal afraid of nothing—this at the very least.

As to Peter's initial vision, it may be said that, while it is everywhere spoken of in the New Testament, it is nowhere described. The reason is that it was not of the same order, and could not be made to fit, with the imaginary experiences by which at a much later date it was sought to prove the resurrection of Jesus as a fact materially verified and verifiable. The message of Jesus was not, in substance, of the kind which lends itself to argumentative polemic or needs long discourses for its delivery, and the same may be said of the message which the Galilean disciples carried back to Jerusalem after his death. Peter's faith is fairly well summed up in the formula given to it by Acts (ii, 36): "Let all the house of Israel, then, know for a certainty that God has made this Jesus whom you crucified into Lord and

Christ"—except perhaps that Peter and his companions clothed it with rather less solemnity. As to the supporting arguments drawn from the Old Testament, they were only gradually discovered as the need arose for them, and by persons more learned than Peter and his band.

Who was the first preacher of the new faith to carry the name of Jesus into the Jewish synagogues and publicly argue for his faith? Exegetes cannot be reminded too often that this preacher was Stephen, a *hellenist* convert of great daring and enterprise, and doubtless the most learned in that category. To those who consider the matter calmly and without prejudice it will be clear that this critical step could not have been taken otherwise.

It is obvious that our information as to the particulars of Stephen's preaching is extremely imperfect. We can only say with confidence that he was filled with the spirit of his group, the group which was soon to admit uncircumcised pagans into the community of believers, and that his trial implies that his preaching had the appearance of being more or less subversive of the Law —for example, that certain rules, held to have been laid down by Moses, would be abrogated in the Kingdom of God. For with Stephen, as with the others, the one question on which everything turned was the coming Kingdom which the Christ would establish at his speedy return. The same holds true of Stephen's former companions who escaped to Antioch, and there founded the first Christian community which admitted Gentiles to the messianic hope without imposing on them the rite of circumcision.

The conditions being such as we now see them to have been, there is no room for astonishment that Paul has nothing whatever to say about the earthly existence of Jesus nor of his characteristic teachings. Paul, like the other believers, knew Jesus as the founder of the Christian hope, as the Messiah to come, but not as Messiah already come and revealer of the Christian mystery. If we consider Paul to be the real author of everything written in the Epistles, and Jesus as the real author of every teaching ascribed to him in the Gospels, even in the Synoptics, Paul's relation to Jesus, as we might gather it from the Epistles, then becomes not only passing strange and at bottom indefinable, but essentially unintelligible. But, in the light we have now gained upon the matter, the relation of Paul to Jesus drops its former character of an unreadable enigma and an insoluble problem. Paul did not teach everything ascribed to him in the Epistles, nor Jesus everything ascribed in the Gospels. With that in mind Paul's eschatological preaching becomes perfectly clear. What, then, was it?

The Real Teaching of Paul

When Paul wrote to the Thessalonians (i, 9–10): "You have been converted from idols to God, to serve the true and living God and to await his Son from heaven, whom he has raised from the dead, Jesus, who saves us from the wrath to come," it is certain that he was not recalling any particular teaching of Jesus; he is proclaiming Jesus as the Christ to come, not as the Christ already come; he is declaring that the conversion of the pagans consists in recognizing the one and only God and Jesus, his Son, who will rescue believers in the day of "the wrath." Paul's catechesis thus implies both moral and eschatological teaching combined with Jewish monotheism and the conception of Jesus raised from death to become the living Christ. In like manner he writes to the Romans (x, 9): "If thou confessest with thy mouth that Jesus is Lord, and if thou believest in thy heart that God has raised him from the dead, thou shalt be rescued." Fundamentally it is the same doctrine as in Thessalonians, and in neither case is there the faintest reference to anything Jesus did or taught before he came to die. But let not the mythologues suppose for one moment that this pleads in favour of their thesis that Jesus never existed. In the same Epistle Paul states explicitly (ix, 5) that the Christ, like the patriarchs, is of Israel's seed; and Paul was a contemporary of Jesus.

Elsewhere, the argumentation by which Paul proves the universality of the messianic rescue is worked out without the slightest dependence on what we are in the habit of calling Gospel tradition. He abstains, for a good reason, from quoting any teaching of Jesus in support of his argument. The story of the centurion of Capernaum and the universalist propositions which the Christ is made to emit on that occasion (Matthew viii, 5–13; Luke vii, 9–10; xiii, 28–29) are entirely ignored by him, and the personality of his Christ derives its significance solely from the Great Event in store for the world. For proof of his thesis he goes indeed to the Scriptures, but the only Scripture he knows and reveres as divine are the Jewish Scriptures which he submits to a wholly irresponsible exegesis, following methods practised by the Rabbis of his time.

It is in these Scriptures that he finds the universal principle laid down of justification by faith, and he not only finds it there but proves it by juggling with words. In the Book of Habakkuk (ii, 4) it is written: "the pious man finds the assurance of his existence in his fidelity to God"; this Paul understood as meaning that by faith alone in God and his Christ any man may become qualified for the messianic rescue from the "wrath" (salvation) without any works of the Law being needed for his qualification; and he pursues the demonstration by bringing forward other texts, although he has begun by announcing, as though it were some trifling commonplace, a principle of plain common sense, namely (Romans iii, 29–31) that God is the God of all men and not only of Jews, to recognize which is not to abolish the Law, but the contrary. But on that he does not dwell; he is only concerned to prove how the scheme of universal salvation by faith was instituted in Abraham, father of all the Jews according to the flesh, father of all believers according to the spirit. The proof is that Abraham was as yet an uncircumcised man when his faith was imputed to him for righteousness—and so on. The imperturbable logic of the apostle, advancing from one absurdity to another, finally comes to this conclusion: that not only to Abraham was faith imputed for righteousness "but also to us who believe in him who raised Jesus our Lord from the dead."

As the argument proceeds we learn what it was that God promised to Abraham and to his posterity. This was not exactly eternal life, the "blessed immortality" of the theologians, but "the heritage of the world" (iv, 13), Genesis having said (xxii, 17) "thy posterity shall inherit the enemies' cities," which Paul understands as promising universal domination over the people of the earth. This shows us that, in the mind of the apostle, the idea of the Kingdom of God and his Christ had not taken the spiritual form. It was still the triumph of God over all nations as predicted by the prophets. Thus the Gospel is still, as it previously was, the proclamation of the coming Reign of God on earth, except for the clause which now offers salvation to pagans who adhere to the saving faith.

Paul added nothing to that belief beyond moral counsels, administered as a cooling draught to the fever of expectation. We have already heard him exhorting the Thessalonians, and that severely, to practise conjugal chastity (iv, 1–8; *supra*, p. 241), and again charging them (iv, 11–12) not to sit idly with crossed arms waiting for the parousia, but "study to be quiet and do your own business and work with your hands . . . that ye may walk honestly towards outsiders and may have need of no man."

The motives which led the apostle to charge his Thessalonian converts to earn their own living and be a burden to nobody becomes clear when we consider the collection he organized for the poor "saints" in Jerusalem. On this affair Paul explains himself rather cautiously in Romans xv, 26–27: "Macedonia and Achaia," he says, "have decided to make a contribution for the poor among the saints at Jerusalem; sharing their spiritual blessings, they ought to help them with material blessings." It is not correct to give the Christians of Hellas the credit of initiating the matter, for we know that Paul had organized the collection at Galatia before calling upon Macedonia and Achaia to put it into effect. The truth must have been that the missionaries to the countries of the dispersion pledged themselves to make the collection when they were at Jerusalem about the year 43–44 on the question of the legal observances.

The question has sometimes been asked whether "the saints" at Jerusalem were really so poor, and, if so, why? The answer is that the saints in question were probably remnants of the little group of earliest Galilean believers which returned with Peter to Jerusalem when the faith that Jesus had risen from death as the Christ was first established and affirmed. We know that they gathered a few recruits, but we know also that their dominant interest was not in propaganda; they had come to Jerusalem to await the second coming of the Lord and to be on the spot where it was due to take place immediately. Their resources were of the scantiest and, the parousia not arriving, were soon exhausted. Thus our saints, whose professed occupation was waiting for the expected event, were really "poor." Their mere existence reveals what faith in the Christ was in its very earliest form. There could be no greater misconception of their mentality than that which takes them to have been the first depositaries and witnesses of what is commonly called the gospel tradition. They were on the watch for the coming of the Lord Jesus and had no other care.

Eschatological teaching could not remain, and did not remain for long, confined to the simple terms professed by the apostle Paul, although it had already received some enlargement from the activity of the hellenist converts and of Paul himself, who together had adapted it to the conversion of uncircumcised pagans. But all these acquisitions became crystallized, so to say, round the original theme of the coming Kingdom. Meanwhile, under the influence of the gnoses which sprang up spontaneously among the recruits to the new faith, the notion of a divine Christ, Saviour of mankind in virtue of his death, in whom the mystery was at once typified and revealed in the course of his earthly career, was gradually leading on to the transformation of the eschatological into the Gospel form of teaching.

Let us note at the outset and never lose sight of the fact that this evolution, from beginning to end, and especially in the early stages, was effected in an atmosphere of superheated mysticism in which there was little room for reflection and none at all for criticism. Christianity was born under the rule of vision and prophecy. Jesus himself, so far as we are able to estimate him, was an ardent visionary, although the worse than meagre information we have about it is hardly sufficient to fix the character of his visions. But what we do know is that he *saw* the Kingdom of God preparing to come by his ministry, and that after him his disciples *saw* the Kingdom ready to come by his act, and himself now living with God as anointed Lord and Christ. These visionaries were of necessity prophets also. We might conjecture as much even if we were not plainly informed of it. Moreover, it is *a priori* certain that these Christian prophets delivered oracles, if not always in Jesus' name, at least about him, and as animated by his spirit.

A few examples of contributions by Christian prophets will

suffice to show how their insertion was effected. What we are about to say is independent of the credit unquestionably due to the statement in Acts xiii, 1 about the five prophet-teachers who presided over the Antioch community before two of them, Barnabas and Paul, were chosen for regular missionary work in that region. We simply assume as a fact beyond question that at an early hour these prophet-teachers, or masters in prophecy, made their appearance in the Christian communities and that they played a great part in the enrichment of the gospel catechesis.

As a type of this teaching-prophecy we choose first the short apocalypse, or allegory of the eschatological Christ, now inserted in Mark xii, 1–11, where it is presented as a specimen of the teaching given by Jesus at Jerusalem, but which, as we have already seen (p. 95), he never gave there, nor could have given.

> A man had planted a vineyard; he had surrounded it with a hedge; he had dug a cellar there for his winepress and built a tower; he leased it to vine-dressers, and went out of the country.

The description of the vineyard is borrowed from Isaiah v, 1–2; the vineyard is Israel and the owner of it is God. The great simplicity of the imagery is remarkable: after miraculously establishing his people in their home, God returns to his.

> And in due season he sent a servant to the vine-dressers to receive part of the produce of the vineyard; but they seized him, beat him and sent him back empty-handed. Thereupon he sent them another servant; to him they gave insults and beat him on the head. He sent them yet another, and this one they killed; and so with many others, of whom some they flogged and some they killed.

Obviously this refers to the sending of the prophets, to whom Israel is supposed to have turned a deaf ear.

> He had still somebody else to send, a well beloved son; he sent him last of all saying "they will respect my son."

Observe that this "son" arrives under the same conditions as the servants; he, no more than they, comes direct from heaven, and he is called "son" in his quality of the Messiah promised to Israel.

> But these vine-dressers said one to another: " 'Tis the heir! Up, let us kill him and ours will be the heritage."

Jesus is "the heir," as having authority to set up the reign of God in the holy land.

> And laying hands on him they killed him and threw his body out of the vineyard.[1] What then will the master of the vineyard do? He will come and destroy the vine-dressers and will give the vineyard to others.

It is obvious that, when this was conceived and put into form, Jerusalem was destroyed and the Gospel preached outside of Palestine, and it is to these believers beyond its borders that "the heritage" will revert; to them will the Kingdom belong, when Christ appears.

> Have you not read this Scripture (Psalm cxviii, 22–23):

> The stone which the builders threw aside has become the corner stone. It is the Lord who has made it so, and the stone is a wonder to gaze upon.

The Son, killed by the Jews, is none the less the Lord Jesus Christ. Plainly this short prophetic allegory is a fragment of anti-Jewish polemic drawn up towards the end of the first Christian century by way of complement to the eschatological catechesis. Thrown back into the earthly life of Jesus it was at first intended to serve as his last discourse at Jerusalem, to be received later into the gospel catechesis. Later still it has been thrown back a stage in Mark's catechesis and placed after the question of the priests about his authority (xi, 27–33) where it stands with nothing logically leading up to it. The other two Synoptics found it there and borrowed it from Mark (Matthew xxi, 33–43;[2] Luke xx, 9–18). But the pushing back of our allegory in Mark's catechesis from its first intended position as the last discourse of Jesus was brought about by the intercalation of a more considerable piece of eschatology, to wit the great apocalypse of the Synoptics, which first came into existence as teaching delivered by the risen Jesus, that is as the utterance of a Christian prophet speaking on his behalf and in his name.

We have already seen that the history of this apocalyptic document is older than that of the allegory of the wicked husbandmen in Mark; but the case requires closer study for its

---

[1] Hardly in keeping with the story of an honourable burial.

[2] Where Jesus, after the final citation from Psalm cxviii, is made to add: "Therefore I say unto you, the Kingdom of Heaven shall be taken from you and given to a nation that will produce the fruits of it."

bearings on the evolution of the Christian catechesis. The kernel of it, as we have remarked above (p. 97) is a short Jewish apocalypse, earlier than the capture of Jerusalem by Titus in the year 70. But the adaptation of it to Christian teaching is later than that event. Moreover it seems clear that the first draft of Mark was ignorant of it as an element of Christian teaching. This conclusion results, not only from the use made of the allegory of the wicked husbandmen in the conditions we have just described, but also from the fact that Mark represents Jesus as delivering the Great Apocalypse almost in secret before the four principal disciples. Mark has the prophecy delivered on the Mount of Olives, the reason being that the source from which he drew it presents it as delivered there by the risen Christ when about to ascend into heaven, that is to say, in the exact condition in which the Apocalypse of Peter presents an analogous revelation. We have equal ground for believing that the artificial introduction to the Book of Acts contains the rudiments of a similar discourse with the scene set exactly as in the Apocalypse of Peter.

Thus our hypotheses are not groundless imaginations; they are inductions as solid as the matter permits of, and based upon texts whose form was under continual alteration until finally fixed in the canonical edition of the New Testament books.

Another point needing careful consideration and easily established, though this is not the place to enter into details, lies in the fact that the revelations about the End in the synoptic apocalypse are accompanied by moral precepts concerning the right attitude, not only in presence of the final catastrophe, but also in meeting the persecutions in store for believers. These precepts are to be found, expressed in almost exactly the same terms, in the instructions given in earlier passages to preachers of the Gospel. The truth is that both the moral instructions and the commission of the apostles were conceived with an outlook to the Second Coming and originally formed part of the teaching about the end of the world. They, also, are instructions given by the risen and immortal Christ. Before the death of Jesus no *apostles* were in existence to receive commission. Strictly speaking apostolic activity did not come into being until the great outbreak of propaganda was let loose by the hellenist believers. All this advice to apostles and victims of persecution, when closely studied, will be seen to have no *raison a"être* in the personal message of Jesus. Most assuredly it does not come from him. It is an utterance of Christian prophecy spoken after Jesus' death in the name of the immortal Christ and with an outlook strictly eschatological.

The Apocalypse of John—a typical Christian Prophecy

That is not all. There is one whole book to attest the long persistence of the view which interpreted the providential mission of Jesus with predominant reference to the coming Reign of God. It is the Apocalypse of John (*circa* A.D. 90). This Apocalypse has only a faint and fugitive allusion (xi, 8) to the crucifixion of Jesus at Jerusalem and refers to nothing else in his earthly career. From beginning to end the figure on which attention is focussed is the Christ-about-to-come; and this whether he speaks himself or by the mouth of his prophet. In the first part of the book the Christ writes to the churches, addressing them directly as the true head of them all; in the body of it he makes his prophet write a kind of eschatological summary concluding with his own triumph. Though doubtless he is mystically the sacrificed Lamb, he never ceases to be the One-who-is-coming. In telling the myth of his own birth (xii) he makes his birth of one piece with the myth of his final exaltation, inasmuch that, for him, being born and being carried up to God, preparatory to his coming triumph over the Beast and Satan, are virtually the same event (xii, 5). In plain truth the author of the Apocalypse would seem to be totally ignorant of the gospel presentation. Is not that significant?

The Mystery of the Lamb

Though the Apocalypse is wholly eschatological in substance, it must not be forgotten that a well-characterized mystery pervades it throughout and brings it into close contact with those whom it attacks so bitterly in the letters to the seven churches. This is the mystery of the Lamb, a Jewish figure. The eschatological character of the book also comes in part from its sources and these, in the body of the work, are purely Jewish, the Christian elements being an added embroidery.

In the letters to the seven churches, written in imitation of the

Epistles, the reward promised to the faithful Christian is as follows: "to eat of the tree of life, which is in the paradise of God" (ii, 7); to be untouched by "the second death," that is, to escape the eternal fire (ii, 11); to eat "the hidden manna" and to possess "a white stone, on which a new name is engraved, known only to him who receives it"—a feature in the mysteries borrowed from paganism (ii, 17); to have the Gentiles in his power "shepherding them with an iron flail and shattering them like a potter's jars" . . . and to possess "the morning star"—this last a feature of astrological magic (ii, 26–29); to be "clothed in white raiments," symbol of purity and of immortality (iii, 5); to be "a pillar in God's temple" and to have inscribed on him "God's name, the name of the new Jerusalem and the new name" (of the Christ)—all features of mystery cults (iii, 12); "to sit with" the Christ "on his throne" as the Christ "sits with his Father on his throne"—a strange enlargement in the perspective of the believer's reward, and hardly in keeping with the idea of the new Jerusalem as coming down to earth (iii, 21). Parallel to this conception of the Christ as enthroned with God is the conception of him as pre-existent, in the preamble to the same letter, where he is entitled "the beginning of the creation of God," which is what the Old Testament says of the Divine Wisdom (Proverbs viii, 23) and is not far removed from "the Logos of God," the name given later on to the conquering Christ (xix, 13). However, it is not impossible that this transcendent mysticism was introduced into the book at the time when the Apocalypse was edited for inclusion in the canon. None the less true is it that the Apocalypse in its earliest form was strongly coloured by astral mysticism.

But here there is another mysticism which is not astral, and has nothing to do with the Ram of the Zodiac. This is the Christ-Lamb, early substituted, as we know, for the Jewish paschal lamb in the quartodeciman Easter, observed to the second century by the Christians of Asia and consecrated by the Johannine Gospel. The Lamb appears as the chief figure in the vision of the book with the seven seals, the book of destiny, which the Lamb only may open. He is first announced (v, 5) as "the lion of Judah" and "stock of David" (Isaiah xi, 1–10)—which reveals the gospel catechesis, at least in process of formation. The description then follows:

And I saw in the midst of God's throne a *lamb* standing upright as *with a cut throat* (Isaiah liii, 7) . . . and he came and laid hold on the book . . . and when he had taken the book, the four Living Ones and the four-score Aged Ones fell down before the Lamb, chanting a new canticle, saying:

> Thou art worthy
> > to take the book and break its seals,
> > because thou hast been cut with the knife
> And by thy blood thou hast ransomed for God
> > men of every tribe, tongue, people and nation,
> And hast made them a Kingdom and priests for God,
> > and they shall be rulers over the earth.

In this passage we have before us a myth of salvation by the Lamb as the redeeming victim. But this is not the mystic gnosis of the Epistle to the Romans. It is a myth of the Christ as the paschal lamb, attached, for consistency with prophecy, to the description of the suffering servant in Isaiah. This Christ-Lamb opens and explains the Book of Destiny, all that is due to happen before the end of the age. The revelation is closely framed in the primitive eschatology, redemption and the revealing of salvation coming to pass by this Kingdom of priests, who are to rule *over the earth*. It is true that, later on, the elect are represented as standing in heaven "before the throne and before the Lamb" (vii, 14–17); but that description refers to a provisional stage of the glorified martyrs before the final triumph to be realized on the regenerated earth.

Elsewhere (xiii, 8) the reprobates, worshippers of the Beast, are described as "those whose names are not written in the book of *the sacrificed Lamb*, since the foundation of the world." The book of the Lamb is the book of the elect, which has existed since the beginning of all things. But this does not mean that the Lamb has been *immolated* since the world's foundation (cf. 1 Peter i, 18–21, written in the same spiritual atmosphere as our passage).

Further on (xiv, 1–5) we next find the Lamb on Mount Sion, with the hundred and forty-four thousand of the elect (from vii). They are those "who have been ransomed from the earth" and "have not defiled themselves with women"; they "follow the Lamb whithersoever he goes." We are again told that the kings who fight for the Beast "will fight against the Lamb, and he will overthrow them" (xvii, 12–14). "The marriage of the Lamb" is announced to follow the destruction of the Beast (xix, 7); but the wife of the Lamb does not appear till after the last judgment. She is the Church of the Blessed (xxi, 2, 9–10), new Jerusalem, where will be the throne of God and of the Lamb (xxii, 1, 3); God and the Lamb will be its temple and its light (xxi, 22–23; xxii, 5). Conclusion (xxii, 16):

> I, Jesus, have sent my angel,
> to give you this testimony in the churches.
> I am the stock and the offspring of David,
> the bright star of the morning.

This can hardly be the star which Balaam predicted would rise out of Jacob (Numbers xxiv, 17). Far more probably it is the planet Venus in her character of a great astral power, so that here, in the concluding note, the element of astral mythology is still present, complicating the Jewish eschatology. On the other hand, the insistence on the Davidic descent of the Christ turns us towards the gospel catechesis, which we must suppose to be now sufficiently developed to make the forms and influence of the gnoses revealed in Gospels and Epistles sensibly felt in the Apocalypse also.

In dating the Apocalypse back to the reign of Domitian (81–96), Irenaeus must have placed it somewhat too early, a consequence of the thesis which attributes its authorship to the apostle John. The last retouching of the book may well be not much earlier than 140. The allusion to "the twelve apostles of the Lamb" (xxi, 14) not only proves that the author cannot himself have been one of the Twelve, but further, and above all, that the myth of Twelve Apostles, founders of the universal Church, and preachers of the Gospel to the whole world, was completely formed at the time this allusion was made. This confirms the remark just made regarding the relatively late date of the Apocalypse.

The Apocalypse of Peter: another Christian Prophecy

Coming now to the Apocalypse of Peter we recall that while, like the Apocalypse of John, it is a revelation delivered by the Risen Christ, it is not dominated to the same extent by pre-occupation with the approaching parousia. After giving instruction parallel to that of the synoptic apocalypse, which seems to prolong the perspective to the time of Barkochba, it describes at length the pains in store for the damned and the blessedness of the elect, coming to an end in the exaltation of the Christ carried up to heaven. This Apocalypse, like most of the others, is a compilation. In the first part it gives us eschatological instruction by the Risen Christ parallel to that of the synoptic apocalypse, of which it reproduces certain elements, and also parallel to the brief summary found at the end of Luke and in the beginning of Acts. But it has certain peculiarities of its own, such as the eschatological explanation of the allegory of the barren fig-tree, of a kind which turns this part of the book into confirmation of our thesis that teachings originally attributed to the Risen Christ speaking through Christian prophets have been transposed into the Gospel story, and there presented as given by Jesus before his death, when preaching in Galilee or at Jerusalem. Another peculiarity is that our Apocalypse, in the last part, and especially in its account of the pains of the damned and the bliss of the elect, describes them as going on in the actual present, as though the fate of men were decided immediately after death by a judgment which classed them for ever as lost or saved. This indicates a point of view entirely different from that of either Jewish or Christian eschatology, but is rather in line with the pagan mysteries, Orphic and Egyptian, in which there was no *general* resurrection.

As to the appearance of Moses and Elijah and the assumption of the Christ to heaven in their company, it is quite clear that our Apocalypse is the original source of the scene which, thrown back into the earthly life of the Christ, became the miracle of the Transfiguration. This explains why the miracle, narrated only in the Synoptics, is said to have been witnessed only by three leading disciples and the injunction laid upon them, according to Mark (ix, 9) and Matthew (xvii, 9), to say nothing about it until the Son of Man be risen from the dead, while, according to Luke, they did keep silence at the time. This is tantamount to saying that the transposition is avowed by the evangelists themselves.

From all this it follows that the gospel legend, as well as the gospel teaching of Jesus, were constructed, in important parts, by a process of transposition and anticipation of elements borrowed from the eschatological catechesis. The fact is significant and by no means lacking in importance. Nor is it in the least surprising, because, however it be explained, it only shows that the teachings of the catechesis, mystic doctrine or seeming narrative, were not dominated by historical considerations but by its own catechetical aim. And this aim, through all its manipulations of the material utilized, which seem so irresponsible to us, was ever one and the same—to exalt the Christ in such manner as to draw men of goodwill to worship him. Had the Gospels been offered as historical tradition one would have to say that those who fixed the form of it were audaciously making sport both of the tradition and of those to whom they would transmit their work.

ESCHATOLOGY FULLY TRANSFORMED INTO GOSPEL LEGEND

Viewing the New Testament literature in its totality, we have now seen how the Christian catechesis, at first eschatological, took the form, in the Epistles regarded as apostolic, of a mystical gnosis *before* it assumed, in the Gospels, the form of a sacred legend by means of which the eager catechumen was initiated into the Christian cult. We have now to consider a little more closely the fortunes of this gnosis before it passed into legend.

For example, we have seen how, in the Epistle to the Romans, a mystical gnosis was hitched on, so to say, to the eschatological theory of salvation expounded by Paul in his original letter to the Christians of Rome. Not only are the two theses (setting aside a few glosses) developed in mutual independence, but each is complete in itself and in contradiction with the other. If, instead of being thus independent and contradictory, the final text presented them as reconciled and fused into one, the mind of the author having thus fused them, then indeed we should have to maintain that this arrangement of the two doctrines was the outcome of spiritual forces at work in Paul himself. But this is not a case of fusion but of juxtaposition, in other words of editorial combination, as anyone who is willing to see what is under his eyes will discover at once on literary analysis of the text.

This is also the right place to recall the further fact that the duality of these two doctrines, the eschatological and the gnostic, is admitted, in principle, by the Epistles themselves. When Paul, that is the pretended Paul, is made to write (1 Corinthians iii, 1–2): "As for me, brethren, I could not address you as spiritual, but as carnal, as babes in Christ; I have given you milk to drink, not solid food; for you were not able to bear it"—when he writes thus about milk and solid food, "milk" can only mean some teaching regarded as elementary, to wit, the eschatological catechesis, while "solid food" is the gnosis of salvation which the author himself is actually in process of addressing to his readers, after having artificially hitched it on to what the real Paul has said about the baptism conferred by him on certain Corinthians (i, 14–16). Now the fact is that the "wisdom" which the mystic or pseudo-Paul declares to be reserved "for them that are perfect," for the fully initiated, wisdom which he teaches "in mystery," because it is "hidden" and which even "the rulers of the world have not known, because if they had known it they would not have crucified the Lord of glory" (ii, 6–9)—the fact is that we have here the very doctrine which he proceeds to expound to the very people whom he declares incapable of understanding it. It would be impossible to avoid the most absurd of contradictions if we remained blind to the double perspective created by this pretended Paul, who now expounds a gnosis in regard to which the teaching formerly given by the real Paul, to wit, the eschatological catechesis, is described as only milk for babes. Whoso is willing to understand, let him understand!

The case of the author of the Epistle to the Hebrews is exactly the same, except that this author gives us explicit information about the elementary catechesis to which he claims that his own gnosis is superior. We have already studied the text which establishes the distinction between the two (vi, 1–2) and made our commentary (*supra*, p. 34). What the author calls "the initial theme of the Christ" is the common catechesis of his time; what he calls "perfection" is gnostic initiation; "the foundation of repentance" is the moral teaching which urges the catechumen to be sorry for the sins of which he will be cleansed by baptism. What is this but the eschatological catechesis, and in a form in which not the least place can be found for the evangelical catechesis of the Gospel story? But, in making this distinction between his own mysticism and the elementary catechism of

Christianity, the author professes the very principle of gnosis and, in proceeding to impart his mystical poetry to people whom he declares to be incapable of understanding it, he falls into the same contradiction as the gnostic who introduces his doctrine into First Corinthians. The sole difference between the two is that the author of Hebrews avows the contradiction. If he really intended to pass himself off as Paul, that is, if it was he who wrote xiii, 19, 23–24, the position of the two gnostics would be exactly the same. In any case, that is the position of the writer who, at the end of the Epistle, speaks in the name of Paul.

The great gnosis developed in the middle part of the Epistle to the Romans (v–viii; see *supra*, p. 253) may have been conceived with no reference to the eschatological theory, and the author does not *himself* pretend to be Paul. But, by incorporation with the Epistle, it is presented as coming from the apostle, and whoever so incorporated it intended it to confront the eschatological Christianity as a higher fulfilment and rectification of its eschatology, just as it is presented in First Corinthians and as the author to the Hebrews presents the gnosis peculiar to his Epistle. The same holds true of the gnostic parts of the Epistle to the Galatians and of Second Corinthians where pretended Paul, Paul the mystic, is represented as the unique depositary of a gospel uniquely true, this gospel being no other than the salvation gnosis preached by him. In the Epistle to the Galatians he prides himself on owing nothing to those who were apostles before him, meaning by that the Elders at Jerusalem. But how often must we repeat that the Twelve, in their lifetime, were never *apostles* and that the real Paul never knew them as such? He also prides himself on having, in a revelation given to himself in particular, received the gospel which he preaches among the Gentiles, to wit, the salvation gnosis summarily taught in the Epistle to the Galatians and, with all the amplitude it merits, in that to the Romans. In Second Corinthians our pseudo-Paul goes as far as to say that since the Christ died "that the living should live no more for themselves but for him who died for them and rose again, henceforth he knew no man after the flesh, and if ever he had known the Christ after the flesh, now he knew him no more." Commentators have been much embarrassed in their attempt to understand what our author means by "the Christ after the flesh." Certainly it was not precisely the Christ of history—for that conception was not in existence at the time. It can only have been the Christ-man of the eschatological catechesis announced by those whom pseudo-Paul condemns as Judaizers—Jesus made Christ by his death and Lord in his immortality. The Christ of Paul the mystic, on the other hand, is the spiritual Man, made flesh to effect redemption by his death and live again as the Lord of his mystery. In this conception, that of the Epistle to the Romans, the revelation of the mystic Christ stands as clearly opposed to the primitive eschatology as in First Corinthians and Hebrews.

Many Forms of Gnosis in the Epistles

Though "the gnosis of Paul" is a phrase freely used, it would be more exact to speak of the gnoses that have been put out under his name. For it is far from true that one and the same gnostic system is professed in all the Epistles, or in all parts of the same Epistle, which have their origin in gnostic mysticism. While there is no ground for making all these gnoses into reflections of Marcion's system, no less unfounded is the fault found with the author of *The Birth of the Christian Religion* for representing them as distinct, since that is precisely what they are when interpreted in the sense conveyed by their own language.

What, for example, is the meaning of the gnostic poem inserted into the Epistle to the Philippians (ii, 6–11; *supra*, p. 264)? Is it not the odyssey of a divine Being, a panegyric of the spiritual Christ, lodged in a moral exhortation penetrated by gnosis, and conceived in complete independence both of the gospel catechesis and the eschatological?

What, again, is the gnostic poem which has got itself enshrined and paraphrased in the Epistle to the Colossians (i, 15–20; cf. *supra*, p. 265) but another definition of the mystery of salvation, analogous to that elaborated in Hebrews as well as to that which underlies the fourth Gospel and, like the foregoing, independent of both catecheses, and perhaps used in the Epistle to counter a pagan mystery with a Jewish colour (ii, 16–23; cf. *The Birth of the Christian Religion*, p. 265).

And is there not yet another gnosis in the Epistle to the Hebrews? And is not this one of the most original, and not the less so because its author presents it as the climax of the revelations made to Israel, apparently lodging it in the frame of the primitive catechesis and giving us a glimpse, through some of its features, of the gospel catechesis in process of formation (cf. *supra*, p, 266).

Finally, we have the brief gnostic poem in the First to Timothy (iii, 16), there offered as a definition of "the mystery of godliness," in which we find a proclamation of the very principle of the gospel catechesis, to wit, "the appearance of the Christ in the flesh." Though of later date than the preceding, does it not seem, in saying that the Christ was "justified in spirit," to retain the original conception of the resurrection as purely spiritual, which is certainly not that of the gospel story in its canonical forms?

In addition to all this, we know how the epistolary teaching made acquisitions of many kinds; how it was not only a depositary for various gnoses, with or without adaptation to the primitive eschatology, but became charged with doctrinal enlargements and compromises, and especially with moral teaching and exhortation, even with rules of church discipline, all this being done by those who believed they had the right to make the apostles give answers on these points whenever conditions in the churches suggested that a ruling was called for.

But, first and foremost, we have only to confront the Epistles attributed to Paul with the seven letters which the Christ of the Apocalypse addresses to the churches of Asia by his prophet-spokesman to satisfy ourselves that in these churches, and chiefly at Ephesus, there were Christian groups which claimed Paul's authority and ascribed it to those whom we may call his literary successors. To such circles as these we owe the creation of the fictitious gnostic Paul who, especially in the Epistle to the Galatians and in Second Corinthians, puts forth the altogether preposterous claim to be, by the special choice and revelation of the Christ, the unique depositary of a unique Gospel, to wit, the revelation of the mystery, under the diverse forms or definitions it assumes in the great epistles and in the lesser. Opposing this fictitious Paul stands the fiction of the Twelve Apostles and that of Peter, the pretended source, original and also unique, of the Christian apostolate. And, combined with this in Asia, we have the fiction of the beloved disciple who, like Paul, is author of a small library, Apocalypse, Gospel and three Epistles. All this in

preparation for the final stage when these more or less contradictory theses will be brought to a synthesis, and their divergences
somewhat smoothed over and apparently reconciled in the
gospel catechesis and the canonical collection of the New
Testament.

The Real Paul and the Fictitious

We have now reached what is, perhaps, the most important
result of this part of our study. This consists in the radical
dissimilation of the Paul who really spoke and the Paul who was
represented as speaking. The first, the historic Paul, was the
preacher of the primitive eschatological catechesis, enlarging it
only, as it had already been enlarged by the Antioch missionaries,
with a view to bringing pagans into the fold by sparing them the
constraint of the legal observances. The second was Paul the
mystic, with his audacious pretensions, his perpetual and tiresome boastfulness, his gross abuse of the old disciples whom he
makes out to be Judaizers. As a personality having a place in
primitive Christian history this second Paul would be wholly
inexplicable, but is intelligible enough as the mouthpiece of
Christian groups which believed themselves heirs of the Pauline
tradition. They it was who, in reality, brought into the tradition,
not indeed the principle of universal salvation by faith in the
risen Christ—from the beginning there had been not great
difficulty in admitting that—but the mystery of salvation by
mystic union with a Saviour who had come down from heaven
and returned to it in glory—a Saviour to whom the ardent
believer was united, not only by knowledge of the mystery,
but in an intimate communion effected by sacraments, with their
ritual of probation, participation and final vision. This point is
reached in the baptismal hymn quoted in the Epistle to the
Ephesians (v, 14) and by Clement of Alexandria:[1]

> Awake, thou sleeper,
>   rise up from among dead men,
> And Christ the Lord shall enlighten thee,
>   the sun of the resurrection,
> Begotten before the morning star (Psalm cx, 3)
>   giving life by his beams.

[1] *Protrepticos*, viii, 84, 1, 2. See *The Birth of the Christian Religion*, p. 228.

As, on the one hand, the mystery retained in substance the ethic of the primitive eschatology and even tended, in certain parts, to improve upon it; as, on the other, it had its own way of understanding the Last Things as the inward and spiritual Reign of God, so it was inevitable that the mystic Paul would be made to deliver oracles on the problems thrown up by the state of the churches and the course of events, and also, when the mounting extravagances of the gnostic Christians made it necessary, on the compromises and the discipline needed to prevent the Church dissolving in a fermentation of sects. Our analysis has already shown the place in the evolution of nascent Christianity which belongs to the documents pretending to be Epistles, and we shall not repeat the exposition here. It is easy enough to understand why Paul was made to deliver oracles on marriage and virginity, on joining pagans in their sacrifices, on the ordering of the Supper, on spiritual gifts, on faith in the resurrection. All that was done spontaneously and under the pressure of circumstances. This it is that explains the differences we encounter in regard both to doctrine and practice, to be found among these lucubrations which, in the view of their authors, seemed required by the needs of the moment.

What could throw a more revealing light on this matter than the intrusion of the Song of Love in 1 Corinthians xiii? If there is one point in the criticism of the Epistles that admits of no doubt, it is that the Song of Love in its primitive form[1] is nothing else than the spontaneous reaction of some highly gifted mystic, of a Christian mind that soared aloft beyond the gnoses and the vulgar eschatology, in presence of the poor display of "spiritual gifts" spread before him in the preceding chapter. We can see how this noble poem got slipped into the Pauline dossier: some scribe or editor, finding it to hand, undertook to place it there as best he could. He has not placed it very happily, but his interpolation has saved it for us, and Christians have good reasons for the profoundest gratitude to its author, who has here bequeathed to us the true "essence of Christianity." How is it that our critics are not impressed by this evident interpolation? The answer is only too plain: if they allowed themselves to recognize it our cause would be won all along the line. The respectable

---

[1] See *Remarques*, 69-74.

311

limitations of their approach to these questions will long prevent them making that admission.

The authoritative pronouncement on the Resurrection in 1 Corinthians xv[1] reveals an attempt to adapt eschatology to gnosis, the material idea of the resurrection to the spiritual, the historic Paul and the mystical Paul to the conventional Paul, who already has almost become the Paul of orthodoxy, full of respect for the Twelve, like the Paul of Acts, and willing to accept the subordinate position imposed upon him by the interest of the Christian communities then in process of unification as the Catholic Church. Here we shall not repeat the detail of what we have said elsewhere on the small retouches and late interpolations this chapter has undergone.

The Remaining Epistles

We have already named the various stages of the Christian movement to which the Pastoral Epistles, the Epistle of James, the two of Peter, Jude's and the three of John, severally correspond. The whole of this literature is as completely fictitious, from the literary point of view, as any writings could be; none of it goes back to the apostolic age; every part of it originated at a moment when it seemed required for the service of a Christianity now established or in process of establishment. The catechesis attributed to James shows that a well-intentioned believer had come to the conclusion that the doctrine of salvation by faith alone, as it had been announced in certain pages of the Pauline *dossier*, might have results reprehensible from the moral point of view. The Pastorals, confronting the gnostic crisis, are concerned with the organization of government in the churches and the crystallization of the traditional deposit of faith. The First of Peter does not look so far ahead; its main interest is in the gnosis which the author finds in the Pauline *dossier* and in the moral consequences it seems to involve, and this is the case of all the other Epistles occasioned or penetrated by gnostic influence. For example, at a given moment between the years 110 and 130 the duty of submission to the established powers became a commonplace with these moralists. The Epistle of Jude betrays a horror of gnostic excesses. The Second of Peter, boldly taking its stand

[1] *Op. cit.*, 74-84.

on the last products of eschatological teaching, also denounces the gnostic peril, but seems mainly preoccupied in presenting a total debâcle of the primitive catechesis by explaining that the delay of the End is a breathing-space of which profitable use should be made, and, strangely enough, points to Paul's Epistles as likely to lead, unless care be taken, to wrong conclusions in this matter. But this pretended Epistle of Peter proves, by the allusion just named, that there existed at the time it was written a collection of letters attributed to Paul, and that these formed part of a body of Scripture, and that it was then possible to speak of a New Testament Canon. As to the Johannine Espistles we have already seen that they shared the fortune of the major writings in that category, the Apocalypse and the Gospel, especially the latter, to which they were intended to serve as convoy. And this leads us to summarize our conclusions regarding the gospel catechesis of which we have already seen glimpses but await a full view.

THE GOSPEL CATECHESIS IN FULL VIEW

We make no apology for repeating, what cannot be repeated too often—that the Gospels were not originally understood as a history of Jesus, of which the material had been furnished by those who had known the Christ in the course of his existence on earth. The primitive catechesis turned on the Last Things; it was eschatological and looked on Jesus not as the Messiah, the Christ, who *had come* (in which case it would have been led to interpret his earthly career as a messianic epiphany), but believed in him solely as the Messiah *about to come*, the effect being to withdraw his earlier existence from the realm of mystical interest and leave the first believers indifferent to it. In consequence, all the interest attaching to the name of Jesus then lay, not in his earthly career, but in his approaching parousia. This in sum was the essential object, if not the unique object, of faith. The Jesus on whom this faith centred was not Jesus as he *had lived* on earth, but Jesus as the Christ *now living* with God, and the conditions needed to make sure of a place in the Great Kingdom he would soon bring in. All the teaching of Jesus known to this catechesis on the Last Things, to this eschatological catechesis, was attributed by it to the immortal Christ in heaven; and we have already seen that it was only at a later period that this teaching was antedated and thrown back into the life of the Christ on earth, and how his exaltation as Messiah was treated in exactly the same manner.

Whence it results that the messianic interpretation of the earthly life of Jesus is not primordial, is not an experience of the age called apostolic; in all strictness of truth it is a *product* of the new faith. It was not with a view to retrieving a forgotten story that the gospel catechesis was drawn up. That was bound to happen, and did happen under a kind of inward necessity resulting, not precisely from the theories of salvation—for mystical speculation was first directed to the death of Jesus as the condition of his exaltation to Messiahship—but from the establishment of the Christian mystery as a *cult* to which initiation was necessary. Of this cult Jesus became, for the faith, not only the divine object, but the founder and master of the mystery, himself the prototype of the salvation which, if we may say so, he had achieved in himself, that he might make it a reality for all who were his. In this way catechesis was transformed into Gospel, into Good News, inasmuch as it showed forth the epiphany of a Saviour, Jesus the Christ. The gospel form of the catechesis, the story form, was non-existent in the first Christian age and cannot go, and does not go, so far back.

This also explains the relative but incontestible poverty of the gospel legend and the perpetual artifice of its construction. Many of our exegetes still speak of it as a selection made from abounding memories. In point of fact, as we have said already and repeat with assurance, neither memory nor selection has anything to do with the matter. The elements of the legend have been taken from various sources; much, and not the least important, has been borrowed, as we have seen, from the eschatological catechesis; and all of it has been adapted, as best might be, to the main object in view, that of setting forth the Christian mystery. The dependence of Matthew and Luke, even of John, on Mark is certainly no indication that a great wealth of material was available; for it is obvious that the Marcan sketch became the base of the other books simply for want of anything better. The workings over and the additions this sketch has undergone, both in Mark's Gospel itself and in the other evangelical writings, have far more the effect upon us of accentuating the artificial character of the story than of disguising it. On a wide view, the first Gospel and the third are a fusion of the sacred legend, sketched in by Mark, with a mass of teaching, mostly moral, whose original place was the eschatological catechesis, while the fourth Gospel is constructed on the model of the other three.

In like manner the documents which exegetes are wont to call "sources" of the Gospels lack the qualities of historical documents, of which use could be made for a biography of Jesus. But that does not prevent the names of places from belonging to a real geography nor the names of persons being those of men who were once alive on earth. Jesus the Nazorean, John the Baptizer, Pontius Pilate belong to the history of their time; but among the actors in this sacred tragedy it may well be that Pontius Pilate is the one about whom history has the most certain, or the least uncertain, information. When human history goes deep into its subject, it finds the rôle played by official persons easier to define than that of others which are often more real and of greater influence on the course of events. But we must not enlarge upon that.

The Catechesis of Mark

Mark's formless sketch is not all of a piece and certainly has been worked over more than once. Memories of Peter? The idea is out of the question. In Mark's Gospel Peter is not a source of information but an object of almost constant abuse. It would seem that the original draft of the Gospel had none of the preliminaries concerning John the Baptist; it began by placing Jesus at Capernaum for the calling of the first disciples, and finished with the exclamation of the centurion on hearing the last outcry of Jesus on the cross: "Verily this man was the Son of God"; at that moment Jesus was deemed to enter upon his eternal life and the tale of his Passion was ended. What follows reflects the relatively late idea of a material resurrection the third day after death, co-ordinated with the Christian celebration of Easter on Sunday. To search for the lost end of Mark is waste of labour, since all endings beyond the centurion's exclamation are only postscripts. The preliminaries of the Gospel, the mission of the Baptist and the baptism of Jesus, are additions borrowed from the source used by Matthew and Luke for the purpose of fixing

John's position as that of forerunner of the Christ, John's rôle, in the messianic epiphany (antedated, as we have seen, to the earthly life of Jesus) being the rôle which the primitive catechesis gave him in regard to the coming Kingdom of God. Then, too, the baptism of Jesus, conceived as the prototype of Christian baptism, served as opening to the catechism of the Christian initiate, and this beginning was the preface to various teachings on the economy of the Christian mystery and its differentiation from Judaism, or what was considered as a Judaizing conception of salvation. For the second part of the Gospel, which begins with Peter's confession at Caesarea Philippi, turns on the mystery of the redeeming death, memorialized in the mystic celebration of the Eucharist.

In one current of this mystic gnosis a point was made of emphasizing Peter's complete lack of understanding in presence of the revealed mystery, to the extent that it was thought fitting to make the Christ characterize him as Satan. His incomprehension is not less complete in presence of the Transfiguration, nor at Gethsemane. It was even thought to be a known fact that, at the trial of Jesus, he had found occasion to deny his master thrice. In presence of the third prediction of the Passion, the sons of Zebedee are not less unintelligent than he; their only response to the prophecy is to ask for the two chief thrones right and left of the Christ's in his Kingdom! But we must not forget that the messianic confession of Peter is the throw-back of what was originally a post-resurrection episode; that the miracle of the Transfiguration is another, and that the whole conception of the mystery in like manner anticipates a later stage in the evolution of early Christian thought. The same may be said of the calling of the fishermen whom Jesus is represented as making into apostles on the spot; of everything, also, that is said about the character of the Son of Man, which, in the gospel tradition, is the definition of the Christ dying for the salvation of mankind. This is the mystery in presence of which the disciples, who knew it not, are said to have shown themselves unintelligent with a perseverance that nothing could overcome. Care also has been taken to inform us that they understood nothing at the two miracles of multiplied loaves (vi, 35–44; viii, 14–21). This also is most sign ficant. For the story of these two miracles is nothing else than the myth of the eucharistic institution at an early stage in the evolution of the mystery at which, without being expressly the symbol of Jesus' saving death, the Supper had come to signify communion in the truth and immortality given by the Christ to his own. This conception has now acquired its mystic character and is no longer purely eschatological.

Lastly we have a feature characteristic of Mark's catechesis and at the same time a revealing light on the general antedating by the Gospels of the divine epiphany: it is as follows.

In the view of the evangelists Jesus is revealed as the Messiah by his miracles, by his own discourses and even by the remarks addressed to him by others. On such occasions the order is given to all to keep silence about what has happened, as if a secret were being violated which ought not to be disclosed until Jesus is dead and risen. Thus we find the demons never fail to cry out that Jesus is the Son of God while Jesus, who continues to drive them out, never fails to bid them hold their peace. The same order is expressly given to the disciples after Peter's confession, and is repeated after the Transfiguration. Nothing could show more clearly that the whole display of messianic signs belongs to a secondary stage in the Christian faith, at which Jesus was consciously invested during his earthly life with a glory originally belonging to him as the Risen Christ.

We conclude, then, that Mark's Gospel, considered as it stands, has a long and complex history. It is impossible to assign precise dates to all the elements it contains. There are details in the compilation which prove a plurality of stages in the drafting of the document. One of these is the note, quite early in Mark (iii, 6), which terminates the series of Jesus' quarrels with the Pharisees, especially those about the Sabbath: "The Pharisees, having departed, took counsel with the Herodians against him how they might destroy him." This half opens the door on the perspective of the Passion, the story of which it may have originally served to introduce.

The facility of the gospel narrator in improvising miracles— and the remark holds good for all the Gospels, and not only for Mark—for no other purpose than to emphasize his exposition and make the point of it clearer, may well cause us some surprise. But it would be a mistake to think that these writers or editors enjoy the invention of the marvellous for its own sake and indulge in it as a pastime or, which would be more serious, that they are boldly taking advantage of the credulous age to which their writings were addressed. The truth is that the stories they tell are, for them, true stories in virtue of the meaning they imply in regard to the spiritual work of the Christ. Unless we take account of this we may be tempted to rank their authors as barefaced purveyors of falsehood. There can be no doubt, however, that they regarded their inventions as justified for the above reason, and we have to take the stories accordingly, attaching more importance to the spirit than to the letter.

Taking the book as a whole, the Gospel according to Mark can hardly have assumed its final form before 130–140, the date at which we find the good Papias acquainted with it. The first drafts of it may go back to the beginning of the second century, the period when the conception of the Christian mystery took definite shape, and the need began to be felt for a catechesis in narrative form embodying the mystery. At an indeterminate stage of its compilation the Gospel must have fallen into the hands of some mystic group in which Peter and the Galilean disciples were no better treated than in certain Epistles attributed to Paul. There is nothing extraordinary in this, but we do well to bear it in mind.

We may accept it as probable that whoever slipped into the Gospel the arrangement of the resurrection stories that authorize the Sunday Easter did so in the interest of that arrangement at a time when the Sunday observance had been accepted by all the groups of the Roman Church; for Mark seems to have been mainly elaborated as a Roman Gospel. It is obvious that the book had no other usage in view than that of public reading in the assembled congregation. Those who think it possible to maintain that the book was written as a chronicle and for private edification are under a radical illusion as to the nature of such literature and the objects for which it was written.

To be sure, no attempt was made to incorporate into Mark the mass of moral instructions more or less closely bound up with the eschatological catechesis. This is what the compilers of Matthew and Luke set themselves to do, for the greater enrichment and efficiency of Christian teaching. The two Gospels, in their traditional form, bear witness to equal concern in a direction opposite to that in which the teaching on the Last Things was turned—that of going *back* to the terrestrial birth of the Christ. This Mark's Gospel had not dared to attempt, the integration it presents of the public life of Jesus with his messianic epiphany being already more than enough to characterize the Gospel as innovating. Preoccupation with this subject would first show itself in Judaizing circles, which had to answer awkward Jewish questions about the person of their pretended Messiah who had no visible claim to be descended from David, as the Messiah must needs be. By some believers this objection had been met by denying that Davidic descent was an essential qualification of the Messiah, quoting Psalm cx as their authority, in which David was said to address the Christ as his "Lord." Mark, Matthew and Luke all record this way of meeting the objection. But the compilers of Matthew and Luke seem to have overlooked the fact that, in this denial of the necessity of Davidic descent recorded by both of them, the genealogies they produce to prove it are rendered superfluous. The compiler who inserted the denial in Mark (xii, 35–37) may have thought it was enough that the Christ should be Son of God. Two genealogies were then invented, both fictitious, and contradictory, as we have seen, to the point of being quite worthless, were it not for the light they throw on other things. Moreover they have not come through without being neutralized and put out of court by the myth of Virgin Conception, from which it would follow that Jesus was only the putative descendant of David by Joseph, who was not his real father, as intermediary. In addition to this, the birth-stories in Matthew are built up on the Virgin Conception, whereas in Luke the Virgin Conception has been interpolated and surcharged (i, 34–35). This divergence, as we have pointed out, is far from furnishing an argument for the priority of Matthew.

The Catechesis in Matthew

The first Gospel may well be of less ancient date than is commonly supposed, not only because its birth-stories are dominated by the Virgin Conception, but also because it has been constructed on Mark in the form given to that Gospel by the oldest manuscripts, and must therefore be later than the literary work which produced the second Gospel. At certain points it may be, and doubtless is, later than Luke, though certainly not dependent on it. Some of the materials collected in it have a Judaizing tendency, though that is not true of its general spirit. Its liking for Old Testament prophecy, of which it never tires of showing the fulfilment, is evidence that this form of argument was of present force with the audience for which it was intended; indeed, the critics are agreed that this Gospel was composed in the East—to be more precise, in Syria. Its dependence on Mark is the more significant on that account; so, too, is the facility with which it has absorbed all that Mark adduces to the discredit of Peter and the Galilean disciples. The reason doubtless is that this part of the story had already taken the form of an accepted tradition.

The remarkable fact remains to be noted that in the solemn episode of the messianic confession the compilers of the Gospel have exalted Peter beyond anything to be read about him elsewhere in the New Testament. To the question propounded by Jesus (xvi, 15): "Who say ye that I am?" Peter not only replies as in Mark (viii, 29): "Thou art the Christ," but "Thou art the Christ, son of the living God." To which Jesus makes answer:

> Blessed art thou, Simon son of Jona,
> > because flesh and blood have not revealed it to thee,
> > but my father who is in heaven.
> But I also say to thee, thou art *Peter*,
> > and on this *rock* I will build my church,
> > and hell's gates shall not prevail against it.
> I will give thee the keys of the Kingdom of Heaven,
> > and what thou shalt bind on earth shall be bound in heaven,
> > and what thou shalt loose on earth shall be loosed in heaven.

Placed beside the "Back, Satan!" etc., by which Peter is crushed in xvi, 23, copied from Mark (viii, 33), these words are simply stupefying. We are told that the play of words on Kepha, "Peter," is possible only in Aramean. That is so; these magnificent propositions were born in the East. Moreover, they are aimed at the mystic Paul with an eye to Galatians i, 11, 15–17: "The Gospel I announce is not according to man . . . I *received it by revelation of Jesus Christ* . . . When it pleased God to reveal his Son in me, *without regard to flesh and blood*, without going to Jerusalem to those who were apostles before me," etc. In our text, he who receives the revelation of Jesus Christ is Peter; he who owes it not to any man is Peter; he who has been appointed foundation of the Church is Peter. But this solemn declaration is no invention of the gospel compiler; he found it complete and ready to his hand. The piece is only the more precious to us for that, but not more authentic nor more ancient. Briefly, it corresponds to the position attributed to Peter in the Book of Acts, and found its way into the first Gospel about the year 140. It would be superfluous to repeat at this point the evidence which forbids us to assign a much earlier date to the *canonical* edition of the whole Gospel, though it was known to Papias along with Mark.

The Catechesis in Luke and Acts

The case of the third Gospel and of the Acts of the Apostles is more complicated than that of Matthew, seeing that the two original books addressed to Theophilus have undergone a process of elaboration of which our two canonical books are the result. It is certain that the writer to Theophilus, like Matthew, knew Mark without further ending than the discovery of the empty tomb by the Galilean women, if indeed he knew it thus, for in that case it could only be the canonical edition of the Gospel. But it is neither certain nor probable that he knew the section of Mark comprised, in the canonical version, between the two miracles of multiplied loaves (vi, 45–viii, 26). In all probability he had no story to tell about the birth of Jesus and began his gospel narrative with the account of John's baptizing. He seems to have known Mark at a stage when it lacked the symbolism of the mystic Supper and of the bread-body and wine-blood of the Christ. Similarly, in the second book (Acts) he seems to have known nothing of the Ascension and its preliminaries nor of the miraculous descent of the Spirit on the first believers at Pentecost. We may infer from this that a long time elapsed between the original composition of the two books and their canonical edition in the form they now have, with its contrivances in favour of the Ephesian legend about John, its set purpose of subordinating Paul to the Galilean apostles (falsely called apostles) and especially to Peter, its grossly material conception of the resurrection and its deliberate reticence about

Simon the Magician, about what happened to Peter after his flight from Jerusalem and, at the end the book, about the fate of Paul.

If we assume that the two books to Theophilus, in their original form as they came from the writer's hand, were earlier than canonical Mark, we might then place their compilation in the first quarter of the second century, between 110 and 120. It is true that the writer to Theophilus supposes that many writings analogous to his own were already in existence. But we must not conclude from this that numerous bipartite expositions of the catechesis, like his, were then in circulation; enough that there were many and varied specimens whether of the eschatological type, which was not yet out of date, and concerned in substance with the origins of the faith and of Christian propaganda, or of sketches more or less rudimentary of the gospel catechesis, such as that which we may continue to call proto-Mark.

As to the date of the canonical edition of the third Gospel and of Acts we may (as indicated above, p. 192) fix it between 135 and 140, with this reservation, that while the third Gospel had, to all seeming, acquired its final form before Marcion, who must have known the *corpus* of the Gospel almost in the form it now has, we have not the same evidence for the date of Acts, though it is certain that one and the same editor gave the two books their characteristic form of apologies for Christianity as the authentic heir of Judaism and the messianic fulfilment predicted in Jewish scripture. It is certain also that features peculiar to the third Gospel and Acts were acquired before Marcion; these features are the symbolic anticipation of Jesus' preaching at Nazareth and of the miraculous draught in the vocation story; the symbolic mission of the seventy or seventy-two forerunners; the representation of the Twelve and chiefly of Peter as the depositaries and authentic apostles of Christian truth. Moreover, Marcion seems to have held that Luke was not free from Jewish contamination. It remains to add that the first edition of this Gospel, like the first of Mark, was adapted to the quartodeciman Easter, and the final edition to the Sunday observance, as was also the final edition of Mark. It would be of great value to the historian if the date could be ascertained when the devices were practised which altered the chronology of the Passion so as to make it support the Roman observance on Sunday; the documentary evidence is lacking that would enable us to fix it with precision (cf. *supra*, p. 75). We know only that between 150 and 160 the Roman bishop Anicetus pretended to authorize the Sunday observance of Easter by citing the practice of his predecessors. We must be resigned, at least provisionally, to be ignorant about certain matters on which our documents were not intended to enlighten us, but rather to keep us in the dark.

The Catechesis in the Fourth Gospel

We have already discussed the origin of the fourth Gospel and seen that the documents on which it rests expound a mystic doctrine which, strictly speaking, is not a gospel doctrine in the sense of the synoptic catechesis, nor strictly eschatological in the sense of the primitive teaching; pieces of gnosis rather, in keeping with the idea of the Christ's continual presence in those who are his own and their participation in his immortal life. The adaptation of it to gospel type sprang from the desire to accommodate mystic gnosis to the teaching pattern of the synoptic catechesis, which was also mystico-gnostic in its own way, though not in its literary form. Nevertheless, the Johannine adaptation remained in keeping with the Easter observance known as quartodeciman, and sublimated into mystic gnosis, as was everything that its catechesis had to borrow from the earlier Gospels, not for the purpose of completing their account, but with a view to displacing them and becoming their substitutes. We have already studied in chapter iii the grandiose and daring fiction that was constructed to invest the new Gospel with the apostolic authority of John. But it arrived too late to supplant the others completely. In the beginning it seems to have had no acceptance beyond the frontiers of the Asiatic province where it saw the light, and where, doubtless, it was at first not unopposed from the side of those who still clung to the synoptic catechesis previously known.

The development of the gnostic crisis seems to have had a great influence in determining the modifications that were soon introduced into this Asiatic Gospel. They were mainly as follows: account was taken of John the Baptist, and even a large use made of his personality; the attempt was made to conform the

document to the general framework of the Synoptics, while
retaining its own chronology; due respect was paid to the traditional eschatology, which the fundamental doctrine of the book
seemed rather to exclude; lastly, without abandoning the fiction
of Johannine authorship nor the somewhat equivocal personality
of the beloved disciple, considerable prerogative was accorded
to Peter, the same that he receives in Matthew and in Acts, to
wit, the charge and function of chief shepherd of Christ's flock.
It follows that, if we date the first writing of the Gospel at
approximately 135, the last working over of its catechesis may
certainly be placed between 150 and 160, that is to say, at the
time when we have good grounds for supposing that the negotiations took place between the chief Christian churches with a
view to fixing the canon of authorized Gospels as a defence
against the dangers of the oncoming gnostic tide.

MARCION'S CATECHESIS

It is generally known, or ought to be, that the first author of
a New Testament canon was none other than the heretic Marcion. Appealing mainly to the authority of the mystic Paul he
sets himself to prove that the Jewish scriptures, made much of
in the common tradition of Christians—and the more so because they had no recognized scriptures of their own to which
appeal could be made—set himself to prove that this Jewish
revelation, together with our bad terrestrial world, were the work
of a hard-hearted and incompetent demiurge, while the Gospel
of the good, transcendent God, who had been unknown to the
world till the epiphany of Jesus, had nowhere been preserved in
its purity. Nowhere; for the gospel books used in the churches
had been contaminated by the Judaizing influences openly denounced by Paul in his Epistles. This was the state of things
which Marcion claimed to have demonstrated in his *Antitheses*.
In his great solicitude for the salvation of all men of goodwill, he
had determined to publish Christian scriptures, cleansed by him
of Jewish poison; to which end he put forth, first, *the* Gospel
(*Evangelion*) which was our Luke *minus* the birth stories, with
such omissions or retouchings as respect for the true doctrine
demanded; and, second, the *Apostolicon*, the collected ten Epistles

then attributed to Paul, their text purified by the same methods and to the same end as that of *the* Gospel.

The Canon becomes a Necessity to the Survival of the Church

It was a great innovation, but one which the Church itself also was bound sooner or later to undertake—meaning by the Church the totality of the Christian communities, then scattered about the Mediterranean world, which continued to await the Reign of God and the coming of the Christ Jesus, while continually exalting their Christ in the direction of the Godhead. It was not only in the Church that the production of Gospels went on apace; many gnostic sects had Gospels of their own; Bastilides had one; Valentinus had another. Nor was Marcion alone in rejecting the Old Testament. Argument about the interpretation of Old Testament texts no longer yielded any profit except against the Jews, not indeed by converting them, but by meeting their objections. An armament was needed against the uncontrolled insurgence of gnostic heresies, and this could only be found in the documents of the faith, which the Church already had in its hands. It remained only to sift them and bring them to a point. This was done. Towards the year 180 the collection of the four Gospels was definitely constituted. To be convinced of that we have only to read Irenaeus.

How the operation was carried through nobody knows and we can only offer conjectures. We are bound to suppose that certain of the leading churches came to an understanding about the Gospels that were to be received to the exclusion of all the many others; failing this, the anarchy which had reigned in the production of Gospels, up to the middle of the second century, might have continued indefinitely. In particular, and chiefly, Asia had to make her own Gospel of John accceptable to the other churches, and in return to give equal consideration to the synoptic catechesis as represented by the Gospels according to Mark, Matthew and Luke respectively. It was an association of members that leaned different ways, in spite of the various retouchings effected to create a sort of harmony, apparent rather than real, between the fourth Gospel and the other three. The mere fact, therefore, that the four were brought together proves that the fourth was introduced into the group as the result of a positive agreement between the churches of Asia, which would never abandon their pretended Gospel of John, with the other churches who held to one or more of the three forms of synoptic catechesis.

The solution that would have been most advantageous, had it been practicable, was to publish a single Gospel containing a synthesis of the four. But this, doubtless, could not be thought of. It is easy to understand, in the urgent need for a rule in the matter, how impossible it would have been to bring the various churches to the point of renouncing the particular Gospel used in their liturgical worship in favour of a revised version of the Gospel to which none of them was accustomed. Tatian might succeed in this, on new and limited ground, with his *Diatessaron*, of which a fragment in the original Greek has lately been discovered at Doura.[1] But an enterprise of that kind for all the churches scattered throughout the Roman empire was quite impossible. The probability is, therefore, that the canon of the four Gospels was fixed, as far as it could be, by positive agreement between the Asiatic church and the Roman.

But when? If we search in the history of the time for an occasion when such transactions may have been set on foot, or the ground prepared for them, the most natural would be that of the conversations which took place in Rome about 150–160 between Polycarp of Smyrna and the bishop Anicetus of Rome. Perhaps we may be permitted to remind apologists of a certain type that Polycarp's journey to Rome was anything but a pious pilgrimage *ad limina*, and that the four Gospels deemed apostolic were not canonized by the sole fact that their supposed authors, apostles or disciples of apostles, themselves made a present of them to the churches and so secured their acceptance as sacred writings. None of the Gospels is apostolic in this rigorous sense, and none was imposed on church usage in the conditions supposed. At a given moment these catechisms were stamped with the authority of an apostolic name to justify the credit they already enjoyed; but neither their origin nor their text was guaranteed by the names chosen to adorn them. Challenged by the gnostic movement, and especially by Marcion's proceedings, the Church found herself summoned to oppose her

[1] Discovered March 5, 1933. See Lagrange, *Revue Biblique*, July, 1933, pp. 326–327.

own texts to those of the heretic. The canon was her answer. It is unlikely, one might even say morally impossible, that in the conversations between the Asiatic and the Roman bishops, when the question of Easter observance was carefully avoided, the two being immovably fixed in their respective practice, that the question of the Gospels to be authorized was not discussed. The hypothesis should not be dismissed as altogether groundless, but the question is, in essence, accessory (cf. *The Birth of the Christian Religion*, p. 342).

The canonization of the four Gospels most in use must have contributed to promote their regular employment in liturgical exercise throughout all the churches, as well as to determine their authority as Scripture by the side of the Old Testament. That is not to say that hitherto they had been regarded as ordinary books and that they were considered as works of the Spirit only in retrospect. All our catecheses had been accepted as works of the Spirit, in this sense, that from the very beginning their content was regarded as animated by the Christ-Spirit. But, for all that, they were not yet official Scriptures in the full and absolute sense in which the term was applied to the sacred books inherited from Judaism. All documents of Christian teaching shared, more or less, in the Spirit. This explains why the writings of certain churchmen, which had found enough credit in the churches to be employed for public reading, enjoyed in their time a sort of provisional canonicity, but lost it when the decision was taken to make apostolicity an indispensable condition for inclusion in the New Testament canon. The Epistle of Clement to the Corinthians and the Pastor of Hermas are cases in point. Certainly these writings were not less worthy of veneration than the Epistles falsely attributed to Peter and to other apostles. But they had no apostolic label, and the door to canonicity was promptly closed against them.

We cannot say what the conditions were under which Alexandria accepted what was soon known as the tetramorphic Gospel. The fact is that she herself made no contribution to the canonical collection and seems to have had no part in the negotiations which prepared it. Nevertheless Clement of Alexandria, who freely quotes the Gospel of the Egyptians, knew the canon of the four Gospels commonly received (cf. *Stromata*, iii, 92–

93), and the Gospel of the Egyptians soon fell into the complete discredit in store for the writings to be henceforth known as apocryphal. As far as we can judge by the known fragments this Gospel was deeply penetrated by gnosticism, of which Alexandria seems to have been a hot-bed in the second century. A more exact description of the situation there would be that there were in Alexandria at this time, not a single church more or less organized, but, as formerly in Rome, various Christian groups without central attachment, of which some were deep in gnosis. Not till after the lapse of considerable time was there unification in Alexandria of the more or less traditionalist groups, and clear differentiation of these from the others which fell into heresy. In the third century it was catholic Alexandria that delivered a damaging blow in the East to the fortunes of the Johannine Apocalypse, the true character of which it had clearly perceived. Later, in the Byzantine Church, the Apocalypse regained the confidence in which it was still held by the more massive faith of the West.

The Catholic Epistles

St. Jerome expresses himself rather freely on some of the catholic Epistles. On James he writes as follows (*De Viris*, 2):

> He wrote only one Epistle, which is one of the seven Catholics.
> It is said that this letter was written by another under his name,
> although it gradually gained authority with the lapse of time.

This is the best that could be said. On Jude he wrote (*De Viris*, 4):

> Jude, brother of James, has left a short Epistle, which is of the
> seven Catholics; and because he brings in a quotation from the
> book of Enoch, which is apocryphal, the letter had been rejected
> by most people; notwithstanding, it deserved credit by its anti-
> quity and by usage, and was counted among the Holy Scriptures.

On Peter he writes (*De Viris*, 1):

> He wrote two Epistles, which are called Catholic: the majority
> deny that the second is from him, in view of the difference in
> style when compared with the first.

These objections soon fell asleep, and the Canon of the New Testament became as solid brass till the time of the Reformation.

But we might almost say of every piece that entered into its composition that it won credit "by antiquity and by usage," not by the real apostolic authorship of its content.

THE FUTURE OF CHRISTIANITY

Putting aside all considerations of supernatural magic, and paying no heed to the narrow prejudice of rationalism, which leads to the denial of all human value in whatever is mingled with historical or literary fiction, dismissing all this, it still remains true that the collection of the New Testament, incomplete and incoherent as it may be in many respects, is the ever-living witness, to those who have ears to hear, of an extraordinary spiritual movement.[1] That movement was the Christian religion in its early youth.

As to the future, we may rest assured that the vitality of this movement, so stagnant at certain stages, so despised and rejected at others, is far from being exhausted. Of the two parties it is hard to say which falls into the deeper error, that which supposes Christianity to be perfect at every point, miraculous and divinely true both in its beginning and in its development to our own day—a theological myth, a dogmatic puerility, old legends converted into absolute dogmas—or that which thinks itself in the way to destroy Christianity and that soon it will be no more—another myth which fancies itself the last word of science and, from the human point of view, is no less childish, no less sterilizing than the other. The distance between mystic illusion and human truth is not as great as such people imagine.

Nothing in nature, so they tell us, ever perishes. Doubtless the same is true in the life of humanity. In the future remaining to man, a future whose end is yet far off, the food on which humanity will live will be, for the better part, the food on which it has lived hitherto. That which happened in "the fifteenth year of Tiberius Caesar," and in the first hundred and fifty obscure and tumultuous years of Christian history, will be matter of consequence to the human race to the last day of its existence on earth, because, while man lives not only upon bread, neither does he live only on science. Before all else he lives on the dynamism

[1] The same is true of the Old Testament.

of the spirit, on the moral electricity of devoted love. Therein lies the true fulfilment of his destiny.

Little does the bare letter matter of what Jesus, Peter, Paul or John, and their interpreters, have had to say on that topic. What matters is the fire they kindled, and it is a fire that will never die till mankind is no more. Men pass away, but humanity remains; religions die, but religion shines for ever. Man would have perished long ago, victim of his own folly, had not the religious ideal of humanity rescued him from the edge of the abyss. May he mend his ways and himself establish this law of his progress on an ever firmer foundation!

INDEX

Library of the Mystic Arts
A LIBRARY OF ANCIENT AND MODERN CLASSICS

APOCRYPHA, The. Intro. by Morton Enslin, Professor of Biblical Languages and Literature, St. Lawrence University. Size 7¼" x 11", xv + 239pp., bound in white and gold, 3-color slipcase. 62-12335. $15.00
REL

"A good book, like a virtuous woman, can be valued for a number of qualities. This makes its initial appeal through the beauty of its binding and printing. Only after one has admired these qualities does he read the familiar passages and move back to the excellent Introduction.

"In 1924 the Nonesuch edition of the Apocrypha appeared, limited to 1325 copies. This new edition is an almost exact facsimile of that very beautiful work, bound in a most attractive cover with stamped gilt design, and boxed. Most marked of its changes from the original, and one that enhances the value of the work considerably, is an Introduction by the editor of this Journal, Dr. Morton S. Enslin, who in brief, concise paragraphs provides excellent prefaces to the work as a whole and to each of the books individually. He places the Apocrypha in its proper context in biblical literature, indicates the inappropriateness of the name when applied to the books as a whole, and shows how it was that Luther split off these writings and placed them 'in the limbo between the Old Testament and the New.' The individual introductions serve to provide the backgrounds, probable datings, and general contents of each of the fourteen pieces. This is a valuable work for both the biblical scholar and the lover of fine books."—*J. Calvin Keene,* JOURNAL OF BIBLICAL LITERATURE

BIRREN, Faber. Color: A Survey in Words and Pictures: From Ancient Mysticism to Modern Science. index. 250 illus. 7⅝" x 10½", slipcased, 224pp. 62-18889. $15.00
PSYCH

In this marvelous encyclopedia of color facts and fancies, Faber Birren, leading consultant in America on the subject, offers a kaleidoscope of information for both the users of color in industry and science and the many who are intrigued by color artistically and psychologically. His contributions to the development of color application in government and industry have influenced us all. Here he offers the results of a lifetime devoted to his studies.

Illustrating his survey with more than two hundred and fifty illustrations in color, Mr. Birren conducts the reader on a leisurely stroll through primitive, ancient, medieval, and modern color conceptions, explaining color's mystic function, its many religious uses, the significance of gem stones, the relation of color to marriage and fertility.

A stimulating section on heraldry precedes an examination of color symbolism today. Color in medicine, from ancient cures to modern diagnoses, is dwelt upon at length, and medieval theories of alchemy are discussed.

The author includes an amusing account of the feud between Goethe and Sir Isaac Newton on color theory, and continues on to a consideration of modern spectroscopy and the wonders of human vision. The human aura is scrutinized, and the language of color, with charming and sometimes unexpected word derivations, dealt with extensively.

The relation of color to music, perhaps less well-known, is the subject of an unusual chapter, giving the history of color scales and color organs. In art, Renaissance artists, Impressionism, and Modern Painting are detailed with excellent illustrations.

CHANG, Garma C. C. Teachings of Tibetan Yoga. Introduction by John C. Wilson. 128pp. 62-22082. $5.00
YOGA

The author-translator who gave us the translation of *The Hundred Thousand Songs of Milarepa* now provides an introduction to the spiritual, mental, and physical exercises of his religion. Tibetan Yoga, or Tantrism, is summarized by the author in the following words: "The divinity of Buddhahood is omnipresent, but the quickest way to realize this truth is to discover it within one's body-mind complex. By spiritual exercises and the application of Tantric techniques one can soon realize that his body, mind, and the 'objective world' are all manifestations of the divine Buddhahood."

DINGWALL, Eric J. Some Human Oddities: Studies in the Queer, the Uncanny and the Fanatical. ill. bibliog. 198pp. 62-14948 $6.00   PSYCH

DINGWALL, Eric J. Very Peculiar People: Portrait Studies in the Queer, the Abnormal and the Uncanny. ill. index. bibliog. 224pp. 62-14949. $6.00   PSYCH

"These reissues of two fascinating books, originally written in 1946 and 1951 respectively, will be welcomed by all the lovers of true tales of the weird, strange and abnormal. Here are stories, scholarly written and scientifically analyzed, of visionary mystics like Emanuel Swedenborg, masochistic saints like St. Mary Magdalene de Pazzi, flying friars like Joseph of Copertino, mediums *extraordinaires* like D. D. Home and Eusapia Palladino, pornographers de luxe like Hadrian Beverland, transvestites like James Allen, and many others."—M.D. PUBLICATIONS

"Dr. Dingwall recounts some real-life stories that rival fiction for strangeness. He views and interprets the lives of these queer folk through the eyes of a psychic researcher—one of great note, indeed, and one with a sound academic background. The author has combined his talents as historian, psychologist and psychic researcher to produce a work for the scholarly with a taste for the macabre."—MEDICAL JOURNAL OF AUSTRALIA

FLOURNOY, Theodore. From India to the Planet Mars; Intro. and final chapter by. C. T. K. Chari. xxxvi+469 pages. 63-16228. $10.00   PSYCH

The passing years have served to confirm the eulogistic estimates of those best fitted to judge this work of the author, who was professor of psychology at the University of Geneva and died in 1921. F. W. H. Myers' *Human Personality* called Flournoy's book, "a model of fairness throughout." William McDougall's *Outline of Abnormal Psychology*, summed up the merits of the book: "Among the many cases of the trance-medium type, one stands out preeminent by reason of the richness and variety of the phenomena presented, of the thoroughness and competence with which it was studied, and of the success attending the endeavor to throw the light of science upon its complexities; I mean the case of Hélène Smith most admirably studied and reported by Th. Flournoy." William James praised it in equally high terms. Recent research into extra-sensory perception and the problems of survival and reincarnation has given a new and decisive importance to this classic. Flournoy's gift for narrative is unquestionable. One learns from him that a popular treatment is consistent with scientific carefulness.

The medium he studied became famous especially for two of her most convincing and most bizarre "incarnations." In the one she re-lived the life of a queen in 15th century India. In the other she was allegedly transported to Mars and described and drew pictures of its flora, fauna and intelligent beings, and wrote in the "Martian language."

Flournoy's critical studies of this medium demolished most of the claims made for her. But what he left standing is amazing enough. Some of what he left is now taken away by the new studies contributed to this volume by Professor Chari, a professor of philosophy and an eminent parapsychologist in India. Even he, however, must testify to the extraordinary verisimilitude of the medium's "memories" of 15th century India.

FOX, Oliver. Astral Projection: A Record of Out-of-the-Body Experiences. xiii + 160 pages. 62-19195. $5.00   OCCULT

The noted psychic researcher, Dr. Hereward Carrington, reports in one of his works: "The only detailed, scientific and first-hand account of a series of conscious and voluntarily controlled astral projections which I have ever come across is that by Mr. Oliver Fox, published in the *Occult Review* for 1920." The articles were expanded into a book. This is its first publication in the United States.

The literature of psychic research includes many instances in which a person has an out-of-the-body experience. Sometimes it arises out of a very serious accident. Sometimes it comes in the course of a profound illness. At other times it results from the shock of tragic information or a harrowing experience. A considerable amount of material on out-of-the-body experiences is found in other books published by us: F. W. H. Myers' *Human Personality and its Survival of Bodily Death*, Mrs. Sidgwick's *Phantasms of the Living*, G. N. M. Tyrell's *Science & Psychical Phenomena & Apparitions*.

FRAXI, Pisanus (pseudonym of **ASHBEE, Henry Spencer**). 3 vols. Each indexed. v. 1. Index Liborum Phohibitorum. intro. by G. Legman. 51+lxxvi+543pp. v. 2. Centuria Liborum Absconditorum. lx+587pp. v. 3. Catena Liborum Tacendorum. lvii+591pp. All bound in buckram and boxed. 63-13985 $35.00 per set   BIBLIOG

"The random bibliographical articles of which the present volumes are composed, sampling and describing at length the more difficult but elusive masterpieces of erotic literature in various languages" is the most important work of its kind in English. A 50-page introduction by G. Legman, whose name will be familiar to many librarians as a great bibliographer in his own right, makes clear the importance of this work, originally privately published a volume at a time (1877, 1879, 1885), of which this edition is a facsimile. "Henry Spencer Ashbee — to quote 'Pisanus Fraxi' by his real name — set out to do only a very limited thing, but in a thorough and profound way. He proposed simply to describe, and copiously to quote, some of the many hundreds of erotic books in various languages that had passed through his hands, and through the hands of some of his friends, during a long and assiduous career as a collector. His striking success, as opposed to the abysmal failure of most of his imitators, rises clearly from the limitations within which he was satisfied to work, without any megalomaniacal vaunting and flaunting of his interests and his evident erudition. Ashbee remains the principal guide-book and source work for the future moral historian of England and the 18th century, and has a great deal to tell any similar historian of England and the rest of Europe as well as America, to nearly the end of the 19th century as well."—*G. Legman*

GRILLOT DE GIVRY, Emile. Picture Museum of Sorcery, Magic and Alchemy. Introduction by Cynthia Magriel. 376 illus. index. 395pp. slipcased. 63-11177. $17.50   OCCULT

By common consent of students of these subjects, the best and most representative illustrations ever gathered in one volume are here. The text, excellently translated from the French, is equal to the illustrations. For the author is one of the great savants in this difficult and complex area of scholarship. Grillot De Givry (1874-1929), after a lifetime largely devoted to translating from Latin into French most of the famous hermetic texts, including Paracelsus, Savanarola, John Dee, Khunrath, Basilius Valentinus, gave the last years of his life to collecting this iconography of occultism.

HARRISON, Jane Ellen. Epilegomena to the Study of Greek Religion [and] Themis: a Study of the Social Origins of Greek Religion. 152 ills. index. lvi + 600 pp. 62-16379. $10.00   REL

"Jane Harrison (1850-1928) symbolizes the meeting between the more traditional classical studies and the disciplines of cultural anthropology and psychoanalytical psychology. She was a contemporary of Sir James Frazer, Sigmund Freud, and C. G. Jung and one of the first classical scholars to identify and discuss the *primitive* bases of the Greek religious tradition. It is largely under her influence that Olympian gods have come to be recognized as relatively late and predominantly literary figures, whereas she maintained the idea that it was the Mysteries, Dionysian and Orphic, that were the core of Greek religion. It is not surprising that the academic world has met her message with scepticism and hostility. In recent years, her books have become scarce on the market. The most recent reprint of "Themis" (1912) was in 1927, and the "Epilogemena" here reviewed is the reproduction of the one edition ever printed at Cambridge, England, in 1921. While she had numerous critics among her academic peers, she has also won the support and admiration of such great scholars as F. M. Cornford and Gilbert Murray, who contribute two long chapters to "Themis." The preface to the present edition, by John C. Wilson, and the "Jane Harrison Memorial Lecture," by Gilbert Murray, with which it concludes, are very helpful for an evaluation of her contribution to classical studies for the less well informed readers. Without taking sides on strictly scholarly issues, which are always open to revision and re-evaluation, one can claim the quality of greatness for Jane Harrison's writings and rejoice at their being made available to the reading public."—LIBRARY JOURNAL

"A book that changed my life — there are times when I think it is the most revolutionary book of the 20th century — has just been reissued, marking the 50th anniversary of its publication. It is *Themis*...Jane Harrison is truly what Edith Hamilton is popularly taken to be, the great lady who found Greece marble and left it living flesh."—*Stanley Edgar Hyman*
THE NEW LEADER

JAMES, William. The Varieties of Religious Experience; A Study in Human Nature; Enlarged Edition with Appendices and Introduction by Joseph Ratner. bibliog. index. 672pp. 63-14505. $10.00   REL

William James (1842-1910) began as a chemist and a physician. The physical side of medicine very soon ceased to interest him and he devoted his life to psychology and philosophy. Very early, too, he understood how shallow and unthinking was the attitude toward science of his colleagues at Harvard Medical School. He introduced Freud to his first American audience at a time when the medical profession anathematised psychoanalysis. He was the first to recognize the epochmaking importance of the discovery of the subliminal parts of the mind by F. W. H. Myers. He spent years studying the mediumship of Mrs. Piper and was the first American to become President of the Society for Psychical Research. He outraged the medical profession by becoming the principal spokesman in a successful fight to prevent requiring medical licenses of mental healers in Massachusetts. Finally, himself free of Christian belief or any other sectarian belief, he yet considered the cental task of his life to defend the legitimacy of religious belief. This is the great theme of this most fascinating and readable book.

James felt himself peculiarly fitted to explain mystics to non-mystics and vice versa and it is this successful role that makes this book a supreme triumph. The present edition of *Varieties* is notable for two things. James always meant to revise and expand it but never did. What Professor Joseph Ratner does now is to provide, in ten Appendices, about 100 pages of William James' other writings which bear on the central theme of *Varieties* and so, in effect, tell us the story of James' ideas on religion up to his death. Second, Professor Ratner provides a long Introduction which serves as a guide to those who may be perplexed by the various misleading interpretations of James foisted upon him during the 60 years since he wrote *Varieties*.

JUNOD, Henri A. The Life of a South African Tribe; 2 vols. intro. by Keith Irvine, Research Officer of the Ghana Mission. 150 ills. photos. index & glossary. 1230 pp. 62-18890. Slipcased. $20.00   AFRICA

"This is the first American edition of a classic anthropological study of an African tribe written by a Swiss missionary and first published in Europe as long ago as 1912 (this is the 1927 revised edition text.) Henri Junod came to what is now Mozambique in 1889, and lived for many years in the interior among the Bathonga people. On his return to Europe he wrote this monumental monograph, surprisingly enough in English when his own language was French. He died in 1934. Junod was inspired by a chance remark of the famed British historian, Lord Bryce, who regretted that no Roman has taken the trouble to investigate fully the ways of the Celtic people. Junod determined to perform this task for the Bathongas, who were still living in what might be described as their primeval state. The book examines in great detail their daily lives as individuals and as members of the tribe, their religion, culture, and social life. It is a massive and masterly performance, all the more valuable now since it represents a way of life that has virtually vanished. Half the Bathonga men now work in the South African mines, and civilization has profoundly affected their traditional customs. The two volumes are illustrated with photographs, maps and diagrams, and come boxed."—*John Barkham*, SATURDAY REVIEW SYNDICATE.

"The finest monograph on any African tribe."

—AFRICA, Journal of Anthropology.

KING, C. Daly. The States of Human Consciousness. approx. 256 pp. 63-10385. $7.50   PSYCH

Science, with all its promise, has diminished the old gods without providing aspirations worthy of twentieth century man. The aimlessness and frustration confronting us today has challenged philosophers to search deeply into the past, and into themselves, for a new approach to the human dilemma. From thinkers as far from us as ancient Egypt, or as near as the Gurdjieff Institute for the Harmonious Development of Man (founded in the 1920's), comes a clue to what we are seeking—a new dimension within man himself. There is an answer—to develop the human consciousness far beyond its present infantile state. In this profound book, the author uses the tools of science as steppingstones to go beyond science.

We know as normal today a Sleep state filled with restlessness and anxiety-ridden dreams; a Waking state of light hypnosis, phantasies and lack of awareness. Using the primary hypothesis of the Gurdjieff Institute, that man as a true individual is still only a potentiality, Dr. King analyzes the various neurological, physiological and psychological states of the organism to find the means whereby consciousness can be changed from a passive entity, capable only of blindly carrying out the body's orders, into an active 'I'-entity: a human "I" controlling every facet of his organism, and through this activity reaching an intimate awareness of the living universe.

Throughout history there have been moments when mankind was aware of abilities beyond those normally experienced. Gurdjieff is the first in modern times to attempt to create a rigorous discipline whereby man can enter states of higher consciousness at will and remain in them at length. The author was a student of Gurdjieff.

That there are different "degrees-of-being" of human beings will be a startling and even threatening idea to many. Yet—hence the great importance of this book—this may lead us to the answer to the human condition.

Dr. King is the author of *Beyond Behaviorism; The Psychology of Consciousness, Integrative Psychology* (with W. M and G. H. Marston), among other books. He received his doctorate in Physiological Psychology at Yale University.

Roy Finch, Professor of Philosophy of Sarah Lawrence College, has written an Introduction on the life and work of Dr. King (who died while this book was in press) ; he has also placed this book in the context of Gurdjieff's work.

LEGMAN, G. The Horn book; studies in erotic bibliography and folklore. index. bibliog. approx. 500pp. $10.00
REF

The Journal of American Folklore, an academic periodical, published last year a special issue devoted to erotic folklore and obscenity. It may be too early to assess the significance of this landmark event, as a sign of America and its higher schools coming of age. Mr. Legman was the principal contributor to that issue of the Journal. Perhaps, then, one can say without irony that it marked the official discovery of Mr. Legman by that part of the academic world occupied with the same subjects to which our author has been contributing for the last twenty-five years. During those years, it has not been easy for Mr. Legman to find himself in print. He had to resort to Samuel Roth's periodical, American Aphrodite, where first appeared the title essay of the present book here expanded and revised. He published some six issues of his own periodical, Neurotica. He is perhaps best known for an essay he published in book form almost 15 years ago, Love and Death. With the exception of the Horn Book, which dates back in its original form to 1953, Mr. Legman has refused to permit us to reprint in this volume any of his work dating back more than a year or two. Except for the essay on Pisanus Fraxi and the three pieces from the Journal of American Folklore, this volume consists of new, unpublished material.

LELAND, Charles Godfrey. Gypsy Sorcery and Fortune Telling: Illustrated by Incantations, Specimens of Medical Magic, Anecdotes, Tales; intro. by Margery Silver. ill. index xxxiii+271pp. 62-22021. $10
ANTHROP

"First published in 1891, this delightfully esoteric work is the product of the prolific American author Leland, who did much of his research abroad where he founded the Gypsy Lore Society, and who, after some 20 years of study and travel, was able to claim, 'I have enjoyed gypsying more than any sport in the world.' And that is certainly the flavor of this reprinted volume which cites the gypsy as the carrier (*colporteur*) of constantly changing witchcraft legends, magic, and memories, as they swept across Europe and around the world from their earliest origins in southern Asia. The description of gypsy lore will charm its readers, much as the gypsy does—with good humor, tolerance, and no sense of patronizing airs (which so frequently spoil George Borrow and others)—in fact the charm may sometimes appear to obscure the authenticity of Leland's fine ethnological studies. Nevertheless, the book remains one of the most important records of the Romany people's passing beliefs. There are numerous drawings and diagrams, and an interesting new Introduction by Margery Silver, a free-lance writer on American history and literature. Recommended for all libraries that may have an interest in gypsy lore or the occult. Can there be any that do not ?"—*Lee Ash*, LIBRARY JOURNAL

"The book is a rare treasure. Rich in knowledge, humor and feeling, it is highly recommended to those who would understand that mysterious tribe who sold good luck when they themselves had none."—*Per Sagereng*, SAN FRANCISCO NEWS—CALL BULLETIN.

LELAND, Charles Godfrey. Etruscan Magic and Occult Remedies; intro. by Margery Silver. index. ill. xxxiii + 385 pp. 63-18491. $10.00   ANTHROP

Etruscan is one of the lost languages. All that remains are a few inscriptions to which no one has yet found the linguistic key. True, archeologists have dug out many remains, especially their magnificent tombs, and we do have literary sources in the literature of the Romans who succeeded the Etruscans as rulers of the land, conquered and assimilated them. But all this is like reading Herodotus on ancient Egypt before we could understand the Egyptian language and use it to support Herodotus, modify him or correct him. In this impasse, the folklorist Leland (author of the gypsy study reviewed above) hit upon a simple but profound truth: that the peasantry of Tuscany, descended from the Etruscans, still preserved basic elements of the ancient Etruscan religion and culture. The Tuscan peasants had remained on the ancient lands, little touched in their rural isolation by the passing conquerors and centuries. They had eventually lost their language when Rome made them Roman citizens. But they had preserved their pagan beliefs. These peasants, of course, call themselves Catholics, but had succeeded in hiding from the priests their continued worship of the pagan deities of their ancestors. One can imagine with what astonishment Leland's first field work from Tuscany was greeted by the Congress of the Folklore Society in London in 1890; the news was reported in the next morning's *Times* as sensational. The original edition of this book, published soon after, was hailed by the serious cultural journals of the day as "a singular achievement" and "a unique accomplishment." Leland had seized his opportunity at a time when Tuscany's rural isolation made his findings of Etruscan remains relatively easy to prove. The clear implication of his work is that even when such remains are overlaid by later accretions they are still to be found. Despite the extraordinary importance of Leland's work and example, he has had few imitators. Jane Harrison (in *Epilegomena* and *Themis*, reviewed on page 8 of this catalogue)similarly marshaled anthropological field work among living peoples to throw new light on Greek religion. John Lawson followed even closer in Leland's footsteps by living among modern Greek peasants and finding there powerful survivals of ancient Greek religion (we shall shortly publish a new edition of his *Modern Greek Folklore and Ancient Greek Religion*). But this method remains anathema to the philologist; the archeologists are neither equipped for it nor interested; and the anthropologists have not learned it. Scientifically, then, Leland's work remains almost as unique an achievement as it was 75 years ago.

Leland was not only a scientific innovator, but a delightful writer and gregarious literary companion. This book is as readable as any of his writings on the gypsies. In those the gypsies speak to us directly; so do the Tuscan peasants and their real priests, their witches and warlocks. In the first part, they tell us about their gods and goblins. In the second part, we are given their incantations, divination, medicine and amulets. The author himself supplied some 60 illustrations, his own drawings.

LOISY, Alfred. The Birth of the Christian Religion [and] The Origins of the New Testament. Intro. by W. Norman Pittenger, General Theological Seminary. index. xix + 768 pp. 62-18073. $10.00   REL

"English readers have not before had access to the writings of Alfred F. Loisy, one of the leaders of the "Catholic Modernism" which disturbed the Roman Catholic Church at the end of the 19th and the beginning of the 20th century. In this volume is presented the excellent translation of his last two books, "The Birth of the Christian Religion" and "The Origins of the New Testament". In them Loisy applies the critical standards regularly employed in the study of non-religious history to the New Testament and other writings of the period, since he believed that unless the faith of men could survive the closest and most rigorous scrutiny by the scientific apparatus available to scholars, men of integrity and honesty could not hold that faith. His own Church excommunicated him for the radical conclusions of his study, and even to readers of this generation Loisy's conclusions are more than a little startling, but the religious spirit with which they are written conveys Loisy's own belief that true religion can always survive the inaccuracies and distortions of the historical record. 'What matters', he wrote, 'is the fire they (the men of the New Testament) kindled, and it is a fire that will never die till mankind is no more.' Students of the development of Christianity and the Church cannot afford to miss this striking and moving contribution to the study in which the last word has by no means been said."—VIRGINIA KIRKUS SERVICE.

MILAREPA. The Hundred Thousand Songs of Milarepa; 2 vols.; tr. from the Tibetan & annot. by Garma C. C. Chang. notes. v. 2, appendix. glossary index. 730 pp. 62-8255. slipcased $20.00   LIT

"*Mila grubum,* probably the most outstanding masterpiece of Tibetan literature, is now available in a Western language. Its form is not unlike *Thus Spake Zarathustra* by Nietzsche; its contents are the teachings of Milarepa (1052-1135), the great Buddhist saint and poet of Tibet. The songs and stories, in which the saint expressed his ideas, abound in Tibetan folklore, traditions, and poetic beauty, as well as philosophical insight into life's mysteries. Mr. Garma C. C. Chang, the translator of this difficult work, should be congratulated on his success in bringing forth this edition in a lucid style, with a sufficient number of competent notes at the end of each chapter. The appendix, including Mr. Chang's background essay at the end of the work, and the index are very helpful. The binding is both practical and beautiful. A work of lasting value and varied interests, this should be available in larger public and all college and research libraries." –LIBRARY JOURNAL

"The Western World has been spiritually enriched by this pioneer translation. To the translator, all Oriental scholars and lovers of the lore of the great teachers owe a debt of gratitude. Herein, in the many yoga-inspired songs and wondrous folk-tales, is revealed, in its mystic splendor, the arcane wisdom of Milarepa's Land of the Snowy Ranges, the land of Saints and Sages." —*W. Y. Evans-Wentz*

"I was overwhelmed by its beauty—beauty in ideas, beauty in expression, and beauty in bookmaking."—*Dr. Wing-tsit Chan,* professor of Chinese culture and philosophy, Dartmouth College.

"For eight centuries the *Mila Grubum* has guided and inspired the Tibetan people as great literature and great teaching. And now through Mr. Chang's presentation it may take its due place in world literature."—*Richard A. Gard,* THE ASIAN STUDENT.

PODMORE, Frank. Mediums of the 19th Century; Introduction by Eric J. Dingwall. index. xxvii + 720 pages, 2 volumes, bound in buckram and slipcased. 63-10384. $20.00   PARAPSYCH

Long famous as the most definitive study of spiritualism and mediumship of the period covered, this work now appears with a long biographical essay by Dr. Dingwall. At his death in 1910 at the age of 54, Podmore was the most distinguished historian and critic that psychical research had produced. This book first appeared in 1902 and is by far Podmore's best and most critical work and, Dr. Dingwall now tells us, is never likely to be superseded.

For a large part of these two volumes, America is the principal stage. Modern mediumship begins here, through the work of the mesmerists, the Shakers, the revelations of such clairvoyants as the Seer of Poughkeepsie (Andrew Jackson Davis), the Swedenborgians, and the Fox family. Podmore shows how the spirit of the frontier spread these beliefs more rapidly in the New World than in the Old; the enterprise of the frontier was active not only in such matters as material success and endeavor but also in the region of social and religious speculation. Mediumship was brought to Europe by a procession of mediums from America, beginning with Mrs. Hayden in 1852, the Davenport brothers, and the most famous physical medium of the century, Daniel D. Home, who arrived from America in 1855 and for ten years or more gave sittings in England, France, Italy, Germany, and Russia.

These were all physical mediums. Podmore is their severest critic, perhaps even unfair, for in effect he denies the genuine character of any physical phenomenon. Dr. Dingwall, who is by common consent the greatest living historian of physical mediumship, indicates the difficulties of Podmore's negative position. But Podmore is eminently fair to all mental phenomena, automatic writings and the productions of the trance mediums. Podmore was only 26 when the Society for Psychical Research was founded. He was soon elected to its Council, where he remained for 26 years, until shortly before his death. His joint work with F. W. H. Myers and Edmund Gurney (all three signed *Phantasms of the Living*) convinced Podmore that telepathy is a fact in nature. He was not, however, convinced as was his friend Myers that the trance communications demanded an explanation which necessitates the theory of spirit interference. Podmore remains the most formidable critical historian that spiritualism has ever encountered; and it is above all in this book that he displays his learning, his fair-mindedness and his critical acumen.

POTTER, Charles Francis. The Lost Years of Jesus. index. bibliog. 160pp. 63-12601. $5.00   REL
A new opportunity for religious liberalism came, in Dr. Potter's opinion, with
the finding of the Dead Sea Scrolls. The new opportunity was bolstered shortly
after by the finding of the Egyptian Gnostic Christian Codices. For these
findings opened up the question once again of what really happened in the
inter-testamentary period, from the end of the Old Testament to the writing
of the New Testament. The lost years, or the so-called "18 silent years"
between the ages 12 and 30, when the Gospels tell us nothing about Jesus, is a
tempting gap to try to fill in. Dr. Potter gives us in this book very good
reasons for believing that Jesus spent those years among the Essenes and
that he was one of them. With the help of the new material, particularly the
writings of the redoubtable French scholar, Dupont-Sommer, Dr. Potter has
tried to fill the gap.

PRINCE, Walter Franklin, Noted Witnesses for Psychic Occurrences; Introduction by Gardner Murphy.
index. x + 336 pp. 63-10387. $10.00   PSYCH
Here are gathered together the stories of supernormal experiences of some
170 men and women; there is hardly one name among them which will not be
known on sight to almost any educated person. They are people who have distinguished themselves in many professions, in many walks of life, and all
testify here to their own experiences of telepathy, apparitions, clairvoyance,
hauntings, precognition—well nigh every kind of psychic experience. This is
the first large collection of "occult" incidents occurring to prominent people.
The emphasis is on what is called, in the language of psychic research, "spontaneous" cases, i.e., experiences occurring usually quite unexpectedly and,
as it were, exploding out of the ordinary course of life. For this reason
there are hardly any incidents with mediums and séances. The selection of
these cases was made by Dr. Walter Franklin Prince when he was 65 years
old, a lifetime of rich study of abnormal psychology and psychic research
behind him. The ministry had led him to social work, and this to abnormal
psychology. He is the author of perhaps the best and most famous study of
multiple personality, the Doris Case. *Noted Witnesses* appeared in 1928 as a
volume of the *Proceedings* of the Boston Society for Psychic Research. Dr.
Prince was one of the renowned and feared investigators of mediums not
only in America but in Europe as well. He mastered the whole field of tricks
developed by professional magicians and conjurors and used this knowledge
to expose fraudulent mediums. One could say with some truth that his
experiments with physical mediums in Europe in 1928 left permanent scars
not only on the particular physical mediums, but on physical mediumship as
well. He had a more receptive attitude toward trance mediums. He came to a
number of positive conclusions, and it is in this book in particular that one
sees him at his most positive. Dr. Prince was the only American, other than
William James, who occupied the position of President of the Society for
Psychical Research (London) which he did for two years, 1930 and 1931.

BIRREN, Faber. Color Psychology and Color Therapy: A Factual Study of the Influence of Color on
Human Life; intro. by Felix Morrow. ill. photogs. biblio. index. xv + 302pp. 61-14266. $7.50
PSYCH

"Faber Birren is a consultant on the use of color in industrial and other
applications, and perhaps without a peer in this field. The book, however, goes
much farther than the mere applications and their psychology. There is
fascinating detail from historical, medical, occult, physiological sources as
well — fascinating and documented . . . Recommended." — LIBRARY JOURNAL

THE BOOK OF THE DEAD: the Hieroglyphic Transcript of the Papyrus of ANI; tr. and intro. by E. A.
Wallis Budge. ill. appendixes. index. xiv + 704pp. 60-12165. $12.50   REL
This is the collection of texts which the ancient Egyptian scribes composed
for the benefit of the dead. A book-length introduction by Sir Wallis Budge,
late Keeper of the Egyptian and Assyrian Antiquities in the British Museum, gives us its history and theology. This is an exact reproduction of the
famous Medici Society edition of 1911 except that the original two volumes
are here bound as one.